From Asylum to Community

From Asylum to Community

MENTAL HEALTH POLICY IN MODERN AMERICA

Gerald N. Grob

PRINCETON UNIVERSITY PRESS

PRINCETON, NEW JERSEY

Copyright © 1991 by Princeton University Press
Published by Princeton University Press, 41 William Street,
Princeton, New Jersey 08540
In the United Kingdom: Princeton University Press, Oxford

Library of Congress Cataloging-in-Publication Data

Grob, Gerald N., 1931–
From asylum to community : mental health policy in modern America
/ Gerald N. Grob.
p.   cm.
Includes bibliographical references and index.
ISBN 0-691-04790-1 (cloth)
1. Mental health policy—United States—History—20th century.
I. Title.
[DNLM: 1. Health Policy—history—United States.   2. Mental
Health Services—history—United States.   WM 11 AA1 GSF]
RA790.6.G76   1991
362.2'0973—dc20
DNLM/DLC
for Library of Congress   90-9178

This book has been composed in Linotron Sabon

Princeton University Press books are printed
on acid-free paper, and meet the guidelines
for permanence and durability of the Committee
on Production Guidelines for Book Longevity
of the Council on Library Resources

Printed in the United States of America by
Princeton University Press, Princeton, New Jersey

10 9 8 7 6 5 4 3 2 1

For David Mechanic and Lawrence J. Friedman

Contents

Illustrations

Tables

Preface

MORE than thirty years ago a colleague asked me a seemingly innocuous question about the history of psychiatry and the mentally ill. The result was a scholarly odyssey that began with a study of a single hospital and state, and concluded with a series of volumes that attempted to provide a comprehensive narrative of the ways in which American society dealt with the human, social, and economic problems associated with mental illnesses.

This volume—the last of three—covers the period from 1940 to 1970. Originally I had planned to deal with many of the same topics as in the previous volumes. While doing research in various archives and libraries, I became increasingly fascinated with the ways in which public policy is defined, formulated, and implemented. Hence this book—which is concerned with the origins of policy and its consequences—differs in significant ways from its two predecessors.

Two caveats are in order. First, my personal belief is that those who are most in need of assistance should have the highest priority. This book, therefore, is deliberately focused on the severely and especially the chronically mentally ill. This is not to argue that mental health services should ignore those who do not fall into these two often overlapping, though distinct, categories. It is only to insist that social support systems are indispensable for the well-being, if not the survival, of many severely and chronically mentally ill.

In centering this historical analysis on the severely and chronically mentally ill, I also recognize that it is not always possible to identify these categories with any degree of precision. In general, however, I have followed the definition used in the formulation of the National Plan for the Chronically Mentally Ill a decade ago. In brief, the chronically mentally ill comprise individuals suffering from "certain mental or emotional disorders (organic brain syndrome, schizophrenia, recurrent depressive and manic-depressive disorders, and paranoid and other psychoses, plus other disorders that may become chronic) that erode or prevent the development of their functional capacities in relation to three or more primary aspects of daily life—personal hygiene and self-care, self-direction, interpersonal relationships, social transactions, learning, and recreation—and that erode or prevent the development of their economic self-sufficiency." The difference between the severely and chronically mentally ill has to do with duration of illness; in the former the signs of illness tend to be episodic rather than persistent and long-term.

Second, I have employed aggregate data where necessary to indicate trends. These data should not be taken literally. I have found gross inaccuracies despite the existence of allegedly sophisticated systems to collect statistical data. Moreover, aggregate national data conceal as much as they reveal; there are incredibly sharp variations between individual states and regions. The statistical data used in this volume, therefore, should merely be regarded as approximations rather than descriptions of reality.

Finally, I should like to call attention to some personal assumptions that undoubtedly influence the ways in which I interpret the past. I have never held to the modern belief that human beings mold and control their world in predetermined and predictable ways. This is not to suggest that we are totally powerless to control our destiny. It is only to insist upon both our fallibility and our inability to predict all of the consequences of our actions. Nor do I believe that human behavior can be reduced to a set of deterministic or quasi-deterministic laws or generalizations, or that solutions are readily available for all problems. Tragedy is a recurring theme in human history and defines the parameters of our existence. I have tried, therefore, to deal sympathetically with our predecessors who grappled—so often in partial and unsuccessful ways, as we still do ourselves—with their own distinct problems.

The research and writing of this book has extended over years, and I have incurred many debts. All scholars benefit from the arduous but indispensable work of the many archivists and librarians who collect and organize materials without which history could not be written. A complete list of such individuals and institutions would be impossible, for my research has carried me to many institutions throughout the United States. I would like in particular to thank William E. Baxter, Director of the American Psychiatric Association Archives in Washington, D.C., who is organizing a superb manuscript collection dealing with American psychiatry since the 1940s.

I am deeply indebted to the National Institute of Mental Health, which supported my research with a research grant (PHS MH 39030), and the National Endowment for the Humanities, which awarded me a fellowship that permitted a leave of absence from teaching to write much of this book. I spent a year in 1985–1986 as a fellow at the Shelby Cullom Davis Center for Historical Studies at Princeton University, where I had an opportunity to continue my research and share ideas with Lawrence Stone and other colleagues.

Many individuals have provided important assistance by answering questions and reading parts of my manuscript at various stages. They include Walter Barton, Alexander D. Brooks, John Clausen, Paul Clemens, Jack Ewalt, Howard H. Goldman, Milton Greenblatt, Gail Hornstein, Allan Horwitz, Morton Kramer, Paul Lemkau, Howard Leventhal, Karl A. Menninger, Jack Pressman, Louise Russell, and Nancy Tomes. Nathan G. Hale, Jr., graciously permitted me to read a draft of his second volume on the history of psychoanalysis in America, which proved an invaluable source; he also read a draft of my manuscript and offered many astute comments. Dr. Alan Miller went over the manuscript from the perspective of a psychiatrist who served in both the federal and New York State governments during these decades and participated in the formulation and implementation of policy. Three close friends and colleagues—George A. Billias, Lawrence J. Friedman, and David Mechanic—commented extensively on the entire manuscript; without their assistance this book would not be in its present form. Finally, Lila K. Grob, my wife and partner, created an atmosphere of patience, understanding, love, and encouragement.

Rutgers University
New Brunswick, New Jersey
June 1990

Abbreviations Used in Text

APA	American Psychiatric Association
AMA	American Medical Association
CIB	Central Inspection Board
CMHC	Community Mental Health Center
CPMSP	Committee for the Preservation of Medical Standards in Psychiatry
CPZ	Chlorpromazine
GAP	Group for the Advancement of Psychiatry
HEW	Health, Education, and Welfare
JCMIH	Joint Commission on Mental Illness and Health
NAMH	National Association for Mental Health
NCMH	National Committee for Mental Hygiene
NCMI	National Committee Against Mental Illness
NIH	National Institutes of Health
NIMH	National Institute of Mental Health
NMHC	National Mental Health Committee
PHS	Public Health Service
SSDI	Social Security Disability Income
VA	Veterans Administration

From Asylum to Community

Prologue

ON THE EVE of World War II the framework of mental health policy in the United States appeared stable. At its center was an extensive system of public mental hospitals whose foundations had been laid in the early nineteenth century. These institutions were responsible for providing both care and treatment for all mentally ill persons irrespective of their ability to pay the high costs associated with protracted institutionalization. By 1940 the resident population of state mental hospitals had reached 410,000; an additional 59,000 patients were in veterans', county, and city institutions. That year 105,000 persons were admitted to state hospitals (82,000 for the first time); 59,000 were discharged (70 percent of whom had either recovered or improved); and 32,000 died. As a group, public hospitals cared for nearly 98 percent of all institutionalized patients. A substantial percentage of many state budgets was devoted to the support of mental hospitals; in 1940 the aggregate budget for such institutions reached $144 million. Although disagreements over details of policy and quality of facilities persisted, there was little disposition to question the concept that the mental hospital was the appropriate location for the care and treatment of the mentally ill. Correspondingly, American psychiatry was still an institutional specialty; more than two-thirds of the members of the American Psychiatric Association (APA) practiced in public institutions as late as 1940.[1]

Within two short decades, however, the consensus on mental health policy virtually vanished. During and after the 1960s the legitimacy of institutional care and treatment was at best problematic. Psychiatric activists and their allies promoted new policies designed to provide care and treatment in the community rather than in the mental hospital. They also insisted that it was possible to identify individuals who were at high risk and for whom preventive therapy would supposedly obviate institutionalization. Indeed, contemporaries often referred to a third or fourth "Psychiatric Revolution" equal in significance to the first "Revolution" when Philippe Pinel allegedly broke the chains of Parisian lunatics in 1793. As was approvingly observed in 1957 by Robert H. Felix (first director of the National Institute of Mental Health [NIMH] from its creation after World War II until 1964), the pendulum had swung "from concentration on improved mental hospitals to outpatient and preventive programs." A decade later he described community psychiatry as "a great movement" destined to make a permanent mark.[2] The new policy, in short, assumed a virtual end of traditional mental hospitals and their replacement by novel community alternatives and a more active role in prevention.

That mental hospitals—institutions that had been the cornerstone of public policy for nearly a century and a half—were beginning to lose their social and medical legitimacy was hardly surprising. Indeed, in the post–World War II decades the prevailing consensus on mental health policy slowly began to dissolve. A number of developments converged to reshape policy during these years. First, the experiences of World War II appeared to demonstrate the efficacy of community and outpatient treatment of disturbed persons. Second, a shift in psychiatric thinking fostered receptivity toward a psychodynamic and psychoanalytic model that emphasized life experiences and the role of socioenvironmental factors. Third, the belief that early intervention in the community would be effective in preventing subsequent hospitalization became popular, a belief fostered by psychiatrists and other mental health professionals identified with a public health orientation. Fourth, a pervasive faith developed that psychiatry was able to identify (and presumably ameliorate) those social and environmental conditions that played an important role in the etiology of mental illnesses. Fifth, the introduction of psychological and biological therapies (including, but not limited to, psychotropic drugs) held out the promise of a more normal existence for individuals outside mental hospitals. Finally, an enhanced social welfare role for the federal government not only began to diminish the authority of state governments but also hastened the transition from an institutionally based to a community-oriented policy. The dreams of psychiatric activists and their supporters were seemingly realized when Congress passed and President John F. Kennedy signed into law the famous Community Mental Health Centers Act of 1963.

Although predictions about the obsolescence of the traditional public mental hospital proved premature, there was little doubt that the status and role of this venerable institution appreciably changed in the postwar decades. That there was a marked difference between intentions and outcome is also obvious. What elements shaped the transformation of policy, and how can we account for many of the unanticipated consequences? The answers to such questions are neither simple nor straightforward. Many explanations offered by contemporary participants reflected personal ideological and professional commitments as well as a desire to legitimate new policy departures. The passage of time, the diminution of passions, and the growing availability of many manuscript collections, however, offers an opportunity to analyze the elements that shaped policy. The chapters that follow seek to delineate and to explain the sources of change in post–World War II America and its consequences.

CHAPTER ONE

The Lessons of War, 1941–1945

WORLD WAR II marked a watershed in the history of mental health policy and the evolution of American psychiatry. Many psychiatrists who served in the military came to some novel conclusions. They found that neuropsychiatric disorders were a more serious problem than had previously been recognized, that environmental stress associated with combat contributed to mental maladjustment, and that early and purposeful treatment in noninstitutional settings produced favorable outcomes. These beliefs became the basis for the claims after 1945 that early identification of symptoms and treatment in community settings could prevent the onset of more serious mental illnesses and thus obviate prolonged institutionalization. The war reshaped psychiatry by attracting into the specialty a significant number of young physicians whose outlook was molded by their wartime experiences and who were attracted by psychodynamic and psychoanalytic concepts. After 1945 many of them assumed leadership positions within the specialty and attempted to forge new community-oriented policies that broke with the traditional consensus on the need for prolonged hospitalization of mentally ill persons. In a sense World War II inaugurated several decades of ferment that eventually led to a profound transformation in mental health policy.

· · ·

Public policies, more often than not, are evolutionary in nature; only rarely do they emerge in some novel form following a cataclysmic event. Mental health policies were no exception: the changes that occurred during and after World War II were linked to earlier trends. The change in the composition of the patient populations of mental hospitals after 1890 was of major significance. Throughout the nineteenth century, patient populations were made up largely of acute cases institutionalized for less than a year. With the exception of such institutions as the Willard Asylum for the Insane in New York State (founded with the express purpose of caring only for chronic cases), the bulk of patients were discharged in twelve months or less. Some elderly persons with marked behavioral signs were institutionalized for longer periods and often remained until they died, but the majority of such cases were sent to almshouses, which served as surrogate old-age homes.

Between 1890 and 1940, however, the proportion of long-term chronic patients increased dramatically. By 1923 more than half of all patients had been institutionalized for five years or more. Many were individuals over sixty-five suffering from conditions associated with aging; others manifested behavioral symptoms that were probably of known somatic origins (e.g., paresis, a tertiary stage of syphilis). The changes in the demographic characteristics of the patient population—often stimulated by the adoption of new public welfare policies—had a marked influence on the structure and function of mental hospitals. Simply put, twentieth-century mental hospitals became institutions that provided long-term custodial care for an overwhelmingly chronic population whose behavioral disorders were often related to an underlying somatic pathology. The presence of so many of these patients contributed to the depressing internal atmosphere characteristic of many public hospitals. Physicians, and especially nurses and attendants, were generally unable to maintain high morale and enthusiasm, given the tragic condition and often bizarre behavior of their patients. Indeed, the character of the patient population contributed to the disruptive forces that were always present; conflict and disorganization lay directly below the surface at many institutions.[1]

As mental hospitals changed, their links with psychiatry became more tenuous. Trained as physicians, psychiatrists clearly preferred a therapeutic rather than a custodial role, and the institutional context in which they traditionally practiced was hardly conducive to the pursuit of the former. The rise of modern "scientific" medicine in the late nineteenth century appeared to accentuate the seeming "backwardness" of psychiatry. Under such circumstances it was understandable that twentieth-century psychiatrists attempted to redefine concepts of mental diseases and therapeutic interventions, as well as the very context in which they practiced. In so doing they implicitly posited a conflict between the traditional mental hospital (which provided custodial care for large numbers of chronic patients) and the imperatives of modern psychiatry.[2]

Receptivity toward innovation was perhaps best illustrated by subtle modifications in psychiatric models of disease. Generally speaking, the traditional model was based on the assumption that there was a sharp distinction between health and disease. The presence of mental disease was indicated by dramatic behavioral and somatic signs that fundamentally deviated from the prior "normal" behavior of that individual. By the turn of the century, however, such representative figures as Sigmund Freud in Europe and Adolf Meyer and William Alanson White in the United States were already challenging this paradigm. They, as well as others, began to argue that behavior occurred along a continuum that commenced with the normal and concluded with the abnormal. Such an approach elevated the significance of the life history and prior experiences of the individual, thereby blurring the demarcation between health and disease. Some who entered the specialty in the interwar years were attracted by psychodynamic or psychoanalytic psychiatry and after 1945 disseminated its virtues among younger colleagues. Psychodynamic psychiatry, wrote John C. Whitehorn, Meyer's successor at Johns Hopkins, emphasized "the study of the 'genetic-dynamic' development of one's personality." Sickness and health, insisted Karl A. Menninger, was "a scale in the successfulness of an individual-environment adaptation." At one end was "health, happiness, success, achievement, and the like, and at the other end misery, failure, crime, delirium, and so forth."[3]

Admittedly, psychodynamic psychiatry did not necessarily reject either the conventional belief that mental disease was a somatic illness or somatic therapies; eclecticism, not consistency, was often characteristic of the specialty. Nevertheless, the implications of psychodynamic psychiatry were striking. If there was a continuum from the normal to the abnormal, then the possibility existed that before the process had run its course *out-patient* psychiatric interventions could alter the outcome. Hence early treatment in community facilities might prevent the onset of the severe mental diseases that had previously required institutionalization. By the 1920s and 1930s signs of modest change were already evident: some psychiatrists were affiliated with child guidance clinics; some were involved with the mental hygiene movement, which had emerged during the first decade of the twentieth century; and some attempted to apply psychoanalytic principles to the practice of psychiatry. The majority of psychiatrists, however, still clung to their traditional base in mental hospitals.

Before 1940 the new psychodynamic psychiatry grew at a slow pace. The specialty was for the most part preoccupied with the severe mental illnesses and identified with traditional mental hospitals. Most state-hospital psychiatrists had little or no interest in psychoanalytic theory and tended to emphasize somatic therapies in conjunction with such directive methods as suggestion, reassurance, advice, and reproof.[4] The preoccupation with institutions was evident in the work of the Mental Hospital Survey Committee, created in 1936 by the APA, U.S. Public Health Service (PHS), and other medical organizations. Under the direction of Samuel W. Hamilton, a prominent psychiatrist, the committee launched a multiyear study of mental hospitals. In an exhaustive survey of mental hospitals published in 1941, Hamilton and his co-workers offered a series of conclusions that were neither striking nor innovative. Their recommendations were traditional and did not in any way suggest that alternatives to mental hospitals be considered. They called simply for higher levels of financial support, greater psychiatric autonomy, and the appointment to hospital boards of disinterested individuals concerned solely with the public good.[5]

. . .

The stability of mental health policy in 1940 was only superficial. The new psychodynamic psychiatry had yet to modify the preoccupation with severe mental illnesses, and the sporadic efforts to create outpatient or general hospital psychiatric facilities were still in their infancy. Nor had the full consequences of the gradual weakening of the links between mental hospitals and psychiatrists been realized. Finally, prewar psychodynamic and psychoanalytic thinking still tended to ignore the influence of broad environmental factors on personality; the prevailing emphasis was on individual and family relationships.

World War II, however, proved a critical catalyst. During that conflict, mental hospitals, which had already been injured by the ravages of the Great Depression of the 1930s, deteriorated still further as other priorities were established. Even as the war drew to a close, revelations of decrepit conditions within hospitals had begun to create an atmosphere in which noninstitutional alternatives would be seriously considered. Equally significant, wartime experiences seemed to provide conclusive evidence that the principles of psychodynamic psychiatry, when linked with new policies and institutions, had the possibility of revolutionizing the ways in which society perceived and dealt with the mentally ill.

Like other public facilities, mental hospitals had been hard hit by the Great Depression of the 1930s. Staff-patient ratios decreased; new construction came to a halt; and normal maintenance was deferred. Under normal circumstances the return of better times might have enabled hospitals to recoup lost ground, just as they had after previous economic crises. The national emergency engendered by the outbreak of a global conflict, however, created more pressing priorities, and the deferred needs of mental hospitals were largely ignored. The rise in the number of patients in state institutions from 410,000 in 1940 to nearly 446,000 in 1946, for example, was not matched by a commensurate expansion of physical facilities. Consequently the excess of population over capacity, according to federal statistics, rose from 9.8 to 16.3 percent. Such data may have even underestimated the magnitude of the problem. An independent study in 1946 estimated that overcrowding ranged from 20 to 74 percent.[6]

Even more significant was the decline in the quality of internal institutional environments during the war years. The induction of large numbers of physicians and staff into the armed forces created acute shortages. By late 1943 New York, which operated the nation's largest hospital system, reported vacancy rates of 31 percent for physicians and 32 percent for ward employees. The consequences of staff shortages throughout the nation were dramatic: restraint of patients became more common; hygienic conditions deteriorated; individualized attention, medical and occupational therapy, and supervised recreation all suffered. Patient care, complained the superintendent of Pilgrim State Hospital in New York in late 1942, "is not what it was a year ago." Replacements for those inducted into the military were "of an inferior grade," and he was forced to employ individuals drawn "from the welfare rolls in New York City and . . . these people are not the type to make good employees." Although such problems were by no means new, there is little doubt that the war exacerbated their impact.[7]

Peacetime failed to bring any immediate improvements. The demobilization of the armed forces and the transition from war to peace took precedence. Few state governments made an effort to deal with nearly a decade and a half of neglect of their mental hospitals. In 1947, for example, there were 12 to 30 patients for each attendant, 176 patients for each nurse, and 250 to 500 patients per psychiatrist. APA standards, by contrast, called for one attendant for every 6 to 8 patients, a nurse for every 4 to 40 patients, and a psychiatrist for every 30 to 200 patients (the variation in the ratios depended on the nature of the patient population at each institution).[8]

· · ·

Crowding of patients, staff shortages, and inadequate facilities and budgets were endemic problems of state mental hospital systems. With variations among states and regions, they had persisted for nearly a century. Indeed, to define problems in such terms was also to identify solutions. Crowding and inadequate facilities could be eliminated through the expansion of existing facilities or the construction of new ones; staff shortages could be alleviated through the employment of additional personnel; meager budgets would disappear with the infusion of new resources. The resolution of existing difficulties, in other words, left intact the basic policy of caring for and treating the mentally ill in traditional public mental hospitals.

The psychiatric experiences of World War II, however, led unerringly to a fundamentally different kind of analysis. By the mid-1940s the wisdom of equating mental illnesses with mental hospitals had become a subject for debate rather than an unquestioned proposition. The psychiatric "lessons" of the war, insisted some, suggested an alternative model based on early identification of individuals who were at high risk or whose mental illness was of recent origin, followed by prompt treatment in outpatient or inpatient *community* settings. In effect, World War II provided psychodynamically oriented psychiatrists (as well as those trained or influenced by Meyer) with an unparalleled opportunity to test new approaches. Out of their encounter with war and the lessons they drew came the outlines of a new paradigm that in the postwar era would prove a potent force for innovation.

On the eve of war there were no indications that psychiatry was on the verge of fundamental change. Although a number of psychiatrists had taken an active part in the military during World War I, their experiences were largely forgotten in the intervening two decades. The outbreak of hostilities in the late summer of 1939 found psychiatrists—much like their compatriots—unprepared for mobilization or war. As early as 1938 the trustees of the William Alanson White Psychiatric Foundation had urged members of the specialty to offer their services to the nation in the impending crisis. In 1939 the Southern Psychiatric Association and, to a lesser extent, the APA added their support. But few responded to these calls at this time.[9]

By the autumn of 1940, however, a number of psychiatrists had become involved in the effort to strengthen the nation's defenses in the event of war. Their initial involvement was with the Selective Service System. The rapid buildup of the armed forces required some mechanism that would assist in identifying in advance individuals unqualified for military service because of neuropsychiatric problems (which at that time included homosexuality). Not only was the induction of such individuals costly in terms of time and money, but it threatened to impair military effectiveness and efficiency. Even before the end of the year, such figures as Harry Stack Sullivan, Winfred Overholser (superintendent of St. Elizabeths Hospital in the District of Columbia), and others were assisting officials of the Selective Service System in setting up procedures to identify individuals ill-suited for the rigors of military life.

The assumption underlying screening, of course, was that knowledge of personality and background could assist in predicting disposition to mental disorders. Indeed, in the emotion-laden atmosphere of the early days of the war, organizations such as the National Committee for Mental Hygiene (NCMH) as well as individuals were speaking in language that implied a sharp expansion in the specialty's boundaries. Not only could psychiatry screen out the unfit and rehabilitate battlefield psychological casualties, but it could also provide indispensable assistance in maintaining military and civilian morale, coping with the dislocations of war, and furthering the social cohesion so vital for the preservation of mental health.[10]

Mass screening, nevertheless, proved more effective in theory than in practice. There was little evidence that available techniques—including personal interviews, tests, and social histories—possessed predictive reliability. Nor was there agreement among psychiatrists on such issues as the ideal attributes required for military life or whether former mental patients should be inducted into the services. Equally important, most psychiatric examinations were at best cursory; often a physician with no psychiatric experience rendered a judgment on the basis of an interview lasting no more than two minutes. Although Sullivan and Overholser championed screening, they met with considerable resistance both within and without psychiatry. Opponents offered a variety of objections: screening was arbitrary and capricious; racial and ethnic factors intruded into the process; rejectees faced discrimination in civilian life; background information about individuals was frequently inaccurate or misleading; and personality tests were both biased and unreliable. Moreover, military authorities were concerned about maximizing manpower resources; the rejection of more than 1.75 million men for neuropsychiatric reasons (including mental deficiency) aroused official anger.[11]

Proponents of screening insisted that predictive techniques could be developed. In mid-1942 an interdisciplinary team headed by two psychiatrists, and including a psychologist and statistician, an internist, and a psychiatric social worker, completed a case study that compared one hundred psychiatric casualties with one hundred normal soldiers (neither having been in combat). They found no fewer than fifteen significant factors that differentiated the patient from the control group, including

> volunteering or volunteering through selective service; shallow friendships; difficulty in making friends; disturbed sex development; under activity; bed-wetting over the age of ten; recognized as a follower in school or later life; not busy and purposeful in terms of general behavior; lacking in initiative; lacking in spontaneity; hypochondriacal before entering the army; overly concerned about general health; overly concerned about energy output or easy fatiguability; and two or more morbid fears.

If any seven indicators had been employed, 94 percent of the patients, but only 10 percent of the control group, would have been excluded from military service. A year later, advocates of screening launched the Medical Survey Program. This venture included a massive national data-gathering process (including criminal, medical, and educational records) and the administration of personality tests to more than three million registrants. Intended to weed out maladjusted individuals, the program quickly aroused controversy. Inaccurate data and vague criteria, critics charged, vitiated the validity of any results, to say nothing about the unwarranted invasion of privacy.[12]

The difficulties of screening, however, were soon eclipsed by the problems arising from breakdowns among military personnel. (Indeed, high battlefield neuropsychiatric casualty rates beginning in 1942 began to call into question the assumptions and effectiveness of screening, since the bulk of those identified as psychiatrically "unfit" had supposedly been excluded from the armed forces.) Some individuals exhibited psychological symptoms following a brief encounter with the rigors of military life, some upon experiencing the threat of potential danger upon arrival in a war zone; and others broke down upon extended exposure to combat conditions. As early as 1942 evidence mounted that prolonged stress associated with warfare led to mental breakdowns even among those who had manifested no prior symptomatology. The results of the Guadalcanal and North African campaigns in particular seemed to confirm the belief that environmental stress played the major role in the etiology of mental maladjustment, and that greater attention had to be given to the neuroses (as compared with the traditional preoccupation with the psychoses). Predisposition, most psychiatrists found, was not a significant factor. In the North African campaign, for example, combat veterans had a higher incidence of psychiatric casualties than did newer and inexperienced servicemen. In the southwest Pacific, on the other hand, the tropical climate, an unfamiliar jungle habitat, an abnormal social and cultural environment, and the absence of a rotation policy appeared to play the major role in neuropsychiatric admissions. William C. Menninger, chief of the army's Neuropsychiatric Division and a figure who would play a significant role in postwar policy, drew an obvious conclusion. The "history or the personality make-up or the internal psychodynamic stresses" were less important in the adjustment process than "the force of factors in the environment which supported or disrupted the individual."[13]

Wartime psychiatric studies suggested that fatigue and the stress of prolonged combat did more to explain psychological malfunctioning than did predisposition; even the healthiest of individuals could break down under the influence of environmental stress. Roy R. Grinker and John P. Spiegel came to such conclusions in their study of the Tunisian campaign in 1943, a work based upon psychoanalytic concepts. Constitutional factors and the individual's life history, though admittedly important, had been given too much weight. "The realities of war," the peculiarities of military organizations, and "traumatic stimuli" could combine "to produce a potential war neurosis in every soldier." By 1945 there was general agreement that intense and protracted exposure to modern warfare gave rise to what in lay terms was referred to as "combat exhaustion" (a term that was used to avoid the dangers of psychiatric stigmatization). "Combat exhaustion," observed a team of five well-known civilian psychiatrists on a tour of the European Theater of Operations in spring

1945, "has meant cumulative stress. Paramount in this stress are the effects of fatigue and hunger, of fear relative to incessant danger, and a series of repeated narrow escapes, following one another in rapid succession. With no adequate recuperative pauses between the repetitive experiences, one's compensatory mechanisms are tried to the limit, especially when fatigue and lack of sleep are coincident. . . . There is left little or no reserve, other than to revert to a less organized, less dangerous pattern at a lower level of human functioning."[14]

Neuropsychiatric disorders during the war posed serious problems for the military. During those years there were 1.1 million admissions to hospitals for neuropsychiatric conditions (although the total number of individuals was smaller, since some were readmissions). Of this number, 15.8 percent were for neurological disorders, 6.1 percent for psychoses, 10.8 percent for character and behavior disorders, and 58.8 percent for psychoneuroses; other diagnoses accounted for 8.5 percent. Slightly over 61 percent of admissions occurred in the United States, and the remainder overseas. Neuropsychiatric admissions, however, were not equally distributed. When fighting was at its peak between July and November 1944, for example, rates in the European Theater of Operations increased significantly. More important, they were far higher among men serving in combat divisions than among those serving in support units. Overall admission rates in the European Theater were 70 per 1,000 mean strength per year; in combat divisions the rate was 250 per 1,000. Admission rates also varied with duration of battle: the longer a unit remained in continuous combat, the higher the admission rate.[15]

Admittedly, admission rates for neuropsychiatric disorders in the military differed fundamentally from those in civilian life. The vast majority of psychiatric cases in the military would never have been considered for hospitalization in civilian life, where diagnoses of psychoneuroses, psychopathic personality, or borderline psychoses rarely led to hospitalization. Military standards of performance, however, differed sharply; "very mild" disturbances, which affected efficiency, caused men to be separated from their units. In the military structure there was nothing between the unit and the hospital. For the armed forces, therefore, admission rates for neuropsychiatric disorders constituted a major problem.[16]

If the rigors of military life and the stress of combat were at least as significant as the structure of personality in contributing to mental breakdown, then it followed that careful and intelligent planning could reduce the number of psychological casualties. Wartime experiences led military psychiatrists to support two strategies: prevention and treatment. The concept of prevention, of course, was long-established and familiar. In the nineteenth century it had been linked with a worldview based on a venerated religious tradition that emphasized natural law, free will, and individual responsibility. Failure to observe stipulated norms was inevitably followed by degradation, disease, and even death. A century later the concept had been redefined in scientific terms and emerged in the form of the mental hygiene movement. But the modern psychiatric concept of prevention had little meaning; it was largely a myth that offered assurance to a wide public and provided the specialty with a measure of legitimacy. Environmental variables, after all, were seemingly endless in number. But even if their relationship to specific mental illnesses could be identified with some precision, it did not follow that individuals would consent to environmental modifications which limited their freedom and autonomy.

Prevention during World War II, however, took on a more concrete and specific meaning. If the neuropsychiatric casualty rate was related to environmental stresses specific to the military, then it might be feasible to introduce innovations that would at least minimize certain risks. The hierarchical and authoritarian nature of military society and its more limited parameters also posed fewer impediments to the introduction of change. By 1943, therefore, psychiatrists had begun to shift their efforts from screening toward prevention and treatment. Herbert X. Spiegel, who served as an infantry battalion medical officer in the Tunisian campaign, called attention to "practical, preventive psychiatric measures" that could be used to minimize psychiatric casualties and thus increase combat efficiency. Spiegel emphasized that a soldier's identification with a group was an important stabilizing influence in combat, and he urged "the advisability of replacing casualties by groups instead of individuals, if at all possible."[17]

In a classic and influential report in mid-1944, John W. Appel provided the military with a set of specific recommendations. In the spring he had been sent to Italy, where he studied several hundred acute psychiatric casualties that had resulted from the bitter fighting at Cassino and Anzio. During these battles no less than 50 percent of the infantry troops attached to the American Fifth Army had either been killed, wounded, or captured, or were missing in action. An extraordinarily high percentage of those who survived sooner or later became ineffective and manifested disabling psychiatric symptoms.

Appel's analysis and conclusions were deceptively simple, but startling. It was not possible, he insisted, to keep men indefinitely in combat. Even line officers had noted that their troops reached their peak of effectiveness in ninety days; thereafter efficiency declined to a point at which the unit was virtually useless. American military commanders, however, had not recognized the risks involved in protracted combat. Unlike the British (who pulled infantrymen out of the line after twelve days for a four-day rest), American commanders provided no respite for their troops. Appel urged military authorities to provide all combat troops with fixed tours of duty. Rotation of entire units, not individuals, would enhance combat effectiveness. Psychiatric breakdowns, he insisted, did not arise from cowardice, laziness, fear, or personality defects; all individuals, placed under sufficient pressure, would sooner or later experience serious and crippling breakdowns.[18]

Appel's observations were echoed and confirmed by colleagues who dealt with neuropsychiatric casualties. By the final stages of the war, therefore, psychiatrists had developed a broad-gauged program to minimize the risks of "combat exhaustion." They urged that troops be provided with periodic rest, that officers be sensitized to the human needs of their troops, and that greater attention be paid to measures that promoted group cohesion. Psychiatrists serving in the United States also called attention to the need for modifying training procedures, some of which were counterproductive and led to breakdowns before combat. The high incidence of neuropsychiatric casualties promoted a more sympathetic response from military commanders. Toward the close of the war, infantrymen in Europe who had served six months or more in combat were granted top priority for rotation to the United States for 30 days of rest and recuperation and were subsequently given the option of base area jobs on their return. By May 1945 the army had adopted a policy that limited combat to a total of 120 days, and shortly thereafter it was decreed that infantry replacements who had been trained together would be sent forward and assigned as units rather than as individuals. Even though such policies were honored more in the breach than in the observance, early reports from the European Theater indicated that rest and rotation policies were effective in minimizing combat exhaustion and maximizing military effectiveness.[19]

While urging the adoption of preventive measures, psychiatrists also took an aggressive therapeutic stance. Their experiences with neuropsychiatric casualties during combat demonstrated that immediate treatment at a battalion or division medical facility was far more effective than removal to a rear-echelon base hospital. In the early stages of the war, there was virtually no provision for psychiatric facilities near the combat zone. In the North African campaign, psychiatric casualties were sent to base hospitals located as much as three to five hundred miles away. Less than 10 percent of those treated were able to return to duty. Gradually modifications were introduced. Under a plan formulated by Colonel Frederick Hanson, the psychiatric consultant for the Mediterranean Theater, and emulated elsewhere, battalion aid-station surgeons were given instruction in "first-aid" psychiatry. The typical course of treatment was mild sedation, a night of sound sleep, and warm food. More seriously troubled soldiers were sent back to the division clearing station two to five miles in the rear, which had a psychiatrist and a treatment center. Men were sedated for twelve to twenty-four hours and given an opportunity to bathe and shave. Those not helped at the clearing station were sent to an "exhaustion center," usually ten to fifteen miles behind the lines, where they were sedated for two days and received psychotherapy or pentothal narcosynthesis. In Europe those who were not sufficiently improved within a week to ten days ended up in a combat-zone neuropsychiatric hospital. Such casualties generally were unable to return to combat, although many were given limited duty assignments.[20] In effect, military psychiatrists modified the continuum concept by adding a form of environmental engineering. The inexorable movement from neurotic to more extreme symptoms could be arrested, if not reversed, by a judicious combination of psychotherapy and environmental changes.

Supportive forms of psychotherapy, when combined with rest, sleep, and food, produced almost instantaneous results. The local setting also ensured that the soldier was not separated for any length of time from his unit and his established social relationships. With prompt treatment about 60 percent of neuropsychiatric casualties were returned to duty within two to five days. The highest success rates were found in forward units, the lowest at rear hospitals. Yet even Grinker and Spiegel estimated that more than 70 percent of patients treated at base hospitals in the rear could be rehabilitated for limited noncombatant service, thus liberating others for combat. Whitehorn, a member of a team of psychiatrists sent to the European Theater of Operations in 1945, concluded that the specific form of treatment—barbiturate narcosis, hypnosis, chemically induced abreaction, subcoma insulin, group therapy, and others—was not the key variable. "Successful treatment," he observed, "seemed to depend less upon specific procedures or specific drugs than upon general principles—promptness in providing rest and firm emotional support in a setting in which the bonds of comradeship with one's outfit were not wholly disrupted and in which competent psychiatric reassurance was fortified, symbolically and physiologically, by hot food and clean clothes and by evidences of firm military support and command of the situation." More than any other element, the success in returning servicemen who experienced psychological problems to active duty renewed a spirit of therapeutic optimism and activism, which was subsequently carried back to civilian life. "Our experiences with therapy in war neuroses have left us with an optimistic attitude," Grinker and Spiegel reported in a chapter for a manual of military psychiatry. "The lessons we have learned in the combat zone can well be applied in rehabilitation at home."[21]

• • •

World War II had a profound effect on American psychiatry. In 1941 the discipline's status, in military as well as civilian life, was marginal. At the time of the Japanese attack on Pearl Harbor, only thirty-five members of the Army Medical Corps were assigned to neuropsychiatric sections in hospitals. During the war, psychiatrists slowly increased their presence and importance. At the beginning of 1944 the specialty was raised to the level of a division in the Office of the Surgeon General and placed on an equal organizational plane with medicine and surgery. William C. Menninger, who directed the division, was the first psychiatrist to be elevated to the rank of brigadier general. By the end of the war about 2,400 physicians had been assigned to psychiatry, although perhaps fewer than a third had prior training in the specialty.[22] In 1940, by way of comparison, the APA had a total membership of only 2,295. The war, in other words, brought into psychiatry hundreds of physicians who might have selected other medical specialties. Their wartime experiences in successfully treating neurotic symptoms in noninstitutional settings (and presumably preventing the onset of more serious psychotic symptoms) created an alluring model that would contribute to the postwar transformation of the specialty.

Military requirements not only increased the number of psychiatrists but, more important, hastened a basic intellectual shift. Before 1940 psychiatry was largely an institutional specialty whose members dealt with chronic and severely ill patients. During World War II, in contrast, there was an overwhelming need for psychiatrists who were capable of understanding and treating war neuroses and psychosomatic disorders. Psychodynamic and psychoanalytic psychiatrists were admirably equipped to meet this need, for their focus had always been on neurotic behavior. Better trained to deal with war neuroses than their institutional brethren, they quickly moved into leadership positions and played key roles in military training programs for psychiatrists. Such psychoanalytically oriented figures as M. Ralph Kaufman, Norman Reider, John Murray, and Roy Grinker trained many young physicians in psychodynamic and psychoanalytic concepts, and thus helped to alter the intellectual foundations of American psychiatry in the postwar era.[23]

More than anything else, the war helped to unify the beliefs that environmental stress contributed to mental maladjustment and that purposeful human interventions could alter psychological outcomes. That so many men had been rejected for military service because of neuropsychiatric disorders suggested that the mental illnesses were a more serious health problem than was generally recognized. The lessons of the conflict thus seemed to confirm the earlier experiences of World War I and the principles of psychodynamic and psychoanalytic psychiatry, neither of which had a significant impact upon public policy before 1940. The claim that environmental factors played a major role in the etiology of mental disorders was to be reiterated by a generation of psychiatrists who served in the military during World War II and assumed positions of leadership in the postwar era. The concept that there was a smooth continuum from health to disease appeared to be confirmed by wartime experiences in treating soldiers manifesting the psychological symptoms associated with severe stress. The relatively low incidence of severe mental illnesses in the military seemed to support the allegation that early treatment in noninstitutional settings represented an effective preventive strategy. Consequently, the continuum theory became an article of faith in the postwar years for those who urged early identification and treatment of individuals in community settings in order to prevent the development of those symptoms that required protracted hospitalization.

Even before the cessation of hostilities, psychiatrists had begun to find civilian analogues. Henry W. Brosin, a young psychodynamic psychiatrist who would become prominent in the postwar decades, for example, spelled out some of the "lessons" learned by the army. The war had demonstrated that neurotics could be functional and that even those who had experienced psychotic episodes could "recover their former integration" within weeks by "environmental manipulation." Although not rejecting the need for hospitalization, Brosin expressed a clear preference for outpatient care. What was required was "an attitude of patient optimism" and a recognition of the stresses that contributed to personality disorders. He called for an expansion in the number of qualified psychiatrists, greater attention to the importance of morale, the application of the lessons of wartime experiences to the home front, and the allocation of sufficient resources to the task at hand. "Good mental health or well-being," he added, "is a commodity which *can be created* under favorable circumstances."[24]

Psychiatric wartime experiences appeared to have significant policy implications. The greatest success in treating soldiers with psychological symptoms occurred at the battalion aid-station level. Conversely, the therapeutic success rate declined as casualties were progressively removed to rear echelon units. In a subsequent analysis of the lessons of World War II, Albert J. Glass, a psychiatrist who spent many years in the army, observed that the therapeutic inefficacy of continued hospitalization during the conflict was confirmed by postwar experiences in civilian mental hospitals.[25] A logical corollary followed: treatment in civilian life, as in the military, had to be provided in a family and community setting rather than in a remote or isolated institution. Just as proximity to their units enabled servicemen to maintain established social relationships and a sense of cohesion and integration, so treatment in a familiar community setting would preclude a break with those structures and relationships around which the lives of individuals were organized. Under such circumstances the disease process would first be halted and then reversed, thus obviating hospitalization. The implication for psychiatry was clear: community and private practice, once the exception, would become the norm and would ultimately replace institutional practice.

At a conference organized by the NCMH in February 1945, the emphasis on community services was already apparent. The meeting, which included representatives from the military, the PHS, the Veterans Administration (VA), and other civilian organizations, focused on the problems of discharged veterans "with psychoneuroses (with or without somatic complaints) and marginal maladjustments, since these problems are the most prevalent, the most neglected, and therapeutically the most promising." One of the key recommendations that emerged from the three-day conference was that psychiatry should give increased attention "to the treatment of the psychoneuroses as they present themselves in both psychiatric and general medical practice, to the care of ambulant patients, to the use of auxiliary personnel (psychiatric social workers and clinical psychologists), and to community services for the promotion of mental health."[26] Although the NCMH had supported such proposals for nearly three decades, the opportunity to implement them emerged only in the postwar era.

Psychiatrists also drew upon their wartime experiences in insisting that the debilitating effects of stress among civilians could be alleviated. If such innovations as rest periods, rotation policies, and measures directed toward the maintenance of group cohesion and social relationships had reduced psychoneurotic episodes in the military, might not corresponding social and environmental changes in the civilian sector optimize mental as well as physical health? Confident that their discipline possessed the knowledge and techniques to identify desirable social and environmental modifications, psychiatrists in the postwar period slowly began to expand the boundaries of their specialty.

But was the analogy of prevention in the military appropriate for civilian society? After all, military psychiatrists dealt less with abnormal men than with normal men in abnormal (i.e., stressful) situations. Most psychiatric activities, conceded John W. Appel, "represented attempts to change the combat situation rather than the combat soldier." The authoritarian structure of the military, moreover, gave its leaders the latitude and power to initiate significant changes; the role of the psychiatrist was simply to demonstrate that such changes were "militarily wise." Appel also conceded that environmental stresses in normal society were "considerably more diverse" and "far less subject to centralized control." Nevertheless, institutions of government, industry, education, religion, and communication possessed sufficient authority to undertake efforts to remove or ameliorate "some of the situational stresses which adversely affect mental health." Appel therefore raised the alluring possibility that psychiatry could contribute to postwar mental health by identifying those stress factors that both promoted mental disorders and were subject to modification or control.[27]

Appel's suggestion that psychiatry might be able to identify such factors was echoed by others. Many postwar psychiatrists, as we shall see, enthusiastically championed efforts to reshape American society, thereby transforming their specialty into a force for change. William C. Menninger, undoubtedly the most influential psychiatrist during the war and the immediate postwar era, was an ardent advocate of a new activist and liberal social psychiatry. The war, he insisted, demonstrated the significance of group cohesion, leadership, and motivation. Every unit in American society, therefore, had to evaluate its program "in terms of the contribution to individual and group mental health." It was vital to determine "the more serious community-caused sources of emotional stress" and thus develop community-oriented strategies to overcome them. Menninger also believed that unemployment, prejudice and discrimination, substandard housing, and delinquency had a deleterious impact on mental health, and he urged the development of constructive policies to deal with them.[28] Nevertheless, his emphasis on the need for environmental change never overwhelmed his psychoanalytic belief that internal psychic factors played a major role in mental maladjustment. Like many psychiatrists of his generation, he never resolved the tensions between an individualistic psychopathology and a more activist social ideology; ambiguity rather than ideological consistency was characteristic.

In *Men under Stress*, Grinker and Spiegel were somewhat more restrained. Their two concluding chapters, however, emphasized the social implications of military psychiatry as well as its applications to civilian society. The two conceded that the method of "brief psychotherapy," though extraordinarily effective for soldiers who had just encountered the stress of battle, might be less useful for civilians whose psychological difficulties were more deep-rooted. Nevertheless, dynamic psychiatry could become less passive and more active "in directing the ego toward mature attitudes in dealing with external pressures and the internal infantile wishes." Both psychiatrists were concerned as well with the millions of servicemen about to be discharged. Although many of their complaints and anxieties were legitimate, others were derived from "displacement and projection from unconscious sources and thus will be irrational and not susceptible to reasonable argument." What had been initiated by combat stress could result in a regressive immaturity. Patience and understanding by families had to be supplemented by "a comprehensive plan for ambulatory medical and psychiatric care, . . . hospitalization, . . . job analysis and placement, . . . and social aid of all types." Psychiatrists could treat individuals but could have "no effect upon the regressive trends within society." Grinker and Spiegel therefore called for a partnership between psychiatrists and those individuals "expert in social, economic and political techniques" to create an optimal environment. Nevertheless, they wrote in a revealing statement, "the principles of this social therapy . . . are the same and are based upon an understanding of dynamic social psychology."[29]

The calls for an expansive and more active social and community psychiatry were by no means limited to those who had served in the military. By the late 1940s such themes had begun to become more commonplace. In a suggestive article in 1948, Felix and R. V. Bowers insisted that mental hygiene had to be concerned "with more than the psychoses and with more than hospitalized mental illness." Personality, after all, was shaped by socioenvironmental influences, and they explicitly alluded to wartime psychiatric experiences. Psychiatry, in collaboration with the social sciences, had to emphasize the problems of the "ambulatory ill and the preambulatory ill (those whose probability of breakdown is high)." The community, not the hospital, was psychiatry's natural habitat. Psychiatrists had to play a vital role in the future in creating a presumably healthier social order. Felix and Bowers pointed to recent epidemiological studies that offered compelling evidence "that both the content and the orientation of personality are powerfully influenced by the social setting" and concluded that the "reintegration of community life" offered the possibility of reducing mental disorders. As early as 1945 Felix argued that psychiatry had an obligation to "go out and find the people who need help—and that means, in their local communities." Nor was Felix speaking merely in abstract terms. Following the passage of the National Mental Health Act of 1946, he worked diligently to reshape public policy by tapping federal resources.[30]

The significance of wartime experiences could hardly be exaggerated, implied Thomas A. C. Rennie and Luther E. Woodward in their optimistic *Mental Health in Modern Society*. World War II demonstrated the importance of environmental factors in health and stability. It revealed how stress could upset normal men, how leadership, morale, and interpersonal relations shaped health and stability, and how vital was an understanding of social and community factors. Employing an analogy drawn from public health, they called upon those concerned with mental health to deal with "ignorance, superstition, unhealthy cultural patterns, and the rigidities and anxieties of parents, as well as with social conditions which foster the development of neuroses and maladjustments." In a similar vein, Nolan D. C. Lewis observed that the war demonstrated the desirability of treating people before they required hospitalization. Thus if potential schizophrenics could be identified before the onset of the acute stage, treatment in a community setting (as in the military) might preclude institutionalization. "We as civilians," he added, "should insist (not merely request) on the establishment of more child guidance centers and treatment clinics in the cities and towns over the country, that corrective measures may be available to those who seek aid."[31]

. . .

When hostilities ceased in 1945, American psychiatry appeared on the threshold of a new era. The experiences of war had not only brought into the specialty a large number of younger individuals but had also strengthened the hands of those who favored the expansion of psychodynamic and social psychiatry and the creation of noninstitutional therapeutic alternatives. That the foundations for change were yet to be laid seemed of little consequence. With a renewed sense of confidence in themselves and their discipline, many eagerly anticipated the immediate future. Although not yet rejecting their institutional legacy, they foresaw the possibility of translating an earlier vision of prevention into concrete policies—policies that would facilitate the identification and treatment of individuals before they reached the acute stage of any of the mental illnesses that had hitherto required institutionalization.

The belief that psychiatry could contribute to the task of individual and social reconstruction reflected the widespread optimism of the immediate postwar years. Americans had weathered a decade and a half of depression and global conflict, and the fabric of their social order had survived intact. A war that had begun with an ignominious defeat had ended on a note of triumph. If the adversity of depression and war had been surmounted, why could not a series of residual social problems be resolved as well? Nor was the anticipation of a brighter future unique to psychiatry. Social and behavioral as well as natural and physical scientists were equally confident in their ability to create a more just social order. Indeed, in the postwar era members of these disciplines would create new careers for themselves in business, government, education, and the public arena, which they would justify in terms of their scientific and professional expertise. That structural changes in government and society were required was self-evident. But given a fortuitous combination of knowledge, will, and the allocation of appropriate resources, there was no reason why the dreams of the past could not become the reality of the future.

Beneath the heady optimism of the postwar years, however, lurked issues and problems that were neither discussed nor confronted. What assurance was there that Americans would accept psychiatric prescriptions for change or provide adequate resources? Equally important, what kinds of evidence could be marshaled in support of prescriptions for change? Would the techniques developed to deal with the psychological casualties of war be as effective in peace? Were health and disease two polar ends of a smooth continuum, thus justifying a blurring of the traditional distinction between the neuroses and the psychoses? Or was there a sharp demarcation between the two, vitiating the claim that early treatment in community settings could prevent the onset of the severe mental illnesses? And even if a psychodynamically oriented therapy in a community setting was as effective as its proponents claimed, what would happen to the nearly half a million persons in traditional mental hospitals? In 1945 such questions for the most part were rarely raised. Psychiatric faith in the wisdom and desirability of change was overwhelming, and members of the specialty moved rapidly to create a structure that would facilitate institutional and therapeutic innovation designed to resolve once and for all the pressing problems associated with mental illnesses.

CHAPTER TWO

The Reorganization of Psychiatry

BEFORE specific substantive policy innovations could even be considered, psychiatrists had to create a more effective organizational vehicle to promote their case for change. Toward the close of World War II, therefore, a group of younger figures—many of whom had served in the military—launched a searching evaluation of the nature and structure of their specialty and began to consider a series of far-reaching proposals for change. At times the intensity of the discussions created rival groups and ruptured long-standing personal and collegial relationships. The dialogue ranged over a variety of issues. What was the etiology and nature of mental illnesses? How and where should the mentally ill receive treatment? Who was qualified to prescribe appropriate interventions for patients? What were the responsibilities of psychiatrists toward the larger society? To what extent did a medical education confer upon the members of the APA authority to deal with larger social, economic, and political issues, such as war, poverty, racism, and the quality of life? What was the appropriate role for a professional organization? How could members be compelled to support programs with which they might disagree?

Between 1944 and 1950 a bitter and acrimonious conflict threatened to fragment the specialty and split the APA into rival factions. At one pole were those who believed that psychiatry had to make a far greater commitment to social activism, to practice in noninstitutional settings, and to psychodynamic and psychoanalytic principles. At the opposite pole were more traditional-minded figures who questioned the wisdom and desirability of social activism and who tended to emphasize a somatic etiology and therapy. Admittedly, the lines between the contending parties were not always clear-cut or coherent; subtle distinctions rather than fundamental principles often separated the protagonists. Psychodynamically oriented practitioners, for example, never excluded somatic elements, and somatic psychiatrists rarely insisted that psychological elements were of no significance. Nevertheless, the effort to apply the experiences of World War II in the postwar years unexpectedly polarized the specialty, and a fierce struggle over its future followed. In the end psychodynamically oriented activists prevailed, and the stage was set for new policies and practices during and after the 1950s.

.   .   .

If psychiatry was to meet new responsibilities, it would require an appropriate organizational structure. Those who believed in the necessity of change turned their attention to the specialty's organizational framework even before they spelled out the nature and rationale of a new program. Their initial focus was on the APA. Founded in 1844 as the Association of Medical Superintendents of American Institutions for the Insane, the organization represented largely, but not exclusively, the interests of hospital psychiatry. More significant, the APA was relatively inactive. It had two basic functions: to hold an annual convention and to publish the *American Journal of Psychiatry*. The association's national headquarters was staffed by only a few individuals; its financial resources were minimal; and elected officials rarely devoted much time to its affairs. The APA Council did little more than receive and then file the recommendations of the more than two dozen committees. Accountability was thus diffused, and the organization never developed systematic or coherent policies.[1]

Dissatisfaction surfaced when certain members endorsed a petition criticizing the *American Journal of Psychiatry* near the end of the war. The petition charged that the journal reached only a narrow audience and that its coverage was dated. The signers called upon the president of the APA to appoint a special committee to suggest changes in the journal's policies "for the betterment of our society" and to publicize its value "to the entire medical profession in order to disseminate psychiatric knowledge." J. K. Hall, a prominent southern psychiatrist and former APA president, expressed a willingness "to ally its contents temporally more intimately with the present and with the future" but rejected any suggestion that its editor be replaced.[2]

In the spring of 1944 the Committee on Psychiatric Standards and Policies suggested that the time had come to modernize the structure of the APA by creating a central headquarters under the direction of a qualified psychiatrist. The committee expressed serious doubts about the value of the APA's contributions to the war effort and about its ability to deal with postwar problems. In late 1944 and early 1945, therefore, the APA Council authorized the president to appoint a Special Committee on Reorganization to recommend the employment of a salaried medical director and to study the organization's structure. The five-person committee was chaired by Karl A. Menninger, a figure whose personality, activities, and writings since the 1920s had brought him fame and a reputation for controversy. The committee clearly favored some kind of change, for a majority were sympathetic to a psychodynamic psychiatry and to psychoanalysis.[3]

In early 1945 the special committee met with the Council. In his opening remarks, Menninger emphasized that the APA's structure was not compatible with its size, and that its mission was vague. For many members the APA existed mainly to hold annual meetings where friends could meet. Others, however, believed that the association had ignored medical education, hospital standardization, and other key issues. Before any decisions were made, Menninger insisted, psychiatry had to define its purposes and goals. In its report the committee as a whole noted that the appointment of a medical director was not "a feasible step." Wide-ranging structural reforms, moreover, required constitutional amendments, and the group lacked a mandate to propose such changes. The committee noted, however, that the council might already have the authority to appoint full-time individuals to improve public relations and psychiatric education, establish clinical standards, and stimulate scientific investigations. Finally, the committee urged that its membership be enlarged to include other eminent figures.[4]

Although the committee had operated openly and had not attempted to impose the views of its members, its deliberations proved controversial. Rumors immediately began to circulate that a small clique was bent on reorganizing and controlling the APA. From the very outset it was evident that opposition to reorganization reflected hostility toward a psychodynamically oriented and socially active psychiatry. Clarence O. Cheyney (medical director of the Westchester Division of the New York Hospital) was opposed to the hiring of a medical director and was especially critical of efforts to broaden psychiatric responsibilities. "The conception that psychiatry and psychiatrists are to take over the function of the guidance of all people not only when they are ill with mental disorders but also in their business and social life and their philosophy," he wrote, "does not appeal to me." Cheyney's views were echoed by others, including William L. Russell (his predecessor at the New York Hospital), James V. May (a former APA president), C. C. Burlingame (psychiatrist-in-chief at the Institute for Living), and Clarence B. Farrar (editor of the *American Journal of Psychiatry*). Farrar feared that appointment of a permanent medical director—as contrasted with a democratically elected president—created the possibility of "dictatorship" and the development of "a potential bureaucracy in our democratic organization." The goal of reorganization, he believed, was "domination by this radical sectarian group." Perhaps the most vigorous criticism came from Russell, who saw the reorganization as "a movement towards control of the association by the psychoanalytical group." As a figure who had been identified with mental hospitals for nearly half a century, Russell endorsed Stanley Cobb's observation that the institutionalized mentally ill constituted the "central problem of psychiatry." J. K. Hall, on the other hand, felt that some change was desirable, but rejected precipitous or radical action.[5]

Surprised by mounting rumors and innuendoes, the committee sent out a questionnaire to APA members. Support for the creation of a new administrative staff, its members noted, reflected the belief that the association faced pressing problems that could not be resolved under the existing structure. Since it was not committed to any particular reorganization plan, the committee decided to poll the membership. It was interested in attitudes toward the APA and especially the reaction to plans that mandated both structural change and increased dues. Much to the dismay of the committee, only about 8 percent of the more than 3,000 members replied. One hundred and twenty-eight individuals responded, and three letters summarized the views of 116 others. Seventy-six of the 128 expressed dissatisfaction with the association, 29 satisfaction, and 23 had no opinion. The group letters expressed no particular dissatisfaction. The query about an expanded program drew a similar response. Although the overwhelming majority of members appeared apathetic or unconcerned, it was clear that a minority—generally composed of the association's elite—held strong convictions. More than half favored change, but about a quarter were opposed. The letters also suggested the possibility that a wide rift in the organization could develop, though there was hope that a reasonable compromise could be reached.[6]

Faced by such ambiguous and seemingly indifferent results, the committee proposed to the APA convention in October 1945 that all plans for reorganization be deferred "pending a further expression of opinion on the part of the membership." Concerned with potential disunity, it recommended that the association arrange a "down-to-earth discussion of the practical problems our members meet in their daily work" at the next national meeting in May 1946.[7]

In the months preceding the convention in 1946, much of the excitement over reorganization appeared to dissipate. The deliberate efforts of the Special Committee on Reorganization to calm angry participants seemed to have had the desired results. At the convention, Karl M. Bowman gave a conciliatory presidential address that included diverse themes designed to appeal to a broad constituency. His address was followed by the open forum on reorganization. After a series of brief statements from a number of prominent figures and an amicable discussion, the convention adopted several resolutions. It endorsed the enlargement of the committee on reorganization to represent a wider constituency and also called upon its members to work with the Program Committee to develop recommendations and a format for discussion at the next meeting. With characteristic bluntness, Karl Menninger expressed doubt that mere enlargement of the committee without guidance would have the desired results. Nevertheless, the adoption of a framework for discussion seemed to have broad support, and it appeared that the threat of conflict had receded, but not disappeared. One participant, for example, conceded that the APA was "oldfashioned" and that it was run by a "clique of elders." Tradition, however, had its place, and he attributed criticism of the status quo to "self-seeking people." Perhaps, he concluded, secession and the formation of a rival group might "prove to be a good thing."[8]

. . .

Until spring 1946 the discussions on reorganization were narrowly focused. There was no indication that the committee was seeking to use the issue to force a more wide-ranging debate. The formation of the Group for the Advancement of Psychiatry (GAP)—an organization dedicated to the creation of an expansive psychodynamic psychiatry that emphasized a broad environmental etiology and defined its mission in terms of social activism—proved to be the catalyst that precipitated an open conflict in the APA.

The day before the APA convention of 1946 officially opened, fifteen psychiatrists held an informal gathering. Among those present were some of the more prominent members of the specialty: William C. Menninger, his brother Karl, Daniel Blain, M. Ralph Kaufman, Marion Kenworthy, Robert Felix, Douglas Bond, Henry W. Brosin, Norman Brill, Laurence Smith, Roy Grinker, John Romano, Thomas A. C. Rennie, and Wilfred Bloomberg. The driving force was clearly William Menninger. As much as any other figure in the postwar era, he was responsible for popularizing psychiatry and psychoanalysis and developing close and warm relationships with leading public figures. Prewar and wartime experiences had confirmed his belief in the significance of the environmental determinants of human behavior. His concern, therefore, was not simply with the background of the individual, but with the social and cultural environment as well. Menninger's vision of psychiatry transcended the care and treatment of the mentally ill. He insisted on the necessity of a "social" psychiatry (the application of psychiatric principles "to many activities which are not concerned with the diagnosis and treatment of illness"). "Can the culture of a race, the Germans for instance, be changed?" he asked. "How can interracial hostilities and fears be bridged? How can nationalistic aggressiveness be best directed and controlled?" Psychiatry, he answered, could help resolve these questions and contribute to such fields of human activity as "education, industry, recreation." Until his death in 1966, Menninger preached the gospel of psychiatry to his colleagues and the American people.[9]

Karl Menninger, who was deeply involved in the reorganization controversy, shared many of his brother's views. Even before 1945 he had published three widely read books that popularized psychoanalytic concepts. Psychiatry, Karl observed in 1940, "had devoted itself in the past too much to the care of a hopeless and hapless few." Indeed, the two brothers made the Menninger Foundation into one of the nation's premier psychiatric centers. Between the 1940s and 1960s the foundation experimented with institutional care, attempted to integrate psychiatry with the social and behavioral sciences and develop interdisciplinary research programs, and trained a large number of young medical graduates in the new psychodynamic and psychoanalytic psychiatry. Although close with his brother, Karl—the elder, and a strong-willed and contentious individual—tended to dominate their relationship. A founding member, Karl was never enamored of GAP, perhaps because he was not in control. When William asked for an evaluation of GAP in 1947, Karl (who knew how proud his brother was of the fledgling organization) gave a negative response and suggested that "it should be quietly and peacefully exterminated." Two years later William expressed distress at Karl's behavior during a GAP meeting and at the "feeling of competition." "Maybe underneath," he wrote in his private diary, "it is the fact that in our theoretical organizational structure he is responsible to me . . . which could stir up unadmitted feelings on his part."[10]

At the first meeting of GAP, those present debated whether the APA could be changed or whether its diversity and unwieldy constitution precluded "decisive action" and thus mandated the formation of "a new militant body." Four individuals tended to favor an alternative organization but went along with the majority, who believed that efforts "to revive the A.P.A. were preferable to beginning a new organization." There was agreement that a new group, limited to 150 members, was the best vehicle to promote change within the association. The following day a slightly expanded group met and decided to nominate from the floor three alternative candidates for the APA Council. This was an unusual step; election to APA bodies had never been contested. Those present settled upon Kenneth Appel (Institute of the Pennsylvania Hospital), Thomas A. C. Rennie (New York Hospital), and William Menninger. All three were elected (although the nominees they ran against subsequently joined GAP). Those who harbored suspicions of reorganization and were opposed to GAP viewed the election results as confirmation of their fear that a minority was plotting to seize control of the association.[11]

The founders of GAP envisaged an activist organization. Each member was assigned to a committee responsible for a particular problem and accepted an obligation to take a meaningful part in its work. Initially the organization had nine committees: their jurisdiction covered therapy, social work, state hospitals, cooperation with government agencies, cooperation with lay groups, public education, racial and economic problems, preventive psychiatry, and medical education. Additional committees were subsequently created. Membership was limited to psychiatrists, even though the organization, because of its emphasis on social action, was committed to cooperation with other disciplines. A poll on the issue of admitting individuals who were not psychiatrists revealed a wide divergence of opinion, and GAP decided to retain its exclusive character and thus preserve organizational unity. Members were expected to contribute time and money and to attend meetings at their own expense. Fortunately, GAP managed to secure a grant of $17,000 from the Commonwealth Fund for the first year of its existence. By 1950 the Commonwealth Fund had provided $109,000 of the $135,000 raised from private foundations.[12]

GAP members functioned on two different levels. All were assigned to working committees charged with the preparation of studies that would clarify internal psychiatric and external social issues. But GAP members also belonged to the APA, which did not necessarily endorse the policies of the newly formed organization. This situation created the perception that GAP was conspiring to dominate the APA. The fact that the committee structures of GAP and the APA generally paralleled each other reinforced this widely held view. GAP members, on the other hand, held very different views. "It is safe to say," Brosin observed, "that the G.A.P. represents a leavening influence which is markedly altering the character of the A.P.A. in the direction of sound leadership and active participation in both the professional and public fields."[13]

In portraying themselves as committed to socially desirable innovation, GAP members inadvertently aroused the ire of those who did not believe that the APA—as an organization—should be in the vanguard of change. Indeed, by criticizing the APA, GAP was indirectly criticizing colleagues with a long history of organizational involvement. Issues aside, there is little doubt that part of the antagonism and conflict between 1946 and 1949 reflected styles and personality as well as substance.

Within six months of the founding of GAP and even before the group had issued position papers, Farrar humorously proposed the formation of an alternative organization—"The Group of Unknowns in Psychiatry" (GUP). Individual members were to be known as "Guppies." Since GUP would be "a very select outfit," members "should be required to grow long beards and wear dark green spectacles; and . . . at meetings . . . wear their coats and vests buttoned up behind." As its slogan, GUP would adopt the cry "Back to Hippocrates"—an obvious allusion to the belief that GAP no longer represented medicine. One requirement for membership in GUP would be an "acceptable thesis" on a prescribed subject, such as "Psychiatric Observations on the Passengers in Noah's Ark," "Group Psychotherapy during Passage in the Ark Which Permitted All Passengers to Land with Sound Minds," or "The Malign Influence of Grandpopism, a Menace to the Future of the Human Race." If a candidate did not prefer "too scientific a subject, he might be let off by writing a good 'Topeka-boo story'" (an obvious allusion to the Menninger Foundation in Topeka). For several years such prominent figures as Farrar, Winfred

Overholser (superintendent of St. Elizabeths Hospital), Samuel Hamilton, and a few others enjoyed corresponding among themselves about GUP and GAP. Indeed, a "constitution" gave preferred membership status to those "who have accepted standpat dogmas." Officers of GUP included the following: a "Grand Bazooka, three Grand Trombones, a Great Dictaphone who shall keep records, and as many Grand Trumpets as there are members." Officers would be "elected casually by attrition." Despite his dislike of GAP, Farrar was willing to publish GAP material in the *American Journal of Psychiatry*.[14]

In 1947 GAP began to issue reports on an irregular basis. The documents were initially drafted by individual committees and then sent out as circular letters to the membership for comment before publication. The first appeared in late 1947 and dealt with electroshock therapy. The report was hardly assuring. It was critical of the indiscriminate use of this technique even while conceding its efficacy in the treatment of depression. Rejecting the use of electroshock therapy outside hospitals, it deplored the fact that this form of treatment was employed to the exclusion of psychotherapy. Nine months later a report on prefrontal lobotomy (a popular procedure in the late 1940s) denigrated not the surgery, but the absence of scientific controls that might shed light on its therapeutic effectiveness. Both of these documents suggested doubts about the efficacy of certain somatic therapies, if not outright antipathy toward those therapies—a position certain to anger those who did not share a psychodynamic orientation. Moreover, GAP was raising, perhaps implicitly, a controversial issue, namely, the right of the APA to define acceptable and unacceptable therapies. Other GAP reports dealt with medical education, psychiatric social work, the improvement of state mental hospitals, community mental hygiene programs, and clinical psychology as a specialty.[15]

Nowhere was the orientation of GAP better revealed than in its reports dealing with the role of psychiatrists in international relations, and with the social responsibility of psychiatry. The first, although specifically disclaiming for psychiatry "sole or special wisdom in settling the problems of nations or the future of society," claimed nevertheless that the specialty had an important role in international relations because of its "specific competence" in "individual motivation." The document on the social responsibility of psychiatry represented a powerful affirmation of psychodynamic principles. Its authors maintained that the "dynamics of personality" could only be understood "in terms of a bio-psycho-social continuum." They rejected out of hand the dichotomy between biological and social causation, the distinction between organic and functional. Psychosocial phenomena required instead a dynamic and unified interpretation of the interaction between individual and society. Consequently, psychiatrists had to be sensitive to both internal psychic factors and external social determinants. In calling for the "development of criteria of social action, relevant to the promotion of individual and communal mental health," the document favored

> the most intensive study of the psycho-social factors influencing human welfare. We favor the application of psychiatric principles to all those problems which have to do with family welfare, child rearing, child and adult education, social and economic factors which influence the community status of individuals and families, inter-group tensions, civil rights and personal liberty.
>
> The social crisis which confronts us today is menacing; we would surely be guilty of dereliction of duty did we not make a conscientious effort to apply whatever partial knowledge we now possess in the interests of counteracting of social danger and promoting of healthier being, both for individuals and groups.
>
> This, in a true sense, carries psychiatry out of the hospitals and clinics and into the community.[16]

GAP members, in addition to issuing published reports, were disproportionately active within the APA. During its first three years 177 individuals joined GAP. Between mid-1947 and mid-1948, 53 of them held 72 APA committee positions. Ten out of the 15 individuals on the APA Council, 4 out of 5 on the Executive Committee, 3 out of 4 national officers, and the medical director belonged to GAP. Thirteen out of 26 APA standing committee chairmen were members, with the expectation that this would increase to 20 by 1949. Other data suggested the prestige of GAP members. Many were directors of institutions or clinics; the bulk were board certified; 120 were engaged in teaching activities, of whom 51 held the rank of professor, 37 associate professor or associate, and 35 lecturer or instructor. GAP members also tended to hold medical degrees from the most prestigious institutions: 20 had studied at Harvard and 16 at Johns Hopkins (out of a total of 126 American medical school graduates). The overwhelming majority were located in urban centers with elite medical schools. Although members were often referred to as "Young Turks," they were by no means youthful. In 1950 the age of members ranged from 28 to 65; the average was 47.[17] Finally and perhaps most significant, virtually all were associated with the psychodynamic and psychoanalytic traditions and tended to be far removed from the daily activities of those psychiatrists employed in state mental hospitals.

. . .

Between 1946 and 1949 the issues raised by the reorganization effort and the founding of GAP became extraordinarily controversial and so polarized the membership that the very existence of the APA was called into question. The fight brought to the surface long-standing differences that touched upon the functions of the APA, the nature and treatment of mental illnesses, and the role of psychiatry. Personality conflicts only exacerbated philosophical and ideological differences. The eventual resolution of the struggle, however, laid the foundation for the dominance of psychodynamic and psychoanalytic psychiatry in the 1950s and 1960s.

After the APA meetings in May 1946, peace and harmony seemed to prevail. In July the Special Committee on Reorganization recommended that the position of a medical director be discussed and decided by the next convention. Indeed, the committee expressed a preference for a medical adviser rather than director, thus assuaging fears that the APA would become less democratic. It also proposed that the Program Committee arrange a series of discussion sections, each dealing with specific structural and substantive issues.[18]

At the convention in 1947 a day was given over to a discussion of APA problems. William C. Menninger served as moderator at the key session devoted to the question of whether the association should employ a full-time psychiatrist in the central office. In his introductory remarks, Menninger noted that wartime and postwar readjustment problems were so pressing that the APA, with its more than four thousand members, could no longer function in a loose and informal manner. The annual budget of $60,000 was inadequate, and its dues were far lower than those of other medical organizations. After a lengthy but not unfriendly debate, a general consensus emerged on the need for a full-time administrative officer and a sharp increase in dues.[19]

That the APA was changing was evident as well in the selection of officers. In deference to the seeming desire of members to exercise a choice, the Nominating Committee presented three names for president-elect, and five for the council. In a split vote, William C. Menninger (who was also president of the American Psychoanalytic Association) was elected with 41 percent of the votes; Nolan D. C. Lewis of the New York Psychiatric Institute received 35 percent and Arthur P. Noyes of the Norristown State Hospital 24 percent. Two of the three individuals elected to the council as well as the secretary and treasurer were GAP members. In Farrar's eyes Menninger's victory was preordained, but not because he was the choice of the majority. On the contrary, the selection of Menninger was due to the divisions among his opponents. Had the contest been between Menninger and Lewis, according to Farrar, the latter would have emerged victorious. Unfortunately, Noyes believed that he could win and hence declined to withdraw.[20]

For Menninger the results were eminently satisfying. Although disagreeing with Albert Deutsch's portrayal of himself and other GAP members as "Young Turks" and the characterization of GAP as a political organization, Menninger interpreted his election as a mandate to change the functions and purpose of the APA. "I think you are on the right track and should be confident as you are to carry out as many of these progressive changes as it is possible to do," Oscar Raeder (secretary of Boston Psychopathic Hospital) wrote to Menninger shortly after the meeting. At the same time Raeder warned of the danger "in overselling psychiatry." But for those who disliked the new spirit that seemed to be infusing the APA, the significance of the meeting was quite different. "There was sort of a wistful sadness about the meeting this year—A tenseness—with perhaps a lessening of the old comradeship of yesteryears," observed Walter L. Treadway.[21]

During the remainder of 1947, lines between the opposing factions hardened. Indeed, mutual suspicions and distrust were so pervasive that both sides used informers to report regularly on the activities of opponents and even to provide copies of key correspondence. By autumn, maneuvering had already begun in the selection of a successor to Menninger. GAP opponents settled on C. C. Burlingame. A staunch proponent of psychosurgery, Burlingame attempted to make the Institute for Living in Hartford a center for this radical procedure. The APA, wrote Cheyney in support of Burlingame, "needs at this time a forceful president who will not be dominated by a minority group and who will uphold the traditions of the association as a scientific medical group and not one that is trying to tell everyone else what to do and how to live." Fearful that the Nominating Committee might indeed select Burlingame as the sole nominee and "do a tremendous amount of damage to our program," Menninger had already undertaken an effort to identify a successor. Failing that, the alternative was to elect two or three additional GAP members to the council. "We could pretty nearly control things," he added, "and force the issue in various areas even if the president was opposed."[22]

As members were lobbying over the election of a new APA president, a weary committee on reorganization continued its deliberations. In October 1947 the committee considered a plan that would transform the association's basic structure. The main feature of the reorganization was the establishment of a House of Delegates with proportionate representation based on district voting areas. Modeled after the organizational structure of the American College of Physicians, the American College of Surgeons, and the American Medical Association, the proposed House of Delegates would presumably become the APA's legislative body. It, in turn, would elect a Board of Trustees with executive responsibilities. The plan, in brief, provided for the election of a representative congress and the transfer to it of all the functions of the council. The committee on reorganization felt that such a structure was more democratic and efficient, and it began to circulate a loose plan for comments and suggestions.[23]

The committee also presented to the council the name of Daniel Blain as its candidate for the position of medical adviser. Blain was then serving as chief of the Veterans Administration Neuropsychiatry Division; he held membership in GAP and had warm relationships with Karl Menninger. Although the specific duties of the office were vague, Blain had a coherent vision of the role of the medical advisor. He observed that such an official should (1) coordinate the association's various elements; (2) prod the APA to consider new issues; and (3) implement established policies. Blain also expressed a clear preference for the title "Medical Director," for the word *Advisor* was "weak [and] without definition or limitation in either direction." The council accepted Blain's recommendation, and on February 20 President Overholser announced the appointment to the membership. The establishment and filling of the new position had wide support. Nevertheless, those most hostile to GAP believed that the creation of the Office of Medical Director confirmed the existence of a conspiracy to seize control of the APA in order to impose the views of a small minority on the entire membership.[24]

At the APA convention in May 1948, long-simmering differences surfaced. The selection of a president-elect and the report of the committee on reorganization exacerbated deteriorating relationships. In the preceding months all sides had engaged in intensive lobbying in hopes of electing their candidate. Opponents of GAP won the first round when they succeeded in persuading the Nominating Committee to recommend Burlingame as the sole candidate, much to William Menninger's dissatisfaction. Many GAP members were reluctant to offer a second name from the floor. Finally, Dexter Bullard—a psychoanalyst not associated with GAP—agreed to nominate George S. Stevenson, head of the NCMH and a longtime proponent of psychiatric activism along a broad front. Bullard was an ardent psychoanalyst and was well known for his hostility toward all somatic therapies. In offering a second candidate, Bullard threw down the gauntlet when he emphasized that Burlingame's current views leaned toward "psychosurgery and lobotomy" (procedures long despised by Bullard), whereas Stevenson had long been associated with "preventive aspects." Bullard's comments drew a sharp rejoinder from Bowman, who felt that a public attack on a colleague was "highly improper." An emotional debate ensued, and in a polarized election Stevenson won by a vote of 389 to 342.[25]

The division was symbolic of the split in the APA. On the one side were those who emphasized psychodynamic and psychoanalytic theories, the significance of the social environment, social activism in a community setting, and various psychotherapies, and who had relatively few links with public mental hospitals. On the other side were those committed to a more traditional institutional orientation, an emphasis on the organic aspects of mental diseases, and somatic therapies (including lobotomy). Even when employing nonsomatic therapies, this faction favored persuasive-directive approaches, as compared with their opponents' preference for psychotherapies designed to help patients develop personal insights into their condition. There were some significant differences of background as well. The psychodynamic group had a high proportion of Jews, whereas traditionalists tended to come from established Protestant families.[26] That there was also overlap between the factions was evident. Many psychodynamic psychiatrists, for example, were not necessarily opposed to such dramatic somatic interventions as lobotomy, nor were their adversaries opposed to psychological therapies. Indeed, many members tended to hold eclectic rather than extremist views, but their choice lay between two polar positions.

Hostilities further intensified with the introduction of a series of tentative constitutional amendments altering the APA's structure: these established a House of Delegates and laid out a provisional geographical district system. Between December 1947 and May 1948 the committee on reorganization had worked on a draft of their plan and called for a year-long debate before a formal vote at the convention in 1949. Members of the committee also addressed a fundamental issue, namely, the degree to which the proposal fostered or diminished organizational democracy. Under a representational plan of government, members elected officers and representatives. In this sense the reorganization was more democratic than the existing structure, which gave the franchise only to those attending the annual meeting. Admittedly, if democracy were equated with a large town meeting, then the new constitution was not democratic. But the size of the APA, the committee insisted, precluded a town-meeting form of organizational democracy.[27]

Curiously enough, the committee on reorganization had been established before the creation of GAP. Moreover, its chairman—Karl Menninger—was never fond of GAP and insisted that GAP and reorganization were not related.[28] Nevertheless, within weeks after the end of the convention the reorganization plan and GAP had become—at least in the minds of opponents—one and the same. Indeed, at the end of the convention Theodore Robie, a New Jersey psychiatrist active in the metropolitan New York area, expressed the belief that Stevenson had obviously been elected by an unrepresentative minority, and that reorganization had to be defeated. He felt that the pendulum had swung too far in the direction of psychoanalysis and recommended the establishment of a new group—the "Psychiatric Democracy Associates or the Friends of Psychiatric Democracy"—to foster a middle-of-the-road position. Robie hoped that a new organization would recognize "any constructive treatment program, pure psychoanalysis at one end of the scale, psychosurgery at the other, and all the various modifications in between, [as] having the proper dignity and recognition worthy of any scientific endeavor."[29]

The dispute was not confined within the APA. The Vidonian Club, a social association of prominent psychiatrists (established in 1914) that met regularly in New York City, found its members embroiled in the controversy. At a special meeting in early June, the informal and often humorous agenda was replaced by a heated discussion of recent events. One member expressed the view that "regimentation was imminent," and that GAP was employing tactics that "smacked of Hitlerism and Stalinism." He opposed any effort to define acceptable therapies and insisted that the freedom of psychiatrists remain inviolate. Burlingame opposed secession, which could only have negative consequences. Joseph Wortis observed that the conflict had three distinctive elements: private practitioners versus hospital psychiatrists; a "feeling that the hospitals were not doing their job"; and a desire of individuals from the Midwest for power.[30]

At the same time, differences over appropriate therapies were aired in public, adding fuel to the fire. In September 1947 GAP had issued its report on electroshock therapy. Despite its moderate tone, the report aroused anger among GAP's enemies because of the implication that electroshock was being improperly employed. The controversy broke into the open when Robert P. Knight, former chief of staff at the Menninger Clinic and director of the Austen Riggs Foundation in Massachusetts, condemned "strong-arm" therapies, including electroshock, injections of sodium amytol, and lobotomy. Knight's comments were reported in the *New York Times*. Robie replied with an angry letter, which the newspaper published in July. Electroshock therapy, insisted Robie, resulted in high recovery rates for depression-related illnesses. Privately Bowman told William Menninger that the GAP Committee on Therapy was primarily "a committee of psychoanalysts and of persons who are interested in psychotherapy," and that these individuals were "obviously ignorant of electro shock therapy." Menninger, on the other hand, insisted that opponents were misreading the GAP report, which had only condemned its indiscriminate use under improper conditions. Electroshock therapy "was a very important part" of the treatment armamentarium at the Menninger Foundation, Menninger claimed, and he issued a joint statement with the president of the Electro-Shock Research Association upholding the efficacy of the treatment, but stressing that it was not a cure-all. In 1950 GAP issued a revised report that sanctioned outpatient electroshock therapy with appropriate safeguards. The new statement, however, reiterated the allegation that "widespread abuses" existed, and insisted on the need for research to gain a better understanding of the procedure. Whatever the medical merits of the therapy, it was clear that the debate had assumed increasing significance because of the broader theoretical polarization that underlay it.[31]

Although both sides made efforts at reconciliation in the late summer and autumn of 1948, the suspicions, hostilities, and mutual distrust of each other's motives precluded any amicable resolution of differences.[32] Even minor issues mushroomed. When *Time* magazine ran an article on American psychiatry, William Menninger's picture appeared on the front cover. Although Menninger insisted that he had been unable to dissuade or prevent the magazine from using his photograph, he came under considerable criticism from opponents who believed he had used *Time* to increase his influence.[33]

In late 1948, Robie, in collaboration with others opposed to GAP and reorganization, decided to form a counterorganization. William Menninger immediately attempted to head off a potential schism, but his conciliatory words fell on deaf ears. By the beginning of 1949 the Committee for the Preservation of Medical Standards in Psychiatry (CPMSP), chaired by Robert McGraw of New York, had come into existence. The new organization first invited all APA members to join in defeating the reorganization plan, which it charged was undemocratic. It demanded an amendment to the APA constitution that provided for a mail ballot on all important issues. What was required was a greater emphasis on "biological investigation and study, and less emphasis on teaching a patchwork of philosophical theories that the public has already rejected as bearing the imprint of neither science nor sense." The CPMSP attacked the medical director's office as both unnecessary and costly. Within weeks its charges grew more and more vituperative. By March the CPMSP *Newsletter* noted that the best thing that could be said about GAP "is that it was conceived on the emotional level of high school days and is reminiscent of the gappa gappa clubs." The worst "is that it was a devious political group established to obtain control" of the APA. The following month the CPMSP published a table that purportedly demonstrated the degree to which GAP had taken over the APA. Burlingame, who remained resentful over his defeat for the presidency, told Jack R. Ewalt that he had been an "innocent bystander" and was uninvolved. More important, Burlingame reported that the CPMSP was considering seeking an injunction against the continuation of Blain's office, beginning a suit against Menninger and other APA officers demanding that the funds expended in support of the office be repaid, spurring a congressional investigation of the relations between the Menninger Foundation and Winter Veterans Administration Hospital in Topeka, and revealing information that would "split G.A.P. wide open."[34]

The charges and language employed by the CPMSP came as a shock. The open airing of intraorganizational differences threatened to undermine public respect and confidence and thus destroy the very legitimacy essential to the well-being of any professional group. Even before the APA Montreal convention in the spring of 1949, the two leading antagonists— Menninger and McGraw—agreed "to do everything possible to prevent reports of dissensions reaching the press."[35]

Although most GAP members vehemently rejected CPMSP allegations, they nevertheless sought ways of defusing the situation before the Montreal meetings. Appel urged that Robie and his followers be permitted to present their views at the convention in order to avoid exacerbating their fears. More important, the meeting should rally the membership to "new goals, ideals, purposes and responsibilities." Maxwell Gitelson, a GAP member and future president of the American Psychoanalytic Association, disavowed the allegations. He expressed his own reservations, however, about the reorganization plan because it disenfranchised the APA's general membership insofar as policy formulation was concerned.[36]

The most diplomatic advice came from Bowman, who was not a GAP member and who had rejected the chairmanship of and membership in the CPMSP. Concerned with the preservation of civility and unity, Bowman insisted that William Menninger had underestimated the resentment created by GAP. Like the CPMSP, GAP was a "small, self-constituted body" that claimed "to speak authoritatively" for American psychiatry. The GAP committee structure paralleled that of the APA, reinforcing suspicion that the former was seeking to control the latter. He urged Menninger—as president of the APA—to separate himself from the issue of reorganization and to do everything possible to avert a schism that could only have disastrous consequences. Bowman addressed an even more critical letter to the CPMSP, scolding them for undermining Blain and his office and distorting facts. Blain himself was sufficiently distressed by the "dirt that is going through the mails these days" that he resigned from GAP to avoid even the appearance of partisanship and seriously pondered leaving the office that he had only recently assumed. He also expressed the hope that GAP would reorganize, broaden its membership, become more democratic, and even change its name.[37]

In the months preceding the Montreal meeting, a number of prominent figures set to work to prevent a schism. The committee on reorganization suggested that the vote on the revised constitution be deferred until significant alterations were made. It endorsed the election of officers by the entire membership and expressed the hope that the committee could finally be dissolved. William Menninger took a more conciliatory approach and prepared several low-key statements that were published in the *American Journal of Psychiatry*. The emergence of a middle-of-the-road group also contributed to the easing of tensions. John C. Whitehorn, head of the Henry Phipps Clinic at Hopkins and soon to become the new president-elect of the APA, decided to resign from GAP in the hope of ameliorating the situation. Whitehorn had never attended a GAP meeting but felt that the group had contributed toward the revitalization of APA committees. In this sense, he argued, GAP had accomplished its mission and should be dissolved. Although recognizing the logic of Whitehorn's position, Menninger defended the organization he had helped found. The heterogeneity of the APA, he observed, made it difficult to take a clear position on such issues as civil rights. GAP, on the other hand, could take a stand on such important problems precisely because it was a small and close-knit organization.[38]

That the stakes in the conflict involved substantive issues, not merely personality differences, was evident. On the first day of the APA meetings in Montreal in 1949, Albert Deutsch—a knowledgeable and perceptive journalist who was sympathetic to GAP—described the differences between the contending factions. There were, he noted, no fewer than three divisions within the APA. The first pitted "neurologically oriented" psychiatrists who stressed somatic factors and the use of drugs, mechanical devices, and surgery against those committed to psychoanalysis and psychotherapy. The second reflected a division between those who believed that the specialty should confine itself to the care and treatment of the mentally ill, and those who insisted that psychiatry had to play an important role in social reform. Finally, there was a split between "old-line psychiatrists" and a newer and more progressive group. In Deutsch's view the conflict among these three distinct but overlapping groups was not a sign of weakness but rather of strength, for it had revitalized the APA. In sympathy with Menninger and his followers, Deutsch implied that the CPMSP ("The Preserves") was seeking to discredit GAP by linking its social and economic activism with communism.[39]

At the Montreal meeting in 1949 the anticipated fight did not take place. Menninger's presidential address was conciliatory but forthright. Differences of opinion, he observed, perhaps had a deeper significance. Was not the real issue the movement of the APA toward social psychiatry? To what extent should the association provide leadership and advice on issues that were not strictly medical? His noncontroversial remarks, the dropping of the controversial reorganization plan, and the dissolution of the committee on reorganization helped to quiet matters. The election of Whitehorn as president-elect also contributed to the relative calm. Further, provision was made for consideration of a series of constitutional amendments that included the election of officers by the entire membership but excluded consideration of an AMA organizational model. The revised constitution adopted the following year did not mandate fundamental structural change. Moderation had seemingly carried the day, and the specter of a permanent split rapidly receded.[40]

After the Montreal meetings, most of the hostility engendered by reorganization and the founding of GAP diminished. GAP itself underwent a series of changes beginning in 1950 that altered its structure and goals. "I have the feeling," Walter Barton (superintendent of Boston State Hospital) wrote, "that G.A.P.'s mission has largely been accomplished." It was time, he added, to confine GAP's work to discussion groups dealing with significant problems. In 1950 GAP adopted a constitution, signifying its organizational independence. Although never explicitly repudiating the idea of transforming psychiatry, it became the vehicle for liberal and activist psychiatrists to express their views on a whole range of social and medical problems. The CPMSP continued in existence for a few years but by 1954 had disappeared from the scene. It had crusaded against a reorganization plan that probably had no chance of adoption, and its attack on the office of the medical director had no results other than to clarify the fact that Blain was an employee but not an officer of the APA.[41]

. . .

The significance of the internecine warfare within psychiatry in the late 1940s can easily be overlooked. Clearly, individual animosities and conflicting personalities played a role. Yet beneath the surface lay more fundamental differences. At one end were the traditional heirs of institutional psychiatry who were committed to a somatic pathology and organic and directive therapies. They did not share the liberal and activist stance of their opponents, and they rejected psychoanalytic concepts. At the other end were those who challenged institutional psychiatry, espoused psychodynamic and psychoanalytic ideas, urged the need for alternatives to traditional mental hospitals, and enthusiastically endorsed social activism.

In a superficial sense the transformation of GAP after 1950 and the failure of reorganization suggested that the effort to reshape American psychiatry had failed. William Menninger and GAP, however, may have lost the battle, but they surely won the war. During and after the 1950s the activism of the APA increased dramatically. The change was achieved less by constitutional means than by a transformation of the association's structure that infused new life into committees and expanded their activities and responsibilities.[42] Under Blain's diplomatic guidance the office of medical director gained in stature and authority. Slowly but surely, the APA began to take a vigorous role in dealing with social as well as medical and psychiatric concerns, which to a large extent mirrored the interests of psychodynamic members. Moreover, by the 1950s psychodynamic and psychoanalytic psychiatrists dominated the specialty. Their control of virtually all university departments of psychiatry ensured that an entire generation that matured in the 1950s and 1960s would share their views.

The significance of the internecine warfare between 1945 and 1950, however, transcended individual or organizational differences. Protagonists, perhaps unknowingly, were debating fundamental issues concerned with the foundations of personality and sources of behavior. For more than a century, psychiatrists had limited their activities to the care and treatment of institutionalized patients with severe psychoses or somatic illnesses with accompanying behavioral signs. For some, institutional inertia may have inhibited receptivity to change. Many, however, recognized the significance of providing care for patients who lacked families or were unable to survive on their own. In spite of some therapeutic successes, however, neither they nor other physiologically oriented medical colleagues had succeeded in identifying many specific disease entities or a clearly demonstrated etiology. Unlike the infectious model of disease (which appeared deceptively simple and clear), psychiatric classifications remained amorphous. Knowledge of brain structure and function was rudimentary, and therapies were empirical and nonspecific. Admittedly, it might have been possible for psychiatrists to concede their inability to explain complex physiological and mental processes. Such a concession, however, would have threatened the legitimacy of the specialty and perhaps opened the door to other groups claiming to possess answers.

In the postwar era a very different conception of the role of psychiatry emerged. Wartime experiences, which also enhanced the public image of the specialty, helped to strengthen an activist psychodynamic and social psychiatry no longer wedded to or identified with mental hospitals. The fight within the APA, to a considerable extent, reflected dissimilar approaches and ideologies. To a generation trained in a psychodynamic and psychoanalytic tradition, the community and society, not the mental hospital, was the arena for psychiatric activity. These activists sought to make the APA a vehicle for altering the location and manner in which psychologically troubled individuals were treated, and also for resolving significant social problems. To emphasize the association's social involvement, as we shall see, is not to imply that the APA ignored the problems of mental hospitals. Nevertheless, the activities and interest of its members were focused elsewhere. By 1957, for example, only about 17 percent of the ten thousand or so members of the APA were employed in state mental hospitals or Veterans Administration facilities; the remainder were either in private practice or employed in government, educational agencies, community clinics, and medical schools.[43] Indirectly, therefore, the APA, as an organization, slowly disengaged itself from public mental hospitals—the same institutions that had brought the association into existence.

What is also striking about the postwar era is the fact that the psychiatric debate was couched in traditional medical and scientific terms.

This was true even though the issues—the sources of behavior and human nature—were not, at least at that time, susceptible to conventional scientific analysis. Equally problematic was the kind of evidence that could shed light on what were perennial but perhaps unresolvable philosophical and ethical problems. Yet so firm was the faith in science and medicine that very few of the protagonists recognized that their respective claims rested on shaky foundations. Karl Menninger was one of the few who questioned the claim that psychiatry rested on a foundation of science and truth; he also recognized that the personal attributes of the psychiatrist played an important therapeutic role. Nevertheless, he was a somewhat idiosyncratic figure whose views often differed from those of his colleagues.[44]

Psychiatric activism carried the day. In the 1950s and 1960s the generation that had served in the military, had created GAP, and were committed to psychodynamic and psychoanalytic concepts came to represent the mainstream of psychiatric thought and practice. Their activities would help to reshape public policies and social attitudes toward the psychologically troubled and severely mentally ill, albeit with unforseen consequences.

CHAPTER THREE

Origins of Federal Intervention

THE EXPERIENCES of World War II and the organizational and conceptual changes within psychiatry, admittedly important, could hardly have promoted major policy and structural innovations by themselves. The lessons of World War II were not fundamentally dissimilar to those of World War I, and even the basic principles of psychodynamic psychiatry had their roots in earlier decades. That change had not occurred prior to 1940 was but a reflection of a quite different context. In 1920 relatively few psychiatrists had been exposed to psychodynamic or psychoanalytic principles, and the ideal of institutional employment still prevailed. More important, the expanded role of the federal government in the formulation of mental health policy was yet to come. Mental health policy thus remained the responsibility of state governments, which continued to pursue traditional institutional solutions.

Structural and intellectual impediments to change, however, had weakened or vanished by the 1940s. During the 1930s the New Deal had legitimated the concept of the welfare state, enlarged in fundamental ways the scope of federal activities, and strengthened the importance of scientists and intellectuals in the formulation and implementation of policy. World War II not only confirmed but accelerated these trends. Indeed, between 1941 and 1945 large numbers of younger social, physical, and natural scientists were employed in federal agencies. Their experiences, when superimposed on the events that occurred during the Great Depression, led them unerringly to the conclusion that national problems required national solutions. Moreover, hereditarian patterns of thought, identified with the horrors of Nazism, fell into disrepute, and environmental ideologies conducive to social activism gained in popularity.[1]

At the end of World War II, many individuals concerned with the problems of mental illnesses shared a passionate belief that changes in public policy were indispensable. Yet the impediments blocking innovation appeared formidable. Traditionally, the care and treatment of the mentally ill was a state responsibility. A century and a half earlier the authors of the federal Constitution had recognized their countrymen's fear of centralized power by restricting the authority of the national government and retaining a large reservoir of power for the states. The divided nature of the American constitutional system in turn placed seemingly insuperable obstacles in the way of those who wanted to deal with social problems on a regional or national basis. One alternative was to create a coalition to persuade state legislatures and governors of the necessity for new policy initiatives. In individual states such a strategy proved successful. During the late 1940s, for example, Karl and William Menninger played forceful and decisive roles in Kansas because of their charismatic personalities and national visibility. By cultivating close relationships with state officials, they made the Menninger Foundation into a potent force for change.[2] Their activities resulted in a dramatic improvement in the state's mental hospitals. But Kansas was not the nation; its example could not be easily emulated. Generally speaking, the sheer number and diversity among the states militated against broad-gauged changes in mental health policy.

Another alternative was to expand the role of the federal government and perhaps create some form of state-federal partnership. The prospects for such a development were not especially bright. Responsibility for care and treatment of the mentally ill still resided with the states. As far back as 1854 a presidential veto of a land-grant bill had ensured that the federal government would play no role in mental health policy. The PHS Division of Mental Hygiene, created in 1930, dealt only with narcotic addiction problems. But the National Mental Health Act of 1946—a key measure that proved a turning point—ended the tradition of federal inactivity. The act provided psychiatric activists with an unprecedented opportunity to introduce changes that they deemed appropriate, and in succeeding decades the federal government would play a prominent, if not a decisive, role in the evolution of mental health policy.

· · ·

That the federal government would assume new responsibilities in mental health was by no means a foregone conclusion. Incremental steps rather than broad policy innovations seemed to offer the best means for transforming the role of the national government. In 1936 the Mental Hospital Survey Committee was created through the collaborative efforts of the NCMH, the APA, and other major medical associations. PHS officials were enthusiastic and agreed to foster cooperative relationships. Assistant Surgeon General Walter Treadway was named chairman, and additional PHS personnel were assigned to the committee. Within several years the Mental Hospital Survey Committee had produced several studies of mental hospitals. Even before World War II, therefore, it was evident that some health officials were receptive to proposals that broadened the responsibilities of the federal government in the mental health field.[3]

At about the same time Lawrence C. Kolb, a psychiatrist in charge of the Division of Mental Hygiene, undertook a quiet campaign to persuade

Congress to establish a National Neuropsychiatric Institute in the PHS modeled somewhat after the National Cancer Institute, established by law in 1937. Kolb believed that "fatalistic" attitudes toward nervous and mental disorders were responsible for the neglect of basic research. The little research that had been done was "superficial, uncoordinated," directionless, and unproductive. Recent findings, however, suggested "a more hopeful line of research." Kolb pointed to work that demonstrated relationships between vitamin deficiencies and mental states, as well as between blood sugar levels and mood. The time was appropriate, therefore, for an expansion of "fundamental research" on the physiological basis of mental and nervous disorders, although he conceded that psychology and criminology ought not to be neglected. Kolb's plan called for the creation of a National Neuropsychiatric Institute that would have authority to conduct research and provide funding for work "at some strategic places."[4]

The initial response among psychiatrists and neurologists was enthusiastic. A few professional associations, including the APA, endorsed the concept. Only the AMA proved recalcitrant. Doubts about the propriety of using federal funds for such a purpose outweighed any merits, and the AMA tabled a motion offered by its Section on Nervous and Mental Disorders supporting the initiative. Preoccupation with war-related issues forestalled congressional action, and the proposal to establish the institute was stillborn.[5]

Between 1941 and 1945 Americans devoted their undivided attention to waging World War II. The demands of combat, of course, magnified medical needs and strengthened the hands of those who believed that the American health care system had to be reorganized. During the war the thrust toward specialization accelerated as it became increasingly clear that general medical practice would decline. At the same time new relationships were forged among the federal government, physicians, and medical institutions. Medical schools received federal subsidies to increase the production of physicians, and research on drugs and technology was spurred by federal contracts. The war also hastened the expansion of the PHS's role. By 1943 Surgeon General Thomas Parran and his colleagues were quietly campaigning to expand their agency's authority to award grants to investigate a variety of diseases, thus building on the legislation that had created the National Cancer Institute. Partial success came in early 1944 with the passage of Public Law 410, which codified several decades of legislation pertaining to the PHS. Parran also moved to assume responsibility for research contracts awarded by the Committee on Medical Research of the Office of Scientific Research and Development. One of the shrewdest federal bureaucrats of his generation, he oversaw the conversion of these wartime research contracts into grants—

a development that became the basis for the phenomenal expansion of the NIH extramural research program. Indeed, the federal health bureaucracy made certain that even the National Science Foundation, established in 1950, would not diminish the research component of the PHS. Hence the latter's extramural research program remained intact, assuring its hegemony in medical research.[6]

By 1945 conditions appeared propitious for dramatic changes in the nation's health care system. A prewar medical coalition that had been seeking to extend health care innovations as widely as possible emerged from the war determined to forge a broad consensus on the need to rationalize the health system by creating formal institutional relationships linking community and teaching hospitals, and to place medical care on a more secure economic footing. Even before the cessation of hostilities the New York Academy of Medicine and the American Hospital Association had established influential commissions to develop agendas for reorganizing health care in the postwar era. Both groups were united in their desire to promote change by consensus rather than conflict. The academy's Committee on Medicine and the Changing Order, for example, urged the adoption of a multifaceted program. Its members recommended that community hospitals be upgraded by developing relationships with larger teaching hospitals and medical schools; that the benefits of modern medicine be made available to all; that the supply of physicians be increased; that voluntary prepayment plans cover as many people as possible; and that federal funds be distributed to solve "many of the problems of medical care." By mid-1946 Congress had enacted the Hill-Burton Act, which provided generous federal subsidies for hospital construction. Under this legislation tens of thousands of new beds were added to hospitals within a short period.[7]

Health care institutions and services were not the only beneficiaries of federal legislation. Biomedical research and medical education were equally affected by new policies and attitudes. The introduction of more sophisticated diagnostic technologies and treatments in the postwar era combined to produce a euphoric faith that the conquest of disease was only a matter of time, given the will and appropriate resources.

Even before the end of the war a lobby to promote federal support of biomedical research was in the making. Between the late 1940s and 1960s this lobby was led by the redoubtable Mary Lasker, a strong-willed and determined woman whose charisma and money were employed in singular pursuit of the goal of conquering disease. The lobby proved extraordinarily successful in reshaping the NIH and making the federal government a major participant in medical research and training. Faith in the redemptive powers of science was equally evident in the deliberations of President Harry S. Truman's Scientific Research Board. Scientific discovery, insisted its members, was "the basis for our progress against poverty and disease." The board devoted an entire volume to medical research and insisted upon the necessity of a "national policy." "The challenge of our times," wrote its members, "is to advance as rapidly as possible the understanding of diseases that still resist the skills of science, to find new and better ways of dealing with diseases for which some therapies are known, and to put this new knowledge effectively to work." To achieve these goals its members called for massive increases in federal support for research and training. In the ensuing decade these and similar recommendations were met with enthusiasm by a bipartisan congressional coalition persuaded that a national health policy could alleviate, if not eliminate, many of the traditional illnesses of humanity.[8]

. . .

After 1945 the structure of the nation's health care system began to undergo significant changes as a result of new federal policy initiatives and programs. During these years, utilization of services and expenditures increased rapidly in response to an enhanced public faith in the efficacy of medical intervention as well as a rising standard of living and general prosperity. Within such an atmosphere, not unexpectedly, an effort was made to ensure that the benefits of new health policies would be distributed as well to the mentally ill. To include mental illness within traditional health policy parameters was no simple task. Care and treatment of the mentally ill was a state function, whereas general medical care—with some exceptions—was a physician/consumer-driven system. Yet the rapid growth in the economy enhanced the prospect of securing additional resources for mental health, for new funding could come out of growth rather than the redistribution of resources.

More than any other individual, Robert H. Felix played the key role in ending the long-standing tradition of federal passiveness in mental health policy. Born in 1904 in Kansas, Felix received his M.D. from the University of Colorado. He then served as a Commonwealth Fund Fellow in Psychiatry under Franklin G. Ebaugh at the Colorado Psychopathic Hospital. Ebaugh was an early proponent of a community-oriented psychiatry. In 1940 he had published an important work emphasizing the need to treat many psychiatric patients in general hospitals and thereby avoid lengthy confinement in mental institutions.[9] After completing his studies under Ebaugh, Felix joined the PHS and eventually was assigned to its narcotic addiction facility in Kentucky. During World War II Kolb offered him an opportunity to attend the School of Public Health at Johns Hopkins. In Baltimore Felix was exposed to the psychobiological concepts of Adolf Meyer and an appreciation of the public health dimension of mental illnesses. Late in the war Felix succeeded Kolb as head of the Division of Mental Hygiene.

At that time the PHS was directed by Thomas Parran, who had been elevated to the position of surgeon general by Franklin Delano Roosevelt in 1936. During Parran's long tenure, the PHS dramatically expanded its role and responsibilities. Perhaps the most influential surgeon general in the history of the PHS, Parran was especially supportive of younger career officers. He urged Felix to think about the outlines of a new program for the Division of Mental Hygiene. Felix immediately resurrected Kolb's proposal for an institute, but in sharply expanded and altered form. Kolb was primarily concerned with research. Although supportive of research, Felix was also persuaded of the necessity of a far broader federal role. A shrewd and knowledgeable individual completely familiar with organizational politics, Felix set to work to create a new bureaucratic structure within the federal government. In brief, his goal was to alter the entrenched tradition of state responsibility for mental illnesses and use the prestige and resources of the national government to redirect mental health policies. Aware of pending changes in federal health policies generally, he was determined that mental health not be excluded.[10]

In late 1944 Felix prepared a memorandum sketching out some of his views. Parran was enthusiastic and promptly put Felix in touch with several key officials at the Federal Security Agency (predecessor of the Department of Health, Education, and Welfare), including Mary E. Switzer, who played an influential role in federal health and rehabilitation policy from the 1940s to the 1960s. They assisted in drafting legislation authorizing the establishment of a National Neuropsychiatric Institute whose functions included but also transcended research. The draft gave the proposed institute responsibility in the training and education of professional personnel, as well as a role in providing psychiatric services. Felix also wanted the bill written in latitudinarian language in order to maximize his ability to shape future policy decisions. Although denying that he was engaged in lobbying (and perhaps violating the provisions of the Hatch Act), Felix was clearly mobilizing the not inconsiderable power of the federal bureaucracy to influence the legislative process in subtle but significant ways.[11]

With a draft in hand and with the support of a small coterie of individuals that included Mary Lasker, Felix had to find a cooperative congressman to propose appropriate legislation. Through Switzer he met J. Percy Priest, a Tennessee congressman interested in psychiatry and the mentally ill. Priest was so aroused by the proposal that he promptly introduced the bill into the House of Representatives in March 1945. Indeed, Switzer and Felix felt that the action was precipitous and premature, since the groundwork to ensure passage had yet to be laid. A few months later

Claude Pepper, the New Deal Democrat from Florida, sponsored similar legislation in the Senate. A number of other prominent congressional figures—many of whom would play important roles in federal biomedical policy in succeeding decades—also lined up in support of the bill.[12]

The passage of legislation, even under the best of circumstances, is fraught with difficulties. Support both within and without Congress had to be mobilized. Members of Congress—few of whom possessed either interest in or knowledge about mental illnesses—had to be persuaded that there were compelling reasons to move in a direction that expanded the role of the national government and implied the commitment of substantial resources. Moreover, in 1945 Congress was inundated by the claims of many interest groups, each arguing that its proposal merited a high priority on the legislative agenda. Felix and his supporters thus faced a formidable task in steering the legislation through a lengthy and complex process and sidestepping numerous pitfalls. The legacy of the New Deal welfare state and growing support for health care legislation, however, provided a favorable atmosphere for mental health policy innovations.

At the outset Felix had to ensure that his psychiatric colleagues would support his initiative. George S. Stevenson and the NCMH were favorable, especially since the bill seemed to endorse community-oriented programs. The APA was slightly more ambivalent, perhaps because the reorganization controversy had begun to fracture professional unity. Winfred Overholser, secretary-treasurer of the APA and superintendent of St. Elizabeths Hospital in the District of Columbia, as well as others, were opposed. Overholser, for example, favored grants to existing institutions—especially his own—and opposed the establishment of another institute within the PHS. The APA initially endorsed the bill's general aims rather than its specific provisions. David Rapaport, the eminent Menninger Foundation psychologist, feared that the bill minimized the crucial role of childhood and would virtually exclude psychologists and other mental health professionals from positions of authority.[13]

The occasional infighting did not discourage Felix and his supporters in the slightest. In the months following the bill's introduction, they worked assiduously to persuade Congress that its passage would ultimately have an extraordinary impact on knowledge about as well as treatment of mental illnesses. In September the Public Health Subcommittee of the House Committee on Interstate and Foreign Commerce, chaired by Priest, held public hearings. Six months later the Health and Education Subcommittee of the Senate Committee on Education and Labor, chaired by Pepper, followed suit. The impressive battery of witnesses included not only psychiatrists and other mental health professionals, but prominent government officials and laypersons as well.

The individuals who testified rarely disagreed among themselves. Indeed, they tended to emphasize similar themes. Mental diseases, observed Parran, equaled physical illnesses in detracting from the nation's total fitness. More than half of all hospital beds were occupied by psychiatric patients. Yet psychiatry was a marginal and grossly understaffed specialty, and training and research programs were hopelessly inadequate. Research expenditures in psychiatry amounted to about twenty-five cents per year for each case of mental illness, whereas the comparable figure for poliomyelitis was one hundred dollars. The vast mental hospital system provided "little more than custodial care." Outpatient clinics had the potential for early diagnosis, effective treatment, and aftercare, but a fivefold expansion in their numbers was required if they were to become effective. Staff shortages compounded existing problems; there was a desperate need for 4,000 more psychiatrists in public institutions alone. Parran estimated that an adequate public mental health program required an additional 1,800 psychologists, 14,000 psychiatric nurses, 6,000 psychiatric social workers, 1,400 occupational therapists, 15,500 attendants, and 3,400 other technical personnel.[14]

Subsequent witnesses supported and added to Parran's testimony. Major General Lewis B. Hershey described the high rates of wartime rejections for military service of individuals with neuropsychiatric problems. William C. Menninger and others stressed the applicability of the lessons of war to the civilian sector. Francis Braceland (chief of the navy's Neuropsychiatric Branch) argued for a multifaceted community educational program that would disseminate psychiatric information among other professional and lay groups. Above all, those who testified emphasized not merely the problems of the present, but the expectation of a brighter future. "The job of tomorrow's psychiatry," according to Braceland, "is large scale prevention. . . . In the same manner in which medicine has overcome such diseases as lockjaw and smallpox by prophylaxis, psychiatry can do likewise by providing information and a public understanding which will prevent much unnecessary unhappiness."[15]

During the hearings some dissatisfaction surfaced over the use of the word *neuropsychiatric* in the draft bill. Karl Bowman, president of the APA, complained that the term was a misnomer, and he suggested that the new agency be named the National Psychiatric Institute. Albert Deutsch proposed that "Mental Health" be substituted for "Neuropsychiatric" in the title. The issue involved more than semantic differences. World War II had clearly stimulated concern with mental disorders, whereas strictly neurological problems (e.g., strokes, brain tumors, multiple sclerosis) had yet to catch public attention. Deutsch's famous exposés of conditions within mental hospitals, which began to appear when the

Senate subcommittee was holding public hearings, had also focused attention on the plight of the mentally ill. Tactical considerations, therefore, suggested an emphasis on mental rather than neurological disorders. Moreover, psychodynamic psychiatrists were clearly the driving force behind the legislation; their preoccupation with environmental and psychological issues made them receptive to a change in terminology.[16]

Only Lawrence Kubie, a psychiatric consultant to the Office of Scientific Research and Development (created by the federal government in 1941 to develop a coordinated wartime policy) expressed reservations. Kubie was not unsympathetic toward the purposes of the bill but was troubled by its essential details. He thought that future funding needs were grossly underestimated. More important, he insisted that the organizational structure of the proposed institute was inappropriate and urged that the research component be separated from the organization responsible for awarding grants. Research required long-term investments rather than fluctuating and uncertain annual appropriations. To make a research institute dependent upon "the changing winds of economics and politics" would inevitably lead to shortsighted rather than long-range projects. He therefore proposed that Congress provide the research component with a permanent endowment and grant it independence. The backwardness of psychiatry as compared with medicine generally, he observed, required that the specialty be singled out for unique consideration and perhaps exempted from congressional oversight.[17]

Both congressional subcommittees were clearly supportive of the intent of the legislation. Concern with health care was pervasive at the time, and there seemed no compelling reasons why mental illnesses should be excluded from impending federal initiatives. The subcommittee members' relative lack of familiarity with psychiatry and mental diseases was probably responsible for their failure to probe in depth the testimony presented by distinguished witnesses. Consequently, they tended to accept rather than challenge substantive claims; their focus was often on peripheral issues of cost and implementation. Only two members indicated possible areas of concern. Senator Robert H. Taft was fearful that all research was becoming dependent on federal funding, and the private sector's involvement was being correspondingly diminished. Congressman Clarence J. Brown had other reservations. An incremental legislative process, he suggested, would ensure steady increases in annual appropriations irrespective of actual needs. More important, he was apprehensive that the federal government might become involved in "routine bed care of mental patients." Although assured by witnesses that such was not the case, Brown believed that the wording of the bill had to be amended to make clear that the role of the federal government would be limited to research and the dissemination of information and advice. Services, he concluded, had to remain a state and local responsibility; federal intervention could only be counterproductive.[18]

The House and Senate committees reported favorably on the bill. Their rationale paralleled the public testimony of prominent witnesses. Both committees also agreed to substitute the term *psychiatric* for *neuropsychiatric*. Nevertheless, their members conceded that the nomenclature of the specialty was "not free from confusion." Hence they accepted the term *psychiatric disorders* but made clear that "diseases of the nervous system which affect mental health" were included. The ensuing debate on the floor of Congress added little to the deliberations. Opposition to the measure came only from critics opposed to any further extension of federal power. Support by such conservative Republicans as Taft and Brown, however, depoliticized the proceedings. The absence of psychiatric dissent precluded criticism or questioning of the analysis or claims of those who supported the legislation. By mid-March the House version passed by a vote of 74 to 10; two months later the Senate followed suit. A conference committee quickly ironed out minor differences, and the legislation passed Congress and was signed into law by President Truman on July 3, 1946.[19]

Although the National Mental Health Act did not lay out a specific blueprint, its very language suggested a break with tradition. Its broad purpose was

> the improvement of the mental health of the people of the United States through the conducting of researches, investigations, experiments, and demonstrations relating to the cause, diagnosis, and treatment of psychiatric disorders; assisting and fostering such research activities by public and private agencies, and promoting the coordination of all such researches and activities and the useful application of their results; training personnel in matters relating to mental health; and developing, and assisting States in the use of, the most effective methods of prevention, diagnosis, and treatment of psychiatric disorders.

The legislation incorporated three basic goals: first, to support research relating to the cause, diagnosis, and treatment of psychiatric disorders; second, to train mental health personnel by providing individual fellowships and institutional grants; and third, to award grants to states to assist in the establishment of clinics and treatment centers and to fund demonstration studies dealing with the prevention, diagnosis, and treatment of neuropsychiatric disorders. During the hearings some concern was expressed that federal funds would be used for the care and treatment of patients at public hospitals. Felix testified that the intent of the legislation excluded such an interpretation, and his view prevailed. The act stipulated the creation of a six-member National Mental Health Advisory Council to provide advice and to recommend grants, and the establishment of the National Institute of Mental Health with an intramural research program. The law authorized $30 million per annum for state programs and research, and $7.5 million for erecting and equipping a physical plant for the NIMH.[20]

. . .

The significance of the National Mental Health Act lay not in its specific provisions, but rather in its general goals and the manner in which they were implemented. The breadth and generalities of its provisions posed more a vision of the future than a specific agenda or policy. Indeed, federal policy in succeeding decades would ultimately be shaped not only by legislation and appropriations, but by the outlook of officials responsible for administering programs and distributing funds.

No individual played a more prominent role in influencing federal mental health policy than Robert H. Felix, who led the NIMH from its formal creation in 1949 until his retirement in 1964. His mastery of bureaucratic and organizational politics was only enhanced by his charismatic, gregarious, humorous, and outgoing personality. Felix used the authority of his position and his personal qualities to work with a variety of individuals and groups to forge new and innovative policies. Neither outwardly combative nor abrasive, he demonstrated an uncanny ability to set legislative and policy-making agendas, thereby reshaping mental health debates along lines of his choosing. His long-standing and cordial relationships with key congressional figures—relationships that were only strengthened by his willingness to provide them with psychiatric assistance in coping with mentally ill relatives—only increased his policy-making effectiveness.

Felix's views were suggestive of the shape that mental health ideology and policy would take in subsequent years. He retained close ties with both psychodynamic and biological psychiatrists but was not identified with either. His orientation rather reflected the belief that mental disorders represented "a true public health problem," the resolution of which required more knowledge about the etiology and nature of mental diseases, more effective methods of prevention and treatment, and better-trained personnel. Felix shared many of the views of Paul V. Lemkau of Johns Hopkins, an able and influential proponent of the public health approach and author of an important text on the subject. Public health, according to Felix, was concerned with the "collective health" of the community. Unlike clinicians who dealt with individuals, public health workers emphasized "the application and development of methods of mass approach to health problems," including mental illnesses. The NIMH's mental health program was designed "to help the individual by helping the community; to make mental health a part of the community's total health program, to the end that all individuals will have greater assurance of an emotionally and physically healthy and satisfying life for themselves and their families."[21]

Although conceding that mental hospitals would be required for the foreseeable future, Felix insisted that the greatest need was for a large number of outpatient community clinics (probably modeled after prewar child guidance clinics) to serve individuals in the early stages of any mental illness. Not only would these clinics avoid the stigmatization associated with mental hospitals, but they would point the way to effective preventive programs. Such clinics, Felix remarked as early as 1945, would provide assistance to nonpsychotic and prepsychotic patients with varying forms of personality disorders. Within a year after the passage of the National Mental Health Act, Felix and Switzer were already exploring the possibility of short-term training courses for physicians and other workers to organize and staff the community mental health program. "The guiding philosophy which permeates the activities of the National Institute of Mental Health," he told his APA colleagues in 1949, "is that prevention of mental illness, and the production of positive mental health, is an attainable goal."[22]

Possessing a vision of the future, Felix was initially confronted with complex organizational problems. The National Mental Health Act had authorized the creation of the NIMH but had been silent about its structure and its location within the PHS. Moreover, Congress failed to provide an appropriation before it adjourned, leaving Felix in the anomalous position of heading an entity without any resources. The immediate need was for funds to convene the newly appointed National Advisory Mental Health Council. Using a relatively minor provision in the legislation permitting the NIMH to accept gifts, Felix persuaded the small New York–based Greentree Foundation to provide a modest grant of fifteen thousand dollars that would enable him to function until the next Congress appropriated money.[23]

A far more important issue was the placement of the NIMH within the PHS. Beneath what appeared to be a strictly organizational problem lay more substantive issues. Organizational location, after all, could play a crucial role in shaping function and significance. One alternative was to attach the NIMH to the Bureau of State Services. Given the goals of the National Mental Health Act, such an affiliation was by no means unlikely. The obvious effect would have been to make the NIMH a service-oriented agency, a development that hardly meshed with Felix's more ambitious agenda. Instead Felix persuaded the surgeon general to place the NIMH within the National Institutes of Health (NIH), thus linking his organization with other research-oriented entities such as the National Cancer Institute. The price for this agreement was modest: NIMH eventually gave up the two federal drug addiction hospitals at Lexington and Fort Worth (except for the Drug Addiction Research Center at the former). The decision to place the NIMH within the NIH proved of considerable importance; it enabled the NIMH to exploit the extraordinarily favorable congressional sentiment in the 1950s that led to higher and higher appropriations each year. That the NIMH (unlike other institutes) was indirectly funding services as well as research and training was largely ignored outside of the PHS. Indeed, officials rationalized funding for demonstration clinics by placing them under the rubric of research. Consequently, Felix was able to exploit the identification of mental health with biomedical science during the 1950s.[24]

In the three years following the passage of the National Mental Health Act, Felix and his associates began to create an organizational structure that culminated with the formal establishment of the NIMH in the spring of 1949, although operations were under way by 1947. In its early days the NIMH had several components, including Professional Services, Publications and Reports, and Biometrics. The Professional Services Branch dealt with long-range program planning and advised other departments. Biometrics was responsible for data gathering and analysis, and in 1947 it took over the task of compiling mental hospital data from the Bureau of the Census, which had begun annual surveys in 1923. Slowly but surely the responsibilities of the Biometrics Branch grew in scope and sophistication as quantitative analysis became a distinguishing characteristic of the social sciences. Under Morton Kramer this division worked to develop standardized classifications for data collection that would in turn create the basis for sophisticated and useful statistical and epidemiological analyses, and the division also sought to persuade states to establish strong statistical bureaus. Publications and Reports was charged with the dissemination of information about mental illness and its prevention. It not only supervised the publication of technical and professional materials but produced films, exhibits, study kits, catalogs, and printed materials intended for use by the general public. Three extramural branches (Research, Community Services, and Training) were responsible for implementing the grants programs (which ultimately accounted for more than three-quarters of the total NIMH annual appropriation). The National Advisory Mental Health Council, composed of external medical, scientific, and lay members, had responsibility for developing policy proposals and reviewing and recommending support of research and training grants.[25]

The NIMH also developed a small but significant intramural research program. When the institute was first established, it acquired the Drug Addiction Research Center at the Federal Narcotic Farm and Hospital in

Lexington. Research on drug addiction continued as an important component in the intramural program and included physiological and psychological studies. The first work on the Bethesda campus was conducted by Wade Marshall, a neurophysiologist interested in cortical function, and in 1953 his unit became the Laboratory of Neurophysiology.

The intramural research program came into its own in 1951 when Felix recruited Seymour S. Kety as scientific director. Personally preoccupied with extramural issues and relations with Congress, Felix gave Kety maximum freedom to develop the intramural program. Cognizant that targeted research on many mental illnesses was somewhat premature, Kety organized the intramural program along disciplinary lines while stressing multidisciplinary cooperation. Indeed, until 1960 the NIMH and the National Institute of Neurological Diseases and Blindness carried on a combined research program because of his belief that knowledge about the nervous system required both biological and behavioral science research. Since his own interests lay more in basic and biological research, Kety recruited Robert A. Cohen from Chestnut Lodge Sanitarium as director of clinical investigations. At about the same time, John A. Clausen became the head of the Laboratory of Socio-Environmental Studies. In 1954 three new laboratories were added: Psychology (David Shakow), Adult Psychiatry (Fritz Redl), and Cellular Pharmacology (Giulio L. Cantoni). A year later the Laboratories of Neurochemistry and Clinical Science came into existence. Overall the intramural program tended to reflect the interests of its staff. Three major kinds of activities were characteristic: biological research, including neurochemistry, biochemistry, neurophysiology, neurobiology, and neuropharmacology; behavioral research in psychology and such subspecialties as sociology and social anthropology; and clinical investigations in psychiatry and medicine.[26]

Organizational structures are merely skeletons, even though particular forms may shape certain kinds of policies. Equally if not more significant are the goals and ideology of individuals who staff and administer their operations. The NIMH is a case in point of an organization whose activities to a large extent were guided by the underlying ideology of its leadership. This is not to imply that legislation, federal executive policies, or appropriations played minor roles, for such was not the case. It is only to insist that policy cannot be understood without some reference to strong-minded individuals determined to push policy in particular directions.

Given his views about the future direction of mental health services, it was hardly surprising that Felix's initial appointments to the National Advisory Mental Health Council represented a broad spectrum but included figures sympathetic to the principles of psychodynamic psychiatry and public health. They included William C. Menninger, Edward A. Strecker (University of Pennsylvania), John Romano (University of Rochester), David Levy (a key New York City figure in child psychiatry and orthopsychiatry), George Stevenson (medical director of the NCMH), and Frank Tallman (commissioner of mental hygiene in Ohio). When the terms of the latter two expired in mid-1947, they were replaced by Karl M. Bowman (Langley Porter Clinic, San Francisco) and Alan Gregg (director of the medical sciences at the Rockefeller Foundation). With the exception of Bowman, all were members of GAP (although their personal views were by no means identical). As a group these figures were sympathetic toward Felix's views about the desirability of moving mental health services away from traditional mental hospitals into the community and reshaping psychiatry along psychodynamic and socially active lines.[27]

The innovative aspects of NIMH policy were evident in three distinct areas: assistance to states, the inclusion of the behavioral sciences and nonmedical mental health professionals in mental health activities, and research grants. The National Mental Health Act of 1946 had included provision for grants-in-aid to states to assist them in establishing and improving their mental health services. Each state was asked to designate a Mental Health Authority to prepare a plan detailing how federal funds would be used and to maintain liaison with the NIMH. By 1947 every state and territory had acted: thirty-two designated their health department; the remainder selected departments of welfare, institutions, mental hygiene agencies, or other agencies. The Community Services Branch of the NIMH in turn sent representatives to meet with each state Mental Health Authority, thus beginning the process of creating a sympathetic national constituency. Although funds could be used for a variety of purposes, it was evident that NIMH officials were determined to use federal resources to persuade states to develop additions, if not alternatives, to traditional mental hospitals. The legislation of 1946, stated Felix in his testimony before a congressional subcommittee in 1949, had explicitly forbidden the use of federal funds for state mental hospitals. State officials, he added, had to develop "an extra-mural type of mental-health program; that is, the development of facilities such as clinics and other similar services." The ideal of the NIMH was one outpatient mental health clinic for each 100,000 of population (with rural areas being served by traveling clinics). In the eyes of their advocates, community clinics were the institutional embodiment of the continuum and psychodynamic model of mental illnesses; the presumption was that early diagnosis and treatment in a community setting would obviate subsequent institutionalization. The ultimate goal of federal officials was the availability of services for a broad range of individuals: emotionally disturbed children; adults not in need of hospitalization; and patients in the early stages of illness when prospects for cure appeared greatest. In addition, clinics would provide follow-up treatment of institutionalized patients on furlough, supervise boarded-out cases, and assume responsibility for mental health education in their respective communities.[28]

At the outset the level of funding for the state grant-in-aid program was relatively small. Indeed, the program never underwent significant growth. For fiscal year 1948 allocations totaled $2 million. The original legislation mandated some state matching funds; NIMH regulations mandated that states provide fifty cents for each federal dollar. By 1958 grants to states had only doubled to $4 million. In spite of modest funding levels, the impact of the program was by no means of minor significance. States used these new resources to move in nontraditional directions. In the first year of the program slightly more than half of the funds was used for mental health clinics; the remainder went to educational work, training, administration, and professional services. Twenty-six states established all-purpose psychiatric clinics, twenty-three children's clinics, and twenty adult clinics. By 1951 the NIMH had assisted 342 clinics that on average served 301 patients (or a total of 109,942). It estimated that about 20 percent (or 22,000 individuals) might eventually have entered a mental hospital if clinic services had not been available. This claim, however, was not based on any data. Indeed, one of the goals of the demonstration project established in Phoenix with NIMH support was to gather data on treatment outcomes in community settings. During the 1950s community-oriented and preventive programs existed in virtually every state, and—as we shall see later—some states had begun to enact legislation providing matching funds to local communities to establish outpatient mental health clinics. Moreover, state matching funds far outpaced federal allocations: by 1954 states were voluntarily providing $2.70 for each federal dollar (as compared with the fifty cents required under federal regulations). When the NIMH conducted its first survey of outpatient psychiatric clinics in the mid-1950s, it found nearly 1,300 in existence. Of these, 277 were associated with state hospitals and 500 others were operated or subsidized by states.[29] State officials in general were enthusiastic about clinics. The claim that early identification and treatment in outpatient community facilities would minimize the need for institutionalization was attractive to public officials faced with constant increases in the size of the hospitalized population.

In its efforts to assist states in developing community programs, the NIMH also established a few demonstration clinics. Such projects had multiple goals: evaluation of methodologies required to measure the mental health needs of communities; the study of environmental etiological factors; the working out of effective staff arrangements; and the testing of new therapies. The first such demonstration project was in neighboring Prince Georges County in Maryland, which already had a tradition of community support and involvement in providing mental hygiene services. The location was desirable on other counts: it could serve as a showplace for members of Congress and could be used to train NIMH personnel. The initial clinic staff consisted of a psychiatrist, two psychiatric social workers, a clinical psychologist, a mental health nurse, and two clerks. The focus was on the problems of children, although the larger goal was to develop community-wide preventive techniques. Much of the staff's time was spent in working with schools, public health nurses, parent groups, and courts and welfare agencies in the hope of preventing the onset of severe mental illnesses. The clinic's activities, the NIMH reported in 1949, "by obviating the need for hospitalization, decreased public expenditures, and by improving personal, marital, and vocational adjustment, conserved human and economic resources in the community."[30]

The most significant impact of the state assistance program, however, was not on the establishment of community clinics. Far more important were the relationships that developed between the NIMH and mental health professionals employed in community institutions. Beginning in the late 1940s the NIMH cultivated close relationships with such individuals by providing advice and assistance. By 1950 it had ten regional offices with seventeen mental health consultants in psychiatry, clinical psychology, psychiatric social work, and mental health nursing. The result was the creation of a new professional constituency with links to the national government as well as to state officials. In subsequent decades its members would contribute to the effort to shift mental health services from traditional state hospitals to community institutions by drawing on the seemingly inexhaustible resources of the federal government. Indeed, the rapid expansion in the number of nonmedical mental health professionals further strengthened community activities, since many were not employed in traditional mental hospitals. The result, noted the National Advisory Mental Health Council in 1954, involved divisions "between agencies administering institutions and those conducting community programs." Although NIMH regional consultants remained neutral, it was evident that a potential for conflict existed between community institutions and state hospitals.[31]

That the NIMH was committed to the development of new and innovative community programs was obvious. Nevertheless, the agency devoted relatively little attention to program evaluation; claims of accomplishments and program effectiveness were rarely, if ever, accompanied by supporting empirical data. As early as 1950 the National Advisory Mental Health Council received from one of its own committees a recommendation that funds be allocated for the investigation of methods and the encouragement of research "for determining the effectiveness of community mental health programs." Guidelines and knowledge about the kind of training required for community mental health personnel were all but nonexistent. By 1955 the members of the council expressed concern over "the vagueness surrounding the whole problem of community mental health, the unclearness surrounding the function and role of the personnel working in this area, and the kinds of preparation these people needed." A study by one of its subcommittees came to the conclusion that mental health evaluation was "necessarily difficult." A "baffling" problem, noted its members, "is how to ascertain the validity of results in the face of elusive variables, both known and unknown, which either influence results or present themselves for their relatedness with undue emphasis." After a survey of the literature, they conceded that there was a "thinness of the efforts at evaluation . . . [and] a confusion of levels of conceptualization."[32]

Innovation was especially evident in the manner in which Felix incorporated the behavioral sciences as integral partners within the NIMH. The National Mental Health Act was silent on the respective roles of disciplines. Much of the testimony before both congressional committees considering the legislation in 1945 and 1946 was given by prominent psychiatrists; the behavioral sciences—with the exception of a few very brief oral presentations and written communications by individual psychologists—were notably absent. Yet the behavioral and social sciences had been growing in significance and vitality since the turn of the century. By the 1930s, as a matter of fact, the publication of several psychiatric epidemiological studies suggested that this kind of research might be relevant to the problems of the mental illnesses.[33] During World War II, moreover, the employment of social and behavioral scientists in the military and the civilian sector of the national government opened new vistas and stimulated interest in research that could be directly related to human welfare.[34] Nevertheless, these disciplines had no institutional base within the federal government until the establishment of the National Science Foundation in 1950 and consequently had little access to the rapidly growing resources available for research.

That Felix would be responsive to an enhanced role for the behavioral and, to a lesser extent, the social sciences, was not surprising. His early training in psychiatry and public health had persuaded him that the social environment played a key role in the etiology of the mental illnesses. In an important and revealing article in 1948 (written largely by his collaborator, R. V. Bowers), Felix spelled out the views that would subsequently be translated into programmatic policies. Psychiatrists—that is, clinicians concerned with the individual—had neither the training, the time, nor the inclination to undertake research that might clarify the role of socioenvironmental factors. Past studies of incidence and prevalence had been limited to hospitalized psychotics and were flawed on a variety of counts:

they dealt with only one segment of the population, the seriously ill; they studied only those seriously ill who were hospitalized; and they took into consideration only those socioenvironmental factors included in hospital records. Data on the neuroses and mild disorders were totally lacking. Recent behavioral science studies of normal personality development, however, had produced "strong presumptive evidence that both the content and the orientation of personality are powerfully influenced by the social setting." What was required was self-evident, concluded Felix. "The community-perceptive techniques of the social scientist" had to be wedded with the "clinical perception of the psychiatrist." Epidemiology represented their logical joining place. It held the means of overcoming barriers that impeded the accumulation of scientific data—data that could illuminate the individual, social, and environmental roots of the mental illnesses and thus facilitate the development of appropriate therapeutic and preventive programs.[35]

Felix's commitment to collaborative interdisciplinary research was by no means merely verbal. Indeed, a substantial proportion of the professional staff was composed of individuals trained in the behavioral sciences and, to a lesser extent, in sociology and anthropology. An external Panel of Social Science Consultants was created and given the task of suggesting ways in which behavioral and social science knowledge and techniques could be employed to shed light on mental health problems. Its membership was revealing: the group included two sociologists (H. Warren Dunham and Robin Williams), an anthropologist (Margaret Mead), a social psychologist (Ronald Lippitt), and an individual whose interests spanned the spectrum of the social sciences (Lawrence K. Frank).[36]

The enthusiasm for the inclusion of behavioral and social science within the NIMH was understandable. In the late 1940s and 1950s the obstacles blocking fundamental biological research into the etiology and physiology of the mental illnesses were formidable. It is entirely possible, after all, to identify significant problems that are not yet at an appropriate stage for study because of the inability to meet specific prerequisites (e.g., lack of a specific technology). This generalization was particularly applicable to psychiatry in the immediate postwar years. Unlike infectious diseases (a classification based on etiology rather than symptomatology), psychiatric nosologies remained for the most part descriptive in character.[37] Symptomatic descriptions, however, were often protean, vague, and shifting, a fact that complicated efforts to design or undertake basic biological or physiological research. In many ways the psychiatric nosologies of these years resembled the medical nosologies of the previous century. Lacking any other basis for classification, mid-nineteenth-century physicians had expended a great deal of energy in an often futile effort to distinguish among various "fevers" (e.g., scarlet fever, yellow fever, rheumatic fever, typhoid fever, etc.). Not until the development of modern bacteriology in the late nineteenth century made possible a shift to an etiologically based nosology did some of the confusion dissipate. To compare psychiatric with earlier medical nosologies is not to imply that psychiatry was "backward." It is only to insist that the problems of undertaking research on the mental illnesses were extraordinarily complex because of the inability to relate pathology with behavior. General medicine faced similar kinds of problems when its focus shifted from infectious to chronic and degenerative diseases where knowledge of specific etiological elements was minimal.

Behavioral, and to a lesser extent social, science research on the mental illnesses (which emphasized broad social, cultural, and demographic elements) did not, at least superficially, face the same kinds of impediments as biological research. Moreover, by the 1940s such disciplines as psychology and sociology claimed to have amassed significant data and derived explanatory theories relevant to the study of normal and abnormal behavior in both individual and social settings. Psychodynamic psychiatrists were sympathetic to these related disciplines that emphasized social and cultural elements that shaped behavior. As clinicians, however, they had relatively little training in evaluating such factors and were even less prepared to judge the efficacy of therapeutic interventions or preventive activities in any kind of systematic or scientific manner. At that time psychiatric training (not unlike medical training) included little or no attention to research design, controlled studies, or statistical methods, all of which played a major role in behavioral and social science training. The conclusion seemed inescapable: research on the mental illnesses had to involve a multidisciplinary effort.

From the very creation of the NIMH, behavioral and social science research occupied an important position. One significant contributory element was the fact that the institute had taken over from the Bureau of the Census responsibility for the annual Census of Patients in Mental Institutions, which provided the most comprehensive data set then available. Equally important, the NIMH had in place a unit (Biometrics Branch) to broaden the collection and standardization of data and to expand coverage by including patients who were not hospitalized. By 1949 its officials were already planning to gather data on individuals under treatment in outpatient facilities and to sponsor studies involving the use of sampling techniques to derive estimates about the prevalence of untreated mental disorders. The scope of the Biometrics Branch steadily expanded. At a conference in 1951 Morton Kramer, the branch's chief, emphasized that the goal was not merely to gather accurate statistical data and to create a Model Reporting Area, but to encourage research that would shed light on such issues—to cite only a few—as therapeutic efficacy, outcomes, and appropriate hospital standards.[38]

That complex methodological problems remained was evident. Clausen, for example, warned that all prevalence studies would continue to "lack precision as long as classification must be based as at present upon overlapping syndromes rather than nosological entities."[39] In any case, in subsequent years the NIMH became the major source for the funding of psychiatric epidemiological studies, some of which played major roles in shaping the ways in which the mental illnesses were perceived and public policy analyzed and formulated.

The multidisciplinary thrust was especially evident in an early research project that involved both the NIMH and the newly established Mental Health Center in Phoenix, a community that lacked psychiatric services. The goal was ambitious: to develop knowledge about the process of implementing both clinical services and an effective preventive program. At the center a group that included psychiatrists, social workers, psychologists, and nurses was seeking to find out, according to Felix,

> (1) what areas of the city the majority of emotional problems come from that are reported to those agencies; (2) what are the problems that these individuals or families present; (3) what has been the disposition of these in the past, and (4) what has been the end result in these individuals.

The presumption was that such knowledge would facilitate the establishment of mental health programs elsewhere. The institute also awarded a grant to the University of Michigan Survey Research Center to assess public attitudes toward mental health and the familiarity of the population with local services.[40]

Nowhere was the broad and innovative nature of the NIMH better illustrated than in its extramural programs, which involved allocation of funds for training and research. By the end of World War II there was a clear recognition that if psychiatry was to play a more prominent and effective role, there would have to be a dramatic increase in the number of qualified medical and nonmedical mental health personnel. In the hearings preceding passage of the National Mental Health Act, as well as in annual testimony before congressional appropriations committees, Felix and other prominent leaders reiterated over and over again their belief in the necessity of increasing both the quality and the numbers of mental health personnel. Congress proved extraordinarily sympathetic, and funding for training gradually but steadily increased.

From the very outset Felix and others, both within and without the NIMH, insisted that funds be used to further both interdisciplinary and psychodynamically oriented training. A Subcommittee on Integrative

Training, appointed in late 1947 and chaired by John C. Whitehorn of Johns Hopkins, recommended that training programs emphasize the necessity for close collaboration among psychiatrists, clinical psychologists, psychiatric social workers, and psychiatric nurses (irrespective of the setting where treatment was provided). Since psychiatrists "had to carry the ultimate responsibility," it followed that their training had to involve the development of collaborative skills. Felix was supportive of such recommendations. Indeed, he wanted to ensure that "the concept of extramural psychiatry, or to term it better, preventive psychiatry . . . be pushed energetically," and that funding be employed to produce a corps of well-trained psychiatrists to work in medical schools that lacked qualified faculty.[41] Such a program would ensure that new psychiatric concepts would be disseminated among future practitioners.

The pattern of NIMH funding for training reflected its multidisciplinary and preventive concerns. Initially the number of awards and funding levels were relatively modest. In 1948 the institute made sixty-two awards and allocated $1,140,079. Within four years the program had nearly quadrupled in awards and allocations. Equally significant was the disciplinary breakdown. In 1948 the bulk of funding went to four disciplines: psychiatry (42.4 percent), psychology (18.4 percent), psychiatric social work (18.6 percent), and psychiatric nursing (18.6 percent). This pattern continued during the succeeding decade. By 1958 psychiatry's share was 39.3 percent, psychology 12.5 percent, social work 13.4 percent, and psychiatric nursing 14.9 percent. The remainder was distributed among the biological and social sciences, public health, and a few other areas. The level of funding, however, increased dramatically: in 1958 the NIMH supported 547 training grants with a total budget of $14.5 million.[42]

There is little doubt that training grants furthered some of the broader goals of the NIMH. The majority of trainees, irrespective of disciplinary affiliation, did not elect to work in traditional mental hospital settings. Admittedly incomplete data on initial employment following completion of training suggest as much. Between 1948 and 1951, 27 percent of NIMH trainees from psychiatry, neurology, and public health mental hygiene entered teaching and 33 percent were employed in psychiatric clinics; the remainder were in government employment or private practice. As time passed, more and more psychiatrists elected to enter private practice; by the 1960s about half had exercised this option. Similar patterns persisted in clinical psychology, psychiatric social work, and psychiatric nursing; employment in mental hospitals was clearly not a preferred choice. Following passage of the National Mental Health Act, therefore, federal funds helped to train a generation of mental health professionals whose career interests and activities lay outside of mental hospitals.[43] The implications of this development were of major significance, for it strengthened mental health policies not wedded to traditional mental institutions.

The awarding of extramural research grants by the NIMH exhibited a slightly different pattern. Research on the mental illnesses, as we have already seen, was confronted with formidable scientific and intellectual difficulties in the postwar era. For this and other reasons, it was virtually impossible for the agency to agree on a consistent and coherent policy that would guide its deliberations. Eclecticism, therefore, became the distinguishing characteristic of policy; the awarding of grants simply reflected the nature of the applications.[44] Research grants were given to those working within the newer psychodynamic and psychosocial as well as the older somatic traditions. Such a policy was understandable. Those who adhered to a biopsychiatric model had never ruled out socioenvironmental determinants; psychodynamic psychiatrists had not repudiated their belief in a somatic component. A few on the extreme fringes found such a blend unfathomable. But many psychiatrists held a moderate position, and the absence of a nosography based on a clearly demonstrated etiology tended to weaken either extreme.

The early appointments to the National Advisory Mental Health Council, which was responsible for both policy and the approval of grants, reinforced a nonexclusive policy. The philosophy of the NIMH, recalled Philip Sapir of the Research Grants and Fellowships Branch, "was to be very broad and to support not only work of direct clinical relevance to the understanding of mental illness, its cure and its prevention, but to provide a broad scientific base in the behavioral and social, and for that matter biological, bases of mental disorder." Indeed, the substitution of the term *mental health* for the older *mental hygiene* symbolized the shift from the earlier preoccupation, "a very narrow clinical concern with psychopathology," to a view that incorporated psychological, social, medical, and biological perspectives.[45] Such eclecticism was most congenial to the behavioral and social sciences, which quickly began to play a mediating role among the various psychiatric schools of thought.

The distribution of research grants during the first four years of the NIMH's existence illustrates its eclecticism. Awards were divided among diverse disciplines and subjects, and grantees' work included projects concerned with the evaluation of such diametrically opposed interventions as lobotomy and psychotherapy, as well as investigations of such diseases as schizophrenia, epilepsy, cerebral palsy, and psychosomatic disorders (table 3.1). In succeeding years, however, behavioral and social science grants became even more significant. In 1964, for example, 55 percent of all NIMH principal investigators came from psychology and 7 percent from sociology, anthropology, and epidemiology. Their com-

TABLE 3.1
Research Grants Awarded by the NIMH, July 1, 1947–March 1, 1951

Research Field	Number of Projects	Amount (dollars)	Percentage of Total
Child personality and development	10	433,100	15.1
Personality studies	4	92,883	3.2
Experimental psychology	16	241,917	8.5
Experimental neurology	16	239,801	8.4
Childhood disorders	6	359,068	12.5
Psychosomatic disorders	10	267,616	9.4
Epilepsy and convulsive disorders	5	114,992	4.0
Schizophrenia	2	41,256	1.5
Mental deficiency	2	37,743	1.3
Physical and sensory handicaps	2	66,608	2.3
Psychotherapy	4	209,685	7.3
Lobotomy	5	201,061	7.0
Sociology and epidemiology	6	136,456	4.8
Preventive techniques	6	246,754	8.6
Diagnostic and prognostic techniques	7	124,136	4.3
Selection and training of personnel	2	14,011	0.5
Miscellaneous	4	36,590	1.3
Total	107	2,863,677	100.0

bined share of the total funds amounted to 60 percent. Only 12 percent of principal investigators came from psychiatry; their share of the budget was 15 percent. Other medical and biological sciences accounted for 21 percent of the dollars distributed.[46]

That the mechanism for awarding grants was imperfect was recognized. As early as 1948 William C. Menninger and Jack R. Ewalt—in their report to the Committee on Federal Medical Services of the Commission on Organization of the Executive Branch of the Government (chaired by Herbert Hoover)—noted that short-term grants militated against long-range planning. Seven years later the commission's Task Force on Medical Services urged that the existing system be replaced by five-year earmarked grants to institutions and agencies in accord with some overall plan for health research. The full commission accepted a modified version of this recommendation that did not refer to a specific number of years. The staff at the NIMH was not unmindful of the issue. By 1957 they were discussing ways in which university administrations might be sensitized to some of the problems identified by the NIMH. Under such circumstances the staff conceded that judicious use of longer-term earmarked grants might be appropriate. Nevertheless, they insisted that the program that funded individual investigators be left untouched. Cognizant of public and political pressures, Felix opposed the fractionalization of his agency's programs "by segregated and earmarked funds."[47] During his tenure the issue remained academic for the most part; the continuous increase in levels of funding vitiated any sentiment for basic changes in the research grants program.

．　．　．

In the two decades following the landmark legislation of 1946, the role and activities of the federal government continued their steady expansion. In its early years the NIMH budget grew at a slow pace. When it came into formal existence in 1949, its appropriation was $9 million; six years later it had only reached $14 million. From this point on, however, the rise was dramatic. By 1959 its appropriation was $50 million, which within five years had tripled to $189 million.

Neither the executive nor legislative branch played a decisive role in shaping policy, although budgetary recommendations and appropriations laid down boundaries and limitations. The key figures rather were Felix and his associates. As the director of the NIMH, Felix developed close contacts with important congressional leaders concerned with health-related issues. Year after year he appeared before congressional committees. Rarely was his testimony challenged or subjected to careful scrutiny; he symbolized the faith of that era in the ability of medical science to uncover the etiology of disease and to develop effective interventions. As laypersons, legislators were not inclined to probe the extent to which the validity of claims could be substantiated by empirical data. Felix's enthusiasm at times proved disconcerting to his NIMH colleagues, some of whom attempted to persuade him to modify exaggerated statements. Nevertheless, under Felix the NIMH became an important component of the biomedical lobby that was so successful in persuading the federal government and the American people that the key to health and longevity lay in the discovery and application of new scientific knowledge. Indeed, its most important contribution was its role in helping to legitimate the importance of psychiatric and psychological services and to develop support for community-based mental health policies.

The political sagacity of Felix and his staff only added to their influence. In public they assumed a neutral stance and rarely criticized or offended those with whom they disagreed. They were particularly adept in building a variety of constituencies. Their support for training brought into the mental health professions thousands of sympathetic supporters, their funding of demonstration clinics and research projects enhanced their influence in higher education and local communities, and their message to the American people was one of hope and optimism. The organization was also cognizant of the value of public relations, and by the early 1950s the Publications and Reports Section was active in disseminating materials for the general public, press, radio, and television.[48]

The influence of the federal initiative, of course, can easily be exaggerated. By the 1950s, as a matter of fact, the expansion of health services was largely consumer-driven. To many Americans, physical and psychological health appeared within reach, and support for an expansion of funding and services became all but irresistible. A favorable environment, therefore, provided the foundation for a remarkable expansion of funding for both research and services, and the leadership of the NIMH was quick to exploit the situation.

That an emphasis on research, expansion in the number of trained personnel, and establishment of a system of community mental health services might not have the anticipated consequences was never considered. In the postwar era federal policies in mental health, with strong public and professional support, were directed away from institutional care. This is not to imply there was overt hostility toward mental hospitals. It is only to insist that federal policy was largely unconcerned with mental hospitals, and its resources were therefore employed in an effort to develop alternatives. Within a decade the pieces would be in place for a profound reversal of the long-standing policy of institutional care and treatment of the mentally ill.

CHAPTER FOUR

Mental Hospitals under Siege

THE IMPETUS for change in the 1940s and 1950s came from individuals and groups somewhat remote from state governments and public mental hospitals. Yet if their hopes and visions were to be realized, they would have to persuade state officials to support and to implement new community-oriented approaches. Such a task presented formidable difficulties. Under America's federal system, power is divided between national and state governments. The Tenth Amendment explicitly provided that powers not delegated to the national government were "reserved to the States respectively, or to the people." Centuries of experience, both preceding and following the adoption of the Constitution, reinforced the belief that responsibility for matters of health and welfare resided with state governments. Not all of them were prepared to surrender their prerogatives and autonomy in this regard. Moreover, states interpreted and carried out their responsibilities quite differently. In 1945, for example, the average annual per capita expenditure for maintenance in state mental hospitals was $386. The range, however, revealed wide variations. Wisconsin and New York spent the most ($563 and $512); Kentucky and Oklahoma the least ($198 and $217).

That a decentralized political system posed major structural impediments to innovation was self-evident. Yet the possibilities for change were by no means lacking. In the immediate postwar era a series of developments converged to create a coalition whose members were unified by their hostility toward existing policy and committed to experimentation. By the mid-1940s a series of exposés in the mass media—newspapers, magazines, novels, and movies—focused public attention on the shortcomings of public mental hospitals. The APA, an increasingly visible organization, as well as GAP, became involved in efforts to restructure institutional care. Toward the close of the decade the Governors' Conference, concerned with allegations of abuses as well as the seemingly endless rise in mental hospital populations and expenditures, authorized some broad-ranging investigations of state institutions and policies. Out of them came a series of proposals intended to reshape the foundations of mental health policy. Additional support for innovation came from private organizations and foundations concerned with improving the quality and availability of health care services.

Slowly, therefore, a powerful coalition made up of diverse elements began to take shape. The overriding objective of its constituent members—most of whom recognized the value of publicity and lobbying—was to forge new mental health policies to deal with the mental illnesses. They were generally united in their belief that state mental hospitals were deficient in crucial aspects, and they believed that publicity would lead to a ground swell of public protest that would force legislative action. Yet in the late 1940s there was no clear consensus on the form that innovation should take. Some critics urged that state mental hospital systems be rebuilt; others favored a shift toward community-based outpatient facilities. Nevertheless, the critique of existing policy prepared the way for change during and after the 1950s.

· · ·

At the end of World War II the nation's public hospitals faced a crisis of unprecedented proportions. State governments between 1930 and 1945, preoccupied with problems growing out of depression and war, paid little attention to the deteriorating conditions within their public hospitals. Despite chronic problems related to aging physical plants and staff shortages, the average daily census rose steadily; by 1945 it stood at 462,000. "Deplorable conditions" in mental hospitals, Dr. Frank Fremont-Smith of the Macy Foundation warned the American Hospital Association in 1946, posed a serious social threat. Discharged patients "will carry back into their communities maladjustments, hatreds, and feelings of aggression accentuated by their experience in our state mental hospitals." The prospect of further deterioration in the near future, he added, could result in "disaster for our patients and dynamite for the politicians."[1]

That conditions within mental hospitals were often deplorable was by no means arcane even if largely unrecognized by the public at large. Before the United States entered World War II, criticisms of mental hospitals were already appearing in the popular media. In the summer of 1941 Edith Stern's "Our Ailing Mental Hospitals" was published in both the *Survey Graphic* and the *Reader's Digest*. In a similar vein Albert Deutsch opened negotiations with the *Reader's Digest* to publish a two-part analysis of conditions in America's mental hospitals. When arrangements fell through, Deutsch prepared a series of columns for *PM*, a recently established New York City newspaper.[2]

State officials were aware of the problems discussed by Stern and Deutsch. In 1940, for example, Governor Herbert Lehman of New York (which had the nation's largest hospital system) appointed a Temporary Commission on State Hospital Problems to suggest ways to reduce admissions as well as to shrink inpatient populations. Concerned with existing conditions, Lehman sought (but without success) to persuade the legislature to place on the ballot a $50 million bond issue, the proceeds to be used to alleviate crowding. In its progress report in late 1942 the temporary commission suggested that expanded use of "shock treatments," parole, and home care could relieve pressure on the state's eighteen hospitals.[3]

The outbreak of amoebic dysentery and the ensuing deaths of a number of patients at Creedmoor State Hospital in Queens early in 1943 caught public attention. Deutsch insisted that the situation at Creedmoor was merely a reflection of what was "happening throughout our State hospital system." The war had lured attendants to higher-paying positions in industry, and the armed forces had inducted many hospital physicians. A weak and ineffectual State Department of Mental Hygiene had done little to alleviate a growing crisis. Deutsch was openly critical of the recommendations of the temporary commission; staff shortages precluded a greater emphasis on therapy. "Our mental hospitals," he concluded, "have returned to their 19th century status as asylums for the custody, rather than the cure, of the mentally sick."[4]

Facing an aroused public, Thomas E. Dewey (Lehman's successor) created yet another special investigatory commission. Dewey also directed the state commissioner of health to take all necessary steps to end the epidemic. The lack of confidence in the Department of Mental Hygiene led to the immediate resignation of its commissioner, Dr. William J. Tiffany, who believed that the governor had deliberately ignored him. Within weeks Dewey, disturbed by "the evidence . . . of long-standing deterioration and breakdown in the Department of Mental Hygiene," appointed another five-member commission under the Moreland Act to conduct an investigation and make recommendations. The commission's final report in 1944 was critical of the Department of Mental Hygiene. Although conceding that many problems were related to the wartime shortage of staff and the fact that mental hospitals were caring for an indigent aged population that more properly belonged elsewhere, its members presented a serious indictment of the existing system.[5] Nor was New York unique; between 1940 and 1944 such diverse states as Louisiana, Connecticut, Massachusetts, and Pennsylvania conducted similar investigations of institutions and policies.[6]

Most states ignored or overlooked the needs of their mental hospitals between 1930 and 1945. But it was not until the end of World War II that the depth of the problem was revealed. In the mid- and late 1940s the public as well as their elected representatives were provided with detailed and graphic accounts of the internal problems of mental hospitals. To be sure, such exposés were hardly novel. In the 1940s, however, intellectual, cultural, and social currents converged to create a receptivity toward innovation. In such an environment, journalistic accounts of institutional shortcomings would have a profound impact.

The opening salvo was fired by Deutsch, the crusading journalist who devoted his energies during and after the 1940s to the cause of psychiatric as well as medical reform. The son of Jewish immigrants, he grew up in harsh poverty and consequently identified with the poor and downtrodden. Although he never attended college, he was a voracious reader. Becoming interested in the mentally ill, he persuaded the NCMH and Clifford W. Beers to subsidize the research and writing of his classic book, *The Mentally Ill in America: A History of Their Care and Treatment from Colonial Times* (1937). In 1941 Ralph Ingersoll, the founder of *PM*, asked Deutsch to write a daily column for his liberal newspaper. Deutsch accepted, and the young historian emerged as a leading journalistic crusader for social justice and an advocate of government support for universal medical care.[7]

In 1944 Deutsch began to examine psychiatric facilities in VA hospitals and subsequently turned his attention to state institutions. In 1946 and 1947 he published several dozen lengthy articles in *PM* exposing the deficiencies in the nation's public hospitals. The city of Detroit, he wrote in graphic and moving language, "pays less attention to its humans, sick in mind, than it does to its machines. I have seen animals better treated and more comfortably housed in zoos than are the mentally sick inmates of Detroit's institution, which is not even an asylum much less a hospital." His personal animus, however, was not directed toward those who administered institutions. Indeed, Deutsch described the chief psychiatrist as a "humane and enlightened" person who conceded his failure to provide active treatment or even decent custodial care because of overcrowding and understaffing. Responsibility for such a dismal situation lay rather with the failure of states and cities to meet their obligations toward the mentally disabled.[8]

In succeeding months Deutsch published similar pieces about conditions in other state institutions. His message was reinforced by dramatic descriptions and photographs of crowded wards and neglected patients. On one occasion he compared California's prisons with its mental hospitals and concluded that he would rather be an inmate at the model state prison at Chino than a patient at Napa State Hospital, an institution that was "short of everything—but patients." Ironically, California—one of the nation's wealthiest states—ranked near the bottom in those categories characteristic of a modern and successful mental hospital.[9]

Deutsch's columns received considerable publicity. Yet their publication in a liberal newspaper that lacked a national audience diminished their potential impact. Deutsch, therefore, decided to use his journalistic investigations as the basis for a full-length book. Published in 1948, *The Shame of the States* bore a title pointedly parallel to that of Lincoln Steffens's famous muckraking exposé of early twentieth-century urban political corruption (*The Shame of the Cities*).

To enhance his credibility, Deutsch persuaded Karl A. Menninger, a friend, to write an introduction. Initially Menninger was reluctant. The book was potentially controversial, and its author had on occasion been labeled by conservatives as a "Red" and an advocate of socialized medicine. Then in charge of a VA hospital in Topeka, Menninger was fearful about engaging in activities that might be construed as partisan or political in nature. Overcoming his initial reservations, he prepared a draft, which he circulated to several prominent psychiatric colleagues. Their responses were generally encouraging, although some were worried that adverse publicity would deter families from sending relatives to hospitals where violence—potential and actual—existed. Only Arthur P. Noyes of the Norristown State Hospital in Pennsylvania expressed a lack of confidence in Deutsch, perhaps because of the journalist's fierce independence. In the end Menninger prepared a warm and appreciative introduction that concluded with the observation that beleaguered hospital administrators would welcome the book, if only because it was a fair and objective analysis of how public apathy and neglect were responsible for institutional shortcomings.[10]

In fact, *The Shame of the States* was intended neither to discredit mental hospitals nor to undermine their legitimacy. On the contrary, it was a clarion call for reform. Not a single public institution met all of the minimum standards set by the APA, Deutsch wrote. Yet the creation of an "Ideal State Hospital" was an achievable dream, and he proceeded to sketch out its attributes. The ideal hospital would be limited in size to a thousand patients; would be funded on a par with general hospitals; would have a competent and well-paid staff; would operate as a "therapeutic community" that utilized psychotherapy, group therapy, hypnosis, hydrotherapy, occupational therapy, and lobotomy (employed "with necessary caution"); would reject mechanical restraint and have more open wards; would make provision for aged patients in satellite colonies; would be affiliated with a nearby medical school; and would retain links with an interrelated chain of mental hygiene agencies, including family counseling services, child guidance centers, and special wards in general hospitals. He called upon an aroused citizenry to join in a coalition to ensure adequate appropriations and to rid society of "prejudices and vague fears that cloud our concepts of mental disease." Deutsch's faith in hospital reform, however, was less than complete. "I really would like to see," he wrote to a California official in late 1948, "far greater emphasis on psychiatric clinics in general hospitals, [and] less emphasis on building state hospitals." He urged the official to persuade the state's political leaders to pursue such a policy, which would "save the state money in the end" and promote the rapid recovery of patients "without having to send them to state hospitals."[11]

At the same time that Deutsch's articles were appearing in *PM*, *Life* published a lengthy piece entitled "Bedlam 1946." Its author was Albert Q. Maisel, who had already written and testified about defects in VA mental hospitals. The article's subtitle was even more graphic: "Most U.S. Mental Hospitals Are a Shame and a Disgrace." Many of Maisel's data were drawn from the personal experiences of several thousand conscientious objectors who, under Selective Service regulations, had volunteered as mental hospital attendants. Maisel compared conditions in mental hospitals to those in Nazi concentration camps and found few differences. He emphasized overcrowding, inadequate diets, widespread restraint, brutality, and poorly trained physicians and staff. Mental hospitals, he proclaimed, were "costly monuments to the states' betrayal of the duty they have assumed to their most helpless wards." Like Deutsch, he called for the public "to put an end to concentration camps that masquerade as hospitals and to make cure rather than incarceration the goal."[12]

One of the most popular magazines of its era, *Life* reached an extraordinarily large and diverse audience. Equally important, it employed visual materials in imaginative ways that often had a far greater emotional impact than the accompanying text. The photographs portraying patients in mental hospitals could hardly have been ignored by readers, for they demonstrated the pervasiveness of restraint, useless or forced patient labor, nakedness, overcrowding, idleness, and obsolete physical plants. Their effect was evident in the pages of such influential religious periodicals as *Commonweal* and *Christian Century*, each of which devoted its editorial columns to an approving discussion of Maisel's analysis.[13]

Many of Maisel's informants came from Quaker and Mennonite backgrounds, and their religious sensibilities were shocked and offended by their experiences. Indeed, their commitment to change was so profound that mainstream organizations like the NCMH were reluctant to become involved with them, perhaps because, as Alan Gregg of the Rockefeller Foundation observed, they "prove unmanageably determined and perhaps even reckless in obtaining their objectives." These conscientious objectors, therefore, formed their own organization, which in 1947 sponsored the publication of Frank L. Wright's *Out of Sight out of Mind*. "Inadequacy, Ugliness, Crowding, Incompetence, Perversion, Frustration. Neglect, Idleness, Callousness. Abuse, Mistreatment, Oppression." Such were the adjectives used by Wright to describe institutional conditions. Yet like Maisel and Deutsch, Wright did not attack the legitimacy of hospitals. Rather he too issued a stentorian call for their reform. He urged laypeople to become more deeply involved in the service of the mentally ill and called for a greater emphasis on training and research. Above all, he insisted that the state meet its obligations by providing adequate funding for both institutional and noninstitutional care, nonpolitical administration, and the involvement of schools, churches, and other community agencies "to promote mental health."[14]

Deutsch and Maisel were familiar with mental hospitals and psychiatry. Mike Gorman, by contrast, had no contacts with the mentally ill before 1946. A native of New York City, he became enamored of Oklahoma and its people during his army service. After his discharge in 1945, he went to work for the *Daily Oklahoman*. In mid-1946 the paper's editor received a complaint about conditions at the state institution in Norman and asked the fledgling reporter to prepare an investigative article. The request was to have a dramatic impact on Gorman's life. His investigations catapulted him to national prominence, and between the 1950s and the 1970s he became, with the financial backing of Mary Lasker, one of the most powerful mental health lobbyists of his generation.

In mid-1946 Gorman's articles began to be serialized by the *Daily Oklahoman*. In brisk prose he described conditions in the state's public institutions, which he conceded were among the worst in the nation. But Gorman was not content merely to criticize. With the support of his paper, he visited the Menninger Foundation in Topeka and the Colorado Psychopathic Hospital in Denver. These institutions, he informed his readers, succeeded where others failed. Their trained personnel were able to identify mental illnesses in early stages and provide restorative therapy. Gorman wrote in glowing terms of the work of the Menninger brothers, who demonstrated at both the Menninger Foundation and the Winter VA Hospital in Topeka the significance of augmented staffs and intensive therapy programs. He was equally impressed with the activities of Colorado's traveling mental health clinics, which successfully treated the "emotional maladjustments" of childhood and thus prevented "chronic mental illness in adulthood." Differing from Deutsch and Maisel, however, Gorman placed far less emphasis on institutional reform; he expressed a clear preference for early treatment in community settings.[15]

After his series in the *Daily Oklahoman*, Gorman began work on a full-length book. He signed a contract with the University of Oklahoma Press to publish "Oklahoma Attacks Its Snakepits" and arranged to have the work serialized in the *Reader's Digest*. When internal problems at the Oklahoma press blocked publication, the *Reader's Digest* published a condensation, and Gorman thereafter lost interest in the book. His articles also caught the attention of Mary Lasker, and she may have been responsible for the decision to designate him the winner of the Lasker Award in mental hygiene for 1948, a prize conferred by the NCMH.[16]

The most dramatic and compelling portrait of the depths to which mental hospitals had allegedly fallen, however, came from the pen of

Mary Jane Ward. In 1946 she published *The Snake Pit*, a novel that quickly caught the attention of a wide audience. Serialized as well in the *Reader's Digest*, *The Snake Pit* was made into a motion picture in 1948 and became one of the five most popular films of 1949.[17]

The theme of both the novel and the motion picture is simple. The heroine (played by Olivia de Havilland, who was nominated for an Academy Award) confronts a severe crisis in her marriage. Unable to accept love from her husband, she is sent to a state mental hospital where life on the wards resembles a snake pit. The picture's message, nevertheless, is more ambiguous. A warm and concerned psychiatrist, by his helpful and sympathetic personality and the use of such techniques as narcosynthesis, enables her to develop insight into her problems. The film thus depicted severe institutional defects, but its underlying message was one of faith in the therapeutic achievements of psychodynamic and psychoanalytic psychiatry.

Both the novel and its motion picture counterpart highlighted the perceived crisis in mental hospital care during the late 1940s. That psychiatrists and their allies were hardly disturbed by such unfavorable publicity was not surprising; they interpreted the harsh portrayal of institutional life as lending credence to their allegations of public and legislative indifference. Deutsch expressed delight when he learned that Anatole Litvak would direct the film version of *The Snake Pit*, for he and his script writers combined "demonstrated ability with social vision." GAP members issued a statement endorsing the accuracy of the film and called upon the public to demand "adequate funds, staff and facilities" for state mental hospitals. Similarly, the editorial board of the *Psychiatric Quarterly* (the official publication of New York's state hospitals) published an approving statement about Ward's novel. They were especially appreciative of her unwillingness to place the blame upon physicians and staff and her insistence that hospitals—in spite of monumental problems relating to a lack of adequate resources—made "a genuine effort to care for and heal the mentally ill."[18]

. . .

The harsh publicity given to institutional defects in the popular media did not arouse anger or concern within psychiatry. To be sure, more and more psychiatrists were finding careers either in noninstitutional settings or in private practice; their links with mental hospitals grew steadily weaker in the postwar years. The difficulty in recruiting young psychiatrists for employment in mental hospitals also aroused considerable anxiety.[19] Even those committed to a social and environmental etiology and psychodynamic therapies in community settings were cognizant of the fact that for the immediate future mental hospitals would continue to play an indispensable role for a patient population that was approaching half a million. Consequently, psychiatric attitudes remained profoundly ambiguous and divided. In theory many believed that community alternatives might eventually obviate traditional mental hospitals. In practice, however, most psychiatrists—irrespective of their ideological preferences—conceded that institutions were necessary, and consequently were active in promoting beneficent and desirable reforms.[20]

In the immediate postwar years the APA—an organization divided by conflicts revolving around the future direction of the specialty—added its voice to the demands for change. In May 1946 its Council issued a public statement calling attention to institutional deficiencies and attributing responsibility to "public . . . [and] legislative indifference." Its members endorsed the demand of the Committee on Standards and Policies that states appropriate a minimum of $5.00 per capita per diem for acute patients and $2.50 for chronic cases. Samuel W. Hamilton, the association's president, called upon the entire membership (including hospital superintendents) "to present forcefully to the public and to their legislators all the shortcomings and deficiencies in the hospitals and to demand the backing necessary to remedy these unsatisfactory conditions."[21]

Similarly, GAP—an organization dedicated to the principles of psychodynamic psychiatry and social activism—was equally committed to the cause of hospital reform. Within months, its Committee on State Hospitals (chaired by Kenneth E. Appel) was already collecting data on institutional deficiencies. Like others, it attributed responsibility to an apathetic and unconcerned public. "The lack of public pressure," the committee observed, "stems from misconception about the nature of mental illness, shame, guilt, fear of the unknown, and irritation with patients and their problems. This has led to a repressive psychology of complacency, indifference and disassociation from responsibility."[22]

By the end of 1947 GAP's Committee on State Hospitals had completed a draft of a lengthy analysis of public institutions. It endorsed APA efforts to rate and to certify hospitals. The committee also called for improvement in the quantity and quality of psychiatric personnel; the development of mechanisms designed to promote cooperation rather than conflict between lay and professional groups; the clarification and rationalization of the respective roles and functions of psychiatrists and other nonmedical professional groups; and efforts to promote research. In April 1948 its report on public hospitals was released in printed form.[23]

That both the APA and GAP supported the legitimacy and importance of institutional care did not imply that the specialty was intellectually unified or that the grounds for conflict were absent. In an analysis of the GAP report (whose recommendations he endorsed), Dr. F. A. Freyhan of the Delaware State Hospital called attention to significant but often ignored issues. American psychiatry was split between the dynamic and descriptive schools, and the differences between them had the potential to vitiate efforts to upgrade the quality of psychiatric practice in traditional institutional settings. The former was often described by such terms as "analytical, sociologic-minded, progressive"; the latter by "organic-minded, institutional, reactionary." Such distinctions, however, distorted psychiatric realities by equating dynamic psychiatry with effective individual psychotherapy and imputing to institutional psychiatry the "static quality of their partly chronic cases." The panenvironmentalist concepts of dynamic psychiatry, moreover, tended to deflect attention from genetic and constitutional factors and minimized the biological basis of personality. Dynamic formulations also undermined "the capacities of psychiatrists to deal with such vital problems as schizophrenia." Psychogenesis, after all, was as artificial an etiological abstraction as physiogenesis; neither described nor explained psychiatric reality.

Freyhan was equally critical of the prevailing emphasis on prevention. Given the absence of "scientifically valid evidence," psychiatrists had to "be more cautious in evaluating our prophylactic potentialities." The undue emphasis on psychological and environmentalist concerns inadvertently diminished the significance and attractiveness of institutional employment, thus hampering recruitment of qualified psychiatrists. "Our intentions were good," he added,

> but the results must be considered catastrophical if the emphasis on psychodynamics and psychodynamics only has produced a radical atrophy of interest in patients who occupy more than 40% of all hospital beds in this country. . . . Many teachers, to arouse interest in modern psychiatry, are in the habit of contrasting the "stagnant" atmosphere of public psychiatric hospitals with the intellectually brilliant environment of teaching institutions. While nobody denies the truth in this, it should not be forgotten that the case material in large mental hospitals is superior to the limited number of patients in teaching institutions and that it can only be favorable for young doctors to get a realistic impression of the totality of pathological phenomena which they usually miss in the refined environment of small neuropsychiatric departments. . . . Realistic and critical analysis of the present psychiatric scene indicates an orientational crisis to be an outstanding reason for the shortage of doctors in public psychiatric hospitals. The advancement of psychiatry may be endangered if the younger generation of psychiatrists specializes exclusively in analytical psychotherapy and turns its back on essential aspects of clinical psychiatry embodied in the case material of mental hospitals.[24]

Such subtle and trenchant observations, however, were generally ignored or submerged in the postwar euphoria. Psychiatric rhetoric about therapeutic possibilities in novel settings prevailed, and the articulation of a theory became the proof of its validity.

In the late 1940s the growing distance between the specialty of psychiatry and mental hospitals was not yet visible. The APA remained a heterogeneous organization in spite of the fact that fewer and fewer members were employed in public hospitals. It was understandable, therefore, that the association's concern with institutions led to two distinct but related developments: the establishment of a Central Inspection Board to evaluate and rate hospitals, and the sponsorship of annual Mental Hospital Institutes.

That the APA was concerned with substandard institutional conditions was evident even before the publication of journalistic accounts. In 1945 it adopted a set of standards and policies for all hospitals and outpatient clinics. The standards were intended to assure that mental hospitals provided the same quality of care and treatment as general hospitals. The financial implications were considerable; implementation required the infusion of substantial resources for staff, specialized facilities, and equipment. Adopted with little dissent, the standards incorporated an underlying ambiguity. On the one hand, they were intended to foster confidence in institutional care and treatment and to persuade the public that mental illnesses did not differ from physical illnesses. On the other hand, they stood as a reminder to state governments and legislators that their public hospitals were barely fit for human habitation. Standards, therefore, could be interpreted in quite different ways.[25]

The adoption of formal standards, of course, raised a further question: what could the APA do to ensure compliance? In 1946 the Committee on Psychiatric Standards and Policies urged the creation of some kind of enforcement machinery. With the endorsement of the Council and a grant from the Psychiatric Foundation, the APA in 1948 authorized the establishment of a Central Inspection Board (CIB). It also concluded an agreement with the American College of Surgeons to assume the latter's responsibility for inspecting hospitals by 1951.[26]

The adoption of standards and an enforcement mechanism created other pitfalls. Even before the APA had acted, Samuel W. Hamilton (whose experiences with the Mental Hospital Survey Committee in the late 1930s had demonstrated the hazards of evaluation) offered some astute comments in his presidential address. Standards that could never be more than aspirations were not helpful; standards that everybody had attained left "no room for striving." Moreover, formal ratings were often deceptive. The APA, Hamilton concluded, would need "great wisdom" in the planning process. As a group, hospital superintendents were not opposed to inspection and rating, but some were fearful that adverse reports would "drive away" employees and physicians.[27]

The early experiences of the CIB demonstrated the wisdom of Hamilton's words. Financing inspections, rating, and hiring of personnel proved troublesome. From the very beginning the board encountered dif-

ficulties in developing rating techniques; it often found an inherent conflict between qualitative and quantitative criteria. Were numerical ratios
by themselves a true measure of the adequacy of an institution? "Mere
number of personnel," noted Addison Duval in his letter transmitting
revision of the standards in 1951, "is not truly indicative of the adequacy
of a hospital program." Indeed, disagreement was even evident within the
committee charged with the revision of the official standards, and the
ambiguities were never clarified. "There is a lack of objective evidence,"
noted Robert C. Hunt in 1959, "as to what level of staffing, etc., is in fact
needed to give good clinical service." Hunt also expressed uncertainty
about the effectiveness of the policy of assisting state hospitals by de-
nouncing them; such an approach generated more pressure to keep raising standards. "One wonders," he added, "whether legislators are asses
enough to go on indefinitely chasing such a carrot on a stick." CIB members were themselves uncertain about the wisdom of releasing their reports to the public.[28]

During its existence the CIB approved fewer than half of the public
hospitals it inspected. By late 1953 it had evaluated 45 hospitals. Only 2
were approved; 10 received contingent approval, and the remainder were
disapproved. The American College of Surgeons, by contrast, found that
25 of these same institutions complied with its standards. Between 1949
and 1960 the CIB approved only 74 out of 176 state hospitals. The ambiguities and problems of inspection and rating ultimately led the APA to
terminate the existence of the CIB in 1960 and turn its functions over to
the Joint Commission on the Accreditation of Hospitals.[29]

Inspection and rating were ambiguous activities. Exposure of shortcomings could be used either as a lever to upgrade institutions or as a
bludgeon to discredit them even further. Despite their problems, however, mental hospitals were the only institutions providing comprehensive
care for the severely mentally ill. Consequently, the APA—most of whose
members no longer had mental hospital affiliations—could ill afford to
ignore completely their beleaguered institutional brethren, many of
whom were located far from urban medical schools and centers. Moreover, the growing significance of VA hospitals—which provided care for
mentally disabled veterans, served as reservoirs for training and employing large numbers of nonpsychiatric professional personnel, and were
funded at far more generous levels than their state counterparts—added
further pressure not to overlook institutional needs.

In late 1948 Daniel Blain proposed that the APA sponsor a meeting of
hospital psychiatrists. The Council and William C. Menninger offered
their support. Organized hastily, the gathering was held in Philadelphia in
mid-April of 1949. The turnout far exceeded expectations, since only
three months had elapsed between the conception and the convening of

the meeting. Nearly two hundred individuals representing thirty-six states, six Canadian provinces, and Puerto Rico were present. The sessions drew enthusiastic audiences and covered such topics as administration, personnel, clinical relations within hospitals, and hospital-community relations. The ardor of the participants left little doubt that the Mental Hospital Institute, as it subsequently became known, would become an annual affair. Shortly thereafter the Commonwealth Fund agreed to provide a grant to launch a new Mental Hospital Service within the APA and the publication of a periodical (*Mental Hospitals*). The result was the creation of a mechanism that maintained formal ties between the APA and mental hospitals.[30]

. . .

The postwar effort to reshape institutional care was not limited to journalists or members of the APA or GAP. Midway between the two stood private organizations with more eclectic constituencies. Such associations had long played significant roles in American society. In the mental health field the National Committee for Mental Hygiene (NCMH)—founded in 1909 by Clifford W. Beers, a former mental patient and author of the classic autobiography, *A Mind That Found Itself* (1908)—was the most famous; its membership included both psychiatrists and laypeople. By the 1920s and 1930s the concerns of the NCMH were already focused on preventive and community programs, child guidance clinics, and efforts to educate the public; its involvement with mental hospitals was marginal.[31] Consequently, its potential role in any coalition seeking fundamental changes in the care and treatment of the severely mentally ill was at best vague.

Immediately following the end of World War II the NCMH joined with the critics of mental hospitals, but with a subtle difference. Figures like Deutsch had called for the reform of hospitals. Dr. George S. Stevenson (longtime medical director of the NCMH) had a more ambivalent attitude. In an article for the influential *New York Times Magazine* in the summer of 1947, Stevenson pointed to the "seriously ailing system of public psychiatry" and the "dreadful mediocrity" of state hospitals. He conceded the need for more and better trained personnel but insisted upon the importance of "a new concept of public psychiatry." There were many individuals "not ill enough to require hospitalization" but who still needed assistance. What was required was a new "community-centered" system with hospitals "*as an adjunct service.*" The American people, he concluded, had two alternatives: "continued atrocities or the development of an enlightened public psychiatric system."[32]

The NCMH was not without its critics. Deutsch had little fondness for the organization and criticized it in *PM.* "I have long felt," he wrote to

Stevenson in friendly but frank words, "that one of the main deficiencies of the mental hygiene movement, as a whole, arises from the creation of personal ties and loyalties that get in the way of public duties." He disparaged the failure of the New York City affiliate of the NCMH (also headed by Stevenson) to expose conditions at Bellevue, Kings County, and other city-operated clinics, insisting that its members had abandoned their moral obligations. The NCMH, he told Harold Maine (author of a book critical of his experiences as a patient in a mental hospital), "just got itself too tied up with vested interests in the field whose stake was in the status-quo. It has also been using a microscope instead of a telescope in carrying out whatever programs it had." By 1947 the NCMH had begun to consider the feasibility of administrative reorganization in order to focus its activities in a clearer and more coherent manner.[33]

That the hegemony of the NCMH in the mental health arena would eventually be challenged was perhaps inevitable. Interestingly enough, the initial challenge came not from within professional ranks, but from without. During World War II, as has been mentioned, a number of individuals had refused to serve in the military for religious reasons. Assigned to the Civilian Public Service, some were placed in mental hospitals as attendants with the cooperation of the NCMH. In 1944 they began publication of a journal (*The Attendant*). Appalled by their experiences, they decided to undertake a major effort to upgrade the quality and status of psychiatric attendants, educate the public, and illuminate the legal rights and responsibilities of families and patients. Unlike the NCMH (which was dominated by psychiatrists), the National Mental Health Foundation, organized formally in late 1946, was overwhelmingly lay in character. Its head was Owen J. Roberts, a former justice of the U.S. Supreme Court, and the organization included prominent figures from nonmedical occupations but only a few physicians.[34]

From its very inception, relations between the National Mental Health Foundation and mainstream psychiatry were hardly close, if only because physicians guarded their authority and autonomy against encroachments by lay groups. William C. Menninger, who maintained friendships with virtually all who came into contact with him, was supportive of the new organization's efforts to improve the quality, role, status, and income of psychiatric attendants, but he was not enamored with its public education program. The APA and the NCMH, though not hostile, were less than friendly. The very existence of the foundation, after all, suggested a partially negative judgment of the achievements and activities of psychiatric organizations. When the foundation applied to the Rockefeller Foundation for a grant, Austin M. Davies, executive assistant at the APA, argued initially to Robert S. Morison against backing "a fly-by-night and irresponsible organization . . . whose program will either encroach too much on the field of medicine or be too limited to be any good." Subsequently

Davies adopted a more moderate position. Rockefeller officials were themselves divided about the wisdom of providing funds for the fledgling organization. Raymond B. Fosdick thought its goals laudable but could not see how the Rockefeller Foundation "can be identified with this kind of approach." Eventually the National Mental Health Foundation received a grant of $50,000, with the proviso that it raise an additional $175,000—a goal that proved unattainable. Despite severe financial problems, the young organization helped to focus public attention on conditions in mental hospitals by supplying journalists like Maisel with data, publishing Frank L. Wright's *Out of Sight out of Mind*, and preparing a series of programs that were aired on various radio stations.[35]

At precisely this same time the APA was creating still another private foundation under its auspices. In 1945 Austin M. Davies pointed out that implementation of the recommendations dealing with research and mental hospitals offered by the Special Committee on Reorganization required substantial financial resources; he urged the establishment of an organization similar to the American Cancer Society and National Foundation for Infantile Paralysis. The following year the Psychiatric Foundation had come into existence. Dominated by psychiatrists (but including wealthy laypersons), the new organization was given the task of raising funds to support the APA's attempts to inspect and rate hospitals and to launch educational programs. Although established as an independent entity, the Psychiatric Foundation, disclaimers to the contrary, was largely an appendage of the APA.[36]

The existence of three distinct paraprofessional organizations in the mental health field quickly became a source of concern. Would the presence of more than one lead to fragmentation and competition, thus vitiating the effort to improve mental health services? In early 1947, therefore, Dr. Frank Fremont-Smith of the Macy Foundation presided over a meeting to discuss relationships among these three foundations as well as the Menninger Foundation. Those present agreed to explore the possibility of forming a federation to coordinate fund raising and other activities and to prevent duplication.[37]

The institutionalization of cooperation, however, proved far easier in theory than in practice. Austin Davies, who also served as executive director of the Psychiatric Foundation, was hostile. When efforts to incorporate a "Federation of Foundations" foundered, the focus shifted in late 1948 toward a formal merger of the three foundations (excluding Menninger) into a single national organization. The ensuing negotiations made it clear that the perennial rift between the professional demand for autonomy and lay insistence upon shared responsibility had not vanished. The NCMH—the oldest organization in mental health—was hardly enamored of the younger upstarts. Ethel Ginzberg, an NCMH staff member, commended the enthusiasm of National Foundation for Mental Health members but deemed their focus on attendants too confining. Their antipathy toward psychiatrists, she charged, led them to espouse "lay domination." George Stevenson observed that neither the Psychiatric Foundation nor the National Foundation for Mental Health (unlike the NCMH) had assets. A merger, therefore, would not represent a union of equals. William L. Russell, a psychiatrist involved with the founding of the NCMH four decades earlier, was equally sensitive to relations among laypersons and professionals. He disparaged the refusal of the National Foundation for Mental Health to accept "medical leadership and direction." "All participants in mental health work," he wrote, "are dependent upon medicine and psychiatry for the greater part of their knowledge and skill which enable them to obtain satisfactory results." Although concerned with professional autonomy, psychiatrists were by no means of one mind. William C. Menninger and other Menninger Foundation personnel, for example, were critical of the NCMH.[38]

Negotiations continued into 1950, and in September the three organizations were merged into the new National Association for Mental Health (NAMH). Of the twenty-three members of its Board of Directors, only four came from the ranks of psychiatry. George S. Stevenson, on the other hand, became its medical director, thus continuing the precedent established by the NCMH. The medical director was assigned responsibility for the administration of all medical and scientific matters and also served as a consultant to the Board of Directors.[39]

The formation of a unified organization, however, did little to resolve existing tensions and problems; no clear consensus on its aims or functions emerged. Indeed, the persistent emphasis on the concept of mental health more often than not was a tacit admission of how little rather than how much was known. Rhetoric confined by neither knowledge nor data became the basis for claims that were subsequently accepted by a public eager to affirm their faith in the efficacy of scientific medicine. That etiology was obscure and disease entities protean and amorphous was all but ignored. Yet if the etiology of mental illnesses remained enigmatic, how was it possible to specify the optimal conditions and circumstances for promoting health? Deutsch, a shrewd yet sympathetic observer, noted as much. In a speech at a training course offered by the NAMH and supported by the NIMH, he offered a devastating analysis. "There is no doubt in my mind too," he observed,

> that a good part of the spread of the mental hygiene movement in the areas that were then unknown, terra incognito as far as psychiatric knowledge was concerned, the rapid spread, the thin spread of the movement into these other areas was partly at least the result of a feeling that mental hospitals were an uncom-

fortable business. It was messy to talk about mental hospitals and fool around with conditions as they were, and so much better to talk about the application of psychiatry to political life and to social life generally in more concrete and narrower terms of the family and the school. . . . How often in my own experience I have come across a gross abuse of that term "positive values"! How much energy have I seen dissipated by people attracted to the movement in the hope of making a concrete contribution by vapid discussions of positive values, or better child-parent relationships, or better social relationships in the community, generalized and meaningless in terms of concrete action, using terms where we have speculated on things we know little or nothing about . . . I do feel so concerned about this tendency in many of these [mental health] societies to drop the mental hospitals, to write them off as if nothing could be done about them anyway, and go off into uncharted seas in very many respects in areas in which we know little or nothing, and areas which are being adequately covered by other types of organizations.

Where should we concentrate the major task of the mental hygiene movement? I think the only answer can be in that area where there are no other organizations. It is messy in many respects, but it is also gratifying in terms of the challenge you have of improving the lot of these hundreds of thousands now in mental hospitals.[40]

Deutsch's analysis of mental hygiene, however harsh, was by no means wide of the mark. Indeed, the early history of the NAMH lent credence to his views. Within a year it had become evident that reorganization was not a panacea. Internal friction, vague lines of authority, and a weak and divided leadership all combined to vitiate whatever role it might have played. Most significant, however, was the vagueness of the association's mission. "I am not sure," observed an individual familiar with its problems, "what is regarded as the primary purpose of the National Association for Mental Health and this obviously has a lot to do with the direction the program can take." The judgment of Rockefeller Foundation officials was not fundamentally dissimilar. In 1951 Arthur H. Bunker, chairperson of the association's Board of Directors, approached the foundation for financial support. The principal function of the NAMH, he wrote to Gregg, "is to guide, service and inspire effective activity in the communities where people live"—a goal that represented "a radical departure from any one of its three predecessors." The vagueness of this claim could hardly have been overlooked by Gregg or Morison, both of whom had been seeking to terminate Rockefeller support for some years. Nevertheless, they agreed to make a final grant of $100,000 for the 1951–1952 fiscal year and subsequently declined to continue funding an organization for which they had little regard.[41]

For a good part of the 1950s the NAMH continued to be plagued by problems that diminished its effectiveness. By 1954 Robert M. Heininger, its executive director, resigned after only two and a half frustrating years in office. Immediately thereafter there were tentative efforts to draft Basil O'Connor, the dynamic and often authoritarian leader who had made the National Foundation for Infantile Paralysis into one of the most famous and effective organizations of its kind. O'Connor had some interest in mental illness and expressed willingness to give up his preoccupation with polio once a vaccine had been developed. For a variety of reasons, however, nothing concrete developed. Aside from financial and administrative problems, conflict persisted between lay members and psychiatrists. In 1955 Thomas A. C. Rennie, a key figure in social psychiatry and psychiatric epidemiology affiliated with the Payne Whitney Psychiatric Clinic at the New York Hospital, also resigned. "I am far from happy as to the direction the National Association is taking," he wrote to Blain. "It is increasingly being talked of as a lay organization. I couldn't stand by and see it get so far removed from medical and psychiatric guidance . . . without finally feeling that I could not really go along with it any longer." Mike Gorman, opinionated and blunt, put the matter very simply. For many years, he recalled in 1972, the NAMH "was a do-goody outfit, more worried about thumbsucking among infants, and putting out pamphlets about what is mental health."[42]

The ineffectiveness of the NAMH stood in sharp contrast to the National Mental Health Committee (NMHC), which subsequently became the National Committee Against Mental Illness (NCMI). Notwithstanding its name and list of eminent sponsors, the NMHC was largely the personal instrument of Mary Lasker, her protégé Mike Gorman, and, to a lesser extent, Florence Mahoney. In 1940 Mary Reinhardt, a Radcliffe graduate, had married Albert D. Lasker, a wealthy advertising executive. Within two years Lasker had liquidated his advertising business and established the Albert and Mary Lasker Foundation. By 1945 Mary and her husband, as well as Mahoney (whose affluent husband had an interest in the Cox newspaper chain) had come to the conclusion that the key to medical progress lay in research, and that the federal government had to underwrite the large costs of research in a major way. Within a short time she and Mahoney developed close ties with influential congressional allies and together created a lobby that was extraordinarily successful in overseeing an unprecedented expansion in federal funding of biomedical research from the 1940s to the 1960s.[43]

During World War II Mary Lasker, still a novice but with a capacity to learn, became involved with the NCMH and subsequently played a role in the passage of the National Mental Health Act of 1946. Her growing contacts with medical and scientific elites and key congressional figures, however, gave rise to disillusionment with the NCMH and the NAMH, both of which had neither a relationship to the newly founded NIMH nor interest in pushing for an expanded federal role. In 1951, therefore, she founded the NMHC and employed Lynn Adams as its secretary. Adams failed to become the dynamic catalyst that Lasker was seeking, and in 1953 she and Mahoney offered the position to Gorman. After his career as a reporter in Oklahoma, Gorman had experienced personal psychological problems and had briefly considered earning a graduate degree in social work. Ultimately he became a staff writer for Truman's influential President's Commission on the Health Needs of the Nation, which had called attention to the growing problem of mental illness among the aged and urged greater expenditures for research and training. After completing its work in 1952, the commission disbanded. Now Gorman immediately accepted Lasker's offer and quickly became the most effective and controversial mental health lobbyist in the nation's capital. His blunt and powerful personality and penchant for taking outspoken and firm stands complemented Lasker's shrewdness and adroitness in shaping legislative agendas. Year after year Gorman testified before House and Senate appropriations subcommittees. He urged increased funding for physiological research and training in psychiatry, and he developed close relationships with key congressional figures. His seemingly indefatigable efforts brought him fame and controversy, and he was identified with the belief that institutional care was outmoded and obsolete.[44]

Although organizations like the NAMH and the NMHC opened the door to lay influence on policy debates and outcomes, their membership, with but few exceptions, excluded actual or former patients. Clifford W. Beers was among the exceptions; yet even he encountered considerable hostility from such figures as Adolf Meyer in the course of his attempt to create the NCMH. The absence of a patient constituency was not surprising. Before the 1960s overt challenges to psychiatric authority were rarely confronted, at least directly. For the mentally ill the problem was even more complex. Many were without families and therefore lacked effective representatives. Alternatively, families—often faced by behavior that threatened their very existence—accepted institutionalization as a last resort and thereafter paid little attention to the quality of care. For professionals the mentally ill—precisely because of their impaired psychological condition—were in no position to make meaningful judgments or contributions.

Nowhere was the dependency relationship of patients and professionals better illustrated than in the less than enthusiastic reception of Recovery, Inc., a self-help organization of former mental patients founded in 1937 by Dr. Abraham Low of Chicago. A Polish-born graduate of the University of Vienna, Low had moved from general practice into neurology and then into psychiatry. In 1937 he began to work with patients in groups and eventually founded Recovery, which was designed to support discharged patients and to fight discrimination against them. The organization grew slowly. A decade after its founding it had about four hundred members; by 1966 it had reached ten thousand and had chapters in more than thirty states. Low argued that such organizations made it possible for psychiatrists to maximize their time by dealing with small groups rather than isolated individuals; he also believed that discharged patients had the capacity to provide mutual psychological support.[45]

Low quickly found that psychiatrists for the most part tended to ignore Recovery. When attention was riveted on its activities, the results were rarely positive. In 1954 internal discussions at the APA suggested concern, if only because some chapters were not under psychiatric supervision. Two years later Blain reported that Low carefully supervised members in the Chicago group. Elsewhere the pattern was somewhat different. Some chapters had "no proper supervision by medical authorities or any connections with psychiatrists." Because of the difficulty of maintaining control, Blain was inclined "to discourage them where possible, or, if they are organized, to see whether it is possible to bring back any semblance of proper professional guidance to the group."[46]

Organizations such as the NAMH and the NMHC were oriented toward the modification of public opinion and public policy; their members attempted to influence policymakers. The Milbank Memorial Fund, by way of contrast, employed its resources in an effort to stimulate scholarly research that had policy implications. An influential private foundation long active in the health arena, the fund turned its attention to the problem of mental disorders in the late 1940s. Between 1949 and 1952 it sponsored three conferences. Two dealt with the relationships between the social environment and mental disorders, one with the biological basis of mental diseases.[47] For the remainder of the 1950s and beyond, the fund's resources were used to bring together prominent psychiatrists and social scientists concerned with stimulating basic and applied socioenvironmental research, thus contributing to the growing debate over the wisdom of basing public policy on a system of traditional mental hospitals.

. . .

Awareness of substandard conditions in the nation's mental hospitals and a belief that change was required were by no means limited to the private sector. On the contrary, in the immediate postwar era a number of state officials began to focus on the problems of their hospitals. A variety of elements contributed to the renewed interest in the institutionalized mentally ill: negative publicity about institutional care; the continuous increase in the total patient population and accompanying budgetary pressures; and faith that alternative modes of care and treatment might prove more effective in returning patients to their communities.

Even during World War II, New York State could not ignore the problems of its mental hospitals, which by 1945 accommodated nearly seventy-five thousand resident patients and suffered from severe overcrowding. With the support of Governor Dewey, the state attempted to modernize its physical plant, promote more active treatment, and increase the number of psychiatrists and other personnel in order to compensate for the sharp decline in staff ratios during the war years. In 1948 officials concluded an agreement with Columbia University that provided for a comprehensive study of all hospitals, general as well as psychiatric, by Eli Ginzberg and his associates. Completed the following year, the report recognized some of the progress in rebuilding institutions but urged an expansion in clinics and other outpatient facilities and programs.[48]

New York State was not alone in seeking to deal with the residual problems rooted in years of neglect. In 1946 the Kansas Legislative Council (composed of the lieutenant governor and individuals from both houses of the legislature) authorized a study of public institutions and policies by two representatives of the PHS. At about that same time William and Karl Menninger were launching a major training and research program that involved both the Menninger Foundation and the Winter VA Hospital in Topeka. During these halcyon days Topeka became the major center of psychodynamic and psychoanalytic psychiatry; graduates of the Menninger School of Psychiatry played important national roles in succeeding decades. The Menninger brothers also established close working relationships with state officials with the aim of rebuilding the public institutional system and creating a more enlightened public opinion.[49]

Similar patterns were evident elsewhere. In California, Governor Earl Warren convened a conference on mental health in early 1949. Its recommendations reflected the growing belief that new policies were required to deal with the complex and often tragic problems associated with mental illnesses. Participants emphasized the role of socioenvironmental factors and insisted that greater attention be paid to education, schools, and the standard of living. Cognizant of the necessity of strengthening a troubled hospital system, they supported an expansion of community treatment and welfare services as well as the establishment of a Division of Community Services in the Department of Mental Hygiene. At about the same time such diverse states as Missouri, Maryland, Washington, and Minnesota were evaluating their own systems.[50] Even where formal investigations were absent, there was mounting evidence that state officials were aware of the problems of their public institutions.

By the late 1940s concern among state officials with mental health policy was pervasive and began to occupy a significant position on the political agenda. Many governors, a Minnesota official observed, preferred to be "off the hot seats they are on as a result of conditions in their state hospitals." In 1949 the Governors' Conference (an annual gathering of the nation's governors) took the unusual step of directing its Council of

State Governments, an influential and respected organization, to prepare a comprehensive and factual analysis of the care and treatment of the mentally ill. The goal was to provide state governments with a body of data to inform public policy discussions. A fourteen-member advisory committee, including ten representatives of the APA, met in the summer to help in the design of the study. The following year the council issued its important report, *The Mental Health Programs of the Forty-Eight States*, a volume that anticipated the activism of states in the mental health field during the 1950s.[51]

The Mental Health Programs of the Forty-Eight States was an extraordinarily comprehensive document. It included a wealth of data on a variety of topics: the growth and composition of the institutionalized population, finances, legal aspects of mental illnesses, state organization and administration, physical plants, personnel, care and treatment, and prevention. Its recommendations were equally striking: construction of additional facilities to alleviate overcrowding and to accommodate such specialized groups as alcoholics, drug addicts, and sex deviants; amendment of obsolete commitment statutes; upgrading of personnel; development of adequate therapeutic programs; greater emphasis on research; modernization of administration; and increased attention to the needs of children. The report noted the special problems posed by the large numbers of aged patients and urged that old-age insurance and public assistance programs be modified to permit such individuals to receive care in specialized community facilities. Cognizant of the interest in community care and treatment, its authors recommended an expansion of mental health clinics and aftercare programs.[52]

At the Governors' Conference in 1950 the report received strong backing; much of the discussion centered on how to secure public support to finance expansion and improvement of services. The following year the governors directed the Council of State Governments to prepare an analysis of training and research. Completed in 1953, the report called for better training of mental health personnel, more emphasis on research, and the establishment of an interstate clearinghouse to disseminate up-to-date information and promote interstate cooperation. The culmination of these developments came in early 1954 when the nation's governors held an unprecedented conference devoted exclusively to mental health and adopted a ten-point program embodying the basic themes of the two studies prepared by the Council of State Governments. "Ultimate reduction of the population in state mental hospitals," proclaimed the governors, "can only be achieved by efforts to *prevent* mental illness." They urged that the amount allocated to research (then limited to $4 million out of a total mental health budget of $540 million) and training be dramatically increased. "State and community mental health organizations," they concluded, "should play important roles in educating the public to the problems of mental health and to the methods of improving psychiatric services. The states should encourage and support mental health education in the schools, good relationships between hospitals and their surrounding communities, and the provision of adequate community psychiatric services." In adopting this platform, the assembled governors committed themselves to the pervasive postwar preventive and community-oriented ideology. They asked relatively few questions; perhaps they believed that solutions to difficult problems were best left to those whose training and experience made them uniquely qualified to provide definitive answers. A program based largely on faith—though one given legitimacy by the impressive credentials of medical science—became the foundation on which public policy would ultimately rest in succeeding decades.[53]

. . .

By the early 1950s the foundations for change were in place. Admittedly, mental hospitals remained the cornerstone of public policy. Yet the hegemonic position they had enjoyed for more than a century was becoming increasingly problematic. The sharp critiques of their shortcomings in the mass media had begun to impact upon both the general public and state officials. The glare of publicity was accompanied by determined efforts by both private organizations and foundations to formulate alternative policies, a development that received substantial support from many of the nation's governors.

In effect, a curious coalition formed in the decade following the end of World War II. Composed of activist psychodynamic and psychoanalytic psychiatrists, journalists, political leaders, and lay and professional organizations, its members endorsed prescriptions for change. This coalition was by no means unified around a common program; disagreement rather than agreement was characteristic. Nor were the consequences of its varied activities immediately apparent; the long-standing commitment to an institution-based system remained outwardly unchanged. Nevertheless, by defining a problem and shaping an agenda, its members helped to set in motion a process that in the future would help to change the ways in which American society apprehended and responded to the problems posed by mental illnesses.

CHAPTER FIVE

The Mental Health Professions:
Conflict and Consensus

THE GROWING HOSTILITY toward a hospital-based policy, the expanding role of the federal government, and the dominance of psychodynamic and psychoanalytic concepts had a profound impact upon the structure of the mental health professions. New concepts of health and disease, an emphasis on psychological therapies, and a commitment to environmental changes implied broadened and more responsible roles for such specialties as clinical psychology, psychiatric social work, and psychiatric nursing. Their growth was also fueled by the gradual weakening of kinship and family networks and religious institutions, which in the past had provided the major supports for individuals requiring some sort of personal assistance. In effect, assistance and support systems became more formalized as they were incorporated into a bureaucratic and organizational society that often justified professional authority in terms of possession of a body of allegedly objective and scientific knowledge.

The growing maturity of new professional groups after 1945 suggested that mental health services would cease to be a purely psychiatric preserve. The nineteenth-century belief that the care and treatment of the mentally ill was an exclusively psychiatric responsibility appeared increasingly obsolete. The continuum theory, which emphasized a social and environmental etiology and belief that the early identification of symptoms and treatment in the community could prevent the onset of serious mental illnesses, provided the basis for an expansion and elaboration of mental health services. Ironically, a concept that strengthened psychodynamic and weakened institutional psychiatry also limited what had been a virtual medical monopoly. The blurring of lines between professional occupations in turn complicated the adjudication of claims involving jurisdiction and authority. The very same forces that promoted the popularization and expansion of mental health services in new social settings, therefore, created circumstances that fostered conflict. After 1945 psychiatric authority was challenged by groups seeking to establish their own claims to legitimacy and autonomy. Consequently, professional and interprofessional rivalries played an increasingly important part in shaping policy deliberations as well as the very structure and delivery of mental health services. These conflicts reflected the needs and perceptions of mental health professionals as much as they did the interests of mentally ill institutionalized patients. In this sense professional rivalries helped to shift attention away from hospitalized patients even as services to individuals experiencing personal and psychological problems were expanding.

. . .

Of all the mental health specialties, psychiatry was probably the most divided in the 1940s. Perhaps no individual more clearly anticipated its future direction than Alan Gregg, director of the medical sciences at the prestigious Rockefeller Foundation. Gregg had received both his undergraduate and medical degrees at Harvard. In Cambridge he came under the influence of Dr. James Jackson Putnam, one of the earliest American supporters of Freud. Instead of following a traditional medical career, Gregg became associated with the Rockefeller Foundation, the most important medical philanthropy of the early twentieth century. By the 1920s changes within the Rockefeller family had altered its preoccupation with a largely biological medicine; in 1923 the Laura Spelman Rockefeller Memorial shifted its support to the social and behavioral sciences, which in turn stimulated interest in psychiatry. During the 1930s Gregg used his influential position in an effort to move psychiatry in an interdisciplinary direction by merging a biologically oriented medicine with psychoanalysis.[1]

Gregg's interest in psychiatry never flagged, and during the 1940s he published a series of influential papers that portended its future course. Unlike many of his medical colleagues, Gregg was sympathetic, though not uncritical, toward psychiatry. The mental illnesses, he wrote in 1942, were not the sole concern of the specialty. Its domain was "bafflingly large" and included "derangements of conduct or behavior often discernable only in terms of the patient's relationships with other human beings in some given intellectual or cultural or social or moral system." Psychology, and especially psychoanalysis, were to psychiatry what physiology was to medicine. To their everlasting credit, therefore, psychiatrists "have laid stress upon the whole personality" within a naturalistic framework.[2]

Two years later Gregg gave a paper at the centennial celebration of the APA that drew widespread attention. No other specialty within medicine, he observed, had to deal with the "confusion of early pathological signs with moral weakness or unethical behavior, and the false distinction between mind and body" or "rescue its patients from persecution, live with them in social ostracism, restore their capacities and then return them to an environment both exigent and suspicious." Nevertheless, psychiatry was not without a measure of culpability. Gregg emphasized its inability to recruit young medical graduates. Equally serious was the absence of adequate training facilities. State mental hospitals were both geographically and intellectually isolated, and young physicians embarking on a career in psychiatry were ignorant of key social and behavioral science disciplines. Such problems did not derive from internal shortcomings alone. On the contrary, the specialty was overburdened, and Gregg pointed to the chilling experiences of those who worked in state hospitals and in the military. Such environments militated against an adequate understanding of human beings as social as well as biological organisms. He castigated psychiatrists for their temerity and inarticulateness in failing to present their burdens to a society all too willing to ignore its mentally ill citizens. Your mission, he told his listeners, was "not only to recognize and treat effectively the major psychoses," but rather to extend "the mission and range of psychiatry" to include an understanding of normal life and to "explain mechanisms and processes at work both in disease and health." Psychiatry had to utilize the insights of psychoanalysis and psychology and apply their findings to the "human relations of normal people—in politics, national and international, between races, between capital and labor, in government, in family life, in education, in every form of human relationship, whether between individuals or between groups." The specialty had to be concerned, he added, "with optimum performance of human beings as civilized creatures."[3]

Gregg's exhortations were to prove remarkably prescient. Even as he was offering his own prescriptions for the future, the social and intellectual foundations of the specialty were being reconstituted. In the postwar era the traditional preoccupation with the severely mentally ill gradually gave way to a concern with the psychological problems of a far larger and more diverse population. Persuaded that there was a continuum from mental health to mental illness, psychiatrists increasingly shifted their activities away from the psychoses in the hope that early treatment of functional but troubled individuals would ultimately diminish the incidence of the more serious mental illnesses. Karl A. Menninger, the charismatic figure who had been pushing for the integration of psychoanalytic insights into psychiatry since the 1930s, was outspoken in his insistence on the need for change. Psychiatric patients, he observed in 1945, could logically be divided into four categories. The first two were composed of children as well as adults with emotional and psychological problems, both of whom could be treated effectively on an outpatient basis. The other two included the acute and chronic mentally ill. In his eyes the former two represented the "most neglected and the most promising," and he insisted that psychiatry readjust its focus accordingly. For too long the specialty had been "satisfied with the custodial status." Early treatment, however, was inconsistent with state hospital psychiatry. The solution was obvious even if difficult; young medical graduates had to be trained for outpatient work. Menninger's views were by no means atypical; they were shared by many of his contemporaries committed to the creation of a new kind of psychiatry.[4]

In emphasizing the need to focus on nonpsychotic but presumably troubled individuals, psychodynamic psychiatrists tended to blur nosological categories. The changing character of the specialty was reflected in its terminology. Traditionally diagnoses were expressed in the language of pathology; the presumption was that changes in behavior (which admittedly might be related to environmental factors) had a somatic foundation. Postwar psychiatrists, by comparison, did not necessarily reject traditional formulations. However, their interest in the nature of personality (normal as well as abnormal), the role of childhood and the influence of parenthood, and the ability of the organism to adjust to the environment in ways that were both effective and satisfying led them to employ a quite different terminology. Their new language emphasized the need to assist unhappy and neurotic individuals, presumably through various psychotherapies. In emphasizing their ability to deal with such varied concerns as parent-child relationships, marriage, emotional maturity, and occupational roles, the specialty appealed to a broad public eager for assistance in dealing with the problems of ordinary life.[5]

Nowhere was the change in the nature of postwar psychiatry better illustrated than in the effort to create definitive diagnostic categories. As late as 1941 American psychiatrists were still utilizing a nosological system that reflected the experiences and needs of public mental hospitals. In 1917 the American Medico-Psychological Association (which in 1921 became the APA) and the NCMH had collaborated to produce a uniform classification of mental diseases in order to overcome the prevailing confusion and disorganization that, as the committee in charge noted, "discredits the science of psychiatry and reflects unfavorably upon our Association." The new nosology, according to its defenders, "substituted system for chaos" and made possible the combination and comparison of data collected in different places at the same time and established a basis for the comparison of present and future data. The new classification was "elastic" and included a provision for revision at five-year intervals. Published in 1918, the *Statistical Manual for the Use of Institutions for the Insane* went through no fewer than ten editions between 1918 and 1942.[6]

During the 1940s, discontent with a classification system prepared more than two decades earlier mounted. Military and VA psychiatrists found themselves using a nomenclature ill-adapted for 90 percent of their cases. Minor personality disturbances—many of which were of importance only because they occurred within a military context—were placed in the "psychopathic personality" category. The "psychoneurotic" label was given to men who had developed symptoms because of the stress of combat. There was virtually no recognition of psychosomatic disorders. Indeed, by the end of the war the army and navy had adopted their own classifications, which subsequently became the basis for revisions of the International Statistical Classification.[7]

The nosological confusion and the proliferation of nomenclatures led the APA Committee on Nomenclature and Statistics in 1948 to postpone further changes in its manual and instead to solicit suggestions for change. By 1950 it had prepared an unpublished revised psychiatric nosology, which was widely circulated to various individuals and organizations. A completed version was presented to the APA Council in 1950 for its approval. In 1952 the APA formally published the first edition of the *Diagnostic and Statistical Manual: Mental Disorders* (which became known as DSM-I).[8]

DSM-I reflected the intellectual, cultural, and social forces that had transformed psychiatry during and after World War II. It divided mental disorders into two major groupings. The first represented cases in which the disturbed mental function resulted from or was precipitated by a primary impairment of brain function. Such brain syndromes were associated with a variety of somatic conditions—infection, intoxication (drug, poison, or alcoholic), trauma, circulatory or metabolic disturbances, intracranial neoplasms, multiple sclerosis, and Huntington's chorea or other diseases of hereditary origin. The second category encompassed disorders resulting from a more general inability of the individual to adjust and in which brain function disturbance was secondary to the psychiatric illness. DSM-I divided this group into psychotic and psychoneurotic disorders. The former included manic depressive and paranoid reactions and schizophrenia. The latter was composed of anxiety, dissociative, conversion, phobic, obsessive-compulsive, and depressive reactions as well as a variety of personality disorders that included emotional instability, compulsiveness, antisocial behavior, sexual deviation, alcoholism, drug addiction, stress, and various reactions associated with different age categories.[9]

The prominence of psychodynamic and psychoanalytic concepts in DSM-I mirrored fundamental changes within psychiatry. The pressure for change, as a matter of fact, was generated largely by analytically oriented psychiatrists who had few ties with public mental hospitals and were largely located in medical schools, clinics, and private practice. Their clientele, to use DSM-I categories, tended to come from the ranks of the psychoneurotic, many of whom seemed to benefit from psychotherapy. Psychodynamic psychiatrists also tended to have a greater commitment to social activism.

The shift toward a psychodynamic orientation was also hastened by changes in medical and postgraduate education. Prior to World War II psychiatry occupied a marginal position in American medical schools, one that improved slightly during the 1930s. The weakness of psychiatric education was confirmed by the fact that many physicians employed in public mental hospitals had little or no formal training in or exposure to psychiatry. By the late 1930s the APA Committee on Psychiatry in Medical Education recommended that two-week institutes, geographically dispersed, be offered to state hospital physicians. Their goal was to encourage more physicians to meet the certification requirements of the American Board of Psychiatry and Neurology; to expand the number of state hospital internships; and to foster closer relationships with medical schools, local and state medical societies, general hospitals, and outpatient clinics.[10]

Concern with the weakness of psychiatry in medical schools led to the publication of a pioneering investigation of the subject by Ralph A. Noble in 1933. A decade later Franklin G. Ebaugh and Charles A. Rymer of the University of Colorado School of Medicine completed an exhaustive and influential study of psychiatric education that provided both an analysis of the present and a prescription for the future. Transitional in character, their work began with the observation that the dominance of the organic point of view in medical education prevented "the proper recognition of the place of psychiatry in the medical curriculum." The concept of organic disease was so pervasive that "functional components are difficult to grasp and appear in the nature of improbability." Other elements contributed to the denigration of psychiatry: a moralistic view of mental disorders; the emotional reaction of medical students to psychiatric concepts; and the seeming hopelessness of mental conditions. Desirable changes, both authors concluded, had to rest on three fundamental principles: the concept of man as a whole; the adoption of "a genetic-dynamic concept of mental disorders"; and the inseparable relationship of psychiatry and medicine (mediated by the psychosomatic approach), and a recognition of the "emotional factors in disease."[11]

After 1945 the number of psychodynamic psychiatrists affiliated with medical schools increased rapidly. The result was predictable: more and more psychiatry was taught in all four years, the expanded curriculum serving as a means of introducing and recruiting young medical students to the specialty. At the same time, psychiatric teaching influenced other departments. NIMH grants in turn subsidized both undergraduate and residency training, and the number of psychiatric residencies expanded rapidly. In 1946 there were 155 residency programs; a decade later the total reached 294. More significant, the number of actual residencies in this period leapt from 758 to 2,983. The rising prestige and attractiveness of psychiatry was accompanied by a dramatic increase in the proportion of medical school graduates selecting the specialty, which in 1954 peaked at 12.5 percent.[12]

Even more important than the increase in actual numbers was the shift in orientation that marked undergraduate and graduate (i.e., residency) training. The Ebaugh-Rymer report of 1942 reflected the influence of Adolf Meyer, who for three decades trained several generations of psychiatrists at Johns Hopkins in what was known as psychobiology, or the genetic-dynamic approach. During the 1940s, by contrast, American psychiatry to an unprecedented degree was influenced by psychoanalytic theory, which emphasized the psychological mechanisms that mediated between instinctual biological drives and the pressures of the external environment. Change was already evident by the end of the war. In 1946 the American Board of Psychiatry and Neurology gave its stamp of approval to psychodynamic principles that anticipated the emergence of a more psychoanalytically oriented psychiatry. Training in the specialty, the board announced, had to include clinical work with psychoneurotic and psychotic patients. Clinical experience had to be integrated "with the study of the basic psychiatric sciences, medical and social psychology, psychopathology, psychotherapy, and the physiological therapies." Psychiatrists had to be taught to collaborate with social workers, clinical psychologists, courts and other social agencies. Finally, residents had to be exposed to neurology to enable them "to recognize and to evaluate the evidence of organic neurological disease."[13]

In 1951 and 1952 the APA and the Association of American Medical Colleges sponsored two significant conferences. The first dealt with psychiatry in medical education and the second with residency training. Both were dominated by the psychodynamic perspective. Anxious to alter the marginal role of the specialty, the participants at the first meeting urged that all medical students be exposed to psychiatric insights in each of the four years. The basic aim was "to equip the student with a reasonably adequate knowledge of the facts of human nature." More specifically, all medical students had to have the ability "to diagnose correctly the condition of patients who are emotionally disturbed and who may be expressing their distress in physical, psychological or social symptoms. . . . [and] a reasonable understanding of the zones of healthy and sick behavior in our society and, more particularly, the ability to differentiate between normal, neurotic, psychopathic, psychotic, and intellectually defective behavior." The deliberations at this conference subsequently led to the preparation of a statement by the APA Committee on Medical Education. It defined the minimum information that all physicians should have about psychiatry, and the means by which medical schools could teach knowledge and skills to their students. Physicians should "treat patients rather than diseases and . . . understand the social and physical environment that affects the patient's health." The committee recommended that during the first two years all medical students be exposed to theories of personality growth, development, structure, and integration; adaptive needs; social and cultural forces affecting personality and behavior; the role of language and mentation; the part played by emotions in physiological functioning; and psychopathology. The curriculum should not attempt to train physicians to become psychiatrists but rather should strive to develop "well-rounded physicians, who, in their relationships with all patients, recognize the importance of unconscious motivation, the role of emotional maladjustment in the etiology and chronicity of illness, the emotional and personality problems engendered by various illnesses; and who habitually see the patient in his family and general environmental setting."[14]

That psychodynamic insights quickly dominated the teaching of psychiatry in medical schools was apparent from a GAP survey in 1959–1960. Out of 93 American and Canadian institutions, 88 taught psychodynamics, 87 personality growth and development, and 77 psychotherapy and clinical syndromes. Further, the number of hours in the curriculum devoted to psychiatry quadrupled between 1940 and 1960. Virtually every chairperson of a department of psychiatry stated unequivocally that the psychodynamic frame of reference (as contrasted with the descriptive or organic) was dominant.[15]

The triumph of a psychodynamic approach also set the stage for the collaboration and cross-fertilization of psychiatry with the behavioral and social sciences during the 1950s. Institutionally this development was reflected in the emergence of the new subspecialty of "social psychiatry." First popularized by such British figures as Maxwell Jones and Aubrey Lewis, social psychiatry reflected the dominant role of environmentalism in postwar thought. In the United States, Thomas A. C. Rennie and Alexander H. Leighton of Cornell University Medical College in New York City as well as prominent social and behavioral scientists began to call attention to the importance of broad environmental factors in the etiology of mental disorders. By 1950 the Social Science Research Council had sponsored two meetings attended by psychiatrists and social scientists. Out of its deliberations came the Committee on Research in Psychiatry and the Social Sciences, chaired by Leighton and including John A. Clausen, Henry W. Brosin, Joseph W. Eaton, Herbert Goldhamer, Ernest M. Gruenberg, Clyde Kluckhohn, Erich Lindemann, Fredrick C. Redlich, James S. Tyhurst, and Edmund H. Volkart. Two years later a Milbank Memorial Fund conference, involving both psychiatrists and social scientists, focused on the interrelations between the social environment and psychiatric disorders. Social psychiatry, Rennie wrote in 1955,

> seeks to determine the significant facts in family and society which affect adaptation (or which can be clearly defined as of etiological importance) as revealed

through the studies of individuals or groups functioning in their natural setting. It concerns itself not only with the mentally ill but with the problems of adjustment of all persons in society toward a better understanding of how people adapt and what forces tend to damage or enhance their adaptive capacities. . . . Social psychiatry is etiological in its aim, but its point of attack is the whole social framework of contemporary living.[16]

The growing interest during the 1950s in social psychiatry paralleled a new kind of psychiatric epidemiology. With only a few notable exceptions, psychiatric epidemiology before World War II focused on the institutionalized mentally ill; the presumption was that data about this group would serve the ends of public policy. The new psychiatric epidemiology that came of age after 1945, by way of contrast, was concerned with the incidence and prevalence of mental disorders in the general population and the etiological role of socioenvironmental factors. The shift represented an extraordinary intellectual leap: it assumed that psychiatric nosology was sufficiently precise to permit the collection of accurate data and also that crucial socioenvironmental variables could be isolated and measured. Psychiatric epidemiologists believed that their research would contribute to both preventive and therapeutic programs.[17]

Admittedly, some of the famous postwar studies were limited in scope. In their influential study of social class and mental illness, August B. Hollingshead and Fredrick C. Redlich sought to link social stratification with the prevalence (and to a lesser extent, the incidence) of mental illnesses and to show how social class was related to therapy. Others, however, took a more global approach. The famous Midtown Manhattan Study, conceived by Rennie in 1950 and continued after his death in 1956 by other colleagues, involved an intensive study of an area with a population of about 174,000. Ultimately the project identified a sample of 1,911 individuals between the ages of twenty and fifty-nine, of whom 1,660 completed a long and detailed questionnaire. The responses were then rated by clinicians according to the severity of psychiatric symptoms and the degree of impairment, and then related to a range of demographic data. The assumptions and conclusions of the study were similar: mental health was in large measure a function of socioeconomic factors.[18]

The emphasis on the etiological role of broad environmental factors promoted a spirit of social activism. In turn, social activism expanded the potential clientele of the specialty, thus diluting psychiatric preoccupation with the needs of the most severely mentally ill. Because of their inability to identify precise environmental boundaries, social psychiatrists in particular defined their specialty in protean terms. To Maxwell Jones, social psychiatry implied "the social factors associated with the living experiences of psychiatric patients or potential patients, whether in

[the] hospital or in the outside world." William Hollister, chief of the NIMH's Community Research and Services Branch, had a more expansive view. "Social psychiatry," he noted, "concerns itself with the impact of the whole social systems of agencies on the mental health of individuals and groups. It is interested in systemwide function and systemic malfunction." In a widely used textbook published in 1966, Redlich and Daniel X. Freedman identified social psychiatry "as the study of the impact of the social environment on the etiology and treatment of abnormal behavior." Virtually all who employed the term conceded that social psychiatry was somehow related to the social and behavioral sciences.[19]

In many ways social psychiatry represented more of an attitude and mood than it did a clinical specialty. In a review of the literature, Norman W. Bell and John P. Spiegel insisted that the term lacked both coherence and logical meaning. Its popularity grew out of the prevailing belief that science held the key to the amelioration of "such vast public problems as mental illness, crime, delinquency, alcoholism, and a good many others." By 1960, more than half of all departments of psychiatry had courses dealing with the contributions of the social and behavioral sciences. At best social psychiatry was a label for cross-disciplinary research training and research procedure; it lacked many of the attributes of clinical practice.[20]

. . .

The emergence of psychodynamic and social psychiatry and the shift from institutional to community practice, however welcomed, inadvertently altered professional boundaries. Traditionally the issue of psychiatric jurisdiction had little or no meaning. In nineteenth-century mental hospitals the supremacy of the superintendent (i.e., psychiatrist) was, at least in theory, unchallenged. With the exception of assistant physicians, the staff consisted of untrained attendants and nurses whose functions were to carry out the directives of their superiors.

During the first four decades of the twentieth century, traditional patterns of authority slowly changed. The creation of a mental hygiene movement, a new "dynamic" psychiatry concerned with social and environmental factors, and an interest in prevention led to such institutional innovations as psychopathic hospitals for acute cases and child guidance clinics. Out of these emerged the concept of the "mental health team"— an interdisciplinary group including psychiatrists, psychologists, and psychiatric social workers concerned with the biological, psychological, and social roots of mental maladjustment. The multidisciplinary theme was even evident in a select number of traditional mental hospitals before 1940. In addition, traditional patterns of authority within state institutions were slowly changing as nurses, social workers, and occupational therapists sought to define professional identities in the hope of upgrading their status and role. These developments had obvious implications for psychiatrists, if only because they posed an incipient challenge to psychiatrists' hegemony over the care and treatment of the mentally ill.[21]

Before 1940 potential interprofessional conflict was muted. The subordinate status of nurses and attendants and the marginal role of occupational therapists (all institutionally based) precluded challenges to psychiatric authority. Psychiatric social workers, many of whom were employed in child guidance clinics, tended to defer to psychiatrists. To be sure, psychiatric social workers were slowly expanding their role beyond the mere gathering of family histories or arranging for services. Their acceptance of a separate but unequal sphere, however, diminished the potential for friction. That psychiatric social work was a predominantly female occupation also made it appear less threatening to the male-dominated specialty of psychiatry. Moreover, some psychiatric social workers had begun to shift their activities into the larger field of social work, where their contacts with psychiatrists were less frequent.[22]

Relations between psychiatry and clinical psychology, by way of contrast, demonstrated a greater potential for friction as early as World War I. During that conflict the widespread use of mental testing in the army had given psychology a new image; testing and service suggested that academic psychology did not provide the only role model. In the interwar years the employment of psychologists as part of the mental health team in child guidance clinics only broadened their responsibilities. Originally their function was to employ their skills to administer and interpret various tests. Their growing belief that psychiatrists lacked psychological training and insight led them to insist upon their qualifications to diagnose and even to engage in a form of psychotherapy. Such claims met with staunch resistance from psychiatrists. The relatively small numbers of clinical psychologists, however, retarded overt conflict. During the 1930s, 1,116 doctorates were awarded in psychology (as compared with 644 in the previous decade), and the membership of the American Psychological Association increased from 393 in 1920 to 2,739 in 1940. These figures, which included all branches of psychology, suggested that the discipline had not yet reached a size at which its influence could expand beyond its academic base.[23]

World War II proved the catalyst that hastened the transformation of clinical psychology from a stepchild into a powerful subdiscipline that offered a variety of practical and applied services. Before 1940 the discipline was dominated by academic psychologists. During the war most psychologists, like professionals generally, volunteered their services to the government, the military, and the private defense sector. They assumed prominent roles in assisting in the mobilization and training of personnel, preparing propaganda and other motivational materials, and conducting research dealing with the relationship between technology and human adaptability. Clinical psychologists also found a friend in Brigadier General William C. Menninger, who was favorably disposed toward utilizing their services in the army's neuropsychiatric service. He emphasized their contributions in developing standardized diagnostic and evaluation tools but was more hesitant about endorsing a therapeutic role.[24]

The experiences of war began to shift the internal balance of power away from academicians and toward applied practitioners. The latter insisted that their discipline, precisely because it rested on scientific knowledge and expertise about human behavior, could assist both the private and the public sector in a variety of ways. In response to the changing nature of psychology, the American Psychological Association underwent a significant reorganization (not unlike the transformation of the APA in the late 1940s). In 1945 it merged with the American Association of Applied Psychologists, an organization founded in 1937 to represent the interests of practitioners who resented the dominant role of academic psychologists in the existing association.

To be sure, conflicting views about the potential role of clinical psychologists existed. However, the shortages of trained psychiatrists and the presence of thousands of neuropsychiatric cases among veterans created grave problems during and after the war. The VA in particular was preoccupied with the dearth of trained medical personnel, since it faced the prospect of a rapid expansion of its hospital and outpatient facilities. Cognizant of the difficulties that impeded a rapid increase in the supply of qualified psychiatrists, it decided to establish a training program in clinical psychology in the hope of meeting some of its own needs. It employed its resources to induce many university departments of psychology to establish rigorous graduate programs with conventional admissions standards. Under this program, degree candidates worked half-time at a VA facility, where they received clinical training. Students were also given stipends, and their educational expenses were covered as well. The attractiveness of the program was enhanced by the virtual guarantee of employment at reasonably good salaries. Aware of the problems posed by status-related issues, VA officials demonstrated political sagacity by insisting that the doctorate, not a lesser degree, become the norm rather than the exception. With federal support from the VA and subsequently from the NIMH, the number of doctorates awarded (a large proportion of which were in clinical fields) rose from 1,253 in the 1940s to 6,412 in the succeeding decade. In the fifteen years following 1945 the membership of the American Psychological Association increased correspondingly from 4,173 to 18,215.[25]

The dramatic increase in the number of clinical psychologists with doctorates was accompanied by rising friction. Somatic therapies (e.g., lobotomy, drugs, and the various shock therapies) were not at issue; they remained exclusively under medical authority. Psychotherapies, on the other hand, presented a quite different problem, if only because they rested on a psychological rather than a biological foundation. That clinical psychologists staked out independent jurisdictional claims was understandable. The training of practitioners in psychology, after all, provided a comparable, if not a superior, basis for asserting a right to offer psychotherapy. In a larger sense the battle over jurisdiction was also one over authority and legitimacy, for the intellectual and scientific foundations upon which the two specialties rested their claims were shaky at best. The practice of psychotherapy was diverse in the extreme; the personalities of both professional and client seemed to play a disproportionately important role; and outcomes were rarely amenable to any precise measurement.

The VA, of course, recognized that the training of nonmedical professionals raised potentially divisive jurisdictional issues. Daniel Blain, who headed the VA Neuropsychiatry Division before becoming the APA's first medical director in 1948, attempted to sidestep this problem. Conceding that clinical psychologists were inadequately trained to undertake therapy, he suggested that attention be focused not on the role of particular mental health specialties but rather on the needs of the patient. "I am quite firm in my conviction," he told the Military Division of the American Psychological Association in 1946, "that anyone properly trained may at any time be given responsibilities commensurate with his background and ability, regardless of his professional category." Privately Blain appeared less sanguine. "I share with you," he wrote to Edward A. Strecker, "the concern about the taking over of psychiatry by psychologists and others."[26]

Well before the VA launched its ambitious program, clinical psychologists had begun to debate issues involving professional training and certification. These discussions took on substantive meaning after the war when in 1947 the newly reorganized American Psychological Association established the American Board of Examiners in Professional Psychology to certify professional psychologists. That same year the association's Committee on Training in Clinical Psychology, chaired by David Shakow, laid down guidelines for graduate programs that endorsed state certification and insisted that no clinical psychologist "can be considered adequately trained unless he has had sound training in psychotherapy." The cumulative impact of the increase in the number of trained psychologists and their growing responsibilities in mental hospitals, outpatient and other public facilities, and the private sector combined to create a self-conscious and confident profession ready to offer its services in a variety of settings. The general receptivity toward and popularity of psychological explanations in the postwar decades only enhanced a profession that had emerged from a relatively isolated academic origin.[27]

Psychiatrists were aware that the growth of clinical psychology offered benefits as well as risks. They were cognizant that psychologists were trained in testing, research design and statistical analysis, vocational and educational counseling, and speech and group therapy, and they were more than willing to integrate these functions into the team approach. The assertion by clinical psychologists that they were qualified to offer individual psychotherapy, on the other hand, was a quite different matter. Even GAP—an organization whose members tended to be liberal and activistic and deeply supportive of collaboration with behavioral scientists—indicated concern. In mid-1947 its Committee on Clinical Psychology circulated a preliminary document. Seventy members (more than half of the total membership) provided comments. Their responses indicated a pervasive hostility toward the concept that clinical psychologists could offer psychotherapy. Fifty-one objected to the private practice of psychotherapy by psychologists; 36 specified that psychotherapy had to be "under the supervision of" rather than "in collaboration with" psychiatrists; 27 emphasized that psychologists could not assume responsibility for medical diagnosis and treatment; 21 defined psychotherapy in medical terms; and 19 expressed doubt about the willingness of psychologists to accept psychiatric supervision. GAP's published report in 1949 expressed strong opposition to the independent private practice of psychotherapy by clinical psychologists; such therapy was acceptable only when "carried out in a setting where adequate psychiatric safeguards are provided."[28]

GAP's position was hardly atypical. As World War II came to a close, the APA's Committee on the Relation of Psychiatry to Psychology had established formal contacts with the American Psychological Association to set high educational standards as a prerequisite for professional certification of psychologists. That broad areas of agreement existed was evident. On such issues as team collaboration, joint training, board certification of psychologists, research, and exchanges of views, there was no conflict. Nevertheless, a report by a joint committee in 1946 that embodied this consensus won only a somewhat ambiguous endorsement from the APA Council. Even at this early date there were fears that clinical psychologists were already engaging in therapeutic activities. James S. Plant, chair of the APA committee, thought it wise to evade the problem and emphasize common training; to do otherwise would accomplish little. In any event, it remained abundantly clear that the issue of who was qualified to provide psychotherapy remained a seemingly insuperable stumbling block to any definitive jurisdictional agreement. Indeed, when the Macy Foundation sponsored a Conference on Training in Clinical Psychology, Lawrence S. Kubie reported that the psychiatric participants thought it impossible "to deal realistically with any of the problems of the clinical psychologist if we try artificially to steer clear of the problem of therapy." In May 1949 the APA, after considerable discussion, adopted a resolution affirming its opposition "to independent private practice of psychotherapy by the clinical psychologists" and insisting that such therapy "should be done in a setting where adequate psychiatric safeguards are provided." At the same time the Council of the American Psychological Association expressed opposition to any practice of psychotherapy by clinical psychologists "that does not meet conditions of genuine collaboration with physicians most qualified to deal with the borderline problems which occur (e.g., differential diagnosis, intercurrent organic disease, psychosomatic problems, etc.)."[29]

That the divisions between psychiatry and clinical psychology were not susceptible to easy solutions was evident. In practice individuals worked together harmoniously. A survey by an American Psychological Association committee in the late 1940s revealed that professional relations between psychiatrists and psychologists on the local level were reasonably good, but that each local group regarded its cooperative relationships as "unusual." These findings suggested that when interprofessional concerns were discussed in the abstract, emotion prevailed and unyielding adherence to principle became characteristic.[30]

Even William C. Menninger, for example, was troubled by existing tensions. More than most psychodynamic psychiatrists, he had been supportive of psychologists both in the military and at the Menninger Foundation. By the late 1940s he was seeking a way to resolve existing tensions. When serving as president of the APA in 1948, Menninger observed that many psychologists were already "doing treatment quite outside a medical group." Psychiatrists, he added, had two choices: "solidifying our relationships, clarifying our misunderstandings, and working closer together; *or* assuming a condemnatory, do-nothing policy." The following year he accepted an invitation to deliver an address before the American Psychological Association. Yet his temperate approach presumed psychiatric leadership. The two disciplines, he noted, were "engaged in a mutually cooperative enterprise." Admittedly, some relationships required clarification, notably the role of the psychologist in treatment. Part of the misunderstanding arose out of the absence of a sharp dividing line "between intensive formal psychotherapeutic sessions with a severely neurotic patient on the one extreme and educational efforts with a child with reading difficulties on the other." "*Any* contact with the patient," he conceded, "has therapeutic implications." Clinical psychologists, therefore, would have to accept that fact "that certain kinds of painstakingly gathered clinical knowledge . . . are prerequisites to carrying on psychotherapy." Hence psychiatrists "will have to be their chief teachers." Menninger looked forward to a time when the psychologist "can accept the psychiatrist as the quarterback of a team that works together, in which neither individual need be concerned with threats from the other. We must reach a stage in our evolution when the bugaboos of status, jurisdiction, equality and subordination become dead issues."[31]

Legal concerns further exacerbated interprofessional tensions. In the postwar years, clinical psychologists began to push for the passage of state certification and even licensing laws. The former provided that only those who satisfied minimum requirements of competency could assume such specified titles as "clinical psychologist." Licensing laws, by contrast, stipulated that only individuals who had satisfied minimum standards of competency *and* obtained a license could render services as a clinical psychologist. In 1945 Connecticut adopted one of the earliest certification laws. A few states followed suit, and at least one made provision for licensing.[32]

The attempt to secure legal recognition of psychologists did not necessarily grow solely out of jealousy of, or rivalry with, psychiatry. On the contrary, psychologists were eager to exclude quacks or charlatans or those who ostensibly lacked appropriate training. By then psychological services, ranging from counseling for the normal to psychotherapy for the emotionally distraught, were common. Bureaucratic and organizational imperatives promoted the concept of adjustment, while cultural norms increasingly incorporated a preoccupation with the self. A variety of individuals and groups eagerly exploited the proclivity of Americans to seek assistance wherever offered, thus threatening the authority of professions. Intraprofessional divisions (e.g., between individuals with doctorates and those with terminal master's degrees) also played a part in the struggle over the passage of laws.[33]

Although psychiatrists were not opposed to certification by the American Board of Examiners in Professional Psychology, they had distinct reservations about the enactment of formal statutes. Medicine had obviously benefited by the passage of medical licensing laws, most of which were intended to regulate the treatment of physical ailments. The problematic nature of mental distress or illnesses, however, created a void, and psychiatrists were fearful that under such conditions the passage of certification and licensing laws would inevitably diminish medical authority. When bills providing for certification and licensing of psychologists were introduced into legislatures, therefore, political conflict inevitably followed.

By 1949, for example, psychologists were promoting legislation in New York State (and elsewhere) providing for the licensing of psychologists. The bill passed the legislature but met with a gubernatorial veto. The APA opposed the bill, Blain wrote, because of its belief that "the treatment and diagnosis of mentally sick people should be called treatment and diagnosis of mentally sick people and the extension of the responsibilities, which some are attempting to put in the hands of clinical psychologists beyond the scope of their training, is against the public interest and more particularly the interest of the people who are sick." In New Jersey, Theodore Robie was active in heading off undesirable legislation by lobbying for a bill that provided for the licensing of psychologists by the State Board of Medical Examiners under the rubric of the Medical Practice Act. The APA was also active in opposing licensure legislation in California and in modifying a description of the qualifications of federally employed clinical psychologists that was under consideration by the United States Civil Service Commission.[34]

On occasion feelings on both sides became so intense that they spilled into the public arena. In 1953 and 1954 (as in 1949), bills had been introduced in the New York legislature amending the state's Medical Practice Act to include the diagnosis and treatment of mental disorders. The ensuing conflict made the pages of the *New York Times*. In a letter to the paper, Rollo May, a highly respected figure and president of the New York State Psychological Association, vigorously criticized the bill. May emphasized that it "would produce chaos among the legitimate facilities in the state for helping people with their emotional and psychological problems" without in any way dealing with quackery. A group of psychiatrists immediately responded in defense of the bill, which they insisted was simply intended to protect the public by ensuring that the diagnosis and treatment of mental disorders remained in the hands of qualified practitioners. In turn, some notable psychologists, social workers, and educators pointed out that the term *mental and nervous disorders* (as contrasted with *mental disease*) was "vague and controversial" and could encompass "conditions ranging, on the one hand, from truancy, behavior disorders in children and undue anxiety in daily living, to organic psychoses, on the other." Responsibility for the former should not be restricted to physicians, they insisted. Human behavior could not be understood in terms of pathology; more relevant were "theories of human development, learning, motivation, cultural conditioning, concepts of personality organization, etc." Two psychiatrists—Theodore Robie and Mildred Pellens—defended the bill by insisting that there was "no justification for the assertion that treating emotional illness does not require medical training and skill." Privately Robie was even more blunt. May's claim that the legislation would wipe out psychological services was "utterly ridiculous" since the APA had repeatedly offered a satisfactory compromise ("psychiatric supervision of psychotherapy by psychologists"). Although the legislation died in committee, the public debate illuminated the seemingly irreconcilable positions of the two groups.[35]

The struggle over certification and licensing was also accompanied by an ongoing dialogue designed to resolve existing differences. Formal and informal contacts between the APA and the American Psychological Association had begun as early as 1946 and continued in subsequent decades. Both sides recognized that political conflicts in the public arena would prove mutually damaging. Yet neither was willing to concede the point that each considered vital, namely, whether or not psychotherapy should remain exclusively within psychiatric jurisdiction. There was agreement that the passage of certification laws for psychologists was desirable (although differences existed on the meaning of certification). Psychologists, however, drew a distinction between the concepts of "supervision" and "collaboration." The supervision of junior clinical psychologists by psychiatrists or psychologists was appropriate. Upon reaching "full professional competence," however, the clinical psychologist no longer required supervision but rather had "to remain in close collaboration with his colleagues of all appropriate professions."[36]

Despite ongoing private negotiations, the governing boards of the APA, the AMA, and the American Psychoanalytic Association adopted a common statement in 1954 that psychotherapy was "a form of medical treatment" and that other professions—admittedly autonomous within their respective spheres—had to concede medical dominance insofar as the diagnosis and treatment of illness was concerned. Such statements, Fillmore H. Sanford (executive secretary of the American Psychological Association) observed, left psychology with only two alternatives: "to submit quietly to the medical profession" or "to oppose openly and vigorously, in whatever ways it can, the move to establish medical hegemony over the field of mental health." Neither was satisfactory, added Sanford. The first represented "an immorally weak submission to medical authority" and would decrease the professional assistance available to millions with personal and emotional problems; the second would harm both professions. Fillmore had no ready solution but expressed the thought that it might be possible "to reinsert the informed citizen . . . into the present dispute" and perhaps find "joint and creative solutions . . . demonstrably consistent with public welfare and with the genuine humanistic concerns of both psychiatrists and psychologists."[37]

At the bottom of the dispute lay some important ideological and professional differences. Psychodynamic psychiatrists believed that inner psychic conflict lay at the base of mental maladjustment. Psychotherapy, by clarifying the origins of conflict, promoted personal insight, which, in turn, ultimately led to behavioral change. Most clinical psychologists, contrastingly, tended to favor behavioral theories and were largely interested in the modification of behavior. Whereas psychodynamic psychiatrists were likely to deal with phobias in terms of inner conflict, clinical psychologists were more prone to employ therapeutic interventions designed to alter external behavior. Psychotherapy, wrote the influential Shakow Committee in 1947, involved the use of "psychological methods based on systematic knowledge of the human personality in attempting to improve the mental health" of patients. The theoretical foundations of psychology, therefore, did not mandate a medical education. Even the "nondirective therapy" of Carl Rogers—one of the most influential psychologists of the 1940s—was closer to behavioral than to psychodynamic theory. Psychotherapy, as Arthur Combs observed in 1953, embodied "a kind of relationship or situation for a client in which he can do something for himself." A colleague put the issue more bluntly: psychiatrists accepted "Medical Omniscience" and were engaged in a form of "Degree Worship." Some psychologists believed that economic issues were involved; psychiatrists simply wanted to maintain their monopoly.[38]

To Lawrence S. Kubie, a psychoanalytically oriented psychiatrist who also served on the APA Committee on Clinical Psychology, the problem required an innovative approach. By 1948 he had come to the conclusion that neither specialty provided adequate training in the use of psychotherapeutic procedures. The solution, Kubie suggested, involved the creation of a new medical-psychological curriculum within medical schools leading to the award of a doctorate in medical psychology. Receiving little support and growing weary of interprofessional tension, Kubie resigned from the APA committee three years later, suggesting that its name be changed to "Committee on Abolishing Relationship between Psychiatry and Clinical Psychology." In 1954 he reiterated his belief in the necessity for novel thinking. "Just as formal psychiatry left the 'lunatic asylum' to enter the community, so we must now face the fact that psychopathology as a discipline, as a theoretical system, as a field of human understanding and as a technique of exploration and of therapy must escape from its confinement in the medical clinic, to offer its knowledge and its skills to all of human culture." Only a doctorate in medical psychology could provide appropriate training for psychodiagnosis and psychotherapy. Kubie met with sharp opposition from his psychiatric colleagues, most of whom were unwilling to consider the merits of his proposal. Indeed, there was even opposition to publishing an explanatory letter written by Kubie to the *American Journal of Psychiatry*.[39]

During 1954 the APA Committee on Relations with Psychology met with its counterpart from psychology and agreed to a moratorium on all legislative actions except those agreed to by both organizations. Privately the APA committee warned that it would be unwise to seek legislative restrictions on the activities of psychologists. Aware that psychology bills of one sort or another were being introduced in perhaps twenty states, the committee proposed that the APA should become active politically to prevent passage of undesirable laws while simultaneously maintaining a dialogue with psychologists. Its members were unalterably opposed to a public debate over certification or licensing, if only because "few members of the public are able to make sound judgments on issues which have divided the professionals themselves." The Council then voted to endorse legal certification. It insisted, however, that laws not include a definition of the practice of psychology; such a statement would be tantamount to licensing. It also recommended the inclusion of a clause stipulating that nothing in the law "shall be construed to give the right to engage in the practice of medicine, or any of the other healing arts."[40]

In actuality it was virtually impossible to separate certification and practice. Moreover, psychologists were aggressively pursuing legislative action to further their own goals. In 1957 the APA responded by rescinding its approval of certification. The following year the American Psychological Association reiterated its opposition to any efforts to restrict the role and practice of psychologists through amendments to medical practice acts; and further, the group offered to join in the legal defense of members engaged in professional practice who were charged "with the practice of medicine in terms of psychotherapy."[41]

The changing social context of the postwar era only exacerbated jurisdictional conflict. During these years, psychological explanations of behavior, fueled by the media, dominated mass culture. In popular thought, psychological insights defined both the problem and its solution. The ensuing pressure for services exerted by a middle-class clientele followed. Psychiatry was unable to meet the demand, given the limited size of medical schools and the proportion of medical graduates selecting psychiatry as their specialty. Nor were its members in a position to impose their will on a public unable to differentiate between professional groups or even to question their claims. For psychiatrists, long accustomed to a kind of hegemony in the mental health field by virtue of their unchallenged authority in mental hospitals, the loss of power came as a distinct shock.

Psychologists, by way of contrast, believed that the time had arrived to confirm their legitimacy and authority. The increase in the number of doctorates, combined with seemingly rapid advances in psychological knowledge, imparted to members of the specialty a sense of mission and confidence. At the same time, the discipline appeared to be in a strategic position to use its knowledge to further socially desirable goals. By the 1950s psychology had lost its purely academic character. A random sample survey of the American Psychological Association in 1960 revealed that 41 percent devoted half of their work schedule to psychotherapy; 17

percent were in full-time practice; and 12 percent had part-time private practices. Four years later a more comprehensive analysis revealed that the principal activity of 68.8 percent of nearly 17,000 psychologists was related to the field of mental health. In addition, more than a dozen states, including New York and California, had passed certification laws during the 1950s.[42]

By 1959 both the APA and the American Psychological Association had begun to retreat from their aggressive stance. Joel S. Handler, chair of the APA Committee on Relations with Psychology, urged that renewed efforts be made to resolve existing tensions and that channels of communication be reestablished. "We do not dismiss patients who disagree with us on moral, scientific or whatever grounds. We try to understand them, we respect them and hope to gain mutual respect and confidence. . . . Psychologists are not our patients, they do not consider *themselves* sick but a good many think *we* are, that we have warped ideas, old fashioned ideas, unscientific, irrational ideas. Can we treat them with less respect than our patients and expect them to respect us?" In early 1960 the two committees, with the endorsement of their respective executive committees, issued a joint report. The document spelled out the major differences, including "the problems of collaboration and supervision" as well as the expressed fear of the APA that psychologists were increasingly moving into private practice despite the absence of "adequate controls."[43]

During the 1960s the two organizations continued their discussions, albeit in a friendlier manner. Nevertheless, the differences were so profound that no satisfactory resolution appeared possible. "I do feel that we have been over concerned about the ambitions, desires and feelings of our colleagues in psychology," APA President C. H. Hardin Branch wrote to Handler in 1962. "Your experience may have been quite different from mine but I do feel that the psychologists with whom I have discussed these problems are inclined to solicit backing from the medical profession in their own drive to do psychotherapy but are not quite ready to accept the fact that the status of the medical position has been achieved after many, many years of relationship with patients and the public and is not something which can be lightly shared with any group." In 1964 the APA adopted a set of principles governing its relations with psychology based on the final report of an AMA committee studying the relations between medicine and allied health professions (McKeown Report), but these proved unacceptable to psychologists.[44]

During the 1960s other developments not only complicated efforts to arrive at mutually satisfactory agreements but actually weakened the ability of psychiatrists to define jurisdictional boundaries. The passage of the Community Mental Health Centers Act of 1963 raised novel questions about interprofessional relationships, and the formal policy statement adopted by the American Psychological Association clearly represented a challenge to medical authority. Indeed, the community mental health center—precisely because its form had not yet been fixed—offered psychology, as Bernard Saper observed, "a fine opportunity for mobility upward and outward from the confining positions it has held in the clinic or mental hospital." Unlike mental hospitals, community mental health centers had neither organizational nor bureaucratic traditions. Because they were relatively autonomous and not under the control of state agencies, their structures tended to be more fluid. The result was an institution in which psychiatrists played important roles but clearly lacked the kind of authority they had in hospitals. That psychologists could and did become clinic directors was but one indication of change.[45]

Disturbingly, the rhetoric, countercharges, and claims of the two groups were exchanged in a partial intellectual vacuum. The debate over psychotherapy was largely symbolic. Neither psychiatrists nor psychologists had ever defined its distinctive attributes or justified their claims to overarching competence. Many groups (including general practitioners), as a matter of fact, were providing psychotherapeutic services to troubled individuals. Above all, there were virtually no adequate evaluations of efficacy, and those that existed generally violated most principles of research design. Neither group considered the possibility of submitting their respective claims to disinterested parties; to do so would be to call into question the very foundations of professional authority and autonomy. A profession that permitted its claims to be adjudicated, William J. Goode observed, "would be comparable to a nation permitting a world court to adjudicate its right to existence." The failure to engage in meaningful evaluation, however, was hardly surprising. An emerging profession, added Goode, "typically survives by faith, not by proof of works." His observation caught the essence of the dispute. Differences could not be resolved by reference to empirical data, if only because the struggle had all the attributes of a confrontation between two religious groups, each persuaded that it had a monopoly on eternal truth and virtue.[46]

. . .

Unlike clinical psychology, the relationships between psychiatry and other nonmedical mental health professions (including psychiatric social work and psychiatric nursing) were relatively tranquil. This is not to imply that social workers and nurses did not harbor grievances or resentments about their subordinate positions, for such was not the case. Whatever their underlying feelings, they did not directly challenge psychiatric authority by seeking to create an autonomous sphere through legislation. Moreover, they accepted, at least in theory, a subordinate role. Certainly the fact that neither of these occupations required a doctorate tended to minimize friction. Perhaps more important, social work and nursing were traditionally female professions whose members did not challenge the male-dominated specialty of psychiatry.

Psychiatric social work was a case in point. During World War II social workers in the military accepted the traditional tasks of taking case histories and assisting servicemen in making effective use of available services. Yet psychiatric services were in such short supply that lines of responsibility were often obliterated in practice, thus providing social workers with expanded therapeutic opportunities. Nevertheless, social workers never questioned the necessity for psychiatric supervision. Indeed, casework—the feature that defined social work—was impregnated with the language and insights of psychiatry, a theme explicitly spelled out by Lawson G. Lowrey (an eminent child psychiatrist) in his book *Psychiatry for Social Workers*, first published in 1946. To a considerable extent, therefore, psychodynamic and psychoanalytic psychiatry became the role model for psychiatric social work.[47]

Contacts between the APA and the American Association of Psychiatric Social Workers generally revolved around the need to define higher educational requirements and achieve greater standardization. That psychiatric social workers were dependent upon psychiatrists was obvious; the former recognized their unequal status even while accepting the benefits that ensued from collaboration with a higher-status medical specialty. Yet the relationship between the two specialties remained problematic. There was general agreement that the goal of casework was not to deal with the internal causes of character disturbances, but rather to assist the client in finding a satisfactory form of social adjustment. In practice the distinction was largely meaningless. Was it possible to differentiate the psychiatric social worker's casework from psychiatry and also from other types of casework? In debating this question in 1942, the Executive Committee of the American Association of Psychiatric Social Workers found itself unable to distinguish between cases appropriate to a psychiatrist and those appropriate to a caseworker. Indeed, its members agreed "that we hardly know what it is we psychiatric social workers do." The relatively small number of psychiatrists employed full-time in clinics and their declining number in mental hospitals, nevertheless, gave psychiatric social workers considerable leeway in their daily activities. By virtue of their intake and administrative responsibilities in clinics and agencies, they used their diagnostic skills to make referrals and to work directly with clients without encountering any resistance.[48]

In the postwar years, psychiatric social workers also began to evaluate their therapeutic role. Their willingness to defer, at least in theory, to psychiatric supervision and guidance minimized the kind of friction that characterized relationships between psychology and psychiatry (although their association agreed to send a "spectator" to a meeting sponsored by the American Psychological Association in 1949 dealing with licensing, since psychiatric social workers might also face that issue in the future). Yet social workers were by no means unaware of the wider implications of the debate over psychotherapy, and they insisted that their profession ought to define its own role rather than having it defined by others. A committee established in 1947 devoted nearly three years to the study of casework and psychotherapy. Members experienced considerable difficulty in separating the two approaches, and several came to the conclusion that they were no more than "differing aspects of the same process." Consequently, the committee expressed the belief that additional training beyond that provided by schools of social work was required.[49]

Although psychiatric social workers sought to create a separate identity, their efforts met with only modest success. Casework in a hospital or clinic setting, after all, was hardly a firm foundation for the creation of professional autonomy and boundaries. The intellectual foundations of casework were unclear and constantly shifted between psychological and sociological extremes. At times, casework was interpreted in psychological and psychiatric terms, thus emphasizing individual psychic adjustment. On other occasions, casework stressed the social and environmental roots of individual disabilities. It was hardly surprising, therefore, that psychiatrists often expressed puzzlement about the precise nature and functions of the specialty. "Social workers," observed a committee of the National Association of Social Workers in 1960, "are not clear about what they have to offer, nor is the medical profession apparently clear about what they want." One psychiatric participant at the Mental Health Institute in 1950 conceded that he was not always able to fathom the nature of the work and therefore urged his colleagues "to arrive at a pretty clear impression . . . as to what we want a social service worker to do." Social service work was commonly confused with psychiatric social work. Walter Barton, head of Boston State Hospital and author of an influential text in administrative psychiatry, expressed similar concerns. The psychiatrist, he wrote, saw the need to assist in getting patients out of hospitals, whereas the focus of social workers was on more casework. Barton also decried the excessive time spent by social workers on "self-analysis and reexamination of their status."[50]

Psychiatric social work was a derivative and synthetic specialty. Its applied character also bespoke the absence of a research tradition, an activity that often lent legitimacy in a society all too willing to accept uncritically the authority of claims that presumably grew out of scientific inquiry. The intellectual constructs of psychiatric social work were for the most part borrowed from other disciplines; overlapping jurisdictional boundaries prevented its members from articulating a clear statement of its distinctive features or unique problems. Casework, precisely because of the personal relationships involved, seemed peculiarly resistant to systematic scientific inquiry or evaluation. Nor were psychiatric social workers trained in research or research methods; the master's degree was directed toward the production of practitioners. Admittedly, several scholarly journals provided the discipline with outlets for publication. These journals, however, addressed largely the practical concerns of the specialty; only rarely did they reflect research in the academic and disciplinary sense of the term.[51]

The social, educational, and occupational characteristics of psychiatric social workers further reinforced an underlying weakness. Within the general field of social work the specialty remained marginal, although NIMH training grants contributed to an expansion in numbers. In 1954, for example, the American Association of Psychiatric Social Workers had 2,115 members. A survey revealed that 90 percent had a master's degree, but only 2 percent a doctorate. The field was predominantly female; males constituted only about a quarter of the total. The settings in which members were employed were hardly conducive to the exercise of independence and autonomy: 29 percent were found in mental hospitals and outpatient clinics; 32 percent in independent psychiatric clinics; 15 percent in family and children's agencies; and 8 percent in colleges and universities. About 43 percent identified casework as their primary job responsibility; 17 percent were engaged in supervision, 18 percent in administration, and 7 percent in teaching. The median salary (slightly over $5,000), though respectable, was not high, and males earned about $400 more than females.[52]

Cognizant of weaknesses within the field of social work generally as well as the ambiguity of psychiatric social work in particular, the American Association of Psychiatric Social Workers began to consider the possibility of a merger with other groups in 1948. These deliberations led to the creation of the Committee on Interassociation Structure, which endorsed the concept of a single national organization. In 1950 the Temporary Inter-Association Council came into existence, and during the succeeding five years this group worked for organizational unity. Success came in 1955 when seven organizations agreed to form the National Association of Social Workers. The merger undoubtedly gave social work more national visibility but hardly strengthened the autonomy or independence of psychiatric social work.[53]

· · ·

Much of the interprofessional rivalry and conflict involved psychiatrists, clinical psychologists, and psychiatric social workers. These specialties were based in part on educational credentials; all required graduate degrees, which helped to provide a rationalization for their authority and legitimacy. Although clearly the most visible part of the mental health force, their actual roles diminished materially when compared with those of the nursing and attendant staff in mental hospitals. The latter were in direct contact with patients virtually every minute of the day and night, and they, along with patients, exercised major influence over the shaping of the institution's internal environment and culture. Insofar as patient care was concerned, the role of nurses and attendants exceeded that of the professional staff. Within certain ill-defined parameters, these groups gave institutions their peculiar ambience.

Before 1940 nurses and attendants, however their services were valued in the abstract, rarely received formal recognition. While they were clearly indispensable to institutional well-being, the normal rewards of service were rarely offered them. Salaries were relatively poor, hours long, and working conditions less than ideal. Annual turnover rates remained consistently high. Nurses received some training in mental hospital nursing schools, which were non-degree-granting entities established solely to prepare individuals for their positions. Attendants, on the other hand, received little or no training; job-related experiences were their introduction to the field.

During World War I the APA created what subsequently became known as the Committee on Psychiatric Nursing. In the interwar years its members prepared a curriculum and began to accredit schools of nursing by employing an annual questionnaire (funds for travel were not available). In 1942 the Rockefeller Foundation awarded the APA a one-year grant of ten thousand dollars to cover the salary and expenses of an eminent nurse. In subsequent years the grant was renewed at somewhat higher levels. Out of the Psychiatric Nursing Project came the publication of a number of guides for the training of both nurses and attendants in mental hospitals.[54]

World War II only exacerbated traditional staffing patterns. Shortages of nurses and attendants were common. Nursing was admittedly a low-status occupation; it was dominated by females and appeared to lack a clearly defined character. Psychiatric nursing had an even more ambiguous status; graduate nurses rarely selected it as their specialty. In 1940 only 4,252 graduate nurses were employed in mental hospitals. A decade later the situation had not changed; of the 56,375 individuals providing care for about 435,000 patients in state mental hospitals, only 4,109 were qualified psychiatric nurses. Oddly enough, female patients were the beneficiaries of the occupation's gender specificity. Since wards—including patients and staff—were structured along gender lines, male patients received care from relatively untrained male attendants, who administered medication and provided postoperative care. "It is rather startling," observed Laura W. Fitzsimmons, the nursing consultant of the APA, in a report to the Rockefeller Foundation in 1943, "that such a standard of nursing care should prevail in our mental hospitals in this modern age of medicine."[55]

After World War II schools of nursing in mental hospitals declined in significance. Increasingly psychiatric nursing began to evolve as a distinct specialty requiring postgraduate training. A crucial element in this development was its inclusion (along with psychiatry, clinical psychology, and psychiatric social work) as one of the four core disciplines within the NIMH. Committed to the concept of a team approach in providing psychiatric services, the NIMH provided funding for the training of graduate psychiatric nurses. In fiscal year 1948 the institute allocated 18.6 percent ($235,824) of its training grants to psychiatric nursing. This percentage declined slightly during the 1950s, but the dollar amount increased sharply. By 1952 the allocation had fallen to 15 percent, but the total had tripled to $697,182.[56]

Although gradually increasing in size, psychiatric nursing remained a marginal occupation: in 1956 no more than 3 to 5 percent of nurses specialized in the care of mental patients. From an economic point of view, there was little incentive to change this pattern; a higher proportion of qualified nurses in the institutional work force would escalate costs. The female character of the specialty, plus the fact that the majority of nurses were married and hence retained familial responsibilities, tended to promote high turnover rates. Thus few psychiatric nurses remained in the field for more than five years, a characteristic that hampered the creation of a professional image.[57]

More important, there was no consensus on the role and functions of psychiatric nurses, or how the specialty could be differentiated from other mental health occupations. "I find the matter of nursing so complex and so uncertain," wrote Harry C. Solomon, professor of psychiatry at Harvard and director of Boston Psychopathic Hospital in 1949, "that I am not sure what a psychiatric committee ought to do about it at this time." Nurses clearly desired to be part of the psychiatric team and hinted that their contacts with patients signified that they played an important part in psychotherapy (under medical supervision and guidance). Their model was understandably derived from medicine. The professional status of psychiatric nursing, wrote Helen Nahm in 1957, implies commitment "to work for the welfare of humanity, to build a body of knowledge by which a special field is defined, to communicate knowledge of this field to others, and to do research which will add to the body of knowledge and will constantly improve the practice." In 1963 the *Journal of Psychiatric Nursing* commenced publication; it stood as a symbol of a new kind of professional identity.[58]

Ideals notwithstanding, nurses in mental hospitals tended to be preoccupied with administrative functions or patient care; a scholarly component was largely absent. A study in 1956 revealed an appreciable disjunction of attitudes and perceptions among physicians and nurses; the result was widespread confusion over roles. Newton Bigelow, editor of the *Psychiatric Quarterly* and an important New York State institutional psychiatrist, expressed unhappiness with trends in psychiatric nursing and the attempt to shift their education from hospital to university schools of nursing. Efforts by nurses to abandon the bedside and move into the university would undoubtedly enhance their status, prestige, and income, he conceded. But was such a trend in the best interests of patients? Bigelow's concerns were not put to the test, however, for the endeavor to alter the nature of psychiatric nursing met with relatively little success. Since the other three mental health professions enjoyed a distinctly superior status, they tended to shift less valued tasks—administration and management—to nurses and thus dilute their significance in the therapeutic program. The conflict that marked the relationships between the other mental health specialties was largely absent; nurses posed no threat to those above them.[59]

At the bottom of the hierarchy was the attendant or, to employ postwar terminology, the psychiatric aide. Numerically this occupational category far exceeded in size all others combined; in 1950 the total numbered about eighty thousand. At the outbreak of World War II there was general agreement that the quality of individuals employed as attendants constituted perhaps the most serious problem facing mental hospitals. "The attendant," wrote Leonard Edelstein (an official with the Civilian Public Service, the organization that supervised conscientious objectors assigned to mental hospitals in World War II), "is the patient's major source of contact with a sane world, yet frequently that contact is made with an indifferent and even psychopathic personality, who subjugates his patients with fear, or undermines attempts at professional treatment by neglect, indifference and even brutality." Patients, according to John M. Grimes, "are still under the care, not of doctors, but of ignorant, short-sighted, bulldozing attendants, whose incompetence, callousness, and brutality beggar description." The comprehensive study conducted by the Council of State Governments reported that in 1949 the average annual turnover rate for attendants was 55 percent, as compared with 28 percent for physicians, 34 percent for graduate nurses, and 17 percent for social workers. Although playing a crucial role because of their close relationships with patients, attendants received little or no training. High turnover rates, therefore, constituted a problem of major proportions, if only because of the adverse impact on patients. Low salaries and long working hours only exacerbated existing problems.[60]

Those World War II conscientious objectors assigned to work in mental hospitals very quickly began to emphasize the need to upgrade the quality of attendants. Psychodynamic psychiatrists were sympathetic with these efforts even though somewhat fearful of working with a group of enthusiastic young men not always willing to defer to professional authority. Yet the difficulties that impeded change were substantial. The NIMH, for example, was unwilling to include psychiatric aides as one of its core disciplines. Aides, explained Felix, were not required in the non-hospital settings upon "which the national mental health program by law places its chief emphasis." Nor did formal training standards for attendants exist. Although holding out hope for future change, Felix was unwilling to commit resources for the training of aides. Moreover, there was considerable hostility, even rivalry, between psychiatric nurses and attendants. Many psychiatric nurses worked in supervisory positions even though they knew less about the job requirements than the attendants whom they supervised. Sustained efforts to improve the status of attendants—a numerically very large group—could easily detract from efforts to upgrade psychiatric nursing.[61]

During the 1950s, nevertheless, there was a gradual improvement in the quality of attendants. Undoubtedly, the general prosperity of the postwar period hastened change because of competition for labor. Yet internal innovations were also important. The development of the concept of milieu therapy and the therapeutic hospital—a concept that placed prime importance on social and environmental interventions—sensitized psychiatrists and others to the importance of the mediating role played by attendants. By the 1940s a number of states had introduced formal training programs. The Menninger Foundation—the most important psychodynamic training institution of the 1940s and 1950s—established an experimental School for Psychiatric Aides in 1949 with a grant from the Rockefeller Foundation. Three years later the foundation published a study of the results. The school had not been able to decide "*how much* of *what material* should be taught and to *whom*," if only because the psychiatric aide's area of competence had not been defined. Indeed, the study found that one of the key problems was the relationship of aides to nurses, a relationship that remained problematic. By 1963 nine out of ten public institutions had their own training programs. The median number of instructional hours was sixty; the number of hours of supervised ward training was thirty-eight. Approximately two-thirds of the 96,000 aides had received some type of instruction.[62]

Postwar demographic data also suggested that beneficial changes had occurred. A comprehensive analysis in 1963 revealed that two-thirds of psychiatric aides were married. Their educational level was slightly higher than the adult population of the country as a whole. Nearly half had a high school education, and 10 percent had completed between one and three years of college. Working conditions had also improved. Most aides worked a standard five-day, forty-hour week, a sharp decline from prewar levels. Provision for vacations and sick leave was general, and virtually all states had established retirement plans. The gender composition was mixed; 60 percent were female. The median salary was $3,550, a figure sharply below the median income for male workers ($5,240), but higher than the female median of $2,447. Women aides earned somewhat more than their male counterparts, perhaps because of their greater longevity on the job. There was some indication that job satisfaction had increased because of the greater emphasis placed on patient care rather than custody. In 1963 the turnover rate—one measure of job satisfaction—had fallen to 30 percent (as contrasted with a rate of 55 percent in 1949).[63]

. . .

During the 1950s and 1960s interprofessional tensions gradually altered jurisdictional boundaries and roles. Federal policy encouraged the training of nonmedical professionals less inclined to accept psychiatric authority in the mental health field. Differing professional perceptions ultimately led to sharp disagreements on the competency of nonmedical personnel to offer psychotherapy without medical supervision. Paradoxically, the debate over psychotherapy—a vague and protean concept that defied any clear definition—was more symbolic than substantive. Evidence demonstrating that psychotherapy as practiced by psychiatrists was superior to that provided by nonmedical professionals was nonexistent. Symbolic conflicts, of course, conceal as much as they illuminate; they are generally bitter and lengthy and often involve status and authority relationships. Such conflicts are especially difficult to resolve, partly because differences cannot be defined or identified in concrete terms. Consequently, professional divisions persisted in the postwar era.

Oddly enough, the friction between the various mental health professions had mixed consequences. Troubled but functional individuals undoubtedly benefited from the expansion of community therapeutic services that followed the growth of the mental health professions. For the severely mentally ill, however, the conflict was in part irrelevant. Most hospitals lacked resources to provide psychotherapeutic services on a large scale. Perhaps the major benefit to institutionalized patients deriving from the debate over psychotherapy was awareness of the importance of attendants, a development that helped to fuel efforts to improve their quality. In essence, the internecine struggle within the mental health professions revolved around services in noninstitutional settings; in this sense some of the basic and most pressing needs of the severely mentally ill (comprehensive and continuous care) were largely overlooked. The debate and struggle over boundaries, therefore, was driven as much by the internal concerns of professional groups as it was by the needs of the severely mentally ill.

CHAPTER SIX

Care and Treatment: Changing Views

MARKED ENTHUSIASM for changes in mental health policy characterized the postwar years. Yet the elements that promoted receptivity toward innovation—the lessons drawn from wartime experiences, the shifts in the structure and ideology of the mental health professions, the altered role of the federal government—did not by themselves define demonstrably more effective ways of providing care and treatment for mentally ill persons. Ideals, hopes, and aspirations had to be translated into concrete programs and policies, and these, in turn, had to be blended and transmuted in the crucible of experience. In the final analysis, the criterion of success was the degree to which such new policies actually benefited the mentally ill both within and without institutions.

Between 1945 and 1960 therapeutic concepts and practices underwent a significant transformation. The simultaneous development of psychotropic drugs and milieu therapy—in addition to electroshock, lobotomy, and psychotherapy—blurred the conventional distinction between psychological and somatic approaches. More important, these new therapies suggested the possibility of integrating community and outpatient facilities with a large but troubled public mental hospital system in imaginative ways, thereby healing the divisions within psychiatry. Such innovations seemed to confirm the hopes and aspirations of a postwar generation driven by the belief that new policies and practices would facilitate the movement of mentally ill persons from institutions into the community.

The differences between rhetoric and expectations, on the one hand, and reality, on the other, were substantial. What kinds of evidence existed to validate claims of greater therapeutic effectiveness? How true was the often-reiterated insistence that more effective alternatives to traditional institutional care were readily available? How was it possible to show that the alleviation of broad social and environmental problems would in fact improve the mental health of individuals when psychiatric disease categories remained protean and of uncertain etiology? Were administrative systems sufficiently developed to permit careful monitoring of patients as they made the transition from hospital to community? That answers to these and other questions were at best tenuous seemed unimportant when placed alongside the excitement, sense of urgency, and optimism characteristic of the postwar years.

. . .

The external confidence and expansiveness of psychiatrists in the years following 1945 masked some feelings of uncertainty. Nowhere were these inner doubts better revealed than in debates over appropriate therapies. It was one thing to talk in general terms about new approaches to care and treatment of the mentally ill or to emphasize the relevance of psychiatric insights to social problems. It was quite a different matter to discuss what kinds of specific therapies were most effective for individual patients.

Psychiatric thinking traditionally incorporated both psychological and somatic elements. Trained as physicians, psychiatrists never abandoned the view that mental illnesses had a distinct biological component. At the same time they insisted that mental disorders could be understood in psychological or functional terms; the inability of human beings to adapt to their environment could lead to aberrant behavioral signs. Admittedly, certain individual psychiatrists identified with positions at the two extreme ends of the spectrum. Nevertheless, most subscribed to a vague consensus that mental illnesses involved both biological and psychological factors, and that human behavior could not be encompassed by monocausal explanations. Having long since abandoned a philosophical dualism that distinguished between mind and matter, psychiatrists—whatever their theoretical allegiances—were receptive to therapeutic latitudinarianism.

The prevailing eclecticism was but a reflection of the inability to demonstrate clear links between symptomatology and pathology. As a matter of fact, when a clear causal relationship between pathology and behavior was demonstrated, jurisdiction for the illness was invariably transferred from psychiatry to another medical specialty. When behavioral symptoms were linked with endocrinological disorders, for example, jurisdiction was transferred from psychiatry to endocrinology. Similarly, paresis—a tertiary stage of syphilis that in the nineteenth century was known as general paralysis of the insane—was incorporated into dermatology, internal medicine, and neurology when the relationship between the *Treponema pallidum* and the disease was demonstrated. Ironically, psychiatrists proved themselves extraordinarily poor tacticians within medicine. By surrendering authority over diseases of known somatic origins marked by disturbed behavior, they were in the somewhat odd position of retaining jurisdiction over all the mental diseases of unknown etiology. Under such circumstances they were vulnerable to accusations by their medical brethren that psychiatry was not part of medicine, and that psychiatric practice rested on superstition and myth.

The psychiatric failure to defend boundaries grew out of unique historical circumstances. Unlike other medical specialties, psychiatry originated in an institutional setting. Its members defined their responsibilities largely in managerial and administrative terms. Consequently, they were somewhat isolated from late nineteenth- and early twentieth-century medicine with its complex web of medical schools, laboratories, and teaching hospitals. Whereas medical leaders were identifying themselves with scientific progress, psychiatrists were managing an extensive system of large public hospitals. Isolation fostered a certain kind of political naïveté: psychiatrists tended to be oblivious to the advantages that accrued from identification with an increasingly popular technologically based medical system. Nor did the situation change in the immediate postwar years. Psychodynamic and psychoanalytic psychiatrists, after all, were for the most part remote from the pharmacological and technological thrust of medical science, and they consequently remained vulnerable to criticism. Yet the differences between psychiatry and other medical specialties should not be exaggerated. In a broad sense, all these subdisciplines were engaged in similar activities. Like other physicians, psychiatrists were seeking to provide explanations for a range of disorders and then to develop therapies that followed logically from these explanations. The belief that general medical practice was "objective" and "scientific"—as compared with the "subjective" character of psychiatry—represented exaggerated rhetoric and somewhat faulty logic. Indeed, many of the standard medical therapies of the 1940s and 1950s were subsequently dropped from practice because of the weakness or absence of data to confirm their efficacy.

. . .

During the 1940s and 1950s the psychiatric armamentarium was extraordinarily varied. At one end were several somatic therapies first developed in the 1930s and employed with increasing frequency during the 1940s and into the 1950s. Such interventions played an important part in furthering the ideal of reintegrating psychiatry and medicine. Somatic therapies, after all, followed the dominant medical analogue; they were based on a technological vision. That efficacy was difficult to determine or theory sometimes wanting was not an important consideration; clinicians in general medicine frequently adopted and remained wedded to empirical treatment where evidence of effectiveness was weak or even nonexistent (e.g., tonsillectomy). The development of somatic therapies, then, had two distinct advantages: they narrowed the gap between psychiatry and medicine; and they held out hope of improvement for tens of thousands of patients hitherto destined to live out shattered lives in dreary institutional settings.

One of the most prominent somatic therapies was developed during the 1930s by Manfred Sakel, a Viennese physician. Sakel administered a large dose of insulin that drastically lowered the sugar content of the blood and thus induced a hypoglycemic state. He and others claimed to have observed significant improvement among schizophrenics, a group traditionally resistant to all known psychiatric interventions. Although hypoglycemic treatment had no basis in theory, its alleged effectiveness promoted its widespread use. At about the same time, metrazol convulsive and then electroshock therapy were also introduced.[1]

Despite encouraging results with insulin, a marked sense of uneasiness persisted among psychiatrists. The puzzle of employing a therapy that could not be reconciled with theory or any known physiological data remained troubling. Solomon Katzenelbogen of Johns Hopkins, for example, pointed out that even favorable outcomes could not be regarded as conclusive evidence without other kinds of data. Along with others, he was sensitive to the therapeutic benefits of any kind of activity involving patients and physicians. It was possible, Katzenelbogen observed, that the major merit of nonspecific treatment lay "in rendering the patient more receptive for the common hospital therapeutic tools, such as occupational therapy, socialization, and other manifold forms of psychotherapy. The ability of the physician and the medical personnel to establish good rapport with the patient and to act, generally speaking, as psychotherapists, plays, therefore, a large part in the outcome of the insulin treatment." Yet even Katzenelbogen was unwilling to recommend discontinuation of a dangerous therapy, one that had a mortality rate ranging from 1 to 5 percent, if it assisted in the recovery or improvement of patients who might otherwise languish in hospitals for most of their adult lives. A study by the New York State Temporary Commission on State Hospital Problems of over eleven hundred schizophrenic patients treated with insulin shock therapy at Brooklyn State Hospital between 1937 and 1942 came to an even more optimistic conclusion. It urged the Department of Mental Hygiene to make the treatment available to all hospitalized patients "who are not ineligible therefor by reason of physical ailments or other factors,—unless and until other forms of treatment of such patients have demonstrated still better results."[2]

By the early 1940s shock therapies were in common use in virtually all mental hospitals, public as well as private. Lawrence C. Kolb and Victor H. Vogel estimated that between 1935 and 1941 more than seventy-five thousand patients had received some form of shock therapy. Because of the risks associated with insulin and metrazol, however, electroshock rapidly became the therapy of choice. Insulin coma therapy, however, persisted well into the 1950s even though existing evidence suggested that it was "irrational and hazardous." The widespread use of electroshock therapy, however, did not diminish skepticism about its efficacy. Stanley Cobb, the eminent Harvard neuropsychiatrist, pointed out that most of the studies evaluating electroshock lacked scientific precision. The diagnoses of diseases were uncertain and their courses unpredictable; adequate controls were absent; and experimentation with animal subjects inadequate. Despite such reservations, the prevailing consensus was that shock therapies, as A. E. Bennett and Bernice Engle wrote in 1947, "furnish a valuable tool with which to alter symptoms and shorten the course of certain psychoses, if the therapy is combined with a complete modern psychiatric program." The previous year Lothar Kalinowsky and Paul H. Hoch published the first edition of their influential text on shock treatment. They were aware that electroshock as well as other somatic therapies did not evolve from basic scientific research. Yet, as Kalinowsky noted nearly thirty-four years later, the findings of clinical observation ought not to be dismissed or written off as "anecdotal." "We are still treating empirically psychiatric disorders we do not understand, with treatments whose mode of action is also unknown."[3]

Electroshock therapy quickly became popular among psychiatrists and the general public. It was relatively easy to administer; it appeared safe; and the results, at least outwardly, were promising. The fact that it caused considerable pain and discomfort and had other undesirable side effects seemed of relatively minor consequence when placed alongside its benefits. Yet the absence of both well-designed evaluation studies (a reflection of the fact that psychiatrists lacked training in scientific methods or quantitative techniques) and a theoretical rationale were disquieting. By 1944 an APA committee reported that electroshock therapy was effective in treating depressions even though there was no consensus on the appropriate intensity or frequency of treatment. It conceded that there were limited data to substantiate the belief that electroshock should be used in combination with psychotherapy. Its members offered a restrained endorsement of shock therapy although agreeing that the subject required far more detailed study.[4]

Electroshock became more controversial after 1945. Faced with tens of thousands of patients and a severe shortage of medical personnel, many institutions turned to electroshock therapy simply as an alternative to complete inaction. "The promiscuous use of E.C.T. [electroconvulsive therapy] without other adequate psychiatric therapies has become a medical scandal," conceded Bennett.

> Many institutions use it wholesale without any other therapy—no proper nursing supervision, no occupational therapy, no psychotherapy—simply a pure physiotherapeutic procedure. They do not follow up patients or note relapses. Patients' fears drive them to suicide because of this failure to incorporate the therapy into a complete psychiatric program. Many poorly trained psychiatrists or non-psychiatrically trained doctors administer the therapy in offices, general hospitals and by non-psychiatric practitioners.[5]

The publication of GAP's report on electroshock therapy in 1947, as we have already seen, only exacerbated internal divisions between psychodynamic psychiatrists and their more biologically inclined colleagues.

The ambivalence that marked psychiatric attitudes toward shock therapies was equally apparent in the reception of psychosurgery or prefrontal lobotomy (its most popular form). The most dramatic innovation of the 1930s, psychosurgery was pioneered by Egas Moniz in Portugal in 1935 and introduced into the United States the following year by Walter Freeman and James W. Watts. Psychosurgery was undoubtedly the most radical therapeutic procedure ever developed in psychiatry; its effects were irreversible and the results not always predictable.

Oddly enough, the procedure had a firmer theoretical foundation than did the shock therapies. Psychosurgery grew in part out of developments in neurophysiology in the 1930s. Following his appointment as chairman of Yale's Department of Physiology in 1929, John F. Fulton spent much of his subsequent career in an effort to understand the nervous system in general and the frontal lobes in particular. As early as 1933 he expressed a desire to create a truly dynamic neurology that could analyze neurological disturbances in terms of brain reflex mechanisms and thus create a sound basis for both diagnosis and therapy. Fulton's own surgical experimentation with chimpanzees only confirmed his faith in a neurophysiological approach to brain function. The concept of functional localization, when combined with the Pavlovian model of "experimental neurosis" (the creation of behavioral abnormalities in animals resulting from traumatic events), led unerringly in the direction of a biological psychiatry. Fulton provided both an intellectual foundation and personal support for the development and dissemination of lobotomy as a significant therapy for dealing especially with the more intractable cases of chronic schizophrenics, a large group seemingly destined to spend the rest of their lives in institutions.[6]

The growing interest in psychosurgery was intimately related to the perceived postwar crisis in institutional care. The nearly half a million patients—many of whom were long-term residents—lived in the deteriorating buildings of overcrowded institutions and were cared for by an inadequate and poorly trained staff. Such a situation created an environment receptive to any therapeutic innovation that held out hope for improvement or recovery. Shock therapies had not demonstrated any appreciable benefits for chronic schizophrenic patients. "In the present state of affairs," observed Amarro M. Fiamberti, an Italian psychiatrist who helped to develop transorbital lobotomy, "if some are critical about lack of caution in therapy, it is on the other hand deplorable and inexcusable to remain apathetic, with folded hands, content with the learned lucubrations upon symptomatologic minutiae or upon psychopathic curiosities, or, even worse not even doing that." A pervasive hopelessness hastened the rapid incorporation of psychosurgery into the psychiatric armamentarium.[7]

That psychosurgery would be perceived as a major addition to hospital-based therapies was not apparent at the outset. Moniz, for example, found that patients suffering from affective disorders benefited the most, and chronic schizophrenics the least. Freeman and Watts were themselves dubious that lobotomy would be effective in cases of schizophrenia (except where "the break from reality" was not "too severe or too prolonged"). Many of the early operations in public hospitals, therefore, were performed on individuals suffering from involutional melancholia or depression. By the early 1940s, however, psychosurgery began to become popular as a treatment for schizophrenia, partly because of successes reported in Missouri and at the influential Institute of the Pennsylvania Hospital. At the latter institution Edward A. Strecker, chairperson of the Department of Psychiatry at the University of Pennsylvania Medical School, reported successful outcomes with such patients in 1940 and 1941; his election as APA president for 1943–1944 only confirmed the growing respectability of lobotomy.[8]

During World War II the number of psychosurgical operations was modest. Between 1940 and 1944, 684 were reported; as late as 1945 the yearly total was only 240. But from this point on, the increase was dramatic. In the peak year of 1949, 5,074 operations were performed. By 1951 no fewer than 18,608 individuals had undergone psychosurgery since its introduction in 1936. More than half of all public hospitals employed psychosurgery; at the remaining institutions, only the lack of proper facilities or staff inhibited its use. Nor was psychosurgery performed merely at marginal institutions. In Massachusetts the prestigious Boston Psychopathic Hospital was designated as the host to which all other state institutions could refer patients for psychosurgery. At this institution—which helped to pioneer the concept of the therapeutic milieu and was a center of psychodynamic psychiatry—surgeons had performed a total of 500 lobotomies by 1950. New York, an influential state with the largest public hospital system in the nation, moved aggressively after 1945 to encourage psychosurgery.[9]

Psychosurgery, of course, was subsequently ridiculed and vilified. A recent critic described it as a "bizarre" treatment "akin more to the early practice of trepanning the skull to allow the demons to escape than to modern medicine."[10] Yet psychosurgery was at least as "scientific" as other medical therapies; by the standards of that era its adoption followed accepted medical and scientific guidelines. Advocates could find adequate and respectable grounds for supporting its judicious use. Psychosurgery was based on the neurophysiological theory of localization of function in the brain. Surgical intervention seemed appropriate if the goal of diminishing or eliminating disordered thinking and behavior was appropriate. Psychosurgery could alter abnormal neuron pathways, thus facilitating the reeducation of patients. A "surgically induced childhood," argued Freeman, ended "extremely rigid autistic attitudes" and created a situation in which psychotherapy could be effectively employed. That the consequences were not always beneficial was not an argument against its continuance; it simply was a reminder of the need for additional research and refinement of the procedure. Disagreeable side effects, after all, were characteristic of many medical therapies; the physician had to employ a cost-benefit calculus to decide whether the gains outweighed the risks. To many the disadvantages of maintaining the status quo in mental hospitals were potent considerations leading them to support this admittedly radical therapy.[11]

The case on behalf of lobotomy was strengthened also by evidence indicating beneficial outcomes. Many of the studies that followed patients after psychosurgery reported that perhaps one-third had been discharged and were living at home. Equally significant, lobotomized patients, previously regarded as highly disruptive or intractable, became more manageable and were able to adjust in ways beneficial to both the individual and the institution. Hospitals, therefore, could resort less to such unpleasant means of managing recalcitrant patients as restraint, seclusion, or sedation. For institutions with thousands of patients, such gains were of no minor importance. A decline in disruptive behavior enhanced the institution's ability to deploy psychological and environmental therapies, which were far less invasive and posed fewer risks. Nor were the economic consequences of negligible importance; society would be less burdened with the care of chronic patients, and hospitals could concentrate more on their therapeutic role. Above all, lobotomy seemed to possess the potential to improve the lives of thousands of patients hitherto confined to back wards by restoring them to at least a partial ability to function in a more normal manner. "There appears to be good evidence," Kolb reported in 1949, that "numerous patients considered chronically and hopelessly ill have been restored to life in the community following operation." Nevertheless, he conceded that the data did not yet distinguish between the surgical procedure and the role of pre- and postoperative psychotherapy, and he called for further large-scale follow-up studies. Milton Greenblatt and Harry C. Solomon, in a review for the prestigious *New England Journal of Medicine*, also emphasized that psychosurgery held out "the hope that the relations of brain, intelligence, emotion and personality may some day be made an exact science."[12]

That psychiatrists accepted such an invasive and radical procedure was hardly surprising. Outward appearances notwithstanding, psychosurgery was not incompatible with the canons of traditional institutional psychiatry. The goal of mental hospitals ever since their establishment in the early nineteenth century had been to rehabilitate mentally ill patients and to facilitate their integration into the community. Such a process traditionally involved psychological and medical therapies, each reinforcing the other. Drugs, for example, were widely used in the nineteenth century to quiet disturbed patients so as to make them more amenable to psychological therapies. Correspondingly, there was general agreement that psychosurgery had to be followed by supportive resocialization, recreational, and occupational therapies to prepare the patient to move from the back to the front wards and ultimately into normal society. Psychiatrists were quick to concede that the majority of patients were not candidates for psychosurgery. Every therapeutic intervention, they maintained, required the diagnostic skills of experienced clinicians, and psychosurgery was no different. Participants at the Third Research Conference on Psychosurgery in 1951 recognized that diagnoses were "variable and notoriously unreliable," and hence of value "only within the experience of a particular hospital group at a particular time." As late as 1955 Milton Greenblatt, who had become involved with a major project designed to demonstrate the significance of the institutional milieu in fostering favorable outcomes, included lobotomy as an acceptable therapy for certain patients. Like many of his contemporaries, he saw no contradiction between somatic and psychosocial treatments.[13]

Despite its later reputation as an abusive therapy, psychosurgery aroused neither extreme controversy nor passionate conflict. Psychoanalysts, of course, tended to be bitterly opposed. Yet even GAP—the institutional embodiment of psychodynamic psychiatry—took a somewhat moderate stance. Many of its members, including William C. Menninger, countenanced the use of the procedure. To be sure, GAP's report on psychosurgery in 1948 was critical of prefrontal lobotomy, which represented "a mechanistic attitude toward psychiatry which is a throwback to our pre-psychodynamic days." The report, however, urged further research based on "careful, controlled observation" so that its usefulness "will not be diluted by utilization in situations where it can do little good and much harm."[14]

Psychosurgery, nevertheless, raised some troublesome problems. If used without discrimination, it had the potential to discredit the medical credentials of psychiatry. Indeed, its radical and irreversible nature only magnified the significance of ordinary psychiatric decision making. What criteria should be applied to the selection of patients for psychosurgery? Which procedure was best suited for an individual case? How were outcomes to be measured? The traditional impressionistic methods of deciding such questions seemed increasingly obsolete at a time when other disciplines were developing more sophisticated research methodologies and techniques. Indeed, psychosurgery only served to highlight the marked deficiencies in psychiatric research, for it demonstrated that clinical judgments rested on slippery foundations. This conclusion was especially evident in the deliberations of three annual conferences on psychosurgery sponsored by the NIMH between 1949 and 1951. The meetings brought together more than two dozen distinguished figures from psychiatry and the social sciences. At the first meeting Dr. Fred Mettler, organizer and chair, identified five rules governing therapeutic evaluation. The contribution of participants was "to point out where necessary basic data are lacking in psychiatry and how it may be possible to go about collecting them." By 1951 he was ready to concede "that the state of psychiatric information is not sufficiently evolved nor clear to allow one to meet the above criteria." Diagnoses lacked precision; statistics were "inadequate, incomplete, and unreliable"; and there was no evidence that "any form" of psychiatric therapy altered the five-year outlook of patients. "Lacking facts," he added, "we must be content to remain in the realm of opinion, for the present at least."[15]

The methodological naïveté of psychiatry became even more apparent because of the growing number of clinical psychologists with extensive training in research design and statistics. Their presence in mental hospitals alerted psychiatrists to the difficulties in measuring therapeutic efficacy. Toward the end of 1951, therefore, the APA decided to establish its own longitudinal study in the hope of developing techniques and guidelines to assess the effectiveness of such different therapies as psychosurgery and psychotherapy. The obstacles to such a study proved overwhelming, and the project never went forward. Indeed, preliminary discussions revealed that it was extremely difficult, if not impossible, to design any methodology capable of measuring the effectiveness of psychotherapy. In 1958, Joseph Zubin—a well-known and respected psychologist who had participated in the three earlier research conferences on psychosurgery—called into question virtually all studies on outcomes. Asked to evaluate a longitudinal study of the results of more than a thousand lobotomies at Pilgrim State Hospital in New York that included a control group, Zubin offered some startling comments. "It is high time that we examine the whole problem of the evaluation of outcome of treatment and of mental illness in general," he stated.

> I have given much thought to this question during years in biometric research, and have come to the conclusion that nothing short of a specific prognosis for each patient under conditions of nonspecific therapy—a prognosis based on objectively-evaluated characteristics—can constitute the basis for a scientific evaluation of a given therapy. This specific prognosis must take into consideration the following areas: the premorbid characteristics of the patient, his morbid status, the course of his illness, and the evaluation of his probable rehabilitation, including rehabilitation after possible return to the community. Once this prognosis for each patient is determined, the outcome for the entire sample under conditions of nonspecific therapy can be predicted.
>
> For a new therapy to be regarded as more efficacious, it must surpass the prognosticated outcome for nonspecific therapy, or for competing therapies.

Zubin's words suggested how far psychiatry had come as well as the distance it had yet to travel in evaluating the effectiveness of its therapies.[16]

By the late 1950s psychosurgery was clearly on the wane. Walter Freeman, its most staunch proponent, had become a lonely voice in the wilderness, regarded by both psychiatric and neurological colleagues as little more than a shadow of the past. The decline of psychosurgery did not occur because of allegations of its brutal and offensive nature—which were rare—but rather because it was replaced after 1954 by the psychotropic drugs, which appeared less invasive and did not initially appear to have irreversible and pernicious consequences. Paradoxically, psychosurgery became a matter of public controversy in the late 1960s and early 1970s only after its disappearance from the psychiatric armamentarium.[17]

· · ·

The psychodynamic orientation in the postwar era stood as a counterweight to somatic interpretations and the use of electroshock and psychosurgery. Both approaches rested partly on situational differences. Psychodynamic psychiatry was associated with medical schools and private and community practices; somatic (or biological) psychiatry was generally (but not exclusively) linked with traditional mental hospitals. The demarcation line between the two, however, remained indistinct and shifting.

Psychodynamic and psychoanalytic psychiatrists were by no means a singular or unified group. Eclecticism was characteristic, and their interventions ranged from individual psychotherapy to various forms of socio- and environmental therapy. Because of the importance of war-related experiences, the initial emphasis was upon individual psychotherapy. The concept of psychotherapy, of course, was not of recent origin, although it was given concrete form in the twentieth century by such figures as Freud in Europe and Meyer in the United States. By World War II the term had come into common use. In 1938 the Association for the Advancement of Psychotherapy was founded by a group of European-born or trained eclectic psychoanalysts who wanted to expand contacts with other disciplines. Two years later Lewellys F. Barker of Johns Hopkins published a volume on the subject in which he defined psychotherapy as a treatment "that attempts to improve the condition of a human being by means of influences that are brought to bear upon his mind (psyche)." In 1947 the *American Journal of Psychotherapy* made its appearance. Psychotherapy, however, was not incompatible with somatic therapies, for structure and function were inseparable. Indeed, Barker noted that experimental work using mescaline and hashish to induce abnormal states of mind offered the prospect that in the future a part of psychotherapy might give way "to new forms of chemotherapy."[18]

Despite its attractiveness, psychotherapy presented intellectual and practical difficulties. That troubled individuals sought assistance and were often helped with their problems by others—lay as well as professional—was a truism. All human beings, after all, require assurance and assistance at various points in their lives. Given its medical context, however, psychotherapy had to involve more than mere human contact and understanding. To delineate the medical features that distinguished this therapy—either in theory or practice—was a formidable task. Many of those making the effort often employed vague language and concepts. The APA's Committee on Psychotherapy (whose members included Harry Stack Sullivan and Oskar Diethelm) conceded in 1944 that "some of the medical thinking about psychotherapy can scarcely be generalized" but insisted that psychiatry was in the midst of "a progressive simplification of theoretic formulae and corresponding increasingly precise and definable types of interaction of physician and patient."[19]

Wartime experiences seemed to confirm the effectiveness of psychotherapy in dealing with stress-related neuropsychiatric symptoms. Whether or not such experiences were an analogue for its use in alternative settings or with other kinds of patients was problematical. There was virtually no agreement on methods or techniques. Moreover, data demonstrating efficacy were virtually nonexistent. Joseph Wilder, an avowed proponent of psychotherapy, conceded as much in a study published in 1945. "Psychotherapeutic statistics are based on different standards," he observed. Available data ignored such categories as spontaneous remissions, demographic variables like age, the possible presence of organic disease, and duration of treatment. Diagnostic categories were imprecise, and follow-up studies nonexistent. "Shrouded in the mystery of the psychotherapist's office, its evaluation is left to the two parties least suited to express objective judgment: the patient and the psychotherapist." For hospitalized patients the situation was equally murky. Even though many patients received little or no treatment in the usual meaning of the word, there were serious reasons "to believe that for many cases hospitalization in itself represents a treatment." Cognizant of profound methodological difficulties, Wilder nevertheless insisted that "a scientific evaluation of psychotherapeutic results simply must be made."[20]

Psychotherapy, of course, became one of the most widely acclaimed psychiatric interventions of the postwar era. It was offered by a multiplicity of professional groups, including psychiatrists and nonpsychiatric physicians, irregular practitioners such as chiropractors and naturopaths, clinical psychologists, social workers, marriage counselors, rehabilitation and vocational counselors, parole officers, clergymen, and others. Its popularity grew out of a fortuitous combination of circumstances: the rise of private and community practice in psychiatry; the general receptivity toward psychological explanations; an economic prosperity that created a middle-class clientele able to pay for and eager to use psychological services; favorable clinical results; and the general popularization of Freudian theories. Although psychotherapy was widely used in a few select private institutions—notably at the Menninger Foundation and Chestnut Lodge[21]—it was more often employed in the treatment of noninstitutionalized psychoneurotic individuals capable of functioning independently. "The pattern of psychotherapeutic practice in America," wrote Jerome D. Frank, an eminent psychiatrist at Johns Hopkins, "is seriously imbalanced in that too many of the ablest, most experienced psychiatrists spend most of their time with patients who need them least." Affluent and well-educated persons were the most numerous candidates for psychotherapy, whereas "lower class, seriously ill patients" received the least attention even though they constituted "by far the greater challenge."[22] For psychiatrists in private or community practice, psychotherapy was generally the treatment of choice; somatic therapies such as lobotomy or shock were rarely employed.

Beneath the surface, however, lurked elements of doubt. "I . . . have been trying to get an adequate definition of psychotherapy," Daniel Blain told Marion E. Kenworthy in 1946, "and, in a broad manner of speaking, for the word therapy itself, attempting to combat the tendency to use therapy in terms of every type of influence on the patient." Psychotherapy, admitted Leo Bartemeier in his APA presidential address in 1952, "still remains a rather vague concept." A year later Jules H. Masserman, a distinguished psychoanalyst and psychiatrist, suggested that psychotherapy might be nothing more than the institutionalization of certain delusions that were "so essential in protecting us against harsh reality that existing without them would be as excruciatingly unbearable as existing without our skin." He was especially critical of gross misunderstandings and popularizations of technique even among better-educated groups. Masserman recounted his tongue-in-cheek lecture on "The Psychosomatic Profile of an Ingrown Toe Nail" before a group of internists. The toenail, he told his audience,

> is the most protuberant part of the body, hard and rounded; in locomotion it describes a most suggestive to-and-fro movement—obviously, then, it is a basic penile symbol displaced, for a change, downward. But let us also remember the anatomic origin of this important little phallus, namely the *nail-bed* . . . a region consummately feminine in its conformation, physiology, and import. . . . But now consider what happens when this normal functioning is disrupted by frustration and conflict: when, specifically, the erect nail is stubbed and traumatized, or is too long opposed by unyielding reality in the form of a repressive shoe. Clinically and perhaps personally we know the effects all too well: the nail, particularly at the peripheral portions of its individuality (or more technically, its "ego boundaries") turns about and digs its way back into the flesh of its origin.

Masserman was chagrined when he was congratulated for his "clinical and analytic perspicacity" in illuminating "the etiology and possible therapy of that hitherto unexplored psychosomatic disorder—onychocryptosis, or ingrown toenail." Nor were doubts absent among psychologists. At the Conference on Graduate Education in Clinical Psychology in 1949 a facetious but revealing statement was made: "Psychotherapy is an undefined technique applied to unspecified problems with unpredictable outcome. For this technique we recommend rigorous training." The protean nature of the term was evident in its myriad forms, which included brief, depth, multiple, social, and group psychotherapy.[23]

Humorous characterizations notwithstanding, psychotherapy presented formidable intellectual and philosophical problems. At its most basic level it involved complex human relationships that could not be easily disaggregated into smaller and presumably more manageable components. It was possible to describe such emotions as love and hate in purely physiological terms (e.g., blood pressure), but to do so in all probability vitiated, if not destroyed, their holistic meaning. Equally significant, psychotherapy brought together a subject and a therapist, and their interaction introduced a new variable. Psychotherapy, therefore, involved more than technique, and to distinguish among its different forms and to measure their respective effectiveness posed a difficult, if not insoluble, challenge.

The absence of serious evaluative research did not go unnoticed. Lawrence S. Kubie noted that members of the National Research Council's Committee on Neuropsychiatry and Sub-Committee on Psychiatry included respected figures. Few of them, he added, had "experimental experience" in psychotherapy. The indiscriminate admixture of neurologists and psychiatrists inhibited any genuine scientific investigation of the subject. "I am not bitter about any of this," Kubie told a colleague.

> It should be a sobering thought to you and all medical educators and Foundation directors that in spite of all of the money that has been poured into American psychiatry during the last 50 years, not a single one of the major psychiatric developments has come from this country. We are surrounded by great and expensive monuments to predictable and in many instances predicted failure: the Phipps, the Payne Whitney, the New York Psychiatric Institute, the Institute of Human Relations, the MGH, etc., etc. Must we go on repeating old follies as these two committees seem bent on doing?

A decade later Benjamin Pasamanick, a noted psychiatrist, observed that too many of his colleagues were more interested in the process than the outcome of psychotherapy. Consequently, relatively little was known about its efficacy, which inhibited efforts to improve current practices.[24]

At a more fundamental level the deficiency of outcome studies was but a reflection of the complexity of the therapy itself. Psychotherapy was not a standardized intervention; innumerable variables had the potential to influence the process. Even control-group studies, as Frank—a noted authority—pointed out, necessitated contacts with the control subjects themselves, contacts that vitiated the precise measurement of any outcome. He also emphasized that the effectiveness of psychotherapy was limited by unmodifiable environmental stresses (e.g., serious illness of family member, stresses arising from racism) and internally set limitations (e.g., biological deficiencies, deeply ingrained maladaptive patterns). The clinician's dilemma, Frank noted in his classic study *Persuasion and Healing* (1961), was that the "practice of psychotherapy cannot wait until research has yielded a solid basis for it." He insisted that virtually all psychotherapies involved persuasion and the restoration of hope. Their effectiveness, he concluded, "may be due to those features that all have in common rather than to those that distinguish them from each other."[25]

The deliberations at the first Conference on Research in Psychotherapy in 1958, sponsored by the American Psychological Association, were also revealing. Though much research had been done, noted Morris B. Parloff and Eli A. Rubenstein in their summation comments, "there has been relatively little progress in establishing a firm and substantial body of evidence to support very many research hypotheses." The most sustained criticism came from Hans J. Eysenck, an influential British psychologist. In exhaustive reviews of research during the 1950s, Eysenck insisted that the therapeutic effects of psychotherapy were "small or non-existent, and do not in any demonstrable way increase the rate of recovery over that of a comparable group which receives no treatment at all."[26]

The difficulties of evaluation were dramatically illustrated in the Menninger Foundation's Psychotherapy Research Project, one of the most detailed and sophisticated longitudinal studies ever undertaken. Begun in 1954 and spanning several decades, the project focused on forty-two adult patients who had entered therapy between 1954 and 1958. The conclusions were scarcely revolutionary: the investigators found that a patient's ego was the critical variable in success or failure, and that psychoanalytic therapy was inapplicable to psychotics. Equally significant, project personnel developed an appreciation of the immense complexities involved in developing a methodology to evaluate the psychotherapeutic process. The majority of their publications, as a matter of fact, dealt with the barriers that impeded scientific measurement of psychotherapy.[27]

. . .

The psychodynamic orientation of American psychiatrists also heightened interest in environmentally oriented interventions. In brief, many psychiatrists developed a sensitivity to the possible role of environmental modifications as a means of treating mentally ill individuals. Of all the approaches that were popular after 1945, "milieu therapy" had the greatest potential to impact upon the lives of tens, if not hundreds, of thousands of severely mentally ill individuals confined in mental hospitals.

The idea that institutionalization could have serious consequences for the patient was by no means novel. Early nineteenth-century mental hospital superintendents had developed "moral treatment" or "moral management"—a therapeutic system that rested on the belief that the institutional environment could be used to reeducate patients in a proper moral atmosphere. Moral treatment, of course, grew out of an entirely different context: many of its basic tenets were derived from religious sources.[28] The change in the nature of the patient population and the emergence of the mental hospital as an institution providing care for geriatric cases and individuals suffering from organically based disorders—groups with little hope of recovery—had dealt the therapeutic ideal a severe setback; by World War II the custodial character of mental hospitals was self-evident.

After 1945 interest in using the institution as a possible therapeutic tool reemerged. Even before World War II Dexter Bullard experimented with new therapies at Chestnut Lodge Sanitarium (a small private psychoanalytically oriented institution in Maryland). He persuaded Frieda Fromm-Reichman to join the staff and employ psychoanalytic techniques in working with psychotic patients, and he encouraged Harry Stack Sullivan to continue his work at the hospital.[29] In many respects Sullivan played a key role during the interwar years. He altered the traditional preoccupation of psychiatry with the individual; his theory of interpersonal relations shifted the focus to interpersonal phenomena, relationships between people, and the social context of behavior. As early as 1930 Sullivan admitted "that it would be a very difficult proposition to show wherein psychiatry is more of a medical than a social science." Personality, he wrote in 1938, "is made manifest in interpersonal situations, and not otherwise." Sullivan's close relationships with members of the Chicago School of Sociology (which shaped the discipline in these years) ultimately transformed both psychiatry and the social sciences. More than any other figure, Sullivan paved the way for the collaboration of psychiatry and social science, and thus facilitated the emergence of socially oriented therapies after World War II.[30]

Unlike the theory of moral management, the concept of milieu therapy (or therapeutic community) was overwhelmingly secular in its origins. The concept of the therapeutic community was partly rooted in psychodynamic psychiatry. If mental disorders had some environmental etiology, might it not follow logically that environmental modifications could play a therapeutic role? Certainly the leading psychodynamic psychiatrists of these years all shared a common belief in the importance of the milieu for therapy.

An equally important contribution came from social and behavioral scientists. Their long-standing preoccupation with the role and function of institutions, interest in the mediating influence of culture and social structure on personality, and environmental and activist ideological orientation were approaches that promoted interest in mental illnesses. During the 1940s and 1950s the social and behavioral science emphasis on the social and cultural roots of behavior became even more pronounced. Bruno Bettelheim's classic analysis of behavior in Nazi concentration camps anticipated a variety of investigations of other kinds of institutions, including mental hospitals.[31] The impact on American psychiatry was dramatic. Postwar changes within academic disciplines in particular and higher education in general, together with a confident and expansive psychodynamic psychiatry, created an environment conducive to cross-disciplinary cooperation between psychiatry and the social and behavioral sciences—a development that rapidly became the norm rather than the exception.

The concept of the mental hospital as a potential therapeutic community was given concrete meaning by Maxwell Jones, a British psychiatrist. During World War II Jones worked with servicemen who had developed neuropsychiatric symptoms during combat as well as with repatriated prisoners of war. He found that group discussions with mutual feedback involving patients and staff assisted the former to view their symptoms more objectively, gain insight, and thus improve sufficiently to return either to their units or to their communities. "In a limited sense," he later recalled, "the treatment was being carried on by the patients in collaboration with the staff."[32]

These experiences led to the establishment at Belmont Hospital in 1947 of what subsequently became known as the Social Rehabilitation Unit. Belmont was a traditional inpatient institution that admitted neurotic and early psychotic patients. The average stay was four to six months, although some remained up to one year. In the new unit the multidisciplinary staff and one hundred patients met daily for an hour, and smaller group meetings were not uncommon. The result was the creation of a "therapeutic culture" that encouraged communication. Patients gained insight and psychiatrists were "taught to speak the patient's language." The lesson to Jones and his associates was clear. Personality disorders resulted from adverse environmental factors. Hence a therapeutic community, organized along democratic and permissive lines, inhibited the reproduction of hostile or repressive responses from society normally anticipated by patients, who, in turn, altered their behavior. It was thus possible, Jones reported in his influential volume, *Social Psychiatry* (1952), "to change social attitudes in relatively desocialized patients with severe character disorders, provided they are treated together in a therapeutic community." The work of Jones and his colleagues, therefore, unerringly led to a heightened appreciation of the impact of the hospital on the individual patient and the possibility of employing the hospital community "as an active force in treatment."[33]

Even as Jones was popularizing the concept of the hospital as a therapeutic community, multidisciplinary teams in the United States were already studying the mental hospital as a social system and the implications for patient care and treatment. One of the earliest was undertaken by H. Warren Dunham, coauthor of an important ecological analysis published in 1939 (*Mental Disorders in Urban Areas*). Dunham arranged with Ohio officials to launch a detailed analysis of the mental hospital as "a special kind of community experience." Completed in 1948, the full study was not published until 1960. Nevertheless, some early articles indicated its basic thrust. In a brief piece in the *American Journal of Psychiatry* in 1948, Dunham and a psychiatric associate reported that the interpersonal relationships and group dynamics of employees and patients created an institutional culture that only aggravated the latter's "existing personality conflicts." Patient welfare was often subordinated to institutional needs. Only when the existing social organization was broken and reoriented in ways compatible with therapy, they concluded, would the situation change.[34]

By the early 1950s an extensive multidisciplinary literature focusing on the hospital as a social organization had appeared in psychiatric as well as social and behavioral science professional journals. In a comprehensive summary, Charlotte Schwartz identified nearly two hundred items, most of which were published between 1945 and 1952. Their authors emphasized not only the treatment of disease per se, but also the need to employ a holistic approach that took into account all of the relevant social and emotional factors relating to mental illnesses. Psychiatric exclusiveness had clearly begun to give way to a multidisciplinary approach that required the integration of sociological, anthropological, and medical knowledge in order to develop a total treatment program. Such a program recognized the significance of the environment, interpersonal relationships, and the social needs of patients. Irrespective of disciplinary affiliation, virtually every researcher found that the attitudes and outlook of staff and patients played a key role in outcome. Understanding the complex elements that shaped the character of mental hospitals, in turn, led to a search for methods and techniques that were effective in promoting meaningful change. Optimistic that new multidisciplinary findings would illuminate the roots of existing problems, researchers were not unmindful of the substantial barriers that impeded beneficial innovations, including the traditional inertia of established routines within institutions and professional fears, as well as the lack of adequate funding.[35]

The concept of the therapeutic community gained new momentum with the publication of a series of volumes in the mid- and late 1950s that reached a wide audience. Most of these studies resulted from collaborations between two kinds of professionals: psychiatrists familiar with the behavior and outlook of patients, and social scientists sensitive to the complexities of social organizations and better trained in research design and methods. One of the first and most influential was Alfred H. Stanton's and Morris S. Schwartz's *The Mental Hospital*, published in 1954. Stanton, a psychiatrist, and Schwartz, a sociologist, designed an intensive two-year sociopsychiatric study of a disturbed ward at Chestnut Lodge. The administration and psychiatric staff at this small psychoanalytically oriented institution provided sympathetic support. The two investigators found that the hospital successfully protected the public and minimally met patient needs but was less effective in "bringing about lasting improvement." Many of the administrative, therapeutic, and nursing procedures reflected the needs of staff rather than patients. The authors' study of administration and interoccupational conflicts led to the observation that staff procedures and attitudes contributed to the maintenance of chronic patterns of behavior. Stanton and Schwartz thus posed a direct challenge to the paternalistic character of Chestnut Lodge, for they emphasized that patients were active participants rather than passive observers even though their influence was not always visible or self-evident. Possessing different characteristics, mental hospitals still tended to emulate the authoritarian structure of general hospitals and thus failed to create a therapeutic environment. The proposition that patient-staff interaction shaped outcomes, they insisted, had to be a guiding principle in organizing mental hospitals. Their work pointed in the direction of a more democratically organized and participatory institution.[36]

The Stanton-Schwartz study was quickly followed by the publication of another significant work by Milton Greenblatt and his colleagues. With the support and encouragement of the Russell Sage Foundation, three Bay State institutions—the Boston Psychopathic Hospital, the Bedford VA Hospital, and the Metropolitan State Hospital in Waltham—designed a joint and collaborative experiment to improve institutional care that involved patients as well as the entire staff. Traditional means of control—seclusion, restraint (mechanical and chemical)—virtually disappeared; the physical environment was made more attractive; socialization therapies—games, music, work, entertainment—became common; patient self-government was encouraged; the therapeutic potential of personnel was fostered; teaching and research opened new possibilities; and close relationships with the community were institutionalized. The combination of intensive physiological treatments (shock, lobotomy, and drug) and environmental changes seemed to have dramatic results. Intensive treatment "necessitated longer stays and fewer cases; yet more patients were treated, more improved, and more were discharged than ever before." Equally striking, the discharge rate to the community in all diagnostic categories rose, "suggesting that no diagnostic label necessarily indicated that a patient had a black future." "The prognosis for the future of psychiatric hospitals," concluded Esther L. Brown and Greenblatt, "is hopeful. . . . With prompt and intensive treatment provided through the somatic therapies, including chemotherapy, individual and group psychotherapy, and the therapeutic use of the social environment, a large proportion of patients admitted to psychiatric hospitals can return to the community within a relatively brief period."[37]

The argument on behalf of such optimism was further elaborated by Otto von Mering, an anthropologist at the University of Pittsburgh School of Medicine. With the support of the Russell Sage Foundation,

Mering visited about thirty institutions that were seeking to alter their traditional custodial role. Too many hospitals, Mering reported, casually accepted what he described as "The Legend of Chronicity," which justified therapeutic passivity toward withdrawn, passive, and hostile patients with no hope of recovery. Yet some institutions were in the process of demonstrating that effective alternatives existed. The primary features of what Mering termed "social remotivation" included the acceptance of the patient "as a worthwhile individual, capable of improvement, regardless of the degree of observable deterioration," and able to take an active role in therapy.

> Social mobilization seeks to mobilize the entire ward routine and program for therapeutic ends. Once the patient has been accepted as worthwhile and as having potential for growth, the daily activities of ward life can take on new meaning. . . . Thus, the social milieu of the ward is mobilized to bring out latent energies toward health, reinforce them through a series of social rewards, looking toward an improved hospital adjustment or eventual return to the community.

In short, improved interpersonal relationships had the potential to alter traditional institutional environments and foster more promising outcomes.[38]

During the latter half of the 1950s multidisciplinary works describing and analyzing the mental hospital in sociological and anthropological terms proliferated. The context and specific subject matter differed, but their underlying methodology and conclusions were remarkably similar. Ivan Belknap's study of a large southern state hospital emphasized the authoritarian and coercive nature of the internal social structure, which militated against effective therapy. William Caudill analyzed the mental hospital in terms of a total social system whose character was shaped by broad historical circumstances over long periods of time. "One of the brightest stars in the social psychiatric firmament," wrote Robert N. Rapoport in 1960, "is the 'therapeutic community' idea. According to this approach, the hospital is not seen as a place where patients are classified and stored, nor a place where one group of individuals (the medical staff) gives treatment to another group of individuals (the patients) according to the model of general medical hospitals; but as a place which is organized as a community in which everyone is expected to make some contribution towards the shared goals of creating a social organization that will have healing properties."[39]

Whatever the specifics, it is clear that the concept of the therapeutic community stood as the obverse of the traditional mental hospital. The former was based on the proposition that patients as well as staff had to take active participatory roles in the therapeutic process; the latter reflected an authoritarian ideology that fostered dependency and actually strengthened pathological symptoms characteristic of the mental illnesses. The emphasis on the therapeutic community was in some ways related to the postwar proclivity to interpret social reality in terms of a perennial struggle of democracy and freedom on the one hand and authoritarianism on the other. Indeed, the reaction against authoritarianism was fostered, if not led, by European-born emigré scholars with firsthand knowledge of Nazism, and by their American counterparts who had served in the military or government during the war. Their experiences facilitated the incorporation of an activist democratic ideology into social and behavioral science theory. Postwar social and behavioral science and psychiatric thinking emphasized the proposition that freedom and democracy, when applied in a setting that promoted participation on more or less equal terms, led to responsible and mature behavior, whereas authoritarian patterns simply reinforced apathy and dependency.[40] The ideology of the therapeutic community also drew part of its inspiration from the optimism of these years; its creators and supporters assumed that administrative and organizational change could lead to the creation of an internal environment conducive to patient recovery. It was hardly surprising that the emphasis on the therapeutic community during the 1950s also led to the rediscovery of the early nineteenth-century formulation of moral treatment and insistence that cure was possible.[41]

Advocates of milieu therapy quickly recognized that their efforts would be in vain if communities were unwilling to accept former mental patients. They therefore moved to blur the demarcation between the hospital and community by creating what in the mid-1950s had become known as the open-door hospital, which had been popularized by T. P. Rees and other British psychiatrists. Advocates of the concept in Britain and the United States believed that the isolation and prisonlike antitherapeutic character of traditional mental hospitals could be altered through the elimination of such features as locked doors and fences. The open-door hospital, like the therapeutic community, represented an institutional deviation. Moreover, supporters of the open-door concept also believed that psychiatric services had to be integrated along an unbroken continuum to ease the release of patients into the community; a range of services was required to meet the needs of a diverse population requiring psychiatric and psychological assistance. An open-door policy and experimentation with novel institutional forms (e.g., the day hospital where patients were treated during the day and returned to their homes in the evening, and the night hospital) would allay public suspicions and mistrust and would facilitate the gradual movement of patients between institutions and communities. "Continuity of care," a New York State legislator observed, "is the heart of the open hospital system" and required the complete integration of psychiatric services—"pre-care, hospital care and after-care." In effect, the open-door, day, and night hospitals represented the fusion of the postwar emphasis on community care with the principles of milieu therapy.[42]

. . .

The prominence of psychodynamic and environmental therapies may have shifted the balance away from a biological orientation, but never to the extent that somatic therapies disappeared. The specialty's syncretism, as a matter of fact, ensured that any therapy—biological or psychological—would be assimilated into the psychiatric armamentarium with little or no resistance if there was some indication of efficacy. Boston Psychopathic Hospital, a major center of training and research, symbolized the eclectic character of American psychiatry. In the postwar era it sponsored a major lobotomy project, helped to pioneer the development of milieu therapy and experimented on patients and Harvard students between 1949 and 1956 with such hallucinogens as lysergic acid diethylamide (LSD) in the hope of developing a better understanding of the genesis of psychosis.[43] When the psychotropic drugs were introduced in 1954, therefore, their acceptance was immediate and rapid even among psychodynamic practitioners. The prevailing view was that drugs were not incompatible with either psychotherapy or milieu therapy and even had the potential to make the most intractable and difficult patients responsive to other environmental and psychological therapies. The majority of psychiatrists endorsed an integrated approach that employed both biological and psychological interventions.

In 1945 it would have been impossible to predict that within a decade scientists would develop substances that had the potential to modify the symptoms associated with such severe illnesses as schizophrenia. The field of psychopharmacology was virtually nonexistent, and there appeared to be no promising ways of undertaking research projects to develop appropriate chemical agents in psychiatry. To be sure, psychiatrists employed a variety of medications, but their use was justified only on empirical and nonspecific grounds; evidence of effectiveness was generally absent.[44] Yet the discovery that chlorpromazine—the first of the psychoactive drugs—had therapeutic properties was not the product of serendipity or accident, even though fortuitous circumstances played a part. Louis Pasteur's famous observation that "chance favors the prepared mind" perhaps more accurately describes the events that inaugurated a new era in psychiatric therapy.[45]

The origins of the introduction of chlorpromazine in psychiatry may be traced to the late nineteenth century. German scientists were then attempting to apply the tools of organic chemistry to the synthetic dye industry, a process that fostered both basic science and industry. One of the early results was the synthesis of phenothiazine in 1883 (the parent compound of chlorpromazine). After 1900 an entirely separate line of inquiry centered on the pharmacological actions of histamine, especially as it related to anaphylactic shock (the dramatic and sometimes fatal reaction of an organism to foreign substances). By the 1930s a number of scientists interested in the central nervous system were working on synthetic antihistamine substances. Within a decade several scientists had begun to focus on the secondary effects of the antihistamines on the central nervous system and their potential use in surgery and the treatment of shock generally. Clinical interest in the life-threatening effects of traumatic and surgical shock, of course, was widespread because of the experiences with battlefield casualties in World War II. By 1949 Henri Laborit, who was seeking a means of preventing shock by inhibiting the autonomic nervous system, had found that promethazine induced a "euphoric quietude" in surgical patients. When compound 4560 RP, subsequently known as chlorpromazine (CPZ), was synthesized a year later in the French laboratory of Rhone-Poulenc, a decision followed to launch a broad clinical study of its possible therapeutic effects.[46]

At the time the team of French scientists recognized that CPZ might have wide applications in surgery, obstetrics, neurology, and dermatology, given its anesthetic, analgesic, and hypnotic effects. There was even the prospect that it might prove useful in psychiatry in modifying the hyperactive behavior of maniacal patients. This hope had a basis in precedent: during the 1940s psychiatrists had sometimes prescribed synthetic antihistamines for their sedative effects on manic-depressives. During 1951 and 1952 clinical testing expanded rapidly. Initially psychiatrists were interested in the capacity of CPZ to enhance the effectiveness of other drugs, and they administered it to patients with a wide variety of neuropsychiatric symptoms. Within a short period of time CPZ was being given by itself. In 1952 Jean Delay and Pierre Deniker published a series of papers giving the results of their clinical trials at St. Anne's Hospital in Paris. CPZ, they reported, not only calmed excited states but had a broad central impact on a range of mental disorders. The following year their enthusiasm was even more evident. CPZ had "important and numerous therapeutic implications, for cases of psychosis as well as neurosis" and had "already brought about a transformation in the atmosphere of the locked wards and definitively relegated the old means of restraint."[47]

Between 1952 and 1954 testing of CPZ expanded beyond the borders of France. In the United States, Smith Kline & French, under license from Rhone-Poulenc, began extensive laboratory and clinical evaluations before marketing CPZ as Thorazine. The relative caution that marked the reception of CPZ in the United States was in part a reflection of the dominant position of the psychodynamic school. Although not opposed to somatic interventions, psychodynamic and psychoanalytic psychiatrists tended to emphasize psychotherapies and environmental treatment. The official journal of the Association for the Advancement of Psychotherapy, for example, editorialized in early 1955 "that the new drugs have only a symptomatic effect on psychic disorders and . . . cannot replace psychotherapy; all they accomplish is to render the patient more amenable to psychotherapy." That the majority of American psychiatrists were found in settings other than mental hospitals also ensured that Thorazine would be introduced gradually, since its greatest potential use was with institutionalized psychotic patients rather than neurotic individuals often seen in noninstitutional settings.[48]

Several of the early clinical evaluations in the United States in 1953 and 1954 indicated that Thorazine was remarkably effective in managing anxiety, agitation, and manic states, and also enhanced patients' receptivity to other psychodynamic therapies. Results from some state and VA hospitals in New York and California offered dramatic evidence of the beneficial changes in the behavior of hitherto intractable patients generally found on the back wards. By 1954 the results of the clinical testing program were so promising that Smith Kline & French decided to go forward with an aggressive marketing program.[49]

Thorazine had two obvious target groups: private practitioners and state hospital systems. The former, committed to personal therapeutic styles, were not quick to embrace the new drugs. The public hospital system, which cared for more than half a million patients, was a more obvious choice. Smith Kline & French representatives, however, quickly found that hospital officials were willing to use Thorazine but were inhibited by their limited institutional budgets. The firm, therefore, decided to form a task force to lobby intensively and persuade state legislatures to provide adequate funding. The political climate was especially propitious; since 1949 the annual Governors' Conferences had been preoccupied with the problems posed by mental illnesses, and most chief executives were receptive to innovations that would somehow arrest the inexorable rise in state hospital populations. By this time as well there was a generalized feeling that perhaps the greatest impact of Thorazine might be on schizophrenic patients, a group that (along with the aged) constituted the largest proportion of the chronic population. The spectacular success of antibiotic drugs in the postwar era undoubtedly created a climate that was sympathetic to the introduction of Thorazine.[50]

At the same time that CPZ was being developed, a second class of "tranquilizers"—the rauwolfia alkaloids—entered psychiatric practice. Long known and used in India, one of the extracts from the plant

Rauwolfia serpentina—reserpine—was isolated in 1953. By 1954 reserpine (marketed as Serpasil by Ciba Pharmaceutical) was being tested and found to have many of the same effects as Thorazine. The latter became the most widely used of the major tranquilizers because of its speed and effectiveness, although the former seemed to have fewer side effects. Once Thorazine and Serpasil (the major tranquilizers) were in use, other psychotropic drugs, including the minor tranquilizers, followed rapidly. By 1956 antidepressants (e.g., iproniazid and imipramine) had made their appearance, and in the succeeding decade dozens of other drugs were developed.[51]

Taken as a group, these drugs appeared to be the harbinger of a new era in psychiatry. That an element of caution was present was obvious. Even the most favorably inclined psychiatrists tended to be realistic in their appraisals. They recognized that unanswered questions persisted concerning the pharmacological action of the new drugs, proper dosage level, risks of long-term usage, and potential side effects. Masserman pointed to the dismal history of psychiatric "breakthroughs" from colectomies to substances that later proved highly toxic. Personally impressed with the new drugs, he nevertheless believed that adequate controlled evaluations were indispensable even though he recognized the difficulty of designing them for a specialty concerned with "the most protean, complex and contingent of all phenomena: human behavior and its vicissitudes." Nor were drugs a panacea. Indeed, in mid-1956 the APA issued a public statement conceding the significance of the tranquilizing drugs for institutionalized patients and, to a lesser extent, for patients seen in private practice or outpatient facilities. On the other hand, the organization expressed deep misgivings about the widespread and casual use of drugs to alleviate "the routine tensions of everyday living," a use that was "medically unsound" and "a public danger." Privately some leading figures were concerned that drug companies were making "excessive claims and pressuring everybody into using a helluva lot more of the drugs than is indicated," and they even questioned some of the evaluation studies.[52]

Yet on the whole the reception of the new pharmacological agents was favorable and enthusiastic. By the end of 1954 and continuing thereafter the APA, in collaboration with other organizations, convened a series of conferences to evaluate the pharmacological aspects of the new tranquilizers and their potential impact on therapy. At an international conference in the autumn of 1955 Winfred Overholser, superintendent of St. Elizabeths Hospital, summed up the prevailing attitude. CPZ improved the behavior and outlook of severely mentally ill patients; the atmosphere of disturbed wards was "completely revolutionized"; staff morale improved dramatically as more hopeful attitudes became common; the hospital as a whole took on a new character; families exhibited optimism about the future; and mental hospitals as medical institutions gained wider public acceptance. Wary of overenthusiasm and cognizant of the need for careful longitudinal evaluations, Overholser nevertheless maintained that there was "no doubt . . . that many new vistas have been opened and that changes have been noted, particularly in hospital psychiatry." "We are living in a moment of excitement, rich in potentialities that can be realized by increased interaction between psychiatrists and pharmacologists," noted Harold E. Himwich in his presidential address that same year before the Society for Biological Psychiatry. "We cannot help but feel that the advances made by chlorpromazine and reserpine, important as they are, represent only the initiation of a new era in psychiatry."[53]

The introduction of the major tranquilizers into state hospitals was not uniform; variability was characteristic. The key elements were the degree of commitment, enthusiasm, and knowledge of state hospital officials and the willingness of legislatures to provide adequate funds. Without doubt New York, which had been among the first of the states to employ drugs on a trial basis, was the leader. By mid-1956 the legislature had provided about three-quarters of a million dollars, and nearly half of its 93,000 patients were given drugs. California, on the other hand, spent about $200,000, and only 21 percent of its patients received tranquilizers. In the early 1960s, on the other hand, the proportion of patients being treated with drugs and the level of funding rose sharply; in many states half of all patients received drug therapy. New York remained the leader: in 1962 it allocated about $3 million, and nearly 57 percent of its patients were receiving tranquilizers.[54]

The development of the major tranquilizers also brought into sharp relief the thorny problem of evaluation. Few of the institutions that tested drugs did so with any degree of methodological sophistication; the overwhelming majority of studies failed to use a control group and did not distinguish between the characteristics of different kinds of patients. Larger aggregate studies had comparable shortcomings. The most influential analyses of the impact of tranquilizing drugs on hospital populations were prepared by Henry Brill and Robert E. Patton of the New York State Department of Mental Hygiene. At the APA meetings in May 1957 the two men reported that their study demonstrated that a decline in the state hospital patient population could only be attributed to the introduction of the tranquilizing drugs, since nothing else had changed. Their conclusion, however, was methodologically flawed: they inferred causation from correlation (a modest decline in the patient population followed the introduction of drugs), and they failed to compare the respective release rates of treated and untreated patients. In a larger study two years later they conceded the difficulty of establishing a causal relationship between the decline of the patient population and the use of new drugs, if only because other variables (open-door hospitals, the decline in use of restraint and seclusion, staff improvement) played a role. Nevertheless, they focused on the beneficial changes that had taken place even if it was "impossible to assign a quantitative role to each factor."[55]

By the mid-1950s there was greater sensitivity toward the methodological problems of identifying and explaining outcomes, if only because of the growing involvement of social and behavioral scientists in mental health research. Morton Kramer, chief of the Biometrics Branch at the NIMH and one of the most important statisticians of the postwar era, was especially cognizant of the problems associated with efficacy studies. In 1956 he offered a series of observations. First, little was known about the safety of tranquilizing drugs, their immediate and long-term effects, or appropriate dosage levels (especially as they related to the various characteristics of patients, including age, sex, and type of psychiatric disorder). Second, hospital admissions and retention rates were governed by a multiplicity of factors, and to attribute apparent declines to the tranquilizers was an error. A longitudinal study at Warren State Hospital in Pennsylvania, for example, suggested that discharge rates, which were by no means constant, were shaped by multiple variables. Because so many factors were involved, Kramer called for well-designed studies to evaluate the various therapies "singly and in combination with each other and with various ancillary programs." Such studies, he added, had to include "carefully defined diagnostic groups of patients, comparable control groups, carefully specified therapeutic plans and staffing patterns, and specific objective criteria for evaluating results of treatment and for determining condition at time of release."[56]

Evaluating the efficacy of the new drugs, as Kramer and others had indicated, was neither simple nor easy even under the best of circumstances. The problem became even more thorny because the new medications raised expectations and led to demands that they be widely distributed and used. The successes of new antibiotic drugs, the activities of pharmaceutical firms, and stories in the mass media created an almost mystical faith in the redemptive powers of medication. During 1955 and 1956 mass circulation magazines including *Time* and *Life* as well as newspapers the *New York Times* published articles implying that the development of chlorpromazine and reserpine was analogous to the discovery of antibiotic drugs that cured infections or the vaccine that prevented polio. Mike Gorman, the indefatigable and influential lobbyist, emerged as the most ardent champion of the new therapy. In his book *Every Other Bed* and especially in his testimony before Congress, he extolled the benefits of the new drugs and castigated those psychiatrists who were raising troublesome questions and preventing their broad use. In 1955 he and

Nathan Kline (the psychiatrist who had pioneered the introduction of reserpine) urged Congress to appropriate funds for a national evaluation project under the aegis of the NIMH, which would be responsible for submitting a summary report in early 1956.[57]

The demand for instant evaluation ultimately led to friction within mental health ranks. Robert Felix moved slowly. His staff, particularly those trained in the behavioral and social sciences, were aware of the methodological difficulties in designing evaluation studies. Indeed, by this time most mental health researchers had been chastened by the previous unsatisfactory efforts to measure the effectiveness of shock therapy and lobotomy, and they were determined to avoid the pitfalls that had led to the rapid deployment of interventions of questionable utility. Felix may also have feared that an overly narrow focus on drugs would prove detrimental to the larger NIMH program. Moving with caution, his first step was to appoint an ad hoc Committee on Psychopharmacology in early 1955 to study the drug issue. Within months its members decided that an interdisciplinary conference to assess the new substances was warranted. Meanwhile the Committee on Psychiatry of the National Research Council was also discussing the problem. In late 1955 both organizations decided to jointly sponsor a conference in the fall of 1956. Additional funding was provided by Congress for an NIMH pharmacological study.[58]

At the conference in September 1956 the participants emphasized the formidable difficulties in designing adequate evaluation studies of the new drugs. Seymour Kety, chief of the Laboratory of Clinical Science at the NIMH, agreed with Louis Lasagna of Hopkins that "psychiatric research was not qualitatively different from research in other fields." Kety nevertheless expressed the belief that psychiatry presented more difficulties than other medical specialties, given the extraordinary complexities of brain function. Yet he was not pessimistic, for the development of adequate evaluation procedures for drugs would serve as a guide for other psychiatric therapies that posed even greater methodological difficulties. The deliberations of the nearly one hundred figures at the conference revealed that they shared Kety's hopes as well as his concerns, and there was substantial agreement that the problem of evaluation would not be solved by the kinds of clinical trials employed in the past.[59]

Gorman was infuriated at the slow pace of events. Neither he nor Mary Lasker was especially understanding of the problems of research and evaluation even though they were extraordinarily successful in persuading Congress to increase annual appropriations. Gorman had never been fond of Felix. In testifying before a congressional subcommittee in the spring of 1956 he accused Felix of "dodging this problem of drug evaluation." Gorman demanded that the new psychotropic drugs—which he believed effective and safe—be introduced as rapidly as possible after a cursory study. By early 1957 his patience reached the breaking point. In a public speech he openly excoriated Felix and described Kramer's monograph on evaluation as "drivel." The NIMH, he charged, "really possesses unmitigated gall in asking for 'reliable experimental evidence' on the efficacy of the new drugs. . . . I respectfully suggest to the Institute that it get about the business of doing the painstaking evaluations ordered by the Congress, and that it cease and desist from using taxpayers' money to conjure up imaginary ghosts designed to alarm both mental patients and their families."[60]

Gorman's attack brought into the open hostilities that lay just beneath the surface. A year earlier, Deutsch had resigned from the NMHC, which he believed was being used by Gorman to express "personal opinions and prejudices." Deutsch also called attention to the history of psychiatric therapies—insulin, metrazol, electroshock, lobotomy—each of which had been heralded as a new miracle. Others, including William C. Menninger, shared Deutsch's concern. To Deutsch's chagrin, many psychiatrists refused to resign from the NMHC, perhaps because Gorman and Lasker retained close ties with many prominent members of Congress. Felix was equally distressed but believed that the NIMH had an obligation to determine efficacy and risks. He insisted that a dual approach was necessary. First, an overall evaluation had to determine whether drugs "are effective in terms of making patients available for earlier release from the hospital than would otherwise be the case." Second, there was need for "more purely clinical information on what the drugs do for and to patients, the kinds of changes they induce that are truly psychiatric in nature as distinguished from physiological only, the differential effects by diagnostic categories, age, sex, etc." The large-scale evaluation studies demanded by Gorman would serve public-relations needs but would not satisfy the "clinician who needs a different kind of information from what fits easily into the Sunday supplement." Felix—perhaps with some reluctance—bowed to growing congressional pressure and agreed to establish the Psychopharmacology Service Center within the NIMH.[61]

The new Psychopharmacology Service Center quickly decided against a large-scale national study. The deliberations of the conference in 1956 proved crucial. Its participants, Felix informed a congressional committee in early 1957, had concluded that "currently available methods are inadequate and new drug study methods must be developed in order to conduct scientifically valid assessments of the benefits and limitations of the tranquilizing and other new psychopharmacological agents." Moreover, the VA was already involved with a large-scale research program. Felix also noted that many improvements attributed to drugs might have been due to other factors. An increase in releases from New York state hospitals, for example, had begun in the late 1940s well before the development of tranquilizing drugs.[62]

Evaluation research proved so problematic that the Psychopharmacology Service Center did not begin its collaborative research project, involving nine institutions, until the spring of 1961, and the results were not published until 1964. The study was a minor landmark in the evaluation of psychiatric therapies and demonstrated the degree to which the methodological debates and controversies of the previous fifteen years had affected research procedures. The group to be studied included only newly admitted schizophrenic patients between the ages of sixteen and forty-five with no history of hospitalization in the preceding twelve months. The double-blind six-week study involved the use of a number of the newer phenothiazines as well as chlorpromazine, and outcome evaluation was based on global clinical judgments as well as clinical judgment of the presence and intensity of specific symptoms and behavior. By prevailing standards, the NIMH study was more than acceptable. The results seemed to demonstrate that phenothiazine therapy in acute schizophrenic psychoses was clearly superior to placebo. Symptoms as well as behavior were affected, and there was a low incidence of serious side effects. "The findings of this study," concluded the participants, "support the increasing confidence in and optimism about the treatment of acute schizophrenic psychoses. Moreover, the efficacy and feasibility of drug treatment have great potential value in the development of a public health approach to the treatment of acute schizophrenic psychoses and the prevention of chronic disability."[63]

. . .

The introduction of chlorpromazine and reserpine in the mid-1950s held out the promise of healing the long-standing division between biological and psychodynamic psychiatrists and promoting the reintegration of the specialty with medicine generally. However the psychiatric scene is characterized, it was clear that by the end of the decade therapeutic optimism was dominant. Biological psychiatrists could take satisfaction in the efficacy of drug therapy; their psychodynamic counterparts could envisage the possibility of employing psychological and environmental therapies with hitherto chronic and intractable patients. The merits of the new drugs, wrote Kalinowsky and Hoch in the third edition of their textbook on somatic treatments, "led to a greater interest in other forms of therapy for them and to an attitude of therapeutic optimism. Their great value in states of acute excitement—without the hypnotic action of the drugs previously used—led to an entirely different atmosphere in the wards of many hospitals, and enabled a larger proportion of such patients to participate in social events and to benefit from the other hospital facilities." Similarly, Jack R. Ewalt, a leading psychodynamic psychiatrist and head of the Joint Commission on Mental Illness and Health, pointed to the impact of drugs upon hospital personnel, who now believed "that the patients can change and that something can be done for them." "Better applications and more knowledgeable combinations of psychological, chemical, and sociological forces," he added, "might result in greater efficiency in treating mental disorders."[64]

More important, drugs initially appeared to have none of the disadvantages of earlier somatic or psychological therapies. Shock, lobotomy, and psychotherapy were individualized procedures that required extensive staff time; many patients were not suitable subjects. Drugs, by contrast, could be used for large numbers of patients, required minimal staff time, and were clearly efficacious and relatively inexpensive. They also seemed to be safer than other more invasive somatic procedures, and quite compatible with efforts directed toward creating therapeutic environments. In short, phenothiazine and its derivatives, the rauwolfia alkaloids, and the antidepressive drugs all seemed to possess ideal therapeutic attributes.[65]

That drug therapy was not without problems was obvious. By the late 1950s heightened public expectations and aggressive marketing by drug companies fostered a more indiscriminate use of psychotropic drugs. Mental hospital medical staffs were relatively cautious in their use of drugs. Physicians in private practice, however, were less aware that drugs did not resolve emotional conflicts and more inclined to prescribe them for patients even in the absence of compelling reasons. The misuse and abuse of the growing psychiatric pharmacopoeia would become more of a problem in ensuing decades.[66]

The introduction of the psychotropic drugs also brought to the fore some long-standing but generally ignored issues: the ethics of therapeutic experimentation and patient consent. Generally speaking, neither had proved troublesome in the past. Prevailing patterns of authority and deference facilitated the development and introduction of innovative medical procedures; there was little disposition to question medical autonomy or to emphasize patient rights. The prestige of the medical profession and reluctance on the part of its members to criticize colleagues in public also served to dampen discussion. The voices of the public and its elected representatives were heard only when publicity riveted attention on dangerous or fatal consequences of therapies. That psychiatrists treated patients with impaired thought processes only heightened their freedom to make decisions without involving patients or families.

In the late 1950s and early 1960s prevailing patterns of deference and authority had begun to weaken. Civil-libertarian concerns, the rise of special pressure groups, and greater dissent both within and without medicine began to result in challenges to medical authority. The decision to engage in large-scale testing of new psychotropic drugs ultimately precipitated debate within the ranks of psychiatry. By 1962 APA officials were discussing some of the ethical problems involved in experimentation with new drugs and the problems associated with written consent. Their deliberations revealed some ambivalence. "Experimentation with new procedures," observed Dana L. Farnsworth, "forms the basis of all advances in medicine." At the same time he insisted upon appropriate animal experimentation, to be followed by trials with human volunteer subjects "who are fully aware of what they are doing and what potential risks are involved." Farnsworth conceded the difficulty of unraveling all of the elements involved. One of his colleagues endorsed an opinion expressed by others, namely, that it was "unwise" to make "an open issue of this matter at the present time." Although the discussions led to no new policy pronouncements, ethical issues of experimentation and patient rights would grow in magnitude during and after the 1960s.[67]

Such problems notwithstanding, the therapeutic innovations of the 1950s seemed to presage a policy capable of realizing the dream of providing quality care and effective treatment for the nation's severely mentally ill population. The simultaneous development of milieu and drug therapy indicated a quite specific direction. Drug therapy would make patients amenable to milieu therapy; a more humane institutional environment would facilitate the release of large numbers of patients into the community; and an extensive network of local services would in turn assist the reintegration of patients into society and oversee, if necessary, their varied medical, economic, occupational, and social needs.[68] The combination of drug and milieu therapy, in other words, blurred the somatic/psychological schism as well as the hospital/community dichotomy. By the end of the decade, logic suggested that public policy focus both on rebuilding a neglected hospital system and promoting its integration with new community services. That logic and the actual course of events would diverge in fundamental ways was unforeseen by an optimistic generation persuaded that a solution to the puzzling dilemmas posed by mental illnesses was finally at hand.

CHAPTER SEVEN

Changing State Policy

THE FERMENT and debates over the proper shape of mental health policy in the postwar years were not simply abstract intellectual exercises. Ideas, after all, often have profound consequences; they can mold policies and shape the thinking of the general public as well as medical and political elites. It would have been surprising, therefore, if newer concepts of mental illnesses, therapies, and alternatives to traditional institutional care had had no impact on public policy.

By the 1950s signs of change were already evident. The postwar exposés of severe deficiencies in the nation's public mental hospitals and their constantly rising patient populations sensitized state officials to the need for change. The broad acceptance of a welfare state ideology led to the enactment of policies that accepted a larger federal and state role in alleviating individual and group distress. Governors who were neither knowledgeable about mental illnesses nor willing to place the issue at the top of their legislative and political agenda nevertheless were receptive to the claims of professionals and influential lay figures that therapeutic and institutional innovations provided the basis for more effective public policies. Slowly states began to pursue policies that at the time were not perceived to be mutually incompatible. On the one hand, they increased resources for a mental hospital system that had been ignored and neglected for nearly two decades. On the other hand, they provided modest funding to create community-based systems of treatment, a development that was compatible with the increasing use of general hospitals for psychiatric purposes. The presumption was that community services would supplement but not replace traditional mental hospital services.

The efforts to improve mental health services reflected widespread public confidence in the ability of professional groups to define the direction in which public policy should proceed. State and federal legislators were rarely disposed to question the competence and knowledge of such professionals or to evaluate their recommendations. Discussions about the manner in which mental hospitals, community clinics, and psychiatric wards in general hospitals related to each other were often vague and general; the practical problems relating to administration and coordination of services were sometimes ignored or dismissed; and evaluation remained an ideal rather than an activity. Consequently, there was a wide discrepancy between the goals of policy innovations and the consequences that followed their implementation. Indeed, by the close of the 1950s the faith in a community-based mental health policy had begun to call into doubt the need for—and therefore the legitimacy of—traditional mental hospitals.

. . .

In 1945 traditional mental hospitals remained the bedrock on which state policy rested. Their average daily resident population at that time was about 430,000; approximately 85,000 were first-time admissions. Of the total, 39,000 died, and 62,000 were discharged (16,000 of whom were listed as recovered and 28,000 improved). About 88 percent of all patient care episodes occurred in mental hospitals, the remainder in general hospital psychiatric units.[1] Such aggregate figures, of course, reveal little about the functions of institutions, the nature of their patient populations, or the outcome and effectiveness of treatment. Yet it is extraordinarily difficult to provide meaningful generalizations, in part because of the imprecision of nosological categories and the generally haphazard, less than precise, and incomplete reporting system of mental hospitals themselves. Moreover, there were wide variations between states and regions; public policies in individual states were not governed by patient needs alone, but also by unique local conditions, practices, and traditions.

The pattern of hospitalization was hardly homogeneous, and rates of institutionalization varied in the extreme. New Mexico had fewer than two mental patients per thousand of population in 1950; twelve states (largely in the South) had between two and three; thirteen states ranged from four to five; and eleven states, largely in the Northeast, had the highest rate (five and over). In general, states with low rates of hospitalization spent the least, states with high rates the most. Curiously enough, there was relatively little relationship between the general revenues of a given state (per person) and maintenance expenditures per patient. For the United States as a whole in 1950, the rank order correlation was only +0.27. The lowest expenditures were in the South and states west of the Mississippi River; the highest were in the Northeast. Massachusetts and New York, ranking first and second, spent on average about 6.5 percent of their general revenues on patient maintenance. Louisiana, which ranked last, spent 0.93 percent. The average for the nation as a whole was 3.06 percent. Generally speaking, rates of expenditure reflected past tradition—states that had always committed substantial resources persisted in doing so over time. The quality of institutional life (as measured by per capita expenditure) was often determined by the state in which a given individual resided. Differentials were striking: in 1950 thirteen states spent less than $2 million each per year; twenty-seven spent between $2 and $8 million; and five states (California, Illinois, Massachusetts, New

York, and Pennsylvania) accounted for nearly 50 percent of the total maintenance budget of $379 million.[2]

The most revealing demographic characteristic of institutionalized patients was their age distribution: the elderly continued to constitute a disproportionately large percentage.[3] Between the 1930s and 1950s the trend toward an older patient population accelerated. The greatest increase occurred in the group sixty-five and older; the largest decline was in the twenty-five to forty-four category. In 1940, 19 percent of all first admissions were sixty-five or older; a decade later the proportion was 25 percent. By 1958, nearly a third of all state mental hospital patients were over sixty-five. Between 1933 and 1956/1958 the rate of first admissions of individuals sixty-five and over increased from 156.6 to 232.7 per 100,000. The prognosis for such persons was hardly promising. A detailed study of 683 admissions of aged persons to Maryland institutions in the early 1940s indicated that most remained institutionalized until they died. About 47 percent died within the first year, and overall only about 10 percent ever left the hospital.[4]

The increasing proportion of elderly patients in public hospitals, however, was not due solely to a rising admission rate. High death rates ensured that the length of stay of newly admitted elderly persons would be limited. At Warren State Hospital in Pennsylvania, for example, 72 percent of such patients died within five years of their admission in the period from 1936 to 1945. The proportion of elderly was instead augmented by the accumulation of schizophrenics admitted at a younger age who grew old in the hospital. The presence of this group accounted for the fact that in 1962 the median length of stay for schizophrenics in twenty-three selected states was 12.8 years, whereas the comparable figure for those admitted with mental diseases of the senium was 3.0 years.[5]

By the mid-twentieth century the mental hospital was serving in part as a final home for aged persons. The depressing institutional environment—a feature noted by virtually all observers—was at least partly attributable to the presence of large numbers of elderly patients whose mental disabilities—as the New York commissioner of mental hygiene observed in 1944—"were more of a physical than a psychiatric nature."[6] The problems posed by the presence of large numbers of aged persons in mental hospitals were by no means unique. Even before World War II there was mounting evidence that the focus of the nation's health care system was shifting away from a concern with acute and infectious diseases and toward chronic illnesses. In this sense mental hospitals merely reflected a development that in subsequent decades would dominate discussions over health care policy in general.

The rising age distribution mirrored a different but related characteristic of the institutionalized population, namely, the presence of large numbers of patients whose abnormal behavior was related to an underlying somatic etiology. Even allowing for the imprecision of diagnoses and the imperfect nature of the statistical reporting system, it was quite evident that a significant proportion of patients were suffering from severe organic disorders for which there were no effective treatments. Many were confined in hospitals because they lacked families or alternative support systems or else because their families could no longer cope with the medical and psychiatric problems involved. In 1946, for example, 43.7 percent of all first admissions (or 41,908 persons) were of individuals with organic brain syndromes (generally associated with senility), and an additional 6.8 percent (6,562) represented cases of paresis. Schizophrenia, by way of contrast, accounted for 19.2 percent and alcoholic disorders for 8.8 percent.[7] The pattern of admissions, therefore, ensured that mental hospitals would provide general custodial and medical care for large numbers of patients who had little hope of returning to their communities.

The large numbers of chronic and aged patients tended to obscure the fact that release rates for nonelderly patients were improving. In a pioneering study of more than 15,000 patient cohorts admitted to Warren State Hospital in Pennsylvania between 1916 and 1950, Morton Kramer and his colleagues found that, for functional psychotics, the probability of release of first admissions within twelve months increased from 42 to 62 percent between 1919/1925 and 1946/1950. These and other data suggested that popular perceptions of mental hospitals were not entirely accurate. To put it another way, a high proportion of chronic and aged patients in public mental hospitals led many to overlook the reality that substantial numbers of patients were admitted, treated, and discharged in less than a year.[8]

The presence in mental hospitals of elderly patients with severe organic disorders posed troubling medical, social, ethical, and economic dilemmas for both public officials and psychiatrists. Was the mental hospital the proper place for such disabled geriatric patients? If not, what alternatives existed? Were elderly patients amenable to psychiatric therapies, or were their needs largely physical? Would their presence in such large numbers conflict with therapeutic goals? These and other questions became increasingly significant as state governments reevaluated their mental health policies. Should admission of aged persons continue, observed a Missouri legislative committee in 1948, "state mental hospitals will tend to become homes for the aged and it will be increasingly difficult to carry on a modern active treatment program." Other states faced fundamentally similar situations.[9]

In addition to fiscal concerns, a deteriorated and overcrowded physical plant, and the presence of large numbers of aged and chronic patients, state officials also faced severe tensions related to the ways in which they administered and managed psychiatric services. That mental health constituted an important concern was obvious. By 1951 states were expending about $5 billion for current operations, a figure that excluded such items as debt servicing and capital outlays. About 8 percent of this budget went to mental hospitals. Some states expended as little as 2 percent; the largest (New York) one-third. In the aggregate, state mental hospitals had about 110,000 employees and nearly half a million patients. Despite such substantial commitments, most states paid relatively little attention to administration; history and tradition—not logic or planning—shaped the ways in which they managed their psychiatric services.[10]

The pattern of administration varied in the extreme. Twenty-two states had boards or commissions to manage mental hospitals; fifteen had a department of welfare or of institutions; ten had a separate or coordinate department of mental health; and one assigned authority to its public health agency. Within each of these broad categories variations were commonplace. When the National Mental Health Act made the federal government a participant in mental health policy, patterns of administration became even more diverse. Under the provisions of this legislation, each state designated a mental health authority to handle federal funds. Some selected the heads of their mental health agencies, but many chose departments of public health or state health officers with few direct links to mental hospitals. The separation of mental hospitals from extramural services was to have a profound impact in future decades. Nor was there consistency in the manner in which departmental commissioners or psychiatric directors of hospitals were selected. Generally speaking, overlapping authority and jurisdiction was the rule rather than the exception. Central agencies often came into conflict with institutional authorities; excessive turnover rates fostered uncertainty about basic goals; and lines of demarcation between policy planning and implementation were amorphous. The diffuse pattern of administration mirrored an underlying confusion about the objectives of public policy. Was mental illness primarily a medical problem? Was it a problem involving dependency or public safety? The absence of clear answers often led to the creation of departments with authority and responsibility in such diverse areas as mental health, public health, welfare, and criminal justice.[11]

. . .

In the immediate postwar era, state officials concentrated initially on rebuilding a deteriorating hospital system. At the outset such efforts were centered in individual states; there was as yet no concerted movement. In Kansas, for example, William and Karl Menninger played significant roles in persuading the governor and legislature to pour resources into their mental health system. Using the Menninger Foundation—a family-dominated institution that had already developed close ties with the Winter VA Hospital in Topeka and was the largest and most important psychiatric training center in the nation—the two brothers, working in cooperation with public officials, helped to transform the ways in which the state cared for its mentally ill citizens. In 1945 Kansas ranked forty-third in terms of its patient-employee ratio (10.1:1); five years later it ranked fifth with a 3.5:1 ratio; and in 1955 it led the nation.[12]

Mounting pressures led the Governors' Conference in 1949, as noted previously, to direct the Council on State Governments to undertake an investigation of the nation's mental hospitals and to submit a report. Finished the following year, *The Mental Health Programs of the Forty-Eight States* detailed the deterioration of the nation's public institutions. The report conceded that its recommendations required massive infusions of new resources but pointed out that half or more of all patients committed to public hospitals, given proper treatment, could return to their communities within a relatively short period of time. The document also alluded to the need for preventive and community-oriented programs, although its focus was on institutions.[13]

The report by the Council of State Governments received a strong endorsement from the governors at their annual meeting in 1950. There was general agreement on the need to rebuild institutional facilities. But the assembled chief executives also accepted the claims by mental health professionals that community and preventive programs had the potential to reduce the need for long-term care. Sympathy toward the claims of the mentally ill, however, was tempered by a recognition of the legitimacy of other priorities. Moreover, states faced an odd dilemma in the postwar era. They were besieged by municipal and county demands for greater state funding for education and other public services. Yet the massive growth in the fiscal role of the federal government—in part the result of the impact of depression and war—had preempted many sources of revenue (excluding the property tax). Faced by pressure from below and above, state officials pursued a variety of strategies. They increased expenditures and taxes; they extended home rule to political subdivisions and transferred to them specific taxation authority; and they attempted to persuade the national government to relinquish or reduce certain kinds of taxes, which could then be used by states themselves. In general, governors responded to pressures in pragmatic terms: they supported increased levels of funding for mental hospitals but were also receptive to policies that promised to contain institutional expenditures.[14]

During the 1950s state mental hospital systems were the beneficiaries of a generally favorable climate. Therapeutic optimism—a product of the development of milieu therapy and new psychotropic drugs—renewed the faith of state officials in the efficacy of hospitalization. The relative economic prosperity of the postwar years and acceptance of a welfare state ideology also made them more willing to commit new resources to an age-old problem. The forging of closer links between state governments, university-affiliated medical schools, and professional and lay organizations, as well as the commitment of funds from the national government for training and research, also facilitated the passage of legislation designed to remedy the severe defects in the nation's public hospital system.

The annual Governors' Conferences called attention to many of the problems and needs of their mental hospital systems. Tending to accept prevailing psychiatric advice, governors played a key role in persuading their legislatures of the need for additional resources. Studies and investigations by legislative committees and other state agencies also added to the pressure for change. By the early 1950s signs of activity were already apparent. During the first half of the decade many states submitted large bond issues to the electorate for ratification; none were disapproved. On average, states allocated about two hundred million dollars a year for capital outlays. A survey of mental hospital construction and renovation in 1955 revealed that about three-quarters of a billion dollars had been appropriated for current projects, of which about 75 percent involved facilities for direct care and treatment of patients. Even in the South—an area that generally lagged behind—there was considerable support for programs designed to upgrade the quality of care and treatment. In 1953 the Southern Governors' Conference, representing sixteen states, adopted a resolution that led to the establishment of the Mental Health Training and Research Project under the aegis of the Southern Regional Education Board. Focusing on training of personnel and research, the project helped to foster more sympathetic attitudes toward the needs of the mentally ill.[15]

Although relatively few of its members were employed in public institutions, the APA played an active role during the 1950s in persuading state officials of the need for greater financial support. It continued to refine a set of standards to evaluate mental hospitals and clinics, and its CIB provided a yardstick by which public officials could judge the relative quality of their public institutions. At the same time the association sponsored annual Mental Hospital Institutes, which brought together superintendents from all regions of the country to familiarize them with new developments. In 1954 the APA also expanded its contacts with state governments by authorizing its medical director to provide assistance in seeking solutions to mental health problems. Out of this evolved a mechanism whereby the APA, in response to an invitation from the governor, would prepare a state survey. The survey commenced with the creation of a local committee composed of both professionals and laypersons selected by the governor. The medical director served as a consultant or chairperson, and the group collected data on the state's mental health program. With such data in hand, the APA's central office prepared an extensive report evaluating the effectiveness of existing facilities, identifying areas of urgent needs, and offering specific recommendations. Following approval by the state committee, the report was sent to the governor. Although most state surveys conducted during the 1950s dealt with both institutional and community programs, they nevertheless performed an important function in persuading state officials of the need to modernize their institutional facilities.[16]

Slowly the quality of patient care in mental hospitals improved. Between 1939 and 1945 the patient-employee ratio worsened, rising from 5.7:1 to 6.8:1, no doubt because of the strain on resources caused by war. In the succeeding decade it improved significantly. By 1950 the ratio had declined to 4.5:1; five years later it stood at 3.8:1. Expenditures showed a corresponding improvement. Between 1946 and 1960 average per capita expenditure for maintenance of patients in mental hospitals for the United States as a whole rose from $437 to $1,679, an increase of 284 percent. If the figures are adjusted to reflect changes in the Consumer Price Index, the increase was still a substantial 153.5 percent. In real dollars, per capita expenditures rose 43.4 percent between 1946 and 1950; 18.3 percent from 1950 to 1955; and 49.1 percent from 1955 to 1960. The conclusion is obvious: state governments substantially augmented their allocations for the care of the institutionalized mentally ill. This could not help but enhance the quality of care.

Nevertheless, the slow improvements in the quality of institutional care tended to be overlooked. The pattern of change was grossly uneven and varied from state to state. Kansas, which ranked first, had a patient-staff ratio of 2.1:1 and an average per capita expenditure of $2,840 in 1955; Tennessee, ranking last, had a 6.9:1 ratio and spent only $562.[17] Those who were critical of institutions, therefore, could always find evidence to justify their claims that the quality of care left much to be desired. Equally significant, the continued presence of a high proportion of aged patients reinforced the identification of hospitals with chronicity. Although state officials were aware of the dilemma posed by therapeutic objectives and the realities associated with large numbers of aged patients, they had few practical solutions. Given other fiscal pressures, there was virtually no chance that they would promote a large-scale effort to develop alternative policies to cope with the growing numbers of aged persons.

Nor did the specialty of psychiatry allay the concerns of public officials responsible for policy formulation and implementation. To be sure, the salaried staff of the APA tended to empathize with institutional members. Psychiatric leaders, most of whom were not affiliated with state hospitals, were somewhat less sympathetic and often emphasized the desirability of noninstitutional alternatives. In his APA presidential address in 1958, Harry C. Solomon described the large mental hospital as "antiquated, outmoded, and rapidly becoming obsolete," perhaps ignoring the improvements during the preceding decade. He urged that separate facilities (colonies or homes) be established for chronic patients not amenable to medical and psychiatric treatment, and that a new discipline be developed to manage them.[18]

Because of his stature and position, Solomon's address received national publicity and became the center of controversy. Robert C. Hunt, director of the Hudson River State Hospital in New York, responded publicly in critical terms and informed Solomon that his "private reactions are still unprintable." Conceding hospitals' shortcomings, Hunt told the APA Commission on Long Term Planning that the organization had not played a constructive role in countering the detrimental effects associated with "the state hospital stereotype." The majority of APA members, he observed, had neither contacts with nor knowledge about mental hospitals and hence were prone to identify prevailing stereotypes with reality. "No serious young professional knowing only this stereotype is willing to acquire or practice his skills in a state hospital setting if he can possibly get anything else." The prevailing conceptual model of psychiatry involved "the psychotherapy of one patient on a couch." Hunt's sentiments were suggestive of the growing isolation of hospital psychiatrists within the specialty.[19]

. . .

The effort to rebuild long-neglected hospital systems was also accompanied by attempts to expand community services. The result was a sharp increase in the number of general hospital psychiatric wards and community clinics. Neither of these alternatives was completely novel, for both had existed in one form or another well before World War II. After 1945, however, there was a dramatic increase in their numbers and size, and this led to significant changes in the nature of the mental health system.

Before 1940 few general hospitals provided direct psychiatric services. As late as 1939 only about 112 of the 4,309 general hospitals in the United States had provision for even the mildest nervous or emotional disturbances (although many psychiatric cases were hospitalized with nonpsychiatric diagnoses).[20] The absence of mental patients in general hospitals was understandable. The number of psychiatrists in private practice was relatively small; third-party insurance plans were as yet in their infancy, and most of them excluded psychiatric illnesses from coverage; and short-term therapies for the most part were nonexistent.

During the 1940s interest in expanding general hospital psychiatry increased markedly. Most practitioners, observed Franklin G. Ebaugh in one of the earliest works devoted exclusively to general hospital psychiatry, gave little attention to the psychogenic and personality aspects of illness, which consequently went unnoticed and untreated. The failure to provide treatment facilities in general hospitals, he added, contributed to sharp increases in chronicity.[21]

In the postwar era, general hospital psychiatric services gradually expanded. The passage of the Hill-Burton Act in 1946 provided substantial federal resources for hospital construction, which in turn facilitated the expansion of psychiatric divisions in general hospitals. In 1950 only 24,000 of the 576,000 general hospital beds were reserved for psychiatric cases; they accommodated about 1 percent of the total mentally ill population. Thirteen years later, however, 467 (5.8 percent) of the 5,291 general hospitals had separate inpatient psychiatric units; 578 others admitted disturbed individuals (without providing separate wards); and 2,137 accepted psychiatric cases for diagnosis and treatment pending transfer to other institutions. That same year 15.6 percent of all patient care episodes occurred in general hospital psychiatric units.[22]

The growing significance of general hospital psychiatry grew out of several interrelated developments. First, the emphasis on community care and treatment required access to some sort of local medical facility. The fact that the general hospital was the center of medical practice made it an obvious choice. Second, the belief that untreated personality disorders led unerringly to the more severe mental illnesses provided a rationale for early treatment in general hospitals in order to avoid protracted institutionalization in the future. Third, the concentration of psychiatrists in private rather than institutional practice provided a ready source of referrals. The urban character of psychiatry also resulted in a concentration of general hospital psychiatric units in the most populated states. Fourth, biological therapies—first electroshock and later drug therapy—often required short-term hospitalization. General hospitals were strategically located to meet such needs, for the average length of stay for psychiatric cases was brief (two weeks was characteristic). Finally, a slow expansion of health insurance psychiatric benefits provided at least minimal coverage.[23]

Paradoxically, the intellectual rationale for general hospital psychiatry came from psychodynamic figures even though in practice biological, rather than psychological, therapies were characteristic. The irony was captured by Karl A. Menninger, an individual long identified with psychodynamic and psychoanalytic theories. When asked to express his views about APA policy on general hospitals, he expressed considerable "misgivings." General hospital psychiatric facilities presented "insuperable problems"; they failed to provide adjunctive therapies (recreational, occupational, educational), emphasized "bed care," and generally served as "emergency detention space" pending recovery or transfer elsewhere. Many patients received electroshock "in the hopes that it would render a more prolonged treatment unnecessary." If this therapy was employed with "selective, diagnostic justification I am all for it," added Menninger, "but I myself have been caught many times with the necessity of doing something quick in an effort to avert administrative shifts to a different kind of treatment situation."[24] Menninger's observations suggested that general hospital psychiatry was not without its own unique problems. The broad ancillary services generally provided by psychologists, social workers, and others in mental hospitals were absent. More important, general hospitals were not integrated with other parts of the mental health system and hence were unprepared to offer supportive services often required by severely mentally ill persons.

The growth of general hospital psychiatry, although presumably relieving the unremitting pressures on mental hospitals, was not directly shaped by state mental health policies. The postwar psychiatric enthusiasm for community clinics, on the other hand, directly involved state governments, which remained the major source of funding for mental health services. That many governors welcomed an expansion of noninstitutional alternatives was understandable. The claims that local clinics would diminish the need for protracted hospitalization appealed to them on several counts: hospitals would diminish in size and lose their "warehouse" characteristics; more humane and effective alternatives, providing both treatment and preventive services, would be put into place; and costs would either stabilize or diminish. Public officials tended to accept such claims without probing their validity or seeking supportive evidence. By this time the prestige of science and medicine had begun to peak, and there was little or no disposition on the part of political leaders to question or challenge professional authority. The few dissenting psychiatric voices were largely ignored if not dismissed. During the 1950s, therefore, the movement away from traditional institutional care and treatment gathered momentum.

Outpatient and community clinics, of course, had existed long before World War II. Massachusetts, for example, inaugurated in 1914 a program designed to broaden the availability of psychiatric services to the general public. During the 1920s the Commonwealth Fund and the NCMH provided resources for the creation of child guidance clinics as demonstration models. On the eve of World War II there were about 372 clinics throughout the country. Most of them dealt with children and occasionally adults, but few focused on the problems or needs of the seriously mentally ill.[25]

The passage of the National Mental Health Act of 1946 proved a watershed. Under its provisions the federal government provided grants to states to support existing outpatient facilities and programs or to establish new ones. The ultimate goal, according to Felix, was to have one outpatient facility for each 100,000 persons. Initially, funding levels were relatively modest. In 1948 states received about $2 million; the following year the level of funding rose to $3.5 million. Nevertheless, the impact was dramatic. Before 1948 more than half of all states had no clinics; by 1949 all but five states had one or more. Six years later there were about 1,234 outpatient psychiatric clinics, of which about two-thirds were state supported or aided.[26]

The belief that clinics prevented hospitalization was but a reflection of the continuum theory of mental illnesses. Deutsch, whose journalistic writings captured the essence of the postwar psychiatric scene with remarkable acumen, urged New York City officials in early 1947 to take advantage of newly available federal funding to expand their outpatient clinic program. "Many emotional disorders have their origin in early childhood," he observed. Similarly, the city could benefit from "a lot more marriage counselling agencies—*with proper standards*—to help straighten out family problems that so often arise from, and in turn create, serious mental unbalance." In a subsequent column he lauded Connecticut officials for providing appropriate resources for outpatient clinics. About 477 children had received outpatient clinic treatment; of these, 66 would have required institutionalization at a cost of about $200,000. The costs of outpatient treatment, on the other hand, were but a fraction of this sum. The conclusion was inescapable: outpatient clinics were cost-effective.[27]

During the late 1940s and early 1950s support mounted for clinics that served the entire community. The 1941 edition of an organizational manual on clinics published by the NCMH was devoted almost entirely to a discussion of services for children. A revised edition eleven years later was indicative of the conceptual change that had occurred. "The psychiatric clinic," wrote its authors,

is an organization established to treat the mental and emotional needs of individual patients and on a broader scale to prevent such ills in the community. . . . The work of a clinic is less limited to helping individual patients and carries responsibility for advancing the mental health of the total community. The clinic discharges its responsibility through consultation and cooperation with a variety of people in the community whose work affects the mental health of those with whom they work, such as physicians, teachers and social workers. Further, the clinic should play an important part in constructive mental health planning through participation in community activities.

The purpose of mental health clinics, insisted Jack R. Ewalt, the Massachusetts commissioner of mental health and clinical professor of psychiatry at Harvard, "is to prepare for living, or . . . to promote health." Detection of "early points of tension or maladjustment or emotional crisis" and early treatment could prevent the onset of psychiatric symptoms.[28]

The interest in community programs was further strengthened by medical philanthropic organizations involved with mental health policy issues. The Milbank Memorial Fund—a foundation long active in health policy issues since its formal creation in 1918—was especially notable. The fund had assisted the NCMH in its early years and continued to provide support for other mental hygiene organizations. In 1948, however, its officers decided to move beyond the awarding of grants and to broaden its activities in mental health. Accordingly, it employed its modest resources in two distinct, albeit related, ways. First, beginning in 1949 it sponsored periodic conferences that brought together figures from both psychiatry and the academic world concerned with the pattern and distribution of mental illnesses and community-based services. Second, it provided financial support for community mental health demonstration projects and for the development of methods for evaluating outcomes.[29]

In 1949 the fund sponsored a conference dealing with the epidemiology of mental disorders. Psychiatric epidemiology at that time was a relatively young subspecialty. Admittedly, interest in statistics dated from the early nineteenth century. The emphasis, however, was on the collection of data dealing with institutionalized patients, and the relationship of such data to an understanding of etiology, incidence, and prevalence was murky. At best, institutional statistics served to establish the legitimacy and utility of mental hospitals, and thus to build broad support among state officials and the public. The new psychiatric epidemiology that developed slowly during the 1920s and came to maturity after World War II, on the other hand, represented an extraordinary intellectual leap; its goal was to study the incidence and prevalence of mental disorders in the community and to isolate a range of socioenvironmental variables, thus enhancing professionals' ability to predict who was at risk and to specify those environmental factors that promoted or prevented the onset of severe symptoms. The importance and popularity of epidemiology was understandable in the postwar milieu. It was compatible with the prevailing emphasis on the role of environment in American thought generally; it suggested the malleability of human behavior; it provided a means of confirming the psychodynamic belief that mental illnesses grew out of various kinds of stress; and it was compatible with prevailing concepts of science.[30]

Participants at the conference—including such figures as Felix, John E. Gordon, Erich Lindemann, Ernest M. Gruenberg, Robert P. Knight, and

Alexander H. Leighton—were clearly concerned with the etiological role of socioenvironmental variables. "The research problem," observed Leighton, "is to analyze a community in order to determine the high and low areas of social-psychological stress and then to determine the distribution of mental disease in these contrasting areas." Knight was less enthusiastic about the feasibility of epidemiological studies of functional mental illnesses. Poor hospital records, psychiatric disagreements regarding diagnosis, and the "unholy mess of nomenclature" led him to question "how an epidemiologist can take figures arising out of such confusion and make anything at all meaningful out of them." Despite such reservations, it was clear that most of the participants believed that epidemiological studies had the potential to identify environmental variables and thereby lay the foundations of more effective prevention and treatment programs. Indeed, the fund began to provide financial support for long-term epidemiological studies in Stirling County (Canada) and midtown Manhattan.[31]

In 1950 the Milbank conference momentarily deviated from its newly articulated goals by focusing on the biology of mental disorders. By and large, the participants were carefully selected in an effort to address the growing imbalance between the psychodynamic and somatic approaches. The subjects that were excluded were striking: sociology, interpersonal relationships, psychotherapy, psychoanalysis, and public health.[32]

By 1952, however, the fund had returned to its original goal of emphasizing the study of socioenvironmental variables and community-oriented programs. In that year it brought together figures from psychiatry and the social and behavioral sciences, virtually all of whom were committed to a psychodynamic and environmental approach. Half of the participants presented papers dealing with the value of sociological and psychological concepts in mental health. The remainder reported on ongoing epidemiological research projects, projects that in subsequent years resulted in a series of famous publications on the role of socioenvironmental variables. Leighton summarized the Stirling County research on the relationship between psychiatric illnesses and sociocultural factors; August B. Hollingshead and Fredrick C. Redlich described their work on the relationship between social class and mental illness; and Thomas A. C. Rennie reviewed the Yorkville (Manhattan) epidemiological project. The conference also provided Lindemann with an opportunity to narrate the novel effort begun in 1948 to create a community agency in Wellesley (Massachusetts) that would provide services, develop means of detecting incipient emotional disorders so as to enhance the possibility of preventive care, and apply mental health principles to community planning in such diverse areas as housing, medical care, education, recreation, and welfare.[33]

Subsequently, Milbank officials continued to support conferences and programs designed to strengthen community mental health programs and agencies. The emphasis on positive mental health and prevention became so overpowering that the needs of the severely mentally ill slowly receded into the background. This is not to argue that those involved with community programs were unconcerned. It is only to suggest that their faith in the efficacy of new approaches led them to overlook many of the intractable problems associated with severely mentally ill persons. The working documents for the conference in 1955, for example, emphasized the need to sensitize a variety of public and private community agencies concerned with physical health, education, and public order to the significance of positive mental health principles; rehabilitation of the severely mentally ill took a distinctly secondary place on the agenda. Succeeding meetings reiterated many of these themes. If the Milbank conferences were not directly linked with policy changes, the deliberations of participants illustrated the growing emphasis on community approaches.[34]

In the immediate postwar years the rhetoric and enthusiasm for a community-oriented program far exceeded any specific achievements. Admittedly, the number of clinics established under the National Mental Health Act increased. The absence of any structure that integrated clinics and mental hospitals, however, precluded fundamental changes in actual practice. Mental hospitals continued to retain responsibility for aftercare, while clinics dealt with a quite different clientele. Given budgetary and personnel pressures, few state hospitals were able to devote resources or staff to monitor or assist discharged patients, a group not served by clinics. Aftercare thus remained largely an ideal; effective services were the rare exception.[35]

Rhetoric and expectations, nevertheless, fueled the desire for innovations. Once again New York—with the largest institutionalized population of any state and officials eager to act—was a catalyst for change. With the support of Governor Dewey, a law was enacted in 1949 that created a State Mental Health Commission composed of the state commissioners of mental hygiene, social welfare, health, correction, and education. Its basic function was to engage in coordinated long-range planning for community mental health programs and to administer funds under the federal act of 1946. By mid-1953 the commission had drafted a master plan for the establishment of community mental health services, the costs of which were to be divided equally between the state and the locality.[36]

Perhaps the greatest barrier blocking a new policy initiative was state officials' fear that budgetary pressures would only be exacerbated. Governor Dewey, for example, was reluctant to endorse the principle of state aid for local initiatives. Faced with an annual increase of three thousand patients in public mental hospitals and a rising budget, however, he finally concluded that only state incentives could induce local communities to provide services that would in the long run reduce the demand for institutional care and treatment. In his message to the legislature in 1954 he endorsed both the establishment of permanent local mental health services dedicated to treatment, rehabilitation, and prevention, and a $350 million bond issue to rebuild mental hospitals and schools. Although some were fearful that local autonomy would be impaired and services further fragmented by the creation of new local agencies, the bill easily passed the legislature and became law in February 1954.[37]

The Community Mental Health Services Act was permissive in nature, although localities that chose not to provide services were ineligible for state aid. Under its provisions, any county or city of fifty thousand or more residents was empowered to establish a nine-member local mental health board, which, in turn, appointed a psychiatrist as director. Two of its nine members had to be the ranking local health and welfare officials; two had to be physicians in private practice; the remainder included individuals employed in local government (including schools and courts) or private voluntary agencies. The premise was that the treatment of mental disorders was a medical responsibility, whereas prevention was a shared responsibility of the service professions and the community. Four services were eligible for reimbursement: outpatient psychiatric clinics; inpatient general hospital psychiatric services; psychiatric rehabilitation for those suffering from psychiatric disorders; and consultant and educational services. Half of all expenditures were eligible for state reimbursement up to a maximum of one dollar per resident per year.[38]

The legislation rested on a clear presumption that the prevention of serious mental illnesses was a major societal goal. The protean nature of the concept of prevention and the lack of a clearly identified target population, however, created administrative difficulties. To define a mental health service by the kind of individual served or the kind of service offered was problematic. The Department of Mental Hygiene—the state agency charged with responsibility for implementing the act's provisions—therefore decided to define a mental health service by the kind of person providing the service. Its regulations stipulated that mental health services were reimbursable only if provided by a qualified psychiatrist or individuals acting under the direction of a psychiatrist. Although simplifying administrative complexities, this decision did not provide for any links between community services and the state's large mental hospital system. Nor did it specify any particular target population to be helped. Hunt, who played an important role in the state, was aware of the problem. He conceded that the location of hospitals and the fact that they drew their patients from a wide geographical area made it extremely difficult to coordinate their activities with those of local mental health services, but he could find no way of resolving this thorny problem.[39]

The impact of the legislation was almost immediate. In less than four years following its passage, twenty-one counties and New York City—which together included more than 85 percent of the state's population—had elected to participate. By 1961 the program covered 159 outpatient clinics, 21 general hospital psychiatric clinics with 2,194 beds, and 7 rehabilitation services, as well as consultation and educational services. In the first eighteen months, state subsidies amounted to $4 million; by fiscal year 1958–1959 the figure was nearly $10.8 million.[40]

The experiences of California, though not identical, paralleled those of New York. By 1950 California's mental hospitals had a resident population of nearly 32,000, on whose behalf the state pursued a somewhat different strategy in providing aftercare services. In the early 1940s Aaron Rosanoff, the first psychiatrist to head the Department of Institutions, formulated a plan to place more patients on leave and created a new office to oversee aftercare. In 1946 the Bureau of Social Work was formally created as a division within the Department of Mental Hygiene (successor to the Department of Institutions) to provide social services in the community for these patients. By the mid-1950s the bureau had 180 employees and was supervising about 8,500 patients on conditional leave.[41]

Interest in new policy initiatives was further stimulated by Governor Earl Warren, who had convened a conference on mental health in 1949. The recommendations of the participants were typical of that era: the establishment of local representative councils; more effective mental health services for children, youths, and adults; a "generalized program for community mental health"; the creation of a Division of Community Services in the Department of Mental Hygiene; an enlarged community clinic program; and expansion and revitalization of state hospitals. During the early 1950s a state-sponsored community services program slowly began to expand local services and preventive programs. By 1953 a trial act provided for state subsidies for some locally operated outpatient services.[42]

Concerned with the seemingly endless rise in the number of hospitalized patients and the commensurate increase in expenditures, the California Senate in 1955 created an Interim Committee on the Treatment of Mental Illness. Publicity about the effectiveness of the new psychotropic drugs played a major role in its establishment, since they appeared to hold out the prospect of sharply reducing the size of the mental hospital system. The passage of New York's landmark law the previous year also reinforced the prevailing faith in the efficacy of prevention.

In the two years of its existence, the interim committee produced a series of influential reports that led to the passage of the Short-Doyle Act in mid-1957. The goals of the act were clear: to promote mental health and to prevent psychiatric illnesses. Under its provisions communities were authorized to establish mental health services. Formal administrative authority was vested in a local administrator; local boards had advisory functions only. The cost of services was divided equally between the state and participating cities and counties; unlike New York, California put no cap on state contributions. The act provided for state reimbursement for three kinds of clinical facilities (outpatient clinics; general hospital inpatient services for a period not exceeding sixty days; and rehabilitation services in clinics, hospitals, or special settings) and two kinds of mental health services (public information to professionals and agencies concerned with mental health, and consultation with schools and other public agencies dealing with individuals before their symptoms became severe enough to warrant psychiatric treatment).[43]

The Short-Doyle Act and subsequent legislative acts in the 1960s slowly shifted the focus of state policy away from a reliance on institutional care and treatment. Counties and cities began to establish facilities and programs that in succeeding years would have a dramatic impact. In 1959 California appropriated $69 million for hospitals and $1.6 million for activities under Short-Doyle; within a decade the figures were $112 and $23.9 million, respectively. By 1966, 115,000 persons were treated in Short-Doyle programs; at the close of the year the caseload amounted to 33,000 individuals (90 percent of whom were outpatients). In that same year, forty-one Short-Doyle programs were operating in areas that included 96 percent of the state's total population. The relationship between Short-Doyle and changes in state hospital populations, however, was not at all clear. There were some striking differences between the groups served. Those under treatment at Short-Doyle facilities came from higher socioeconomic groups and had less serious mental disorders. The decline in state hospital resident populations (as of June 30) between 1959 and 1966 from 37,592 to 26,567, moreover, did not necessarily occur because of the establishment of local clinics. During this same period, for example, admissions to mental hospitals increased from 20,105 to 25,300.[44]

New York and California were by no means alone in seeking to redefine their traditional reliance on hospitalization by creating local facilities and programs that could presumably prevent mental illnesses and identify and treat individuals with early warning symptoms. Other states, while not adopting such comprehensive legislation, nevertheless began to provide support for community services and programs. In 1957 Minnesota and New Jersey passed similar laws. Although the details differed, their underlying principles were similar. These laws permitted rather than mandated local action; they supported local planning while providing for consultation and advisory services by state employees; they placed operating responsibility at the community level; and they provided for cost sharing by both levels of government.[45]

Even in states that did not follow suit, it was evident that officials—persuaded by the claim that untreated mental disorders led to more serious mental illnesses—were placing greater emphasis on the preventive aspects of their mental health programs. In many areas the demands placed on clinics exceeded their capacities, and requests for educational materials and consultative services from schools, physicians, probation officers, and parent groups could not be met. Most State Mental Health Authorities (mandated under the provisions of the National Mental Health Act of 1946) emphasized a litany of needs: the lack of local diagnostic and treatment facilities for adults and children; the need for more social services; the shortage of trained psychiatrists and other mental health personnel; and the scarcity of funds for community programs.[46]

That outpatient clinics and mental hygiene services in schools, courts, and social agencies grew rapidly was hardly surprising. When the NIMH inaugurated its reporting system of outpatient clinics in 1954, it identified 1,234 clinics, of which 508 were state operated (268 by mental hospitals), and 286 others state aided. Five years later there had been a 16 percent increase in the total number of clinics; all states were now represented. Admittedly, sharp differences between and within regions were characteristic: the Northeast and the north central states had the highest concentration, the South the lowest; and services in urban areas were far more extensive than those in rural areas.[47] Nevertheless, there was a growing consensus that future policy would rest on the primacy of outpatient and community services.

.   .   .

During the 1950s the twin ideologies of prevention and faith in community care and treatment found a receptive audience among a public enamored with psychological explanations and eager to take advantage of psychological services. Similarly, political leaders and officials in populous states were also supportive; they accepted at face value the claims that prevention and early treatment in community facilities would be effective and more economical.

The enthusiasm for community-oriented programs did not go completely unchallenged; from time to time dissenting voices were heard. Deutsch felt constrained in 1956 to add to his generally optimistic evaluation of recent developments some cautionary words. He specifically pointed to the distressing tendency of mental health advocates to ignore "disgraceful and remediable conditions" in public mental hospitals and to "expend their zeal rather in promoting ambiguous and often fleeting concepts about 'mental health,' along with confusing and mutually contradictory theories unsupported by solid scientific knowledge." "I see, in too many states," he added, "a virtual abandonment of mental hospital patients by societies especially entrusted with the task of mobilizing public support for improved institutional conditions. . . . It remains a capital irony that the traditional neglect of hospitalized mental patients is too often supplemented by neglect on the part of groups supposedly dedicated to better care and treatment."[48]

In the heady atmosphere of the 1950s Deutsch's warnings were all but ignored. During this decade rhetorical claims became so powerful that they acquired a life of their own. The assertions that community programs and services were inherently superior to institutional care and treatment, and that prevention could diminish the incidence of serious mental illnesses, became articles of faith rather than hypotheses to be investigated. Rhetoric proved so pervasive and powerful that it literally overwhelmed meaningful evaluations of programs and policies.

Equally important, rhetoric often overshadowed data that questioned prevailing beliefs. That many individuals could be treated more effectively in outpatient clinics was an article of faith during the 1950s that fueled demands for community-based policies. Yet supporting data were all but absent. Admittedly, the results of providing brief therapy for soldiers with neuropsychiatric symptoms seemed promising. But were military experiences an appropriate analogy on which to base public policy? Were the stress-related symptoms associated with war similar to the kinds of symptoms that in civilian life led to hospitalization in public institutions? Was it possible to predict whether untreated persons experiencing personal and psychological problems would require treatment in mental hospitals? Answers to these and other questions had obvious implications for public policy.

More significant, data that contradicted prevailing beliefs were all but ignored. In the mid-1950s a group of California researchers decided to study the effectiveness of hospital and clinic treatment in comparable psychiatric cases. The project involved three California hospitals and two state community clinics. From a sample of state mental hospital admissions, the investigators screened 504 patients in the hope of referring half to clinics. Their actual experiences were quite different. Only 57 were identified as candidates for clinic referral; 20 of the 57 were referred; and 6 were accepted by the clinics for treatment, of whom only 2 kept appointments and demonstrated any improvement. The investigators concluded that there were "marked discontinuities in functions" of hospitals and clinics. Those who required an extensive social support network were not candidates for clinics, which provided no assistance in finding living quarters or employment. In other words, the kinds of patients seen in clinics were not similar to those admitted to hospitals. According to the investigators, the study did not contradict the view that early treatment in clinics could prevent hospitalization. On the other hand, they pointed to the need for "substantiation by control-group design."[49]

The California study did not challenge the viability of clinics. But the evidence suggested that the ways in which clinics were conceptualized required modification, and that far greater attention had to be paid to the development of links between clinics and hospitals.[50] Although relevant to policy issues, such findings were largely ignored. Moreover, many of the discussions about evaluation focused on individual patients or else were global and impressionistic in character.[51] Neither state legislators nor members of Congress questioned the claims of professionals, perhaps because of the prestige of medicine. The annual hearings before the House and Senate appropriations subcommittees during the 1950s, for example, offer dramatic evidence of the degree to which professional assertions assumed an aura of omniscience.[52]

Rhetoric not only shaped policy but actually impeded evaluation research. That techniques existed to test with any degree of precision some of the major elements in psychodynamic and psychoanalytic ideology was dubious. To be sure, a number of social and behavioral science disciplines by the 1950s had developed a sophisticated awareness of research design and statistical analysis. Whether their methodologies could be employed in evaluating mental health ideology was more problematical. Mental health, a subcommittee of the National Advisory Mental Health Council observed in 1954, was an elusive concept and embraced a variety of beliefs, including:

> More treatment [should be provided] for more patients in the community;
> Community clinics will save many patients from State hospitals;
> More psychiatrists, clinical psychologists, social workers, and psychiatric nurses are the answer to the mental health problem;
> The basis of prevention is correction of faulty child-rearing practices and the treatment of emotional disorders in childhood;
> Knowledge of the psychological development of the child by professionals and laity is the keystone of mental health;
> Ministers, school teachers, recreational workers, and mental hygiene societies can stave off tendencies to mental disorder;
> Mental health is a state for which individuals can be educated by disseminating knowledge about emotional processes through pamphlets, popular books, movies, posters, exhibits, radio, television, and lectures;

The problem of mental and emotional disorder should be attacked broadside on a mass scale reaching as many of the population as possible, irrespective of the current state of mental health of any individual or family;

Unconscious psychological determinants are the major explanation of maladaptive reactions; and

An understanding of causality in human behavior is more effective in improving mental health than is emphasis on surface effects.

These beliefs, noted the subcommittee, often reflected a desire to deal with perceived problems rather than to develop a research program to test the validity of these perceptions.[53]

It cannot be denied that the design of research projects to test psychiatric claims faced formidable difficulties. Indeed, Simon Flexner, director of the Rockefeller Institute for Medical Research, even before 1920 expressed doubts about the ability to conduct neuropsychiatric research because "there were no problems in a fit state for work." His comments, made in a quite different context, were echoed by Alan Gregg, his successor. "Perhaps the sum and substance of what seems to me to be the difficulty is this," Gregg wrote to William Menninger: "first-class research work in psychiatry and human psychology is extremely difficult and rare."[54]

Yet evaluation research was by no means impossible. In 1961, for example, Benjamin Pasamanick and his associates began a classic two-and-a-half-year study to determine the relative value of hospital versus home treatment for schizophrenic patients. They randomized 152 schizophrenic patients referred to a state hospital into three groups: a drug home care group; a placebo home care group; and a hospital control group. The first group was seen regularly by a public health nurse and less frequently by a staff psychiatrist, psychologist, or social worker. The results were striking: over 77 percent of the drug home care patients, as compared to only 34 percent of the placebo home care cases, remained continuously at home. After an average institutional stay of eighty-three days, the control group required hospitalization more often than did the drug home care patients. Pasamanick and his colleagues were critical of the fact that the vast majority of psychiatrists were in private practice, where they provided psychotherapy for "predominantly nonpsychotic patients, of middle-class status, in the professional occupations, and with college education." They emphasized the importance of supportive, continuous, coordinated, and comprehensive services. "Schizophrenia and other forms of mental illness," they concluded, "affect not only the psychological but the economic, social, and familial functioning of the patient, and . . . psychiatric care alone, however adequate, will sometimes do very little to improve functioning and reduce incompetence in these other areas." Their findings, as a matter of fact, were hardly supportive of the global claims of those who were urging the adoption of a community-based mental health policy, but who seriously underestimated the administrative difficulties in integrating and coordinating various kinds of services.[55]

Rhetorical statements were hardly the only impediment to evaluation. Funding levels remained minimal. In 1953 the Council of State Governments estimated that federal and state expenditures for research amounted to about $5.7 million out of a total of nearly $800 million (or 0.7 percent). The resources available for evaluation research were only a fraction of this small research budget. State and hospital officials were preoccupied with care and treatment; evaluation had a low priority. NIMH-sponsored research in part redressed the balance. But the institute's leadership was as much concerned with services and policy issues as with evaluation and research; in this sense it played a role quite different from that of other NIH institutes. Even had greater resources been made available, however, it was doubtful that a different state of affairs would have prevailed. Psychiatry remained a largely clinical specialty; few of its members were trained in evaluation or research. Indeed, the protean and inclusive character of the psychodynamic model may actually have inhibited the development of evaluation techniques with adequate controls. "Verbal unreality," observed Jurgen Ruesch, "retards psychiatric progress."[56]

. . .

During the 1950s sentiment among both professional and lay groups gradually shifted as receptivity toward community alternatives modified the long-standing commitment to mental hospital care and treatment. The shift was not strictly linear; at the outset considerable resources were devoted to the rebuilding of a long-ignored hospital system. The presumption, at least in the early part of the decade, was that community and mental hospital services each occupied a legitimate sphere, although there was an underlying feeling that a serious imbalance had been created by the manner in which resources had been allocated. The passage of community mental health services acts in New York and California was intended in part to redress the balance; they did not imply the eventual destruction of traditional mental hospitals. The ideal, at least in theory, was an integrated system that included preventive services, treatment, and care in different kinds of settings depending upon the severity of the problem or illness. The discussion at the thirty-eighth annual conference of the Milbank Memorial Fund in 1961 dealt with the very real problems of bringing mental hospitals and community mental health programs "into closer working relationship in the interest of providing better clinical services to patients." At the close of the conference Dr. John D. Porterfield, a PHS official, captured the spirit of the 1950s in his comments. "The patient with his comprehensive if not integrated balance of chemistry and psychodynamics," he told his colleagues, "continues to await your resolution of these problems of the reorganization of state hospital procedures as it moves into the community, the reorganization of community services as it receives this integrated operation and the achievement of the objective of continuity of care for the continuity of problems."[57]

In less than a decade, however, community mental health would be reconceptualized in ways that polarized policy choices and laid the foundations for a concerted attack on the very legitimacy of traditional mental hospital care. A curious alliance of individuals and groups from a variety of disciplinary and occupational backgrounds having quite different agendas would emerge from the vortex of the political and social ferment of the 1960s. Even before the decade had come to an end the goal of integrating mental hospitals and community services would be partially modified by a new policy whose long-range goal included the eventual replacement of traditional mental hospitals with new community institutions.

CHAPTER EIGHT

A National Campaign:
The Joint Commission on Mental Illness
and Health

THE PACE of change in the decade following 1945, however rapid, seemed cumbersome and slow to impatient contemporary activists. The decentralized nature of the American political system meant that the struggle to transform public policy had to be fought in each individual state. A unified campaign was extraordinarily difficult, given the fact that policy and appropriations were the responsibility of state legislatures and governors. Success might come in New York and California where a large concentration of psychiatric personnel and services existed and where a commitment to the welfare of the mentally ill had a long-standing tradition. In other states, however, different conditions prevailed, and the barriers to change remained formidable.

The experiences of the New Deal, World War II, and the steadily growing role of the federal government in health and welfare suggested to postwar psychiatric activists an avenue for fundamental change. They concluded that the time was ripe for a new initiative that would shift, at least in part, authority and responsibility in mental health policy from the states to the national government. The passage of the National Mental Health Act in 1946 had been an important first step; what was required was legislation that provided direct federal subsidies for mental health services. Federal appropriations for other health-related activities (e.g., biomedical research and hospital construction) had already demonstrated the power of the purse to modify and reshape public policy.

That a biomedical lobby with intimate congressional ties was flourishing also implied that new policy initiatives would receive a sympathetic reception in the nation's capital. Public receptivity for psychological explanations and services, along with a generalized faith in medical and even social and behavioral science, moreover, augured well for those who promoted a greater federal role. The continuum model of mental health and corresponding faith in the efficacy of preventive and therapeutic interventions was especially attractive to a broad middle-class public eager to exploit psychological services. Finally, many psychiatric activists shared the prevailing view that social policy would benefit from a diminution of state responsibility and a commensurate increase in federal authority. Indeed, during the 1950s the pervasive faith in the national government and a corresponding belief that states were backward, parsimonious, and reactionary helped to shape many social policy debates. The transformation of mental health policy was slowly incorporated into the program of a coalition dedicated to altering the traditional boundaries between the national and state governments.

To alter governmental functions and boundaries was not an easy task. Long-standing political traditions and customs as well as regional, state, and local loyalties remained powerful. Moreover, the idea that the national government could play an effective role in the delivery of services remained problematic. To overcome impediments to change, psychiatric activists turned to the past for guidance. Their model was the famous report by Abraham Flexner for the Carnegie Foundation for the Advancement of Teaching. Published in 1910 under the title *Medical Education in the United States and Canada*, the Flexner report played a significant role in confirming changes in medical education and setting the stage for the subsequent preeminence of the United States in medical research and practice. Why could not a comparable report on mental health policy ultimately lead to fundamental changes in the ways in which American society acted toward its mentally ill citizens? Success came in 1955 with the formal creation of the Joint Commission on Mental Illness and Health (JCMIH). During the six years of its existence, the commission sponsored a series of significant scholarly studies. More important, it helped to create an atmosphere conducive to the discussion of new policy initiatives and ultimately to the passage of federal legislation that would undermine the traditional emphasis on institutional care and treatment of the severely mentally ill.

. . .

The idea of a Flexner-type report was first raised by Kenneth E. Appel, then APA president and professor of psychiatry at the University of Pennsylvania School of Medicine. In an address in 1953 dealing with the need for mobilizing public support (hitherto largely absent), Appel called for "a sociological study of the breakdown crisis in the administration of state mental hospital functions" modeled along the lines of the Flexner report on medical education. In subsequent speeches he reiterated this theme. One of his underlying concerns was to study "the political troubles" faced by mental hospital superintendents and administrators because the frequent changes in state administrations often brought inexperienced figures into high-level positions. "Planning on a nationwide, long-term scale is essential," he told the Symposium on Directions of Current Progress in Psychiatry in the autumn of 1954. Moreover, leadership had to be taken by psychiatrists. Appel's suggestions received a warm reception by several APA committees, which supported the concept of a Flexner-type study.[1]

In arguing for a national study of mental illness, Appel and others misunderstood the Flexner report but may have intuitively grasped its significance. In their eyes the Flexner report had led to the modernization of medical education. In reality, Flexner had built on a conceptual revolution that had its roots in the late nineteenth century when medical educators had transformed the ways in which physicians were educated; his report confirmed but did not originate the changes that followed. More important, Flexner's career illustrated the ways in which early twentieth-century private philanthropy used its resources to hasten the rationalization of medical schools, universities, and hospitals into a functionally related national system. In organizing knowledge and expertise, these private foundations played the same role in the United States as the nation-state played in Europe. By the 1930s, however, foundations had lost much of their authority to the federal government and to those hierarchies that constituted the core of the new organizational society.[2]

Mental health policy, by contrast, lacked national cohesion; each of the forty-eight states retained autonomous decision-making authority. If policy were to be rationalized, a way would have to be found to overcome the fragmentation of a society marked by organizational power yet lacking a central core of authority. In the decade after 1945 the groundwork for change was slowly prepared. During these years the public was sensitized to the failure of traditional mental hospitals; the revitalized specialty of psychiatry defined new and presumably more effective policies; and the federal government became a participant in the policy-making process. Hence a Flexner-type *national* investigation seemed the appropriate mechanism to centralize decision making, thus facilitating the implementation of a reform agenda.

In early January 1955 the APA Executive Committee and the AMA Council on Mental Health (composed of psychiatrists who were also prominent APA members) met to discuss Appel's proposal. There was strong sentiment in favor of establishing a joint commission with two overriding objectives: first, to undertake a national survey of all resources and methods employed in the diagnosis, care, and treatment of the mentally ill and retarded; and second, "*to formulate*, on the basis of this survey, a *feasible program*" of improvement. There was unanimous agreement that a commission would be more effective if it were *not* sponsored by the federal government (although financial assistance from a grant-making agency would be welcomed). The primary sponsors would be the APA and the AMA, although the support of other national organizations would be sought. The participants authorized the formation of a Planning

Committee of twenty-three, including eight from the APA and the AMA, with the remainder coming from such groups as the American Hospital Association, the Council of State Governments, the VA, the NIMH, the Social Science Research Council, and organizations representing nurses, psychiatric social workers, and clinical psychologists.[3]

At the same time a drive was launched to secure the approval (and financial support) of the federal government. In January 1955 several bills and resolutions were introduced in both houses of Congress. One resolution endorsed the establishment of a Commission on Mental Health, which would conduct a thorough investigation into the problems of mental illnesses and recommend a comprehensive national mental health program. Other bills sought to expand federal funding for mental health programs involving training, construction of research facilities, and special projects demonstration grants. Pressure for an expanded role for the national government was generated by a biomedical lobby composed not only of private and professional groups, but also of key congressional leaders and federal officials. J. Percy Priest, the original sponsor of the National Mental Health Act of 1946, took the lead in the House; his counterpart in the Senate was Lister Hill, who played a major role in health policy issues in the postwar era. Within weeks a number of prominent members of Congress from both parties lent their names as cosponsors—an indication of the popularity of legislation designed to promote the health of the American people. In a special message, President Dwight D. Eisenhower also expressed support for health-related programs. His administration's modest fiscal recommendations, however, led Congress to take a leadership role.[4]

In March and April both the House and Senate held public hearings. The objective was not to mobilize Congress; by this time bipartisan support for health-related legislation was so strong that actual appropriations often exceeded presidential recommendations. Moreover, the funding levels envisaged in all of the proposals were—by the standards of that era—modest. The goal of the hearings was rather to focus public attention on mental health policy, and thus to strengthen support for an enhanced federal role and to promote policy innovations. In this respect, the hearings had a largely symbolic character; the testimony of the witnesses and the favorable reaction of members of Congress recapitulated the annual hearings on the NIMH budget.

The hearings before a House subcommittee began with testimony by six federal officials, including Health, Education, and Welfare (HEW) Secretary Oveta Culp Hobby, Surgeon General Leonard A. Scheele, and Felix. Their agenda reflected the concerns of their own organization. They emphasized the need to broaden the provisions of the National Mental Health Act of 1946, and they supported higher appropriations for the training of personnel, improvements in community mental health services, and pilot projects to upgrade mental hospital care and treatment. Felix called attention to the need for outpatient facilities and foster homes for discharged patients. The large number of aged patients in mental hospitals, he added, represented a "nursing problem"; he suggested that the Hill-Burton legislation fund construction of a "new type of institution . . . half way between the home and the mental hospital."[5]

A familiar litany of witnesses repeated themes that by the 1950s had become the conventional wisdom. The tireless Mike Gorman supported the concept of a national study as well as increased levels of federal funding. Daniel Blain, APA medical director, echoed Gorman. "There is a crying need," he testified,

> to reexamine our basic assumptions in the field, to see what actually takes place in hospitals with high discharge rates as compared to others with low discharge rates; to assist the factors which account for the tragic lag between the development of psychiatric knowledge and its application in the public mental hospitals; to determine the extent to which community services pay off in keeping people out of mental hospitals; to discover the most effective ways of utilizing present personnel; to find out more about the epidemiology of mental illness; to discover why it is that young professional students resist entering the field of mental illness; to find out exactly what our personnel needs are; to review our whole statistical system for gathering data on mental illness; to assess the contribution that psychiatry can make to the various social ills in which mental illness is a component, such as alcoholism, drug addiction, juvenile delinquency and crime, misfits in industry, accident proneness on the highways, suicides, and so on.

Leo Bartemeier, a former APA president representing the AMA Council on Mental Health, called attention to therapies and research findings, which "together with other noncustodial treatment techniques . . . will prove to be the beginning of a new and successful approach to the staggering problem of mental illness."[6]

Only Fillmore H. Sanford, executive secretary of the American Psychological Association, expressed a more cautious note. The friction between psychologists and psychiatrists shaped some of his views. Although supportive of the concept of a national survey, he warned that the enumeration of shortages of beds and staff was not sufficient. Surveys, he insisted, had to capitalize on the skills of behavioral scientists; mental health was "not exclusively a psychiatric problem" but involved the "whole social fabric." Nor should a survey "concentrate exclusively on the hospital problem or the problem of the mentally ill." The real hope, he added, "lies in prevention—in finding ways to promote the growth of creatively healthy American personalities."[7]

The hearings before the Senate subcommittee were virtually identical to those of its House counterpart. The same witnesses appeared (e.g., Hobby, Felix, Gorman, Blain, Bartemeier), and their testimony was unchanged. Both subcommittees provided a warm and sympathetic environment. Their members tended to be deferential, and the testimony was generally treated as though it embodied statements that had a firm basis in fact. Occasional critical comments tended to reinforce rather than contradict the witnesses. Senator Herbert Lehman, for example, chastised the Eisenhower administration for its parsimonious budgetary recommendations for mental health.[8]

Not a single governor appeared before either subcommittee. In many respects this was a surprising omission, given the fact that responsibility for mental health policy lay with the states. That no governor appeared before or communicated with either subcommittee suggests that states were not seeking a greater federal role merely to transfer their fiscal responsibilities. Representing the Council of State Governments, Sidney Spector submitted a written document emphasizing the growing burden on states occasioned by the continuous rise in hospital populations. He noted the dramatic increases in state appropriations for mental hospitals between 1945 and 1953, the corresponding improvements in staff and per capita patient expenditures, and the renewed commitment to therapeutic care. Spector also called attention to the ten-point program adopted by the first Governors' Conference on Mental Health the previous year recommending more resources for training, research, prevention, and community psychiatric services. In urging the federal government to expand its role, the council was not supporting a change in federal-state relationships. On the contrary, it was simply urging the national government to use the massive resources at its disposal to supplement the already large state investments in mental health.[9]

Both subcommittees reported favorably on the joint resolution to endorse a national study and to authorize grants totaling $1.25 million over a three-year period for support. The ensuing congressional debate was equally supportive, if largely superficial. By the end of July the Mental Health Study Act passed Congress and was signed into law by President Eisenhower. Under its provisions the JCMIH, although a nongovernmental body, received federal endorsement and a modest level of funding.[10]

The events that led to the passage of the Mental Health Study Act also played a role in subsequent legislation. During the spring of 1955 Mike Gorman and the APA lobbied on behalf of federal appropriations for the construction of health research facilities (a bill opposed by the AMA). A year later the Health Research Facilities Act authorized up to $30 million per year for construction. More significant was the Health Amendments Act of 1956, a law designed to increase the supply of nurses and other public health personnel. Title V—which drew little or no attention—authorized a new program of federal grants to state and local agencies and other public or nonprofit institutions "for investigations, experiments, demonstrations, studies, and research projects with respect to the development of improved methods of diagnosing mental illness, and of care, treatment, and rehabilitation of the mentally ill, including grants to State agencies responsible for administration of State institutions for care, or care and treatment, of mentally ill persons for developing and establishing improved methods of operation and administration of such institutions." Title V, although having little bearing on federal-state relationships, modified the National Mental Health Act of 1946, increased federal funds for mental health, and magnified the subsequent importance of the NIMH in mental health policy.[11]

Even before formal congressional endorsement, the APA and the AMA moved forward to establish the JCMIH on a permanent basis. In early April their Planning Committee held a two-day meeting in New York City. More than two dozen individuals representing eighteen national organizations came to quick agreement. Three months later the commission was legally incorporated in the District of Columbia, and in September a formal set of bylaws was adopted.[12] The stage was now set for a major national study. Those involved hoped that the results would approximate those of Abraham Flexner's famous study nearly half a century earlier. Just as his activities placed medical education upon a scientific foundation, so too might the JCMIH alter the ways in which American society dealt with their mentally ill citizens.

· · ·

The creation of the JCMIH was but a modest beginning. Much remained to be done: the appointment of a director; the recruitment of a staff; and the formulation of goals and a plan of action. Given diverse and often competing beliefs and ideologies, it was clear that the forging of a consensus would face daunting obstacles. Those who had lobbied on behalf of such a commission tended to rationalize their efforts in vague and elusive terms (perhaps because of an understandable desire to avoid controversy). Their success, however, meant that rhetorical statements and claims had to be translated into a concrete plan of action—a task that was considerably more difficult.

Virtually all of the individuals associated with the JCMIH subscribed to the continuum concept, according to which there was no sharp demarcation between mental illness and mental health. Within this consensus, however, there was considerable variation. At one end were those who were committed to a more extreme social and behavioral science environmentalist perspective that emphasized the external elements that shaped behavior. At the other end were those who were closer to the more traditional individual patient medical model. They did not exclude socio-environmental factors but instead tended to emphasize the importance of individual psychopathology. To be sure, common elements far out-weighed differences. Nevertheless, within the context of the deliberations of the JCMIH (which largely excluded biological psychiatrists), the differences became significant, if only because the policy implications were not identical. The first group was receptive to preventive activities and services for the nonmentally ill; the second emphasized the necessity of providing adequate care and treatment for the mentally ill but did not exclude broadening the availability of psychiatric and psychological services.

When a broad planning session took place in April, it was evident that there were unresolved issues. The participants came from a variety of disciplines and represented organizations whose interests reflected the occupational concerns of their members. Psychiatric social workers and nurses recommended demonstration studies that would shed light on social services and hospital practices that affected nurses; behavioral and social scientists were concerned with the effects of social, environmental, cultural, and psychological influences; and lawyers emphasized the personal and property rights of the mentally ill. There was both support for and criticism of the concept of a national survey of existing practices.[13]

Faith in national planning may have given an appearance of unity to the deliberations, but on specific details wide differences remained. Nowhere were the differences better expressed than in the discussion about basic objectives. Should the JCMIH focus on the problems of the mentally ill, or should it emphasize prevention and the promotion of mental health? Was it possible to study mental illness without an explicit concept of mental health? If the mentally ill were to be the prime target of the investigation, what specific issues merited analysis?

The ensuing debate illuminated the barriers that impeded the development of a specific research agenda. M. Ralph Kaufman, an eminent New York psychiatrist affiliated with Mount Sinai Hospital and a member of the AMA Council on Mental Health, offered a trenchant criticism of those who emphasized prevention. "As I look around the room," he observed, "I would challenge anybody to tell me what, on the basis of present-day knowledge, we know about preventive psychiatry. . . . And what are the techniques? What knowledge do we have which would indicate that we are in a position to get up such a program?" Kaufman hinted that psychiatrists were prone to exaggeration, and he argued that relatively little was known about nosology, etiology, treatment, and cure. He was equally scornful about the value of most quantitative studies, given the extraordinary variability and unreliability of psychiatric diagnoses.

Warning against the pursuit of some "Utopian fantasy," Kaufman insisted that the JCMIH had to delimit its activities.[14]

Most of those present endorsed the idea of a limited study that emphasized the mentally ill. Yet there was considerable difficulty in spelling out precise forms and details. Nicholas Hobbs from Peabody College and the representative of the American Psychological Association noted that participants were often "talking about different things" and insisted on the need for greater precision and specificity. He then suggested a two-part effort: first, "a staff study of existing knowledge" that could answer some of the questions that had been raised; second, studies designed to lead to new knowledge. Hobbs offered some specific examples: better epidemiological investigations; evaluations of the relative efficacy of the new psychotropic drugs combined with psychotherapy; examinations of the impact on communities saturated with psychiatric services; and more attention to the formulation of "basic theory."[15]

Most of the participants agreed with the observations of Kaufman and especially Hobbs. Yet an element of uncertainty persisted. Was it feasible—given the limitations posed by the pending legislation in Congress that authorized funding for a three-year period—to provide answers to problems that had resisted solutions for decades? What kinds of studies were feasible, given the imprecision of psychiatric etiology and nosology? Above all, were there significant and important questions that could not be answered because of the lack of knowledge or appropriate technologies? In the end the faith in the redemptive authority of science and medicine so characteristic of the postwar years proved irresistible. The participants simply agreed to push ahead with the expectation that existing problems would ultimately be resolved.

The JCMIH's official goals, adopted formally in September 1955, were so broad as to conceal potential differences. First, to study mental illness and health and the various "medical, psychological, social, economic, cultural and other factors that relate to etiology." Second, to discover, develop, and apply appropriate methods for the diagnosis, treatment, care, and rehabilitation of the mentally ill and mentally retarded.[16] Third, to evaluate and to improve the recruitment and training of personnel. Fourth, to conduct a national survey of the problems of mental illness and mental health and to formulate a comprehensive program. Finally, to furnish to the federal and state governments as well as to the public the results of all the studies and surveys. Curiously enough, these goals ran somewhat contrary to the deliberations of those who had participated in the planning conference the previous April. Their adoption suggested that the rhetoric employed by the commission was intended largely to influence a broad public and their elected representatives. Nevertheless, rhetoric acquired a life of its own. It was not without influence, moreover, on both the strategy adopted by the commission and the eventual outcome.[17]

The structure of the JCMIH was designed both to insure medical dominance and to mobilize a broad national constituency. Initially about twenty-five organizations (subsequently expanded to thirty-six) were represented on the commission. In addition to a number of medical and non-medical professional associations, the JCMIH included as members the American Legion, the Council of State Governments, and such federal agencies as the NIMH, the Department of Defense, and the VA. Each organization was entitled to one representative; the APA and the AMA sent five each. In turn, the commission elected a Board of Trustees, which was responsible for administration and the hiring of personnel. Not all psychiatrists believed that the APA and the AMA should have proportionately more authority, for they were concerned that the traditional hostility of the AMA toward psychiatry might prove troublesome.[18]

The crucial position within the JCMIH was that of director (or principal investigator). Given the somewhat vague and amorphous goals and an elaborate and complex governing structure, it was evident from the outset that the individual chosen for this job would have a major role in shaping the commission's agenda and therefore the outcome. The director had a relatively free hand in selecting the members of advisory committees, staff, areas to be studied, and the general nature of the final report.

Even before the formal incorporation of the JCMIH, Daniel Blain, APA medical director, indicated his interest in the position. His failure to be selected left him embittered. In October the directorship was offered to Harry C. Solomon, whose long and distinguished career in Massachusetts government and at the Harvard Medical School had brought him to national prominence. Solomon declined because of uncertainty about his ability to "undertake this with conviction and honest belief that I could do it well." The trustees, therefore, settled on Jack R. Ewalt, then commissioner of mental health in Massachusetts. After training under Ebaugh at the University of Colorado, Ewalt had joined the faculty of the medical school of the University of Texas at Galveston and had also served as one of the psychiatric representatives on the Hoover Commission studying the organization of the federal government after World War II. Ewalt believed his selection to be the result of a compromise; the trustees represented a "very large and heterogeneous group of organizations" and could not "find anybody they could all trust." Ewalt offered to resign as commissioner of mental health but, with the support of the governor, worked out an arrangement with the Commonwealth that involved a reduced work load and salary, thus permitting him to hold two positions simultaneously.[19]

At the outset much of Ewalt's time was devoted to organizational matters. The complex structure of the JCMIH as well as occasional personality conflicts created tension. The Executive Committee and Board of

Trustees were responsible for business and administration. Substantive issues (e.g., identifying the specific areas to be studied, organizing investigations, and shaping the final report), Ewalt suggested, were his responsibility. The role of the Scientific Planning and Study Committee (appointed by the director) was to provide advice rather than supervision. Blain, on the other hand, believed that the director ought to have somewhat less autonomy, a view that Ewalt attributed to Blain's disappointment in not being offered the position. By the autumn of 1956 many of the initial problems had been resolved.[20]

During the six years of its existence, the JCMIH was plagued by financial problems. The projected cost of the study was about $4 million; in reality the commission had to operate with a budget of $1,548,000. More than 90 percent ($1.4 million) of its total income came from the NIMH, which had been authorized to provide grants under the Mental Health Study Act of 1955. On its own the JCMIH was able to raise only $137,000. Initially the commission assumed (erroneously, as it turned out) that it would be able to tap private foundations for support (just as Abraham Flexner was funded by the Carnegie Foundation). However, both the Ford Foundation and Commonwealth Fund declined to provide assistance. Ford officials felt that the commission was "attempting too ambitious a program" and proceeding at a pace that was "too hard and fast." The only substantial private funds came from the Rockefeller Brothers Fund ($60,000 for the study of the role of religion in mental health), the Smith Kline & French Foundation ($25,000), and the Benjamin Rosenthal Foundation ($20,000).[21]

That the study was directed toward changing public perceptions and behavior was indisputable. In Ewalt's view, prevailing public attitudes constituted perhaps the most important impediment to progress. He cited Shirley Star's well-known (although unpublished) study of public impressions about mental illnesses conducted at the National Opinion Research Center at the University of Chicago. Star had found that Americans supported expenditures for psychiatric care, treatment, and research, but tended to think in stereotyped terms that blurred the distinction between mental illnesses and socially reprehensible behavior. Furthermore, only extreme behavior predisposed the public to think of mental illnesses. There was little recognition, for example, of the behavior of the simple schizophrenic, alcoholic, anxiety neurotic, emotionally disturbed child, or compulsive phobic. Hence the very designation of mental illnesses was equated with an aura of pessimism and hopelessness. The preference of the public for segregation of the mentally ill "in some asylum safe from harm to themselves or to others" was therefore understandable.[22]

From the very beginning it was evident that the JCMIH would define its mandate in the broadest manner possible. Ewalt and his colleagues had two objectives. First, they sought to amass data that would describe "the prevalence of mental disorders, and the existing resources for and methods of dealing with the diagnosis, treatment, care and rehabilitation of patients suffering from these illnesses." Second, they wanted to use these data as the basis for a "radical reconceptualization of the institutions so that resource-use might be more economical and mental health better served." Just as the Flexner report had reformed medical education and led to the closure of a large number of medical schools, so too would the JCMIH lead to "the complete reform of a system."[23]

The JCMIH began its work with a relatively clearly defined model of mental illnesses that emphasized the role of environment in the shaping of personality. The model began with the assumption that there were two kinds of forces operating on individuals and society: "health-promoting, growth promoting and integrative" and "regressive, illness-producing and disruptive." The goal was to identify both categories. This was to be done by dividing the population into three "criterion" categories designed to measure "bio-psycho-social functioning": effective, borderline, and ineffective. In turn, the study of these groupings would illuminate those causal factors—including "family, community institutions, cultural values, and peer and reference group relationships"—that molded personality. In this sense the study was equally concerned with the elements that promoted mental health and those that created mental illnesses.[24]

To categorize the population was only a beginning. Ewalt and his colleagues were especially concerned with those individuals who fell into the borderline or ineffective categories. Some of them had sufficient insight into their condition that they sought help from social welfare agencies, clergymen, pediatricians, and family physicians. Others were identified as problems by their peers and subjected to pressure to seek assistance. Still others were labeled as psychiatric clients or patients and were often referred (sometimes involuntarily) to clinics, psychiatrists, and mental hospitals. Finally, there were individuals who were not functioning effectively and yet were not identified as such. The commission hoped to gather empirical data that would illuminate the effectuality of all individuals, agencies, and institutions providing services. In turn, these data would serve as the basis for wide-ranging policy recommendations.[25]

Ewalt and his staff conceded that underlying all of the processes of health lay a "biological substratum of organic and chemical factors." To be sure, such an admission rested on a foundation of faith rather than data. In the 1950s knowledge about physiological mechanisms and processes that helped to shape human thought and behavior was at best rudimentary. The theoretical and methodological difficulties that impeded biologically oriented research on abnormal behavior tended to direct the commission's activities toward the study of social and environmental variables that did not require such sophisticated technological and scientific capabilities. For the staff to have minimized or overlooked the theoretical and methodological difficulties of analyzing the relationships between individual behavior, on the one hand, and global variables, on the other, was hardly surprising. In the postwar years Americans generally exuded a startling confidence in their ability to reshape the world along predetermined lines. All that seemed to be required was a judicious combination of intelligence, knowledge, and volition. Most professional groups—including psychiatrists and individuals from allied disciplines—shared this optimistic outlook and acted accordingly.

That the JCMIH became a largely social and behavioral science operation was perhaps inevitable. In the postwar era these disciplines enjoyed an almost explosive growth. Increases in funding for research, broader occupational opportunities in government and universities, and higher prestige tended to enhance their significance. The commission's members were sanguine that their research findings would contribute in meaningful ways to the development of more effective public policies. Nor was social and behavioral science environmentalism necessarily incompatible with many of the principles underlying psychodynamic and social psychiatry. Cross-disciplinary collaboration was a natural consequence. The problems that lent themselves to research and analysis—the epidemiology of mental disorders, evaluation of therapies, development of instruments to measure behavior, study of institutions and organizations—were relevant to both psychodynamic psychiatry and social and behavioral science; the physiology of mental illnesses, by way of contrast, seemed to be largely beyond existing capabilities.

The staff and advisory committees of the JCMIH reflected its interdisciplinary character. Fillmore H. Sanford (former executive secretary of the American Psychological Association) served as the consultant for scientific studies, and Gordon W. Blackwell (director of the Institute for Research in the Social Sciences at the University of North Carolina at Chapel Hill) as the consultant on the social sciences. Two physicians (John E. Gordon in epidemiology and Richard J. Plunkett in administration) and one lawyer (Charles S. Brewton) rounded out the professional staff. Greer Williams, a professional writer and former director of public relations at the American College of Surgeons, became director of information and played an important role in preparing the final report in a form that made it accessible to federal officials and a broad public. The roster of the various advisory committees and consultants read like a veritable *Who's Who* in American psychiatry and social and behavioral science.[26]

Ewalt and his staff initially decided to sponsor studies that would serve as the basis for the preparation of a final report. By mid-1957 a number of individuals had been commissioned to investigate such topics as manpower, patterns of patient care, the role of schools in the production of mental health, community resources in mental health, epidemiology, research, popular attitudes, economics, and concepts of mental health. Ewalt's original blueprint called for more extensive studies involving law, effects of mass communications on mental health, penology, mental health of the aged, mental health in industry, and others. But budgetary considerations forced a sharp cutback in the scope and number of projects.[27]

The selection of topics illuminated a peculiar ambivalence within the JCMIH about its basic goals. "By far the larger part of our total study," Ewalt stated in 1956, "will concern itself, inescapably, with the mentally ill who need definitive care in a psychiatrist's office, a mental health clinic or a mental hospital, private or public." Yet even this statement was by no means unambiguous, for it rested on the undemonstrated presumption that individuals seen in private practice or mental health clinics represented the same kinds of cases as those found in traditional mental hospitals. By accepting the continuum model of mental illness and mental health, the commission vacillated between two kinds of policies. The first was concerned with the needs of the mentally ill, the second with the delivery of services to a broader clientele in the hope that early treatment would prevent a progression toward more serious mental illnesses.[28]

Commission members were rarely without ambivalence; their confidence and hopes were always tempered by an element of uneasiness. A range of views was evident at a meeting in 1956 which dealt in part with the nature of mental illnesses and target populations. Appel wanted to look beyond the hospitalized patient; Ewalt expressed the opinion that there was too much emphasis "on positive signs of pathology without getting information of instances of people who don't become defined as patients"; and Harvey Tompkins had reservations about a "panoramic view" that would dissipate any "major focus." The entire discussion suggested that the very inclusiveness of the continuum model was itself a source of confusion. Equally striking, there was little or no awareness of the possible risks for the severely mentally ill if new policies shifted resources in order to provide services for nonmentally ill persons. Those in favor of new and broader community-oriented programs believed that in the long run the incidence and prevalence of mental disorders would be reduced by preventive activities.[29]

· · ·

By early 1958 Rashi Fein of the University of North Carolina at Chapel Hill and Marie Jahoda of New York University had completed their respective studies of the economics of mental illness and current concepts of positive mental health. Both reports were published within months by Basic Books, the publishing house selected by the JCMIH to issue its monographs.[30] Fein's report aroused little controversy; it was an economic analysis of the direct and indirect costs of mental illness, which he estimated at approximately $2.5 billion. He warned against a purely economic analysis that incorporated the assumption that large direct costs were undesirable. Public institutions, after all, had to remember the purposes for which they had been established. Within that framework it was appropriate to evaluate the cost-effectiveness of alternative strategies. Even if increased expenditures resulted in higher discharge rates, long-term savings would not necessarily follow. More people might seek hospital treatment. Alternatively, new medical therapies might increase the life expectancy of elderly persons (including those in mental hospitals) and thus cause a rise in the number of resident patients. Fein concluded that the issue of how much a society could afford to spend on mental illnesses was not a question that could be answered by economists. "An economy," he observed,

> can afford to spend whatever it desires to spend. All that is necessary in order to spend more on one thing is that we spend less on something else. . . .
>
> What society can spend (and ultimately what society should spend) depends on the value system that society holds to. It is obvious that society *can* spend much more on mental illness (or on anything) than it presently is doing. Whether or not it chooses to do so is another question.[31]

Jahoda's monograph on current concepts of positive mental health proved more controversial, for it embodied some of the same ambiguities confronting the JCMIH. Written by a social psychologist, the study largely ignored mental illnesses and focused instead on mental health. Jahoda described its ambiguities and complexities, and identified at least six major approaches ranging from self-perception to an ability to accept and master the givens of life. She specifically rejected the idea that the absence of disease implied the presence of health. Conceding the difficulties that impeded a unified concept of mental health, she called for more research on the subject.[32]

Jahoda's monograph was largely concerned with the psychological and, to a lesser extent, sociological components of mental health. The absence of any clear medical or organic frame of reference troubled several members of the Committee on the Studies. Walter Barton in particular was dismayed at the omission of any mention of biochemical and biopsychiatric elements; he noted that Jahoda had ignored the recently introduced psychotropic drugs. His concerns were echoed by John R. Seeley, who observed that the report had virtually no implications for clinical practice. Barton then prepared a statement that was included as an appendix to the book. Physicians, he wrote, operated on the assumption that the absence of illness denoted health, whereas Jahoda believed that illness and health overlapped but did not coincide. To a clinician like Barton, the study of mental health, although legitimate, was too far removed from conventional medical concerns. "There would be no Joint Commission," he added, "if there were no mental illness." Indeed, mental illness was "the primary threat to positive psychological health."[33]

Less controversial was George W. Albee's analysis of mental health manpower trends. A psychologist by training, Albee had perhaps the easiest task, for the shortage of professional and nonprofessional personnel was well-documented. What Albee did was to detail in systematic form shortages and geographical maldistribution of personnel in all categories, along with the barriers that blocked efforts to alleviate the problem. He was not sanguine about the future: other professions competed with mental health for recruits; deficiencies in the nation's educational system discouraged able younger persons from pursuing careers in science; salaries and working conditions were less than attractive; and prevailing social and cultural values were not conducive to the pursuit of the intellect or a commitment to service professions. "Our country," he concluded, "will continue to be faced with serious personnel shortages in all fields related to mental illness and mental health for many years to come. Barring the possibility of a massive national effort . . . or the possibility of a sharp breakthrough in mental health research, the prospects are pessimistic for significant improvements in the quantity or quality of professional services in these fields." Albee's report received a generally favorable reception in the Committee on the Studies, although minor disagreements on details were evident.[34]

At the outset the JCMIH had emphasized the severely mentally ill. Yet with the passage of time its focus blurred because of its concern with mental health and its tendency to juxtapose individuals experiencing psychological or personal problems with those who were severely mentally ill. Nowhere was this better illustrated than in the decision to sponsor four studies dealing with public attitudes and community resources in mental health (including schools and religious institutions). Taken as a group, these studies were suggestive of the ambivalence within the JCMIH that led its staff and consultants to vacillate between their desire to improve the care and treatment of the mentally ill, on the one hand, and their interest in prevention of mental illnesses and promotion of mental health, on the other hand.

By 1956 Ewalt and his staff had arranged with the University of Michigan's Survey Research Center to investigate the ways in which Americans viewed their mental health. In the planning stage it became abundantly clear that the survey would be only tangentially concerned with mental illnesses. In describing the study, the first annual report of the commission expressed criticism of the traditional "preoccupation with pathology" and called instead for the development of an "epidemiology of trouble" that illuminated the worries and personal problems of ordinary Americans and the means by which they contended with them. "Freedom from mental illness has taken on a social importance somewhat equivalent to freedom from want or freedom from fear, and the right to mental health is achieving a status like that of the right to work." The overriding need, therefore, was for a systematic program designed "to facilitate the growth of robust and resilient personalities."[35]

Conducted by Gerald Gurin, Joseph Veroff, and Sheila Field, the study surveyed a representative sample of nearly twenty-five hundred individuals over the age of twenty-one and living at home; transients and all individuals in hospitals, prisons, or other institutions were excluded. The group interviewed constituted "an accurately proportioned miniature of the 'normal,' stable, adult population." The goals were simple: to ascertain the ways in which Americans perceived their own adjustment to life and their attitudes toward marriage, parenthood, and work; and to survey the ways in which people coped with their problems. Nearly one in four Americans on occasion felt the need for help, and one in seven actually sought some form of counseling or treatment. The study emphasized how such factors as age, sex, marital status, income, and education determined both the self-perceptions of individuals and the means of assistance they selected. Those with higher levels of education had greater insight into the psychological nature of their problems and hence were more likely to seek professional help; lower-status individuals were far less likely to use available facilities. Such epidemiological findings, concluded the investigators, could assist in the design of programs to make help "available to the maximum number of people in trouble."[36] They omitted any analysis of the precise relationship between "people in trouble" and the mentally ill, or the impact of an expansion of services for the former on the latter.

Three other projects sponsored by the JCMIH analyzed and described the mental health activities of communities, schools, and religious institutions. Two explicitly accepted the prevailing ideology that placed problems in general living and mental illnesses as points along an unbroken continuum; their authors could thus range globally on the assumption that environmental stresses of any kind could impact upon mental health. In *Community Resources in Mental Health*, Reginald Robinson, David DeMarche, and Mildred Wagle emphasized the gross neglect of the welfare of millions of children, including those from broken homes; the weaknesses of local public health, child welfare, day service, and recreational programs; the disabilities faced by aged and unemployed persons;

and the fact that less than one-quarter of the nation's counties had mental health clinics. Only an amalgamation of mental health forces with those involved in public welfare, schools, courts, child welfare, public health, and recreation programs could create "a balanced mental health program giving proper weight to prevention." Similarly, Wesley Allinsmith and George W. Goethals insisted that teachers, without overburdening themselves or subverting their educational obligations, could "at times contribute to the avoidance or alleviation of mental illness" and thus forward the improvement of society "through increasing individual maturity." They defined at least eight areas as providing the potential for effective action by teachers: detection, diagnosis and prognosis, first aid, referral, treatment, rehabilitation, follow-up, and prevention.[37]

Only Richard McCann took a more cautious approach in his monograph on religious institutions and mental health. He did not examine religion as a source of either mental health or illness. Instead, he confined himself largely to an examination of the role of the clergy. Their work with the mentally ill, he noted, was only of peripheral significance. At best, they provided pastoral counseling and could therefore function only on a secondary level of prevention. McCann's study offered relatively little hope that religious bodies could become effective participants in mental health programs.[38]

The three remaining studies—dealing with psychiatric epidemiology, research, and patient care, respectively—were somewhat more directly related to mental illnesses. The first was prepared by Richard J. Plunkett and John E. Gordon, both trained in medicine. The former was associate director of the JCMIH and secretary of the AMA's Council on Mental Health; the latter professor emeritus of epidemiology at the Harvard School of Public Health. In many respects their monograph on psychiatric epidemiology offered little support for the concept of prevention. Indeed, the two men emphasized the limitations rather than the extent of psychiatric knowledge about mental disorders. They called attention to the difficulties that hindered the development of an adequate and defensible classification of mental disorders, especially the absence of any real comprehension of causality (which was "fundamental to the prevention and control of disease"). Existing data on prevalence and incidence were therefore virtually useless. Diagnoses were governed largely by the "interpretations and preferences" of clinicians and hospitals; extreme variability was the norm. The range of rates in most community surveys of prevalence was "so great as to defy generalization." Epidemiology, Plunkett and Gordon wrote, traditionally contributed to an understanding of infectious diseases only after the accumulation of scientific knowledge provided grist for the interpretive mill. A "comparable degree of knowledge concerning mental illness does not now exist," they added. Although suggesting the construction of "orderly, well-controlled field experiments designed to identify and quantitate, one by one, the various factors that have been advanced as being involved in causality," they offered little to substantiate the more confident claims of those associated with the JCMIH. Indeed, the commission's final report, which summarized in great detail all of the other monographs, omitted any mention of the Plunkett and Gordon contribution.[39]

William F. Soskin's report on research resources in mental health was traditional and aroused no controversy. He pointed out that the major share of systematic mental health research was conducted by psychologists; psychiatrists generally were neither trained for nor interested in research. Much of his report described patterns of funding, identified areas most in need of work, and analyzed the distinction between basic and applied research. His recommendations were hardly novel. "Unglamorous as it may sound," he wrote, "the only realistic approach seems to lie in a long-term program of basic and clinical research equally well supported in the broad spectrum of medical, biological, psychological, and social science disciplines and conducted in universities, in hospitals, in clinics, and in a variety of other settings."[40]

In establishing parameters for the individual studies, the commission's staff also made provision for a volume on patterns of patient care. The project was headed by Brandeis University sociologist Morris S. Schwartz (with Charlotte Schwartz as the associate director) and included six other individuals drawn with but one exception from the ranks of the social and behavioral sciences. Because of its more inclusive character, the study was available only in draft form at the time that the JCMIH was preparing its final report; a published version did not appear until 1964.[41]

The Task Force on Patterns of Patient Care was given a triple mandate: to describe existing mental patient care systems; to look for new and promising leads; and to develop a series of specific and general recommendations. The group in turn divided into three teams charged with the responsibility for examining outpatient, inpatient, and ex-patient care, respectively. Their members visited a large number of facilities devoted to patient care that were experimenting with promising, novel, or unconventional programs. In addition, they interviewed 179 "experts in the mental health field."[42]

At the outset Schwartz and his colleagues faced a thorny issue, namely, the problem of specifying the kinds of individuals who needed treatment. Was it important, for example, "to distinguish among those not mentally ill those who are mentally *healthy* from those who are not just mentally *ill*?" The continuum model of mental illnesses itself promoted disagreements not merely between the "organicists" and the "psychodynamicists," but between these two and a more sociologically oriented group that projected the problem beyond the individual and upon the family, community, and society. Theoretical conflict, in turn, fostered professional and disciplinary disagreements over the qualifications of those who engaged in therapy. The very difficulty in conceptualizing the problem, the authors conceded, was but a reflection of the lack of knowledge about the nature of human beings and human relationships.[43]

The deliberations of the members of the task force reflected their social and behavioral science affiliations. They believed that institutions (e.g., mental hospitals) could be understood only as complete social systems, and they were persuaded by Harry Stack Sullivan's emphasis on the significance of interpersonal relationships. Their theoretical beliefs led them to denigrate the "medical-clinical frame of reference" that governed the interpretation of disturbed behavior. Admittedly, the medical model of mental illnesses rationalized psychiatric hegemony. Yet this very same model blinded biological and psychodynamic psychiatrists alike "to the social sphere" and to the relevance of "networks of interpersonal relations." Disturbed behavior, argued Schwartz, could be interpreted "as a defect in socialization or education as well as organic or psychodynamic impairment." If this were true, then the role of nonmedical disciplines and staff would be clearly enhanced, and that of psychiatrists diminished.[44]

The body of the report was devoted to a description and analysis of the three subsystems of services: outpatient, inpatient, and ex-patient. The outpatient system included public and voluntary clinics, as well as services provided by private practitioners drawn from the ranks of psychiatry and other mental health professions. Its inadequacies made it difficult for persons with emotional problems to secure immediate assistance. Overspecialization and the absence of coordination often limited access on the basis of such variables as age, income, education, and type of psychiatric problem, to cite only the more obvious. The inpatient system, which included state, VA, and small private hospitals, presented even more serious problems. State institutions were used as a "dumping ground" for "troubled and troublesome individuals" from the lowest socioeconomic classes. Their presence, together with the high proportion of aged and chronic patients, created an "apathetic atmosphere." Finally, the ex-patient system was relatively underdeveloped.[45]

The recommendations of the task force were far-ranging but also diffuse. Its members supported a broadened concept of help and an expansion of outpatient services. The needs of mental hospitals were equally pressing: individualization of care and treatment; breaking down of barriers between institutions and community; and creation of a therapeutic milieu. Finally, systems of care for ex-patients had to be redesigned to meet their specific needs, and services had to be linked and continuous. The improvement of the system as a whole depended upon the creation of planned, comprehensive, and diversified services. The preconditions for improvement were clear: greater funding for personnel, training, and research; the replacement of political by professional control; and changes in public perceptions and attitudes to facilitate innovative programs and policies. These recommendations, Schwartz added, were premised upon a continued separation of inpatient, outpatient, and ex-patient services. Even their integration within a unified mental health center would merely perpetuate a medical model that identified disturbance as "illness," labeled persons as "patients," and offered physician-directed "treatment." A more radical reconceptualization might involve substituting "psycho-social disabilities" for mental illnesses and redefining assistance as an effort to reeducate or resocialize individuals in a "resocialization center."[46]

Schwartz's report aroused some controversy. Warren T. Vaughan, the only physician on the task force, was so annoyed with the draft report that he resigned (but subsequently relented). Vaughan believed that Schwartz was "anti-psychiatrist." The theme of "medical-clinical *versus* socio-psychological" denigrated the work and accomplishments of psychiatry. Vaughan was not opposed to a concept of treatment that included a consideration of "psychological and social factors." Schwartz and his colleagues, however, set up "old dichotomies anew" instead of fostering "a holistic approach."[47]

Barton also echoed Vaughan's criticisms. Contrary to the authors' intentions, Barton found the work conventional rather than innovative and felt that they had overlooked interesting ongoing experiments in patient care. Moreover, the discussion about aftercare was presented in a vacuum and all but ignored eighty years of history. Barton reserved his most severe criticism for the assertion that mental illnesses were not illnesses at all but social disorders, and that physicians had no business treating them. In particular, he resented the underlying "tone of hostility" even more than the substance. Together with M. Ralph Kaufman, he filed a dissent that began with a list of mental disorders of somatic origin. Many psychoses, they observed,

frequently require management in a mental hospital. The chronically ill may require prolonged care. Research offers hope that additional disorders, now classified as functional, may be understood and more effectively treated. . . .

The authors of the volume attack the assumption that psychoses are illnesses and occur in persons called sick . . . [and] challenge the assumption that the physician is the appropriate individual to carry out treatment of the psychotic. Presumably the writers were not thinking of psychoses in the broad context of patients who require hospital care, when they suggested that milieu therapy was the principal tool effective in changing social behavior. It might be easier to teach psychiatrists the social dynamics necessary for group work than it would be [to] teach social scientists the medical knowledge essential to total treatment of hospitalized patients.

We recognize the desirability of experimentation by social scientists in a more active therapeutic role to test in the field their belief that they can cure more patients than have those with a medical clinical orientation. We know of no proof that social scientists have been more effective than psychiatrists in curing mental disease.[48]

The cumulative impact of the ten individual studies sponsored by the JCMIH was striking. The absence of a consensus on specific details was obvious; disagreements were by no means absent. Yet the areas of agreement were striking. Most of the authors shared the belief that the pervasiveness of psychological and environmental stresses mandated an expansion of therapeutic services both within and without institutions; that early interventions would prevent the onset of more serious illnesses; that the efficacy of social and psychological therapies was a matter of fact rather than a subject to be investigated; and that a concerted attack on the problems posed by psychological disturbances and mental illnesses required the creation of a broad coalition of professional and lay groups. Most significant, the thrust of the reports—though little noticed at the time—further blurred the distinction between individuals with problems on the one hand and the mentally ill on the other. In the ensuing policy debates, the central focus shifted inexorably from the latter toward the former. This is not in any way to insist that the JCMIH consciously or deliberately downplayed or ignored the problems of the mentally ill. It is only to maintain that the consequences of its activities proved to be somewhat at variance with its original goals.

. . .

By late 1958 the members of the JCMIH and the Committee on the Studies were discussing the form and substance of the final report. It was frankly recognized that there were two distinct audiences. The first was the commission itself, which had a largely professional constituency. But the second included Congress, which had the power to enact legislation and provide the large resources required for substantive policy changes. In the eyes of some, the distinction was between a scientific and a popular document. At its third annual meeting the members of the full commission agreed that Ewalt, with the advice of the Committee on the Studies, would prepare a draft document that would be circulated for comments. Nicholas Hobbs, vice-chair of the Board of Trustees, expressed his belief that the final report could not be presented as a staff document but rather had to receive the endorsement of all of the members of the JCMIH even though some of its recommendations might prove uncongenial to selected individuals.[49]

The rough draft was prepared by Ewalt with the assistance of Greer Williams. The initial reaction was somewhat less than enthusiastic, partly because Ewalt's language was tailored to a professional constituency and lacked the fervor and passion that might appeal to Congress or the public. Williams, a science journalist with considerable experience in writing for a popular audience, believed that the circulation of the draft was a "mistake." An admirer of Ewalt, he nevertheless concurred with the views of some of the members of the JCMIH that the document had to be "big and bold" and incorporate recommendations that neither the APA nor the AMA would completely approve. Ewalt slowly was persuaded that Williams was on the right track. The two men then began a fruitful collaboration, and Williams supplied much of the language to dramatize and popularize what might otherwise have been a dull document. Ewalt, Williams wrote in approving terms, "shows definite signs of ceasing to be an able politician and becoming a great statesman."[50]

By the late summer of 1960 the nearly completed draft was submitted to a subcommittee of the JCMIH for comment and advice. Generally speaking, there were no fundamental criticisms. Indeed, its members (including Appel, Bartemeier, and Barton) were supportive of the view that mental health services were interdisciplinary in nature and that rivalries and competition over who was qualified to provide therapy were counterproductive. There was some concern that the draft "overemphasized the language in our knowledge of mental health" because of the need to increase research funding. On the other hand, the description of psychiatry as an "inexact science" required clarification in order to minimize any negative consequences. The discussion mirrored a broad consensus; differences were expressed only on marginal details.[51]

In March 1961 the final report of the JCMIH—*Action for Mental Health*—was transmitted to Congress and the nation's governors and released to the public with considerable fanfare. The document could have been released months earlier. The delay was probably the result of a calculated political judgment. Specifically, there was some sentiment that the Eisenhower administration would not prove overly sympathetic to the far-reaching recommendations and fiscal implications of the report. The hope of a more receptive administration was realized when John F. Kennedy defeated Richard M. Nixon in the fall of 1960. Hence the release of the report came shortly after the inauguration of a young Democratic leader whose youth and vision seemed to inspire those individuals and groups seeking fundamental changes in some of the nation's social policies.[52]

Written in lay rather than medical or technical language, the document dramatically portrayed the shortcomings of the mental health service system while at the same time sketching out its potentialities. The opening chapter noted the progress that had been made in providing facilities for care and treatment but also emphasized that mental health programs lagged behind programs designed to deal with other acute and chronic diseases. "If we are to be wholly honest with ourselves and with the public, then we must view the mental health problem in terms of the unmet need—those who are untreated and inadequately cared for. . . . [T]he information we have leads us to believe that more than half of the patients in most State hospitals receive no active treatment of any kind designed to improve their mental condition."[53]

Therapeutic failures could not explain the lag in providing services. Existing data, as a matter of fact, revealed that the prognosis for functional psychoses was considerably better than that of many types of malignancies. *Action for Mental Health* took note of the successes of nineteenth-century moral treatment and called attention to more recent outcome studies of social, psychological, and somatic therapies in both inpatient and outpatient settings that offered *"new hope."* Indeed, the reversal of the upward trend in the resident population of state mental hospitals was indicative of what increases in hospital personnel, improved social treatment, more liberal parole and discharge policies, and the use of the new psychotropic drugs could accomplish.[54]

Given successful interventions, why had *"efforts to provide effective treatment for the mentally ill lagged?"* The basic problem, insisted the JCMIH, was that many people, including physicians, failed to recognize psychological illness as illness. Moreover, the mentally ill, precisely because of their behavior, aroused little sympathy in others. Madness, unlike other illnesses, tended to break the bonds that defined humanity and thus set the mentally ill as a group apart. Consequently, state mental hospitals, founded to provide therapy, evolved into dumping grounds for individuals outside the pale of normal society.[55]

Nearly half of *Action for Mental Health* was devoted to a summary of the ten monographic studies. Their findings bore out the belief "that, with conscious effort, negative attitudes can be overcome and are, among better-educated people, already in the process of reversing themselves." Curiously enough, the commission members seemed unaware that their basic goal—to develop a national program that met the "individual needs of the mentally ill people of America"—was not entirely compatible with the underlying ideology and analytic concepts of the individual monographs. The latter had clouded the distinction between troubled individuals and the severely mentally ill; their recommendations in part anticipated a redirection of policy and funding patterns away from the severely mentally ill and toward individuals with psychological problems. The impact of such a shift on the former was largely overlooked. The JCMIH's final report was somewhat more ambivalent. It criticized the mental hygiene movement for diverting attention "from the core problem of the major mental illness" by emphasizing "primary prevention" (eliminating the causes of disease) and instead endorsed "secondary prevention" or "early treatment of beginning disturbances to ward off more serious illness." Yet the document also stipulated that the "need in its largest, theoretical dimension is to provide every person with the chance to develop a personality or character of sufficient strength to cope with the stresses life imposes upon him, or, to provide those persons who find the stress too great with the benefits of proper diagnosis, adequate treatment, and rehabilitation."[56]

Having identified issues and problems, the commission offered a comprehensive national program composed of four distinct but related elements. First, it called for larger investments in basic research; for the allocation of venture or risk capital to support both individuals and concepts; for an expansion in the educational and research activities of the NIMH; and for federal funding for the establishment of research centers or institutes, geographically dispersed. Effective policies required that "the large gaps in our scientific knowledge about the fundamentals of mental illness and mental health" be diminished.[57]

Second, *Action for Mental Health* proposed a series of recommendations relating to manpower and services that were intended to maximize the effectiveness of existing knowledge and experience. A "national manpower recruitment and training program" was needed to remedy the existing shortfall. The adoption of "a broad liberal philosophy" of treatment could diminish the dangers of jurisdictional rivalries among the various mental health disciplines. Certain somatic interventions could only be provided by those with commensurate medical training. Similarly, the practice of psychoanalysis and "depth psychotherapy" had to be limited to physicians, psychologists or other professionals with relevant educational training and experience. On the other hand, nonmedical mental health workers, if qualified, could provide "general, short-term psychotherapy . . . under the auspices of recognized mental health agencies." Since the demand for services by individuals experiencing psychological stress would always exceed the supply, other occupational groups— teachers, clergymen, social workers, family physicians, pediatricians, nurses, and others—could, with some training, assume the role of mental health counselors.[58]

In dealing with services, the JCMIH sketched out a national program that reflected postwar mental health ideology. Acutely ill mental patients required access to emergency care and treatment in general and mental hospitals as well as community clinics. The community mental health clinic, however, was a main line of defense in reducing the need for prolonged and repeated hospitalization. Serving children and adults, such clinics could operate as outpatient departments of general or mental hospitals or as independent agencies. The commission recommended one full-time clinic for each 50,000 of population. Finally, general hospital psychiatric units and state-run regional intensive psychiatric treatment centers (with space for no more than 1,000 acute patients) would supplement the services provided by clinics.[59]

The logic of the report also led to a radical and controversial recommendation, namely, that no state mental hospital with more than 1,000 beds be constructed, and that existing institutions with more than 1,000 beds "be gradually and progressively converted into centers for the long-term and combined care of chronic diseases, including mental illness." Such institutions would require fewer psychiatrists and more nurses, occupational therapists, and attendants to work with patients and "create a stimulating day-to-day life for the patient." The commission also insisted on the integration of aftercare and rehabilitation with all services in order to limit the need for either hospitalization or rehospitalization.[60]

Third, *Action for Mental Health* identified a need to disseminate information concerning mental illness among the public. The stigma attached to mental illness had to be fought and the idea conveyed that a pervasive defeatism often blocked effective treatment. Modification of attitudes and beliefs went in both directions, and the report recommended that the APA transmit to its members an accurate perception of the public image of the psychiatrist. Professional legitimacy rested on public trust, which could be threatened if the specialty overvalued, overreached, and oversold itself and assumed "attitudes of omniscience or superiority."[61]

Having sketched the outlines of a broad national program, the JCMIH faced the final and most sensitive task, namely, to estimate costs and to suggest how funds would be raised. The issue, it insisted, was not economic but moral. "In conserving useful life, civilized man achieves his most glorious moments. It is our creed that life is sacred, that bodies should be healed when sick. . . . Every living man has a right to be treated as a human being." The prevailing philosophy of humanitarianism, nevertheless, did not achieve its full expression in the mental health service system. Mentally ill people were kept physically alive, but their mental life was all but ignored. Nor was it feasible to expect that desired changes could depend upon the ability of the individual to pay for the costs of care and treatment or to assume that voluntary health insurance could be extended to the mentally ill; the costs of major mental illnesses were too large.[62]

What was required, therefore, was a doubling of expenditures for public mental patient services in five years and a tripling in ten. Such a goal could only be met through a massive increase in federal funding. In arguing for an enhanced federal role, the members of the commission were following in the footsteps of many who had come to the conclusion that states and localities possessed neither the willingness nor the resources to resolve pressing social and medical problems. The experiences of the New Deal and World War II had fostered the belief that a national perspective invariably led to more enlightened policies. Hence a slow but steady transfer of authority from communities and states to the federal government was a desirable policy objective. That the JCMIH shared such views was evident from the fact that its members regarded federal cost sharing as a lever with which to elevate standards of care and treatment. They urged a gradual increase in the federal share, which would be distributed according to "criteria of merit and incentive" formulated by an expert advisory committee appointed by the NIMH. States would be required to make professionally acceptable treatment as well as custody a requirement in mental hospitalization; to alter patient commitment laws that minimized compulsion and promoted voluntary admission and discharge; to cease to differentiate between residents and nonresidents; to distinguish between facilities providing care for acute mental patients and those caring for the chronically ill or disabled, including the aged; to integrate mental hospitals with outpatient and aftercare facilities; to provide for training of mental health personnel; and to cease allocating funds for the construction of mental hospitals with more than 1,000 beds or admission of patients to hospitals having more than 1,000 patients. Federal funding would also be used to encourage greater local participation in providing services. The share assumed by the federal government in the first year would be 10 percent of the state total, rising in equal increments to reach parity at the end of a decade. A slightly different scale would apply for local funding: at the end of a decade the federal share would be three times the local share. *Action for Mental Health* offered the following example. Assuming a total expenditure of $3 billion in the tenth year (exclusive of inflation), the federal government would provide $1.75 billion, states $1 billion, and local communities $250 million. "*We believe,*" the JCMIH concluded, "*that the time is at hand and their courage is such that modern legislators may make history by adopting a new policy of action for mental health.*"[63]

Action for Mental Health received a warm endorsement from the members of the JCMIH. Only three members dissented from some of its specific recommendations. Two had reservations about the propriety of offering proposals to alter tax laws; one criticized the proposal to convert state hospitals with more than 1,000 beds into chronic long-term treatment centers.[64] Although representing the contributions of many individuals, the report reflected Ewalt's influence and thinking. More than any other individual, he had directed the work of the commission and molded the final document along lines he thought appropriate. At the same time he was flexible enough to accept criticism and thus managed to create a broad consensus among commission members.

Action for Mental Health was not without ambiguity. Its staff and members hoped to reshape conditions affecting the nation's severely mentally ill and to provide them with a greater range of therapeutic and support services both within and without institutions. The report also appealed to those urging an expansion of services for troubled but not mentally ill persons. The goals, improving services to both groups, of course, were not mutually exclusive, particularly in view of the claim that early treatment of nonmentally ill persons diminished the incidence of mental disorders. But if the latter claim proved fallacious, a serious dilemma would follow. If large resources were used for services to troubled persons, programs and facilities for the more severely mentally ill might suffer correspondingly. Under these conditions mentally ill persons might find themselves cut off from social support systems. Equally significant, the commission did not take into account the different kinds of patients admitted to mental hospitals. Thus its broad recommendations were not always directly related to the needs of a diverse and changing patient population.

At the time that the JCMIH's final report was made public, such issues were rarely discussed, nor were the potential consequences of new policy initiatives explored. Indeed, the publication of *Action for Mental Health* was accompanied by feelings that bordered on euphoria. If enacted into law, the recommendations of the JCMIH would "revolutionize public care of persons with major mental illness—the nearly 1,000,000 patients who pass through State hospitals and community mental health clinics each year."[65] The stage was now set for a broad public debate over a document that urged fundamental changes in the ways in which American society dealt with the problems of severely mentally ill persons.

CHAPTER NINE

From Advocacy to Policy

THE IDEALS that people pursue in seeking social change and the realities that subsequently emerge rarely correspond. This generalization is particularly applicable to the evolution of mental health policy in the 1960s. *Action for Mental Health* represented the work of individuals determined to improve the lives of the mentally ill and the psychologically troubled. Its authors believed the time was ripe for dramatic changes; their goal was not merely to reshape traditional mental hospitals, but to dramatically expand community services. Aware of the rapidly growing role of the federal government in health and biomedical research, they sensed a golden opportunity to transform mental health policy and to develop new sources of funding. Congress was sympathetic to programs designed to bring the benefits of modern medicine to as many people as possible. The election of John F. Kennedy in 1960 also augured well. The new president, unlike his predecessor, appeared committed to the pursuit of more activist policies.

The case for change made by the JCMIH seemed compelling. Yet its final report failed to offer a precise blueprint that could serve as the basis for legislative action. It suggested instead a general direction. What was required was the translation of these broad goals and objectives into a specific legislative agenda that would include adequate levels of funding.

To move from advocacy to policy was neither simple nor easy. The absence of fundamental conflict within the commission did not imply that its proposals would not arouse controversy. The individuals and groups that constituted the JCMIH represented a relatively narrow constituency and generally were not forced to choose between competing priorities. *Action for Mental Health*, after all, was based on the politics of distribution rather than redistribution; it assumed that in an expanding economy new resources could be found to achieve desirable social goals. Distributive politics, moreover, muted intergroup conflict; all groups could simultaneously benefit (as contrasted with high levels of conflict that often resulted from redistributive politics in which a gain for one meant a loss for another).

In the larger world of American politics, however, the situation was quite different. Mental health advocates had to compete with a variety of other interest groups, all seeking support for their own programs. Any political consensus, therefore, would have to be created rather than assumed. The commission's program also had important implications for federal-state relationships. Not all were prepared to concede the wisdom of shifting authority to the federal government. Finally, the broad and encompassing nature of the commission's program did not always meet with a favorable reception. If the JCMIH were to succeed in mobilizing support, it would have to make a compelling case in a complex and divided political system where clear choices between policy alternatives were the rare exception.

Two and a half years after *Action for Mental Health* was made public, Congress enacted and the president signed the Community Mental Health Centers Act of 1963. Hailed by enthusiastic supporters as the harbinger of a new era, the act in reality departed from the complex recommendations in the commission's final report. The JCMIH favored in part the rebuilding of state mental hospitals. Supporters of the legislation, by way of contrast, believed that the new community-oriented policy would provide better and more effective services for the mentally ill and ultimately eliminate an institution that provided obsolete custodial care. In practice the law—in conjunction with other developments—magnified many of the problems faced by some severely mentally ill people who did not have access to care and treatment, and often lacked homes or families. Paradoxically, the recommendations of the JCMIH were altered almost beyond recognition between 1961 and 1963. In the end a policy designed to improve the lives of the mentally ill had unforeseen and sometimes unwelcome consequences.

. . .

When *Action for Mental Health* was nearing completion, members of the JCMIH assumed that a broad coalition would be mobilized in support of its program. In turn, a friendly Congress and new president would look with favor on proposals to expand federal participation in the mental health field. Indeed, the language employed in the commission's final report suggested that its appeal was not to mental health professionals, but rather to a broad constituency aware of, and sensitive to, the needs of the severely mentally ill and to individuals experiencing personal difficulties.

Yet the reception of *Action for Mental Health*, though generally favorable, was by no means uncritical or one-sided. Given the report's "global" recommendations, a dearth of dissent would have been surprising. Responding to a series of criticisms by Francis Braceland, Kenneth E. Appel expressed the belief that unanimity was not a requirement for action. "I should think that if 75–80 percent of the recommendations were satisfactory to an individual that would be all we could expect."[1]

The formal reaction of the APA revealed the ideological diversity that existed on a variety of issues. Upon receiving *Action for Mental Health*, the APA Council commended Ewalt. Its members then referred the document to the membership and to committees whose reactions were to provide the basis for the official response. During the remainder of 1961, intensive discussions took place within the major standing committees as well as the District Branches. A curious reaction followed. There was considerable enthusiasm overall for many specific recommendations of the commission. Nevertheless, there were dissenting voices on particulars. The APA Council expressed its "enthusiasm for the essence of the program" but also affirmed its responsibility "to render such constructive professional criticism of specific findings and recommendations and omissions in the Report as it thinks may guard against misinterpretations and therefore misguided efforts from a professional point of view."[2]

Dissent was wide-ranging. Some were concerned that psychiatric legitimacy and authority might be called into doubt by a shift of functions to "Mental Health Counsellors." Walter E. Barton took note of these concerns when he informed Ewalt that there were "doubts as to the wisdom of lowering standards and abandoning the strict medical definition of psychotherapy to include lay persons treating minor disorders." Similar feelings were expressed by members of the Commission on Long Term Policies, the District Branches, and other standing committees. Indeed, discussions in twenty-nine out of fifty-three District Branches indicated dissatisfaction with the inference that psychotherapy and social therapy were "the answers to the prevention and cure of mental illness." The failure "to give due credit to pharmacological and physical therapeutic procedures" risked placing "a shadow of charlatanism over psychiatry." Nor did the District Assemblies agree with the recommendations by the JCMIH that the size of institutions be limited or that hospitals for chronic patients be established. The claim that *"largeness"* was synonymous with *"badness"* was also open to dispute; and the proposals that every hospital with 100 or more beds have a psychiatric unit and that there should be one mental health clinic for every 50,000 of population were deemed unrealistic. Such criticisms were echoed in the deliberations of a number of APA standing committees.[3]

A similar pattern emerged when the committee charged with advising the APA on means of implementing *Action for Mental Health* polled a representative sample of twenty-four state commissioners of mental health. Although only thirteen replied, their comments reflected the same kind of ambivalence. Some questioned whether a national program could take local differences into account; some noted that the report had received virtually no exposure within their respective jurisdictions; some argued in favor of full federal funding without matching state contributions; some were opposed to any federal funding; some expressed the belief that the report might widen the cleavage between mental hospitals on the one hand and community programs on the other; some suggested that the report was "anti-climactic" since their states had already incorporated most of the recommendations into their programs; and others were more positive.[4]

The most vociferous criticism of the JCMIH came from individuals long identified with traditional state hospitals. The leading critic was Newton Bigelow, editor of the *Psychiatric Quarterly* and a major official in the New York state hospital system. In a series of article-length editorial comments, Bigelow spelled out his concerns. Many hospitals, he insisted, played a vital role in caring for and treating psychotic patients—a group all too often ignored, especially by psychiatrists in private practice. Nor was size by itself a crucial variable; far more significant was the medical staff-patient ratio. Bigelow was especially critical of the proposal to create institutions for chronically ill persons. "To send a 'chronic' mental patient to a custodial, second-class hospital half full of 'physical incurables' is more barbaric," he wrote in 1961.

> Who will say that there is no hope for this person as opposed to that one in this day of remission of chronic illness? Who will serve on the medical, nursing, occupational therapy or attendant staff of such a hospital? Who will face the patients' relatives in the matter of such "disposition"? There have been "receiving" state hospitals and "secondary" state hospitals in the dim past. Let us not resurrect them! We need to raise standards!

Bigelow was equally derisive of the omission of any "humane planning" in *Action for Mental Health* for the large proportion of aged persons with major mental illnesses in mental hospitals.[5]

Bigelow's public criticism was shared by other hospital superintendents who felt that the JCMIH had mounted an attack on them and their institutions. At the APA Mental Hospital Institute in the fall of 1961, the predominant tone was one of hostility. Most of those attending were employed at public hospitals, and their experiences led them to reject many recommendations of the commission. They employed a number of arguments: the claim that community services would promote the secondary prevention of mental illnesses was unproven; suggested size limitations were "too arbitrary"; the conversion of large hospitals into chronic care facilities was unsound and was based on an inappropriate dichotomy between the acutely and chronically ill; the achievements of many hospitals had been slighted; and many of the data in *Action for Mental Health* represented "personal opinions and biases."[6]

Those more favorably inclined toward the commission expressed some concern that the superintendents might "possibly act as a very potent obstructive force" because of their political connections. Indeed, William C. Menninger warned that state hospital psychiatrists were even thinking of running an opposition candidate if Ewalt were nominated for the APA presidency. John Cumming, a psychiatrist and director of the Mental Health Research Unit in the New York State Department of Mental Hygiene, believed that the fears of hospital superintendents were not entirely groundless. He (in collaboration with his wife Elaine) had published an influential work on mental health education and was sympathetic toward a psychodynamic etiology and therapy. Cumming conceded that Bigelow had done himself a disservice by identifying all critics of large hospitals as a single undifferentiated group. Nevertheless, many of the smaller hospitals associated with teaching centers admitted "not too sick, nearer upper than lower class patient[s] which approximates what their residents will meet in private practice." Such institutions ignored the kinds of patients found in state hospitals. Cumming also observed that some large hospitals had made significant efforts to improve themselves. At the same time he expressed serious reservations about overselling the "adult outpatient clinic idea" whose supporters had never dealt with patients most likely to be treated in mental hospitals.[7]

After nine months of internal debate and discussion, the APA Council finally issued a position paper. The document was generally laudatory and supportive of the objectives of *Action for Mental Health*. It endorsed the recommendations pertaining to research, personnel and training, the expansion of community treatment facilities, and federal financing. Nevertheless, the Council was unwilling to accept at face value all of the JCMIH proposals. The proposed 1,000-bed limitation on intensive treatment centers, for example, was "not [to] be taken too literally." Nor did the group necessarily agree with the suggestion that large state hospitals be converted into chronic care facilities. Conceding that some institutions might profit from such a conversion, the Council urged a continuation of efforts to upgrade rather than to change the character of large state institutions. Indeed, overly specific numbers ran the risk of assuming "the character of rigid standards or slogans," which, in turn, could "impede and hamper adoption of sound principles to actual needs and circumstances." The document closed on a note of enthusiastic support, although conceding that the JCMIH had ignored the mentally retarded—a group that was gaining increased prominence because of the involvement of President Kennedy and his family.[8]

The reaction of the AMA to the JCMIH was somewhat more guarded and ambiguous. In mid-1961 its Board of Trustees resolved that *Action for Mental Health* was "a basis for a program" that merited support. The AMA Council on Mental Health adopted a strongly supportive document (although it reaffirmed its opposition to "the independent private practice

of psychotherapy by nonmedical persons") and urged its parent organization to do likewise. In the autumn the AMA convened a special conference to develop a comprehensive mental health program based upon
work of the joint commission. The following summer the AMA adopted
a program recommended by its Council on Mental Health couched in
general terms that differed in significant respects. The AMA was more
disposed to retain local government fiscal responsibility, although it expressed a preference for integrated and coordinated services designed to
maximize preventive activities and to promote community care and treatment. In October 1962 it convened a national congress designed to develop state programs to implement these recommendations. Close to two
thousand persons attended; 38 percent were psychiatrists, 15.5 percent
nonpsychiatric physicians, 13 percent hospital administrators, 12.5 percent lay workers, and the remainder represented social work, psychology,
nursing, education, religion, and law. The deliberations emphasized the
need to involve state and local medical societies in developing community-oriented services that brought together nonpsychiatric physicians
and psychiatrists. The diffuse nature of the meeting, however, fulfilled
Robert T. Morse's prediction that "little ultimate good comes from such
congresses."[9]

The Board of Directors of the American Psychological Association also
endorsed *Action for Mental Health* but added a significant caveat. Its
members were critical of the document's failure to provide a "fundamental reformulation" of the problem by not taking into account "recent
basic criticism of the medical model of health and illness." The absence of
any consideration of mental retardation was also unfortunate. In the future, the statement concluded, greater attention would have to be paid
"to creative human functioning, and to ways in which society can contribute to goals beyond mere health and illness."[10]

The strongest support, as might have been expected, came from the
National Association for Mental Health—the nation's foremost citizens'
advocacy organization. It endorsed the emphasis on research; the expansion of the pool of trained personnel; the need for smaller mental hospitals (although insisting that the 1,000-bed limitation was an "arbitrary
goal"); the desirability of expanding and integrating community services with traditional hospitals; and broad financial support from "all
levels of government." On the other hand, the organization virtually ignored the proposal to transform large hospitals into chronic care institutions and urged instead that such institutions be divided into "multiple,
self-contained smaller units each related to its own community or
communities."[11]

The divisions among organizations in many ways mirrored differences
among individuals. John C. Whitehorn emphasized the need for "profes-

sional psychiatric leadership" as contrasted with "amateurish social leadership in dealing with patients' problems." William C. Menninger disliked the manner in which *Action for Mental Health* identified psychiatry with the severely mentally ill and ignored the neuroses and character disorders. He was also wary of segregating chronic cases because of his concern about substandard conditions. Ewalt responded by pointing out that the definition of mental illness "is one of semantics" and he dismissed its significance. The commission, he added, focused on the seriously mentally ill and not on problems relating to alcoholism, crime, and geriatrics, partly because it lacked adequate resources to broaden its focus. Ewalt also defended his proposal for institutions for chronically ill persons. "Psychiatrists," he observed, "have long since demonstrated that most of them are not interested enough in chronic disease to do anything but store such patients on back wards. It is my belief the patients would get a better shake if psychiatrists acted as consultants and allowed people with great involvement and commitment to rehabilitation of all types of chronic disorders to take charge." The internal debate suggested that a general consensus on broad and vague principles and on the need for action was matched by an equally striking disunity on specifics.[12]

The support of professional associations was obviously important. Yet by themselves such organizations—even assuming their unity (and such was not the case)—lacked the power to design public policy. Mike Gorman was cognizant of the need to forge a broad-based coalition. By early 1961 he began to consider the possibility of mobilizing the nation's governors, scheduled to meet in June.

Gorman initially attempted to persuade William C. Menninger (with whom he had recently had a falling-out) to act as a spokesperson because of his close affiliations with state officials throughout the country. Menninger was somewhat reticent, partly because he was not in full agreement with the report. Upon receiving assurances from Ewalt that unanimity on all points was unnecessary, Menninger responded positively. At the Governors' Conference, an entire session was devoted to "The States and the Mentally Ill." Menninger, Gorman, and Ewalt made presentations before a sympathetic audience. The participants at the close adopted a resolution that authorized a special Governors' Conference on Mental Health in the autumn to discuss ways in which the recommendations of the JCMIH could be translated into policy.[13]

That conference, in November 1961, attracted only about a third of the nation's governors, although many states sent other representatives. A number of prominent psychiatrists and other interested parties attended. Menninger spoke and Gorman provided a draft statement generally supportive of the JCMIH. The policy statement finally adopted by the governors reflected some of the thinking of that era: the need for a wide range of community services; the importance of continuity of treatment; inpatient treatment in small mental hospitals and an expansion of psychiatric facilities in general hospitals; the decentralization of large hospitals "to ensure the best patient-care and maximum efficiency"; greater attention to research and training; and cost sharing among local, state, and national governments. The conference also arranged for representatives of the Advisory Commission on Intergovernmental Relations to contact the White House in order to draft appropriate legislation.[14]

. . .

The persistence of disagreements over the specific recommendations of the JCMIH did not dampen enthusiasm for some form of positive action. The time for change seemed propitious. The political climate was sympathetic. Equally significant, public sentiment appeared supportive. Concern for the mentally ill through much of American history generally had been confined to two groups: families with members whose aberrant behavior threatened the existence of the household; and public officials responsible for providing some form of care. In the postwar era, however, psychological interventions—notably psychotherapy—to deal with personal problems had become increasingly popular. The continuum model of mental health and mental disease stimulated pressure for an expansion of psychiatric and psychological services for nonmentally ill persons. All of the elements for a new policy now appeared favorable; the remaining task was to tap the massive financial resources of the federal government.

That those committed to new policies turned to the federal government was not at all surprising. The experiences of the New Deal and the acceptance of the idea of the welfare state had persuaded many that the federal government was better qualified than its state counterparts to deal with pressing social problems. By the 1960s the prevailing consensus was that states had failed to meet their social welfare responsibilities. Hence many activists, even though paying homage to the idea of a federal-state partnership, promoted policies designed to bypass state governments. The tendency to denigrate state governments was accompanied by an idealization of local community institutions and attitudes. The result was a curious effort to shift political authority toward both the federal government and local communities, and thus implicitly to weaken the authority of state governments.

Critics of state social policy-making received indirect support from federal agencies, notably the NIMH. Led by Felix, many of the key personnel within this organization did not believe that states had either the knowledge or the capacity to institute meaningful changes, and that this accounted for their continuing to focus on their obsolete mental hospital systems. Hence NIMH officials were supportive of legislative initiatives that favored community services and alternatives to mental hospital care. Committed to a public health approach, they were eager to create a system capable of providing therapeutic and preventive services to an entire population within a defined geographical area. Seeking to improve care and treatment of the mentally ill and to expand psychological services for nonmentally ill persons, they foresaw no negative consequences that might follow a diminution in the mental health activities of states.

The internal reaction to Ewalt's early draft version of the JCMIH's final report was suggestive of the thinking of NIMH officials. When asked in early 1959 to provide comments, their reactions were generally hostile or noncommittal. Philip Sapir, chief of the Research Grants and Fellowships Branch, responded sharply that many statements were "pedestrian, platitudinous, rehashes of previous statements, half-truths, or untruths." The draft was "so incredibly bad that there seems almost no point in making specific criticisms." Richard H. Williams of the Professional Services Branch used more polite language but echoed Sapir's sentiments. The "sad feature" of the document, he added, is that it "fails, largely, to bring much *wisdom* to the material available."[15]

Felix was aware that the recommendations of the JCMIH had major implications for the NIMH. His dual agenda, however, had somewhat different goals. He hoped to expand community mental health services for both the mentally and the nonmentally ill. Thus he informed John R. Seeley of the Alcoholism Research Foundation in Toronto that his agency did not believe that the emphasis should be completely "on the problems of the mentally ill." The "scope of our interest," he added,

> has been changed from concerns with patients and hospital treatment situations, to the family, and to the community and its institutions. As our program develops, I can visualize increasing demands for personnel for these new non-treatment areas. Are we training the needed personnel now? Should we retain those we have? or change their original training? or even train new kinds of personnel? or develop new skills? Should the funds we have available have a reshuffle of emphasis between treatment, and community adaptive activities? Should the promotion of health have as much emphasis put upon it as prevention and treatment of disease?

Felix subsequently recalled that both he and his staff believed that the commission had placed too much emphasis on "hospital care of patients" and had ignored the importance and effectiveness of community-based therapeutic facilities. In a speech at the Special Governors' Conference in 1961 he predicted that the proposal to create hospitals for chronically ill patients would be "obsolete before this Report is well along the way to total implementation." Felix was also cognizant of political realities and recommended that any program "should provide for sharing the costs of mental health services with the States (and with local units through the States)."[16]

NIMH officials, despite their lack of enthusiasm about the program of the JCMIH, lacked a specific legislative agenda of their own before 1961. State officials were less reticent than their federal counterparts. At the annual conference with the surgeon general in 1959, they recommended that federal officials establish an ad hoc committee of state mental health and Hill-Burton authorities to work with the PHS in formulating treatment and administrative guidelines that could be used to develop state-wide comprehensive plans. In August the surgeon general acted accordingly by creating the Ad Hoc Committee on Planning for Mental Health Facilities, composed largely of state health officials. In January 1961 its members offered a series of recommendations that differed fundamentally from the program presented by the JCMIH.

Simply put, the members of the ad hoc committee recommended a plan that followed the examples of New York and California. Both had in place programs providing for partial state support for community mental health services. The committee urged that "community-based mental health facilities be established as part of a coordinated system of state-wide health services." This proposal anticipated one of the most striking developments of the 1960s, namely, the idea of providing services within specific geographical areas (subsequently designated as "catchment areas"). What was required was a detailed study of the population to be served, followed by a plan that divided the state into "logical community service areas." Within this framework "need-criteria" could be employed to determine "the nature and size of the facilities required to provide adequate service to the area population." At the same time the committee insisted that "construction and expansion of large mental institutions should be strongly discouraged, and State activities should be directed toward replacement of existing institutions of this type by smaller community or regional facilities offering a wide spectrum of services." The group also suggested that mental health services be coordinated with other state and federal welfare programs, but they did not propose a massive infusion of new federal funds. They endorsed instead a slight increase in Hill-Burton funding for mental health construction as well as an expansion of state grants-in-aid programs to encourage local communities to expand their facilities and thus diminish the pressure on state institutions. Their report did not envisage any fundamental change in the prevailing pattern of federal-state relations but instead pointed toward the expansion of community institutions within a state-planned, coordinated, and administered system.[17]

The inauguration of President Kennedy in early 1961 and his call for a New Frontier appeared promising in the eyes of those committed to an expanded federal role in mental health policy. Indeed, the Democratic party platform in 1960 included a plank pledging federal support for research, training, and community mental health programs. Unlike Eisenhower, Kennedy seemed favorably disposed. His staff, including Theodore C. Sorenson and Myer Feldman, as well as members in the Bureau of the Budget, believed that the recommendations of the JCMIH could serve as the basis for "broadened Federal activity." Yet Kennedy's basic concern—and that of his family—was with mental retardation. His younger sister Rosemary had been diagnosed as mildly retarded and had undergone a lobotomy that appreciably worsened her condition. In the years following the end of World War II, the family established the Joseph P. Kennedy, Jr. Foundation. By the late 1950s the foundation was seeking to use its resources to further research into retardation at such leading institutions as the Harvard Medical School.[18]

Eunice Kennedy Shriver, the president's sister, became a crucial figure within the administration and emerged as an outspoken advocate of federal action in the field of mental retardation. From the outset Kennedy was confronted with divisions and conflicts. The advocates of the mentally retarded were by then an organized and vocal pressure group. They were especially critical of the psychiatric preoccupation with the psychologically troubled and mentally ill. In their eyes *Action for Mental Health* was evidence of the characteristic lack of concern, if not overt hostility, of psychiatry toward the mentally retarded. Consequently, there was growing political tension over the allocation of resources in the mental health field; each side feared that the success of the other could come only at their expense. Trivial issues were magnified. On one occasion Feldman (the key presidential assistant dealing with mental health and retardation) urged the president to accede to a request to recognize Mental Health Week because he had already recognized Mental Retardation Week; at the same time Eunice Shriver wanted her brother to see only one mental health representative rather than two. Despite these internal pressures, the president did not move rapidly during 1961, partly because of the constraints facing the new administration in formulating its legislative agenda, and partly because of the preoccupation with retardation and the potential for divisive political conflict.[19]

Shortly after the election, Kennedy and his staff decided to form "task forces" to make recommendations on major policy issues. To avoid any presidential embarrassment, they directed the Bureau of the Budget to estimate the economic costs of new legislative initiatives. In late winter and early spring of 1961 the new administration began to plan for the creation of the President's Panel on Mental Retardation, which became a reality in October. During these months, pressure mounted on the White House to take corresponding action in the mental health field. Lasker and Gorman both had access to Kennedy. Abraham Ribicoff, the new secretary of HEW, seemed supportive of the JCMIH, although he believed that the "hospital system [should] eventually be replaced by a constellation of psychiatric resources in the heart of the community." Wilbur Cohen, assistant secretary of HEW, began to draft legislation incorporating the major recommendations of the commission. In Congress, Hill and Fogarty were likewise pushing a draft bill.[20]

Despite enthusiasm for action, there was as yet no agreement on a clear policy that could serve as the basis of specific legislation. The recommendations of the JCMIH were extraordinarily broad, and many remained controversial. Faced with pressure to do for mental health what he had done for retardation, Kennedy followed Feldman's advice. He created an Interagency Task Force on Mental Health in December 1961 to consider the recommendations of the JCMIH. Chaired nominally by Ribicoff (and then by his successor, Anthony Celebrezze), the group included several other high-level officials from the Department of Labor, the VA, the Council of Economic Advisers, and the Bureau of the Budget. The real work, however, was done by a group of insiders: Boisfeuillet Jones, a special assistant at HEW and the unofficial chair, Felix and his deputy Stanley Yolles from the NIMH, Daniel Patrick Moynihan from the Department of Labor, Robert Atwell from the Bureau of the Budget, Robert Manley from the VA, and Rashi Fein from the Council of Economic Advisers.[21]

Charged with analyzing *Action for Mental Health*, the task force was instructed to deal with "the desirable alignment of responsibility among Federal, State and local agencies and private groups; the channels through which federal activities should be directed; the rate of expansion possible in light of trained manpower availabilities; and the balance which should be maintained between institutional and non-institutional programs." Felix and Yolles represented the professional psychiatric point of view, whereas Jones, Moynihan, and Fein were the link with the administration and thus would presumably advise the president on what was politically and economically feasible. Robert Atwell, the Bureau of the Budget's examiner for the NIH, occupied a particularly crucial niche. His agency evaluated the budgets and programs of the various federal agencies and advised the executive branch on all legislative proposals.[22]

Months before the creation of the interagency task force, Atwell was pushing the NIMH to respond to the JCMIH and to develop a specific mental health program that could serve as the basis for legislation. He believed that *Action for Mental Health* had discredited state mental hospitals even though the commission recommended their revitalization. Conceding that institutional services had to be improved, Atwell believed that it was more important to stress noninstitutional services. By November 1961 the NIMH had produced a position paper that reflected the organization's unique character. Most of the institutes within the NIH tended to pursue basic biomedical research. The NIMH, by way of contrast, was interested in service delivery systems as much as, if not more than, it was in research. Admittedly, the lion's share of its appropriation was for the support of research. A substantial portion of its research budget, however, went to the behavioral and social sciences, thus linking it more directly with the evaluation and delivery of services. Its service orientation reflected both the public health background of many of its staff and their aversion to traditional mental hospital care. Indeed, a few NIMH officials had been involved with the demonstration project (created in 1949) in adjacent Prince Georges County in Maryland, a project that emphasized community mental health services.[23]

The position paper of the NIMH on *Action for Mental Health* began with a complimentary statement and was strongly supportive of many of the commission's specific recommendations. Nevertheless, it disagreed with the underlying presumption of the JCMIH that the core of the problem was the care and treatment of the mentally ill. The commission could have focused more attention on "the prevention of mental illness and . . . maintenance of mental health." The position of the NIMH was clear: "The proper focus for any mental health program, Federal, State or local, should be upon the improvement of the mental health of the people of the country through a continuum of services, not just upon the treatment and rehabilitative aspects of these programs." The document was also critical of the assertion that no hospital of more than 1,000 beds be constructed, and it completely rejected the recommendation that large state hospitals be converted into centers for the care of chronic patients. Accepting the need for larger expenditures and a greater federal role, the NIMH offered a somewhat different proposal: it recommended the creation of a federal subsidy program that encouraged states and communities to upgrade their activities in prevention and treatment of mental illnesses.[24]

At this time some divisions were evident in the upper echelons of the federal health establishment. In responding to the NIMH, the PHS concurred with the Bureau of the Budget and the National Mental Health Advisory Council that discussion of federal funding was premature. The council feared that federal funds would "freeze State and local fiscal efforts," and budget bureau staff wanted "more specific proposals" that addressed intergovernmental relationships and manpower shortages. Although the NIH generally endorsed the PHS reaction, it supported the NIMH proposal to provide federal subsidies to the states for the care of mental patients. Unlike the PHS, the NIH believed that the goal of expanding services should not be dependent on finding a solution to the manpower problem.[25]

In the spring of 1962 two internal NIMH task forces completed their work. The first, chaired by Robert T. Hewitt, dealt with the status of state mental hospitals. "Despite improvements," the group reported, "the traditional large State mental hospital continues to be the focal point of negative attitudes toward psychiatric treatment." Moreover, such institutions fostered dependency and were governed by an archaic administrative system. The task force urged that new approaches be identified and that federal funds be used to assist states in formulating new policies.[26]

A second task force, headed by Yolles, developed a comprehensive proposal that reflected its own preference for a community-oriented public health approach. Its members began with the presumption that progress in the prevention of mental illnesses and the growing acceptance of community responsibility for care, treatment, and rehabilitation of the mentally ill led to an inescapable conclusion: that comprehensive community mental health programs would make it possible "*for the mental hospital as it is now known to disappear from the scene within the next twenty-five years.*" In referring to *centers* (as compared with clinics), Yolles and his colleagues conceptualized a radically new kind of institution. "A complete mental center," they wrote, "is a multi-service community facility designed to provide early diagnosis and treatment of mental illness, both on an inpatient and outpatient basis, and serve as a locus for aftercare of discharged hospital patients." Such a center provided a broad spectrum of services and programs: diagnosis and evaluation; inpatient care; day and night care programs; twenty-four-hour emergency services; rehabilitation; consultative services to community agencies; public information and education; and supervision of foster care. Ultimately, all services within communities and regions—preventive, therapeutic, educational—would be absorbed into comprehensive centers serving a designated population within a specific geographical area. The creation of such centers, the task force noted, required careful and thoroughgoing state planning. Its members also projected a dramatic increase in federal funding on a continuing basis to support planning, training of personnel, research, and construction. The role of the NIMH would also undergo a major expansion. Its mission to provide advice and oversee the creation of these new centers required a corresponding increase in the size of its regional staffs. Yolles's plan, however, was not completely consistent. Despite its general rhetoric, it left a continuing albeit modest role for traditional mental hospitals.[27]

While the NIMH was developing its recommendations, the administration continued to demonstrate its interest in mental health. In January 1962 the surgeon general and state mental health authorities discussed the recommendations of the JCMIH. Ribicoff offered the prospect for an expanded federal role that would hasten the introduction of community programs and would diminish the role of large mental hospitals. The following month William C. Menninger met privately with Kennedy and came away persuaded that the president was sincere and receptive to meaningful change. Kennedy's special message to Congress at the end of February was equally supportive.[28]

The failure of the administration to develop a specific legislative agenda disturbed such figures as Gorman, who undoubtedly had used his congressional contacts to create pressure for action. Fearing that the hiatus following the release of *Action for Mental Health* might end hope for legislative action, he used his influence to persuade Hill and Fogarty to include in the HEW budget for 1963 the sum of $4.2 million for states to develop "long-range, community based plans for comprehensive mental health programs." Indeed, Fogarty expressed astonishment at the irony of the situation. Like Gorman, Fogarty was disappointed at the inability of the administration to provide leadership. The Committee on Appropriations, he noted in March 1962, "was disappointed that the budget did not include any plans for implementing the [JCMIH] Report. . . . The committee feels that the Executive Branch has been remiss in its duties in not yet having a plan for implementation before the Congress." Fogarty's comments suggested that congressional pressure for some kind of presidential policy recommendation was mounting.[29]

In April the presidential task force began to consider the NIMH proposals. In general, members were enthusiastic, for the NIMH—unlike the JCMIH—had defined an institution that seemed to offer an attractive alternative. The group readily accepted the assertion that new knowledge about diagnosis, treatment, and prevention offered the potential for an exciting new policy departure that could "really make a difference in length and severity of illness, in prevention of illness, and in eliminating the necessity for the institutionalization of individuals." In less than a decade the state hospital population could be halved. "I have checked the NIMH views with independent experts," Fein told Walter W. Heller of the Council of Economic Advisers, "and they agree that the program is desirable and—in terms of medical knowledge—feasible. They do *not* consider the NIMH as 'visionary.'"[30]

During the deliberations of the task force, it became increasingly evident that some members were receptive to a strategy of diminishing the role of state governments in providing mental health services because of their close identification with traditional mental hospital care. They were also supportive of the welfare state ideology that increasingly dominated the political agenda during the 1960s. In this sense they shared the pervasive liberal belief that states were in part obsolete entities because they had impeded or opposed programs designed to assist disadvantaged groups to achieve greater equality. Indeed, they were persuaded that modern and effective social policies required federal leadership and action. They were prepared, therefore, to recommend policies that implied not only federal funding but a measure of federal control. But differences over details persisted. Felix, Moynihan, and Jones did not want to bypass the states; they hoped that informal persuasion and education might achieve the desired goal of altering mental health policy. Atwell, on the other hand, believed that tighter federal controls were necessary.[31] A number of other serious issues also remained unresolved. What kind of financing mechanisms, regulations, and standards were appropriate? Was there a sufficient supply of trained personnel to staff the two thousand centers that would be required to meet projected needs? How would an enhanced federal role impact upon traditional federal-state-local relationships?

In the end, the task force agreed that the comprehensive community mental health center approach should become the basis for the president's policy. Its members conceded that they had departed from the recommendations of the JCMIH "in a major respect, namely, in the proposal that there be a major effort to eliminate the State mental institution as it now exists in a generation, in favor of establishing comprehensive community-centered mental health programs." Specifically, the group recommended that federal grants assist in the construction of such centers and that a decreasing federal subsidy cover initial operating costs. The goal was to have five hundred centers by 1970 and an additional fifteen hundred a decade later. The group also urged that the federal program include planning grants to states; modest levels of federal support for improved patient care in state mental hospitals; greater psychiatric coverage in voluntary health insurance plans; and continuing high levels of federal support for training and research.[32]

That the president's interagency task force had partly ignored—if not rejected—the recommendations of the JCMIH was evident. Even more significant, however, was the absence of any evaluation of the claims that comprehensive centers could obviate mental hospital care within a generation. Assumptions rather than evidence became the basis on which new policy proposals were formulated. Indeed, by the 1960s rhetorical claims about community superiority had created their own irresistible momentum. Though unrecognizable at the time, the paradoxes and contradictions were profound. Federal beneficence and wisdom, on the one hand, and community enlightenment, on the other, would combine to create a new kind of institution that would overcome the myopic inability of states to formulate and implement effective mental health policies. The interagency task force had developed a paradoxical synthesis that rationalized centralized control and local autonomy while implicitly weakening the mediating role of state governments.

A discordant note sounded when Celebrezze indicated his opposition to the use of federal subsidies for operating funds for the new centers. Task force members (as well as officials in the Department of Labor, the Bureau of the Budget, and the Council of Economic Advisers) were "extremely disturbed" at Celebrezze's reaction. Without federal subsidies, they argued, state and local governments might not build centers. Even if such centers were built, they would be unable to function effectively. Raising fees would only discourage use by lower- and middle-class groups, and transferring funds from the general budget might impact negatively on other important social priorities. Fein, in particular, was not impressed by the argument that temporary subsidies would tend to become permanent. He argued instead that declining state hospital budgets would free resources. The negative reaction forced Celebrezze to reverse himself, and he agreed to recommend favorably on the staffing issue.[33]

In the late autumn Celebrezze submitted a series of far-reaching recommendations to the White House. Rejecting the emphasis placed by the JCMIH on the need to increase services to the severely mentally ill within the state hospital system, he insisted that the "primary interest in future mental health programs should be improvement of the mental health of the people of the community through a continuum of local services." Public policy had to incorporate two overriding objectives. The first was the development of measures "to promote mental health and prevent mental illness." The second was an emphasis on cure rather than incarceration. Recent progress in therapy had rendered traditional arrangements for patient care "outmoded, unnecessary and inefficient." Hence the time had come "when almost all the mentally ill could be cared for in treatment centers in their own communities."[34]

Celebrezze therefore endorsed the creation of a "comprehensive community mental health center—a comparatively new concept which offers exciting possibilities for upgrading mental health services."

> Such centers, replacing the traditional institutions, should be the foci of future mental health activities. They would be close to the patient's home, and would provide preventive, early diagnostic, and outpatient and inpatient treatment, and transitional and rehabilitation services. They would include psychiatric units in general hospitals, thereby providing the patient with the opportunity of being treated within his community environment. These facilities would be conveniently located in population centers and could provide patients with a continuity of care not now available. As his needs change, the patient in such a center could move quickly to appropriate services such as those for diagnosis, treatment, and rehabilitation; inpatient, outpatient, day or night programs; foster care, sheltered workshop, and industry.

Construction of such centers would follow the cost-sharing arrangements of the Hill-Burton program, which had led to a rapid expansion of general hospitals in the postwar years. Although operating costs of community mental health centers would be borne by state and local governments and the private sector, Celebrezze recommended that the federal government provide financial support for staffing (50 percent in the first year and a decreasing amount for two additional years). Such assistance would stimulate communities "to undertake reasonably comprehensive programs quickly, and, at the same time, will afford them opportunity to find long-term, non-Federal sources of operating support." Conceding that the transition from hospital to community care would take time, the secretary also supported modest funding for upgrading institutional care and treatment and for training the additional personnel required by the new policy initiatives.[35]

The recommendations of the interagency task force and HEW raised a number of important and controversial issues that required White House adjudication. There were, after all, fundamental differences between the JCMIH, on the one hand, and the task force and HEW, on the other. The JCMIH had envisaged a far more significant fiscal role for the federal government. HEW, by way of contrast, combined fiscal prudence with policy radicalism. Indeed, Celebrezze had gone beyond Hill-Burton in reluctantly endorsing transitional support for staffing. Moreover, issues of feasibility remained unresolved. Michael March of the Bureau of the Budget, for example, insisted that the task force–HEW program was not feasible because of the shortage of qualified personnel to staff the projected two thousand community mental health centers. HEW's own estimates confirmed March's analysis. Whether schools of social work or nursing had the capacity to meet projected needs was problematic. Equally significant, the goal of dramatically increasing the number of psychiatrists might have the inadvertent effect of reducing the supply of general practitioners and specialties providing services to the nonmentally ill, thereby exacerbating other health problems.[36]

When the Panel on Mental Retardation offered its own recommendations in the autumn of 1962, the stage was set for some form of presidential decision. In December mental health and mental retardation leaders met with officials from Kennedy's staff, the Bureau of the Budget, HEW, the PHS, and the Council of Economic Advisers. Kennedy subsequently agreed to support a major federal initiative. In his State of the Union message in early January he included a reference to a new national program that would receive extensive elaboration in a subsequent special message to Congress. Within the administration a number of successive drafts were prepared that involved the NIMH and such figures as Gorman, Feldman, and Bertram Brown. All those involved recognized that they were entering a political mine field because of the mutual distrust of the mental health and mental retardation advocates. Ultimately Kennedy agreed with Feldman that it would be prudent to prepare a single message recommending legislation dealing with mental illness and mental retardation. Such a tactic, recalled Feldman, would result in a "more saleable" program.[37]

When Kennedy was shown the draft of his message to Congress, he offered neither significant comments nor substantive modifications. He simply accepted the recommendations of his task force and advisers. This passivity was somewhat uncharacteristic; his normal pattern was to make changes. In this instance Kennedy accepted Feldman's and Eunice Shriver's assurances that the substance and form of the message was appropriate. On retardation matters he deferred to his sister; on mental health he relied on the recommendations of his advisers.[38]

. . .

On February 5, 1963, Kennedy forwarded his mental illness and mental retardation message to Congress. After a brief review of the dimensions of the problem and the cost to the nation, he called for a "bold new approach" based upon "new knowledge and new drugs" that made it possible "for most of the mentally ill to be successfully and quickly treated in their own communities and returned to a useful place in society." The centerpiece of his new policy was to be the comprehensive community mental health center, which would integrate "diagnostic and evaluation services, emergency psychiatric units, outpatient services, inpatient services, day and night care, foster home care, rehabilitation, consultive services to other community agencies, and mental health information and education." The role of the federal government was to stimulate "State, local, and private action." The president urged Congress to authorize construction grants and short-term subsidies for staffing as well as $4 million for state planning. Since it would take more than a decade to fully implement the new policy, he also endorsed a modest appropriation of $10 million for demonstration projects to improve patient care and staff training in mental hospitals. Kennedy noted that the shortage of professional personnel could be alleviated by an increase in funds for training. His proposals dealing with retardation followed similar lines of thought.[39]

The president's message received national publicity and aroused little overt opposition. The *New York Times*, for example, immediately published a warm and favorable editorial. The APA began work to mobilize legislative support for the new initiative.[40] Yet the barriers that blocked decisive action remained formidable. The administration was pushing a number of other major legislative initiatives dealing with health policy, and mental health and retardation had to compete in a Congress that was increasingly wary of the deepening federal involvement in such matters. Nor was the administration especially effective in its relationships with the House and Senate, and several major initiatives remained stalled. Moreover, even the NIH biomedical research program—which during the previous decade had received enthusiastic congressional support and was seemingly immune to criticism—was coming under legislative scrutiny because of underlying managerial problems.[41]

The administration, however, was fortunate because several key congressional figures came to its support. Immediately following Kennedy's message, identical bills were introduced in the Senate by Lister Hill and in the House by Oren Harris. Under the terms of both bills, the federal government would provide matching subsidies for the construction of community mental health centers ranging between 45 and 75 percent and funding for staffing on a declining basis for a four-year period. The bills also mandated broad governmental and nongovernmental involvement in state planning. The mental retardation recommendations initially came before Congress in a separate bill. Hill, who chaired both the Committee on Labor and Public Welfare (to which the bills were referred) and the Committee on Appropriations (which recommended funding) became the crucial figure in the Senate. A long-standing proponent of federal activism in health policy issues, he accepted professional claims about the effectiveness of community mental health centers. Well-versed in political strategy, he quickly scheduled public hearings, thereby inhibiting the emergence of any cohesive opposition.[42]

The testimony before Hill's committee was orchestrated by organizations and individuals long active in the mental health field: the APA, the AMA, the NAMH, Gorman, Ewalt, Blain, and others. HEW secretary Celebrezze was the first witness; he compared the seemingly obsolete custodial state mental hospital with the new community mental health center (CMHC), an institution that represented "a dramatic advance in our capacity to cope with mental illness." He stressed that the legislation did not in any way envisage a shift of administrative and fiscal responsibility to the federal government. The role of the federal government would be to act as a catalyst for change; states and local communities would retain "this basic health responsibility." If Congress acted favorably, Felix told the committee in impassioned words,

I am certain as I am that I am sitting here that within a decade or two we will see the size of these mental hospitals, the population of these mental hospitals, cut in half. I wish to God I could live and be active for 25 more years, because I believe if I could, I would see the day when the State mental hospitals as we know them today would no longer exist, but would be a different kind of institution for a selected few patients who needed specialized types of care and treatment.

Dissent was virtually absent. The three representatives of the AMA were supportive but conceded that their organization had yet to consider the propriety of using federal funds for staffing.[43]

Perhaps the most striking testimony was offered by Ewalt, who now insisted that the bill had grown out of the recommendations of the JCMIH urging the creation of "facilities to provide early diagnosis, treatment, and rehabilitation near the patient's home." Hospitalization, he added, "is to be used as one phase of treatment rather than as the principal treatment resource." In point of fact, *Action for Mental Health* had been directed largely at the improvement of care and treatment for the severely mentally ill—though it did not rule out additional services for nonmentally ill but troubled individuals. The bill, by way of contrast, was designed to create a novel kind of institution with a less clearly defined but comprehensive focus. Ewalt's testimony (which he later repeated before a House subcommittee) conferred legitimacy upon the new policy. He also contributed to the subsequent creation of a myth that the focus of the JCMIH had been on the establishment of community mental health services, and that the act of 1963 was a logical outgrowth of the commission's recommendations.[44]

Supporters of the bill faced a somewhat different situation in the House. Oren Harris, chair of the Committee on Interstate and Foreign Commerce, had few links to the mental health lobby. Admittedly, his committee had supported the National Mental Health Act of 1946 and the Mental Health Study Act of 1955. During these deliberations, however, Priest, an enthusiastic champion of the legislation, had presided over the public hearings. Gorman, quickly emerging as the major link between the committee and the mental health lobby, helped to orchestrate support. Nevertheless, he and his allies encountered more difficulties in the House than they had in the Senate.

The problems became evident during the public hearings before a House subcommittee chaired by Kenneth A. Roberts. Celebrezze's testimony, according to Gorman, was so ineffectual that Harris thought it necessary to excise a large part of it from the printed record. Fortunately, the statements by Wilbur Cohen and Boisfeuillet Jones compensated in part for the shortcomings of their superior. In the course of the deliberations several committee members raised serious concerns. Paul Rogers, a knowledgeable figure, expressed doubts about the feasibility of staffing the projected number of centers with qualified personnel. "I just wonder where we are going to get them all if we build these facilities and I don't see much point in building them unless we have an adequate staffing, because it seems to me that the staffing is more important than going around building buildings." Jones and Surgeon General Luther L. Terry assured Rogers that the impending legislation was designed to increase the supply of trained personnel and would mitigate the problem. Lindsay E. Beaton (vice-chair of the AMA Council on Mental Health) suggested that the creation of centers would be matched by a decline in the size of mental hospitals, thereby creating a reservoir of professionals to meet staffing needs. During the hearings, fears surfaced that the legislation would involve an unacceptable degree of federal involvement and control. One committee member observed that the reverse might occur, since there would be a shift of authority from centralized state agencies to local communities. There was also considerable concern over whether the temporary financial support for staffing could actually be phased out in the future. Ancher Nelson, a subcommittee member, repeated the old adage that "there is nothing so permanent as something temporary." An internal memorandum in the Bureau of the Budget expressed serious doubts about the allegation that federal support was merely a transitory mechanism. "The real question is who is going to finance operating costs once the federal subsidies are ended or indeed if they can be ended."[45]

Governor Frank G. Clement of Tennessee summarized the sentiments of the Special Governors' Conference on Mental Health eighteen months earlier and also spoke about his own state. Less certain that centers would render mental hospitals obsolete, he believed that they would at the very least alleviate institutional crowding and thus foster individualized care. Daniel Lieberman of the California State Department of Mental Hygiene, as a matter fact, proposed that existing mental hospitals be utilized "as focuses of community mental health centers of the future." Neither Clement nor any other witness suggested that the goal of the legislation was to transfer onerous state fiscal burdens—with the exception of the staffing issue—onto the shoulders of a more affluent national government.[46]

Taken together, the hearings in both chambers took on some of the characteristics of a rhetorical exercise. The claims about the alleged superiority of centers were asserted but not demonstrated. "We think," Jones told the House subcommittee, that enactment of the bill would "encourage and . . . stimulate communities to develop the comprehensive center that will make possible caring for the emotionally disturbed, the mentally ill, and to assist in preventing mental illness through the training of ministers, of social workers, of teachers, of police officers, of juvenile court representatives in the community in order that mental health will be promoted."[47] Such testimony was accepted uncritically by congressional figures who were not inclined to question professional authority. A peculiar partnership of professional omniscience and political deference dominated the proceedings. There was no effort to evaluate the claims that centers could deal with severely mentally ill persons requiring a wide range of support services. Nor was there any discussion about the practical difficulties of integrating former mental patients into society. Assertions about continuity of care and integration of services were at best thematic statements that did not address the administrative and organizational problems involved in implementing a community-oriented policy. The result was the creation of a euphoric atmosphere that ultimately facilitated favorable congressional action.

Even before the House subcommittee held hearings, Hill recognized that the legislation might encounter more opposition in the lower chamber than in the Senate—particularly over the issue of providing federal funds for staffing. He therefore persuaded the administration to support the merger of mental health and mental retardation into a single bill. This strategy ensured that the administration would not sacrifice mental health in favor of retardation. In an omnibus bill, moreover, the staffing issue might recede in significance, given the popularity and noncontroversial nature of the retardation provisions. Eunice Shriver and others were willing to go along with this strategy, largely because of assurances that the mental health bill might not pass if it were not combined with the more popular mental retardation bill. Feldman, who was supportive of the strategy, conceded that if a combined bill encountered difficulties, "mental health will be stripped away leaving retardation to go through." Friction persisted despite the combined bill. The two groups, however, had no recourse but to compromise, given Hill's influence. The strategy proved eminently successful in the Senate; on May 27 the upper chamber passed the bill by the overwhelming vote of 72 to 1.[48]

Despite this victory, the bill quickly encountered a serious roadblock. Originally the AMA Council on Mental Health had supported federal funding for construction and staffing. But the AMA Council on Legislative Activities was strongly opposed to the staffing provision, and in June the AMA House of Delegates voted to disapprove the bill. Opposed to any kind of legislation leading toward what it defined as "socialized medicine," the AMA employed its political power in an effort to defeat the bill in the form in which it was presented. The action by the AMA caught many of the bill's supporters by surprise.[49]

Initially the House subcommittee conducting the public hearings had unanimously voted in favor of the legislation. But the House Republican Policy Committee decided to follow the AMA; it opposed the staffing provisions because they ran counter to the ideological outlook of many GOP members. Hitherto marked by consensus, the legislative deliberations were now transformed by partisan conflict. When the bill was referred back to the House subcommittee for technical reasons, Congressman Roberts decided to hold additional hearings in early July. Jones, Terry, and Felix repeated much of their earlier testimony that federal funding for staffing would stimulate community action that would transform the nature of public policy on the care and treatment of the mentally ill. An initial staffing subsidy would enable centers to develop an optimal pattern of services and also gain sufficient operating experience on which to base future budgetary projections. In turn, third-party health insurance plans would accumulate the necessary actuarial experience to provide comprehensive coverage for mental illness. The result would be a broadened financial base that would support services for the mentally ill in the same manner as services for other illnesses. A number of states sent representatives to urge Congress to take favorable action.[50]

Although the subcommittee reported favorably, it was clear that the bill faced powerful opposition. Mental health proponents attempted to rally support during the summer. The National Association of Counties adopted a resolution urging Congress to pass the bill with the staffing provisions, and expressions of support came from governors and officials in about forty states. The full House committee remained sharply divided, however, and in mid-August reported out a different version of the Senate bill. The House version omitted the staffing provisions and reduced the authorization for appropriations from eight to three years (although with the assumption that if the program was successful, Congress would extend the authorization period). Within the committee the staffing provisions had been deleted by a vote of 15 to 12 (with three Democrats joining twelve Republicans). Oren Harris (who personally favored the original bill) conceded that he could persuade a sufficient number of colleagues to change their votes and restore the staffing authorization, but he declined to do so because he feared a floor fight might imperil the entire bill. Nor was the administration inclined to jeopardize the bill by engaging in a protracted conflict. The result was an agreement to accept the amended bill and to leave the staffing issue for a more propitious occasion.[51]

In early September the revised bill was brought before the House of Representatives. The same arguments employed by supporters were recapitulated during the debate. The underlying assumption was that state mental hospital care was inadequate and obsolete. Community mental health centers, one representative stated, "will help to phase out the 50-year-old, antiquated, overcrowded, and obsolete State mental institutions and bring the patients back into their own community to clinics or centers where they can be diagnosed, treated, and rehabilitated; where they can consult and obtain professional guidance; where their problems can be spotted early and nipped in the bud before institutionalizing becomes necessary; where local schools and institutions can come for advice; and where local doctors and psychiatrists can follow through with their own patients." Harris, despite his personal views, opposed any effort to restore the staffing authorization. Several of his colleagues disagreed; they feared that without financial assistance for staffing, many states would be reluctant to undertake broad construction programs. George M. Rhodes, a subcommittee member, was critical of the AMA for rejecting the recommendations of its own Council on Mental Health and expressed regret that his colleagues had chosen to follow its lead. Toward the end of the debate, Harris promised to defend the deletion of the staffing provisions in the conference with his Senate counterparts. With these assurances the amended bill passed by a vote of 335 to 18.[52]

A House and Senate conference committee held several hearings to reconcile their differences in October. Cohen, representing the administration, worked assiduously to arrange a compromise on the staffing issue. Supporters of the legislation increased their lobbying activities, and an NAMH poll purportedly demonstrated that a narrow majority in the House would support an amendment to restore the staffing authorization. But Harris was unyielding; he believed that such a tactic might backfire and send the entire bill down to defeat. He also chastised those supporters who indicated that a bill without the staffing provisions was unacceptable. "I just do not see how they could mean it," he told his colleagues, "because we know from our years of experience here that there have been so many things that we could not have just like we wanted them, each of us, and therefore we have had to do the best we could." In the end Harris prevailed; both the House and Senate adopted the compromise version. The bill was signed into law by President Kennedy on October 31.[53]

The mental health provisions of the Mental Retardation and Community Mental Health Centers Construction Act of 1963 were relatively simple. It provided a three-year authorization for grants totaling $150 million for fiscal years 1965 through 1967 for construction; the federal share ranged between one-third and two-thirds. To be eligible, states had to submit a comprehensive plan; designate an agency to administer the plan, as well as an advisory council with broad representation; and establish a construction program based on a statewide inventory of existing facilities and needs. The designated state agency would forward individual construction applications to Washington for final approval. The legislation, proclaimed Felix,

reflects the concept that many forms and degrees of mental illness can be prevented or ameliorated more effectively through community oriented preventive, diagnostic, treatment, and rehabilitation services than through care in the traditional—and traditionally isolated—state mental hospital. The act is designed to stimulate state, local, and private action. It is based on the belief that it will be possible to reduce substantially, within a decade or two, the numbers of patients who receive only custodial care—or no care at all—when they could be helped by the application of one or more of the modern methods of dealing with emotional disturbances and the mental illnesses.

Felix's optimistic comments were echoed by others who shared his belief that the act represented a new departure in public policy, one that would ultimately transform the ways in which American society dealt with the massive problems presented by mental illnesses.[54]

. . .

The context of policy-making between 1961 and 1963 was marked by paradox and ambiguity. Professional and political leaders accepted claims that a community-oriented policy could overcome the intrinsic and unchangeable defects of mental hospitals. Their policy discussions, however, rarely included any consideration of a large body of empirical data that was not always compatible with prevailing policy assumptions.

Beginning in the 1950s, the Biometrics Branch of the NIMH, headed by Morton Kramer, had collected and studied new kinds of data about the nature of the institutionalized population. In a series of significant (but neglected) studies, Kramer and his colleagues analyzed the experiences of patient cohorts to illustrate changes over time that had important policy implications. They pointed out that longitudinal data revealed declining lengths of stay for particular diagnoses. Between 1940 and 1950, for example, first admissions for schizophrenics—the core of the seriously mentally ill—increased. Yet the length of stay for such patients had been declining for more than thirty years. In 1948, 56 percent of all schizophrenics admitted to state hospitals were discharged within twelve months, as compared with only 33 percent in 1914. In the same period the rise in the number of resident patients with mental diseases of the senium, from 24 to 42 percent, reflected declining mortality rates (a favorable development that created new problems). Such data suggested that the often-repeated generalizations about the "warehousing" functions of public mental hospitals were somewhat inaccurate, and that policy had to begin with an understanding of a diverse patient population with a variety of disorders, each with its own specific prognosis. Significant variations among the institutionalized populations of different states, furthermore, called into doubt the wisdom of a unitary national policy. Kramer also insisted that policy analysis required a consideration of demographic trends that were changing the age structure of the general population, which in the future would greatly impact on patterns of institutional utilization.

Other data raised even more serious questions. A community policy was based on the expectation that patients could be treated in noninstitutional settings. Underlying this belief were several assumptions: that patients had a home; that patients had a sympathetic family or other person willing and able to assume responsibility for their care; that the organization of the household would not impede rehabilitation; and that the patient's presence would not cause undue hardships for other family members. In 1960, however, 48 percent of the mental hospital population were unmarried, 12 percent were widowed, and 13 percent were divorced or separated. A large proportion of patients, in other words, may have had no families to care for them. The assumption that patients could reside in the community with their families while undergoing rehabilitation was hardly supported by such findings. Indeed, a community-based policy had to incorporate supportive services that included, but were not limited to, housing. Such data (which were obviously known to Felix and others who set the agenda and developed a rationale for the CMHC concept) were barely considered during the political and legislative deliberations between 1961 and 1963, even though they were crucial to the implementation of the new policy departure.[55]

When the JCMIH was created, the central concern had been with the severely mentally ill found in the nation's public hospitals. Eight years later Congress enacted a law that dramatically shifted the focus to a new kind of institution that presumably represented a radical break with the past. The underlying assumption was that the traditional policy of institutional care was responsible for a national disaster of the first magnitude. What was required, therefore, was not an incremental policy of reform and change, but a new beginning that swept away the vestiges of a dismal past. Hence the analyses and recommendations of the JCMIH were either ignored or reinterpreted in such a way as to alter their original meaning. What had begun as an effort to improve the lot of the severely mentally ill had concluded with a dramatic new policy initiative.

The new departure had major implications for the pattern of intergovernmental relations. Historically, health care services were under the aegis of state and local governments. Even when the federal role in health policy increased after World War II, it rarely included direct services (excepting the VA, which dealt with a special population). The Hill-Burton legislation, for example, provided subsidies for hospital construction. The act of 1963, by contrast, differed in fundamental respects. The increasing concentration of federal fiscal capacity, Alan D. Miller of the NIMH noted in an address in September 1963 at a meeting of Northeastern State Mental Health Authorities, heightened "the need for a reexamination of the relationships between the Federal, State, and local governments." In effect, the federal government undertook to shape policy by forging more direct links with local communities, which inadvertently tended to diminish the authority and policy-making role of state governments. Such an administrative procedure heightened the policy-making role of professionals and federal officials, few of whom had direct links with mental institutions. Rather than providing services in more centralized public mental hospitals, states would forward construction applications conceived and developed at the local level as part of a comprehensive plan to regionalize mental health services.[56]

Even before passage of the act of 1963, Congress had appropriated funds for statewide planning. Yet the planning process under this legislation was somewhat vague and included so many groups that the final documents produced in many states lacked specificity and focus. Indeed, the guidelines for planning reflected the thinking of the NIMH and other federal officials, who preferred a community-based policy and disliked traditional mental hospitals. The initial guidelines (adopted in January 1963) stipulated that each state "must work with its communities, toward programs which have their roots in those communities. Such community based mental health programs should provide a broad spectrum of mental health services emphasizing a continuum of care, should assure coordination among all relevant community resources, and should work toward the prevention of mental illnesses, and for promotion of mental health." The result was a planning process that managed to mobilize a broad statewide constituency and simultaneously to increase the involvement of state governments while somewhat weakening their policy role.[57]

Federal officials were probably aware of the impact of their activities on intergovernmental relations. The Hospital Improvement Program, proposed by the NIMH and modestly funded by a sympathetic Congress, also had the outward appearance of assuring harmony. For fiscal year 1964, Congress appropriated $6 million; by 1983 a total of about $41.5 million had been committed for projects at 183 hospitals. The goal of the program was clear: to enable institutions to fulfill a transitional mission until such time as their functions could be assumed by the new centers. The Hospital Improvement Program, Felix told Congress in 1964, was designed to assist hospitals to "achieve a more positive role as an integral part of the comprehensive community programs in mental illness and mental retardation, and to help the communities benefit from the unique contributions the institutions can make in comprehensive community programs." The modest levels of funding assured that the impact on the nation's mental hospital system would not be extensive. The efforts made by mental hospitals to improve themselves, two psychiatrists employed by the state of Illinois charged in 1968, "have received little support from the professional planners." Whereas the federal government would provide several million dollars to construct and staff centers, Hospital Improvement Program grants were limited to $100,000 per year. Planners, they wrote, seem to be operating on the assumptions that state hospitals cannot be significantly improved and that imposing the new model of the community mental health center will obviate the need for state hospitals. Thus the professional planners seek to add new facilities rather than to modify existing ones. . . .

The problem inherent in this situation is that we may create two worlds of mental health care. The modern and better staffed facility will be available to the select few who meet stringent intake criteria. It will become a showcase, treating selected patients, while the majority of people needing mental health services will continue to be relegated to the state hospitals, where they will receive only a small fraction of the treatment resources.[58]

Aside from the consequences for intergovernmental relationships, the act of 1963 was designed to create a novel institution—the CMHC—that would be the foundation of a new departure in mental health policy. Yet what is especially striking in retrospect is the ill-defined nature and function of *centers*, as compared with existing clinics (which had more focused goals). The potential clients of centers were generally described in global and protean terminology, and they included the non- as well as the severely and chronically mentally ill. More important, the administrative relationships between such centers and traditional mental hospitals were not spelled out with any degree of precision, nor was serious consideration given to the ways in which centers would or could assume the caring functions of existing mental hospitals. That mental hospitals had major shortcomings was indisputable. Yet at the very minimum they were the only institutions that were prepared to provide the basic care required by many severely mentally ill persons. How would centers assure minimum levels of care (food, clothing, shelter) as well as support mechanisms that enabled such individuals to cope with their environment? Indeed, the legislation dealt with the construction of physical structures but was largely silent on the basic functions of centers. Nor did the law deal with the problem of adequate staffing levels, which Rogers and others had identified during the committee hearings. If inadequate levels of staffing were responsible for mental hospital shortcomings, what assurances were there that centers would not face the same problems?

Equally significant, the legislation did not spell out in detail linkages between CMHCs and other local medical institutions. To be sure, rhetorical statements abounded concerning the importance of integrating psychiatric and medical services with rehabilitation and support services in defined geographical areas. Yet a substantial gap remained between rhetorical goals and the actual implementation of a complex and decentralized policy. Indeed, local institutions such as CMHCs were relatively immune to state oversight, while the NIMH clearly lacked the administrative machinery to reach local officials and institutions. The subsequent evolution of centers, therefore, was shaped as much by local interests and groups as by concerns with the needs of severely and chronically mentally ill persons.[59]

The advocates of community care and treatment—whose visions surely represented an effort to institutionalize humanitarian concerns— had offered an ideal but had not spelled out in any detail the substantive, administrative, and financial mechanisms required to translate an abstract concept into concrete terms. In the early 1960s community mental health assumed the character of a social reform movement driven by a utopian vision of a society whose members took for granted their ability to deal effectively with the problems faced by severely mentally ill and psychologically troubled individuals. The pervasive confidence of these years grew out of a conviction that medical and scientific advances, combined with new institutional forms and an enlightened federal leadership, provided the mechanisms that would overcome the existing defects of public mental hospitals. That the consequences of the new policy departure would not always reflect the initial aspirations and expectations of its creators would only become apparent in future years.

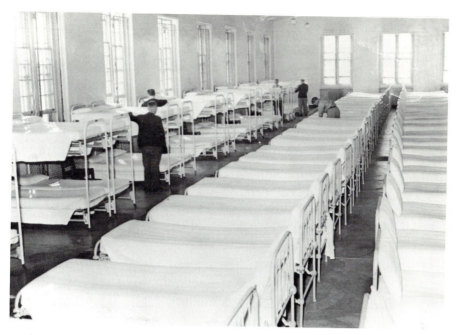

1. The increased number of patients at Byberry (Philadelphia State Hospital) in 1941 necessitated double-decker beds and a center row in one of the men's dormitories.

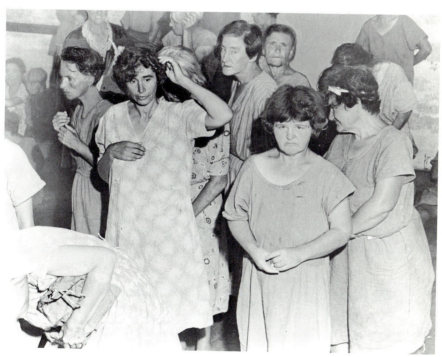

2. With no place to sit except on the floor, female patients wander aimlessly in an overcrowded ward at Byberry in 1946.

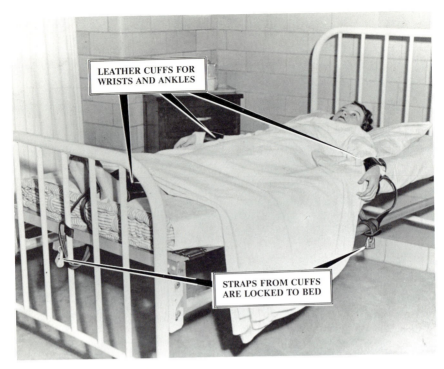

LEATHER CUFFS FOR
WRISTS AND ANKLES

STRAPS FROM CUFFS
ARE LOCKED TO BED

3. Physical restraint at Byberry in 1950.

4. St. Elizabeths Hospital, East Campus, 1941. At its peak, the hospital had
an inpatient population that exceeded 7,000 by the 1950s.

5. Occupational Therapy Department, Phipps Psychiatric Clinic,
Johns Hopkins Medical Institutions, ca. 1939.

6. A scene from the Twentieth Century–Fox production of *The Snake Pit* (1948).

7. Female patient in a New York City mental hospital, 1956.

8. Female patients in a New York City mental hospital ward, ca. 1971.

9. Group therapy session, Phipps Psychiatric Clinic,
Johns Hopkins Medical Institutions, ca. 1965.

10. John F. Kennedy meeting with William C. Menninger at the White House,
February 9, 1962.

11. John F. Kennedy signing into law the Mental Retardation Facilities and Community Mental Health Centers Construction Act, October 31, 1963. Representative Paul Rogers (center) and Senator George Smathers (left).

12. Karl A. Menninger (left) and William C. Menninger (right), 1960.

13. John C. Whitehorn.

14. Robert H. Felix, 1958.

15. Daniel R. Blain.

16. Harry C. Solomon.

17. Jack R. Ewalt.

18. Walter E. Barton.

19. Stanley Yolles, 1961.

CHAPTER TEN

From Institution to Community

COMMUNITY mental health centers represented a radical policy innovation. In many respects they were an outgrowth of the continuum concept of mental illnesses and the prevailing faith in the superiority of community care and treatment. Indeed, by the early 1960s the term *community psychiatry* had come into use to describe the intellectual and institutional changes that were transforming mental health policy and practice. The presumption was that a national program to construct centers would ultimately make available integrated and coordinated mental health services in defined geographical areas. Centers would facilitate early identification of symptoms, would offer effective preventive treatments that would diminish the incidence of mental disorders, and would provide integrated and continuous services to seriously mentally ill persons in the communities in which they resided.

Reality rarely corresponds with ideals sought. Human beings have an almost limitless capacity to conceptualize change. Their ability to ensure that there is a direct relationship between policy and eventual outcome is more circumscribed and tenuous. The developments that followed the passage of the Community Mental Health Centers Construction Act of 1963 offer compelling proof of this generalization.

The goals of mental health policy in the 1960s were relatively clear: namely, to expand community mental health services and to diminish sole reliance upon mental hospitals. Although the increase in the number of centers was slower than anticipated, there was little doubt that the act of 1963 and the authorization of funds for staffing two years later had a dramatic impact. Yet CMHCs did not replace traditional mental hospitals, nor did they focus on the severely and chronically mentally ill. Many centers devoted much of their attention and many of their resources to the treatment of individuals experiencing less serious psychological disturbances or problems in living. Unlike mental hospitals, they rarely provided an integrated system of care and treatment. Relatively few CMHCs, as a matter of fact, were linked with mental hospitals, and the centers in general did not offer comprehensive support services that dealt with all of the varied needs of the mentally ill. Whatever their contributions, centers neither replaced mental hospitals nor assumed responsibility for providing longitudinal care for discharged or other mentally ill individuals. Some of these generalizations were equally applicable to general hospitals, which treated ever-increasing numbers of psychologically troubled and mentally disordered individuals.

To be sure, resident populations of mental hospitals declined rapidly after 1965, and the institutions' therapeutic role increased correspondingly. This dramatic change, however, was not related to the establishment of centers. On the contrary, the transformation in the character and functions of mental hospitals was shaped by other developments. The passage of Medicaid and Medicare led to a sharp decline in the number of aged chronic patients. At the same time the cumulative impact of new therapies, recognition that long-term hospitalization was undesirable, and improved conditions that followed a reduction in the number of chronic resident patients enhanced hospitals' therapeutic role. Consequently, most mental institutions experienced a steep increase in admissions and shortened lengths of stay. The expansion of their acute services, nevertheless, was not accompanied by the development of community support systems. Many discharged patients, therefore, often found themselves living in communities unprepared to provide comprehensive care. In effect, the nineteenth-century unification of care and treatment in mental hospitals was largely, if inadvertently, dismantled by the policy and administrative innovations of these years.

.   .   .

Although the newfound faith in the inherent superiority of community care and treatment had its roots in the 1940s and 1950s, it was invested with new vigor during the tumultuous 1960s. John F. Kennedy may have brought to the White House an energetic, youthful, and activist image, but it was Lyndon B. Johnson's Great Society program that stimulated the extraordinary growth of federal social programs. Before the Vietnam War overshadowed domestic issues, Congress—prodded by a shrewd and dominant president—enacted in rapid succession a series of laws designed to diminish economic inequalities, address racial issues, and ensure that all Americans would have access to quality medical care. Much of the legislation between 1964 and 1966 reflected the pervasive belief that state governments were reactionary and were best bypassed in favor of a federal-community partnership.

Enacted before Johnson succeeded Kennedy, the Community Mental Health Centers Construction Act bore a striking ideological resemblance to other Great Society legislative landmarks. They all rested on the assumption that federal leadership and funding, on the one hand, and an enlightened and activist community, on the other hand, would combine to create more effective social and medical policies capable of resolving seemingly intractable problems.

In the optimistic atmosphere of the 1960s mental health rhetoric and ideology paralleled newly enacted federal social and economic programs. Both grew out of the belief that the origins of most social problems could be found in a deficient environment. The emphasis on community mental health services was also compatible with a new community-oriented ideology that stressed the empowerment of individuals and small groups and their involvement in all decisions that impacted on their lives. Moreover, the belief that mental hospitals were obsolete also fitted with the growing anti-institutionalist sentiment that idealized human beings while condemning arbitrary bureaucratic organizations.

Community psychiatry was the term that perhaps best defined some of the distinguishing characteristics of these years. It drew its inspiration from a variety of sources. Faith in the redemptive qualities of modern psychiatry was fused with demands for social justice, for an end to structural barriers that impeded individuals' realizing their full potential, and for the realignment of mental health services at the community level where a professional-public partnership could function effectively. In many respects community psychiatry also mirrored the noninstitutional and urban character of the specialty. Sensitive to the problems of urban life and committed to an environmental etiology, psychiatrists tended—unlike their colleagues in other medical specialties—to support legislation designed to assist less fortunate individuals and groups.[1]

What were the attributes of community psychiatry? To Louis Linn of Columbia University's School of Public Health and Administrative Medicine, community psychiatry constituted a fourth psychiatric revolution. Psychiatry, linked with the "principle of districting," aimed at "the saturation of a given geographical area with medical services aimed at all levels of prevention and treatment for the families who reside therein." Such a restructuring of services rested upon the postwar development "of effective symptom control." Community psychiatry, according to Leonard J. Duhl of the NIMH, was concerned "with optimizing the adaptive potential and psychosocial life skills, as well as lessening the amount of pathology, in population groups (communities, functional groups, etc.) by population-wide programs of prevention, case finding, care, treatment and rehabilitation." The tools of community psychiatry, according to the staff at the Langley Porter Neuropsychiatric Institute in San Francisco, included consultation, in-service training, and general public education. The population targeted comprised "key groups and individuals in the community whose behavior and attitudes have broad influence over the lives of others."[2]

Because of its all-encompassing nature, community psychiatry defied precise definition. Gerald Caplan of the Department of Psychiatry at the Harvard Medical School argued that community psychiatrists—unlike their brethren in traditional clinical practice, who dealt only with individual patients—accepted responsibility for all those "who manifest abnormalities of behavior or thinking which most psychiatrists would diagnose as being due to mental subnormality, psychosis, neurosis, psychosomatic disorder, personality disorder, and the other illnesses listed in the *A.P.A. Manual of Mental Disorders*, whether or not the individuals concerned, or others, have already defined these people as mentally disordered." The community psychiatrist, he added,

> needs a chart which emphasizes not the individual peculiarities of a single patient, but broad issues of mental disorder and its causation which apply to populations of patients. His task is to investigate widely occurring harmful factors and their pathological consequences, and also to plan programs of intervention which will significantly affect many people not only by his direct interaction with them, but also indirectly through the mediation of other caregivers and by altering social and cultural influences which affect them.

In his popular *Principles of Preventive Psychiatry*, Caplan joined community with preventive psychiatry and insisted upon the viability of primary, secondary, and tertiary preventive programs. Critical of the rehabilitation emphasis of the JCMIH, Caplan insisted that prevention held the key to future progress.[3]

That community psychiatry was identified with social and political activism was undeniable. Indeed, Saul Alinsky—a charismatic organizer of poor and powerless people during the 1960s—urged psychiatrists to involve themselves in the harsh social realities of the poor and to work with and not upon them. But if such social problems as poverty, racism, and unemployment were detrimental to mental health, how could the specialty reconcile its claims to professional authority and legitimacy with its commitment to democratic politics in which partisanship and competing ideologies played a significant role? "The psychiatrist," insisted Harold Visotsky, "must spurn the role of the sole community expert who solves all social ills." Yet to limit the boundaries of community psychiatry might vitiate its central elements. All that he could suggest, however, was an alliance with other professional groups "to intervene in and face up to the major social ills of our community and the implications of these for our major concern: mental health and mental illness." Such expressions of concern were common during these years. "If we are to make any substantial progress in promoting mental health and preventing mental and social disorder," Jack and Patricia Ewalt observed, "we must involve ourselves in informed activism to change our national goals and priorities. We cannot afford to have health, welfare, and education programs cut to give higher priority to highways, wars, farm support, and missiles."[4]

Community psychiatry, however popular, was not without critics. John C. Whitehorn, by this time one of psychiatry's elder statesmen, emphasized the dilemmas. When groups or governments called upon psychiatrists for guidance and leadership in social action (e.g., antipoverty) programs that impacted upon mental health, how was it possible to draw a line "between the psychiatrist as a medical specialist and the psychiatrist as a citizen." Different individuals, he conceded, would draw the line in different ways. In 1968, Lawrence S. Kubie, a sympathetic critic, pointed to some fallacious beliefs that underlay community psychiatry: that treatment near home was necessarily good; that residential treatment facilities belonged in urban general hospitals; that the shorter the period of hospitalization the better; that the CMHC could be led by young psychiatrists with relatively little experience; and that psychopathology was due to either poverty or affluence. In reflecting upon his career two years later, Kubie emphasized the importance of what he termed "clinical maturity"—a trait that could only develop out of sustained contacts with "the intransigent patient." Administration, research, teaching, and the application of psychiatry to massive social problems were in themselves laudable but could never substitute for the meaningful clinical experience, maturity, and wisdom that came out of patient contacts. Kubie's paper—appropriately entitled "The Retreat from Patients"—posed a friendly yet trenchant criticism of many of his colleagues. Leon Eisenberg also called attention to the need for evaluating programs. Otherwise, he warned, "we will face a succession of psychiatric 'revolutions,' each of which will be based on the rediscovery of moral treatment but none of which will have advanced beyond the starting point of its predecessors."[5]

One of the most hostile evaluations of community psychiatry came from H. Warren Dunham, coauthor of the classic *Mental Disorders in Urban Areas* (1939), a work that attempted to demonstrate a relationship between different types of hospitalized psychoses and community conditions. By the 1960s Dunham had reversed his position. Schizophrenia, he believed, was a biological entity that created disabilities and thus resulted in a lower social class position.[6] A common element among the diverse definitions of community psychiatry, Dunham noted, was the belief that a community psychiatrist was an individual "skilled in the techniques of social action." Such claims, however, rested on faith rather than evidence. He was equally caustic about prevention: "How are we going to take the first preventive actions if we are still uncertain about the causes of mental disorders?" The numerous efforts to grapple with juvenile delinquency since the 1920s suggested the problematical nature of preventive programs. Nor was the rush to treat individuals with minor emotional disturbances a welcome development; it followed the rise of office psychiatry and the frustrations arising out of the inability to treat severely mentally ill persons. Community psychiatry, therefore, mirrored the cherished American belief that all problems could be solved "if we can just discover the key by means of the scientific methodology at our disposal." "I am most skeptical," he added, "concerning the adequacy of our knowledge to develop significant techniques for treating social collectivities or for developing techniques on the community level that will really result in a reduction of mental disturbances in the community."[7]

Such criticisms notwithstanding, community psychiatry assumed the character of a social movement during the 1960s. In this sense it paralleled the adoption of the melioristic social policies that helped to reshape the welfare and health care delivery systems during this decade and also contributed to the diminution of poverty and discrimination. The pervasive activism associated with community psychiatry impacted upon the APA as well. In the fall of 1964 its Council met at Arlie House, a conference center outside of the nation's capital. Out of its deliberations emerged a series of "Propositions" designed to reorganize the structure of the association to make it a more effective vehicle for social change. Before the close of the decade the association had revised its constitution, created a series of task forces to deal with a variety of social problems and to study in depth the new CMHCs, and adopted a series of official policy statements on a wide range of social issues.[8]

· · ·

At the same time that the rhetoric of community psychiatry was giving the specialty a visible and activist aura, communities were preparing to implement the provisions of the Community Mental Health Centers Act of 1963. Its provisions were somewhat vague, although the goal—as Kennedy remarked when he signed the bill into law—was to replace custodial hospitals with local therapeutic centers. The act did not define the essential services that CMHCs were required to provide but left that responsibility with HEW. The meaning and actual operation of the legislation, therefore, would reflect the views of those HEW officials responsible for writing the regulations and standards.

At the very outset an internal bureaucratic struggle took place within the PHS. The Hill-Burton staff in the Bureau of Medical Services wanted jurisdiction, since responsibility for hospital construction resided in this division. Felix and his associates, on the other hand, interpreted the act as mandating a service system. In their eyes the legislation was the capstone of a process begun by the National Mental Health Act of 1946, which had authorized the creation of the NIMH and given it responsibility for research, training, and service. In the ensuing struggle Felix easily prevailed; responsibility for writing the regulations and administering the program remained within the NIMH.[9]

The writing of regulations was completed by the end of April 1964. The specific provisions, prepared by a small group that included Felix, Bertram Brown, and four other individuals, defined five essential services that each CMHC was required to provide: inpatient services; outpatient services; partial hospitalization services (including day care at the minimum); twenty-four-hour emergency services within at least one of the previous three services; and consultation and educational services for community agencies and professional personnel. No center would be eligible for funding without these services. The regulations were also designed to encourage states to offer in their comprehensive plans not only the five essential services, but also diagnostic, rehabilitative, precare and aftercare services (including foster home placement, home visiting, and halfway houses), training, research, and evaluation.[10]

The regulations addressed other concerns as well. Which professional group would have primary responsibility for administering centers? On this issue the law was silent. The regulations, however, mandated psychiatric control of the clinical program and stipulated that nonpsychiatric professionals had to work under psychiatric supervision. Similarly, the legislation employed the term *community* but did not define its meaning. In seeking a consensus, those responsible for drafting the regulations found that political, geographical, ethnic, or socioeconomic boundaries did not work; hence they fell back on sheer numbers. Ultimately they defined what a community was by stipulating a population range of 75,000 to 200,000. These figures had been arbitrarily developed by Felix and his colleagues and represented a compromise designed to avoid high costs associated with a large number of small units or the chaos that might accompany organizations serving populations over 200,000. Finally, the regulations shrewdly mandated that applications for funds be accompanied by a complete budgetary breakdown of the center's proposed staffing pattern, a regulation that was ultimately used to justify subsequent legislation providing staffing grants.[11]

In many respects the regulations that governed the new centers embodied the concepts and visions held by both NIMH officials and advocates of community care and treatment for nearly two decades. The legislation of 1963 provided them with an unparalleled opportunity, and they did not hesitate to act. The final regulations were issued without their having solicited comments, criticisms, or alternative views. Nor were state governments assigned a central role. To be sure, state officials were required to develop comprehensive plans, to divide their jurisdiction into geographical areas, and to rank and approve locally developed proposals for funding. In practice, however, the regulations diminished state authority by creating a more decentralized system that enhanced the role of communities.

The most curious aspect of the new regulations was the omission of any mention of state hospitals. In one sense this was understandable, given the fact that CMHCs were designed in part to replace institutions deemed obsolete. Nevertheless, the absence of linkages in many states between the new centers and the mental hospital system was striking. If centers were designed to provide comprehensive services and continuity of care, how could they function in isolation from a state system that still retained responsibility for most of the nation's severely and chronically mentally ill population? Indeed, the absence of specific linkages facilitated the development of an independent system of centers that ultimately catered to a quite different clientele.

The final element in the new community-oriented system—legislation providing for federal support for staffing CMHCs—was in place within fifteen months after the promulgation of the new regulations. But it was a convergence of fortuitous events that led to the rapid reversal of the funding provisions of the act of 1963. The assassination of Kennedy shortly after he signed the CMHC bill brought to the White House an individual extraordinarily well versed in the intricacies of congressional politics. Lyndon B. Johnson was a shrewd, determined, forceful, effective, and often ruthless president. Unlike his predecessor (whose legislative program was languishing), Johnson used his remarkable talents to push Congress to enact many of the elements that made up his Great Society program. Committed to civil rights and to programs designed to alleviate the burdens of poverty and ensure access to health care, he oversaw a legislative program that had a profound impact upon the lives of millions of Americans. The nomination and subsequent defeat of Senator Barry Goldwater by a wide margin in the election of 1964 only strengthened Johnson's hand and gave his program the appearance of moderation when placed alongside the seemingly militant antigovernment ideology of his opponent.

Johnson's elevation to the presidency mobilized the NIMH. In the summer of 1964 Robert Atwell (who had left the Bureau of the Budget to become first deputy to Bertram S. Brown, the official with administrative responsibility for the centers program in the NIMH) prepared a document urging his superiors to push for federal support for staffing. Atwell predicted that Johnson would be elected by a wide margin, that the new Congress would be supportive, and that the strength of the AMA would be substantially reduced. Yolles, by then acting director of the NIMH, was initially hesitant. He had been persuaded by Gorman that further legislative initiatives should await the actual construction of centers. The slowness of the states to prepare master plans and the reluctance of less affluent states to embark on extensive construction projects without assurances of adequate operating funds, however, ultimately led Yolles to reverse himself. By the fall of 1964, he had reached an understanding with Wilbur Cohen, the influential assistant secretary of HEW, that the administration would introduce the staffing bill.[12]

Shortly thereafter Yolles and his staff developed a proposal that went much further than the section on staffing support that had been deleted from the act of 1963. They were aware that budgetary pressures precluded any substantial infusion of state funds for centers. Nor was it likely that resources for state hospitals could be redirected to centers, psychiatric units in general hospitals, or outpatient clinics. Third-party insurance held "some promise," but restrictions on coverage for mental illnesses posed a major impediment even though they were slowly diminishing. The argument for action was overwhelming, and Yolles proposed federal funding not merely for staffing centers, but for added mental health services in local communities. In deference to Celebrezze (who opposed a permanent system of subsidies), he also offered a provision for a declining system of subsidies for five years, after which time support would be limited to 25 percent with no cutoff date. Nor was Yolles, as compared with Felix, sensitive to state governments, for he proposed that funding go directly to local communities with virtually no state control.[13]

Mental health leaders mobilized their constituencies even before the close of 1964. Nevertheless, it was evident that a current of dissatisfaction was present. At the annual conference of state mental health authorities and the surgeon general in early January 1965, Dr. David Vail of Minnesota insisted that CMHCs could not alleviate "social ills." What was needed was a strengthening of the state hospital system and the filling in of program gaps at the community level. He was also critical of the NIMH policy that favored general over state hospitals and the tendency of its officials to ignore their state counterparts. At the close, the conference called for more program flexibility. At about the same time the Board of Directors of the National Association of State Mental Health Program Directors endorsed the program but called for greater federal financial support for operating expenses even if new construction was not involved. Some dissent, however, appeared in the private discussions. One official was critical of the effort to bypass state authorities, and another argued that the center concept was poorly conceived. Their views, however, were largely ignored. In February, an APA-sponsored conference brought together about five hundred individuals, many of whom were prominent in the mental health professions, politics, and public life. The group threw its weight behind the proposed bill, which by then had received presidential sanction. Circumstances augured well for the bill's passage. Weakened by the results of the national election, the AMA was a less formidable opponent. Its officials were more preoccupied with the impending Medicare bill than with the staffing issue, and private negotiations between the APA and the AMA ensured that the latter's opposition would be muted and therefore ineffective.[14]

Oren Harris's House committee conducted hearings on the bill in early March. Like the earlier hearings on the CMHC act of 1963, the proceedings were largely orchestrated and many of the same individuals were involved. Celebrezze began the proceedings by insisting that the failure to establish centers because of a lack of operating funds would result in "the further entrenchment of existing trends in the usage of State mental hospitals," which until recently "were rather disgraceful." Some committee members expressed concern that no centers had been built and suggested that states were dragging their feet in anticipation of federal funding of operating costs. Celebrezze and Yolles, however, insisted that such was not the case. Faced with a variety of priorities, states needed subsidies in order to gain time to readjust their budgets. That the NIMH had the freedom to allocate funds on a nonformula basis—thereby bypassing states—also came under legislative scrutiny. When queried about the risks that states would reduce their mental health expenditures and substitute federal funds, Yolles responded that the legislation was intended to assist community mental health services and thus to hasten the disappearance of mental institutions. "There is no direct link between the community program and the State hospital program," he added. Several governors expressed a preference for channeling federal resources through existing state agencies on a formula basis, but they were not unalterably opposed to a system that left the decision in the hands of the NIMH. The testimony of several AMA representatives proved ineffective, and committee members manifested little sympathy with their position.[15]

Within a month Harris's committee, without dissent, forwarded the bill to the House, which in turn approved it by a vote of 389 to 0. Confident perhaps that passage seemed assured, Hill's Senate Committee on Labor and Public Welfare did not hold public hearings, and in late June its version easily passed the full Senate. Several significant differences between the two bills had to be reconciled by a conference committee in late July. After favorable action by both chambers, President Johnson signed the bill into law on August 4.[16]

Under the terms of the act, HEW was authorized to provide grants for staffing new centers and new services. Awards were to be based on relative needs of states for services, their financial situation, and their population. In effect, this stipulation departed from a formula based system (such as Hill-Burton) and gave NIMH officials considerable decision-making authority while bypassing their state counterparts (the final regulations governing the act simply asked state authorities to evaluate applications but denied them a right to disapprove). The bill authorized an expenditure of $73.5 million for three years (although funding could be spread over fifty-one months to ensure that new centers receiving grants in the second and third years of the program would have full funding). Congress also mandated a declining level of support beginning with 75 percent and ending at 30 percent. Interestingly enough, the law—although authorizing funding for three years—did not provide a specific termination date (the Senate had insisted that no such provision be included). An extension of the program, therefore, remained a possibility.[17]

In the ensuing discussion over the regulations, the National Mental Health Advisory Council wanted to encourage both flexibility and innovation. The final regulations, however, followed essentially the same pattern as those governing the act of 1963—even though its members were not altogether happy with the overly broad definition of the scope and mission of centers. The mission still remained both broad and ambiguous; centers had responsibility for the "mental health of the community, . . . the prevention of mental illness and the more rapid and complete recovery of persons affected with mental illness in the community, . . . [and] the development of improved methods of treating and rehabilitating the mentally ill."[18]

. . .

The act of 1965 put into place the final elements of a *national* program designed to transform public policy. Laws assume a static universe; a legal innovation presumably alters individual and group behavior to produce a stipulated result. Reality is more complex. Confronted with a legal mandate, individuals and groups often adjust their behavior. In so doing they transform laws in unforeseen and unpredictable ways. The evolution of CMHCs after 1965 is a case in point.

The effort to construct and staff centers initially moved at a relatively slow pace. By the spring of 1967 the NIMH had funded 173 projects (100 for construction, 47 for staffing, and 26 for both); the projected total by the end of that fiscal year was 286. Harley O. Staggers, chair of the House Committee on Interstate and Foreign Commerce and a supporter of the legislation, expressed some concern. Only a limited number of communities with a large enough population could support centers. The shortage of professional personnel, even in urban areas, was a limiting factor; many smaller communities did not have a single person trained in mental health. Finally, Staggers pointed to increasing competition for funding from other health programs. The goal of 2,000 centers, therefore, was unrealistic on several counts, and Staggers suggested the desirability of concentrating "our efforts in a different manner."[19]

By this time the endeavor to build a national system of centers was encountering the same kinds of fiscal difficulties as other Great Society programs. In 1965 national politics was dominated by Johnson's vision of social justice for all. Two years later Johnson and the American public were preoccupied with the war in Vietnam. Domestic concerns quickly receded into the background. The political coalition forged in 1964 had all but disintegrated, and the rise in military spending heightened pressure for cuts in domestic programs.

Under such circumstances it was hardly surprising that the CMHC program, along with others, suffered. Internal recommendations for funding, Gorman charged in 1967, had been "chopped down considerably" by the administration. By the end of the third year of the program, fewer than 200 centers would have been built—a figure that made the original goal of 2,000 centers unrealistic. Although in 1967 Congress extended the construction authorization for two years and staffing for three, a wide discrepancy between expectations and achievements existed. When testifying on behalf of another extension two years later, Gorman noted that the amount appropriated was only about 40 percent of the total authorization. An interim study by the Joint Information Service of the APA also emphasized the differences between authorizations, appropriations, and actual expenditures. Between 1964 and 1968 federal funding for construction and staffing totaled $232 million. This broke down to an average of $0.30 per capita per year, or slightly less than 5 percent of the annual per capita expenditure for state mental hospitals (which in 1966 amounted to $6.64).[20]

That financial problems posed serious obstacles to the effectiveness of a national system of CMHCs was obvious. Indeed, the issue of adequate operating funds was probably a more important concern than construction, which involved only a single initial outlay. Although third-party insurance coverage for psychiatric illnesses was slowly increasing, many centers found themselves in a precarious financial state. As early as 1967 the American Hospital Association had concluded that the concept of temporary federal support was unrealistic, and it urged Congress to consider a long-range commitment to finance local mental health services in partnership with states and local communities. By 1969 testimony before two congressional committees considering legislation to extend the life of the program made it clear that alternative funding to replace declining levels of federal support had not materialized. Conceding as much, Creed C. Black (an assistant secretary for legislation in HEW) suggested a partial retrenchment. Fewer but more effective centers would be preferable to larger numbers of substandard centers. Income from fees for service to private patients, health insurance reimbursements, state subsidies, and other miscellaneous revenues, insisted Dr. James N. Sussex (the APA representative), "is not sufficient to maintain even the five essential services, let alone offer other services." Centers located in poverty areas—which had greater needs—were even worse off. A number of center directors appearing before both House and Senate committees painted a bleak picture of their finances.[21]

Two decades later, Senator Daniel Patrick Moynihan (who had served on Kennedy's original task force) charged that the failure to construct and staff the projected 2,000 centers by 1980 and the concomitant discharge of patients from mental hospitals were responsible for the creation of a large population of "homeless, deranged people." In 1989 there should have been 2,400 centers (to compensate for population growth); only 768 existed. The implication was obvious: had the federal government and American people not reneged on their commitment, deinstitutionalization would have been successful. "What ever became of our capacity to govern ourselves?" he concluded.[22]

Moynihan's observations, however informed, are hardly sustained by a careful analysis of the activities of centers that were created. The euphoria and rhetoric surrounding the acts of 1963 and 1965 concealed an inner ambiguity about the precise nature and functions of centers. Such terms as *mental illness*, *mental health*, and *community mental health* were hardly models of clarity; they meant different things even to professionals. To some the terms implied the care and treatment of the mentally ill in the community; others believed that they were synonymous with preventive interventions; and still others emphasized changes in environmental conditions that presumably promoted mental disorders. Each of these meanings in turn led to fundamentally different kinds of organizational functions and structures. A reservoir of experience with the effectiveness of different kinds of models might have served as a guide. Yet instruments that might have measured effectiveness were absent. An APA study of eleven community facilities established between 1950 and 1962—all of which met the subsequent federal criteria for centers even though there were important differences between them—conceded that there was no "means of determining the effectiveness of their services." Rhetoric often obscured a more complex reality. "The community mental health movement," Herbert Modlin of GAP told Barton,

is at present handicapped by overenthusiasm, partly because of much childishly gullible fascination with the new and adolescent rejection of the old. We have been through these phases many times before—remember! In the beginning, two-thirds of schizophrenic patients were "cured" by insulin coma; sixty percent of paranoid schizophrenics were improved by convulsive therapy; and similarly rosy results were initially attributed to psychoanalysis, lobotomy, tranquilizers, and the therapeutic community. This enthusiasm is not necessarily all bad: the new must be tested, applied with mild indiscrimination; sustain a shakedown cruise, be pushed to the limits that inform what it can and cannot accomplish, where it fits and where it rattles. Furor therapeutics has its value if one does not lose perspective and indulge in chauvinistic adherence to an innovation.[23]

Nor was there a clear consensus on the kind of clientele that would be served by centers. The continuum theory of mental illnesses—widely accepted by those who believed in the viability of a community-oriented policy—was a source of confusion. This theory assumed the feasibility of identifying troubled individuals who, if untreated, would be at high risk to become mentally ill and therefore candidates for admission to mental hospitals. Left out of the equation, however, was any consideration of the behavior of those consumers who used the mental health system. In the postwar decades, Americans became enthusiastic users of medical services; their faith in the efficacy of medical science and the development of third-party insurance plans combined to alter traditional utilization patterns. Might not the use of CMHCs by the general public differ appreciably from the expectations of their supporters and staff? In their study of urban community mental health in 1968, Robert H. Connery and his associates warned that the discovery of new categories of individuals with emotional disturbances might "absorb much of the energies of the new centers," thereby redirecting their focus away from the severely mentally ill. David Mechanic expressed a similar concern when he called attention to a growing dichotomy between the goals and practices of CMHCs. Centers, he added,

> should be encouraged to deal with difficult and unattractive cases as well as with those that fit their preferences. If the ideology of community care of mental patients is to flourish, the community mental health center must take its share of the responsibility for providing a coordinated pattern of aftercare services and continuing help to chronic mental patients as well as for dealing with the more common and less serious psychological disturbances and problems in living. . . . If we are going to encourage the early release of mentally ill persons from hospitals and attempt to maintain chronic psychiatric patients in the community, we must be ready to deal with the problems resulting from such policies.[24]

Equally problematical were the therapeutic activities of centers. The APA study of eleven centers found that eclecticism was characteristic; most used all of the customary modalities, including individual and group psychotherapy, drugs, electroshock, and milieu therapy. The treatment of choice, however, was individual psychotherapy, an intervention especially adapted to a middle-class educated clientele and congenial as well to professional staff. Yet it was equally clear that if this practice became the foundation of new centers, their mission would be profoundly transformed. "There simply are not enough therapists—nor will there ever be—to go around, nor are there enough hours, nor is the method suited to the people who constitute the bulk of the problem—the uneducated, the inarticulate," M. Brewster Smith and Nicholas Hobbs pointed out in a document that became the official policy of the American Psychological Association in 1966. Even if there were sufficient staff, they added, the "superior effectiveness" of psychotherapy was not an established fact.[25]

The existing chasm between psychiatry and mental hospitals enhanced the possibility that centers might have only tenuous relationships with the severely mentally ill. In their classic community study in 1958 Hollingshead and Redlich provided some striking data. Psychiatrists in private practice tended to treat more affluent neurotic patients, whereas psychotic individuals from lower-class backgrounds were found in mental hospitals. By the mid-1960s the linkages between the specialty and traditional state hospitals were remote. Few psychiatrists, experienced or inexperienced, pursued institutional careers. Nationally, about 25 percent of budgeted positions for staff psychiatrists in state mental hospitals remained unfilled, and more than a third of all positions were held by foreign physicians, few of whom were trained in psychiatry. Indeed, many foreign physicians accepted institutional employment because of their inability to get regular medical licenses.[26]

Among the most significant elements that shaped the actual development of CMHCs were the weakness of linkages among the various levels of government and the increasing diversity and complexity of the mental health field. If the frailty of regulation gave centers the autonomy with which to experiment, it also left them free to move in directions not always conducive to the welfare of the severely mentally ill. Many centers, for reasons that were quite understandable, ultimately serviced a quite different population. The severely mentally ill, after all, presented daunting problems. They were not always easy to manage; they often required comprehensive care; and many were poor candidates for psychotherapies, the approach most favored by center personnel. Needs that in mental hospitals were minimally satisfied were not as easily met in a community setting. Who would ensure that mentally ill persons would have access to housing, food, support systems, and jobs? To provide for the mentally ill in the community, in other words, was time-consuming and arduous, and the available means of administration—despite the confident rhetoric of these years—were not always adequate. Under such circumstances, centers were free to respond to local pressures for services to nonmentally ill constituencies.

A novel effort to integrate state mental hospitals and community institutions occurred in California, which in 1967 enacted the Lanterman-Petris-Short Act (but delayed its effective date until 1968) and then amended the Short-Doyle Act to finance the new system. Designed to protect the civil rights of the mentally ill by ending indefinite commitments, this legislation gave county governments major responsibilities for community programs, although the state assumed 90 percent of the costs. The new departure, curiously enough, was a product of what was described as "an unholy alliance of liberals and conservatives"; concern with the welfare of the mentally ill was fused with a desire by figures like Governor Ronald Reagan to reduce the role of the state by possibly eliminating all state hospitals. The results of the California experiment were mixed. Variability among counties was striking. Three counties developed community programs that incorporated special services for former hospital patients, while others all but ignored this group.[27]

During the 1960s, friction between states and the federal government began to impact on the mental health system. Indeed, by 1966 a number of Democratic governors meeting with President Johnson expressed concern about the growing conflict between the two levels of government that resulted from the massive increase in federal funding for Great Society programs.[28] Yolles faced similar complaints. When the NIMH was reorganized in 1966, he appointed an Ad Hoc Committee on State Mental Health Program Development. In the autumn the NIMH convened a meeting that brought together representatives from ten states (West Virginia, New Hampshire, Pennsylvania, Delaware, California, New York, Maine, Colorado, Illinois, and Tennessee) with fourteen staff members (including Yolles and Brown). The discussions immediately focused on the problems growing out of the absence of coordination. Some of the state representatives maintained that a change in the respective roles of the federal and state governments was undesirable, and they expressed concern about the growing "dichotomy between state hospital[s] and community programs." They were not opposed to the CMHC concept but pointed out that many centers had made no plans "for accepting responsibility for the seriously ill." State mental hospitals could not be left out of planning; they were "an appropriate part of the system" and many provided "comprehensive services of high quality to a community." "There is need," they added, "for a single system of services with staff interaction between all resources and levels to effect quality and total care. The comprehensive Center should provide the opportunity to pull the two together. This requires deliberate planning at both the State and local level."[29]

The subsequent evolution of CMHCs during and after the 1970s fulfilled few of the expectations prophesied by their advocates. To be sure, the inpatient population of state mental hospitals dropped dramatically after 1965. Between 1955 and 1965 the inpatient population fell by about 15 percent, in the succeeding decade by 59 percent. Yet the decline had little to do with centers, which generally serviced a quite different clientele. In many urban areas CMHC clients, as compared with inpatient mental hospital populations, tended to be younger, poorer, less well educated, and disproportionately drawn from minority and nonwhite backgrounds. Many of these individuals were referred to centers because of alcoholism and drug addiction, conditions that had aroused public concern and apprehension. That substance abuse during the 1960s was already subsumed under the category of mental health only enhanced the possibility that many centers would take on new responsibilities. Indeed, much of the testimony before various congressional committees considering the financing of centers during and after 1965 dealt with alcoholism and drug addiction. Satisfied that centers had already contributed to the reduction of inpatient mental hospital populations, Congress passed a series of amendments between 1968 and 1974 expanding their therapeutic responsibilities to include the prevention and treatment of alcoholism and drug addiction. Although understandable, such legislation only served to blur still further the role and responsibilities of centers toward the severely mentally ill.[30]

Despite prevailing beliefs, early evaluations of CMHCs offered little evidence that their activities had any significant relationship to the decline in inpatient mental hospital populations. The APA's Joint Information Service study in 1969 found that five out of the eight centers evaluated were doing little to reduce mental hospital admissions from their catchment areas. Nor did some of the centers studied evince any concern with developing community-based rehabilitation and maintenance programs "that would attempt to prevent the exacerbation of acute illness in the chronically mentally ill." Other studies during the 1970s called into doubt the claim that centers had an appreciable effect on state hospital admissions. At best, the available data suggested that centers which coordinated their activities with state hospitals played a modest role in reducing admissions; those without linkages had no impact. Whatever functions centers were serving and however valuable their contributions, most—with some notable exceptions—did not provide an alternative to mental hospital care.[31]

Some community mental health centers were also caught up in the social and political conflicts of the 1960s and early 1970s, thus further vitiating their already marginal involvement with the severely mentally ill. These years saw a rise in the popularity of antiorganizational ideologies that emphasized the importance of activism undertaken by the very groups that lacked power and occupied a marginal role in society. The emphasis on community empowerment was reflected in the legislation creating the Office of Economic Opportunity. This agency was dedicated to the proposition that conditions could be improved if poor and powerless groups rejected middle- and upper-class paternalism and took an active role themselves in shaping urban community programs. Although the

concept of CMHCs antedated the emergence of community-oriented ideologies, many urban centers responded to community pressures by shifting the emphasis from treatment and rehabilitation of the mentally ill
toward the improvement of social conditions. Brown and an NIMH colleague put the issue quite succinctly in early 1967. "The success of a mental health program," they wrote, "is no longer simply a function of the
clinical skills of the program staff; the success of a program is equally
dependent on skills in coping with, and adapting to, and sometimes even
changing the local political, social, and economic environment."[32]

The most famous example of political activism occurred at the Lincoln
Hospital Mental Health Services in the southeast Bronx, a neighborhood
that seemed to symbolize all the problems of urban America. Organized
at the end of 1963 under a contract between New York City and Albert
Einstein College of Medicine of Yeshiva University, the new organization
(with a three-year grant from the Office of Economic Opportunity in
1965) undertook an experiment. With the use of neighborhood service
centers staffed by trained indigenous nonprofessionals to stimulate social
and community action programs, the hospital sought to deal with the
chronic problems of urban ghettos. In March 1969 nonprofessional staff
workers went on strike, occupied administrative offices, and demanded
that power be transferred from professionals associated with a predominantly white university power structure to the poor, blacks, and disfran-
chised persons. The confrontation at Lincoln Hospital was perhaps an
extreme example. Nevertheless, internecine conflict, particularly in urban
centers, was common, given the ideology of community control and the
demand for actions that would transform an environment that allegedly
produced high rates of psychiatric pathologies.[33]

Within a decade after the passage of the act of 1963, it had become
clear that CMHCs, whatever their original purposes, had neither replaced mental hospitals nor provided alternative services for the severely
mentally ill. Indeed, the relationship between the specialty of psychiatry
and centers became problematical. Rather than increasing, the number of
psychiatrists affiliated with centers declined sharply. In 1970 the average
number of full-time psychiatrists per center was 6.8; seven years later the
number was 4.2. In 1973, 56 percent of all centers had psychiatrists as
directors; by 1977 the comparable figure was 22 percent. Centers were
largely staffed by clinical psychologists, social workers, or nonprofessional staff—groups that in general had neither interest in nor experience
with the severely mentally ill.[34] The decline in the number of psychiatrists
in CMHCs paralleled a comparable decrease in their numbers in mental
hospitals—further evidence that the links between psychiatry and the
public mental health system had become less significant.

Created as alternatives to or replacements for mental hospitals,
CMHCs by the 1970s were serving quite different purposes. Most of

them, APA president Donald G. Langsley charged in 1980, were offering "preventive services that have not yet been proven successful" and "counseling and crisis intervention for predictable problems of living." "A critical consequence of these events," he added, "has been the wholesale neglect of the mentally ill, especially the chronic patient and the deinstitutionalized." "By endorsing and funding psychiatry's more grandiose claims," David F. Musto wrote in 1975 in a devastating epitaph, "the CMHC program's most enduring contribution may have been to lead the profession to a clearer sense of reality and of its own areas of greatest competence."[35]

. . .

At the same time that the federal government was seeking to forge a new community-based policy, the shape of mental health services was changing rapidly. In the postwar era mental health services became both more diverse and more diffuse. The continuum model, eradicating the sharp demarcation between mental health and mental illness, justified the creation of new services for a range of individuals whose characteristics often differed in the extreme. The changing occupational patterns of psychiatrists also played an important role. In private practice and community employment, they were less likely to come into direct contact with the severely mentally ill. Consequently, the very shift in the locus of psychiatric practice helped to foster demands for services among nonmentally ill persons from middle- and upper-class backgrounds, many of whom accepted the prevailing faith in the ability of professional elites to resolve a variety of pressing personal problems. The expansion of services reflected both provider and consumer pressure; each reinforced the other. Finally, the availability of funding from private foundations and organizations promoted experimentation with novel forms of service.[36]

Nowhere were the changes in the mental health system during the 1960s more visible than in the aggregate data dealing with patient care episodes.[37] In 1955 there were 1,675,352 patient care episodes; 379,000 (22.6 percent) occurred in outpatient facilities, 818,832 (48.9 percent) in state mental hospitals, and the remainder in other institutions. Of 3,380,818 episodes in 1968, 52.7 percent occurred in outpatient facilities (of which 8 percent were in CMHCs), 23.4 percent in state hospitals, and 23.9 percent in other institutions. To put it another way, 77.4 percent of episodes occurred in inpatient facilities in 1955 and 22.6 percent in outpatient settings; thirteen years later the respective figures were 47.3 percent and 52.7 percent. In sum, there was a definitive shift in the location of services as well as an increase in the *rate* of episodes. In 1955 there were 1,028 episodes per 100,000; by 1968 this figure had risen substantially to 1,713 (table 10.1).[38]

TABLE 10.1
Number, Percent Distribution, and Rate per 100,000 of Inpatient and Outpatient Care Episodes in U.S. Selected Mental Health Facilities, 1955, 1965, 1968, 1971

		Inpatient Service						Outpatient Service		
	Total All Facilities	All In-Patient Services	State and County Mental Hospitals	Private Mental Hospitals	General Hospital Units (Non-VA)	VA In-Patient Services	CMHCs[a]	All Out-Patient Services	CMHCs[a]	Other
		Number of Patient Care Episodes (in thousands)								
1955	1,675,352	1,296,352	818,832	123,231	265,934	88,355	—	379,000	—	379,000
1965	2,636,525	1,565,525	804,926	125,428	519,328	115,843	—	1,071,000	—	1,071,000
1968	3,380,818	1,602,238	791,819	118,126	558,790	133,503	—	1,778,590	271,590	1,507,000
1971	4,038,143	1,721,389	745,259	126,600	542,642	176,800	130,088	2,316,754	622,906	1,693,848
		Percent Distribution								
1955	100.0	77.4	48.9	7.3	15.9	5.3	—	22.6	—	22.6
1965	100.0	59.4	30.5	4.8	19.7	4.4	—	40.6	—	40.6
1968	100.0	47.3	23.4	3.5	16.5	3.9	—	52.7	8.0	44.7
1971	100.0	42.6	18.5	3.1	13.4	4.4	3.2	57.4	15.4	42.0
		Rate per 100,000 of Population								
1955	1,028	795	502	76	163	54	—	233	—	233
1965	1,376	817	420	65	271	60	—	559	—	559
1968	1,713	812	401	60	283	68	—	901	138	763
1971	1,977	843	365	62	266	87	64	1,134	305	829

[a] Federally assisted CMHCs only.

The change in the location of services, however, did not mean that public mental hospitals were on the road to extinction and that community outpatient centers and clinics were assuming their functions. On the contrary, outpatient facilities grew rapidly because they were used by new groups that in the past had had no access to the mental health system and who were for the most part not in the severely mentally ill category. Thus while the rate of inpatient care episodes at public hospitals declined from 502 to 401 per 100,000 between 1955 and 1968, outpatient care episodes leaped from 233 to 901. In absolute terms, inpatient care episodes at public institutions in the same period fell from 818,832 to 791,819, whereas outpatient care episodes increased from 379,000 to 1,778,590. These data demonstrate that the growth in outpatient services did not come at the expense of inpatient ones. Many of the changes in the mental health system, in other words, occurred because of the expansion of services and recruitment of a new clientele rather than the substitution of one service for another.

The dramatic growth of outpatient facilities diminished the relative significance of public mental hospitals, which for more than a century had been central to the mental health system. The number of resident patients fell slowly in the period from 1955 to 1965, and more rapidly thereafter. Yet at the same time the number of admissions was increasing. In 1955, 178,003 persons were admitted to state and county mental hospitals. A decade later the figure was 316,664. The rapid decline in the resident population after 1965 did not alter this pattern; in 1970 there were 384,511 admissions (table 10.2). These figures suggest that an important change in the function of state hospitals had taken place. During the first half of the twentieth century these institutions cared for large numbers of chronic cases drawn from several categories, including schizophrenic patients admitted during youth and early maturity, who remained for the rest of their lives, along with paretics and senile aged persons. By the late 1960s the number of aged and chronic patients began to fall, and mental hospitals then began to provide more short- and intermediate-term care and treatment for severely mentally ill persons.[39]

To be sure, the number of patient care episodes in general hospitals (with and without psychiatric units) and federally funded CMHCs increased, although there were sharp variations from place to place. The available (and imperfect) data, however, indicate that these facilities did not generally treat individuals previously admitted or likely to be admitted to mental hospitals. There were, for example, some striking differences in diagnostic categories. In 1969 state hospitals had a higher proportion of patients with schizophrenic reactions, a group that constituted the core of the severely mentally ill group. Nearly 30 percent of its admissions were in this category; 11 percent were in the organic brain syn-

TABLE 10.2
Resident Patients, Admissions, Net Releases, and Deaths in
U.S. State and County Mental Hospitals, 1950–1971

	Resident Patients at End of Year	Admissions	Net Releases[a]	Deaths
1950	512,501	152,286	99,659	41,280
1951	520,326	152,079	101,802	42,107
1952	531,981	162,908	107,647	44,303
1953	545,045	170,621	113,959	45,087
1954	553,979	171,682	118,775	42,652
1955	558,922	178,003	126,498	44,384
1956	551,390	185,597	145,313	48,236
1957	548,626	194,497	150,413	46,848
1958	545,182	209,823	161,884	51,383
1959	541,883	222,791	176,411	49,647
1960	535,540	234,791	192,818	49,748
1961	527,456	252,742	215,595	46,880
1962	515,640	269,854	230,158	49,563
1963	504,604	283,591	245,745	49,052
1964	490,449	299,561	268,616	44,824
1965	475,202	316,664	288,397	43,964
1966	452,089	328,564	310,370	42,753
1967	426,309	345,673	332,549	39,608
1968	399,152	367,461	354,996	39,677
1969	369,969	374,771	367,992	35,962
1970	337,619	384,511	386,937	30,804
1971	308,983	402,472	405,681	26,835

[a] Net Releases equals the resident patients at the beginning of the year, plus admissions, minus deaths and resident patients at end of year.

drome and 10.2 percent in the depressive categories. General hospital inpatient services treated different kinds of patients. More than a third of their admissions suffered from depressive disorders; schizophrenic reactions accounted for 17.2 percent and organic brain syndromes 6.5 percent.[40]

The differences between state mental and general hospitals with specialized units becomes even clearer from length-of-stay data. The mean and the median stay in general hospitals in 1963 were 20 and 17 days respectively. These figures fell slightly during the 1960s, the former to 17 in 1969 and the latter to 11 in 1971. By 1975 the mean stay was only 11 days and the median 6.7.[41]

The pattern in state mental hospitals differed substantially. Unfortunately, length-of-stay data were not reported before 1970. Other data, however, shed light on the functions of these institutions. Before 1965 public mental hospitals had a large chronic population. Data from twenty-three states in 1962 revealed that the median stay for patients resident at the end of the year was 8.4 years. The distribution was even more striking: 18.4 percent of patients were institutionalized for less than a year; 22 percent from 1 to 4; 14.6 percent from 5 to 9; 20.4 percent from 10 to 19; and 24.6 percent 20 years or more. Such data, however, tended to conceal the fact that release rates for newly admitted patients had been rising for several decades. In an important study of 15,472 patients admitted for the first time to Warren State Hospital in Pennsylvania during the period 1916–1950, Morton Kramer and his associates found a marked improvement in the release rates during the first year of hospitalization of the cohorts of 1936–1945 and 1946–1950, as compared with those of 1916–1925 and 1926–1935. A comparison of the earliest and latest cohorts indicated that the probability of being released within a year of admission increased from 42 to 62 percent. The probability of release in the first year for patients with functional psychosis in 1946–1950 was considerably greater than that in the three earlier periods. Subsequent studies revealed that the experiences of Warren State Hospital were by no means atypical.[42]

After 1965 the number of long-term patients at public institutions fell precipitously, largely because changes in funding patterns led to a sharp decline in elderly and chronic patients. This is not in any way to imply that state hospitals no longer provided long-term care. On the contrary, state hospitals remained what three investigators termed "the place of last resort" for perhaps 100,000 individuals for whom no alternative facility was available. Thus in 1969 the mean stay of discharged patients at public hospitals was 421 days; six years later the corresponding figure was 270 days. Median length-of-stay data, however, reveal a quite different situation. In 1970 the median length-of-stay for admissions (and excluding deaths) was 41 days; five years later this figure had dropped to 25 days. These data suggest that public institutions continued to treat and care for more severely and chronically ill persons than any other kind of institution. Indeed, in 1969 and 1975 they accounted for 79.4 and 67.2 percent, respectively, of all days of inpatient psychiatric care.[43]

Perhaps the most startling feature of the institutional scene was the weakness of coordination or cooperation between the various kinds of institutions responsible for providing care and treatment. Continuity of care remained the prevailing ideal; reality was quite different. The slow increase in the number of CMHCs and their often freestanding character virtually ensured that in many areas they would not be linked to state hospitals. A more important role might have been taken by general hospital psychiatric inpatient units, which by the mid-1960s accounted for nearly 20 percent of all inpatient care episodes. Yet these units were not for the most part geared toward meeting the long-term needs of chronically mentally ill persons. It is true that about 70 percent provided after-care programs for former patients. But the components of aftercare, as defined by general hospitals, had little to do with the basic and everyday needs of chronic and severely mentally ill persons. Of the 70 percent of general hospitals that had aftercare programs in 1963, 84 percent reported that the program included psychotherapy, 52 percent electroshock, 37 percent group psychotherapy, and 25 percent drug therapy. Surveys of general hospital psychiatric units in 1963 and 1972 revealed that links with mental hospitals or concerns with the varied needs of severely and chronically mentally ill patients were all but absent.[44]

Interestingly enough, small-scale aftercare experiments were by no means lacking. For more than a century, state and hospital officials had been aware of the problems of patients returning to the community. During the 1860s interest in decentralized mental hospitals—institutions that permitted a gradual movement from institution to community—and the hope of emulating a Gheel-like precedent[45] set off a prolonged debate among state officials and hospital superintendents. In the 1880s Massachusetts pioneered the boarding out of quiet and chronic mentally ill patients in private homes; in 1914, 2.4 percent of all mentally ill persons under its jurisdiction lived outside of hospitals. By 1943 eight states had followed the Massachusetts model. During the 1950s family care grew at a modest pace; in 1960 thirteen states and the VA had placed 9,610 patients with families. Despite its promising beginnings, family care remained a marginal activity. The difficulties in administration and supervision appeared so imposing that foster home care never became a significant component of the mental health system. Moreover, community resistance to the placement of patients posed additional impediments not easily overcome.[46]

Foster home care was not the only program designed for discharged patients. By the 1940s the New York State Department of Mental Hygiene was administering aftercare clinics under the auspices of its mental hospitals for patients convalescing at home and requiring additional assistance. In 1954 the department created four aftercare clinics in New York City to deal with the more than 7,000 patients on convalescent status. The same period witnessed the genesis of "halfway houses"—institutions designed to assist discharged patients in making the transition from hospital to community. Such institutions grew out of the concern with discharged patients evinced by such figures as Dr. Abraham Low, experiences with military convalescence hospitals during World War II, and the belief that the new psychotropic drugs would facilitate the release of hospitalized patients.[47]

Halfway houses did not have a shared set of characteristics. Some were organized under professional auspices; some had direct links with hospitals; and others were founded by lay volunteers. One of the most famous—Fountain House in New York City—evolved out of an informal organization of former Rockland State Hospital patients in the 1940s. In 1948 it acquired a clubhouse and acted as a support group. During the 1950s it expanded its scope by establishing a transitional employment program and acquiring residential apartments for members.[48]

By 1970 there were perhaps 170 or so halfway houses throughout the country with the capacity to serve nearly 3,000 individuals. Most of their clients fell into the schizophrenic category and had a history of prior hospitalization. The average length-of-stay was about four to six months. In a given year, therefore, halfway houses served between 6,000 and 9,000 individuals. Their facilities were used for a variety of functions: to smooth the absorption of discharged patients into the community; to provide more or less permanent placement for individuals who no longer required hospitalization, but who lacked the ability to live independently; to serve as an alternative to hospitalization; and to shorten the length of inpatient stays.[49]

Halfway houses—at least in their original form—never became a significant component within the mental health system. The system for financing mental health services made few provisions for such institutions. States supported hospitals and local clinics; federal funds were directed toward CMHCs; and third-party health insurance plans limited psychiatric coverage and excluded halfway houses. On the other hand, many halfway houses received funds from the federal/state rehabilitation program under which Washington reimbursed 80 percent of the costs of services provided by state Divisions of Vocational Rehabilitation. Another source of revenue—rents and fees—was limited, if only because many former patients were dependent on welfare, Social Security Disability Insurance (SSDI), and Vocational Rehabilitation maintenance stipends. But all of these funds at best provided only modest levels of support. Many houses, therefore, had to rely on private contributions. Consequently, their financial state was always precarious. More important, halfway houses never addressed the fundamental problem of how to provide long-term care for chronically and severely mentally ill persons in the community. "Many mental health professionals," observed Raymond Glasscote and his associates in their study of rehabilitation for the APA, "do not have much knowledge of, interest in, or commitment to the importance of rehabilitative and supporting resources that must be available on an intermediate or long-term basis to the seriously ill people that they seek to retain in the community."[50]

The relative weaknesses of aftercare for the severely (and especially chronically) mentally ill and the deficiencies in the mechanisms designed to ensure that services would be coordinated pointed up the sharp contradictions within the mental health system. In theory the increase in the number of CMHCs and general hospital psychiatric services should have been matched by a corresponding decline in the numbers and size of state mental hospitals. Actual practice, however, was quite different. CMHCs provided services to new categories of untreated patients seeking assistance for a variety of problems ranging from alcoholism and drug addiction to personal and marital difficulties. This is not to imply that CMHCs ignored the severely mentally ill. In 1970, 15.1 percent of all of its admissions were from the schizophrenic category. Five years later the percentage dropped to 10 percent but only because the rate of increase in the admission of individuals with other conditions exceeded the increase in the number of schizophrenics. Thus CMHCs played a role in providing services to some of the severely mentally ill but did not in any way supplant public hospitals.[51]

General hospital inpatient units also dealt with the severely mentally ill, but they did not resolve the issue of how to provide supportive care and services after discharge. The broadening of the boundaries of the mental health system, therefore, was accompanied by a diffusion of responsibility toward the severely and chronically mentally ill. To be sure, the increase in admissions at state mental hospitals implied that they would continue to be the primary provider of services for these persons. Yet the decline in length-of-stay meant that their role as a provider of care (as distinct from treatment) would weaken. Consequently, severely and chronically mentally ill persons were now scattered throughout the mental health system, but no single organization accepted longitudinal responsibility to provide for their basic needs. Hence for many individuals some of the basic changes in the mental health system during and after the 1960s only exacerbated their problems.[52]

. . .

The changing nature of the mental health system in the 1960s was in part shaped—as it had been in the past—by funding mechanisms. On the eve of World War II, responsibility for the severely and chronically mentally ill still lay with the states. The high costs associated with protracted hospitalization made it impossible for most families to assume the financial burden. Yet even the public sector presented a diverse picture. As late as 1959 twelve states required local counties to pay for part or all of the costs of hospitalizing residents, and most states demanded payments from families with some resources.[53] Only affluent families could afford the luxury of using private mental hospitals, which in 1940 accounted for 2.2 percent of the resident patient population.[54] Psychiatric clinics (largely for juveniles) were financed by a mix of fees, public funds, and private donations. Psychiatrists in private practice dealt with relatively well-to-do persons, since third-party health insurance rarely covered mental health services.

During the 1950s and 1960s the financing of the mental health system underwent far-reaching changes that ultimately transformed its basic configuration. In the private sector third-party health insurance coverage expanded rapidly after World War II. By 1970 about 80 percent of the population was covered to some extent for hospitalization; 77.7 percent for surgical services; 71.7 percent for in-hospital visits; and 45.1 percent for office and home visits. Nevertheless, insurance plans—particularly in the decade following 1945—did not treat all illnesses equally. Many Blue Cross as well as private insurance company plans severely circumscribed coverage for mental disorders, alcoholism, drug addiction, and self-inflicted injuries. Such exclusionary practices reflected a variety of factors: fears that the high incidence of psychiatric illnesses and long hospital stays would generate excessive pressure on costs; a belief that diagnostic categories were vague and that the line between oddity and illness was difficult to ascertain; and the absence of reliable actuarial data. "We are not going to use subscribers' money," a Blue Cross official informed an APA committee studying the problem in 1954, "to pay for rest cures, to buy sobering-up vacations for drunks, or to coddle a hypochondriac who wants nothing better than to be waited on in a hospital bed."[55]

The APA in the 1950s took an increasingly strong position against discriminatory insurance coverage. It feared that the absence of coverage would undermine psychiatric legitimacy at a time when the specialty was seeking to persuade the public that effective treatment in community settings could eventually lead to an end of protracted custodial care in out-of-date public mental hospitals. Moreover, the movement of psychiatrists into private practice and the growing importance of general hospital psychiatric units and outpatient clinics only exacerbated fears that fiscal constraints would abort efforts to transform the mental health system. By the latter half of the decade, a gradual diminution in exclusionary practices was evident. In 1955 only 39 of 79 Blue Cross plans offered 21 days of hospitalization for mentally ill persons; by 1960, 62 out of 85 plans offered 21-day coverage. Progress, however, was unequal; alcoholism and drug addiction were often excluded, and reimbursements to psychiatrists lagged behind those to other physicians.[56]

During the 1960s insurance coverage for mental illnesses gradually expanded, even though discrimination persisted. By 1971 all 74 Blue Cross plans in the United States offered some psychiatric benefits. Most limited coverage for mental illnesses to about 30 days (as compared with 125 days for general illnesses) but excluded public mental hospitals. Many employees were also covered for outpatient psychiatric benefits under group plans offered by private insurance companies. Oddly enough, during the 1950s benefits for outpatient psychiatric services were similar to those for other services. When total charges for outpatient psychiatric care became a substantial part of physicians' charges for care of all conditions, many companies began to reduce benefits, although the range of practices varied considerably.[57]

Because of the critical importance of insurance for inpatient care in general hospitals as well as for outpatient care, the APA was active in monitoring and attempting to influence developments. Its involvement grew out of two distinct but related concerns. First, community outpatient and inpatient treatment required appropriate fiscal supports. To exclude or to limit psychiatric coverage unfairly might in the intermediate or long run have a decidedly negative impact. Second, self-interest was not absent. Because psychiatrists saw fewer patients per week than other specialists, each patient tended to carry a heavier share of the cost. If insurance plans limited coverage, their potential clientele would be limited to affluent individuals. Hence both psychiatrists and potential patients had an interest in ensuring nondiscriminatory benefits. It is worth noting that the financial burdens of patients receiving treatment did not imply that psychiatry was the highest-paid specialty. In 1966, for example, psychiatry ranked fifth among ten fields of practice in terms of net income. Radiology ranked first ($38,560), followed by orthopedic surgery ($37,120), ophthalmology ($36,450), general surgery ($30,950), and psychiatry ($29,050); the bottom five included anesthesiology ($28,700), obstetrics/gynecology ($27,790), internal medicine ($24,380), pediatrics ($23,230), and general practice ($23,010).[58]

In the 1960s the APA's newly created Commission on Insurance issued an official set of guidelines in an effort to ensure that coverage for psychiatric services would achieve parity. It also sponsored a series of scholarly studies and engaged in broad lobbying efforts to ensure an end to discriminatory practices. When the United Automobile Workers negotiated a contract with the automobile companies that included restrictions, the APA, fearful that others might use this as a precedent to reduce psychiatric coverage, expressed its concerns. The Subcommittee on Prepaid Health Insurance called attention to the important role that mental health played "in the performance and productivity" of workers, and their report emphasized that "unions, management, and psychiatry have a common interest."[59] The slow liberalization of psychiatric benefits undoubtedly played a significant role in broadening the availability of services in the community and expanding the potential clientele. The benefits to the severely and chronically mentally ill, however, were somewhat more problematical. Health insurance plans were not designed to provide either care or supportive services. Moreover, the most severely impaired often lacked coverage, which was generally a function of regular employment.

Changes in federal funding also had a major impact on the mental health system. The CMHC act of 1963 and staffing amendments of 1965 were obvious examples of how the availability of funds could direct policy. Equally important was the passage of amendments to the Social Security Act of 1935. This landmark legislation, although best known for its old age assistance and insurance programs, included provisions dealing with health and welfare: aid for dependent children and the blind; grants to states for maternal and child welfare and public health; and provision for federal-state unemployment compensation. Incremental changes altered and broadened the act in subsequent years. The passage of amendments in 1956 creating SSDI provided benefits for people fifty years and older who were unable to hold a job because of their physical or mental condition. Four years later this age limitation was deleted. Nevertheless, federal regulations sometimes distinguished between more and less worthy handicapped persons; individuals who were handicapped because of mental illness were often the objects of discrimination.[60]

During the 1960s a series of far-reaching changes in the Social Security system had a dramatic, though inadvertent, impact on mental health policy. In 1960 an amendment to the old-age assistance and medical assistance for the aged program permitted payment for short-term treatment in public mental hospitals for up to forty-two days. Two years later, HEW revised its regulations to permit welfare payments to conditionally discharged psychiatric patients, a move designed to facilitate their return to the community (previously individuals carried on the books of mental hospitals had been ineligible to receive federal welfare payments). The most important change came in 1965 when Congress, with presidential encouragement, enacted a series of amendments to the Social Security Act. Two programs in particular—Medicare and Medicaid—were designed to provide medical care for the aged and the poor. Title 18, Part A (Medicare) dealt with hospital insurance for the aged; Part B dealt with insurance for physicians' services. Title 19 (Medicaid) involved grants to states for medical assistance programs for indigent persons. The most surprising feature of these amendments was the inclusion of psychiatric benefits.[61]

The changes in the Social Security system and the inclusion of psychiatric benefits were extraordinarily complex. In the proceedings that led to the passage of the bill, there was an effort to incorporate a clause that would have excluded hospitals and nursing homes caring for the mentally ill. A vigorous campaign by the APA and the biomedical lobby within Congress was successful in deleting this clause. Title 18, nevertheless, stipulated a lifetime limit of 190 days for inpatient services in psychiatric hospitals; no such limitation was placed on the treatment of psychiatric illnesses in general hospitals. The underlying premise was that general hospitals provided active treatment, whereas mental hospitals more likely offered custodial care. Moreover, less favorable treatment was accorded patients already in state mental hospitals, and fees for physicians for outpatient psychiatric treatment were also limited. Title 19 removed the long-standing denial of federal assistance to patients of sixty-five and over in mental hospitals, although matching funds had to be used to improve treatment. It permitted as well the use of federal funds for the treatment of indigent persons of all ages in general hospitals. To qualify for matching funds, states had to develop an individualized plan for each eligible aged person in a mental hospital as well as suitable alternatives to hospital care. Title 19 specifically excluded financial support for mental hospital patients under the age of sixty-five.[62]

The consequences for mental health policy that followed the enactment of Titles 18 and 19 were both profound and paradoxical. Medicaid in particular became an important source of funding for the care of elderly patients in mental hospitals. In fiscal year 1969 Medicaid paid $161 million out of a total of $307 million for the care of persons age sixty-five and over in state mental hospitals in thirty participating states. New York was by far the largest beneficiary, receiving $61 million. California, with almost the same population, received only $9.3 million. This and other variations were a function of differing policy decisions by individual states. Since the 1940s California's administrative policy had discouraged admissions of aged persons to mental hospitals, and in 1963 the state established a Geriatric Screening Program to reduce commitments of such persons and find suitable alternatives. New York, on the other hand, had what amounted to an open-door policy for mentally ill persons of any age.[63] Thus federal funds slowly became an increasingly significant element in financing the state mental hospital system.

More important, there was a dramatic shift after 1965 in mental hospital populations.[64] In 1962, for example, 153,309 (29.7 percent) of 504,604 resident patients were sixty-five or older; in 1969 the comparable figures were 111,420 (30.1 percent) and 369,969. By 1972 the number of such patients had fallen to 78,479 (28.6 percent) out of a total of 274,837. This is not to suggest that aged persons were no longer institutionalized, for such was not the case. The decline in the number of aged patients in state hospitals was accompanied by a sharp increase in the number of aged mentally ill individuals in nursing homes. In 1963 nursing homes cared for 221,721 individuals with mental disorders, of whom 187,675 were sixty-five or older. Six years later the comparable figures

TABLE 10.3

Number and Rate per 100,000 of First Admissions to U.S. State and County Mental Hospitals, 1962, 1965, 1969, and 1972

	Number of First Admissions				Rate per 100,000			
	1962	1965	1969	1972	1962	1965	1969	1972
Under 15	3,460	4,510	6,553	7,661	6.0	7.5	11.0	13.5
15–24	19,473	25,878	37,507	35,111	76.9	88.6	114.4	95.1
25–34	22,761	25,625	26,614	27,767	105.1	118.5	111.4	103.8
35–44	23,146	25,669	30,779	24,069	96.0	106.6	134.3	107.2
45–54	19,243	21,205	24,676	19,618	91.2	96.6	106.8	83.3
55–64	13,280	14,597	18,264	12,097	82.4	86.1	100.3	63.3
65 +	28,335	26,606	19,591	14,490	163.7	146.5	100.6	69.2
Total	129,698	144,090	163,984	140,813	70.6	75.1	82.1	68.2

were 426,712 and 367,586. What had occurred in effect was a lateral shift. Aged (as well as younger) persons diagnosed as mentally disordered were now sent to nursing homes rather than state hospitals. In large measure this shift followed the passage of Titles 18 and 19. By limiting the use of Medicaid and Medicare funds for aged patients in state hospitals, the legislation tacitly encouraged states to send such individuals to nursing homes because of more generous federal payments. By 1977, 14 percent of the total Medicaid funds spent on mental health supported elderly patients in state hospitals, and 53 percent elderly and nonelderly individuals in nursing homes. Although other elements played a role in the decrease in long-term aged patients in state hospitals, federal funding of nursing home care was of crucial importance.[65]

The percentage of individuals aged sixty-five and over in public mental hospitals, to be sure, changed but little over these years. Nevertheless, the decline in first admissions of such persons was far more rapid than for any other age group. Indeed, first admissions for younger people actually showed an increase (table 10.3).[66] What was clearly beginning to happen was that the length-of-stay, which had begun to drop much earlier, dropped even more rapidly as the proportion of aged admissions fell. Public mental hospitals, in effect, were admitting more individuals and releasing them more quickly.

The reduction in the admission of elderly long-term patients in state and county mental hospitals undoubtedly improved the quality of acute care and treatment. Between 1960 and 1970 average per capita expenditure for maintenance rose from $1,679 to $5,435, an increase of 224 percent. Even when adjusted for inflation, the average per capita expenditure rose 147 percent. States, of course, did not necessarily increase their appropriations by this amount; the decline in the inpatient resident population meant that more resources were available for the remaining patients. That conditions in many public hospitals improved during and after the mid-1960s is indisputable. The improvement in the internal institutional atmosphere fostered a more hopeful outlook. A variety of factors obviously played a role: a greater emphasis on therapy (somatic and psychological); recognition of the negative consequences of long-term hospitalization; enhanced efforts to prevent chronicity and reduce lengths of stay; and improved staff-patient ratios. Whatever the reasons, there is little doubt that mental hospitals had changed dramatically by the 1970s. Admittedly, diversity, not unity, was the rule rather than the exception; in some states the quality of mental hospitals left much to be desired. Yet in the aggregate, conditions improved markedly. Between 1970 and 1982 the average number of patients per employee fell from 1.7 to 0.7, as compared with 6.8 in 1945, 3.83 in 1955 and 2.42 in 1965. By 1980 the median stay in public institutions was 23 days, although sharp differences for specific diagnoses existed (for alcohol- and drug-related conditions the median stay was 12 days, for organic disorders 71, for affective disorders 22, and for schizophrenia 42). That public hospitals remained a place of last resort for certain chronic and severely mentally ill patients is evident from that fact that the mean length-of-stay in 1980 was 165 days.[67]

. . .

For the seriously mentally ill the decade of the 1960s represented a watershed. In the preceding century, mental health policy had rested on the presumption that the care and treatment of the mentally ill should take place in public hospitals financed and administered by the states. During the 1960s this consensus gradually dissolved. New community-oriented and socially activist ideologies, novel federal medical and welfare policies, and the rise of prepaid health insurance slowly but surely combined to diminish the centrality of public mental hospitals and to expand alternative services. In a decade noted for social and economic innovation, the pace of change in mental health policy was striking.

Nevertheless, the expectation that the creation of community-oriented policies would lead to the decline and perhaps eventual demise of public mental hospitals proved premature. To be sure, the growing importance of general hospital inpatient units, CMHCs, and chronic care nursing homes diminished the relative significance of public mental hospitals within the mental health system. Yet these new institutions (with the exception of chronic care nursing homes) often catered to new categories of previously untreated groups. Innovative policies and institutions, therefore, did not necessarily serve all mentally ill persons, many of whom remained dependent upon services provided at public mental hospitals.

The consequences of the innovations that transformed the mental health system, like those of all human activities, were at best mixed. The expansion of the range of mental health services undoubtedly met the needs of many persons seeking assistance in dealing with their personal problems. Similarly, the decline in the number of long-term aged patients enabled mental hospitals once again to focus on therapeutic services for the severely mentally ill. Indeed, the creation of alternatives to long-term institutionalization, a recognition that chronicity was not inevitable, and therapies that held out the hope of more effective functioning enhanced the possibility that seriously mentally ill persons could be treated in the community and subsequently lead a more or less normal existence.

The chasm between possibilities and reality, however, remained wide. When the emphasis on treatment in the community was combined with an expansion of services to new groups, the result was a policy that often overlooked the need to provide supportive services for the seriously and chronically mentally ill. In this sense, mental health activists all but ignored what their nineteenth-century predecessors had perhaps instinctively grasped, namely, that care and treatment, although conceptually separate, were not mutually exclusive. Under certain conditions, for example, care was a form of treatment.

A policy that emphasized therapy, while leaving care unassigned, appealed to both the public and mental health professionals. Americans generally have had a favorable perception of those medical therapies that are linked with the objective findings of medical science. Their view of care (often equated with welfare) has been more ambivalent and has reflected the pervasive belief that dependency is in part a function of character deficiencies, which in turn result in social and economic failure. It was not surprising, therefore, that mental health professionals identified themselves with medicine rather than welfare. Moreover, professional services required relatively simple organizational structures. Welfare services (excluding the distribution of money), by way of contrast, depended on extraordinarily complex administrative systems, few of which came close to approximating the goals of their designers.

Thus one of the driving forces of these years—antipathy toward traditional mental hospitals and a faith in community-oriented policies and institutions—gave rise to a bifurcated system with weak institutional linkages or mechanisms to ensure continuity and coordination of services. Severely and chronically mentally ill persons were often released from public hospitals after relatively brief stays into communities without adequate support mechanisms. The implications of the absence of longitudinal responsibility for meeting some of their basic needs in the community—including housing, medical care, welfare, and social support services—would become painfully evident during the 1980s when the contraction of public welfare and housing programs exacerbated an already difficult situation.

CHAPTER ELEVEN

Challenges to Psychiatric Legitimacy

BY THE EARLY 1960s psychiatric activists seemed on the verge of achieving their long-sought goals. A combination of federal action and third-party insurance had seemingly created a series of alternatives to mental hospital care and treatment. New therapies—psychological, psychosocial, biological—offered hope to those who had traditionally languished in the back wards of public hospitals. "We are now in a period of hopeful change," observed Harry C. Solomon in his APA presidential address in 1958 in which he described the present and future trends that were transforming the very structure of the specialty. "An atmosphere of greater optimism about the outcome of psychoses" enhanced the prospect for reducing the number of chronic patients and virtually eliminating an "antiquated, outmoded, and . . . obsolete" mental hospital system.[1]

Indeed, in the postwar era the prestige of psychiatry reached unprecedented heights. Both the number and the proportion of medical school graduates entering the specialty increased rapidly. At the same time the public's affinity for psychological explanations and professional assistance enhanced the role and authority of practitioners. "Present-day society in the United States has accepted psychiatry as a catalytic force in the culture," wrote Howard P. Rome of the Mayo Clinic and APA president in 1965. "This means that not only has the language of psychiatry acquired a portmanteau character as witnessed by the extended meaning given technical words as they are used in everyday conversation, but also its theories of behavior and practices have led to many attitudinal derivatives which extend its influence beyond the limited boundaries of diagnostic and therapeutic medicine." One indication of the specialty's status was the manner in which its members were depicted in motion pictures, a medium that often reflected prevailing cultural norms and attitudes. Between 1957 and 1963 Hollywood produced at least twenty-two films that presented psychiatrists—the purveyors of reason, knowledge, and well-being—in glowing and idealized terms.[2]

Yet at precisely the time that the social legitimacy of the specialty peaked, a series of disquieting elements were already eroding its very foundation. The challenges to its authority came from a variety of sources. Within the specialty the hegemony of psychodynamic and psychoanalytic psychiatrists came under attack from more biologically oriented colleagues. To internal controversies were added sharp criticisms of both the theory and practice of psychiatry by individuals and groups from without.

Equally significant, psychiatry was unable to distance itself from the strains and fissures characteristic of the larger society. The willingness of members to assert personal opinions and offer prescriptions for social change that were presumably justified by their training and expertise tended to merge the voices of professional competency on the one hand and citizenship on the other. Expansion of the professional sphere beyond traditional boundaries, however, only heightened the specialty's vulnerability. Moreover, its increasingly close relationships with the social and behavioral sciences proved a mixed blessing; academic research and clinical practice were not always compatible. Finally, the growing challenges to previously accepted authority and orthodoxies of all sorts during and after the 1960s, combined with an active civil rights movement that focused part of its concerns on the institutionalized mentally ill, posed new problems.

Internal disunity and external hostility combined to diminish the elevated status and popularity enjoyed by psychiatry in the postwar decades. More important, the virtual abandonment of the older commitment to mental hospitals and severely and chronically mentally ill persons—a commitment that had given members their raison d'être for more than a century—removed crucial elements that had both defined psychiatry's unique character and enhanced its social legitimacy. In an era in which services were fragmented, boundaries vague, policy diffuse, and public welfare under attack, the absence of a unifying focus and the weakening of an obligation to assume responsibility for care as well as treatment—a distinctive characteristic of the biological approach—blurred demarcations between psychiatry and other medical specialties. For some severely and particularly chronically mentally ill persons in need of medical and support services, however, such changes were not necessarily to their advantage.

. . .

American psychiatry in the postwar decades was led by individuals whose outlook had been shaped by psychodynamic and psychoanalytic concepts and training as well as a commitment to a public health approach. In their view the etiology of mental disorders was perhaps best explained in terms of individual psychology and interpersonal relationships. Psychotherapy, in one form or another, was the favored treatment. These very same individuals also tended to be politically liberal. The sources of their liberalism were varied. An environmental ideology and close ties with equally liberal social and behavioral scientists were important. The decline of anti-Semitism after 1945, moreover, led to an increase in Jewish medical graduates, of whom a significant number selected psychiatry as their specialty. These individuals brought with them the political progressivism characteristic of the American Jewish community. The specialty's liberal cast was further strengthened by members committed to a public health approach. From the 1940s through the 1960s the commitment to social and environmental reforms never wavered; psychodynamic and psychoanalytic psychiatry (but not necessarily orthodox psychoanalysis) was entirely compatible with liberal and activist politics.

Nowhere was the specialty's political liberalism better revealed than in the activities of GAP. Before 1950 its members were preoccupied with an effort to reshape and revitalize the APA. In the succeeding two decades, on the other hand, the organization's focus shifted, and its members staked out positions on racism, desegregation, international relations, homosexuality, industrial relations, and urban poverty. That a conflict might exist between a psychodynamic psychiatry that emphasized individual psychology and a broad social etiology was rarely confronted. Just as tuberculosis required an understanding of both the bacillus and the environmental conditions under which it thrived, so too mental disorders had to be studied within an individual and a social framework. Despite its broad social agenda, GAP remained within the mainstream of American psychiatry. Of the seven individuals who served as president between 1946 and 1965, five (Menninger, Ewalt, Barton, Brosin, and Bartemeier) were also elected to the presidency of the APA.

Social action, insisted GAP's Committee on Social Issues in 1950, "implies a conscious and deliberate wish to foster those social developments which could promote mental health on a community-wide scale." Psychiatric principles, therefore, had relevancy for "all those problems which have to do with family welfare, child rearing, child and adult education, social and economic factors which influence the community status of individuals and families, inter-group tensions, civil rights and personal liberty." Recent psychiatric theory "with its emphasis on ego psychology," observed Leonard J. Duhl more than a decade later at a GAP discussion of the planning of mental health services in urban America, "has increased our knowledge of the relationship between the individual and the significant environment around him. Thus, the concerns of the psychiatrist have increasingly placed the ill in a broader social context both in understanding etiology and in attempting treatment." In considering the future role of GAP, Herbert C. Modlin emphasized three distinct psychiatric contributions to psychosocial problems: a knowledge of individual psychology; an understanding of family dynamics; and knowledge of the irrational. The last, he added, "is perhaps the most important: I cannot think of any other organized discipline which can claim equal expertise."[3]

In favoring a socially active psychiatry, GAP members recognized that there was an important distinction between their professional competence and general citizenship. Personal preferences, insisted one of the organization's committees, had to be disassociated from professional judgments. That psychiatrists had the same rights as other citizens to express their views was self-evident. Nevertheless, the results of a questionnaire circulated among members focusing on three important issues of the late 1960s—fair housing, guaranteed annual wage, and the war in Vietnam—suggested "role uncertainty" among many respondents. Moreover, the opinions of professionals were invariably "accorded more weight" than nonprofessional opinions. Hence there existed a pressing need to clarify the nature and limits of professional competency.[4]

Intellectual awareness that an impression of professional omniscience or omnipotence posed risks, however, did not deter psychiatrists from the all-too-human proclivity of expressing judgments on a broad range of contemporary issues. During the decade of the 1960s psychiatric social activism was by no means limited to small organizations like GAP. On the contrary, the NIMH and even the larger and more diverse APA became deeply involved in issues whose relationships to mental illnesses were tenuous or problematic. Under Yolles's leadership the NIMH defined a multifaceted role for the new federally funded CMHCs that implied approval of efforts to upgrade the social and physical environment. Yolles decried "the professional isolation in the ivory tower of the private practice of yesterday." He was equally enthusiastic toward younger persons entering the specialty for their involvement in "social action" and their desire to use their expertise "to effect changes to improve the communities in which they live and work."[5]

Nor were the experiences of the APA different from those of other professional organizations whose members were unable to maintain neutrality on domestic and foreign problems that threatened to divide American society along class, racial, age, and gender lines. At its annual meetings the association sponsored sessions that dealt with psychiatry and a variety of social problems. Its Committee on Research organized a conference specifically on contemporary social issues and published its deliberations. Toward the end of the decade the APA issued a series of position papers dealing with homosexuality, drugs, abortion, violence, and health policy. The adoption of a new constitution in 1969 provided an even more potent mechanism for greater social activism.[6]

To be sure, there were striking differences among association members. Walter E. Barton (president in 1961–1962, and subsequently medical director) believed that the APA should focus on the needs of the mentally ill, especially those who were elderly. Others insisted that linkages between socioenvironmental conditions and mental health mandated social and political activism on ethical as well as scientific grounds. In his widely-read work on preventive psychiatry, Gerald Caplan implicitly insisted on an avowedly political role. Seymour L. Halleck of the University of Wisconsin's Department of Psychiatry went even further when he argued that the search for political neutrality was "illusory"; all psychiatric roles had some implications for the status quo. The stresses caused by poverty and discrimination, for example, imposed suffering upon individuals. "Where it is clear that the patient's suffering is to a considerable degree being imposed upon him by others," he observed,

> the psychiatrist has some obligation to consider the means by which he might alter the environment which is hurting the patient. . . .
>
> As long as mental illness is even partially related to social processes the physician must involve himself in preserving or changing the status quo. To deny the issue, or to cloak it under medical cliches merely compounds the problem. Psychiatry needs to conceptualize the means by which medical values can be integrated into a political system.[7]

Halleck's position was not atypical. Psychiatry, wrote Gerald L. Klerman of Yale, faced both dangers and opportunities. American society had become polarized in the confrontations between black and white, inner city and suburb, and the poor and the prosperous. Traditionally rational and liberal, the mental health professions found themselves under attack from both extreme wings of the political spectrum. The challenge, he concluded, was to change rapidly enough to meet the needs of hitherto ignored groups and yet retain "professional values and integrity." Robert L. Coles of Harvard turned his entire attention to some of the major social ills of this era: the uneasy relations between psychiatry and the poor, the adjustment of black and white children to school desegregation, the impact of poverty on children, and migrant workers. "A dirty, ugly environment," he wrote in *Wages of Neglect* in 1969,

> reinforces the ghetto child's sense of worthlessness, which he has already acquired through his parent's overly desperate moralism and plaintively rigid lecturing.
>
> Thus the once rural, now urbanized and rapidly disintegrating family combines with an ugly, unsafe environment to prepare the child of poverty for a life without hope and without self-esteem, a life which he may well help to perpetuate, alas, a "world without end"—unless, that is, we all care enough to make all sorts of changes in our society.[8]

In adopting a more activist stance, the APA by no means ignored more traditional issues. It sponsored a study of long-term care of mental patients and issued a not unfriendly position statement in response to the decision by the U. S. Court of Appeals for the District of Columbia that an individual found not guilty by reason of insanity, but institutionalized, had a right to treatment. Nevertheless, the long-standing strains between state hospital psychiatrists and their brethren in noninstitutional settings persisted, albeit in muted form. In testimony before a Senate subcommittee, a state hospital psychiatrist was critical of the APA for ignoring the needs of institutionalized patients. Similarly Lawrence S. Kubie—who had moved into hospital psychiatry after his retirement from office practice—found his new experience unusually rewarding. Although not hostile toward social and community psychiatry or political activism, he was concerned nevertheless at the undesirable consequences that followed "the retreat from patients."[9]

Psychiatric activism, of course, had provocative and potentially divisive consequences. In extreme forms it could imperil the very legitimacy of the specialty. The most embarrassing incident occurred during the presidential election of 1964. In the early autumn *Fact Magazine* polled more than 12,000 psychiatrists about the psychological fitness of Senator Barry Goldwater. Slightly more than 2,400 responded: 1,189 thought the Republican candidate unfit for the presidency; 657 pronounced him fit; and 571 believed that they lacked sufficient information to render a judgment. A humiliating controversy followed, for those who had replied had confused political preference with psychiatric diagnosis. APA officials even debated the possibility of disciplining the respondents.[10]

That social activism, however laudable its goals, posed risks was well understood. Like virtually all other professional groups during these years, psychiatrists were of two minds. On the one hand they were aware of the consequences of poverty, substandard housing, unemployment, malnutrition, prejudice, discrimination, and inadequate schooling; all were destructive to emotional well-being much as air and water pollution were to physical well-being. On the other hand, they recognized the distinction between their role as professionals and that as citizens. To conflate the two could either damage professional authority or could imperil democratic and representative government. The resolution of this dilemma was by no means obvious, and disunity was common. Differences of opinion were generally not substantive but focused rather on the location of the parameters that defined professional competency. In the charged atmosphere of the late 1960s and early 1970s, the debate became impassioned; that few of the figures who argued over the political stance of their specialty provided any compelling empirical data merely gave them extraordinarily wide latitude. Indeed, Joseph Wortis, a prominent psychiatrist identified with a biological rather than a psychoanalytic orientation since the 1930s, felt impelled to warn his colleagues about the danger of rationalizing social action in professional terms. The record of psychiatric social pronouncements was mixed, he noted.

Jung defended the Nazis, Reich regarded the plough as a phallic symbol and tried to found a new science of sexoeconomics, Freud ascribed war to aggressive instincts and took sides with the Germans in World War I; psychiatry has been invoked to support individualism and collectivism, progress and reaction, and to smear or incarcerate political opponents. In a democracy, the general population should be the final judge and main instigator of social action. Psychiatrists can make an important contribution by directing attention to the basic social factors that can cause or aggravate mental disorder, and by treating their patients in accordance with these insights, but it is presumptuous for psychiatrists to base their claims for leadership in the broader arena of social action on their technical credentials.[11]

. . .

The debate about the propriety of social activism during the 1960s assumed that the status of psychiatry, like that of medical science in general, was secure. Yet during these very same years the foundations on which its claims to legitimacy and authority rested were slowly being eroded. Some of the dissent came from psychiatrists who did not share the dominant liberal ideology. Most, however, came from diverse external sources, including social and behavioral scientists, civil rights activists, and individuals and groups. Representing all shades of the political spectrum, these critics were united in their belief that there were fundamental flaws in the mental health system. Their critique ultimately contributed to the breakdown of the consensus around the psychodynamic model that had dominated the specialty since the 1940s.

The criticisms of American psychiatry during the 1960s were neither unprecedented nor novel. From its very inception in the early nineteenth century, the young specialty faced challenges from those who believed that its members had not lived up to their stated ideals. Many of these criticisms of institutional psychiatry, as a matter of fact, echoed the dissatisfactions of psychiatrists themselves with the system over which they presided. Searching though they were, these critiques rarely questioned the raison d'être of the specialty or the legitimacy of institutional care. Their focus was rather on the unsatisfactory implementation of a basically acceptable policy.

Psychiatrists in the postwar decades were often attacked for their allegedly atheistic or communist leanings. In 1947 Monsignor Fulton J. Sheen, the prominent Catholic publicist, described psychiatry as "irreligious." Four well-known Catholic psychiatrists (Edward A. Strecker, Leo Bartemeier, Frank J. Curran, and Francis J. Gerty—all GAP members) issued a vigorous rebuttal. Two years later *Sign* (a Catholic periodical) published an article by John O'Connor charging that the specialty was dominated by a Freudian group led by the Menninger brothers. The members of this cabal, he wrote, "have the backing of people of affluence and influence . . . [and] are the shock troops of Sigmund Freud, atheist and anti-Christian, in their ordered attack upon the mind and soul of man." Dr. D. Bernard Foster, a practicing Catholic and neurologist on the staff at the Menninger Foundation, sent a lengthy protest to members of the church hierarchy.[12]

During the 1950s and 1960s the specialty was also the object of bitter attacks from the extreme anticommunist right. When Congress began to consider legislation to establish some mental hospital facilities in Alaska in 1955 (then a territory without a single mental hospital), a group of Californians mounted a campaign to ensure its defeat. They charged that the proposed bill was intended to brand anticommunists as mental cases and exile them to an American Siberia. They claimed the bill was being pushed by a Zionist conspiracy bent on spreading communism throughout the world. Other right-wing groups and publications quickly took up these themes, which were repeated continuously in the late 1950s and 1960s by such organizations as the John Birch Society, the D.A.R., and Gerald L. K. Smith's Christian Nationalist Crusade. Although receiving widespread publicity and generating considerable anger and anxiety among psychiatrists and other mental health professionals, such attacks had little, if any, impact upon either public policy or the mental health professions.[13]

Of far greater significance was the appearance of a critical literature that attacked the very basis of psychiatric legitimacy and authority.[14] The best-known internal critic of psychiatry was Thomas S. Szasz. After migrating from Hungary in 1938, he attended the University of Cincinnati and was awarded his M.D. by that institution in 1944. Subsequently he received psychoanalytic training at the Chicago Institute for Psychoanalysis. He eventually became a professor of psychiatry at the State University of New York's Upstate Medical Center in Syracuse while simultaneously maintaining a part-time private practice in psychiatry and psychoanalysis.

A prolific, articulate author and popular speaker, Szasz initially presented his unorthodox views in professional journals. During and after the 1960s, however, he published a series of provocative and popular books that quickly made him the enfant terrible of psychiatry. Although part of what quickly became known as the antipsychiatry movement, Szasz actually represented an idiosyncratic strain during an era in which liberal and radical activism was characteristic. In many respects he was an intellectual heir of the nineteenth-century liberalism that began with the proposition that individual liberty was the highest good. Conversely, any government activity that infringed upon the liberty of the individual—no matter how nobly motivated—only had detrimental consequences. Szasz's hostility toward social programs to benefit disadvantaged groups did not necessarily indicate a probusiness stance but rather embodied a deeply held faith in the virtues of voluntarism rather than compulsion. His commitment to a puristic libertarian ideology, however, made him popular with conservative and right-wing groups.

Szasz focused on several distinct but interrelated themes including the "myth of mental illness" and the role of psychiatry in suppressing nonconformity. In his eyes there were fundamental differences between the concepts of mental and nonmental (i.e., organic) illnesses. Defined in conventional medical terminology, mental illness was a form of social labeling that had dramatic and drastic consequences for individuals. Indeed, psychiatry was little more than a pseudoscience. Its nosology lacked reliability and validity, and embodied a set of value judgments that imposed a particular view of bourgeois reality (with all of its vested interests) upon a minority. Commitment laws, ostensibly intended to promote the welfare of patients, actually enhanced what Szasz called the "Therapeutic State." Psychiatry, therefore, was merely an instrument of social control. As such, it constituted a threat to individual liberty in a free society precisely because of its rejection of such values as personal autonomy, volition, liberty, and responsibility. By the close of the decade Szasz's attack on the specialty had grown even more vituperative. "To maintain that a social institution suffers from certain 'abuses,'" he wrote in what purported to be a historical work, "is to imply that it has certain other desirable or good uses. This, in my opinion, has been the fatal weakness of the countless exposés—old and recent, literary and professional—of private and public mental hospitals. My thesis is quite different: Simply put, it is that there are, and can be, no abuses *of* Institutional Psychiatry, because Institutional Psychiatry *is*, itself, an abuse."[15]

This attack on psychiatry from the libertarian right was accompanied by one led by a small group of younger psychiatrists influenced by or affiliated with the New Left. Employing an avowedly political analysis and confrontational tactics, they demanded nothing less than a series of far-reaching and fundamental changes in individual and social relations. Radical psychiatry—the name they adopted—meant different things to different people. To some it meant an emphasis on individual freedom and antiauthoritarianism that placed patients and therapists on an equal plane; to some it involved a savage critique of capitalist society as a whole and its dehumanizing technology. To most, however, it involved an almost complete abandonment of the medical model of mental illnesses. Although the number of radical psychiatrists was always small, their clarion calls for basic social change conferred upon them a visibility out of all proportion to their size or influence. They were to become a significant element in the antipsychiatry movement.[16]

The emergence of a psychiatric counterculture in the 1960s was not an isolated or even indigenous movement. On the contrary, it crossed national boundaries and defied clear ideological categorization. If Szasz attacked orthodox psychiatry because of his commitment to principles derived from nineteenth-century liberalism, figures such as R. D. Laing in England developed an equally powerful critique more compatible with the social activism and political radicalism of that decade. Laing and his associates were initially concerned with making intelligible the thought and feelings of schizophrenics, and subsequently on understanding their behavior within the context of disturbed interpersonal relationships in the family. Laing agreed with Szasz and others that concepts of sanity and insanity often reflected moral rather than medical or scientific judgments. Indeed, to Laing the difference between sanity and insanity was merely a question of adaptation to social and cultural norms; those who refused to adapt were consequently labeled insane.

More important, Laing insisted that the concept of sanity was based on a statistical statement of normality. Those who defined insanity in such terms failed to question or to criticize dominant cultural values and therefore accepted an unsatisfactory status quo. "There is no such 'condition' as 'schizophrenia,'" he wrote in 1967, "but the label is a social fact and the social fact a *political event*." In a vivid analogy he described a formation of planes observed from the ground. One plane could be out of formation and hence perceived as "abnormal, bad or 'mad' from the point of view of the formation." There was a distinct possibility, on the other hand, that the formation was "bad or mad," and that the errant plane was actually on a truer course than all the others. By insisting that madness might be a rational response to an irrational world, Laing and his colleagues aligned themselves with a radical politics and thus became part of the antipsychiatry movement. "Perhaps," Laing wrote in a romantic vein,

> we will learn to accord to so-called schizophrenics who have come back to us, perhaps after years, no less respect than the often no less lost explorers of the Renaissance. If the human race survives, future men will, I suspect, look back on our enlightened epoch as a veritable age of Darkness. . . . The laugh's on us. They will see that what we call 'schizophrenia' was one of the forms in which, often through quite ordinary people, the light began to break through the cracks in our all-too-closed minds.[17]

Equally, if not more, significant were external challenges to psychiatric legitimacy. The most prominent and influential came from the social and behavioral sciences. In the postwar era the prestige of these disciplines reached unprecedented heights. Its members exploited (and were exploited by) popular media eager to translate scholarly research for the general public. The process of popularization was hastened by the implicit (and sometimes explicit) claim that the social and behavioral sciences could not merely explain but could predict human behavior as well. If this were true, it followed that scholarship had to inform and guide policy and politics.[18]

Before 1940 a few psychiatrists—notably Harry Stack Sullivan—had emphasized the affinity between psychiatry and the social and behavioral sciences. The blossoming of this relationship, however, occurred in the postwar decades. The psychodynamic emphasis on the relationship among personality, culture, and environment created a milieu in which interdisciplinary themes were characteristic. The absorption of a social science perspective into psychiatric education was but one indication of the significance that both groups attached to interdisciplinary approaches.[19]

Despite their intellectual affinity, the possibility of conflict between psychiatry and the social sciences was always present. During the 1960s a number of social and behavioral scientists raised fundamental questions about the nature of psychiatry. Among the earliest and most famous social science works whose insights were incorporated into the antipsychiatry movement, as well as into the counterculture of the 1960s and 1970s, was Erving Goffman's *Asylums*. After receiving a Ph.D. in sociology from the University of Chicago in 1953, Goffman was a visiting member of the Laboratory of Socio-environmental Studies at the NIMH. During his stay he undertook some fieldwork at St. Elizabeths Hospital in Washington, D.C., the famous federal institution with more than seven thousand patients. Goffman published some of the results of his research as early as 1957. Issued in paperback form in 1961, *Asylums* presented the views of a scholar with an acute sense of observation and an ability to generalize in unique and provocative ways. By conventional academic standards the book was idiosyncratic; it embodied the results of personal observations rather than quantitative analysis.

An independent, if not eccentric, scholar with a firm belief in the overriding importance of personal autonomy, Goffman was concerned with the impact of institutions such as mental hospitals upon the personality and behavior of patients. He began by identifying a "total institution"— "a place of residence and work where a large number of like-situated individuals, cut off from the wider society for an appreciable period of time, together lead an enclosed, formally administered round of life." Goffman's concept of the total institution was not his invention. Bruno Bettelheim's study of Nazi concentration camps (published in 1943) had already emphasized the ways in which extreme situations could shape and mold the collective behavior of inmates, a theme that resonated through some of the sociological and historical literature of the 1950s. Goffman's own portrait was devastating; he described the ways in which a humiliating institutionalization stripped individuals of their self-identity and esteem and induced deviant responses. Expressions of hostility toward hospitals by patients were regarded as evidence that their commitment was proper and that they had not sufficiently recovered to be released. Mental hospitals, Goffman insisted, were staffed and administered in order to affirm the legitimacy of a medical service model. The result created a paradox. "To get out of the hospital, or to ease their life within it, they [patients] must show acceptance of the place accorded them, and the place accorded them is to support the occupational role of those who appear to force this bargain."[20]

Asylums was the product of a gifted and perceptive observer. Its literary and intellectual qualities overshadowed methodological issues, and the book proved immensely popular among social activists, intellectuals, academics, and counterculture figures, many of whom were persuaded that established institutions served only the rich and powerful. Curiously enough, Goffman's commitment to individual autonomy conferred upon him a remoteness from public issues. Nor did he offer any prescriptions for better and more effective ways of dealing with individuals designated as mental patients, and he even conceded that the closing of all hospitals would "raise a clamor for new ones" by relatives and public authorities. Yet his work was absorbed into both popular and professional thought and became a significant element in the antipsychiatry movement.[21]

At about the same time that Goffman's critique appeared, others were developing themes that were implicitly or explicitly critical of psychiatry. During the 1950s, sociologists by and large accepted the medical model of mental disorders: they were concerned with identifying etiological mechanisms and the extent of pathology in large populations. A decade later, epidemiological research was accompanied by an examination of the underlying concepts that shaped psychiatric thought and practice. In developing what became known as "labeling" (or societal reaction) theory, a number of sociologists called into question the very validity of the medical model of mental illnesses and, by indirection, the legitimacy of psychiatry.

Labeling theory did not emerge in an intellectual vacuum; there had long been sociological interest in the ways in which society identified deviant behavior. During the 1960s, however, labeling theory assumed new prominence, partly because it could be used as a form of social criticism. Thomas J. Scheff, a scholar who helped to popularize labeling theory, argued that psychiatric diagnoses were merely convenient labels attached to individuals who violated conventional behavioral norms. The breaking of norms, he conceded, was common. But when certain kinds of rule breakers generated adverse reactions, they were placed within a specific category that mandated a response by agents representing dominant social groups. A label of mental illness, therefore, led to commitment to a mental hospital. In turn, the process of institutionalization altered self-conceptions and created a form of secondary deviance in which behavior reflected a new deviant self-image. The labeling or stigmatizing of individuals as mentally ill produced disturbed behavior. A diagnosis of mental illness, in other words, said less about the individual patient than about the social system itself, the reaction of others to unconventional behavior, and the official agencies of control and treatment.[22]

The implications of labeling theory were obvious. Concepts of mental illnesses were not "neutral, value-free, [or] scientifically precise terms." They were rather, as Scheff observed, "the leading edge of an ideology embedded in the historical and cultural present of the white middle class of Western societies." The real use of psychiatric labels such as *schizophrenia* was to reify and legitimate the existing social order. Psychiatrists were in reality fulfilling a social control function rather than a medical purpose. Labeling theory was especially conducive to those who were critical of psychiatry and persuaded that fundamental social change was long overdue. Indeed, labeling theory proved appealing to a variety of activists, including civil rights advocates, feminists, and radicals of all persuasions.[23]

The attack on psychiatric legitimacy, however, was not limited to sociologists who followed or whose thinking was shaped by Goffman or Scheff. Equally influential, if more subtle, critiques came from those directly involved in the delivery of services but who lacked medical degrees. Such individuals were hostile toward the presumption that mental illnesses were necessarily medical and biological in character. Beneath a seemingly esoteric debate, of course, were practical concerns that involved power, status, and income. The growing significance of alternatives to mental hospital treatment—including outpatient clinics, CMHCs, and private practice—as well as the liberalization of third-party insurance regulations to include psychiatric coverage gave new meaning to the older controversy about the practice of various psychotherapies and sociotherapies by mental health professionals without medical degrees. If mental illnesses continued to be subsumed under psychiatric jurisdiction, other mental health professionals would remain in a subservient position.

Psychologists in particular were irritated by a medical model that in their view was deficient. Having made the Ph.D. their terminal degree, they were less likely to defer to psychiatric hegemony. During the 1950s the two groups had come into conflict on the issue of licensing and certification. A decade later, clinical psychologists were directly challenging the validity of the medical model. When the JCMIH issued its recommendations in *Action for Mental Health*, the Board of Directors of the American Psychological Association was supportive. Nevertheless, its members expressed regret that the document ignored "recent basic criticisms of the medical model of health and illness." "We anticipate that, in the long run," they added, "a different way of conceiving the relative success or failure with which people confront their problems of living may turn out to be more appropriate." In testimony before a congressional committee considering community mental health legislation, Nicholas Hobbs, representing the American Psychological Association, was equally critical of the prevailing medical model. Mental disorders, he observed, differed in fundamental respects from other illnesses; they both grew out of and contributed to "family and community disorganization." Public policy had to rest on a frank recognition that mental disorders were "inextricably bound up with child rearing practices, education, employment, recreation, health, religion—in sum, with the totality of family and community life." Effective policies, therefore, had to go beyond a model that emphasized "illness or disease and that simply extends or duplicates current predominant trends of medical care."[24]

In 1969 Roy R. Grinker, Sr., and George W. Albee used the pages of the *American Journal of Psychiatry* to debate the issue. The former, a distinguished psychiatrist, took a moderate position. "The biopsychosocial field," he insisted, "cannot be fractured into the social or medical." Nor was psychotherapy synonymous with psychiatry. Grinker called for a moratorium on conflict and for genuine collaboration, and he expressed the hope that evolutionary experimentation could replace confrontation. Albee, a well-known psychologist who had prepared a JCMIH monograph dealing with manpower, was not in a compromising mood. He rejected the illness model and substituted one based on the presumption that disturbed behavior reflected "the results of social-developmental learning in pathological environments." The destruction of the "emotional integrity of the family," for example, had a negative impact on mental health. Effective interventions, he added, had to be social and educational in nature; one-to-one therapeutic relationships were essentially futile. Albee's analysis—which dismissed the intellectual and scientific foundations of psychiatry—left little room for compromise or even debate.[25]

The attack on psychiatry was not limited to those involved in clinical practice or the study of mental illnesses. On the contrary, the specialty found itself under siege by intellectuals, radical activists, and civil rights advocates, all of whom challenged the very foundations of professional autonomy and legitimacy. Gaining a wide audience, these disparate critics were nevertheless united in their belief that medical hegemony over mental illnesses had to be ended.

Foes of psychiatric orthodoxy drew heavily upon the work of Michel Foucault. Born and educated in France, Foucault flourished in a postwar revolutionary Parisian environment that produced such intellectuals as Jean-Paul Sartre and Claude Lévi-Strauss. This group changed twentieth-century thinking by breaking down the barriers between staid academic disciplines and synthesizing insights drawn from Marx and Freud. Its members were fascinated by the role of language in seeing or reconstituting reality, and they altered the very framework of intellectual discourse. Foucault's work, like that of others of this group, defied neat categorization; it spanned a variety of disciplines and ranged over centuries of human experience. In a series of influential and widely read books, he attempted to penetrate into the inner meaning of ideas.

In 1961 Foucault published his famous *Histoire de la Folie* (translated into English a few years later in abridged form). This provocative and idiosyncratic book sought to describe the changing inner meaning of madness from the late Middle Ages to the birth of the asylum in the eighteenth century. Unlike liberal scholars who saw the asylum as an indication of progress, Foucault had a quite different interpretation of this ubiquitous institution. The creation of asylums, he averred in language that was both elliptical and prophetic in tone, represented an attempt to conquer madness by imposing a new system designed to enforce conformity. In Pinel's hands, he wrote, the asylum became "an instrument of moral conformity and of social denunciation." The new understanding of insanity required that mad persons assume responsibility for their condition. Nor was moral therapy a synonym for kind and humane treatment; it was rather an effort to force insane persons to develop an understanding of their own moral transgressions and then to alter their behavior by internalizing the values of their keepers. The physician thus became the "essential figure of the asylum." His authority, however, did not derive from science, but rather from the moral and social order associated with bourgeois society and its values. Foucault's writings tended to demythologize psychiatry because of his insistence that the specialty's appeal was to be found not in its contribution to an understanding of human behavior, but in its relationships to the sources of power and domination.[26]

Ever changing and often obscure, Foucault's writings became one of the pillars of dissenting and counterculture thought during the 1960s and 1970s. His work seemed to strip away the melioristic and idealistic veneer of an alleged medical specialty and presumably benevolent institutions and to lay bare their role in enforcing a universal conformity. By the late 1960s Foucault had already become one of the patron saints of a group of historians and social scientists who rejected the idea that mental hospitals were symbols of progress. Their scholarly studies often emphasized the social control functions of psychiatry and mental hospitals, the abuses inherent in institutionalization, and the demands generated by a capitalist social order that insisted on conformity to a unitary standard of citizenship and behavior.[27]

A more subtle but equally significant critique of psychiatry came from both the legal profession and civil rights advocates. The tension between psychiatry and law, of course, had a long history. In the nineteenth century the two often came into conflict on the questions of involuntary commitment and the insanity plea. Elizabeth P. W. Packard, for example, led a crusade against the dangers of arbitrary commitment procedures, and the trial of presidential assassin Charles Guiteau revolved entirely around the issue of responsibility. Yet the legal constraints on nineteenth-century psychiatric authority and autonomy were relatively minor. This is not to suggest that members of the specialty were free to do as they chose. On the contrary, informal norms and standards of conduct qualified and limited professional autonomy. Such norms reflected a society that valued deferential and paternalistic relationships, which implied that those in positions of authority had clearly defined responsibilities toward those under their charge.

During the 1960s, by contrast, patterns of authority and deference came under attack. The postwar civil rights movement, initially concerned with racial inequality, quickly broadened its scope to include gender and class, as well as the rights of the mentally ill. The attack on a variety of inequalities inevitably weakened professional demands for autonomy and freedom.

The impact on the mental health system was immediate and profound. In the past, a leading student of mental health law wrote, the study of the relationship between law and psychiatry was regarded as an "elitist and relatively esoteric pursuit." By the 1960s, on the other hand, social and legal developments had converged to infuse "new dynamism and significance" into the subject. Mental health law emerged as an important subject in its own right. The identification of new legal issues had significant consequences for psychiatry and mental hospitals. Before World War II, for example, discussions about the ethics of therapeutic experimentation, informed consent, and patient rights were extremely rare. The change in the postwar decades was striking. During and after the 1960s a series of important judicial decisions, the passage of new legislation, and the publication of a body of scholarly literature converged to alter the legal framework and transform the status of mentally ill persons. The shift from a preoccupation with professional needs toward a concern with patient rights resulted in a more critical stance toward psychiatry and mental hospitals.[28]

The postwar concern with patient rights was related in part to the perceived crisis of mental hospitals. The exposés in the immediate postwar years and the growing involvement of the nation's governors with mental health policy issues implicitly posed troublesome questions. If society had authority to enforce involuntary commitment, did it not have a commensurate responsibility to provide treatment, as contrasted with custodial care? What circumstances justified involuntary commitment, and who was qualified to make such decisions?

After 1945 such organizations as the American Bar Association, the American Civil Liberties Union, and GAP began to study commitment laws and offer recommendations. The important policy analysis sponsored by the Governors' Conference and published in 1950 devoted a chapter to traditional procedural issues such as commitment, release, and the degree to which institutionalized patients could exercise their personal rights. The interest in commitment laws by private and public groups, however, produced few substantive changes; their activities were at most a prelude to future developments. Much the same held true for the drafting of a model act. Acting on the advice of its National Mental Health Advisory Committee, the NIMH established a group in 1949 to prepare such an act. Completed in 1952, the model act included provision for simplified voluntary admission procedures. Its suggestions for involuntary commitment required a finding that the patient was mentally ill and, because of illness, was likely to injure himself or others if left at liberty, or that he was in need of custody, care, and treatment in a mental hospital but, because of illness, lacked the insight or capacity to make a responsible decision with respect to hospitalization. The draft also included a clause stipulating that every patient had a right to humane care and treatment. Such a statement was by no means radical; lawyers and courts had always accepted the argument that patients retained certain personal rights. Adopted in one form or another by a number of states, the draft act actually enhanced rather than diminished psychiatric discretion and authority, for in many cases it eliminated trial by jury in sanity proceedings.[29]

In the mid-1950s the American Bar Association sponsored a lengthy study of the rights of the mentally disabled, the results of which were published in 1961. The volume (subsequently revised) was more a compendium of law than a call for change. Its analysis, although not overtly critical of psychiatry and hospitals, subtly shifted the focus from professional authority to patient rights. Indirectly the study suggested shortcomings in the system responsible for the care and treatment of institutionalized patients.[30]

That same year the Subcommittee on Constitutional Rights of the Senate Judiciary Committee held public hearings dealing in part with commitment procedures in the District of Columbia. Sam J. Ervin of North Carolina (subcommittee chair) probably had personal reasons for convening the hearings, for there was little or no indication of widespread concern with constitutional issues relating to the mentally ill.[31] Much of the testimony, however, began to focus on broader issues, specifically the *constitutional* rights of patients. By emphasizing the constitutional rights of patients, the Ervin subcommittee subtly shifted the debate to more fundamental issues that impacted significantly upon public and professional authority. In this sense the hearings both anticipated and reflected the growing efforts during the decade of the 1960s to define a new legal relationship between established authority and disadvantaged groups generally, be they defined by race, gender, ethnicity, disability, or income.

Although not conducted in an adversarial manner, the proceedings—precisely because they were concerned with the constitutional rights of patients—suggested that mental hospitals were not meeting all of their responsibilities. "One of the paramount questions confronting us today," Ervin stated, "is whether society, which is unable or unwilling to provide treatment, has the right to deprive the patient of his liberty on the sole grounds that he is in need of care." Indeed, Morton Birnbaum, who was trained in both medicine and law and appeared as a witness before the committee, had already argued the previous year in an influential article in the *American Bar Association Journal* that patients had a constitutional right to treatment. He focused on the shortcomings of hospitals and argued that courts should be prepared to rule that failure to provide treatment for involuntarily committed patients was sufficient grounds for discharge regardless of the severity of the illness. "An institution that involuntarily institutionalizes the mentally ill without giving them adequate medical treatment for their mental illness," Birnbaum insisted, "is a mental prison and not a mental hospital; and . . . substantive due process of law does not allow a mentally ill person who has committed no crime to be deprived of his liberty by indefinitely institutionalizing him in a mental prison." Birnbaum's yardsticks were relatively simple and included such things as staff-patient ratios. Sensitive to clinicians, he did not argue that courts were competent to judge appropriate therapies, and he even placed blame on governments for their failure to provide adequate resources. Nevertheless, his analysis contained an implied criticism of mental hospitals, if not of the psychiatrists who administered them.[32]

Despite an enthusiastic editorial in the *American Bar Association Journal*, Birnbaum's arguments had no immediate judicial impact. Indeed, the apparent thrust to establish alternatives to mental hospital care during the early 1960s deflected attention away from strictly legal issues, although a number of states enacted legislation that restricted commitment procedures and thus expanded patients' rights. In 1966, however, Birnbaum's argument was adopted by Judge David Bazelon in the famous *Rouse v. Cameron* case. Although the litigant's case did not address the issue of constitutional rights, Judge Bazelon brought it up on his own, thus raising the subject before the public. He found a right to treatment in his interpretation of District of Columbia statutes. More important, he suggested that constitutional rights were involved as well. Bazelon alluded to cruel and unusual punishment (Eighth Amendment) as well as due process and equal protection of the laws (Fourteenth Amendment). The decision, however seemingly radical, was carefully worded. Bazelon demanded neither cure nor improvement; he simply required that hospitals make a bona fide effort to provide patients with an individualized treatment program and periodic evaluations. Two years later the Massachusetts Supreme Court enunciated a right to treatment for individuals judged incompetent to stand trial and whose return to competency was required if the case were to resume. In its decision the court employed the due process and equal protection clauses.[33]

The major challenges to the procedures governing commitment, hospitalization, and treatment came from lower federal and state courts during the 1970s. During that decade public-interest lawyers, representing clients previously without access to traditional legal services, challenged many long-standing doctrines that governed mental hospitalization. They argued that commitment statutes were vague and arbitrary; that courts and legislatures should be required to follow a least-restrictive alternative approach to civil commitment; that all persons facing the prospect of involuntary hospitalization should be provided with maximum due process of law to ensure that they would not be deprived in arbitrary ways of their liberties; and that hospitalized patients should retain certain basic rights, including a right to treatment, a right to refuse (within certain limits) some controversial or undesirable treatments, and confidentiality of records.[34] In a series of landmark decisions, courts accepted many of these arguments, thereby limiting the discretionary authority of psychiatrists, public officials, and other mental health professionals. Although the precise impact of changing doctrine was not always clear, there is little doubt that legal and judicial developments tended to weaken the legitimacy and authority of both psychiatry and mental hospitals. The changes in mental health law, however, did not directly lead to a decline in public mental hospital inpatient populations. The major judicial decisions relating to mental hospitals came after 1971 and had only a limited impact before 1975. By 1975 the average resident population had already declined to 191,000 (as compared with 475,000 a decade earlier). The concern with patient rights, in other words, significantly reinforced and perhaps even made irreversible (but did not inaugurate) the decline in both resident populations and average lengths of stay.

The multifaceted attack on psychiatric theory and practice was also mirrored in the appearance of new images in the press and media. In the late 1950s and 1960s Hollywood consistently presented an idealized and favorable image of psychiatry. John Huston's *Freud* in 1962 was the culmination of this tradition: the creator of psychoanalysis was presented in almost Christlike terms. Thereafter a remarkable shift occurred. Just as psychiatry came under unfavorable scrutiny by individuals and groups who questioned its claims and achievements, so Hollywood produced a series of motion pictures depicting the specialty in a negative light. By the mid-1960s mental hospitals were portrayed as institutions that tortured inmates by employing electroshock and other invasive procedures that represented punishment rather than therapy. Frederick Wiseman's vivid documentary *The Titicut Follies* (1967) used live footage of Bridgewater State Hospital in Massachusetts that in effect recreated the snake pit image current in the late 1940s. The *Diary of a Mad Housewife* (1970) presented the psychiatrist as an unpleasant male figure seeking domination over females. Similarly, such popular novels as Ken Kesey's *One Flew Over the Cuckoo's Nest* (1962) and Elliot Baker's *A Fine Madness* (1964) used fiction as the means to describe psychiatrists as evil egomaniacs.[35]

. . .

To be sure, psychiatrists were not passive; they were quick to respond to the allegations of their critics. The writings of such well-known figures as Szasz, Laing, Goffman, Scheff, Foucault, and others were subjected to equally careful scrutiny and often found wanting.[36] Nevertheless, the attack on psychiatry—whether on the psychodynamic or the biological school—slowly took its toll. Fragmentation and retrenchment perhaps best described the specialty after the halcyon era from the 1940s to the 1960s. The decline in psychiatric authority and unity created a partial vacuum, which subsequently added to the difficulties in defining a clear and unambiguous mental health policy after 1970.

Although the psychodynamic school shaped and dominated the evolution of the specialty in the two decades following World War II, its hegemony had never been absolute. Admittedly relegated to a minority position, the older biological tradition persisted in one form or another. As early as 1946 a small group of organically oriented psychiatrists, neurologists, and neurophysiologists led by George Thompson, Abram Bennett, and Johannes Nielson, and including Percival Bailey, Harry Solomon, Stanley Cobb, Samuel Wortis, and Karl Bowman, formed the Society of Biological Psychiatry. Representing a variety of medical specialties, its members were united by a belief in the neuronal basis of psychiatry. Without ruling out completely the relevance of psychological factors, they insisted nevertheless on the necessity of adding "substance to psychological concepts" by tracing "the anatomical structures which made these concepts possible." Rejecting dualisms of all sorts and reiterating the older belief that the brain was the organ of the mind, its members tended to favor such somatic therapies as electroshock and lobotomy in the late 1940s, and the psychotropic drugs in the succeeding decade. In the APA's Academic Lecture in 1956, Bailey berated his psychodynamic colleagues and suggested that psychoanalysis was a religion rather than a science. "Yet there is no proof that the system is true," he observed. "It is an intellectually closed world, but the argument that it is internally coherent is no proof . . . and is, moreover, demonstrably false. Another proof sometimes adduced is its triumph over opposition. This is the proof theologians sometimes use to prove the truth of Christianity which the analysts disdain. It can be used with equal cogency to prove the truth of Mohammedanism or Buddhism." Toward the close of his lecture he urged his colleagues to return to "asylums and laboratories which they are so proud to have left behind them, and prove, by established criteria, that their concepts have scientific validity."[37]

Biological psychiatry, however, occupied a distinctly subordinate position in the two decades following 1945. The widening chasm between psychiatry and neurology only enhanced the dominance of psychodynamic practitioners. Whereas Adolf Meyer had insisted upon the interdependence of the two specialties, his postwar successors all but eliminated neurological training in psychiatry. In 1959 the AMA gave de jure recognition to this situation: the *Archives of Neurology and Psychiatry* (first issued in 1919) ceased publication and was replaced by two new journals (*Archives of Neurology* and *Archives of Psychiatry*). Stanley Cobb—a figure who spanned the interwar years and remained in the Meyerian psychobiological tradition—was distressed by the split as well as by the overdrawn claims of both psychodynamic and biological psychiatrists. "We really don't know very much," a former resident recalled Cobb saying about 1954. "We let them all shout and then hope that some truth will come out of it all." Cobb's humility was atypical; the majority of his colleagues, whatever their views, believed themselves to be on the threshold of fundamental breakthroughs.[38]

During the 1960s psychodynamic psychiatry began to lose its dominant position. In particular, its control over the psychotherapies became more tenuous. Several studies had made it abundantly clear that proposed increases in the number of CMHCs would more than drain the pool of qualified psychiatrists needed to staff them. In addition, psychotherapies were time-consuming and labor-intensive and therefore could not be used to treat hundreds of thousands of seriously mentally ill persons. These facts alone accounted for a further jurisdictional expansion of such nonmedical specialties as clinical psychology, whose members offered psychotherapeutic services independently of medical supervision. As the role of mental health professionals without medical training grew, the arena of psychiatric expertise inevitably diminished. Such developments strengthened biological psychiatry, given the fact that somatic therapies, especially drugs, remained under medical control.

More important, psychodynamic and psychoanalytic psychiatrists were ill-equipped to respond to a series of challenges by more somatically oriented colleagues. After World War II, controlled clinical trials for new therapies became the norm. Psychodynamic practitioners were thus faced with demands for the same kinds of sophisticated evaluations employed in judging the efficacy of all therapies, psychiatric or otherwise. These evaluations had to include matched samples of individuals with uniform diagnoses randomly assigned to treatment and control groups and given standardized therapies. The results of these evaluations, furthermore, had to be judged by external impartial observers rather than therapists. Such standards posed extraordinarily difficult problems for psychiatrists accustomed to dealing with individuals on a case-by-case basis and who routinely related environmental influences to individual pathology without identifying or demonstrating causal links. One of the most detailed and sophisticated longitudinal evaluations—the Menninger Foundation's Psychotherapy Research Project (begun in 1954 and spanning more than two decades)—in fact met none of the conventional standards.[39]

In a classic epidemiological study begun in 1961 and completed six years later, Benjamin Pasamanick and his associates concluded that much psychiatric training was already obsolete. Basic biological interventions had previously appeared to be secondary to psychodynamics, psychotherapy, and individual analysis. Their randomized study (which included two control groups) seemed to demonstrate that excellent results could be achieved with drug therapy in a home-care setting for schizophrenic patients. Yet psychiatrists were "being prepared to practice a form of medicine which is already archaic, utilizing knowledge and skills which daily approach obsolescence." The Pasamanick study implicitly undermined a number of the cherished claims of psychodynamic and psychoanalytic psychiatry.[40]

The social context of psychodynamic psychiatric practice also suggested that those most in need of services tended to be the most neglected. An extensive study of private office practice in the early 1970s revealed that psychiatrists (most of whom had been trained in the psychodynamic tradition) treated affluent professional and managerial groups. Blue- and white-collar workers were underrepresented, while blacks and Spanish-speaking groups were virtually absent from their patient populations. The neuroses (especially depression) and other personality disorders accounted for a large proportion of office patients, whereas schizophrenia and other severe mental illnesses were underrepresented. Individual psychotherapy, with or without adjunctive chemotherapy, remained the dominant therapeutic approach.[41]

As the psychodynamic consensus began to dissolve, biological psychiatry became more prominent. The preoccupation with social and psychological factors, somatic psychiatrists argued, had only widened the gap between psychiatry and other medical specialties. Whereas other medical specialties had benefited from the therapeutic applications of science and technology, psychiatry had ignored the importance of somatic therapies (e.g., psychotropic drugs) and had neglected the study of basic biological processes. A portent of things to come was the creation in 1959 of the short-lived American Society of Medical Psychiatry and the *Journal of Neuropsychiatry* by Ladislas Meduna, who had introduced metrazol convulsive therapy in the late 1930s. "Our basic tenet," he wrote in the first issue, "is that the mind and the so-called mental functions are functions of the brain, wherefore a disturbance in these functions must be caused by a physical disturbance in the substance of the brain, and therefore is amenable to pharmacological and other physical treatments."[42]

Meduna's extremist views were unpalatable even to those sympathetic to a somatic orientation. The views of members of the Society of Biological Psychiatry, on the other hand, were more acceptable. By 1959 its members launched the publication of the annual proceedings of their scientific sessions under the title *Recent Advances in Biological Psychiatry*. A decade later the annual volumes were replaced by a new journal (*Biological Psychiatry*). Such activities suggested a renewed interest in the neurophysiology of the mental illnesses. Biological psychiatry, insisted Paul H. Hoch in his presidential address before the society in 1960,

> is not only important from the point of view of research and treatment, but is very important as a philosophy of psychiatry. Biological psychiatry is fully aware of the fact that the psyche does not have an independent existence such as the soul, but it is a function of the organism and it is the product of nervous system action. This does not mean that we are not aware of other philosophies in psychiatry and that we do not acknowledge the existence of motivational forces or social relationships which cannot be expressed today in organic terms. Nevertheless, it is important to stress that the most productive approach in psychiatry will be as it has proved to be—the approach which fully realizes the biological organization of the organism and understands that the biological laws governing the organism's existence also apply to its psychic functioning.[43]

During the 1960s and 1970s, interest in finding a somatic etiology for such conditions as schizophrenia gradually increased. The confession by two leading psychiatrists in a textbook published in 1966 was revealing. Despite thousands of publications in their field, they concluded that

> the important questions of diagnosis, prognosis, etiology, and therapy are still unanswered and constitute psychiatry's greatest challenge. Can the behavioral

processes and changes be described with any precision and order? Is schizophrenia a group of ill-defined syndromes, or is it a true nosological entity? Is it a disease? A maladjustment? A way of life? Is the irrationality of schizophrenia transmitted by genes or by interpersonal relations? What are the best methods of treatment?

That such issues were even raised suggested the growing disillusionment with largely psychosocial explanations. Consequently, more and more figures, in psychiatry as well as other specialties, began to focus on the role of genetic factors, neurotransmitters, aberrant metabolisms, and a variety of somatic therapies.[44]

The growing strength of biological psychiatry did not necessarily lead to a new consensus. On the contrary, differences persisted even among those who accepted somatic premises. The absence of persuasive or conclusive evidence to support strongly held theories created more controversy. A case in point involves the rise of what became known as orthomolecular psychiatry in the late 1960s. During the 1950s Humphry Osmond and Abram Hoffer began giving niacin to patients diagnosed as schizophrenic. Their experiments were based on the model of pellagra, a disease related to a vitamin deficiency. Its symptoms included forms of psychotic behavior; in the early part of the twentieth century, southern mental hospitals had admitted significant numbers of individuals suffering from "pellagrin insanity." Osmond and Hoffer published a series of studies purportedly showing that megavitamin therapy resulted in significant improvements in mental patients even when this group was compared with a control group receiving a placebo.[45] Nevertheless, their work was largely ignored by psychodynamic and biological psychiatrists alike, who dismissed their studies and results as flawed and insignificant.

In 1968, however, Linus Pauling, the distinguished Nobel laureate in chemistry, threw his influence behind their work. Already controversial because of his claim that vitamin C could prevent many respiratory infections, Pauling argued in the pages of *Science* that orthomolecular therapy was perhaps the best treatment for many mentally ill persons. "Orthomolecular psychiatric therapy," he wrote, "is the treatment of mental disease by the provision of the optimum molecular environment for the mind, especially the optimum concentrations of substances normally present in the human body." Schizophrenia was probably the result of a genetic factor that led to deficiencies in vital substances in the brain; appropriate treatment involved the administration of megadoses of vitamins. Pauling's claims received wide publicity and stimulated interest in this approach. Molecular psychiatrists quickly founded a national organization and commenced publication of a journal.[46]

Pauling's claims, as well as those of orthomolecular psychiatrists, came

TABLE 11.1
Numbers and Percentages of American
Medical Graduates Entering Psychiatry,
1925–1973

Years M.D. Obtained	Average Number per Year	Average Percentage per Year
1925–1929	57	2.7
1930–1934	118	3.6
1935–1939	192	4.7
1940–1944	285	5.1
1945–1949	369	7.1
1950–1954	396	6.7
1955–1959	476	7.1
1960–1964	526	7.0
1965–1969	493	6.4
1970–1973	461	5.0

under immediate attack. Donald Oken of the NIMH's Clinical Research Branch pointed to serious methodological flaws in the studies cited by Pauling: inappropriate sampling methods, inadequate controls, loose diagnostic criteria, and observer bias. Pauling responded by charging that fear of losing patients and income was behind the opposition of "old guard" psychiatrists. Although molecular psychiatry quickly disappeared from public view, its short-lived popularity offered testimony to the growing receptivity toward biological explanations.[47]

The shift toward biological explanations of mental disorders was hastened by a growing disillusionment with psychodynamic psychiatry rather than by any new medical breakthroughs. Many psychiatrists were troubled by the tenuous relationship of their specialty to the rest of medicine; they were also concerned with the decline in the number of medical graduates entering the specialty. Between 1945 and 1965 about 7 percent had selected psychiatry; by the early 1970s only 5 percent entered the specialty (see table 11.1). According to George Engel of the University of Rochester's School of Medicine, in a widely discussed editorial in the *American Journal of Psychiatry*, psychiatry was failing in its responsibilities toward medicine. He pointed to the statement by the American Board of Psychiatry and Neurology suggesting that the traditional internship was a waste of time for the would-be psychiatrist. Moreover, too many departments of psychiatry endorsed programs that permitted students to enter residency programs with a minimum of experience in other clinical disciplines. Engel insisted that the traditional medical model incorporated both biological and psychosocial elements, and to permit the latter to overshadow the former simply resulted in the weakening or destruction of the links between psychiatry and medicine. His provocative editorial drew an unusually large number of letters, suggesting that his sentiments had struck a responsive chord among colleagues.[48]

Two years later Richard Schwartz expanded upon Engel's views. The drift of psychiatry away from its medical moorings, he wrote, grew out of a variety of postwar developments. The concept of psychiatric illnesses had become "increasingly vague, diffuse, and overly inclusive," thus obliterating the distinction between mental illness and deviant behavior. Psychiatrists were too much involved with nonmedical service programs. Those employed in state mental hospitals occupied administrative and supervisory positions and had few contacts with patients; others provided long-term psychotherapy or psychoanalysis and treated troubled but not sick individuals; and still others were in CMHCs or other community agencies not directly involved in the treatment of psychiatrically ill persons. "By neglecting its basic responsibilities for the care and treatment of nervous and mental patients in favor of many kinds of nonmedical activities," charged Schwartz, "the psychiatric profession has greatly overextended itself and has gotten into a position where it has promised far more than it can hope to deliver. The result is that in many respects its performance record is poor, which has led to decreased public trust and confidence." He concluded by urging his colleagues to adopt a more strict definition of psychiatric illnesses, to limit their professional work to the care and treatment of the mentally ill, and to disengage from psychoanalytic and psychotherapeutic practices intended to reconstruct personality.[49]

After 1970 the gulf between psychodynamic and biological psychiatrists narrowed. In the 1950s Maciver and Redlich identified two competing kinds of practitioners. The directive-organic psychiatrist employed biological tools (psychosurgery, electroconvulsive therapy, and drugs) combined with persuasive-directive methods; analytic-psychological practitioners favored one of the dynamic psychotherapies. Twenty-five years later a follow-up study found that a significant therapeutic homogenization had occurred. The predominant treatment technique involved a combination of individual, group, and milieu therapies in conjunction with drugs. Psychiatrists who did not employ drugs were the exception to the rule; eclecticism once again was characteristic. Indeed, the "sharing" of forms of psychotherapy among a variety of occupational groups precluded its use as a means of defining jurisdictional boundaries. Consequently, somatic therapies—particularly drugs—differentiated psychiatrists from other mental health professionals. The trend even affected those in strictly psychoanalytic practice; a survey in 1976 revealed that about 60 percent of psychoanalysts prescribed medication for some of their patients.[50]

The decline of the psychodynamic or psychoanalytic school corresponded to a shift in the ways in which psychiatrists were educated. In the two decades following 1945 virtually all chairs and professors in departments of psychiatry were either trained psychoanalysts or sympathetic to psychoanalytic theory. Consequently, an entire generation of psychiatrists were educated in the precepts of their mentors. As late as 1962 the Conference on Graduate Psychiatric Education agreed that psychoanalytic theory was one of the specialty's "basic frames of reference" and hence merited a significant place in the core curriculum. Participants recognized that psychoanalytic theories rarely remained neutral elements when presented as part of the basic knowledge of psychiatry. Indeed, such theories often engendered reverberations that made it difficult "to see other basic aspects of psychiatry and thus may lead ... [residents] to substitute psychoanalysis for everything else in the field." Nevertheless, most training programs continued to emphasize psychodynamics and psychotherapy. Although dissent was evident, the debate suggested that the psychoanalytic or psychodynamic consensus remained unshaken.[51]

During the 1960s there was mounting concern that the preoccupation with the psychodynamics of neurotic patients had led to "a neglect of the psychotic, and in particular inadequacy in the teaching, epidemiology, and physiology of the major psychiatric diseases."[52] Psychiatry seemed somewhat dated because it was not directly affiliated with the technological and pharmacological changes in medicine that had raised public expectations to unprecedented (even if unrealistic) heights. Indeed, the rapid development of the neurosciences held out the potential threat that psychiatry as a specialty might become obsolete as the etiology of mental disorders was traced back to physiological and biochemical components.

By the 1970s psychodynamic concepts no longer dominated psychiatric education. Bernard Bandler, for example, pointed to a "de-emphasis of the importance and contribution of psychoanalytic understanding" in psychiatric education. Although personally persuaded that psychoanalysis was still "the method par excellence for gaining understanding of one's self," he conceded its many shortcomings. As a therapy, psychoanalysis was inapplicable on a large scale; evaluations were lacking because the problems of "criteria, controls, and variables" remained unsolved; and as a research instrument its reliability and validity remained in doubt. By the middle of the decade few departments of psychiatry were headed by psychoanalytic psychiatrists, and some of the more promising younger figures identified themselves with a biological tradition even though practice tended to be more eclectic.[53]

· · ·

In the nineteenth century, psychiatry's inseparability from mental hospitals had defined its essential character. In effect, psychiatrists functioned within a system that linked care and treatment. After World War II a new synthesis took shape. The specialty was now identified with psychodynamic and psychoanalytic concepts, a public health orientation, a hostility toward mental hospitals, an affinity for community-based treatment, an awareness of the role of broad environmental factors in the shaping of personality, and a commitment to social and political activism.

The very attributes that gave psychodynamic psychiatry popularity and influence in the postwar decades were also in part responsible for its eclipse beginning in the late 1960s. The broadening of the specialty's boundaries increased its vulnerability to critics representing the entire political spectrum. Nor were psychiatrists strategically situated to mount a firm defense. Failing to define precisely their distinct professional role, they were unable to draw a line between their responsibilities as physicians and their role as citizens. Equally important, the specialty lost its once-clear identification with the severely mentally ill—an identification that had contributed to its social and medical legitimacy.

The changes of these years were reflected in the career of Bertram S. Brown, who succeeded Stanley Yolles as director of the NIMH in 1970. Brown had entered federal service on the eve of Kennedy's inauguration. Both he and Yolles spoke for the community-oriented and socially active psychiatry of the 1960s.[54] By the 1970s Brown's position had shifted. In 1972 he conceded that the comprehensive mental health planning of the 1960s "was one of the most fundamental failures" of that decade. In an address before the APA three years later he addressed a series of questions about the "role, definition, scope, and boundaries of psychiatry." Had the specialty become too involved with broad social and political issues and unduly expanded its boundaries? Who were its logical clientele? Had the specialty erred in shifting its focus away from the severely mentally ill in order to provide services to individuals experiencing emotional and psychological disturbances or problems in living? Did the breaking of the links between psychiatry and public mental hospitals have beneficial consequences? That such questions were even asked was emblematic of the distance that separated the 1960s from the 1970s.[55]

After 1970 the character of American psychiatry underwent a marked transformation. As psychodynamic and psychoanalytic leaders who had dominated the specialty for nearly a quarter of a century retired, their places were taken by those more committed to biological explanations of mental disorders. Less concerned with the role of broad environmental and psychological factors in the shaping of personality, these individuals stressed the importance of integrating psychiatry and medicine and exploiting new medical technologies that might eventually illuminate the biology of mental disorders. Psychiatric attention increasingly was riveted on problems of pathology and diagnosis, and interest in psychosocial rehabilitation correspondingly diminished.

The growing significance of biological psychiatry gave rise to a series of paradoxical consequences. The preoccupation with pathology and diagnosis shifted interest back toward the severe mental illnesses; in this respect late twentieth-century biological psychiatrists were somewhat closer to their nineteenth-century ancestors than to their immediate post–World War II predecessors. Nevertheless, biological psychiatrists were more likely to compartmentalize the medical and social aspects of mental illnesses; they were for the most part neither involved nor concerned with psychosocial rehabilitation or community support systems. Moreover, the fragmented and uncoordinated nature of the mental health system that grew out of the policy changes of the 1960s only reinforced the distinction between psychiatry, on the one hand, and support and rehabilitative services on the other. Tragic consequences followed for some severely and chronically mentally ill persons living outside of institutions in communities where support systems and linkages between mental health services were either weak or nonexistent. *need for continuum of care*

Epilogue

IN THE EARLY nineteenth century, Americans pursued institutional solutions to resolve complex social problems. To activists such as Horace Mann and Dorothea L. Dix, the mental hospital symbolized the means by which society fulfilled its moral and ethical obligations to mentally ill persons requiring assistance. Such institutions, they insisted, benefited the community, family, and afflicted individual by providing care and treatment irrespective of ability to pay the high costs associated with protracted hospitalization. In the succeeding century the mental hospital became the foundation of a policy that guaranteed access to care and treatment for the mentally ill. From modest beginnings, the number and size of mental hospitals increased with each passing decade. At their peak they contained a resident population in excess of half a million and accounted for a substantial proportion of state welfare budgets.

Paradoxically, a century later public mental hospitals had come to be perceived as the problem rather than the solution. At the end of World War II many institutions were suffering from nearly two decades of neglect. A deteriorated physical plant, shortages of psychiatrists and other staff, overcrowding, and a preoccupation with the need to provide custodial care for large numbers of chronically mentally ill persons were characteristic. Faced with an institutional policy that appeared inhumane and bankrupt, a coalition of professional and lay activists launched a crusade to transform mental health policy. Their goal was simple but radical, namely, to begin a process that would culminate in the replacement of traditional mental hospitals with new forms of community care and treatment.

The dramatic policy shifts of the postwar decades had important consequences. Robert H. Felix's crusade to confer legitimacy upon mental health services and to incorporate them within the framework of health care was largely successful. Community psychiatric and psychological services grew rapidly; general hospitals expanded their psychiatric capabilities; and acute services for the severely mentally ill expanded both quantitatively and qualitatively. Public mental hospitals were relieved of the burden of caring for large numbers of chronic and especially aged patients, which facilitated their conversion into more active treatment centers. Finally, mental health services grew somewhat less stigmatized, thus enhancing their popularity and use among both nonmentally and mentally ill groups.

The consequences of human activities, however, tend to be complex and unpredictable; ambiguity—not clarity or consistency—is often characteristic. This is especially true for the changes in the mental health system since World War II. Prior to 1940 the focus of public policy had been almost exclusively on the severely and chronically mentally ill. This policy was based on the assumption that society had an obligation to provide such unfortunate persons with both care and treatment in public mental hospitals. The policies adopted during and after the 1960s rested on quite different assumptions. That public mental hospitals continued to play an important role is indisputable. The creation of a decentralized and heterogeneous system of services, however, diminished their relative significance. Equally important, the target population became more diffuse and variegated; the mental health system was no longer concerned solely with the severely and chronically mentally ill. Even those professionals involved in providing services were less likely to deal with a group that presented formidable and sometimes insoluble problems. Ironically, the growing availability, variety, and popularity of mental health services sometimes worked to the detriment of those most in need of assistance.

Perhaps one of the most striking results of the postwar shift in policy was the severing of the traditional and previously unbreakable ties between care and treatment. Despite monumental shortcomings, mental hospitals had provided at least a basic level of care for many individuals incapable of functioning as independent and self-reliant human beings. Moreover, mental hospital care had derived legitimacy from its identification with medical science. Thus these institutions did not have to bear the burden of being tied to a welfare system grounded in part on the belief that dependency was self-inflicted, and that poverty, misfortune, and illnesses were consequences of character deficiencies rather than environmental or biological circumstances.

The community mental health policies that emerged during the postwar decades inadvertently distorted priorities by strengthening the distinction between care and treatment. Admittedly, these policies paid rhetorical homage to the need for care. Reality, however, was quite different. The main focus was on providing therapeutic services in outpatient settings to a broad, rather than a defined, population. Consequently, the social and human needs of the most severely and especially chronically mentally ill—particularly assistance in dealing with the subsistence tasks of daily life—were often ignored or overlooked. The identification of mental health policy with therapeutic services was understandable, given the obvious advantages of being included within the medical health care system. Caring and support services, by way of contrast, were affiliated with a welfare system that by the 1970s and 1980s was under attack by a political constituency bent on diminishing governmental responsibilities and activities.

The subtle shifts in the mental health system were to have tragic consequences for many chronically and severely mentally ill persons most in need of assistance. In the 1970s and 1980s they were often cast adrift in communities without access to support services or the basic necessities of life. For such persons the transition from an institutional to a community-based system proved devastating. By the 1980s the presence of homeless mentally ill persons in many communities served as a stark reminder that the new mental health policies had negative as well as positive consequences.[1]

In their desire to improve the lives of the severely mentally ill, psychiatric and lay activists had helped to lay the foundation for a new policy. Like others before them, they dismissed out of hand the experiences of the past. A peculiar blend of indignation at the continued existence of mental hospitals and a faith in a professionally grounded ideology combined to lay the groundwork for ending what to them was an obsolete and bankrupt policy. Ironically, overstated claims, enthusiasm for change, and an inability to appreciate the complexity of noninstitutional life for many severely and chronically mentally ill persons led these activists to overlook the difficulties that impeded the creation of support systems capable of providing care outside of institutions.[2]

Human triumphs invariably incorporate elements of tragedy as well. The generation that reached maturity during and after the 1940s firmly believed that the adoption of new mental health policies would lead to dramatic improvements. Their efforts played a major role in reshaping the mental health system by shifting the focus away from an institutional system plagued with severe problems. At the same time they sometimes failed to understand the human and social needs of the very persons they wanted to help, and they consistently overestimated their ability to shape administrative mechanisms, institutions, and policies. Although a broad constituency benefited from their innovative policies, many who required the most assistance—especially the chronically mentally ill—lost. More than a century and a half after a system of public mental hospitals was created, Americans had yet to define a mental health policy that integrated decent and humane *care* with access to medical services for severely and chronically mentally ill persons.

Notes

PROLOGUE

1. Unless otherwise noted, all statistical data have been drawn from the annual volumes *Patients in Mental Institutions,* 1940–1966 (through 1946 the data in these volumes were gathered by the U.S. Bureau of the Census; beginning in 1947 the NIMH assumed responsibility). The data on psychiatrists have been compiled from *List of Fellows and Members of the American Psychiatric Association 1940/ 1941* (n.p., 1942). In this directory, 1,458 members listed an institutional address and 841 a private address (which did not necessarily imply private or noninstitutional practice).

2. Louis Linn, "The Fourth Psychiatric Revolution," *AJP,* 124 (1968): 1043–48; Frederick A. Lewis, "Community Care of Psychiatric Patients versus Prolonged Institutionalization," *JAMA,* 182 (1962): 323–26; H. G. Whittington, "Is Community Psychiatry Revolutionary?" *AJPH,* 55 (1965): 354; Robert H. Felix, "Evolution of Community Mental Health Concepts," *AJP,* 113 (1957): 674, and "Community Mental Health: A Great and Significant Movement," ibid., 122 (1966): 1057.

CHAPTER ONE
THE LESSONS OF WAR, 1941–1945

1. For more detailed information on the changing nature of mental hospital populations in the early twentieth century, see Gerald N. Grob, *Mental Illness and American Society, 1875–1940* (Princeton, 1983), chap. 7.

2. Ibid., chaps. 3, 5–6, 11.

3. John C. Whitehorn to Jacob Meislin, Feb. 16, 1948, Whitehorn Papers, APAA; KAM, address in 1958, published in *A Psychiatrist's World: The Selected Papers of Karl Menninger* (New York, 1959), 526–28. Menninger advanced many of the same arguments in his popular and influential *Man against Himself* (New York, 1938).

4. In a study done in the early 1950s John Maciver and Fredrick C. Redlich used this description to distinguish between directive-organic psychiatrists (most of whom were employed in state hospitals) and those adhering to an analytic-psychological orientation. See their article "Patterns of Psychiatric Practice," *AJP,* 115 (1959): 692–97.

5. Samuel W. Hamilton et al., *A Study of the Public Mental Hospitals of the United States 1937–39* (Public Health Reports Supplement No. 164: Washington, D.C., 1941), 13–16, 81, 89–90; Grob, *Mental Illness and American Society,* 310–15.

6. GAP Circular Letter No. 12 (Nov. 20, 1946), GAP Papers, AP. See also National Committee for Mental Hygiene, *State Hospitals in the Depression* (New York, 1934).

7. N.Y.S. Commission to Investigate the Management and Affairs of the Department of Mental Hygiene . . . and the Institutions Operated by It, *The Care of the Mentally Ill in the State of New York* (Albany, 1944), 15, 111; Albert Deutsch columns in *PM,* Mar. 18 and 19, 1943; Harry J. Worthing to J. K. Hall, Nov. 26, 1942, Hall Papers, University of North Carolina Library, Chapel Hill, N.C.;

Dorothy Deming, "Mental Hospitals in Wartime," *American Journal of Nursing,* 43 (1943): 1013–17; *New York Times,* Jan. 22, 1945. That many of the problems of mental hospitals were endemic rather than war-related can be seen from the following studies of four state systems: T. L. McCulloch, "A Report on the Survey of the Louisiana State Institutions by the U.S. Public Health Service," *News-Letter of the American Association of Psychiatric Social Workers,* 12 (Summer 1942): 42–47; *Care of Patients in the State Mental Institutions of Connecticut: A Report to . . . the Governor* (Hartford, 1942); U.S. PHS, *A Survey of the Mental Institutions of the State of California* (Washington, D.C., 1943); Pa. Department of Welfare, *Report of the Committee Appointed by Honorable Edward Martin to Make a Complete Study of the Mental Hospitals of the Commonwealth of Pennsylvania, July, 1944* (Harrisburg, 1944).

8. "Public Psychiatric Hospitals," GAP *Report No. 5* (Apr. 1948): 1.

9. *Psychiatry,* 2 (1939): 133–35, 3 (1940): 326–27, 483–92, 619–27; *AJP,* 98 (1941): 296–98; Albert Deutsch, "Military Psychiatry: World War II 1941–1943," in *One Hundred Years of American Psychiatry,* ed. J. K. Hall (New York, 1944), 419–41. The experiences of World War I are detailed in the U.S. Surgeon General's Office publication, *The Medical Department of the United States Army in the World War,* vol. 10, *Neuropsychiatry* (Washington, D.C., 1929).

10. J. K. Hall to Henry L. Stimson, Aug. 20, 1941, Hall Papers, University of North Carolina Library; NCMH, "Request to the Rockefeller Foundation for Support of a Process Designed to Improve Selective Service," Sept. 3, 1942, Alan Gregg to George S. Stevenson, Jan. 7, 1943, Rockefeller Foundation Papers, RG 1.1, Series 200A, RAC; C. M. Campbell, "Selective Service and Psychiatric Issues," *JAMA,* 116 (1941): 1883–87; Franklin G. Ebaugh, "The Role of Psychiatry in National Defense," ibid., 117 (1941): 260–64; George S. Stevenson, "The National Committee's Part in the War Effort," *Mental Hygiene,* 27 (1943): 33–42. The pages of *Mental Hygiene* and the *AJP* during the war offer further confirmation of the generalizations in this paragraph.

11. See Rebecca S. Greene, "The Role of the Psychiatrist in World War II" (Ph.D. diss., Columbia University, 1977), 59–208, and U.S. Army Medical Department, *Neuropsychiatry in World War II,* 2 vols. (Washington, D.C., 1966–1973), 1:153–91, 740–44, 768. The latter work was collaborative; most of the chapters were written by prominent psychiatrists who played key roles in the military during World War II.

12. Research Project M-704 for the Committee on Medical Research of the Office of Scientific Research and Development ("Analysis of One Hundred Psychiatric Casualties and One Hundred Apparently 'Normal' Soldiers," July, 1942), copy in John C. Whitehorn Papers, APAA; Greene, "Role of the Psychiatrist," 323–50; U.S. Army Medical Department, *Neuropsychiatry in World War II,* 1:177–85.

13. U.S. Army Medical Department, *Neuropsychiatry in World War II,* 1:390–91, 406–7, 2:995, 1017–21; WCM, "Psychiatric Experience in the War, 1941–1946," *AJP,* 103 (1947): 580; Greene, "Role of the Psychiatrist," chap. 7.

14. Roy R. Grinker and John P. Spiegel, *War Neuroses* (Philadelphia, 1945), 70; Office of Scientific Research and Development, "Report of Special Commission of Civilian Psychiatrists Covering Psychiatric Policy and Practice in the U.S.

Army Medical Corps, European Theater, 20 April to 8 July 1945," 15, and Whitehorn, "Combat Exhaustion," Whitehorn Papers, APAA. The special commission's report by Leo H. Bartemeier, L. S. Kubie, KAM, J. Romano, and J. C. Whitehorn was published under the title "Combat Exhaustion," *Journal of Nervous and Mental Disease*, 104 (1946): 358–89, 489–525.

15. U.S. Army Medical Department, *Neuropsychiatry in World War II*, 1:376–82, 2:1003ff.; Malcolm J. Farrell and John Appel, "Current Trends in Military Neuropsychiatry," *AJP*, 101 (1944): 12–19.

16. Farrell and Appel, "Current Trends in Military Neuropsychiatry," 14–15; WCM, "Psychiatric Experience in the War," 580.

17. See Herbert X. Spiegel, "Psychiatric Observations in the Tunisian Campaign," *American Journal of Orthopsychiatry*, 14 (1944): 381–85, "Preventive Psychiatry with Combat Troops," *AJP*, 101 (1944): 310–15, and "Psychiatry with an Infantry Battalion in North Africa," in U.S. Army Medical Department, *Neuropsychiatry in World War II*, 2:111–26.

18. Appel's report was subsequently published in collaboration with Gilbert W. Beebe, "Preventive Psychiatry: An Epidemiologic Approach," *JAMA*, 131 (1946): 1469–75. See also John B. Dynes, "Mental Breaking Points," *New England Journal of Medicine*, 234 (1946): 42–45.

19. Appel and Beebe, "Preventive Psychiatry," 1475; "Report of Special Commission of Civilian Psychiatrists . . . 1945," 77–78.

20. WCM, *Psychiatry in a Troubled World: Yesterday's War and Today's Challenge* (New York, 1948), 293–319; U.S. Army Medical Department, *Neuropsychiatry in World War II*, 2:275–333. The latter source includes lengthy descriptions of psychiatric treatment in the military. See also Abram Kardiner and Herbert Spiegel, *War Stress and Neurotic Illness* (New York, 1947), chaps. 2–5.

21. WCM, "Psychiatric Experience in the War," 579; Whitehorn, "Combat Exhaustion," 6; Grinker and Spiegel, *War Neuroses*, 113–14; Grinker and Spiegel chap. in *Manual of Military Neuropsychiatry*, ed. Harry C. Solomon and P. I. Yakovlev (Philadelphia, 1944), 539. See especially Nolan D. C. Lewis and B. Engle, eds., *Wartime Psychiatry: A Compendium of the International Literature* (New York, 1954).

22. U.S. Army Medical Department, *Neuropsychiatry in World War II*, 1:33–66; WCM, "Development of Psychiatry in the Army in World War II," *War Medicine*, 8 (1945): 230–31.

23. My discussion has been greatly informed by Nathan G. Hale's analysis of World War II developments in his as yet unpublished manuscript on the history of American psychoanalysis since 1917.

24. Henry W. Brosin, "The Army Has Learned These Lessons," *Modern Hospital*, 64 (1945): 45–47. The optimism that grew out of the war was dramatically illustrated in an army documentary film approved by William C. Menninger in late 1945 and written and directed by John Huston. Completed in early 1946 under the title *Let There Be Light*, the film portrayed the manner in which battlefield experiences tested individual breaking points. It called attention to the role of earlier childhood experiences and dramatically illustrated the successes of narcosynthesis, occupational and physical therapy, individual and group psycho-

therapy, and hypnosis. The film was quickly withdrawn, partly because the use of actual patients raised ethical issues involving privacy.

25. U.S. Army Medical Department, *Neuropsychiatry in World War II*, 1:749. The lessons of World War II drawn by some British military psychiatrists were fundamentally the same as those gleaned by their American counterparts. See especially John R. Rees (an individual who played a major role in the organization of the psychiatric division of the British Army Medical Service), *The Shaping of Psychiatry by War* (New York, 1945).

26. "Conference on Post War Psychiatric Needs Called by the National Committee for Mental Hygiene, February 1–3, 1945," foreword and recommendations, typescript copy, Whitehorn Papers, APAA. See also George S. Stevenson, "Contributions of War Experience to Our Knowledge of Mental Hygiene," *AJPH*, 36 (1946): 1129–32.

27. Appel and Beebe, "Preventive Psychiatry," 147.

28. WCM, *Psychiatry in a Troubled World*, 410–37.

29. Grinker and Spiegel, *Men under Stress* (Philadelphia, 1945), 427–60.

30. Robert H. Felix and R. V. Bowers, "Mental Hygiene and Socio-Environmental Factors," *Milbank Memorial Fund Quarterly*, 26 (1948): 125–47; Felix, "Mental Public Health: A Blueprint," presentation at St. Elizabeths Hospital, Apr. 21, 1945, Felix Papers, NLM; *New York Times*, Apr. 4, 1947. The following articles by Felix are illustrative of his views in the late 1940s: "Psychiatric Plans of the United States Public Health Service," *Mental Hygiene*, 30 (1946): 381–89; "Developing a Federal Mental Health Program," National Conference of Social Work, *Proceedings*, 73 (1946): 547–55; "State Participation in the National Mental Health Program," ibid., 74 (1947): 461–68; "State Planning for Participation in the National Mental Health Act," *Public Health Reports*, 62 (1947): 1183–91; "Psychiatry in Prospect," *AJP*, 103 (1947): 600–606; "Mental Hygiene and Public Health," *American Journal of Orthopsychiatry*, 18 (1948): 679–84; "Mental Disorders as a Public Health Problem," *AJP*, 106 (1949): 401–6.

31. Thomas A. C. Rennie and L. E. Woodward, *Mental Health in Modern Society* (New York, 1948), vii–xi and passim; Nolan D. C. Lewis, "What the Wars' Experiences Have Taught Us in Psychiatry," in N.Y. Academy of Medicine, *Medicine in the Postwar World* (New York, 1948), 65.

CHAPTER TWO
THE REORGANIZATION OF PSYCHIATRY

1. KAM, "History of the Reorganization Program" (Aug. 1, 1948), 1, in RMDO, 200-20, APAA. See also KAM's remarks in APA Council Proceedings, Feb. 26–27, 1945, 3–11, APA Board of Trustees Papers, APAA.

2. Undated petition in "President's Correspondence 1948–1949," Box 2 (W. Overholser File 1944–1945), APAA; J. K. Hall to Karl Bowman, Dec. 18, 1944, Hall Papers, University of North Carolina Library, Chapel Hill, N.C.

3. "Proceedings of Societies," *AJP*, 101 (1944): 248–49, "Reports of Committees," ibid., 102 (1945): 117, 119. The members of the committee included Leo H. Bartemeier, A. E. Bennett, Spafford Ackerly, and Thomas A. Ratliff.

4. "Report of the Special Committee . . . October 27–28, 1945," *AJP*, 102 (1946): 694–95 (a preliminary draft copy of this report can be found in the KAM Papers, MFA); APA Council Proceedings, Feb. 26–27, 1945, 3–11, APA Board of Trustees Papers, APAA.

5. Cheyney to Samuel W. Hamilton, Jan. 17, Farrar to Cheyney, Feb. 11, Russell to Farrar, Feb. 26, Mar. 12, Farrar to Russell, Feb. 15, Mar. 8, Russell to Winfred Overholser, Feb. 26, Mar. 9, Burlingame to Farrar, Mar. 19, Abraham Myerson to Farrar, Mar. 2, Farrar to Myerson, Mar. 7, May to Farrar, Apr. 27, 1945, Fararr Papers, APAA; J. K. Hall to Ross M. Chapman, Jan. 31, 1945, notebook, "Palmer House Chicago. Special Meeting Council of the American Psychiatric Association, February 26–27, 1945," Burlingame to Overholser, Feb. 15, 1945, Hall Papers, University of North Carolina Library.

6. Karl M. Bowman to APA members, Apr. 9, with enclosed letter from Special Committee on Reorganization, William Sandy to Farrar, Apr. 21, 30, Farrar to Sandy, Apr. 25, James V. May to Bowman, Apr. 20, R. C. Montgomery to Bowman, May 4, Russell to Bartemeier, May 4, Farrar to Bowman, June 9, 1945, Fararr Papers, APAA; "Report of the Special Committee . . . October 27–28, 1945," *AJP*, 102 (1946): 694–700.

An earlier survey by Samuel W. Hamilton (president-elect of the APA) revealed a comparable split. Sixty-three favored a full-time medical director, and an equal number were opposed. Fifty-three favored an increase in dues, and seventy expressed opposition. Austin M. Davies to Farrar, Feb. 25, 1945, Farrar Papers, APAA.

7. "Report of the Special Committee . . . October 27–28, 1945," *AJP*, 102 (1946): 698–700; Minutes of the Meeting of the Committee on Reorganization, Feb. 10, 1946, RMDO, 200-19, APAA.

8. Karl M. Bowman, "Presidential Address," *AJP*, 103 (1946): 1–17; "Reports of Committees," ibid., 268–69, "Proceedings of Societies," ibid., 400–414; Robert H. Hutching to Farrar, June 14, 1946, Farrar Papers, APAA.

9. GAP, Minutes of the First Informal Gathering, May 26, 1946, GAP Papers, AP; WCM, "Psychiatric Experience in the War, 1941–1946," *AJP*, 103 (1947): 582, and "Psychiatry and the Army," *Psychiatry*, 7 (1944): 175–81. See also the following works of WCM: "The Promise of Psychiatry," *New York Times Magazine*, Sept. 15, 1946, 10, 53–54; "Psychiatry Today," *Atlantic Monthly*, 181 (Jan. 1948): 65–72; (with Munroe Leaf) *You and Psychiatry* (New York, 1948); *Psychiatry: Its Evolution and Present Status* (Ithaca, N.Y., 1948); *A Psychiatrist for a Troubled World: Selected Papers of William C. Menninger* (New York, 1967).

10. KAM, *The Human Mind* (New York, 1930), *Man against Himself* (New York, 1938), and (with Jeanette Lyle Menninger) *Love against Hate* (New York, 1942); KAM, "Psychiatry Must Emerge," unpublished manuscript, May 10, 1940, KAM Memo to Mildred Law, July 14, 1947, KAM to Lawson W. Lowrey, Apr. 22, 1950, KAM Papers, MFA; WCM Diary, Apr. 22, 1949, manuscript in possession of Catherine Menninger, Topeka, Kans. See also *A Psychiatrist's World: The Selected Papers of Karl Menninger, M.D.*, ed. Bernard H. Hall (New York, 1959). Lawrence J. Friedman's *Menninger: The Family and the Clinic* (New York, 1990) is an indispensable source for the history of the Menninger Foundation.

11. GAP, Minutes of the First, Second, and Third Informal Gatherings, May 26–28, 1946, GAP Papers, AP; "Proceedings of Societies," *AJP*, 103 (1946): 388–89. See also Henry Brosin's "Historical Remarks on the First Eighteen Years of GAP," address delivered at the 1963 meeting of GAP (second draft), 4–5, copy in WCM Papers, MFA. For a generally accurate—but highly favorable and partisan—analysis, see Albert Deutsch, *The Story of GAP* (New York, 1959).

12. GAP, Circular Letters 1, 2, 3 (June 1946), 170 (Jan. 1950), 189 (Mar. 1950), 250 (May 1954), Minutes of the First Formal Meeting, Nov. 3–6, 1946, Statement of Aims, Apr. 9, 1949, with reactions, GAP Papers, AP.

13. Draft of letter by Brosin to Mildred Scoville (Commonwealth Fund), ca. May 1947, Brosin-GAP Papers, MFA.

14. Farrar to Overholser, Dec. 20, 1946 (with enclosed constitution), Overholser to Farrar, Feb. 15, June 26, 1947, May 11, 1949, June 6, 1951, Overholser to Treadway, July 3, 1951, Burlingame to Farrar, Nov. 26, Dec. 19, 1947, Farrar to Burlingame, Dec. 2, 1947, WCM to Farrar, Dec. 2, 1946, Jan. 18, 1947, Farrar to Menninger, Dec. 6, 1946, Mar. 6, 1947, Farrar to Hamilton, Dec. 6, 1946, Jan. 31, 1947, Hamilton to Farrar, Feb. 17 (two letters), Feb. 28, Mar. 6, 1947, Fararr Papers, APAA.

15. GAP, *Reports Nos. 1–10* (Sept. 15, 1947–July 1949).

By the 1940s electroshock had largely replaced insulin shock therapy, which had been introduced by Manfred Sakel in the 1930s. Although widely employed, shock therapies in general created unease, especially among those critical of somatic therapies. Shock therapies could not be reconciled with any theory or known physiological data, and there were few valid studies of their effectiveness. Nevertheless, they were widely employed and received favorable publicity in the popular media. See Gerald N. Grob, *Mental Illness and American Society, 1875–1940* (Princeton, 1983), 296–303.

16. "The Position of Psychiatrists in the Field of International Relations," GAP *Report No. 11* (Jan. 1950); "The Social Responsibility of Psychiatry, A Statement of Orientation," GAP *Report No. 13* (July 1950): 1–5. The preliminary draft of this document was even more strident. "We are not ashamed," the draft stated, "to confess to a mission of social reform, qualified by all the reasonable limitations intrinsic in the status of our profession. Within these limits, we feel not only justified, but ethically compelled to advocate those changes in social organization which have a positive relevance to a program of mental health." GAP Circular Letter 154 (Sept. 16, 1949), 7, GAP Papers, AP.

17. GAP Circular Letters 88 (May 11, 1948), 102 (June 9, 1948), 311 (July 7, 1961), app. A p. E, "Degree of Integration of GAP and APA Committees," undated (ca. 1948), GAP Papers, AP; Deutsch, *Story of GAP*, 31.

18. Special Committee on Reorganization, Minutes, July 14, 1946, RMDO, 200-19, APAA.

19. Transcript of the Meeting of Section I, APA, May 20, 1947, copy in WCM Papers, MFA; "Reports of Meetings of the Council," *AJP*, 104 (1947): 205.

20. "Proceedings of Societies," *AJP*, 104 (1947): 333–34; Farrar to Burlingame, Dec. 2, 1947, Farrar Papers, APAA.

21. KAM to Albert Deutsch, June 2, WCM to Deutsch, June 9, Deutsch to KAM, June 18, 1947, Deutsch Papers, APAA; Oscar Raeder to WCM, July 24,

1947, Daniel Blain Papers, APAA; Walter L. Treadway to Farrar, May 30, 1947, Farrar Papers, APAA.

Deutsch used the term *Young Turks* as early as 1946. See his columns in *PM*, May 29, Nov. 18, 1946. Nevertheless, as he wryly informed WCM, "I know a lot of young 'Jerks' and a lot of old 'Turks,' but chronological age has nothing to do with it." Deutsch to WCM, June 25, 1947, Deutsch Papers, APAA.

22. Copy of letter from Cheyney to Douglas Thom, Nov. 28, 1947, Farrar Papers, APAA; WCM to M. Ralph Kaufman, Oct. 27, 1947. See also WCM to Kaufman, Nov. 18, WCM to Bartemeier, Nov. 18, WCM to Charles A. Zeller, Oct. 27, 1947, WCM Papers, MFA.

The hostility toward psychiatric activists was evident in Burlingame's correspondence. "I have such a tremendously high regard for you and for your scientific ability and horse sense," he told Farrar, "that to be mixed up with you in any capacity gives me a clean, wholesome feeling in these days when I feel that I need a psychiatric bath, or house cleaning." Burlingame to Farrar, Dec. 23, 1947, Farrar Papers, APAA.

Burlingame attended the First International Congress on Psychosurgery, which was organized in honor of Dr. Egas Moniz (who introduced the procedure) by Dr. Walter Freeman, the American pioneer of psychosurgery. Burlingame characterized psychosurgery as "a powerful instrument of therapeutic advance that must not be neglected." Burlingame, "First International Congress on Psychosurgery," *AJP*, 105 (1949): 550–51.

23. "Report of the Committee on Reorganization," Dec. 11, 1947, with attached "Basis for Constructing Districts," RMDO, 200-20, APAA.

The creation of district areas reflected the concentrated geographical distribution of APA members. Of the nearly 4,000 members residing in the United States, 957 (24.1 percent) were in New York, 319 (8.0 percent) in California, 241 (6.1 percent) in Massachusetts and an equal number in Pennsylvania, and 220 (5.5 percent) in Illinois. Only six other states had between 100 and 200 members. The eleven states with 100 or more members accounted for 68 percent of the total membership.

24. "Report of the Committee on Reorganization," Dec. 11, 1947, RMDO, 200-20, APAA; Bartemeier to Frank Fremont-Smith, Nov. 13, 1947, WCM Papers, MFA; Blain to KAM, Feb. 11, 1948, KAM Papers, MFA; Blain to Overholser, Feb. 6, 1948, Overholser to APA Members, Feb. 20, 1948, RMDO, 100-28, APAA; "Appointment of Dr. Blain," *AJP*, 104 (1948): 581. See also Blain to Overholser, Jan. 19, Overholser to Blain, Jan. 22, 1948, RMDO, 100-28, APAA.

25. WCM to George S. Stevenson, Feb. 7, 1948, RMDO, 200-4, APAA; WCM to Douglas A. Thom, Apr. 12, 1948, WCM Papers, MFA; Dexter Bullard interview, August 5, 1964, Oral History 148, 31–34, APAA; "Proceedings of Societies," *AJP*, (1949): 858–60. The most authoritative history of psychosurgery in this period is Jack S. Pressman's "Uncertain Promise: Psychosurgery and the Development of Scientific Psychiatry in America, 1935–1955" (Ph.D. diss., University of Pennsylvania, 1986). Elliot S. Valenstein's *Great and Desperate Cures: The Rise and Decline of Psychosurgery and Other Radical Treatments for Mental Illness* (New York, 1986) is less satisfactory.

26. For an analysis of these differences in the early 1950s, see John Maciver and Fredrick C. Redlich, "Patterns of Psychiatric Practice," *AJP*, 115 (1959): 692–97.

27. "Report of Meeting of the Committee on Reorganization," Mar. 16, 1948, "Report to the A.P.A. Council Meeting of 15 May 1948, from the Committee on Reorganization," KAM to Presidents and Secretaries of the Affiliate Societies of the APA, June 10, 1948, WCM Papers, MFA; "Constitution and By-laws," *AJP*, 105 (1948): 132–47, "Proceedings of Societies," ibid., 860–63, 933–34; Letter to APA Members from Committee on Reorganization, Aug. 9, 1948 (with attachment), RMDO, 200-20, APAA.

28. For KAM's angry response to those who identified reorganization and GAP, see his letter to Lawson G. Lowrey, Apr. 27, 1950, and his Memo to Mildred Law, July 14, 1947, KAM Papers, MFA. WCM also felt impelled to correct Maxwell Gitelson's views. "Actually I had nothing to do with the way the special committee on reorganization was set up," he wrote in quite accurate terms. Gitelson to WCM, Mar. 3, WCM to Gitelson, Mar. 10, 1947, Gitelson Papers, Manuscripts Division, Library of Congress, Washington, D.C.

29. Robie to Burlingame, 21 May 1948, Farrar Papers, APAA.

30. Minutes of the Vidonian Club, June 6, 1948, Vidonian Club Papers, AP. The minutes of the club in the late 1940s offer evidence of the pervasiveness of internal divisions in American psychiatry (see the Minutes for the meetings of Oct. 30, 1948, Oct. 29, 1949).

31. "Shock Therapy," GAP *Report No. 1* (Sept. 15, 1947); *New York Times*, June 6, July 12, 1948; Bowman to WCM, May 27, WCM to Bowman, June 7, WCM to Robie, June 7, WCM to Robert P. Knight, June 7, 1948, RMDO, 100-16, APAA; "Joint Statement on Electroshock by the Presidents of the American Psychiatric Association and the Electro-Shock Research Association," *AJP*, 106 (1949): 152; Robert B. McGraw to Brosin, Dec. 12, 1949, Brosin-GAP Papers, MFA; "Revised Electro-shock Therapy Report," GAP *Report No. 15* (Aug. 1950). Robie defended both inpatient and outpatient ambulatory electroshock therapy in a paper delivered in 1949 and published as "Is Shock Therapy on Trial?" *AJP*, 106 (1950): 902–10.

32. APA Council Meeting, Minutes, Nov. 16, 1948, 160–76, APA Board of Trustees Papers, APAA; Bowman to WCM, June 21, Felix to WCM, July 23, WCM to Felix, July 28 (200-27), WCM to Hamilton, Sept. 28 (same letter sent to Overholser, Stevenson, Edward A. Strecker, and Earl D. Bond), Bowman to WCM, Oct. 4 (200-13), Blain to WCM, Sept. 30, 1948 (100-8), RMDO, APAA; Rennie to WCM, Aug. 2, WCM to Rennie, Aug. 5, 1948, WCM Papers, MFA; Burlingame to Farrar, Aug. 11, Nov. 4, 6, 17, Robie to Farrar, Sept. 1 (two letters), Nov. 19, Robie to Burlingame, Sept. 1, Burlingame to KAM, Nov. 17, Farrar to H. C. Baugh, Nov. 24, 1948, Farrar Papers, APAA.

33. "Are You Always Worrying?" *Time*, 52 (Oct. 25, 1948): 64–66, 69–72; WCM to Henry Luce, Sept. 4, T. S. Matthews to WCM, Sept. 12, Strecker to WCM, Sept. 25, WCM to Strecker, Sept. 28, Burlingame to WCM, Sept. 29, WCM to Burlingame, Oct. 4, Bowman to WCM, Sept. 28, WCM to Bowman, Oct. 13, Transcript of telephone conversation with Miss Doherty of *Time*, Oct. 18, Rennie to WCM, Oct. 21, WCM to Rennie, Oct. 27, Carl Binger to WCM,

Oct. 26, WCM to Binger, Nov. 1, Deutsch to WCM, Oct. 29, Burlingame to J.D.M. Griffin, Oct. 24, Griffin to Burlingame, Oct. 29, WCM to Griffin, Nov. 1, 1948, WCM Papers, MFA; WCM to Burlingame, Oct. 4, 1948, RMDO, 100-8, APAA; Burlingame to Farrar, Nov. 1, 1948, Farrar Papers, APAA.

34. WCM to Robie, Nov. 8, Dec. 1, 1948, Ewalt to WCM, Mar. 5, WCM to APA officers and Council members, Mar. 18, 1949, WCM Papers, MFA; form letter from Robie and letter from CPMSP to all APA members, n.d. (ca. late Dec. 1948 or early Jan. 1949), CPMSP to WCM (similar letter widely circulated), Jan. 5, 1949, RMDO, 200-25, APAA; CPMSP *Newsletter*, No. 1 (Jan. 1949), No. 2 (Mar. 1949), No. 3 (Apr. 1949), copies in GAP Papers, AP.

35. D. Ewen Cameron to Blain, Apr. 26, May 12, 1949, RMDO, 100-3, APAA.

36. Appel to WCM, Jan. 17, 1949, WCM Papers, MFA; Gitelson to KAM, Jan. 10, 1949, Gitelson Papers, Library of Congress.

37. Bowman to WCM, Jan. 20, Mar. 7, WCM to Bowman, Feb. 7, Mar. 9, 24, 1949, Bowman to McGraw, Mar. 17 (this letter was circulated, with Bowman's permission, to all APA members on Apr. 28 by five psychiatrists), WCM to Blain, Feb. 7, 1949, WCM Papers, MFA; Blain to WCM, Apr. 5, WCM to Blain, Apr. 21 (100-16), Blain to Burlingame, Apr. 19 (100-2), Blain to Harry Solomon, May 12, 1949 (100-10), RMDO, APAA.

38. APA Council Meeting, Minutes, Nov. 16, 1948, 160–76, APA Board of Trustees Papers, APAA; "Report to the Council from the Committee on Reorganization," May 1949, RMDO, 200-20, APAA; WCM, "President's Page," *AJP*, 105 (1949): 548–49, 704–5, 794; Whitehorn to Brosin, Jan. 15, Brosin to Whitehorn, Jan. 17, Brosin to WCM, Jan. 17, 19, WCM to Whitehorn, Jan. 19, Feb. 10, Whitehorn to WCM, Jan. 24, 1949, WCM Papers, MFA. See also Whitehorn to John A. P. Millet, Feb. 11, Whitehorn to Brosin, Dec. 8, 21, Brosin to Whitehorn, Dec. 14, 21, 1949, Whitehorn Papers, APAA.

39. *New York Daily Compass*, May 24, 1949. Robie sent a furious letter to CPMSP members on the Deutsch column, noting that the committee included psychoanalysts, social psychiatrists, and others of progressive political affiliations. See Robie to CPMSP members, n.d., copy in Deutsch Papers, APAA. There is no evidence that members of GAP were sympathetic toward the Communist party.

40. WCM, "Presidential Address," *AJP*, 106 (1949): 1–12; "Proposed Amendments to Constitution," ibid., 228–32; "Proposed Constitutional Amendments," ibid., 472–74; "Proceedings of the American Psychiatric Association . . . 1949," ibid., 196 (1950): 771–74; "The Detroit Meeting," ibid., 107 (1950): 70; "Constitution and By-laws . . . 1950," ibid., 138–43; Whitehorn, "A Message from the President," ibid., 145–46; "Proceedings of the American Psychiatric Association . . . 1950," ibid., 283–97; WCM letters dated June 2, 1949, to Cameron, Hamilton, Bowman, Ewalt, and Brosin, in APA President's Correspondence Box 1941–42, 1948–49, WCM File, 1948–49, APAA. See also Whitehorn's "Presidential Address: The Individual Psychiatrist and Social Psychiatry," *AJP*, 108 (1951): 1–6.

Suspicions of GAP did not die easily. In January 1950 critics charged that the Mental Health Study Section of the NIMH gave preferential treatment to grant applications from GAP members. The data did not substantiate the charge. Memo, C. V. Kidd to Mary E. Switzer, Jan. 11, 1950, Switzer Papers, Schlesinger Library, Radcliffe College, Cambridge, Mass. See also Lowrey to Bartemeier, Mar. 2, Bartemeier to Lowrey, Mar. 20, 1950, Whitehorn Papers, APAA.

41. Barton to Ewalt, Mar. 16, 1950, Whitehorn to WCM, Feb. 3, WCM to Whitehorn, Feb. 7, 1950, Brosin, "Historical Remarks," passim, WCM Papers, MFA; Deutsch, *Story of GAP*, 28–34; GAP Constitution and By-Laws (ca. 1950), copy in GAP Papers, AP.

42. See D. Ewen Cameron, "The Committee Structure of the American Psychiatric Association," *AJP*, 109 (1952): 386–88. The need to provide a link between the members and the APA led to an expansion of the district branches and the creation of an assembly. For an analysis of the evolution of this system, see the following: WCM to Cameron, Jan. 26, George Stevenson to Cameron, Jan. 26, Ewalt to Cameron, Jan. 30, 1951, Cameron, "Notes on the Development of the District Branch and Assembly System" (Sept. 1958), and "The Assembly of District Branches of the American Psychiatric Association," Cameron Papers, APAA.

43. This generalization is based on a 10 percent (n = 943) sample of the total membership of the APA for 1957, using the *Biographical Directory of Fellows & Members of the American Psychiatric Association as of October 1, 1957* (New York, 1958).

44. Cf. KAM, "A Psychiatric Fable," *Bulletin of the Menninger Clinic*, 14 (1950): 129–30.

CHAPTER THREE
ORIGINS OF FEDERAL INTERVENTION

1. World War II had a dramatic impact upon the social sciences, for it strengthened faith in the efficacy of social engineering. See especially Peter Buck, "Adjusting to Military Life: The Social Sciences Go to War, 1941–1950," in *Military Enterprise and Technological Change: Perspectives on the American Experience*, ed. Merritt Roe Smith (Cambridge, Mass., 1985), 203–52.

2. See especially Lawrence J. Friedman, *Menninger: The Family and the Clinic* (New York, 1990).

3. Gerald N. Grob, *Mental Illness and American Society, 1875–1940* (Princeton, 1983), 308–15. The development of federal biomedical research policy can be followed in Victoria A. Harden's *Inventing the NIH: Federal Biomedical Research Policy, 1887–1937* (Baltimore, 1986).

4. Lawrence C. Kolb, "The Need for a Neuropsychiatric Institute in the U.S. Public Health Service for the Study of Nervous and Mental Diseases," ca. late 1939, Samuel W. Hamilton to Kolb, Dec. 18, 1939, NIMH Papers, Subject Files 1940–51, Box 75, WNRC.

5. C. C. Burlingame to Lawrence Kolb, Sept. 15, Kolb to Burlingame, Sept. 23, Franklin G. Ebaugh to Kolb, Oct. 13, Kolb to Ebaugh, Oct. 25, 1940, S. Bernard Wortis to Kolb, Apr. 16, 1963, Kolb Papers, NLM; *AJP*, 97 (1941): 1244–45, 98 (1941): 285; *JAMA*, 114 (1940): 2570, 116 (1941): 2790, 2796.

6. Daniel M. Fox, "The Politics of the NIH Extramural Program, 1937–1950," *Journal of the History of Medicine and Allied Sciences*, 42 (1987): 447–

66. My analysis of health policy in the postwar era is based on Fox's *Health Policies, Health Politics: The British and American Experience, 1911–1965* (Princeton, 1986), chaps. 5, 7.

7. New York Academy of Medicine, *Medicine in the Changing Order* (New York, 1947), 221–32; American Hospital Association Commission on Hospital Care, *Hospital Care in the United States* (New York, 1947); Fox, *Health Policies, Health Politics*, 115–31.

8. President's Scientific Research Board, *Science and Public Policy*, 5 vols. (Washington, D.C., 1947), 1:3, 113–18; Fox, *Health Policies, Health Politics*, 158–60; Stephen P. Strickland, *Politics, Science, and Dread Disease: A Short History of United States Medical Research Policy* (Cambridge, 1972), chaps. 2–3.

9. Franklin G. Ebaugh, *The Care of the Psychiatric Patient in General Hospitals* (Chicago, 1940).

10. See especially Robert H. Felix interview by Harlan Phillips, Feb. 8, 1963, and interview by Jeanne Brand, April 2, 1964, NLM; Felix interview by Daniel Blain, May 15, 1972, Blain Papers, APAA; Felix interview by Milton J. E. Senn, March 8, 1979, Senn Collection (OH76), NLM; John A. Clausen conversation with Gerald N. Grob, May 3, 1988.

11. Felix interview by Brand, NLM; Alanson W. Willcox to Felix, Jan. 22, Feb. 20, 1945 (with draft bill), Mary E. Switzer Papers, Schlesinger Library, Radcliffe College, Cambridge, Mass.

12. Felix interview by Brand, NLM; Switzer to Martin H. Miller, Mar. 12, Switzer to Lasker, Mar. 13, Switzer to KAM, Mar. 14, Lasker to Switzer, Mar. 14, Switzer to Lasker, Mar. 17, 1945, Switzer Papers, Schlesinger Library; 79-1 Congress (1945), *Congressional Record*, 1991, 6205.

13. George S. Stevenson, "National Neuropsychiatric Institute Bill," Apr. 3, 1945, Winfred Overholser to Burlingame, Apr. 28, 1945, RMDO, 200-18, APAA; Burlingame to C. B. Farrar, Apr. 26, 1945, Farrar Papers, APAA; Willcox to Switzer, June 8, David Rapaport to Switzer, July 24, Felix to Switzer, Aug. 3, 1945, Switzer Papers, Schlesinger Library.

14. 79-1 Congress, *National Neuropsychiatric Institute Act. Hearing before a Subcommittee of the Committee on Interstate and Foreign Commerce, House of Representatives . . . 1945* (Washington, D.C., 1945), 8–17, and 79-2 Congress, *National Neuropsychiatric Institute Act. Hearings before a Subcommittee of the Committee on Education and Labor, United States Senate . . . 1946* (Washington, D.C., 1946), 7–19.

15. 79-1 Congress, *National Neuropsychiatric Act. Hearing . . . House*, 29–30, 35–54; 79-2 Congress, *National Neuropsychiatric Institute Act. Hearings . . . Senate*, 47–61.

16. 79-1 Congress, *National Neuropsychiatric Act. Hearing . . . House*, 109–10; 79-2 Congress, *National Neuropsychiatric Act. Hearings . . . Senate*, 107; Felix interview by Brand, NLM.

The bulk of Deutsch's articles on the plight of institutionalized patients appeared in the newspaper *PM* between March and June of 1946. "Publication of these articles," Pepper wrote, "was an important public service in explaining the falseness of our thinking on the mentally ill and in revealing the barbaric and degrading conditions which prevail in our mental health institutions." Pepper to Deutsch, June 13, 1946, Priest to Deutsch, May 11, 1946, Deutsch Papers, APAA.

17. 79-2 Congress, *National Neuropsychiatric Act. Hearings . . . Senate*, 76–88.

18. 79-2 Congress, *National Neuropsychiatric Act. Hearings . . . Senate*, 13–16; 79-1 Congress, *National Neuropsychiatric Act. Hearing . . . House*, 12, 60–61, 68–69, 77, 84, 100–101.

19. 79-1 Congress, *House Report No. 1445* (Dec. 14, 1945); 79-2 Congress, *Senate Report No. 1353* (May 16, 1946); 79-2 Congress, *House Report No. 2350* (June 26, 1946); 79-2 Congress (1946), *Congressional Record*, 2283–2300, 2347–48, 5069, 6936, 6995–96, 7155, 7163, 7584, 7925–26, 7957, 8015, 10104.

20. Chap. 538, *U.S. Statutes at Large*, 60:421–26, 1946; 79-1 Congress, *National Neuropsychiatric Act. Hearing . . . House*, 82ff.; 79-2 Congress (1946), *Congressional Record*, 2284ff.; Felix interview by Daniel Blain, May 15, 1972, 5–6, Blain Papers, APAA.

21. Felix, "Mental Disorders as a Public Health Problem," *AJP*, 106 (1949): 401–6; Paul V. Lemkau, *Mental Hygiene in Public Health* (1949; 2d ed., New York, 1955).

22. For Felix's views, see the following: "Developing a Federal Mental Health Program," National Conference of Social Work, *Proceedings*, 73 (1946): 447–55; "State Participation in the National Mental Health Program," ibid., 74 (1947): 461–68; "Psychiatry in Prospect," *AJP*, 103 (1947): 600–606; "Mental Disorders as a Public Health Problem," ibid., 106 (1949): 401–6; Felix and R. V. Bowers, "Mental Hygiene and Socio-Environmental Factors," *Milbank Memorial Fund Quarterly*, 26 (1948): 125–47; "The Relation of the National Mental Health Act to State Health Authorities," *Public Health Reports*, 62 (1947): 41–54; "The National Mental Health Program: A Progress Report," ibid., 63 (1948): 837–47; "Mental Public Health: A Blueprint," presentation at St. Elizabeths Hospital, Apr. 21, 1945, Felix Papers, NLM. The discussion about training personnel for work in community mental health clinics can be followed in Switzer to WCM, June 3, Switzer to Felix, June 2, Switzer to Edward A. Strecker, June 2, WCM to Switzer, June 9, 1947, WCM Papers, MFA. In *Mental Illness: Progress and Prospects* (New York, 1967), Felix summarized his views about post–World War II developments in an account that was partly autobiographical and partly historical.

Many of Felix's articles were actually prepared by NIMH staff members even though their names—with some exceptions—did not appear on the title pages. The views expressed in these publications, however, accurately reflected Felix's thinking.

23. Felix interview by Brand, NLM; Felix, *Mental Illness*, 49–50.

24. See Felix interview by Brand, NLM.

25. Jeanne L. Brand and Philip Sapir, eds., "An Historical Perspective on the National Institute of Mental Health," February, 1964, mimeograph document prepared as sec. 1 of the NIMH Report to Dean E. Woolridge, chairperson, NIH Study Committee, copy provided by Jeanne L. Brand; NIMH, *Mental Health Series*, No. 4 (PHS *Publication 20:* rev. ed., 1950), 1–20.

The National Mental Health Act of 1946 originally stipulated that the National Advisory Mental Health Council should consist of six medical and scientific members. Four years later an amendment expanded its membership to twelve (six professional and six lay representatives).

26. Seymour Kety interview by Daniel Blain, May 14, 1973, 1–19, Blain Papers, APAA; John Clausen interview by Senn, Mar. 30, 1973, 5ff., Senn Collection (OH20), NLM; Brand and Sapir, "An Historical Perspective on the National Institute of Mental Health," 69–79. See also Clausen, *Sociology and the Field of Mental Health* (New York, 1956).

Since this book is concerned with the history of policy, I have not dealt with the NIMH intramural research program. Its activities can be followed in the many publications of the staff as well as in Felix's testimony during his annual appearances before the House and Senate subcommittees of the Committees on Appropriations.

27. 80-2 Congress, HR Subcommittee of the Committee on Appropriations, *Department of Labor—Federal Security Agency Appropriation Bill for 1949. Hearings* (Washington, D.C., 1948), Pt. 2, 267; GAP Circular Letter 102 (June 9, 1948), 3–9, GAP Papers, AP.

28. PHS Mental Hygiene Division, "Annual Report for Fiscal Year 1947," 5–6, typed copy in NIMH Records, Subject Files, 1940–51, Box 82, WNRC; 80-2 Congress, HR Subcommittee of the Committee on Appropriations, *Department of Labor–Federal Security Agency Appropriation for 1949. Hearings*, Pt. 2, 271; Felix, "The Relation of the National Mental Health Act to State Health Authorities," *Public Health Reports*, 62 (1947): 46–47; idem., "The National Mental Health Program—A Progress Report," ibid., 63 (1948): 837–39; *New York Times*, Apr. 4, 1947.

29. PHS Mental Hygiene Division, "Annual Report, Fiscal 1948," 4, NIMH, "Annual Report, Fiscal 1949," 9 and table 5, typed copies in NIMH Records, Subject Files, 1940–51, Box 82, NIMH, "Objectives and a Balanced Program for the NIMH," draft, Oct. 15, 1951, 15, Central Files 1951–54, Box 10, WNRC; 81-2 Congress, HR Subcommittee of the Committee on Appropriations, *Department of Labor–Federal Security Agency Appropriations for 1951. Hearings* (Washington, D.C., 1950), 539; 83-1, HR Subcommittee of the Committee on Appropriations, *Department of Labor–Federal Security Agency Appropriations for 1954. Hearings* (Washington, D.C., 1953), pt. 1, 1034; Jerry W. Carter, "The Community Services Program of the National Institute of Mental Health, U.S. Public Health Service," *Journal of Clinical Psychology*, 6 (1950): 113–14; Anita K. Bahn and V. B. Norman, *Outpatient Psychiatric Clinics in the United States 1954–55* (PHS, *Public Health Monograph No. 49*: 1957), 40.

30. Mental Hygiene Division, "Annual Report, Fiscal 1948," 8–9, NIMH, "Annual Report, Fiscal 1949," 12, typed copies in NIMH Records, Subject Files 1940–51, Box 82, WNRC; Felix interview by Senn, 13–15, NLM; 80-2 Congress, HR Subcommittee of the Committee on Appropriations, *Department of Labor–Federal Security Agency Appropriation Bill for 1949. Hearings*, pt. 2, 282–83.

31. Carter, "Community Services Programs," 14; National Advisory Mental Health Council, Minutes of Meeting, Nov. 8–9, 1954, 8, RG 90, National Ar-

chives, Washington, D.C. See especially the Community Services State Files 1949–1954, and the Annual Summaries of State Mental Health Programs 1947–60, in NIMH Records, WNRC.

32. National Advisory Mental Health Council, Minutes of Meeting, Dec. 11–12, 1950, 11–14, Mar. 9–11, 1955, 5–7, RG 90, National Archives, Washington, D.C.; NIMH, *Evaluation in Mental Health . . . Report of the Subcommittee on Evaluation of Mental Health Activities, Community Services Committee, National Advisory Mental Health Council* (PHS *Publication 413*: 1955), 1, 3, 57.

33. 79-1 Congress, *National Neuropsychiatric Act. Hearing . . . House*, 25, 114; 79-2 Congress, *National Neuropsychiatric Act. Hearings . . . Senate*, 26, 88; Felix interview by Brand, NLM. For a discussion of psychiatric epidemiology, see Gerald N. Grob, "The Origins of American Psychiatric Epidemiology," *AJPH*, 76 (1985): 229–36.

34. See Buck, "Adjusting to Military Life," 203–52; John A. Clausen, "Research on the American Soldier as a Career Contingency," *Social Psychology Quarterly*, 47 (1984): 207–13 and "Health and the Life Course: Some Personal Observations," *Journal of Health and Social Behavior*, 28 (1987): 337–44.

35. Felix and Bowers, "Mental Hygiene and Socio-Environmental Factors," 124–47. See also 82-1 Congress, HR Subcommittee of the Committee on Appropriations, *Department of Labor–Federal Security Appropriations for 1952. Hearings* (Washington, D.C., 1951), pt. 2, 799–800.

36. John A. Clausen, "Social Science Research in the National Mental Health Program," *American Sociological Review*, 15 (1950): 404.

37. For the state of psychiatric classification in the postwar period, see *Diagnostic and Statistical Manual: Mental Disorders* (often referred to as DSM-I), prepared by the Committee on Nomenclature and Statistics of the APA (Washington, D.C., 1952). See also the editorial comment ("Back to Babel") by Newton Bigelow in *Psychiatric Quarterly*, 24 (1950): 385–90, and Paul Haun, "A Rational Approach to Psychiatric Nosology," ibid., 23 (1949): 308–16.

38. Clausen, "Social Science Research," 405; NIMH, *Proceedings of the First Conference of Mental Hospital Administrators and Statisticians* (Feb. 26–28, 1951) (PHS *Publication 295*: 1953), 1–12.

39. Clausen, "Social Science Research," 405.

40. Ibid., 405–6; 81-2 Congress, HR Subcommittee of the Committee on Appropriations, *Department of Labor–Federal Security Agency Appropriations for 1951. Hearings*, pt. 1, 539.

41. Felix to WCM, Feb. 11, enclosed with "Report of the Sub-Committee on Integrative Policy to the Committee on Training, Division of Mental Hygiene, U.S. Public Service," Felix to WCM, July 23, 1948, WCM Papers, MFA.

42. William C. Jenkins to R. R. Willey, Sept. 6, 1952, NIMH Records, Central Files 1951–54, Box 7, WNRC; NIMH, *Training Grant Program Fiscal Years 1948–1961* (PHS *Publication 966*: 1962), 4–7.

43. The data for 1948–1951 are included in Jenkins to Willey, Sept. 8, 1952, NIMH Records, Central Files 1951–54, Box 7, WNRC. The data are suggestive rather than definitive. The NIMH had data on only about 60 percent of trainees, and the information was limited to the first position accepted by individuals. Nor did the data delineate situations that included multiple employment. Information

for the 1960s can be found in the following: *Current Professional Status of Mental Health Personnel Supported under National Institute of Mental Health Training Grants* (PHS *Publication 1088*: 1963); *A Study of the Current Status of Mental Health Personnel Supported under National Institute of Mental Health Training Grants* (PHS *Publication 1541*: 1966); and Franklyn N. Arnhoff, B. M. Shiver, and R. M. VanMatre, "Subsequent Career Activities of National Institute of Mental Health Trainees in Psychiatry," *Journal of Medical Education*, 42 (1967): 855–62.

44. Lawrence C. Kolb, "Research and Its Support under the National Mental Health Act," *AJP*, 106 (1949): 409; Philip Sapir interview by Senn, Nov. 30, 1977, 6ff., Senn Collection (OH76), NLM; Brand and Sapir, "An Historical Perspective on the National Institute for Mental Health," 27–28.

45. Sapir interview by Senn, 6, 13, Senn Collection (OH76), NLM.

46. "Research Grants Awarded by the National Institute of Mental Health July 1, 1947 to March 1, 1951," typescript copy in RMDO (200-20), APAA; NIMH, "Annual Report, Fiscal 1949," 2–4, in NIMH Records, Subject Files 1940–51, Box 82, WNRC; NCMHI, *The Research Grant Program of the National Institute for Mental Health . . . Fiscal Year 1964* (PHS *Publication 1423*: 1966), 11–12.

47. Commission on Organization of the Executive Branch of the Government, app. E, "Report of the Subcommittee on Psychiatry and Neurology Committee on Federal Services," November, 1948, 35–36, typescript copy, Hoover Institution, Stanford, Calif.; idem., *Report on Federal Medical Services . . . by the Task Force on Federal Medical Services February 1955* (Washington, D.C., 1955), 115; *Federal Medical Services: A Report to the Congress by the Commission on Organization of the Executive Branch of the Government February 1955* (Washington, D.C., 1955), 66; Richard H. Williams, "Some Issues of Planning and Policy in the National Institute of Mental Health: Report of Discussions of the Executive Staff April 8, 1957," 1–4, 16, NIMH Records, Mental Health Subject Files 1957–60, Box 14, WNRC.

48. See Memo of Harold P. Halpert to Robert Felix and Staff, October 3, 1952 ("Draft of Long-Range Plan for P & R Section"), NIMH Records, Central Files 1951–54, Box 11, and Richard H. Williams, "Some Issues of Planning and Policy in the National Institute of Mental Health," Mental Health Subject Files 1957–60, Box 14, WNRC.

CHAPTER FOUR
MENTAL HOSPITALS UNDER SIEGE

1. Frank Fremont-Smith, "New Opportunities for the Improvement of Mental Hospitals," *Mental Hygiene*, 31 (1947): 354–62; *New York Times*, Oct. 3, 1946.

2. Edith Stern, "Our Ailing Mental Hospitals," *Survey Graphic*, 30 (1941): 429–32, also summarized in *Reader's Digest*, 39 (Aug. 1941): 66–69; Albert Deutsch to Charles W. Ferguson, Jan. 20, 1941, Deutsch Papers, APAA; *PM*, Aug. 4, 5, 6, 7, 8, 1941.

3. *New York Times*, Apr. 3, 4, 1941; *Mental Hygiene*, 25 (1941): 145, 27 (1943): 146–51; *JAMA*, 116 (1941): 62, 120 (1942): 1327; *Diseases of the Ner-*

vous System, 4 (1943): 25–29; *Modern Hospital,* 60 (Mar. 1943): 69–70. See also Temporary Commission on State Hospital Problems, *Insulin Shock Therapy* (Albany, 1944).

4. *PM,* Mar. 18, 19, 1943.

5. *New York Times,* Mar. 13, 14, 15, 24, 31, May 25, 27, July 14, 1943, Mar. 16, 1944; J. K. Hall to Arthur H. Ruggles, Mar. 27, Hall to James W. Vernon, Aug. 13, 1943, Hall Papers, University of North Carolina Library, Chapel Hill, N.C.; *JAMA,* 126 (1944): 33; N.Y. State Department of Mental Hygiene, *Annual Report,* 56 (1943–1944): 13–17; Commission to Investigate the Management and Affairs of the Department of Mental Hygiene of the State of New York and the Institutions Operated by It, *The Care of the Mentally Ill in the State of New York* (Albany, 1944).

6. T. L. McCulloch, "A Report on the Survey of the Louisiana State Institutions by the U.S. Public Health Service," *News-Letter of the American Association of Psychiatric Social Workers,* 12 (Summer 1942): 42–47; *Care of Patients in the State Mental Institutions of Connecticut: A Report to His Excellency the Governor by the Public Welfare Council* (Hartford, 1942); *Report of the Committee Appointed by Honorable Edward Martin to Make a Complete Study of the Mental Hospitals of the Commonwealth of Pennsylvania July 1944* (Harrisburg, 1944); Charles H. Watkins, Charles W. Greenough, Clifton T. Perkins (committee appointed by the governor of Massachusetts to make a survey of all public institutions) to Governor Leverett Saltonstall, June 1, 1942, Saltonstall Papers, Massachusetts Historical Society, Boston, Mass.

7. Jeanne Brand, "Albert Deutsch: The Historian as Social Reformer," *Journal of the History of Medicine and Allied Sciences,* 18 (1963): 149–57.

8. Ibid., 153; *PM,* Mar. 11, 12, Oct. 7, 1946.

9. Ibid., May 12, 13, 1947. The bulk of Deutsch's articles appeared in the spring of 1946. See ibid., Mar. 11, 12, Apr. 17, 23, 24, 26, 28, 29, 30, May 2, 6, 7, 9, 10, 12, 14, 15, 16, 20, 22, 23, 30, June 9, 10, 18, 21, Oct. 7, Nov. 21, Dec. 28, 1946, Feb. 2, 6, Sept. 25, 28, 1947.

10. Memos from KAM to P. Lundgren, June 15, 16, and Lundgren to KAM, June ? (two memos), KAM to WCM and reply, June 17, Harry Levinson to KAM, June 27, Harvey J. Tompkins to KAM, July 2, J. R. Stone to KAM, July 6, Malcolm J. Farrell to KAM, July 6, 20, Deutsch to KAM, July 22, M. A. Tarumianz to KAM, July 22, Edward A. Strecker to KAM, July 24, Arthur P. Noyes to KAM, July 26, Karl M. Bowman to KAM, July 27, Clifton T. Perkins to KAM, July 28, C. A. Bonner to KAM, July 29, 1948, KAM Papers, MFA; KAM, "Introduction," in *The Shame of the States,* by Albert Deutsch (New York, 1948), 15–24.

11. Deutsch, *Shame of the States,* 182–88; Deutsch to Dora S. Heffner, Dec. 21, 1948, Deutsch Papers, APAA. *The Shame of the States* received generally favorable reviews in newspapers, magazines, and medical journals. A list of these reviews can be found in the Deutsch Papers, APAA. See also Deutsch, "Recent Trends in Mental Hospital Care," National Conference of Social Work, *Proceedings,* 77 (1950): 143–59.

12. Albert Q. Maisel, "Bedlam 1946," *Life,* 20 (May 6, 1946): 102–18.

13. "Growing Outcry over Mental Hospitals," *Christian Century,* 63 (1946): 611–12; "The Naked 'Innocents,'" *Commonweal,* 44 (1946): 107.

14. Alan Gregg to John D. Rockefeller, Jr., Mar. 18, 1946, RG 1.2, Series 200A, Rockefeller Foundation Papers, RAC; Frank L. Wright, Jr., *Out of Sight out of Mind* (Philadelphia, 1947), 123–51.

15. Gorman's articles in the *Daily Oklahoman* were reprinted in pamphlet form under the following titles: *Misery Rules in State Shadowland* (Norman, ca. 1946), *Let There Be Light* (Norman, 1947), and *If We Can Love* (Norman, 1947). See also the transcript of the interview of Gorman by Michael Barton, Apr. 7, 1972, copy in Daniel Blain Papers, APAA.

16. "Oklahoma Attacks Its Snakepits," *Reader's Digest*, 53 (Sept. 1948), 139–60; Mike Gorman to Gerald N. Grob, July 11, 1986; *Daily Oklahoman*, April 25, 1948; KAM to George Stevenson (with enclosure), Apr. 16, 1948, KAM Papers, MFA.

17. Mary Jane Ward, *The Snake Pit* (New York, 1946), serialized in *Reader's Digest*, 48 (May 1946): 129–68. See also Krin and Glen O. Gabbard, *Psychiatry and the Cinema* (Chicago, 1987), 68–71.

18. *PM*, May 27, 1947; GAP Circular Letter 125 (Jan. 19, 1949), GAP Papers, AP; "The Root of Our Evils," *Psychiatric Quarterly*, 20 (1946): 332–44. For a different reaction to the novel, see Walter B. Pitkin, "Facts behind 'The Snake Pit,'" *Reader's Digest*, 49 (Dec. 1946): 121–24.

19. See, for example, George H. Preston, "The New Public Psychiatry," *Mental Hygiene*, 31 (1947): 177ff.; Harvey J. Tompkins and Lucy D. Ozarin, "Changing Concepts of the Role of the Institutional Psychiatrist," *Psychiatric Quarterly, Supplement*, 24 (1950): 23–34; Minutes of the Vidonian Club, Jan. 28, 1950, Vidonian Club Papers, AP; D. Blain to Gov. William G. Stratton, June 4, Nov. 25, 1953, Jan. 18, 1954, Stratton to Blain, Dec. 30, 1953, Feb. 3, 1954, Blain to Paul R. Hawley, Jan. 18, 1954, RMDO, 100-22, APAA; DeWitt Dominick to Lauren H. Smith, Jan. 25, enclosed with "Report of the Joint Committee from the Senate and House on . . . the Wyoming State Mental Hospital at Evanston," Dominick to KAM, Jan. 25, KAM to Dominick, Feb. 4, 1955, KAM Papers, MFA.

20. See, for example, KAM, "The Future of Psychiatric Care in Hospitals," *Modern Hospital*, 64 (May 1945): 43–45, and Minutes of the Vidonian Club, Mar. 29, 1947, Vidonian Club Papers, AP.

21. Samuel W. Hamilton to APA members, ca. 1946, with enclosed "Addenda to Report of May 26 of the Committee on Standards and Policies" and Press Release of APA Council Statement, RMDO, 200-25, APAA; *PM*, May 30, 1946.

22. GAP Circular Letter No. 12 (Nov. 20, 1946), GAP Papers, AP.

23. GAP Circular Letter No. 22 (Mar. 20, 1947) and No. 55 (Dec. 5, 1947), GAP Papers, AP; "Public Psychiatric Hospitals," GAP *Report No. 5* (Apr. 1948).

24. F. A. Freyhan to Hugh T. Carmichael, June 17, 1948, Carmichael Papers, APAA.

25. "Standards for Psychiatric Hospitals and Out-Patient Clinics Approved by the American Psychiatric Association (1945–46)," *AJP*, 102 (1945): 264–69; "Report of the Committee on Psychiatric Standards and Policies May 26, 1946," ibid., 103 (1946): 257–59; Robert C. Hunt, "APA Standards for Public Mental

Hospitals," in "Exploratory Conference to Review Standards for Public Mental Hospitals . . . June 3, 4, 1959," 7–9, RMDO, 200-25, APAA.

26. Hunt, "APA Standards for Public Mental Hospitals," in "Exploratory Conference . . . 1959," 10, and Leo Bartemeier to Hans H. Reese, Mar. 1, 1947, RMDO, 200-25, APAA; M. A. Tarumianz, "The Background and Development of the Central Inspection Board of the American Psychiatric Association" (Apr. 1960), 1–4, Box 17, CIB Papers, APAA; *AJP*, 105 (1948–1949): 391–92, 932; Ralph H. Chambers, "Inspection and Rating for Mental Hospitals," ibid., 106 (1949): 250–54.

27. Blain to Walter E. Barton, June 25, 1948, with summary of meeting of hospital superintendents, May 17, 1948, RMDO, 200-25, APAA; Samuel W. Hamilton, "Our Association in a Time of Unsettlement," *AJP*, 104 (1947): 5.

28. Hunt's paper, "APA Standards for Public Mental Hospitals," and the ensuing discussions can be found in "Exploratory Conference . . . 1959," RMDO, 200-25, APAA; "Reformulation of A.P.A. Standards Proposed," *Mental Hospitals*, 11 (May 1960): 37–38; Minutes of the Executive Committee of the CIB, Apr. 19, 1950, Jan. 11, 1954 (Box 17), "Report on the Program of the Central Inspection Board," ca. 1959, Box 16, CIB Papers, APAA; "Hospital Standards," Mental Hospital Institute, *Proceedings*, 3 (1951): 18–32; APA, *Standards for Hospitals and Clinics* (1956; rev. ed. Washington, D.C., 1958).

29. Tarumianz, "Background and Development of the Central Inspection Board," passim (Box 17), "List of Hospitals Inspected by the Central Inspection Board . . . 1949 through 1960," Box 16, CIB Papers, APAA; "Preliminary Report of the Ad Hoc Committee to Program Future of Central Inspection Board February 16, 1960," Braceland Papers, APAA.

30. Daniel Blain, "The Mental Hospital Institute—an Appraisal," *Mental Hospitals*, 6 (Nov. 1955): 5–6; Robert L. Robinson, "The First APA Mental Hospital Institute: A Reminiscence," *Hospital & Community Psychiatry*, 21 (1970): 317–19; APA Mental Hospital Institute, *Proceedings*, 1–6 (1949–1954). Beginning in 1955, the proceedings were published in *Mental Hospitals* and its successor (*Hospital & Community Psychiatry*). *Mental Hospitals* was originally issued under the title *APA Mental Hospital Service Bulletin* and in 1960 was renamed *Hospital & Community Psychiatry*.

31. For background material on the NCMH from the early twentieth century to World War II, see Gerald N. Grob, *Mental Illness and American Society 1875–1940* (Princeton, 1983), chap. 6, and Norman Dain, *Clifford W. Beers: Advocate for the Insane* (Pittsburgh, 1980).

32. George S. Stevenson, "Needed: A Plan for the Mentally Ill," *New York Times Magazine*, July 27, 1947, 11, 18–19.

33. *PM*, Feb. 18, 1947; Deutsch to Stevenson, Feb. 12, Deutsch to Harold Maine, Nov. 19, Sol W. Ginzberg to Deutsch, Feb. 21, 28, 1947, Deutsch Papers, APAA; Memo from Ethel L. Ginzberg to Stevenson, July 29, 1947, WCM Papers, MFA.

Maine's book, *If a Man Be Mad* (Garden City, N.Y., 1947) was an autobiographical account by an alcoholic of his experiences with treatment. His reminiscences of institutional life were harsh.

34. Alan Gregg Diary, Apr. 24, 1945, Mar. 8, 1946, Rockefeller Foundation Papers, RG 1.2, Series 200A, RAC; *The Attendant*, 1–2 (1944–1945), continued as *The Psychiatric Aide*, 3–9 (1946–1952); *New York Times*, May 6, July 22, Oct. 11, 1946.

35. WCM to Charles Dollard, Jan. 4, 1947, Gregg Diary, Apr. 24, 1945, Jan. 16, 1947 (with grant award attachment), Raymond B. Fosdick Inter-Office Memo, June 3, 1946, Norma Thompson to Harold Burton, Jan. 16, 1947, Robert S. Morison interview (i.e., office diary), Oct. 8, Nov. 1, 1946, Feb. 17, May 6, 1947, Feb. 6, 1948, Gregg to John D. Rockefeller, Mar. 18, 1946, Rockefeller Foundation Papers, RG 1.2, Series 200A, RAC.

36. Leo H. Bartemeier, "The Psychiatric Foundation," *AJP*, 104 (1947): 145–47; *American Journal of Psychotherapy*, 1 (1947): 96–97; form letter from Bartemeier, Feb. 18, 1947, Farrar Papers, APAA; WCM to Blain, Sept. 13, 1948, RMDO, 100-8, APAA.

37. "Materials Pertaining to Federation Discussions between Menninger Foundation, Psychiatric Foundation, National Committee for Mental Hygiene and National Mental Health Foundation," Rockefeller Brothers Fund Papers, Box 64, RAC; WCM to Mary Switzer, Aug. 26, 1947, Switzer Papers, Schlesinger Library, Radcliffe College, Cambridge, Mass.

38. WCM to Mary E. Switzer, Nov. 14, 1947, Nov. 29, 1948, Switzer to Richard C. Hunter, Nov. 22, Hunter to Switzer, Nov. 23, with enclosed "Minutes of the Annual Meeting of the Members Held on November 16, 1948," Mildred Law to Switzer, Nov. 26, 1948, "Purpose and Plan of the Mental Health Study and Planning Committee," Mar. 30, 1949, Elling Aannestad to Switzer, June 6, 1949, with "Preliminary Memorandum on Voluntary Mental Health Organization," Hunter to Law, Jan. 7, 1948 (actual date is 1949), Law to Hunter, Jan. 12, 1949, with "Suggestions for a Federation of Organizations Interested in Mental Health" (written by WCM, Jan. 12, 1949), Switzer Papers, Schlesinger Library, Radcliffe College, Cambridge, Mass.; Switzer to WCM, Nov. 19, WCM to Switzer, Nov. 26, 29, 1948, WCM Papers, MFA; "Memorandum" (with enclosed correspondence) from President Arthur H. Ruggles to the Board and Council of the NCMH, Jan. 11, 1949, KAM Papers, MFA; WCM to Stevenson and Blain, Sept. 24, 1949, RMDO, 100-8, APAA; William L. Russell to Edward W. Bourne, Nov. 7, 1949, WCM Papers, MFA.

39. Memorandum from Arthur Ruggles to Elected Members of the NCMH, June 23, 1950, with enclosed Notice of Special Meeting, WCM Papers, MFA.

40. NAMH/NIMH Training Course, 1953, 84–89, Deutsch Papers, APAA. See also Harry Milt to Deutsch, Dec. 27, 1954, ibid.

41. "Points for Investigation of the Internal Structure of the National Association for Mental Health," Nov. 1951, Thomas A. C. Rennie to WCM, Nov. 26, 1951, WCM Papers, MFA; Arthur H. Bunker to Gregg (with enclosed budget), Mar. 12, 1951, Morison to Bunker, Apr. 18, 1951, Flora M. Rhind to Oren Root, June 22, 1951, RF 51113 (grant), June 22, 1951, Morison interview (i.e., office diary), Feb. 26, 1952, Morison to H. W. Elley, Oct. 24, 1952, Rockefeller Foundation Papers, RG 1.1, Series 200, RAC.

42. Robert M. Heininger to WCM, July 9, Sept. 23, WCM to Heininger, July 13, Sept. 29, 1954, H. W. Elley to WCM, Apr. 19, WCM to Elley, Apr. 22, 1955,

WCM Papers, MFA; Blain to Rennie, Apr. 21, Rennie to Blain, Apr. 26, 1955 (100-9), Blain to Paul V. Lemkau, June 14, Lemkau to Blain, June 17, 1955 (100-6), Blain to Harvey J. Tompkins, June 2, 1956 (100-11), RMDO, APAA; Gorman interview by Michael Barton, 43, Stevenson interview by Blain, May 8, 1972, 27–28, both in Blain Papers, APAA; Leo Bartemeier interview No. 3 (Mar. 2, 1967), 19–21, APA OH115, APAA; Charles Schlaifer to Deutsch, Feb. 6, Mar. 19, 1957, Deutsch Papers, APAA. The Marion E. Kenworthy Papers at the AP are particularly good for the internal problems of the NAMH during the 1950s.

43. For background on Lasker, see "Moving Force in Medical Research," *Medical World News*, Nov. 20, 1964, 83–89; Elizabeth B. Drew, "The Health Syndicate: Washington's Noble Conspirators," *Atlantic Monthly*, 220 (Dec. 1967): 75–82; and Stephen P. Strickland, *Politics, Science, and Dread Disease: A Short History of United States Medical Research Policy* (Cambridge, Mass. 1972), 32–54.

44. Gorman interview by Blain, Oct. 7, 1942, 1–4 and passim, Gorman interview by Michael Barton, passim, copies in Blain Papers, APAA; KAM telegram to A. H. Gottesman, Nov. 28, KAM to Gottesman, Dec. 23, "Psychological Study T. Gorman," Dec. 1, 3, Gottesman to KAM, Dec. 20, 1949, Jan. 16, 27, Betty H. Andersen to KAM, May 26, KAM to Andersen, June 1, Milton Chernin to KAM, May 23, KAM to Chernin, May 27, 1950, KAM Papers, MFA; President's Commission on the Health Needs of the Nation, *Building America's Health: A Report to the President*, 5 vols. (Washington, D.C., 1953), 1:41, 58–60, 2:48–54, 89–98, 152–55, 206, 5:457–83. See especially Gorman's *Every Other Bed* (Cleveland, 1956).

45. Abraham A. Low and Alberta H. Brown to John C. Whitehorn, Oct. 9, Whitehorn reply, Oct. 30, 1940, Whitehorn Papers, APAA; Low, "Lost and Found," *Modern Hospital*, 54 (Feb. 1940): 59–60; Lulu Wendel, "How Former Patients Help Themselves," ibid., 69 (July 1947): 56; Low to Deutsch, June 18, 1949, Deutsch Papers, APAA; Low, "Recovery Inc., A Project for Rehabilitating Postpsychotic and Long-Term Psychoneurotic Patients," in *Rehabilitation of the Handicapped: A Survey of Means and Methods*, ed. William H. Soden (New York, 1949), 213–26; Low, *Mental Health through Will-Training* (Boston, 1950); Jack Alexander, "They 'Doctor' One Another," *Saturday Evening Post*, 31 (Dec. 6, 1952): 31, 182–84, 186; 89-2 Congress (1966), *Congressional Record*, 10322.

Low's *Mental Health through Will-Training* went through eighteen editions by 1972.

46. Rennie to Blain, June 22, Blain to Rennie, June 25, 1954 (100-9), Charlotte Watkins to Blain, Feb. 28, Blain to Watkins, March 13, 1956 (100-12), RMDO, APAA.

47. Milbank Memorial Fund, *Epidemiology of Mental Disorder* (New York, 1950), *The Biology of Mental Health and Disease* (New York, 1952), and *Interrelations between the Social Environment and Psychiatric Disorders* (New York, 1953).

48. *New York Times*, Apr. 15, 1944, Apr. 28, May 7, 1947, Sept. 14, 15, 1948; New York State Department of Mental Hygiene, *Annual Report*, 57 (1944–1945): 12–16, 59 (1946–1947): 4–6; William L. Russell to C. B. Farrar,

Jan. 22, 1945, Farrar Papers, APAA; *Psychiatric Quarterly Supplement*, pt. 1, 19 (1945): 83–84; *Mental Hygiene*, 30 (Oct. 1946): 684–87; E.H.L. Corwin and T. Pierce, "Some Aspects of the Problem of the New York State Mental Hospitals System," *New York State Journal of Medicine*, 48 (1948): 529–34; Eli Ginzberg, *A Pattern for Hospital Care: Final Report of the New York State Hospital Survey* (New York, 1949), 24–29, 222–79.

49. "Study of Psychiatric Facilities in Kansas," Kansas Legislative Council, *Publications 143, 146* (Nov. 1946); *A Psychiatrist for a Troubled World: Selected Papers of William C. Menninger, M.D.* (New York, 1967), 770–81. See especially Lawrence J. Friedman's *Menninger: The Family and the Clinic* (New York, 1990).

50. *The Governor's Conference on Mental Health . . . Sacramento, California March 3 and 4, 1949: Preliminary Report* and *Final Report* (Sacramento, 1949). See also Missouri General Assembly, *The Mentally Ill: Their Care and Treatment in Missouri*, Missouri Committee on Legislative Research, *Report No. 8* (1948); idem., *The Mentally Ill: Their Care and Treatment in Four Selected States*, Missouri Committee on Legislative Research, *Report No. 10* (1949); *Report of the Joint Senate and House Committee to Study the State Mental Hospitals, State of Maryland, March 1949* (1949); *Mental Institutions in the State of Washington: A Report of a Survey by Roger Nett* (1948); *Care and Treatment of Mental Patients*, Minnesota Legislative Research Committee, *Publication No. 19* (1948).

51. Justin G. Reese to Blain, Jan. 9, 1950, RMDO, 100-9, APAA; *AJP*, 106 (1949): 233; Council of State Governments, *The Mental Health Programs of the Forty-Eight States: A Report to the Governors' Conference* (Chicago, 1950).

52. Ibid., 4–13 and passim.

53. "Mental Health," *State Government*, 23 (1950): 183–84; Council of State Governments, *Training and Research in State Mental Health Programs: A Report to the Governors' Conference* (Chicago, 1953); "A Ten Point Program on Mental Health" and "The National Governors' Conference on Mental Health," *State Government*, 27 (1954): 48–52, 64–66.

CHAPTER FIVE
THE MENTAL HEALTH PROFESSIONS:
CONFLICT AND CONSENSUS

1. Theodore M. Brown, "Alan Gregg and the Rockefeller Foundation's Support of Franz Alexander's Psychosomatic Research," *Bulletin of the History of Medicine*, 61 (1987): 155–82.

2. Gregg, "What is Psychiatry?" *Bulletin of the Menninger Clinic*, 6 (1942): 137–46.

3. Gregg, "A Critique of Psychiatry," *AJP*, 101 (1944): 285–91. See also Gregg's "Psychiatry in Public Health," ibid., 107 (1950): 330–33 and "The Limitations of Psychiatry," ibid., 104 (1948): 513–22, as well as Robert S. Morison's Alan Gregg Lecture, "Some Illnesses of Mental Health," *Journal of Medical Education*, 39 (1964): 985–99.

4. KAM to Mary E. Switzer, Apr. 7, 1945, Switzer Papers, Schlesinger Library,

Radcliffe College, Cambridge, Mass. See also KAM's *Man against Himself* (New York, 1938).

5. For typical expressions, see Thomas A. C. Rennie to WCM, Jan. 20, 1948, WCM, "Psychiatry for Everyday Needs," Laity Lecture at the New York Academy of Medicine, Feb. 26, 1948, WCM Papers, MFA; and WCM, "The Role of Psychiatry in the World Today," *AJP*, 104 (1947): 155–63.

6. Gerald N. Grob, *Mental Illness and American Society, 1875–1940* (Princeton, 1983), 118–19; *Statistical Manual for the Use of Institutions for the Insane, Prepared by the Committee on Statistics of the American Medico-Psychological Association in Collaboration with the Bureau of Statistics of the National Committee for Mental Hygiene* (New York, 1918); *Statistical Manual for the Use of Hospitals for Mental Diseases Prepared by the Committee on Statistics of the American Psychiatric Association in Collaboration with the National Committee for Mental Hygiene*, 10th ed. (Utica, N.Y. 1942).

7. APA, *Diagnostic and Statistical Manual: Mental Disorders* (Washington, D.C., 1952), v–vii.

8. *AJP*, 105 (1949): 930, 109 (1953): 548–49; APA, *Diagnostic and Statistical Manual*, vii–x.

9. APA, *Diagnostic and Statistical Manual*, 9–43.

10. Preliminary Report (Dec. 15, 1938) and Report (n.d.) of the Committee on Psychiatry in Medical Education to the APA Council, Rockefeller Foundation Papers, RG 1.1, Series 200A, RAC; *AJP*, 97 (1940): 470–72.

11. Ralph A. Noble, *Psychiatry in Medical Education: An Abridgement of a Report Submitted to the Advisory Committee on Psychiatric Education of the National Committee for Mental Hygiene* (New York, 1933); Franklin G. Ebaugh and Charles A. Rymer, *Psychiatry in Medical Education* (New York, 1942), 486–508. For a general overview, see Jeanne L. Brand, "Neurology and Psychiatry," in *The Education of American Physicians: Historical Essays*, ed. Ronald Numbers (Berkeley, 1980), 226–49.

12. David A. Boyd, "Current and Future Trends in Psychiatric Residency Training," *Journal of Medical Education*, 33 (1958): 341–43; Charles E. Goshen, "Psychiatric Training and Its Relation to Medical Education," ibid., 35 (1960): 363. Data on NIMH training grants can be found in William C. Jenkins to R. R. Willey, Sept. 8, 1952, NIMH Records, Central Files 1951–54, Box 7, WNRC, and Roger L. Robertson and E. A. Rubenstein, *National Institute of Mental Health Training Grant Program Fiscal Years 1948–1961* (PHS *Publication 966*: 1962).

13. Conference on Psychiatric Education, *Report*, 1952, 3. See also the "Report on Medical Education," GAP *Report No. 3* (1948).

14. Conference on Psychiatric Education, *Report*, 1951, 42; APA Committee on Medical Education, "An Outline for a Curriculum for Teaching Psychiatry in Medical Schools," *Journal of Medical Education*, 31 (1956): 115–28. See also Theodore Lidz, "The 1951 Ithaca Conference on Psychiatry in Medical Education," ibid., 30 (1955): 689–97.

15. "The Preclinical Teaching of Psychiatry," GAP *Report No. 54* (1962): 16, 22, 35.

16. Alexander H. Leighton, J. A. Clausen, and R. N. Wilson, *Explorations in Social Psychiatry* (New York, 1957), v–vii and passim; Milbank Memorial Fund, *Interrelations between the Social Environment and Psychiatric Disorders* (New York, 1953); Rennie, "Social Psychiatry: A Definition," *International Journal of Social Psychiatry*, 1 (1955): 12.

The growing significance of social psychiatry was evident in the appearance in the 1954–1955 edition of the *Year Book of Neurology, Psychiatry and Neurosurgery* of a chapter entitled "Psychosocial Medicine (Social Psychiatry)." That same year the *International Journal of Social Psychiatry* began publication.

17. For an expansion of this theme, see Gerald N. Grob, "The Origins of American Psychiatric Epidemiology," *AJPH*, 75 (1985): 229–36.

18. August B. Hollingshead and F. C. Redlich, *Social Class and Mental Illness: A Community Study* (New York, 1958); Leo Srole, T. S. Langner, S. T. Michael, M. K. Opler, and Rennie, *Mental Health in the Metropolis: The Midtown Manhattan Study* (New York, 1962). The psychiatric epidemiological literature of the 1950s is extensive. A useful summary can be found in Myrna M. Weissman and G. L. Klerman, "Epidemiology of Mental Disorders," *Archives of General Psychiatry*, 35 (1978): 705–10. See also H. Warren Dunham, "Methodology of Sociological Investigations of Mental Disorders," *International Journal of Social Psychiatry*, 3 (1957): 7–17; Benjamin Pasamanick, ed., *Epidemiology of Mental Disorder* (Washington, D.C., 1959); and Paul H. Hoch and J. Zubin, eds., *Comparative Epidemiology of the Mental Disorders* (New York, 1961).

19. Maxwell Jones, *Social Psychiatry: In the Community, in Hospitals, and in Prisons* (Springfield, Ill., 1962), ix; William Hollister, "New Approaches in Social Psychiatry," in NIMH, *Mental Health Career Development Program . . . 1964* (PHS *Publication 1245*: 1964), 82; Redlich and D. X. Freedman, *The Theory and Practice of Psychiatry* (New York, 1966), 823. See also Walter Reed Army Institute of Research, *Symposium on Preventive and Social Psychiatry . . . April 1957* (Washington, D.C., 1958); Julia W. Mayo, "What Is the Social in Social Psychiatry?" *Archives of General Psychiatry*, 14 (1966): 449–55; and Joseph Zubin and F. A. Freyhan, eds., *Social Psychiatry* (New York, 1968).

20. Norman W. Bell and J. P. Spiegel, "Social Psychiatry," *Archives of General Psychiatry*, 14 (1966): 337–45; GAP, "The Preclinical Teaching of Psychiatry," 22.

21. For discussions of pre–World War II patterns of professional relationships, see Grob, *Mental Illness and American Society*, chaps. 9–10; Nancy Tomes, "The Rise of the Mental Health Professions," unpublished paper in possession of author; Kathleen W. Jones, "As the Twig Is Bent: American Psychiatry and the Troublesome Child 1890–1940" (Ph.D. diss., Rutgers University, 1988); and John C. Burnham, "The Struggle between Physicians and Paramedical Personnel in American Psychiatry, 1917–41," *Journal of the History of Medicine & Allied Sciences*, 29 (1974): 93–106.

22. Grob, *Mental Illness and American Society*, 244–60; Lois M. French, *Psychiatric Social Work* (New York, 1940), passim; Tomes, "The Rise of the Mental Health Professions."

23. Grob, *Mental Illness and American Society*, 260–64; Conference on Psychiatric Education, *Proceedings*, 4 (1936): 199–203; James H. Capshew, "Psy-

chology on the March: American Psychologists and World War II" (Ph.D. diss., University of Pennsylvania, 1986), 19, 21. See also Donald S. Napoli, *Architects of Adjustment: The History of the Psychological Profession in the United States* (Port Washington, N.Y., 1981) and Michael M. Sokol, ed., *Psychological Testing and American Society 1890–1930* (New Brunswick, N.J., 1987).

24. Capshew, "Psychology on the March," 104–7 and passim. See also Napoli, *Architects of Adjustment*, chaps. 5–6, and U.S. Army Medical Department, *Neuropsychiatry in World War II*, 2 vols. (Washington, D.C., 1966–1973), 1:567–603.

25. James G. Miller, "Clinical Psychology in the Veterans Administration," *American Psychologist*, 1 (1946): 181–89; Jenkins to Willey, Sept. 8, 1952, NIMH Records, Central Files 1951–1954, Box 7, WNRC; Robertson and Rubenstein, *National Institute of Mental Health Training Grant Program*; Capshew, "Psychology on the March," 19–21; Tomes, "The Rise of the Mental Health Professions"; Napoli, *Architects of Adjustment*, chaps. 6–7.

26. Daniel Blain, "The Psychiatrist and the Psychologist," *Journal of Clinical Psychology*, 3 (1947): 4–10; Edward A. Strecker to Blain, Nov. 15, Blain to Strecker, Dec. 9, 1948, RMDO, 100-10, APAA.

27. "Report of Committee on Clinical Training of Psychologists," *American Journal of Orthopsychiatry*, 10 (1940): 166–71; David Shakow, "The Training of the Clinical Psychologist," *Journal of Consulting Psychology*, 6 (1942): 277–88; "Proposed Program of Professional Training in Clinical Psychology," ibid., 7 (1943): 23–26; APA Committee on Training in Clinical Psychology (Shakow Committee), "Recommended Graduate Training Program in Clinical Psychology," *American Psychologist*, 2 (1947): 539–58; John M. Reisman, *A History of Clinical Psychology*, enl. ed. (New York, 1976), chap. 7.

28. GAP Circular Letters No. 26 (May 16, 1947), 64 (Dec. 10, 1947), 140 (May 4, 1949), GAP Papers, AP; GAP, "Meeting of Committee on Therapy," Nov. 9, 1947, 5–8, G. N. Raines to George E. Gardner, Aug. 21, 1947, Blain Papers, APAA; "The Relation of Clinical Psychology to Psychiatry," GAP *Report No. 10* (July 1949); Paul E. Huston to WCM, Sept. 12, WCM to Huston, Sept. 14, Gardner to WCM, Oct. 6, WCM to Gardner, Oct. 11, 1949, WCM Papers, MFA.

29. James S. Plant to Karl M. Bowman, Sept. 20, 1945, "Excerpt from Stenotypists Minutes, [APA] Council Meeting," Dec. 14–15, 1946, David M. Levy to WCM, May 11, 1948, enclosed with copies of Levy to Plant, Nov. 24, 1944, June 9, 1945, WCM to Levy, May 25, 1948, APA Committee on Relation of Psychology and Psychiatry, "Committee Functions," June 21, 1948, "Report of the Committee on the Relation of Psychiatry with Clinical Psychology," ca. Feb. 26, 1949, RMDO, 200-14, APAA; Lawrence S. Kubie, "Memorandum to Participants of Conference on Training in Clinical Psychology," Apr. 7, Blain to Kubie, Apr. 19, 1948, Blain Papers, APAA; John C. Whitehorn to Joe M. Harris, May 15, 1950, Whitehorn Papers, APAA; *American Psychologist*, 4 (1949): 445.

30. "Report of the Committee on the Relation of Psychiatry with Clinical Psychology," ca. Feb. 26, 1949, Appendix, ix, RMDO, 200-14, APAA.

31. WCM, "Psychiatry and Psychology," *AJP*, 105 (1948): 390, and "The Relationship of Clinical Psychology and Psychiatry," *American Psychologist*, 5

(1950): 3–15, also printed in the *Bulletin of the Menninger Clinic*, 14 (1950): 1–21.

32. *New York Times*, Jan. 19, 1949; "Regulation of Psychological Counseling and Psychotherapy," *Columbia Law Review*, 51 (1951): 474–95.

33. See especially John C. Burnham, "Psychology and Counseling: Convergence into a Profession," in *The Professions in American History*, ed. Nathan O. Hatch (Notre Dame, Ind., 1988), 181–98.

34. Blain to Norman A. Cameron, May 3, 1951, and copy of "Newsletter. Division of Clinical and Abnormal Psychology" (American Psychological Association), 4 (Apr. 1951), Mimeograph document headed "This material on the general subject of clinical psychologists has been collected by the Medical Director's Office of the American Psychiatric Association," 1951, George S. Stevenson to Chairman, Civil Service Commission, May 5, 1950 (200-14), D. Ewen Cameron to Lewis A. Alesen, Nov. 25, 1952, (100-22), RMDO, APAA; Theodore R. Robie to Whitehorn, Nov. 9, 21, Whitehorn to Robie, Nov. 16, Dec. 3, 1951, copy of draft of proposed New Jersey bill, Aug. 1951, Whitehorn Papers, APAA; Francis J. Gerty and J. W. Holloway, Jr., "Licensure or Certification of Clinical Psychologists," *JAMA*, 148 (1952): 271–73.

35. *American Journal of Psychotherapy*, 3 (1949): 207–12, 8 (1954): 215–18; *New York Times*, Mar. 4, 7, 17, 23, 1953, Feb. 16, 18, 21, 23, 24, Mar. 9, 11, 15, 16, 17, 1954; Robie to Kenneth Appel, Feb. 19, 25, Edward Adelson to Blain, Mar. 18, 1954 (200-17), Fillmore H. Sanford, "Relations with Psychiatry," ca. 1953 (200-15), RMDO, APAA; CPMSP, *Bulletin*, n.d., ca. 1953 (sent to all APA members), copy in GAP Papers, AP.

36. *AJP*, 111 (1954): 385–86; *Mental Hospitals*, 5 (Dec. 1954): 7; *JAMA*, 159 (1955): 1662; Sanford, "Relations with Psychiatry," ca. 1953, RMDO, 200-15, APAA, also published in the *American Psychologist*, 8 (1953): 169–73.

37. *AJP*, 111 (1954): 385–86; "Report of the Committee on the Relation of Psychiatry with Clinical Psychology," ca. Feb. 1949 (200-14), Memorandum from the APA Committee on Clinical Psychology to the American Psychological Association Committee on Clinical Psychology, 1951 (200-24), Blain to Sanford, Apr. 1, 25, June 12, Sanford to Blain, Apr. 16, June 3, 1952, APA Committee on Clinical Psychology, "Report to the Officers and Council," Feb. 4, 1953, "Notes on Conference on the Relations of Psychology and Psychiatry . . . July 31, 1953," "Memorandum of Conference between Officers of the American Psychiatric Association and of the American Psychological Association, July 31, 1953," (200-15), RMDO, APAA; Sanford, "Relations with Psychiatry," *American Psychologist*, 8 (1953): 169–73.

38. Carl Rogers quoted in Reisman, *A History of Clinical Psychology*, 291; "Recommended Graduate Training Program in Clinical Psychology," *American Psychologist*, 2 (1947): 548; Arthur W. Combs, "Problems and Definitions in Legislation," ibid., 8 (1953): 562, "Comment," ibid., 590–97; David P. Ausubel, "Relationships between Psychology and Psychiatry: The Hidden Issues," ibid., 11 (1956): 99–105.

39. Kubie, "Medical Responsibility for Training in Clinical Psychology," *Journal of the Association of American Medical Colleges*, 23 (1948): 100–107

and "The Pros and Cons of a New Profession: A Doctorate in Medical Psychology," *Texas Reports on Biology and Medicine*, 12 (1954): 692–737; Kubie to Leo Bartemeier, Apr. 26, Gardner to Bartemeier, Apr. 30, Bartemeier to Gardner, May 10, 1951, RMDO, 200-14, APAA; Kubie to Clarence B. Farrar, May 27, June 21, Farrar to Kubie, June 16, Farrar to Arthur P. Noyes, June 16, 28, July 19, Noyes to Farrar, June 21, 28, July 6, 13, 23, Sept. 29, Frank J. Curran to Noyes, June 22, Karl M. Bowman to Noyes, July 8, D. Ewen Cameron to Noyes, July 9, Whitehorn to Noyes, July 9, Appel to Noyes, July 15, 19, Noyes to Huston, July 20, Kubie to Noyes, Sept. 23, 1954, Farrar Papers, APAA.

Kubie's letter to the *AJP* was apparently not published. Instead, a version appeared in *JAMA*, 157 (1955): 466–67, 1434.

40. Noyes to Walter B. Martin, Jan. 17, 1955 (100-14), APA Committee on Relations with Psychology, "Relations with Psychology," Feb. 15, 1955, and "Report to Council," May 9, 1955, (200-15), RMDO, APAA; *AJP*, 112 (1955): 219; *American Psychologist*, 10 (1955): 93–95.

41. APA Committee on Relations with Psychology, "Report to Council," May 13, 1957, and "A.P.A. Policies Regarding the Practice of Medicine by Non-Physicians and the Role of Psychologists," Oct. 23, 1957, RMDO, 200-16, APAA; *American Psychologist*, 13 (1958): 610–11, 761–63.

42. John C. Burnham, *How Superstition Won and Science Lost: Popularizing Science and Health in the United States* (New Brunswick, N.J., 1987), chap. 3; Bernard Lubin, "Survey of Psychotherapy Training and Activities of Psychiatrists," *Journal of Clinical Psychology*, 18 (1962): 252–56; NIMH, *Psychologists in Mental Health: Based on the 1964 Register of the National Science Foundation* (PHS *Publication 1557*: 1966); Reisman, *A History of Clinical Psychology*, 354.

43. Joel S. Handler, "Summary of Report to Council . . . on Present Status of Relations with Psychology," ca. 1959, RMDO, 200-16, APAA; *AJP*, 116 (1960): 950–52; *American Psychologist*, 15 (1960): 198–200.

44. *AJP*, 118 (1961): 268, 119 (1962): xiv, 121 (1964): 290; C. H. Hardin Branch to Handler, Dec. 27, 1962 (100-35), APA Committee on Relations with Psychology, "Report, May, 1963," Robert H. Thrasher communication on relationship of psychiatry and psychology, Apr. 16, 1963, "Principles Underlying Interdisciplinary Relations between the Professions of Psychiatry and Psychology: A Position Statement by the Council of the American Psychiatric Association February, 1964," "Combined Meeting Committee on Relations with Psychology [APA] and Committee on Relations with Psychiatry [American Psychological Association] October 30, 1965," APA, "Summary Statement of Major Developments in Psychology-Psychiatry Relationships," June 24, 1966, "Meeting of the Committee on Relations of the American Psychiatric Association with the Corresponding Committee of the American Psychological Association," Oct. 29, 1966 (200-32), "Comments on American Psychiatric Association's Position with Respect to Relations with Psychology," Feb. 1966, MDO Papers, Box 906, APAA.

45. "Summary Statement of Major Developments in Psychology-Psychiatry Relationships," June 24, 1966, RMDO, 200-32, APAA; M. Brewster Smith and N. Hobbes, *The Community and the Community Mental Health Center* (statement adopted Mar. 12, 1966, by the Council of Representatives as an official

position paper of the American Psychological Association) (Washington, D.C., 1966).

46. William J. Goode, "Encroachment, Charlatanism, and the Emerging Profession: Psychology, Sociology, and Medicine," *American Sociological Review*, 25 (1960): 902–14.

47. Report of Committee on Government and Psychiatric Social Work, ca. 1941, "Verbal Report of the Work of the War Service Office," Nov. 17, 1943, Elizabeth H. Ross, "What's So Different about Army Psychiatric Social Work?" Feb. 18, 1946, American Association of Psychiatric Social Workers Papers, Social Welfare History Archives, University of Minnesota, Minneapolis, Minn.; Clara Rabinowitz and E. H. Ross, "The Military Psychiatric Social Worker," *News-Letter of the American Association of Psychiatric Social Workers*, 14 (1944): 14–26; Daniel E. O'Keefe, "Casework in the Armed Forces," National Conference of Social Work, *Proceedings*, 73 (1946): 312–18; "The Responsibility of the Psychiatric Social Worker," Imogene S. Young, "I: In Civilian Life," Saul Hofstein, "II: In the Armed Forces," Bertram M. Beck, "III: Discussion of the Problem," Grace F. Marcus, "IV: A Further Consideration of Psychiatric Social Work," ibid., 319–41; U.S. Army Medical Department, *Neuropsychiatry in World War II*, 1:605–30; Henry S. Maas, ed., *Adventure in Mental Health: Psychiatric Social Work with the Armed Forces in World War II* (New York, 1951); Lawson G. Lowrey, *Psychiatry for Social Workers* (1946; 2d ed.; New York, 1950).

48. *AJP*, 97 (1940): 467–69, 98 (1941): 281–82, 288–92, 99 (1942): 137–39; Executive Committee Minutes, Sept. 18–19, 1942, 11, American Association of Psychiatric Social Workers Papers, Social Welfare History Archives; *Journal of Psychiatric Social Work*, 19 (1949): 33–36; Charlotte S. Henry, "Growing Pains in Psychiatric Social Work," ibid., 17 (1947–1948): 88–90; Celia S. Deschin, "How Can Social Work Make a Major Contribution to Psychiatric Theory?" ibid., 20 (1950): 43–52; Alan A. Lieberman, "A Psychiatrist Views the Role of the Psychiatric Social Worker in the Mental Hospital," ibid., 22 (1953): 195–99; Grete L. Bibring, "Psychiatry and Social Work," *Journal of Social Casework*, 28 (1947): 203–11.

49. Executive Committee Minutes, Apr. 23, 1949, 4–5, American Association of Psychiatric Social Workers Papers, Social Welfare History Archives; "Report of the Committee on the Role of the Psychiatric Social Worker as Caseworker or Therapist," *Journal of Psychiatric Social Work*, 19 (1950): 87–90.

50. Report of the Medical and Psychiatric Social Work Sections of the Joint Committee on Participation in Medical Education of the National Association of Social Workers, 1960, cited in William A. Rushing, *The Psychiatric Professions* (Chapel Hill, N.C., 1964), 7; Mental Hospital Institute, *Proceedings*, 2 (1950): 112; Walter E. Barton, *Administration in Psychiatry* (Springfield, Ill., 1962), 37.

51. Cf. Jean M. Arsenian, "Research in Psychiatric Social Work," *Social Service Review*, 26 (1952): 15–29.

52. Robertson and Rubenstein, *National Institute of Mental Health Training Grant Program*, passim; Marcene P. Gabell, "Salient Characteristics of AAPSW Members," *Journal of Psychiatric Social Work*, 24 (1955): 196–203.

53. *Journal of Psychiatric Social Work*, 18 (1948–1949): 129–34, 24 (1955): 70, 188; Ethel L. Ginzberg, "The Temporary Inter-Association Council and Its Meaning for Psychiatric Social Work," ibid., 22 (1952): 35–37.

54. *AJP*, 98 (1941): 286–87; APA, "A Report to the Rockefeller Foundation on the Psychiatric Nursing Project July 1, 1942–June 30, 1951," Rockefeller grant awards, Jan. 19, 1945, Oct. 17, 1947, Rockefeller Foundation Papers, RG 1.1, Series 200A, RAC.

55. Laura W. Fitzsimmons, "Report of a Survey of Nursing in Mental Hospitals in the U.S. and Canada," Apr. 1943, Rockefeller Foundation Papers, RG 1.1, Series 200A, RAC; idem., "A Searchlight on Psychiatric Nursing," *Modern Hospital*, 64 (May 1945): 59–61; APA, *Psychiatric Nursing Personnel* (Washington, D.C., 1950), 17.

56. Francis H. Sleeper, "Present Trends in Psychiatric Nursing," *AJP*, 109 (1952): 203; GAP, "The Psychiatric Nurse in the Mental Hospital," GAP *Report No. 22* (May 1952), 1; Robert H. Felix to WCM, Feb. 11, 1948, with "Report of the Sub-Committee on Integrative Policy to the Committee on Training," WCM Papers, MFA; Jenkins to Willey, Sept. 8, 1952, NIMH Records, Central Files 1951–54, Box 7, WNRC; Robertson and Rubenstein, *National Institute of Mental Health Training Grant Program*, 7.

57. See Harry W. Martin and I. H. Simpson, *Patterns of Psychiatric Nursing: A Survey of Psychiatric Nursing in North Carolina* (Chapel Hill, 1956).

58. Harry C. Solomon to WCM, June 16, 23, 1949, with enclosed notes, WCM Papers, MFA; Helen Nahm quoted in John V. Gorton, "Trends in Psychiatric Nursing," *Journal of Psychiatric Nursing*, 1 (1963): 435; Helen Huber, "Defining the Role of the Psychiatric Nurse," ibid., 2 (1964): 595–610; "Physicians, Nurses Often Fail to Communicate," ibid., 3 (1965): 446–49.

59. Martin and Simpson, *Patterns of Psychiatric Nursing*, passim; Newton Bigelow, "The Enema Giver," *Psychiatric Quarterly*, 41 (1967): 144–54; Thomas Hale, "Cliches of Nursing Education," *Psychiatric Quarterly Supplement*, pt. 1 (1968), 40–56 (reprinted from *New England Journal of Medicine*, Apr. 18, 1968).

60. Walter H. Baer, "The Training of Attendants, Psychiatric Aides and Psychiatric Technicians," *AJP*, 109 (1952): 291; Leonard Edelstein, "Obstacles to Care and Treatment," *The Attendant*, 1 (1944): 1, 4; John M. Grimes, *When Minds Go Wrong* (Chicago, 1949), 112; Council of State Governments, *The Mental Health Programs of the Forty-Eight States* (Chicago, 1950), 156–65; "Public Psychiatric Hospitals," GAP *Report No. 5* (1948): 13.

61. WCM to Charles Dollard, Jan. 4, 1947, Rockefeller Foundation Papers, RG 1.2, Series 200A, RAC; KAM to Felix, Feb. 14, KAM to Oscar Ewing, Feb. 14, Felix to KAM, Mar. 1, 1951, KAM Papers, MFA; Frank F. Tallman to Albert Deutsch, Sept. 18, 1952, Deutsch Papers, APAA.

62. Baer, "The Training of Attendants," 293–94; Council of State Governments, *Training and Research in State Mental Health Programs* (Chicago, 1953), 96–104; Bernard H. Hall, M. Gangemi, V. L. Norris, V. H. Vail, and G. Sawatsky, *Psychiatric Aide Education* (New York, 1952), 115 and passim; NIMH, *The Psychiatric Aide in State Mental Hospitals* (PHS *Publication 1286*: 1965), 4.

63. NIMH, *The Psychiatric Aide*, 1–5; Richard L. and I. H. Simpson, "The Psychiatric Attendant: Development of an Occupational Self-Image in a Low-Status Occupation," *American Sociological Review*, 24 (1959): 389–92; Richard L. Simpson, *Attendants in American Mental Hospitals: An Interim Report and Research Prospectus* (Chapel Hill, N.C., 1961), passim.

CHAPTER SIX
CARE AND TREATMENT: CHANGING VIEWS

1. The therapeutic innovations of the 1930s are discussed in Gerald N. Grob, *Mental Illness and American Society, 1875–1940* (Princeton, 1983), 291ff.

2. Solomon Katzenelbogen, "A Critical Appraisal of the 'Shock Therapies' in the Major Psychoses, I—Insulin," *Psychiatry*, 2 (1939): 504; New York State Temporary Commission on State Hospital Problems, *Insulin Shock Therapy* (Albany, 1944), 81 and passim.

3. Lawrence C. Kolb and Victor H. Vogel, "The Use of Shock Therapy in 305 Mental Hospitals," *AJP*, 99 (1942): 90–100; Harold Bourne, "Insulin Coma in Decline," ibid., 114 (1958): 1015–17; "Electroshock: A Round Table Discussion," ibid., 100 (1943): 362; Leon Salzman, "An Evaluation of Shock Therapy," ibid., 103 (1947): 669–79; A. E. Bennett and B. Engle, "A Critical Review of Recently Advocated Technics in Psychiatric Shock Therapy," *Quarterly Review of Psychiatry and Neurology*, 2 (1947): 1–5; Lothar B. Kalinowsky and P. H. Hoch, *Shock Treatments and Other Somatic Procedures in Psychiatry* (New York, 1946), second edition entitled *Shock Treatments, Psychosurgery and Other Somatic Treatments in Psychiatry* (New York, 1952), and in 1961 issued under the title *Somatic Treatments in Psychiatry: Pharmacotherapy; Convulsive, Insulin, Surgical, Other Methods* (New York, 1961); Kalinowsky, "The Discoveries of Somatic Treatments in Psychiatry: Facts and Myths," *Comprehensive Psychiatry*, 21 (1980): 434.

The use of metrazol can be followed in Miriam R. Geller, *The Treatment of Psychiatric Disorders with Metrazol 1935–1960: A Selected Annotated Bibliography* (PHS *Publication 967*: 1963).

4. *AJP*, 101 (1944): 267–69.

5. A. E. Bennett, "Evaluation of Progress in Established Physiochemical Treatments in Neuropsychiatry," *Diseases of the Nervous System*, 10 (1949): 200.

6. The description of Fulton is based on Jack D. Pressman, "Sufficient Promise: John F. Fulton and the Origins of Psychosurgery," *Bulletin of the History of Medicine*, 62 (1988): 1–22. See also Fulton's *Frontal Lobotomy and Affective Behavior* (New York, 1951). My discussion of the history of lobotomy is heavily indebted to Pressman's outstanding "Uncertain Promise: Psychosurgery and the Development of Scientific Psychiatry in America, 1935 to 1955" (Ph.D. diss., University of Pennsylvania, 1986), which will be published in revised form by Cambridge University Press.

7. Fiamberti (1937), quoted by George W. Kisker, "Remarks on the Problem of Psychosurgery," *AJP*, 100 (1943): 180.

8. Elliott S. Valenstein, *Great and Desperate Cures: The Rise and Decline of Psychosurgery and Other Radical Treatments for Mental Illness* (New York,

1986), 107; Pressman, "Uncertain Promise," 95–98; Walter Freeman and James W. Watts, *Psychosurgery* (Springfield, Ill., 1942), 311.

9. Morton Kramer, "The 1951 Survey of the Use of Psychosurgery," in *Proceedings of the Third Research Conference on Psychosurgery* [1951] (PHS *Publication* 221: 1954), 159–68; Council of State Governments, *The Mental Health Programs of the Forty-Eight States* (Chicago, 1950), 304–10, 346; Milton Greenblatt, R. Arnot, and H. C. Solomon, *Studies in Lobotomy* (New York, 1950), 4–5; Harry J. Worthing, H. Brill, and H. Wigderson, "350 Cases of Prefrontal Lobotomy," *Psychiatric Quarterly*, 23 (1949): 617–56; *New York Times*, Sept. 14, 1948.

10. Valenstein, *Great and Desperate Cures*, 3–4. Pressman's "Uncertain Promise" is by far the best historical study of lobotomy.

11. Freeman quotation from *Proceedings of the Third Research Conference on Psychosurgery* [1951], 151; Pressman, "Uncertain Promise," 140–41.

12. Kolb, "An Evaluation of Lobotomy and Its Potentialities for Future Research in Psychiatry and the Basic Sciences," *Journal of Nervous and Mental Disease*, 110 (1949): 112–48 (quotation from 142); Milton Greenblatt and Solomon, "Psychosurgery," *New England Journal of Medicine*, 248 (1953): 19–27, 59–66 (quotation from 66). Much of this section is based on Pressman, "Uncertain Promise," chap. 2.

13. *Proceedings of the Third Research Conference on Psychosurgery* [1951], 146; Greenblatt, R. H. York, E. L. Brown, and R. W. Hyde, *From Custodial to Therapeutic Patient Care in Mental Hospitals* (New York, 1955), 102–5.

14. "Research on Prefrontal Lobotomy," GAP *Report No.* 6 (June 1948): 2.

15. *Proceedings of the First Research Conference on Psychosurgery* [1949] (PHS *Publication No.* 16: 1951), 5; *Proceedings of the Third Research Conference on Psychosurgery* [1951], 4.

16. Pressman, "Uncertain Promise," 350–66; APA Mental Hospital Institute, *Proceedings*, 5 (1953): 78–91; Kenneth E. Appel, J. M. Myers, and A. E. Scheflen, "Prognosis in Psychiatry," *Archives of Neurology and Psychiatry*, 70 (1953): 459–68; H. S. Barahal, "1,000 Prefrontal Lobotomies—a Five-to-10-Year Follow-up Study," *Psychiatric Quarterly*, 32 (1958): 653–78; Joseph Zubin, "Discussion of '1,000 Prefrontal Lobotomies,'" ibid., 683–90. See also Zubin, "Evaluation of Therapeutic Outcome in Mental Disorders," *Journal of Nervous and Mental Disease,* 117 (1953): 95–111.

17. See letter by Freeman and response by Peter R. Breggin in *AJP*, 128 (1972): 1315, 129 (1972): 97–98; William H. Sweet, "Treatment of Medically Intractable Mental Disease by Limited Frontal Leucotomy—Justifiable?" and Kolb, "Psychosurgery—Justifiable?" *New England Journal of Medicine*, 289 (1973): 1117–25, 1141–43; *JAMA*, 225 (1973): 1035–37, 1041–44; *Journal of Nervous and Mental Disease*, 157 (1973): 151–52; Stephan L. Chorover, "The Pacification of the Brain," *Psychology Today*, 7 (May 1974): 59–60, 63–64, 66, 69–70.

A study of the incidence of psychosurgery in the three years from 1971 to 1973 found that neurosurgeons performed a total of 476 procedures for intractable pain and 1,039 for psychiatric conditions. Excluding the procedures reported by four neurosurgeons who performed more than 20 psychosurgical procedures in any one of the three years, the number of psychosurgical procedures dropped to 575 for the three years or 125 per year. John Donnelly, "The Incidence of Psychosurgery in the United States, 1971–1973," *AJP*, 135 (1978): 1476–80.

Somatic therapies were by no means confined to shock or psychosurgery. Individual psychiatrists, admittedly atypical, experimented with a range of techniques and substances. The value of most of these remained unproven. Among the techniques employed were continuous sleep, fever, nitrogen inhalation, and refrigeration therapies; certain substances, such as tuberculin, estrone, methyl guanidine, and dilantin were also used. See Joseph Wortis, "Physiological Treatment of Psychoses," *AJP*, 103 (1947): 538–42; Kalinowsky and Hoch, *Shock Treatments and Other Somatic Procedures in Psychiatry*, chap. 5; Kalinowsky and Hoch, *Shock Treatments, Psychosurgery and Other Somatic Treatments*, chap. 6.

18. Joseph Wilder, "Twenty-Five Years of the Association for the Advancement of Psychotherapy," *American Journal of Psychotherapy*, 18 (1964): 452–57; "Editorial," ibid., 1 (1947): 125–28; Lewellys F. Barker, *Psychotherapy* (New York, 1940), 2, 181–82. See also Barker's article "Psychotherapy—A Modern Medical Science," *American Scholar*, 11 (1942): 201–7.

19. *AJP*, 101 (1944): 266.

20. Wilder, "Facts and Figures on Psychotherapy," *Journal of Clinical Psychopathology and Psychotherapy*, 7 (1945): 311–47.

21. See Harold Maine, "We Can Save the Mentally Sick," *Saturday Evening Post*, 220 (1947): 20–21, 160, 162, 165–66, and *If a Man Be Mad* (Garden City, N.Y., 1947). Lawrence J. Friedman's *Menninger: The Family and the Clinic* (New York, 1990) provides detailed descriptions and analyses of one of the nation's most important postwar psychiatric institutions.

22. Jerome D. Frank, *Persuasion and Healing: A Comparative Study of Psychotherapy* (Baltimore, 1961), 11–13, 231–32.

23. Daniel Blain to Marion E. Kenworthy, Nov. 12, Kenworthy to Blain, Nov. 12, 1946, Kenworthy Papers, AP; Leo H. Bartemeier, "Presidential Address," *AJP*, 109 (1952): 1–7; D. Ewen Cameron, "Postgraduate Instruction in Psychotherapy in the University," *Journal of the Association of American Medical Colleges*, 25 (1950): 338–44; Jules H. Masserman, "Faith and Delusion in Psychotherapy," *AJP*, 110 (1953): 324–33; Samuel H. Hadden, "Historic Background of Group Psychotherapy," *International Journal of Group Psychotherapy*, 5 (1955): 162–68; American Psychological Association, Conference on Research in Psychotherapy, *Proceedings*, 1 (1958): 292.

24. Kubie to Lewis Weed, Apr. 14, WCM to Kubie, June 20, 1950, WCM Papers, MFA; Albert Deutsch interview with Benjamin Pasamanick, May 10, 1960, Deutsch Papers, APAA.

25. Frank, "Problems of Controls in Psychotherapy as Exemplified by the Psychotherapy Research Project of the Phipps Psychiatric Clinic," in Conference on Research in Psychotherapy, *Proceedings*, 1 (1958): 10–26, and *Persuasion and Healing*, 223, 231–32.

26. Parloff and Rubenstein, "Research Problems in Psychotherapy," Conference on Research in Psychotherapy, *Proceedings*, 1 (1958): 292; Hans J. Eysenck, "The Effects of Psychotherapy: An Evaluation," *Journal of Consulting Psychology*, 16 (1952): 319–23, and "The Effects of Psychotherapy," *International Journal of Psychiatry*, 1 (1965): 99–144 (see also the discussion by various individuals

on 144–78); Herbert J. Cross, "The Outcome of Psychotherapy: A Selected Analysis of Research Findings," *Journal of Consulting Psychology*, 28 (1964): 413–17. Eysenck's "The Effects of Psychotherapy," cited above, contains a lengthy bibliography on the subject (138–42). See also American Psychological Association, Conference on Research in Psychotherapy, *Proceedings*, 2–3 (1961–1966).

27. The Menninger Foundation's Psychotherapy Research Project generated numerous publications. The most detailed summary was Robert Wallerstein's *Forty-Two Lives in Treatment: A Study of Psychoanalysis and Psychotherapy* (New York, 1986). For a history of the project, see Friedman, *Menninger*, 287–89.

28. For varying interpretations of moral treatment, see Norman Dain, *Concepts of Insanity in the United States 1789–1865* (New Brunswick, N.J., 1964); David Rothman, *The Discovery of the Asylum: Social Order and Disorder in the New Republic* (Boston, 1971); Gerald N. Grob, *Mental Institutions in America: Social Policy to 1875* (New York, 1973); Nancy Tomes, *A Generous Confidence: Thomas Story Kirkbride and the Art of Asylum-Keeping, 1840–1883* (New York, 1984); and Constance McGovern, *Masters of Madness: Social Origins of the American Psychiatric Profession* (Hanover, N.H., 1985).

29. Dexter M. Bullard, "The Organization of Psychoanalytic Procedure in the Hospital," *Journal of Nervous and Mental Disease*, 91 (1940): 697–703; Robert A. Cohen, "The Hospital as a Therapeutic Instrument," *Psychiatry*, 21 (1958): 29.

30. Helen S. Perry, *Psychiatrist of America: The Life of Harry Stack Sullivan* (Cambridge, Mass., 1982), 258; Sullivan, "The Data of Psychiatry," *Psychiatry*, 1 (1938): 121, reprinted in *The Fusion of Psychiatry and Social Science* (New York, 1964), 31–55. See especially Sullivan's article, "A Note on the Implications of Psychiatry, the Study of Interpersonal Relations, for Investigations in the Social Sciences," *American Journal of Sociology*, 42 (1937): 848–61, reprinted in *The Fusion of Psychiatry and Social Science*, 15–29.

31. Bruno Bettelheim, "Individual and Mass Behavior in Extreme Situations," *Journal of Abnormal and Social Psychology*, 38 (1943): 417–52. See also Bettelheim and E. Sylvester, "A Therapeutic Milieu," *American Journal of Orthopsychiatry*, 18 (1948): 191–206, and Bettelheim, *Love Is Not Enough* (Glencoe, Ill., 1950).

32. Jones, "The Treatment of Personality Disorders in a Therapeutic Community," *Psychiatry*, 20 (1957): 212–13. See also Milton and M. Silverman, "Asylums without Bars," *Saturday Evening Post*, 231 (Oct. 25, 1958): 110.

33. Jones, "Treatment of Personality Disorders in a Therapeutic Community," 213–17; idem, *The Therapeutic Community: A New Treatment Method in Psychiatry* (New York, 1953), 156–57 (this work was first published in England under the title *Social Psychiatry*). See also Deutsch's interview with Jones and Harry Wilmer, Aug. 29, 1959, Deutsch Papers, APAA.

34. J. Fremont Bateman and H. Warren Dunham, "The State Mental Hospital as a Specialized Community Experience," *AJP*, 105 (1948): 445–48. See also *Bulletin of the Menninger Clinic*, 10 (1946): 65–100, which contains a series of articles by British psychiatrists dealing with what subsequently became known as the therapeutic community concept.

The book-length study by Dunham and S. K. Weinberg was based on data collected at Columbus State Hospital in 1946 and completed in 1948. By the time that it was published in 1960, its methodology and conclusions were commonplace, given the appearance of other institutional studies during the 1950s. Essentially, Dunham and Weinberg argued that the employee culture that shaped the institution was directed toward "the complete subjection and control of patients" (249). Patients, on the other hand, created their own culture to facilitate their adjustment to hospital life and their eventual release. Most therapies had meager results precisely because they were interwoven with the institutional culture. A dramatic change in the cultural climate was essential if recovery was to become the hospital's primary goal. Dunham and Weinberg, *The Culture of the State Mental Hospital* (Detroit, 1960), chap. 12.

35. Charlotte G. Schwartz, *Rehabilitation of Mental Hospital Patients: Review of the Literature* (*Public Health Monograph No. 17*, issued as PHS *Publication 297*: 1953). See also the bibliography in Greenblatt et al., *From Custodial to Therapeutic Patient Care*, 431–84.

36. Alfred H. Stanton and Morris S. Schwartz, *The Mental Hospital: A Study of Institutional Participation in Psychiatric Illness and Treatment* (New York, 1954).

37. Greenblatt et al., *From Custodial to Therapeutic Patient Care*, passim (quotations from 237, 424).

38. Otto von Mering and Stanley H. King, *Remotivating the Mental Patient* (New York, 1957), 51.

39. Ivan Belknap, *Human Problems of a State Mental Hospital* (New York, 1956); William Caudill, *The Psychiatric Hospital as a Small Society* (Cambridge, Mass., 1958); Robert N. Rapoport, *Community as Doctor* (London, 1960), 10; Greenblatt, D. J. Levinson, and R. H. Williams, eds., *The Patient and the Mental Hospital* (Glencoe, Ill., 1957); Morris S. Schwartz and E. L. Shockley, *The Nurse and the Mental Patient: A Study in Interpersonal Relations* (New York, 1956). The literature on the therapeutic community is immense; the above-mentioned examples are only offered as illustrations. For a more extensive bibliography listing relevant citations through the beginning of 1957, see Mering and King, *Remotivating the Mental Patient*, 201–7.

40. Cf. T. W. Adorno, E. Frenkel-Brunswik, D. J. Levinson, and R. N. Sanford, *The Authoritarian Personality* (New York, 1950).

41. See especially J. Sanbourne Bockoven, "Moral Treatment in American Psychiatry," *Journal of Nervous and Mental Disease*, 124 (1956): 167–94, 292–321; Greenblatt, *From Custodial to Therapeutic Patient Care*, 407–14; Earl D. Bond, "Therapeutic Forces in Early American Hospitals," *AJP*, 113 (1956): 407–8.

42. Bertram Mandelbrote, "An Experiment in the Rapid Conversion of a Closed Mental Hospital into an Open-Door Hospital," *Mental Hygiene*, 42 (1958): 3–16; George R. Metcalf, "The English Open Mental Hospital: Implications for American Psychiatric Services," *Milbank Memorial Fund Quarterly*, 39 (1961): 586; "Observations on the British 'Open' Hospitals," *Mental Hospitals*, 8 (1957): 5–9, 12, 14, 16; "Laying the Foundations for an Open Mental Hospital" and "Legal Implications of the Open Hospital" (discussions at the ninth APA Mental Hospital Institute in 1957), ibid., 9 (1958): 10–12, 24–26; Milbank Memorial Fund, *An Approach to the Prevention of Disability from Chronic Psycho-*

ses: The Open Mental Hospital within the Community (New York, 1958); APA, Proceedings of the 1958 Day Hospital Conference (Washington, D.C., 1958).

See also Mike Gorman, "'Open Hospitals' for the Mentally Ill," New York Times Magazine, Dec. 29, 1957, 12, 26; Silverman, "Asylums without Bars," Saturday Evening Post, 231 (Oct. 25, 1958): 28–29, 110, 112–16, 118; "Open Door in Psychiatry," Time, 74 (Nov. 16, 1959): 85–86, 88.

43. For the work on LSD at Boston Psychopathic, see Max Rinkel, R. W. Hyde, and H. C. Solomon, "Hallucinogens: Tools in Experimental Psychiatry," Diseases of the Nervous System, 16 (1955): 229–32, and Dana L. Farnsworth to Solomon, Dec. 12, Solomon to Farnsworth, Dec. 14, 1956, Solomon Papers, APAA.

44. See Mortimer D. Sackler et al., "The Newer Biochemotherapies in Psychiatry," Quarterly Review of Psychiatry and Neurology, 7 (1952): 59–69.

45. My discussion of the development and introduction of psychoactive drugs is based on Judith P. Swazey's excellent monograph, Chlorpromazine in Psychiatry: A Study of Therapeutic Innovation (Cambridge, Mass., 1974).

46. Ibid., chaps. 1–4.

47. Ibid., 111–41. The quotation from Delay and Deniker (taken from ibid., 137) appeared in their article "Les neuroplégiques en thérapeutique psychiatrique," Thérapie, 8 (1953): 361.

48. Swazey, Chlorpromazine in Psychiatry, chaps. 6–8; Editorial, American Journal of Psychotherapy, 9 (1955): 193–95.

49. Swazey, Chlorpromazine in Psychiatry, chap. 8. The most significant of the early American clinical evaluations included N. William Winkelman, Jr., "Chlorpromazine in the Treatment of Neuropsychiatric Disorders," JAMA, 155 (1954): 18–21, and Vernon Kinross-Wright, "Chlorpromazine—A Major Advance in Psychiatric Treatment," Postgraduate Medicine, 16 (1954): 297–99.

50. Swazey, Chlorpromazine in Psychiatry, chap. 8.

51. Ibid., 191–95; Norman Rosenzweig, "Developments in Psychiatry over the Past Decade," Bulletin of the Sinai Hospital of Detroit, 10 (1963): 304–68 (this article contains an extensive bibliography on psychiatric drugs). See also Fredrick C. Redlich and D. X. Freedman, The Theory and Practice of Psychiatry (New York, 1966), chap. 11.

52. APA, An Evaluation of the Newer Psychopharmacologic Agents and Their Role in Current Psychiatric Practice (APA, Psychiatric Research Reports, 4 [1956]), 125–29); APA, "A Statement on the Contribution of the Tranquilizing Drugs ... and the Dangers Inherent in the Casual Use of These Drugs by the Public for the Relief of Everyday Tensions," press release, June 7, 1956, RMDO, 200-21, APAA; New York Times, July 6, 1956; Norman Reider to Deutsch, May 17, 1956, Jan. 29, 1957, Deutsch Papers, APAA; Francis J. Braceland to Solomon, D. Ewen Cameron, Jack Ewalt, and William Malamud, Nov. 23, Solomon to Braceland, Nov. 28, 1956, Solomon Papers, APAA.

53. Nathan S. Kline, ed., Psychopharmacology: A Symposium ... December 30, 1954 (Washington, D.C., 1956); APA, Pharmacologic Products Recently Introduced in the Treatment of Psychiatric Disorders (APA, Psychiatric Research Reports, 1 [1955]); "The New Drugs," discussion at the seventh Mental Hospital Institute (1955), in Mental Hospitals, 6 (1956): 30–34; Harold E. Himwich, ed., Tranquilizing Drugs: A Symposium ... December 27–28, 1955 (Washington,

D.C., 1957); APA, *An Evaluation of the Newer Psychopharmacologic Agents*; Harold E. Himwich, "Prospects in Psychopharmacology," *Journal of Nervous and Mental Disease*, 122 (1955): 422; International Symposium on Chlorpromazine, in *Journal of Clinical and Experimental Psychopathology*, 17 (1956): 15–80, 129–88; Winfred Overholser, "Has Chlorpromazine Inaugurated a New Era in Mental Hospitals?" ibid., 197–201.

54. Data on drug usage and expenditure can be found in California Senate Interim Committee on the Treatment of Mental Illness, *First Partial Report* (1956), 19 and passim; Council of State Governments, *Action in the States in the Fields of Mental Health, Mental Retardation and Related Areas* (Chicago, 1963), 18–22.

55. Henry Brill and R. E. Patton, "Analysis of 1955–1956 Population Fall in New York State Mental Hospitals in First Year of Large-Scale Use of Tranquilizing Drugs," *AJP*, 114 (1957): 509–17, "Analysis of Population Reduction in New York State Mental Hospitals during the First Four Years of Large-Scale Therapy with Psychotropic Drugs," ibid., 116 (1959): 495–508, and "Clinical-Statistical Analysis of Population Changes in New York State Mental Hospitals since Introduction of Psychotropic Drugs," ibid., 119 (1962): 20–35; Patton, "What the Tranquilizing Drugs Are Doing to the Population in Mental Hospitals," American Statistical Association, *Proceedings of the Social Statistics Section*, 1958, 79–85.

56. Morton Kramer, *Facts Needed to Assess Public Health and Social Problems in the Widespread Use of the Tranquilizing Drugs* (*Public Health Monograph No. 41*, issued as PHS *Publication No. 486*: 1956), and Kramer et al., *A Historical Study of the Disposition of First Admissions to a State Mental Hospital. Experience of the Warren State Hospital during the Period 1916–50* (*Public Health Monograph No. 32*, issued as PHS *Publication No. 445*: 1955).

57. *Time*, 65 (Mar. 7, 1955): 63–64; *Life*, 41 (Oct. 22, 1956): 119–24, 126, 131, 133–34, 139–40, 142; *New York Times*, Jan. 15, 16, 17, Apr. 6, 1956; Mike Gorman, *Every Other Bed* (Cleveland, 1956), 89–132; 84-1 Congress, *Labor–Health, Education, and Welfare Appropriations for 1956. Hearings before the Subcommittee of the Committee on Appropriations . . . Senate* (Washington, D.C., 1955), 751–70.

58. 84-1 Congress, *Labor–Health, Education, and Welfare Appropriations for 1956. Hearings . . . Senate*, 473–92; 84-2 Congress, *Labor–Health, Education, and Welfare Appropriations for 1957. Hearings before the Subcommittee on Appropriations . . . Senate* (Washington, D.C., 1956), 562, 593–94, 597–600; Jonathan O. Cole and R. W. Gerard, eds., *Psychopharmacology: Problems in Evaluation* (Washington, D.C., 1959), 1–5.

59. Cole and Gerard, *Psychopharmacology*, 1–19, 650.

60. Gorman to KAM, ca. 1953, KAM Papers, MFA; 84-2 Congress, *Labor–Health, Education, and Welfare Appropriations for 1957. Hearings . . . Senate*, 1298–1300, 1308ff.; Gorman speech, Trenton, N.J., Feb. 4, 1957, copy in Gorman Office Files, now at NLM; *New York Times*, Feb. 5, 1957. Gorman's dislike of Felix is evident in the Michael Barton interview of Gorman, Apr. 7, 1972, 37ff., and the Blain interview of Gorman, Oct. 7, 1972, copies in Blain Papers, APAA.

61. WCM to Deutsch, Feb. 28, Deutsch to Mary Lasker, Mar. 5, 1956,

Deutsch to Norman Reider, Feb. 16, Deutsch to David Rapaport, Feb. 17, 1957, Deutsch Papers, APAA; Gorman to Felix, Feb. 21, with copy of Paul Lemkau to Theodore R. McKeldin, Feb. 15, and McKeldin to Lemkau, Feb. 19, 1957, NIMH Records, Mental Health Subject Files, Box 67, WNRC; WCM to Gorman, Feb. 25, Robert T. Morse to WCM, Mar. 12, 22, WCM to Morse, Mar. 20, Felix to WCM, Mar. 5, WCM to Felix, Mar. 11, Felix Memo to Surgeon General, PHS, Re. Public Attack by Mr. Mike Gorman, Feb. 13, 1957, WCM Papers, MFA; Felix to Gorman, Feb. 28, 1957, RMDO, 100-18, APAA; KAM to Felix, Mar. 1, Felix to KAM, Mar. 18, 1957, KAM Papers, MFA; Jack Ewalt to Leverett Saltonstall, May 21, 1957, Ewalt Papers, CLMHMS; Blain to C. B. Farrar, Dec. 17, 1964, Blain Papers, APAA; Philip Sapir interview by Milton J. E. Senn, Nov. 30, 1977, 22–23, Senn Collection (OH76), NLM.

62. 85-1 Congress, *Departments of Labor and Health, Education, and Welfare Appropriations for 1958. Hearings before the Subcommittee of the Committee on Appropriations House of Representatives* (Washington, D.C., 1957), 851–78.

63. NIMH Psychopharmacology Service Center Collaborative Study Group, "Phenothiazine Treatment in Acute Schizophrenia," *Archives of General Psychiatry*, 10 (1964): 246–61.

64. Kalinowsky and Hoch, *Somatic Treatments in Psychiatry*, 3d ed. (New York, 1961), 6; Jack R. Ewalt, "Evaluation of the New Drugs from the Viewpoint of a Medical Executive," in Cole and Gerard, *Psychopharmacology*, 146–47.

65. For a listing of drugs in use by the end of the decade, see James P. Cattell, "Psychopharmacological Agents: A Selective Survey," *AJP*, 116 (1959): 352–54.

66. Cf. summary of discussion between NIMH officials and the [Blatnik] Subcommittee of the House Government Operations Committee, Aug. 15, 1957, and Felix to Surgeon General, Jan. 28, 1958, NIMH Records, Mental Health Subject Files 1957–60, Box 13, WNRC; Don D. Jackson, "Beware Ataraxes in the Attic," *New Republic*, 135 (Oct. 22, 1956): 22, (Nov. 19, 1956): 3, 31; Ian Stevenson, "Tranquilizers and the Mind," *Harper's Magazine*, 215 (Aug. 1957): 21–27; Frank Orland, "Use and Overuse of Tranquilizers," *JAMA*, 171 (1959): 633–36.

67. Dana L. Farnsworth to Greenblatt, May 16, Greenblatt to Farnsworth, May 24, Greenblatt to Committee on Research, May 23, Farnsworth to Bartholomew W. Hogan, June 6, George A. Ulett to Greenblatt, June 7, 1962, RMDO, 200-22, APAA.

68. For an extraordinarily optimistic assessment of an integrated system of services for chronic schizophrenic patients developed between 1955 and 1961, see Donald M. Eldred, G. W. Brooks, W. Deane, and M. B. Taylor, "The Rehabilitation of the Hospitalized Mentally Ill—The Vermont Story," *AJPH*, 52 (1962): 39–46.

CHAPTER SEVEN
CHANGING STATE POLICY

1. Unless otherwise noted, all statistical data are derived from the NIMH's annual *Patients in Mental Institutions*. Data on patient care episodes are taken from Morton Kramer, *Psychiatric Services and the Changing Institutional Scene,*

1950–1985 (DHEW Publication No. [ADM] 76-374: Washington, D.C., 1976), 75.

The term *patient care episode* represents the sum of two numbers: residents at the beginning of the year or on the active roll of outpatient clinics; and admissions during the year. The first is an unduplicated count; the second includes duplications, since some individuals had multiple admissions.

2. Data compiled from 84-1 Congress, *Mental Health Study Act of 1955. Hearings before a Subcommittee of the Committee on Interstate and Foreign Commerce House of Representatives . . . 1955* (Washington, D.C., 1955), 141; "Maintenance Expenditures in Public Mental Hospitals in Relation to General Revenues of States," *Public Health Reports*, 67 (1952): 681–85.

3. The increase in their number represented a dramatic change from earlier patterns. Before 1890 relatively few elderly persons had been sent to mental hospitals. Patient populations were composed of younger persons who remained institutionalized for only three to nine months. Aged persons unable to care for themselves or who lacked families and/or financial resources were generally sent to local almshouses—the nineteenth-century equivalent of an old-age home. Toward the turn of the century, most states (Wisconsin being a notable exception) began to end a system developed during the nineteenth century that provided for shared responsibility for the mentally ill with local communities. With the assumption of total state responsibility for the mentally ill, local officials redefined senility in psychiatric terms and transferred the aged from almshouses to mental hospitals. The advantages to the local community were obvious: fiscal burdens were shifted to the state. For a discussion of the change in the nature of the patient population before 1940, see Gerald N. Grob, *Mental Illness and American Society, 1875–1940* (Princeton, 1983), chap. 7.

4. The increase in the proportion of aged patients was not merely one of numbers; age-specific rates also changed. In 1885 age-specific first admission rates in Massachusetts for males sixty and over was 70.4 and for females 65.5 (per 100,000); in 1941 the corresponding figures were 279.5 and 223.0. In 1919–1921, 13.6 percent of all first admissions to New York State hospitals were individuals aged sixty-five years or over even though this category only accounted for 4.7 percent of the population; by 1949–1951 the figures were 33.3 and 8.6 percent, respectively. Nationally a similar trend was apparent. See Herbert Goldhamer and Andrew W. Marshall, *Psychosis and Civilization: Two Studies in the Frequency of Mental Disease* (Glencoe, Ill., 1953), 54, 91; Benjamin Malzberg, "A Comparison of First Admissions to the New York State Civil Hospitals during 1919–1921 and 1949–1951," *Psychiatric Quarterly*, 28 (1954): 314; U.S. Bureau of the Census, *Fourteenth Census of the United States*, vol. 2, *Population 1920* (Washington, D.C., 1922), 248; idem, *Census of Population: 1950*, vol. 2, *Characteristics of the Population*, pt. 32 (Washington, D.C., 1952), 58; 84-1 Congress, *Mental Health Study Act of 1955*, 137; APA, *Report on Patients over 65 in Public Mental Hospitals* (Washington, D.C., 1960), 5; Earl S. Pollack, B. Z. Locke, and Kramer, "Trends in Hospitalization and Patterns of Care of the Aged Mentally Ill," in *Psychopathology of Aging*, ed. Paul H. Hoch and J. Zubin (New York, 1961), 24; Oswaldo Camargo and G. H. Preston, "What Happens to Patients who Are Hospitalized for the First Time When over Sixty-Five Years of Age," *AJP*, 102 (1945): 168–73.

5. Pollack, Locke, and Kramer, "Trends in Hospitalization and Patterns of Care of the Aged Mentally Ill," 36; Kramer, H. Goldstein, R. H. Israel, and N. A. Johnson, *A Historical Study of the Disposition of First Admissions to a State Mental Hospital: Experience of the Warren State Hospital during the Period 1916–50* (PHS *Publication 445*: 1955), 12; Kramer, Pollack, R. Redick, and Locke, *Mental Disorders/Suicide* (Cambridge, Mass., 1972), 27–28.

6. *Psychiatric Quarterly Supplement*, 18 (1944): 201; *New York Times*, Mar. 28, 1944. During the 1940s interest in the psychiatric problems of geriatric patients increased dramatically. See Winfred Overholser, "The Problems of Mental Diseases in an Aging Population," National Conference of Social Work, *Proceedings*, 68 (1941): 455–63; William Malamud, "Current Trends and Needs in Research on Problems of the Aged," *Diseases of the Nervous System*, 2 (1941): 37–42; Benjamin Simon and S. H. Kaufman, "Psychiatric Problems of the Aged," ibid., 2 (1941): 62–65; Harold W. Williams et al., "Studies in Senile and Arteriosclerotic Psychoses," *AJP*, 98 (1942): 712–15; Harold D. Palmer et al., "Somato-Psychic Disorders of Old Age, ibid., 99 (1943): 856–63; Samuel W. Hartwell, "Mental Diseases of the Aged," in *New Goals for Old Age*, ed. George Lawton (New York, 1943), 132–43; Oscar J. Kaplan, ed., *Mental Disorders in Later Life* (Stanford, 1945); and Howard A. Rusk, "America's Number One Problem—Chronic Disease and an Aging Population," *AJP*, 106 (1949): 270–77.

7. Kramer, *Psychiatric Services and the Changing Institutional Scene*, 82.

8. Kramer, Goldstein, Israel, and Johnson, *A Historical Study of the Disposition of First Admissions to a State Mental Hospital*, 16.

9. Missouri General Assembly, *The Mentally Ill: Their Care and Treatment in Missouri*, Missouri Committee on Legislative Research, *Report No. 8* (1948), 58, and *The Mentally Ill: Their Care and Treatment in Four Selected States*, Missouri Committee on Legislative Research, *Report No. 10* (1949), 17.

10. Raymond G. Fuller, "A Study of the Administration of State Psychiatric Services," *Mental Hygiene*, 38 (1954): 181–82.

11. Ibid., 177–235; Clifton T. Perkins to WCM, May 14, 1948, with enclosed "Report of the Committee on Public Health to the Council of the American Psychiatric Association," May 12, 1948, RMDO, 200-18, APAA; Council of State Governments, *The Mental Health Programs of the Forty-Eight States* (Chicago, 1950), 70–104; George Stevenson to State Mental Health Associations, Nov. 25, 1952, WCM Papers, MFA. For an analysis of the evolution of state administrative policies and structures dealing with the mentally ill, see Grob, *Mental Institutions in America: Social Policy to 1875* (New York, 1973), and *Mental Illness and American Society, 1875–1940*. Descriptions of state administrative structures in the postwar era are to be found in the Council of State Governments, *Book of the States*, which was issued biennially.

12. "Study of Psychiatric Facilities in Kansas," Kansas Legislative Council, *Publications 143, 146* (Nov. 1946); *A Psychiatrist for a Troubled World: Selected Papers of William C. Menninger, M.D.* (New York, 1967), 770–81; "Changes in Patient-Employee Ratios in Public . . . Mental Hospitals . . . 1939–1955," JIS *Fact Sheet*, 1 (1957): 2. See especially Lawrence J. Friedman, *Menninger: The Family and the Clinic* (New York, 1990).

13. Council of State Governments, *Mental Health Programs of the Forty-Eight States*, esp. 4–13, 195–96.

14. *State Government,* 23 (1950): 4–5, 183–84.

15. Sidney S. McMath, "Arkansas's Mental Health Plan," *Bulletin of the Menninger Clinic,* 14 (1950): 153–56; *Welfare: Mental Hospitals* (Kentucky Legislative Research Commission, *Research Publication No.* 24: 1951); *The Minnesota Mental Health Program January 1951 [by] Ralph Rossen, M.D.* (n.p., 1951); *Report of the Special Commission on Commitment, Care and Treatment of Mental Health Hospital Patients* (Mass. *Senate Document No. 735* [May 2, 1955], and Mass. *Senate Document No. 700* [Apr. 18, 1956]); *Report to the Special Commission on Audit of State Needs: Massachusetts Needs in Mental Health and the Care of the Retarded* (Mass. *House Document No. 3250* [July 30, 1958]); *New York State's Needs in Mental Health Research, Training and Community Services: Proceedings of the Public Hearing on Mental Health Held by the New York State Senate Committee on Public Health . . . 1956* (Albany, 1956); Washington State Mental Health Survey Committee, *The End of the Beginning: A Report on Mental Health Problems in the State of Washington* (n.p., 1956); 83-2 Congress, *Departments of Labor and Health, Education, and Welfare Appropriations for 1955. Hearings before the Subcommittee of the Committee on Appropriations House of Representatives* (Washington, D.C., 1954), 262–63; *Mental Hospitals,* 6 (1956): 29–32; *Mental Health Training and Research in the Southern States: A Report to the Southern Governors' Conference . . . 1954* (Atlanta, 1954).

16. Robert C. Hunt, "APA Standards for Public Mental Hospitals: History, Development and Present Status," in "Exploratory Conference to Review Standards for Public Mental Hospitals . . . 1959," 7–18, RMDO, 200-25, APAA; APA, *Standards for Hospitals and Clinics* (1956; rev. ed., Washington, D.C., 1958); Mental Hospital Institute, *Proceedings,* 1–6 (1949–1954); APA, "List of Hospitals Inspected by the Central Inspection Board from 1949 through 1960," CIB Papers, Box 16, APAA; M. A. Tarumianz, "The Background and Development of the Central Inspection Board of the American Psychiatric Association," April, 1960, ibid., Box 17, APAA; Harvey J. Tompkins, "State Surveys," Mental Hospital Institute, *Proceedings,* 6 (1954): 86–88; "State Surveys of Mental Health Needs and Resources," Nov. 1955, RMDO, 100-25, APAA. The following state surveys are in the APA State Surveys, APAA: Indiana (1955), Iowa (1956), Kentucky (1955), Louisiana (1954), New Hampshire (1958), Ohio (1957), Pennsylvania (1956), Alabama (1959).

17. Statistics for this and the preceding paragraph drawn from "Changes in Patient-Employee Ratios," 2; expenditure data compiled from the NIMH's *Patients in Mental Institutions.* See also *State Government,* 28 (1955): 86–87, 95, and *Book of the States,* 11 (1956–1957): 307–12.

18. Harry C. Solomon, "The American Psychiatric Association in Relation to American Psychiatry," *AJP,* 115 (1958): 1–9.

19. *New York Times,* May 13, 16, 1958; Robert C. Hunt to Solomon, June 17, Solomon to Hunt, June 19, 1958, Solomon Papers, APAA; Hunt, "The State Hospital Stereotype" (statement before APA Commission on Long Term Planning, Oct. 30, 1959), in "Minutes . . . Commission on Long Term Policies," Oct. 30, 1959, and Memo from D. Ewen Cameron to Commission, Nov. 9, 1959, Jack R. Ewalt Papers, CLMHMS; "Resume of Actions of the Long Term Planning Committee," Oct. 30, 1959, RMDO, 200-11, APAA.

20. Lawrence S. Kubie, "The Organization of a Psychiatric Service for a General Hospital," *Psychosomatic Medicine*, 4 (1942): 253–54; Franklin G. Ebaugh, *The Care of the Psychiatric Patient in General Hospitals* (Chicago, 1940), 17.

21. Ebaugh, *Care of the Psychiatric Patient in General Hospitals*, 14–18.

22. A. E. Bennett, E. A. Hargrove, and B. Engle, "Psychiatric Treatment in General Hospitals," *JAMA*, 147 (1951): 1020; idem, "Present Status and Future Needs of Psychiatric Facilities in General Hospitals in the United States and Canada," *AJP*, 107 (1951): 321–27; Raymond Giesler, P. L. Hurley, and P. H. Person, Jr., *Survey of General Hospitals Admitting Psychiatric Patients* (PHS *Publication 1462*: 1966), 2; Kramer, *Psychiatric Services and the Changing Institutional Scene*, 75. See also Raymond M. Glasscote and C. K. Kanno, *General Hospital Psychiatric Units: A National Survey* (Washington, D.C., 1965).

23. Giesler et al., *Survey of General Hospitals*, 9–10; Texas Division of Mental Health, *Psychiatric Inpatient Units in Texas General Hospitals* (n.p., 1958), 19, 21, 27–31; Glasscote and Kanno, *General Hospital Psychiatric Units*, vi–vii, 11–12, 16–23, 29–37.

24. KAM to Matthew Ross, Feb. 12, 1959, KAM Papers, MFA.

25. Gerald N. Grob, *The State and the Mentally Ill: A History of Worcester State Hospital in Massachusetts 1830–1920* (Chapel Hill, N.C., 1966), 349ff.; Anita K. Bahn and V. B. Norman, *Outpatient Psychiatric Clinics in the United States 1954–55* (PHS *Public Health Monograph 49*: 1957), 3; Maurice J. Shore et al., *Twentieth Century Mental Hygiene: New Directions in Mental Health* (New York, 1950), 80ff.

26. *New York Times*, Apr. 4, 1947; NIMH, "Annual Report, Fiscal 1949," 9–10, NIMH Records, Subject Files, 1940–51, Box 82, WNRC; Bahn and Norman, *Outpatient Psychiatric Clinics . . . 1954–55*, 38.

27. Deutsch, "More Mental Clinics Mean Fewer Patients in Mental Hospitals," and "State-Aid Plan for Mental Clinics Saves Money in Connecticut," *PM*, Feb. 19, 20, 1947.

28. A. Z. Barhash, M. C. Bentley, M. E. Kirkpatrick, and H. A. Sanders, *The Organization and Function of the Community Psychiatric Clinic* (New York, 1952), 10 (the first edition was written by Kirkpatrick and published in 1941 by the NCMH); Ewalt, "Principles for the Mental Health Clinic," *State Government*, 27 (1954): 136–39, 152–53. For similar statements, see George S. Stevenson, "Dynamic Considerations in Community Functions," *Mental Hygiene*, 34 (1950): 531–46; National Conference of Social Work, *Proceedings*, 77 (1950): 119–42; Mabel Ross, "A Community Mental Health Program," *AJPH*, 41 (1951): 950–53; and Leonard T. Maholick, "The Mental-Health Clinic as a Therapist in the Community," *Mental Hygiene*, 37 (1953): 61–65.

29. See Frank G. Boudreau, "Programs and Policies of the Milbank Memorial Fund in the Field of Mental Health," in *Programs for Community Mental Health: Papers Presented at the 1956 Annual Conference of the Milbank Memorial Fund* (New York, 1957), 14–21.

30. Gerald N. Grob, "The Origins of American Psychiatric Epidemiology," *AJPH*, 75 (1985): 229–36.

31. Milbank Memorial Fund, *Epidemiology of Mental Disorder* (New York, 1950), 114, 132 and passim; Boudreau, "Programs and Policies of the Milbank Memorial Fund," 15–16. For a summary of epidemiological studies of mental

disorders in the 1950s and 1960s, see Myrna M. Weissman and G. L. Klerman, "Epidemiology of Mental Disorders: Emerging Trends in the United States," *Archives of General Psychiatry*, 35 (1978): 705–12.

32. *The Biology of Mental Health and Disease: The Twenty-seventh Annual Conference of the Milbank Memorial Fund* (New York, 1952).

33. Milbank Memorial Fund, *Interrelations between the Social Environment and Psychiatric Disorders* (New York, 1953).

34. The following publications of Milbank conferences held between 1955 and 1961 illustrate some of these generalizations about the thrust of the fund's activities during these years: *The Elements of a Community Mental Health Program* (New York, 1956); *Programs for Community Mental Health* (New York, 1957); *An Approach to the Prevention of Disability from Chronic Psychoses* (New York, 1958); *Planning Evaluations of Mental Health Programs* (New York, 1958); *Progress and Problems of Community Mental Health Services* (New York, 1959); *Steps in the Development of Integrated Psychiatric Services* (New York, 1960); and *Decentralization of Psychiatric Services and Continuity of Care* (New York, 1962).

35. See Donald M. Carmichael, "New York State Aftercare Clinics in New York City," *American Journal of Orthopsychiatry*, 31 (1961): 642.

36. N.Y.S. Department of Mental Hygiene, *AR*, 61 (1948–1949): 43, 62 (1949–1950): 43–45, 63 (1950–1951): 46–48; Hunt and H. M. Forstenzer, "The New York State Community Mental Health Services Act: Its Birth and Early Development," *AJP*, 113 (1957): 680; Forstenzer and Hunt, "The New York State Community Mental Health Services Act: Its Origins and First Four Years of Development," *Psychiatric Quarterly, Supplement*, pt. 1, 32 (1958): 41–54.

37. *New York Times*, Jan. 5, 7, 26, Feb. 2, 14, 1954.

38. Hunt and Forstenzer, "The New York State Community Mental Health Services Act," 680–81; Hunt, "Pooling Resources for Mental Hygiene," *State Government*, 29 (1956): 17.

39. Hunt and Forstenzer, "The New York State Community Mental Health Services Act," 682–84; Hunt, "Pooling Resources for Mental Hygiene," 18–21.

40. Forstenzer and Hunt, "The New York State Community Mental Health Services Act," 54–56; N.Y.S. Department of Mental Hygiene, *AR*, 73 (1960–1961): 5. See also *New York State's Needs in Mental Health Research, Training and Community Services*, and N.Y.S. Department of Mental Hygiene, *A Guide to Communities in the Establishment and Operation of Psychiatric Clinics* (Albany, 1959).

41. This paragraph is based on Uri Aviram's analysis of postwar mental health policy in California, "Mental Health Reform and the After Care State Service Agency: A Study of the Process of Change in the Mental Health Field" (D.S.W. diss., University of California, Berkeley, 1972). See also Eugene Bardach, *The Skill Factor in Politics: Repealing the Mental Commitment Laws in California* (Berkeley, 1972).

42. *The Governor's Conference on Mental Health . . . Sacramento, California March 3 and 4, 1949: Preliminary Report* and *Final Report* (Sacramento, 1949); California Senate Interim Committee on the Treatment of Mental Illness, *Partial Report*, 2 (1956), 36ff.; Aviram and S. Segal, "From Hospital to Community

Care: The Change in the Mental Health Treatment System in California," *Community Mental Health Journal*, 13 (1977): 159–60.

43. California Senate Interim Committee on the Treatment of Mental Illness, *Partial Report*, 1–5 (1955–1958); Portia B. Hume, *The Short-Doyle Act for Community Mental Health Services* (Sacramento, 1957), 13ff.

44. California Senate Interim Committee on the Treatment of Mental Illness, *Partial Report*, 5 (1958): 16–17; Bardach, *Skill Factor in Politics*, 18–28.

45. JIS, "Highlights of Recent Community Mental Health Legislation," *JIS Fact Sheet*, 8 (Jan. 1959), passim.

46. See *State Mental Health Programs . . . 1954 and 1955* (PHS *Publication 374*: 1954).

47. Bahn and Norman, *Outpatient Psychiatric Clinics in the United States 1954–55*, 5; "Gains in Outpatient Psychiatric Services, 1959," *Public Health Reports*, 75 (1960): 1092–93; Carol L. McCarty et al., "Trends in Outpatient Psychiatric Clinic Resources, 1959," *Mental Hygiene*, 45 (1961): 483–93; Reginald Robinson, D. F. DeMarche, and M. K. Wagle, *Community Resources in Mental Health* (New York, 1960), passim.

48. Albert Deutsch, "States Astir against Mental Disease," *Mental Hygiene*, 40 (1956): 16–17.

49. Harold Sampson, D. Ross, B. Engle, and F. Livson, *A Study of Suitability for Outpatient Clinic Treatment of State Mental Hospital Admissions* (California Department of Mental Hygiene, *Research Report No. 1*: 1957). A briefer version appeared under the title "Feasibility of Community Clinic Treatment for State Mental Hospital Patients," *Archives of Neurology and Psychiatry*, 80 (1958): 71–77.

50. Sampson et al., "Feasibility of Community Clinic Treatment," 77.

51. See especially the proceedings of the following Milbank Memorial Fund conferences: *Elements of a Community Mental Health Program* (1956); *Programs for Community Mental Health* (1957); and *Steps in the Development of Integrated Psychiatric Services* (1960).

52. The testimony of mental health professionals and the reaction of members of Congress can be found in the hearings before the House and Senate Subcommittees on Appropriations dealing with the budget of the Department of Health, Education, and Welfare.

53. *Evaluation in Mental Health . . . Report of the Subcommittee on Evaluation of Mental Health Activities, Community Services Committee, National Advisory Mental Health Council* (PHS *Publication 413*: 1955), 5–6.

54. Ibid., 6–31; GAP Committee on Research, "Some Observations on Controls in Psychiatric Research," GAP *Report No. 42* (1959): passim. Flexner's observations were noted in E. E. Southard to Thomas W. Salmon, July 24, and Salmon to Southard, July 21, 1919, Salmon Boxes, American Foundation for Mental Hygiene Papers, AP; Alan Gregg to WCM, Dec. 4, KAM to Gregg, Dec. 21, 1950, KAM Papers, MFA.

55. Benjamin Pasamanick, F. R. Scarpitti, and S. Dinitz, *Schizophrenics in the Community: An Experimental Study in the Prevention of Hospitalization* (New York, 1967), vii–x, 267–70.

56. Council of State Governments, *Training and Research in State Mental*

Health Programs: A Report to the Governors' Conference (Chicago, 1953), 10; Lawrence S. Kubie, "Research in Psychiatry Is Starving to Death," *Science*, 116 (1952): 239–43; Jurgen Ruesch, "The Trouble with Psychiatric Research," *Archives of Neurology and Psychiatry*, 77 (1957): 96.

57. Milbank Memorial Fund, *Decentralization of Psychiatric Services and Continuity of Care*, 5, 172.

CHAPTER EIGHT
A NATIONAL CAMPAIGN: THE JOINT COMMISSION
ON MENTAL ILLNESS AND HEALTH

1. Kenneth E. Appel, "A Program for Public Support," APA Mental Hospital Institute, *Proceedings*, 5 (1953): 1–8; "Summary of Joint Meeting" (AMA Council on Mental Health and APA Executive Committee), Jan. 7–8, 1955, Box 6, and "Proceedings of Meeting of Joint Commission . . . April 7–8, 1955," 213–15, Box 5, JCMIH Papers, APAA; William Malamud to Walter Barton, June 22, 1954 (with notes), RMDO, 100-2, APAA; *Mental Hospitals*, 16 (1965): 62; Daniel Blain to Malamud, June 28, 1965, Blain Papers, APAA.

2. The most authoritative analysis of Flexner and the role of foundations in medical education is Steven C. Wheatley, *The Politics of Philanthropy: Abraham Flexner and Medical Education* (Madison, Wis., 1988). For discussions of the background to Flexner's report, see Robert P. Hudson, "Abraham Flexner in Perspective: American Medical Education 1865–1910," *Bulletin of the History of Medicine*, 56 (1972): 545–61, and Kenneth M. Ludmerer, *Learning to Heal: The Development of American Medical Education* (New York, 1985), 166–90.

3. "Summary of Joint Meeting," Jan. 7–8, 1955, Box 6, JCMIH Papers, APAA. At this time the name Joint Commission on Mental Health and Illness was adopted; shortly thereafter "Health" and "Illness" were reversed.

4. 84-1 Congress (1955), *Congressional Record*, 712–13, 1021–22, 1091, 1705, 1706, 2007, 2483; "Message of the President of the United States Transmitting Recommendations Relative to a Health Program," 84-1 Congress, *House Document No. 81* (Jan. 31, 1955); Lister Hill interview by Harlan B. Phillips, Jan.–June, 1967, 309–10, NLM. The text of the bills and resolutions introduced in early 1955 can be found in the House and Senate hearings, cited below.

In the section of his presidential message relating to mental health, Eisenhower asked that aid to states for preventive and community programs be strengthened; that additional resources be provided for training; and that a new program of mental health project grants be inaugurated to improve the quality of care in, and administration of, mental hospitals.

5. 84-1 Congress, *Mental Health Study Act of 1955. Hearings before a Subcommittee of the Committee on Interstate and Foreign Commerce House of Representatives . . . 1955* (Washington, D.C., 1955), 4–22.

6. Ibid., 35–83, 106–11.

7. Ibid., 145–51.

8. 84-1 Congress, *Mental Health. Hearings before the Subcommittee on Health of the Committee on Labor and Public Welfare . . . Senate . . .1955* (Washington, D.C., 1955), 107–8 and passim.

9. Ibid., 145–49; 84-1 Congress, *Mental Health Study Act of 1955. Hearings*, 157–61.

10. 84-1 Congress, *House Report No. 241* (Mar. 21, 1955), *Senate Report No. 870* (July 14, 1955), *Congressional Record* (1955), 3004–5, 3113, 4899, 4919–26, 4942–43, 5116, 10704–6, 11129, 12723–24; chap. 417, *U.S. Statutes at Large*, 69:381–83, 1955.

11. Mike Gorman to Robert P. Knight, Apr. 5, Robert T. Morse to Gorman, Apr. 7, R. Finley Gayle to Lister Hill, May 13, 25, 1955, RMDO, 100-27, APAA; 84-1 Congress, *Senate Report No. 869* (July 14, 1955); 84-2 Congress, *Health Amendments Act of 1956 . . . Hearings before a Subcommittee on Interstate and Foreign Commerce House of Representatives . . . 1956* (Washington, D.C., 1956); 84-2 Congress, *Congressional Record* (1956), 8558, 9147, 9963, 9989–10001, 12227–28; 84-2 Congress, *House Report No. 2086* (May 2, 1956); chaps. 779 and 871, *U.S. Statutes at Large*, 70:717–21, 923–30, 1956.

12. Blain, "Memorandum of Conversation with Dr. Appel on Long-distance Telephone . . . March 7," Mar. 10, 1955, Jack R. Ewalt Papers, CLMHMS; "Proceedings of Meeting of Joint Commission . . . April 7–8, 1955," "Summary Report [of] Meeting of Planning Committee for the Joint Commission on Mental Illness and Health . . . April 7–8, 1955," Blain Memo to Members of JCMIH, Apr. 29, Minutes of the JCMIH, May 26, Minutes of the Organizational Meeting of the Board of Trustees, JCMIH, Sept. 11, 1955, Box 5, JCMIH Papers, APAA.

13. "Proceedings of Meeting of Joint Commission . . . April 7–8, 1955," and "Summary Report . . . April 7–8, 1955," Box 5, JCMIH Papers, APAA.

14. "Proceedings of Meeting of Joint Commission . . . April 7–8, 1955," 114–21, 123–26, Box 5, JCMIH Papers, APAA.

15. Ibid., 125, 135, 145–50.

16. Although the original mandate of the JCMIH was to study both mental illness and mental retardation, the latter was deleted relatively early. The care and treatment of the mentally retarded had been of marginal concern to psychiatrists, and by the 1950s there was clear evidence of friction between mainstream psychiatry and those involved with retardation. Indeed, the American Association on Mental Deficiency (which held membership in the commission) opposed the inclusion of retardation, favoring instead a separate study (which, because of the death of a key figure, ended up as a work on research into mental deficiency). Jack R. Ewalt taped remarks, Nov. 1985, transcript in possession of Gerald N. Grob.

17. Minutes of the Organizational Meeting of the Board of Trustees, Sept. 11, 1955, Box 5, JCMIH Papers, APAA.

18. Blain Memo to JCMIH, Apr. 29, Minutes of the JCMIH, May 26, Appel to Ewalt, July 19, Minutes of the Organizational Meeting of the Board of Trustees, Sept. 11, 1955, Box 5, JCMIH Papers, APAA.

19. Robert T. Morse to Ewalt, Apr. 11, Ewalt to Morse, Apr. 14, Ewalt to Carl A. Sheridan, Dec. 29, 1955, Ewalt to Russell A. Nelson, Apr. 6, 1956, Ewalt Papers, CLMHMS; Harry C. Solomon to Leo H. Bartemeier, Oct. 21, 1955, Solomon Papers, APAA; Blain to Greer Williams, Dec. 5, 1955, RMDO, 100-12, APAA.

20. Nelson to Ewalt, Apr. 3, 25, Ewalt to Nelson, Apr. 6, May 7, Harvey J. Tompkins to Ewalt, July 6, Ewalt to Tompkins, July 10, 1956, Ewalt Papers, CLMHMS; Ewalt to Felix, Sept. 13, 1956, NIMH Papers, Mental Health Subject Files, 1957–60, Box 6, WNRC.

21. Draft letter from Bartemeier (prepared by Ewalt) to Felix, Oct. 14, 1955, Ewalt Papers, CLMHMS; Bartemeier to Ewalt, Jan. 14, 1957, Bartemeier Papers, APAA; Memo from Harry C. Meserve to R. B. Fosdick Files, June 20, 1957, Rockefeller Brothers Fund Papers, Box 54, RAC; *Action for Mental Health: Final Report of the Joint Commission on Mental Illness and Health 1961* (New York, 1961), 316.

22. *Action for Mental Health*, 6–9. Shirley Star's study of mental health was completed in 1950. Parts of it circulated in mimeograph form, but the entire manuscript (running to several hundred pages of text) was never published. Professor Jack Elinson has graciously permitted me to examine his copy of Star's influential study.

23. Ewalt, "Evaluating Mental Health Programs," 12–14, presentation at the National Opinion Research Center, Aug. 9, 1956, copy in Box 2, JCMIH Papers, APAA.

24. JCMIH, *AR*, 1 (1956): appendix D (mimeographed), 4–5, appendix F, 2–8, copy in CLMHMS. See also Ewalt, "Goals of the Joint Commission on Mental Illness and Health," *AJPH*, 47 (1957): 19–24.

25. JCMIH, *AR*, 1 (1956): appendix F, 10–12, copy in CLMHMS.

26. For a complete listing of staff, committee, and advisory personnel see *Action for Mental Health*, 309–15.

27. Ewalt, Staff Memo, June 5, 1957, Box 6, JCMIH Papers, APAA.

28. Ewalt, "Evaluating Mental Health Programs," 15, Box 2, JCMIH Papers, APAA; Ewalt, "Goals of the Joint Commission," 22.

29. JCMIH, "Summary of Minutes [of] Meeting," May 11, 1956, Box 2, JCMIH Papers, APAA.

30. See the Memo from Greer Williams to Ewalt, Oct. 14, 1957, Box 3, JCMIH Papers, APAA.

31. Rashi Fein, *Economics of Mental Illness* (New York, 1958), 123–39 and passim; "Summary of the Minutes of the Meeting of the Committee on the Studies," Mar. 9, 1958, 2–10, Box 1, JCMIH Papers, APAA.

32. Marie Jahoda, *Current Concepts of Positive Mental Health* (New York, 1958).

33. "Summary of Discussion of the Meeting of the Committee on the Studies," Nov. 15, 1957, 2, 23, "Summary of the Minutes of the Meeting of the Committee on the Studies," Mar. 9, 1958, 10, Box 1, JCMIH Papers, APAA; Barton, "Viewpoint of a Clinician," in Jahoda, *Current Concepts*, 111–19.

34. George W. Albee, *Mental Health Manpower Trends* (New York, 1959), 259 and passim; "Summary of the Minutes of the Committee on the Studies," Oct. 25, 1958, 1–19, Box 1, JCMIH Papers, APAA. See also Albee's two articles (each with the same title), "The Manpower Crisis in Mental Health," *AJPH*, 50 (1960): 1895–1900, and National Conference on Social Welfare, *Mental Health and Social Welfare* (New York, 1961), 22–36.

35. JCMIH, *AR*, 1 (1956): appendix J, 2–7, copy in CLMHMS.

36. Gerald Gurin, J. Veroff, and S. Field, *Americans View Their Mental Health* (New York, 1960), 406 and passim.

37. Reginald Robinson, D. F. DeMarche, and M. K. Wagle, *Community Resources in Mental Health* (New York, 1960), 392 and passim; Wesley Allinsmith and G. W. Goethals, *The Role of the Schools in Mental Health* (New York, 1962), 36, 131 and passim.

38. Richard V. McCann, *The Churches and Mental Health* (New York, 1962).

39. Richard J. Plunkett and John E. Gordon, *Epidemiology and Mental Illness* (New York, 1960), 4–5, 25, 91, 95. For a discussion of some of the preliminary analysis of the Plunkett and Gordon project, see "Summary of the Minutes of the Meeting of the Committee on the Studies," 23ff., Mar. 9, 1958, Box 1, JCMIH Papers, APAA.

40. Soskin's report was never published. My description is based on the summary in *Action for Mental Health*, 193–224.

41. Memo from Ewalt to the Committee on Research in Mental Health, Apr. 30, 1956, included with "Notes on Proposal for a Study of Patterns of Patient Care," Box 6, JCMIH Papers, APAA; Morris S. and C. G. Schwartz et al., *Social Approaches to Mental Patient Care* (New York, 1964).

There were substantial differences between the draft submitted to the JCMIH in 1961 (summarized in *Action for Mental Health*, 166–92) and the published volume.

42. Schwartz, *Social Approaches to Mental Patient Care*, 20–21.

43. Ibid., 12–19.

44. Ibid., 192–97.

45. Ibid. For a brief summary of the work of the task force, see Warren T. Vaughan and M. G. Field, "New Perspectives on Mental Patient Care," *AJPH*, 53 (1963): 237–42.

46. Schwartz, *Social Approaches to Mental Patient Care*, 291–308.

47. Warren T. Vaughan to Barton, Aug. 21, 1961, Barton Papers, APAA.

48. Ewalt to Members of the Committee on the Studies, June 12, Barton to Ewalt, July 5, Ewalt to Barton and M. Ralph Kaufman, Aug. 8, Barton to Vaughan, Aug. 14, Barton to Kaufman, Aug. 14, 1961, Kaufman and Barton, "Dissent," Barton Papers, APAA. The "Dissent" by Kaufman and Barton did not appear in *Social Approaches to Mental Patient Care*. Unlike the other monographs, this volume was not published by Basic Books (which had a formal agreement with the JCMIH) but was rather issued by Columbia University Press in 1964.

49. "Summary of the Minutes of the Third Annual Meeting Joint Commission," Oct. 24, 10–14, Box 2, "Summary of the Minutes of the Committee on the Studies," Oct. 25, 1958, 19–38, Box 1, JCMIH Papers, APAA.

50. Greer Williams to Albert Deutsch, Dec. 9, 1959, Deutsch Papers, APAA; Ewalt taped remarks, Nov. 1985, transcript in possession of Gerald N. Grob.

51. "The Joint Commission on Mental Illness and Health, Inc. . . . Boston . . . August 20–21, 1960" (typed stenographic transcript), 105–47, 158–71, Box 2, JCMIH Papers, APAA.

52. Mike Gorman interview by Michael Barton, Apr. 7, 1972, 28–29, copy in Blain Papers, APAA.

53. *Action for Mental Health*, 22–23.
54. Ibid., 8, 26–55.
55. Ibid., 56–85.
56. Ibid., xxv, 93, 228, 241–43.
57. Ibid., 213–41.
58. Ibid., 241–60.
59. Ibid., 260–68.
60. Ibid., 267–75.
61. Ibid., 275–81.
62. Ibid., 282–85.
63. Ibid., 285–95.
64. Ibid., 330–31.
65. JCMIH Press Release, Mar. 24, 1961, in R. L. Robinson File *Action for Mental Health*, Box 6, JCMIH Papers, APAA.

CHAPTER NINE
FROM ADVOCACY TO POLICY

1. Francis J. Braceland to Kenneth E. Appel, Nov. 9, Appel to Braceland, Dec. 6, 1960, Braceland Papers, APAA.
2. APA Council Meeting, May 6–7, 22, November 24–26, 1961, 5–6, plus backup item No. 2, APA Executive Committee Meeting, June 16, 1961, 1, plus backup item No. 2, APA Board of Trustees Papers, APAA.
3. Walter E. Barton to Jack Ewalt, Nov. 14, 1961, Ewalt Papers, CLMHMS; Reactions of APA Committees to JCMIH report, n.d. (ca. 1961–1962), Bartholomew Hogan Box, JCMIH Papers, APAA; APA Commission on Long Term Policies, Minutes, Jan. 19, 1962, 3, D. E. Cameron Papers, APAA; "Report to the Council . . . of the Policy Committee of the Assembly of District Branches," Nov. 14–16, 1961, 3, R. L. Robinson File *Action for Mental Health*, JCMIH Papers, APAA; "Committees on Professional Standards Comments on the Report of the Joint Commission," n.d. (200-24), Minutes of the Committee on Public Health, Nov. 3–4, 1961, 200-33, RMDO, APAA.
4. "Private Communication for Use of the APA Committee to Advise on Implementation of the Joint Commission Report," Oct. 23, 1962, R. L. Robinson File *Action for Mental Health*, JCMIH Papers, APAA, and summary of "Private Communication," RMDO, 200-9, APAA.
5. Newton Bigelow's criticisms, which appeared throughout the decade of the 1960s, appeared in the *Psychiatric Quarterly*, 33 (1959): 148–65, 35 (1961): 576–85 (quotations from 581–82), 777–84, 36 (1962): 151–64, 754–67, 37 (1963): 153–65, 39 (1965): 347–54, 40 (1966): 357–66, 43 (1969): 568–73.
6. "Chronology and Abbreviated Commentary on Follow-up Actions on the Final Report of the Joint Commission . . . up to July 23, 1962," 2, RMDO, 200-9, APAA; Francis J. Gerty, "Summation," and Henry W. Brosin, "Summation," *Mental Hospitals*, 13 (1962): 84–86, 88–89, 114–16.
7. Warren S. Williams to Matthew Ross, Oct. 30, Ewalt to Williams, Nov. 6, 1961, Ewalt Papers, CLMHMS; Ewalt to Ross, Oct. 18, 1961, RMDO, 100-35, APAA; Ewalt to WCM, Oct. 31, WCM to Ewalt, Nov. 6, 1961, WCM Papers,

MFA; Albert Deutsch to Bigelow, Jan. 7, John Cumming to Deutsch, Feb. 24, Mar. 10, 1960, Deutsch Papers, APAA. See also Elaine and John Cumming, *Closed Ranks: An Experiment in Mental Health Education* (Cambridge, Mass., 1957).

8. Memo by Barton, with revised draft of APA Council statement, Dec. 22, 1961, JCMIH Papers, APAA; APA Executive Committee Minutes, Jan. 15, 1962, 4–6, APA Board of Trustees Papers, APAA; APA Council, "A Position Statement with Interpretive Commentary and Commendation," *Mental Hospitals*, 13 (1962): 68–69, 72.

9. AMA Council on Mental Health Minutes, July 15, 1961, and "Official Statement of the Council on Mental Health on the Report of the Joint Commission," both in MDO Papers, Box 608–9, APAA; AMA, *National Congress on Mental Illness and Health October 4–6, 1962* (Chicago, 1962), passim; "Chronology and Abbreviated Commentary," 1–2, 10, RMDO, 200-9, APAA; Robert T. Morse to WCM, Feb. 15, 1961, WCM Papers, MFA.

10. "Statement on Report of Joint Commission on Mental Illness and Health," *American Psychologist*, 18 (1963): 307–8.

11. "Report on the Joint Commission Report by the National Association for Mental Health," in R. L. Robinson File *Action for Mental Health*, JCMIH Papers, APAA; "Chronology and Abbreviated Commentary," 4, 9, RMDO, 200-9, APAA; *New York Times*, Nov. 19, 1961.

12. John C. Whitehorn to C. H. Hardin Branch, June 13, Hardin Branch to Whitehorn, June 27, 1962, Whitehorn Papers, APAA; WCM to Mike Gorman, Feb. 17, Ewalt to Greer Williams, Mar. 10, 1961, WCM Papers, MFA. See also *AJP*, 118 (1961): 369–71; Leo Bartemeier, "The Future of Psychiatry: The Report of the Joint Commission on Mental Illness and Health," ibid., 118 (1962): 973–81; Benjamin Pasamanick, "Action for Mental Health," *American Journal of Orthopsychiatry*, 32 (1962): 539–50; and Brosin, "Action for Mental Health—Blueprint or Beacon?" *Pennsylvania Psychiatric Quarterly*, 3 (1963): 3–10.

13. Gorman to WCM, Feb. 14, WCM to Gorman, Feb. 15, 17, Ewalt to WCM, Feb. 15, Mar. 7, WCM to Ewalt, Mar. 3, 10, Morse to WCM, Feb. 15, 20, WCM to Morse, Feb. 17, 23, Mar. 6, Robinson to WCM, Feb. 17, WCM to Robinson, Mar. 1, WCM Papers, MFA; *Proceedings of the Governors' Conference 1961* (Chicago, 1961), 10–40, 148.

14. Bernard Crihfield to WCM, Aug. 17, Oct. 6 (with enclosed policy statement by Gorman), WCM to Crihfield, Aug. 31, WCM to Gorman, Sept. 18, 1961, WCM Papers, MFA; *State Government*, 35 (1962): 2–19; *Mental Hospitals*, 13 (1962): 6–9; Frank Bane to Frederic C. Dutton, Nov. 14, 1961, White House Central Files, Box 338, HE 1-1, JFKL; Gorman, "Mental Illness: Legislative and Economic Considerations," *AJPH*, 53 (1963): 403–8.

15. Philip Sapir to Robert H. Felix, Oct. 23, Richard H. Williams to Felix, Oct. 22, Joseph M. Bobbitt to Felix, Oct. 22, Lauren Wispe comments, Oct. 23, Ewalt to Robert T. Hewitt, July 29, Harold P. Halpert to Ewalt, Aug. 17, 1959, NIMH Records, Mental Health Subject Files 1957–60, Box 7, WNRC.

16. John R. Seeley to Felix, Jan. 22, Felix to Seeley, Feb. 25, 1959, NIMH Records, Mental Health Subject Files 1957–60, Box 7, WNRC; Felix interview,

Aug. 5, 1964, 8 (OH120), APAA; Felix, "Implications and Implementation of the Joint Commission Report at the Federal Level," speech at Governors' Conference, Nov. 1961, Felix Papers, NLM; Felix to Special Assistant to Secretary, Health and Medical Affairs, DHEW, Sept. 27, 1961, Bertram S. Brown Papers, NLM.

17. *Planning of Facilities for Mental Health Services: Report of the Surgeon General's Ad Hoc Committee on Planning for Mental Health Facilities* (PHS Publication 808: 1961), ii–v, 2–5, 25–34.

18. Theodore C. Sorenson to Secretary Abraham Ribicoff (HEW), Apr. 6, 1961, Records of DHEW Selected for Deposit at the JFKL; Memo, Director of the Bureau of the Budget for the President Regarding the Report of the JCMIH, ca. Nov. 1961, White House Central Files, Box 338, Folder HE 1-1, JFKL; George P. Berry to McGeorge Bundy, Mar. 6, Aug. 11, Bundy to R. Sargent Shriver, Mar. 7, Shriver to Bundy, June 4, Berry to Ewalt, Mar. 11, 26, Aug. 11, Ewalt to Berry, Mar. 16, Berry to Shriver, Aug. 10, 1958, Ewalt Papers, CLMHMS. See also Edward D. Berkowitz, "The Politics of Mental Retardation during the Kennedy Administration," *Social Science Quarterly*, 61 (1980): 128–43.

19. Gorman to Myer Feldman, Feb. 20, Feldman to Kenneth O'Donnell, Mar. 1, 1963, President's Office Files, Box 102, JFKL. The following provide much background material: Feldman interview, Sept. 21, 1968, vol. 14, 1–30, Eunice Kennedy Shriver interview by John F. Stewart, May 7, 1968, Stafford Warren interview by Ronald Grele, June 7, 1966, Seymour S. Kety interview by John F. Stewart, May 2, 1968, JFKL.

20. Feldman interview, vol. 7, 304–7, vol. 14, 3–10, JFKL; Gorman to Ewalt, May 10, with enclosed Address by Ribicoff, May 3, 1961, WCM Papers, MFA; Henry A. Foley, *Community Mental Health Legislation: The Formative Process* (Lexington, Mass., 1975), 33.

21. Kennedy to Ribicoff, Dec. 1, 1961, White House Central Files, Box 338, Folder HE 1-1, JFKL; Foley, *Community Mental Health Legislation*, 33–37.

22. JFK Special Message on Health Care, Feb. 27, 1962, in *Congressional Quarterly Almanac*, 18 (1962): 899; Kennedy to Ribicoff, Dec. 1, 1961, White House Central Files, Box 338, Folder HE 1-1, JFKL; Foley, *Community Mental Health Legislation*, 35–37.

23. Foley, *Community Mental Health Legislation*, 35–36.

24. "National Institute of Mental Health Position Paper on the Report of the Joint Commission on Mental Illness and Health," Nov. 1961, passim, NIMH Records, Miscellaneous Records 1956–67, Box 1, WNRC. See also Felix to Special Assistant to Secretary, Health and Medical Affairs, HEW, Oct. 6, 1961, Brown Papers, NLM.

25. James A. Shannon to Surgeon General, n.d., copy in Brown Papers, NLM.

26. "Report of [NIMH] Task Force on the Status of State Mental Hospitals in the United States," Mar. 30, 1962, Brown Papers, NLM.

27. "Preliminary Draft Report of NIMH Task Force on Implementation of Recommendations of the Report of the Joint Commission on Mental Illness and Health," Jan. 5, 1962, and "A Proposal for a Comprehensive Mental Health Program to Implement the Findings of the Joint Commission on Mental Illness

and Health," Apr. 1962, 10, 12, 34–35, and passim, NIMH Records, Miscellaneous Records, 1956–67, Box 1, WNRC.

28. *Proceedings 1962 Annual Conference Surgeon General Public Health Service with State and Territorial Mental Health Authorities* (PHS *Publication 916:* 1962), 1–2, 19–31; WCM, "Memorandum for the Record," Feb. 9, 1962, WCM Private Papers in possession of Cay Menninger, Topeka, Kans.; "A Visit with President John F. Kennedy," in *A Psychiatrist for a Troubled World: Selected Papers of William C. Menninger* (New York, 1967), 795–97; JFK Special Message on Health Care, Feb. 27, 1962, in *Congressional Quarterly Almanac,* 18 (1962): 897–900.

29. Gorman to Feldman, Feb. 19, 1962, White House Central Files, Box 338, Folder HE 1-1, JFKL; 88-1 Congress, *Departments of Labor and Health, Education, and Welfare Appropriations for 1964. Hearings before a Subcommittee of the Committee on Appropriations House of Representatives* (Washington, D.C., 1963), pt. 3, 473–77; Gorman interview by Daniel Blain, Oct. 7, 1972, 27–29, Blain Papers, APAA; John E. Fogarty speech, "The Responsibility of the Federal Government in the Fight against Mental Illness," Mar. 6, 1962, copy in WCM Papers, MFA; 87-2 Congress, *House Report No. 1488* (March 23, 1962), 34–35.

30. Fein to Walter W. Heller, Nov. 21, 1962, Heller Papers, JFKL.

31. Foley, *Community Mental Health Legislation,* 39–40; Lisa Reichenbach, "The Federal Community Mental Health Centers Program and the Policy of Deinstitutionalization," 63, unpublished manuscript in possession of Professor Lawrence E. Lynn, Jr., of the University of Chicago.

32. Robert H. Atwell to Director, "Proposals for the President's Mental Health Program—A Report of the Interagency Group Appointed by the President," draft dated Nov. 1, 1962, Daniel Patrick Moynihan to Boisfeuillet Jones, Aug. 21, 1962, Brown Papers, NLM; Foley, *Community Mental Health Legislation,* 40–41.

33. Fein to Heller, Nov. 21, 1962, Heller Papers, JFKL. Celebrezze's memorandum to JFK was sent to the White House in preliminary form. The original draft did not include funding for the staffing of centers; such a proviso was added only at the behest of the administration. See the draft of the Celebrezze memorandum dated Nov. 14, 1962, in the Feldman Papers, Box 12, JFKL; Stanley Yolles interview, Sept. 23, 1977, 9, Senn Collection (OH76), NLM. The final version included funds for staffing. See Celebrezze, W. Willard Wirtz, and J. Gleason to JFK, Nov. 30, 1962, White House Central Files, Box 338, Folder HE 1-1, JFKL.

34. Celebrezze, Wirtz, and Gleason to JFK, Nov. 30, 1962, White House Central Files, Box 338, Folder HE 1-1, JFKL.

35. Ibid.

36. 88-1 Congress, *Mental Health. Hearings before a Subcommittee of the Committee on Interstate and Foreign Commerce House of Representatives . . . 1963* (Washington, D.C., 1963), 100–106; Foley, *Community Mental Health Legislation,* 41–44.

37. *Wall Street Journal,* Jan. 15, 1963; Feldman interview, vol. 14, 13–15, JFKL. See also Brown interview by John F. Stewart, Aug. 6, 1968, 23, ibid., and Felix interview, Aug. 5, 1964, 11 (OH120), APAA.

38. Feldman interview, Sept. 21, 1968, vol. 14, 24–25, JFKL; Brown interview, Aug. 6, 1968, 24, ibid.

39. "Message from the President of the United States Relative to Mental Illness and Mental Retardation," 88-1 Congress, *House Document No. 58* (Feb. 5, 1963).

40. *New York Times*, Feb. 8, May 7, 1963; APA Executive Committee Meeting Minutes, Mar. 17–18, 1963, 21–22, APA Council Minutes, May 4–5, 37–38, plus backup item 15B, 2–3, APA Board of Trustees Papers, Box 20, APAA. The *New York Times* published a critical letter (Feb. 25, 1963) by a former college student who had done volunteer work in a mental hospital. The correspondent argued that the presidential initiative had ignored the plight of the chronically mentally ill.

41. See especially "Health Research and Training: The Administration of Grants and Awards by the National Institutes of Health," 87-1 Congress, *House Report No. 321* (April 28, 1961); 87-1 Congress, *Health Research and Training: Hearings before a Subcommittee of the Committee on Government Operations House of Representatives . . . August 1 and 2, 1961* (Washington, D.C., 1961); 87-2 Congress, *The Administration of Grants by the National Institutes of Health. Hearings before a Subcommittee of the Committee on Government Operations House of Representatives . . . March 28, 29, and 30, 1962* (Washington, D.C., 1962); 87-2 Congress (1962), *Congressional Record*, 12843–46, 13949–56, 14789–92, 15285–92.

42. The provisions of the bills can be found in 88-1 Congress, *Mental Illness and Retardation. Hearings before the Subcommittee on Health of the Committee on Labor and Public Welfare United States Senate . . . March 5, 6, and 7, 1963* (Washington, D.C., 1963), 1–15. See also Hill to Hardin Branch, Feb. 25, 1963, RMDO, 100-35, APAA.

43. 88-1 Congress, *Mental Illness and Retardation. Hearings . . . Senate*, 17–19, 87–88, 191 and passim; "Briefing Book for Secretary [HEW] on Community Mental Health Centers Act of 1963," and "Background Material Supporting the Testimony of the Secretary of Health, Education, and Welfare before the Senate Committee on Labor and Welfare Regarding S755, Community Mental Health Centers Act of 1963," Sept. 4, 1963, Brown Papers, NLM.

44. 88-1 Congress, *Mental Illness and Retardation. Hearings . . . Senate*, 41–44; 88-1 Congress, *Mental Health. Hearings . . . House*, 239–43.

45. Gorman interview by Blain, 35, Blain Papers, APAA; 88-1 Congress, *Mental Health. Hearings . . . House*, 99–106, 341–42; Bureau of the Budget Memorandum, Dec. 12, 1962, cited in Reichenbach, "The Federal Community Mental Health Centers Program," 77.

46. 88-1 Congress, *Mental Health. Hearings . . . House*, 147–55, 237–38.

47. Ibid., 97.

48. Foley, *Community Mental Health Legislation*, 60; Brown, "Aide Memoire," Apr. 22, 1963, Brown Papers, NLM; Eunice Shriver interview by John F. Stewart, May 7, 1968, 23, JFKL; Gunnar Dybwad to Mrs. R. Sargent Shriver, June 20, 1963, Feldman Papers, JFKL; 88-1 Congress (1963), *Congressional Record*, 9519; *New York Times*, May 28, 1963.

49. AMA Council on Mental Health Minutes, June 14, 1963, 106–8, copy in

APA MDO Papers, Box 608–9, APAA; Hamilton Ford to WCM, July 16, WCM to Ford, July 18, 1963, WCM Papers, MFA; *JAMA*, 186 (1963): 349.

50. 88-1 Congress, *Mental Health (Supplemental). Hearings before a Subcommittee of the Committee on Interstate and Foreign Commerce House of Representatives . . . July 10 and 11, 1963* (Washington, D.C., 1963).

51. "Initial Staffing Grants for Community Mental Health Centers," Sept. 1963, Feldman Papers, JFKL; Gorman interview by Blain, 34–35, Blain Papers, APAA; *Mental Retardation Facilities and Community Mental Health Centers Construction Act of 1963: Report of the Committee on Interstate and Foreign Commerce House of Representatives*, 88-1 Congress, *House Report No. 694* (Aug. 21, 1963); Foley, *Community Mental Health Legislation*, 68–70.

52. 88-1 Congress (1963), *Congressional Record*, 16650–97.

53. 88-1 Congress (1963), *Congressional Record*, 17492–98, 19845–47, 19954–65, 20162; 88-1 Congress, *House Report No. 462* (Oct. 21, 1963); Foley, *Community Mental Health Legislation*, 74–76.

54. Public Law 88-164, *U.S. Statutes at Large*, 77:282–99, 1963; Felix, "A Model for Comprehensive Mental Health Centers," *AJPH*, 54 (1964): 1965. See also Felix's "The National Mental Health Program," ibid., 1804–9, and "Community Mental Health: A Federal Perspective," *AJP*, 121 (1964): 428–32.

55. Data in this and the preceding paragraph are drawn from a sample of studies produced by the staff of the Biometrics Branch during these years that were relevant to policy. See Kramer, "Long Range Studies of Mental Hospital Patients, an Important Area for Research in Chronic Disease," *Milbank Memorial Fund Quarterly*, 31 (1953): 253–64; Kramer, H. Goldstein, R. H. Israel, and N. A. Johnson, *A Historical Study of the Disposition of First Admissions to a State Mental Hospital: Experience of the Warren State Hospital during the Period 1916–50* (PHS *Publication 445*: 1955); Kramer, *Facts Needed to Assess Public Health and Social Problems in the Widespread Use of the Tranquilizing Drugs* (PHS *Publication 486*: 1956); Ben Z. Locke, Kramer, C. E. Timberlake, B. Pasamanick, and D. Smeltzer, "Problems in Interpretation of Patterns of First Admissions to Ohio State Public Mental Hospitals for Patients with Schizophrenic Reactions," APA, *Psychiatric Research Reports*, 10 (1958): 172–208; Earl S. Pollack, P. H. Person, Kramer, and Goldstein, *Patterns of Retention, Release, and Death of First Admissions to State Mental Hospitals* (PHS *Publication 672*: 1959); Kramer, Pollack, and R. W. Redick, "Studies of the Incidence and Prevalence of Hospitalized Mental Disorders in the United States: Current Status and Future Goals," in *Comparative Epidemiology of the Mental Disorders*, ed. Paul H. Hoch and J. Zubin (New York, 1961), 56–100; Kramer, *Some Implications of Trends in the Usage of Psychiatric Facilities for Community Mental Health Programs and Related Research* (PHS *Publication 1434*: 1967); Kramer, "Epidemiology, Biostatistics, and Mental Health Planning," in APA *Psychiatric Research Reports*, 22 (1967): 1–68; Kramer, C. Taube, and S. Starr, "Patterns of Use of Psychiatric Facilities by the Aged: Current Status, Trends, and Implications," in APA, *Psychiatric Research Reports*, 23 (1968): 89–150.

56. Alan D. Miller, "Common and Unique Features in State Plans," Sept. 1963, copy provided by Dr. Miller. For a sensitive and insightful analysis of mental health policy in the 1960s by a shrewd observer, see Alfred J. Kahn, *Studies in*

Social Policy and Planning (New York, 1969), 194–242. Kahn's book anticipated with remarkable accuracy some of the developments of the 1970s and 1980s.

57. For the process and consequences of planning, see the following: Raymond Glasscote and Charles Kanno, *"The Plans for Planning": A Comparative Analysis of the State Mental Health Planning Proposals* (Washington, D.C., 1963); *Digest Progress Reports on State Mental Health Planning 1964* (PHS Publication 1248: 1964); *1966 Final Reports: State Mental Health Planning* (PHS Publication No. 1685: 1966), quotation from 182; Harold P. Halpert, *Comprehensive Mental Health Planning in Six States* (PHS Publication 1686: 1967).

58. Miller, S. L. Buker, and R. N. Elwell, "The Hospital Improvement Project Grant Program," *Mental Hospitals*, 15 (1964): 526–28; NIMH, *Better Care for Mental Patients: A Progress Report: The First 5 Years of a Hospital Improvement Program 1963–1968* (PHS Publication 1896: 1969); 88-2 Congress, *Departments of Labor and Health, Education, and Welfare Appropriations for 1965. Hearings before a Subcommittee of the Committee on Appropriations House of Representatives* (Washington, D.C., 1964), pt. 3, 242; Arthur A. Woloshin and H. C. Pomp, "The Gulf between Planning and Implementing Mental Health Programs," *Hospital & Community Psychiatry*, 19 (1968): 60–61.

59. Paul Lemkau to Gerald N. Grob, Mar. 9, 1987.

CHAPTER TEN
FROM INSTITUTION TO COMMUNITY

1. Demographic data on psychiatrists can be found in the following: JIS, *Fact Sheet 10* (1959); NIMH, *Mental Health Manpower, Current Statistical and Activities Report*, No. 9 (Feb. 1966): 12; NIMH, *The Nation's Psychiatrists* (PHS Publication 1885: 1969); and Franklyn N. Arnhoff and A. H. Kumbar, *The Nation's Psychiatrists—1970 Survey* (Washington, D.C., 1973).

2. Louis Linn, "The Fourth Psychiatric Revolution," *AJP*, 124 (1968): 1043–48; Stephen E. Goldston, ed., *Concepts of Community Psychiatry: A Framework for Training* (PHS Publication 1319: 1965), 195–97.

3. Gerald Caplan, "Community Psychiatry," in *Concepts of Community Psychiatry*, ed. Goldston, 4, 10; idem., "Current Issues Relating to the Education of Psychiatric Residents in Community Psychiatry," in *Mental Health Career Development Program . . . 1964* (PHS Publication 1245: 1964), 12–30; idem., *Principles of Preventive Psychiatry* (New York, 1964), 16ff.

Primary prevention, according to Caplan, involved a reduction in the incidence of mental disorders; secondary prevention meant a reduction of the duration of those disorders which occurred; and tertiary prevention meant a reduction in the impairment which resulted from those disorders.

4. Saul D. Alinsky, "The Poor and the Powerful," *International Journal of Psychiatry*, 4 (1967): 304–9 (discussion on 309–15); Harold M. Visotsky, "Community Psychiatry: We Are Willing to Learn," *AJP*, 122 (1965): 693; Jack R. and P. L. Ewalt, "History of the Community Psychiatry Movement," ibid., 126 (1969): 51.

The literature dealing with community psychiatry is extensive. The *AJP* published several issues devoted to the subject (122 [1966]: 977–1017, 1056–57, 124

Supplement [Oct. 1967]: 1–11). For additional examples, see Leigh M. Roberts, "Expanding Role of the Psychiatrist in the Community," *Diseases of the Nervous System*, 26 (1965): 147–55; Alvin Becker, N. M. Murphy, and M. Greenblatt, "Recent Advances in Community Psychiatry," *New England Journal of Medicine*, 272 (1965): 621–26, 674–79; *Current Psychiatric Therapies*, 6 (1966): 299–305, 7 (1967): 225–30, 9 (1969): 284–91; "Education for Community Psychiatry," and "Education for Community Psychiatry," GAP *Reports No. 64* (1967) and *No. 69* (1968); and Arthur J. Bindman and A. D. Spiegel, eds., *Perspectives in Community Mental Health* (Chicago, 1969).

5. John C. Whitehorn, "Thoughts on 'Issues' in Regard to Our Expanding 'Community Psychiatry,'" Dec. 1965, Whitehorn Papers, APAA; Lawrence S. Kubie, "Pitfalls of Community Psychiatry," *Archives of General Psychiatry*, 18 (1968): 257–66, and "The Retreat from Patients," *International Journal of Psychiatry*, 9 (1970–1971): 693–722; Leon Eisenberg, "The Need for Evaluation," *AJP*, 124 (1968): 1700–1701.

6. See H. Warren Dunham, P. Phillips, and B. Srinivasan, "A Research Note on Diagnosed Mental Illness and Social Class," *American Sociological Review*, 31 (1966): 223–27, and Dunham, *Community and Schizophrenia: An Epidemiological Analysis* (Detroit, 1965).

7. Dunham, "Community Psychiatry: The Newest Therapeutic Bandwagon," *Archives of General Psychiatry*, 12 (1965): 303–13. See also Dunham's exchange of correspondence with John R. Seeley in ibid., 13 (1965): 288–90.

For a perceptive analysis of social and community psychiatry, see Alfred J. Kahn, *Studies in Social Policy and Planning* (New York, 1969), chap. 6.

8. *Psychiatric News*, 1 (Jan. 1966): 1, 18–19, 3 (Jan. 1968): 5, 4 (May 1969): 3, 8; "The Arlie House Propositions," Jan. 1966, issued by the APA Publications Department; Henry W. Brosin to Whitehorn, June 13, 1967, Whitehorn Papers, APAA; Daniel Blain interview, 3–14, APA OH135, APAA; *AJP*, 124 (1968): 1015–16, 126 (1970): 1490–92, 1543–54.

9. The bureaucratic maneuvering is ably traced in Henry A. Foley, *Community Mental Health Legislation: The Formative Process* (Lexington, Mass., 1975), chap. 4.

10. The regulations can be found in the *Federal Register*, 29 (1964): 5951–56.

11. Ibid. For an insightful analysis of the writing of the regulations, see Foley, *Community Mental Health Legislation*, 89–98.

12. Foley, *Community Mental Health Legislation*, 103–5.

13. Stanley F. Yolles to Asst. Surgeon General for Plans, Nov. 16, 1964, in NIMH Records, Miscellaneous Records 1956–67, Box 2, WNRC; Foley, *Community Mental Health Legislation*, 104–6.

14. Annual Conference of the Surgeon General Public Health Service with State and Territorial Mental Health Authorities, *Proceedings*, 1965, 10–11, 39 (PHS *Publication 1355*: 1965); APA Conference for Leaders in State Mental Health Planning, *Planning for Mental Health: A Report to the Nation* (Washington, D.C., 1965); Foley, *Community Mental Health Legislation*, 107–10.

15. 89-1 Congress, *Research Facilities, Mental Health Staffing . . . Hearings before the Committee on Interstate and Foreign Commerce House of Representatives . . . 1965* (Washington, D.C., 1965), 28–59, 152, 168, 180–81, 213–28.

16. 89-1 Congress, *House Report No. 248* (Apr. 15, 1965) and *No. 678* (July 23, 1965), *Senate Report No. 366* (June 24, 1965); 89-1 Congress (1965), *Congressional Record*, 6160–61, 9391–99, 14949–52, 18215, 18428–30.

17. Public Law 89-105, *U.S. Statutes at Large*, 79:427–30, 1965.

18. *Federal Register*, 31 (Mar. 1, 1966): 3246–48; Foley, *Community Mental Health Legislation*, 113–16.

19. 90-1 Congress, *Mental Health Centers Construction Act Extension. Hearings before the Subcommittee on Public Health and Welfare . . . House . . . 1967* (Washington, D.C., 1967), 13, 18; 90-1 Congress (1967), *Congressional Record*, 13060.

20. 90-1 Congress, *Mental Health Centers Construction Act Extension. Hearings . . . House*, 13, 82–89; Public Law 90-21, *U.S. Statutes at Large*, 81:79–80, 1967; 91-1 Congress, *Community Mental Health Centers Amendments of 1969. Hearings before the Subcommittee on Health . . . Senate . . . 1969* (Washington, D.C., 1969), 58; Raymond M. Glasscote, J. N. Sussex, E. Cumming, and L. H. Smith, *The Community Mental Health Center: An Interim Appraisal* (Washington, D.C., 1969), 5–7.

21. 91-1 Congress, *Community Mental Health Centers Act Extension. Hearings before the Subcommittee on Public Health and Welfare . . . House . . . 1969* (Washington, D.C., 1969), 18–21, 96, 107–40, 148–62; 91-1 Congress, *Community Mental Health Centers Amendments of 1969. Hearings . . . Senate*, 17–18, 98–102, 121–34, 140–50; 90-1 Congress, *Mental Health Centers Construction Act Extension. Hearings . . . House*, 171–72.

22. *New York Times*, May 22, 1989.

23. Glasscote, D. S. Sanders, H. M. Forstenzer, and A. R. Foley, *The Community Mental Health Center: An Analysis of Existing Models* (Washington, D.C., 1964), 28–30; Herbert C. Modlin to Walter E. Barton, June 29, 1966, GAP Papers, AP; Harvey J. Newton, "The Comprehensive Mental Health Center: Uncharted Horizons for Inpatient Services," *AJP*, 123 (1967): 1210–19.

24. Robert H. Connery et al., *The Politics of Mental Health: Organizing Community Mental Health in Metropolitan Areas* (New York, 1968), 479; David Mechanic, *Mental Health and Social Policy* (Englewood Cliffs, N.J., 1969), 148–49.

25. Glasscote, *The Community Mental Health Center: An Analysis of Existing Models*, 22; M. Brewster Smith and N. Hobbs, *The Community and the Community Mental Health Center* (Washington, D.C., 1966), 15.

26. August B. Hollingshead and F. C. Redlich, *Social Class and Mental Illness: A Community Study* (New York, 1958), 258 and passim; 89-2 Congress, *Labor—Health, Education, and Welfare Appropriations for Fiscal Year 1967. Hearings before the Subcommittee of the Committee on Appropriations . . . Senate . . . 1966* (Washington, D.C., 1966), pt. 2, 2185.

27. Donald G. Langsley and J. T. Barter, "Treatment in the Community or State Hospital: An Evaluation," *Psychiatric Annals*, 5 (1975): 163–70. See also Uri Aviram, "Mental Health Reform and the After Care State Service Agency: A Study of the Process of Change in the Mental Health Field" (D.S.W. diss., University of California, Berkeley, 1972); Steven P. Segal and Aviram, *The Mentally Ill in Community-Based Sheltered Care* (New York, 1978), 44–49; Eugene Bardach,

The Skill Factor in Politics: Repealing the Mental Commitment Laws in California (Berkeley, 1972); and Paul Lehrman, *Deinstitutionalization and the Welfare State* (New Brunswick, N.J., 1982). Developments in other states are described in *Financing Mental Health Care in the United States* (DHEW Publication No. [HSM] 73-9117: 1973), 78–92.

28. Bertram S. Brown, P. L. Sirotkin, and J. W. Stockdill, "Psychopolitical Perspectives in Federal-State Relationships," *American Journal of Psychotherapy*, 23 (1969): 645–56. See also the comments of Dr. Addison M. Duval (director of the Georgia Division of Mental Health) before the American Public Health Association, reprinted in 90-1 Congress (1967), *Congressional Record*, 35975–76.

29. "Report of the Meeting of the Ad Hoc Committee on State Mental Health Program Development October 10–11, 1966," NIMH Records, Subject Files, 1963–66, Box 12, WNRC.

30. William Gronfein, "Incentives and Intentions in Mental Health Policy: A Comparison of the Medicaid and Community Mental Health Programs," *Journal of Health and Social Behavior*, 26 (1985): 196; "Whom Are Community Mental Health Centers Serving?" NIMH *Statistical Note 67* (1972), passim; Lisa Reichenbach, "The Federal Community Mental Health Centers Program and the Policy of Deinstitutionalization," chaps. 4–5, unpublished manuscript in possession of Professor Lawrence E. Lynn, Jr., of the University of Chicago.

31. Glasscote, *The Community Mental Health Center: An Interim Appraisal*, 12; Charles Windle and D. Scully, "Community Mental Health Centers and the Decreasing Use of State Mental Hospitals," *Community Mental Health Journal*, 12 (1976): 239–43. For a useful summary of the studies dealing with the relationship between the decline in inpatient residents in state hospitals and the activities of centers, see Charles A. Kiesler and Amy Sibulkin, *Mental Hospitalization: Myths and Facts about a National Crisis* (Newbury Park, Calif., 1987), 143–46, and Peter Braun et al., "Overview: Deinstitutionalization of Psychiatric Patients, a Critical Review of Outcome Studies," *AJP*, 138 (1981): 736–49.

32. Alan I. Levenson and Brown, "Social Implications of the Community Mental Health Center Concept," paper delivered before the meetings of the American Psychopathological Association, Feb. 17, 1967, Brown Papers, NLM. See also Geoffrey Tooth to Brown, Nov. 10, 1969, ibid.

33. *New York Times*, Mar. 5, 6, 7, 9, 15, 18, 19, 21, 1969; Harris B. Peck, "A Candid Appraisal of the Community Mental Health Center as a Public Health Agency: A Case History," *AJPH*, 59 (1969): 459–69; Robert Shaw and C. J. Eagle, "Programmed Failure: The Lincoln Hospital Story," *Community Mental Health Journal*, 7 (1971): 255–63.

34. Rosalyn D. Bass, "Trends among Core Professionals in Organized Mental Health Settings: Where Have All the Psychiatrists Gone?" NIMH, *Mental Health Statistical Note No. 160* (1981); Walter W. Winslow, "The Changing Role of Psychiatrists in Community Mental Health Centers," *AJP*, 136 (1979): 24–27; Paul J. Fink and S. P. Weinstein, "Whatever Happened to Psychiatry? The Deprofessionalization of Community Mental Health Centers," ibid., 136 (1979): 406–9; John A. Talbott, "Why Psychiatrists Leave the Public Sector," *Hospital & Community Psychiatry*, 30 (1979): 778–82.

35. Donald G. Langsley, "The Community Mental Health Center: Does It Treat Patients?" *Hospital & Community Psychiatry*, 31 (1980): 815–19; David F. Musto, "Whatever Happened to 'Community Mental Health'?" *Public Interest*, 39 (Spring 1975): 53–79.

36. See Jeanne L. Brand, *Private Support for Mental Health* (PHS *Publication 838*: 1961), and John E. Hinkle, *Private Funds for Mental Health* (PHS *Publication 1985*: 1969).

37. For the definition of *patient care episode*, see chap. 7, n.1.

38. Data taken from NIMH, *Statistical Note 23* (Apr. 1970): 1–4, and *Statistical Note 154* (Sept. 1980): 12. Slight differences in totals are due to the rounding out of fractions. It should be noted that NIMH data usually did not count patient care episodes in general hospitals without specialized psychiatric units.

39. NIMH data in Morton Kramer, *Psychiatric Services and the Changing Institutional Scene, 1950–1985* (DHEW Publication No. [ADM] 77–433: 1977), 78.

40. NIMH, *Psychiatric Services in General Hospitals 1969–1970* (NIMH, *Mental Health Statistics*, Series A No. 11 [1972]), 21; Charles Kanno and P. L. Scheidemandel, *Psychiatric Treatment in the Community: A National Survey of General Hospital Psychiatry and Private Psychiatric Hospitals* (Washington, D.C., 1974), 35; Kramer, *Psychiatric Services and the Changing Institutional Scene*, 17. See also James W. Thompson, R. D. Bass, and M. J. Witkin, "Fifty Years of Psychiatric Services: 1940–1990," *Hospital & Community Psychiatry*, 33 (1982): 714.

41. Glasscote and C. K. Kanno, *General Hospital Psychiatric Units: A National Survey* (Washington, D.C., 1965), 16; Kanno and Scheidemandel, *Psychiatric Treatment in the Community*, 34; NIMH, *Statistical Note No. 70* (Feb. 1973); Texas Division of Mental Health, *Psychiatric Inpatient Units in Texas General Hospitals: A Report . . . 1958* (n.p., 1958), 21.

42. Kramer, E. S. Pollack, R. W. Redick, and B. Z. Locke, *Mental Disorders/Suicide* (Cambridge, Mass., 1972), 28; Kramer, H. Goldstein, R. H. Israel, and N. A. Johnson, *A Historical Study of the Disposition of First Admissions to a State Mental Hospital: Experience of the Warren State Hospital during the Period 1916–1950* (PHS *Publication No. 445*: 1955), and the same authors' "Application of Life Table Methodology to the Study of Mental Hospital Populations," in APA, *Psychiatric Research Report*, 5 (1956): 49–87. See also Pollack, P. H. Person, Jr., Kramer, and Goldstein, *Patterns of Retention, Release, and Death of First Admissions to State Mental Hospitals* (PHS *Publication 672*: 1959), and NIMH, *Statistical Note 74* (1973).

43. Howard H. Goldman, N. H. Adams, and C. Taube, "Deinstitutionalization: The Data Demythologized," *Hospital & Community Psychiatry*, 34 (1983): 133; Kiesler and Sibulkin, *Mental Hospitalization*, 86, 95; NIMH, *Mental Health, United States, 1985*, ed. Carl A. Taube and S. A. Barrett (DHHS Pub. No. [ADM] 85–1378: 1985), 33, 53. See also NIMH, *Statistical Note 74* (1973), and Fritz Redlich and S. R. Kellert, "Trends in American Mental Health," *AJP*, 135 (1978): 24.

44. Glasscote and Kanno, *General Hospital Psychiatric Units*, 23; Kanno and Scheidemandel, *Psychiatric Treatment in the Community*, 16ff.

45. The colony system in Gheel, Belgium, dated back about a millennium. Large numbers of mentally ill persons lived with the residents, and the colony was governed by a formal administrative structure that included medical and psychiatric supervision.

46. Gerald N. Grob, *Mental Institutions in America: Social Policy to 1875* (New York, 1973), chap. 8, and *Mental Illness and American Society 1875–1940* (Princeton, 1983), 83–86; Hester B. Crutcher, *Foster Home Care for Mental Patients* (New York, 1944); Hans B. Molholm and W. E. Barton, "Family Care, a Community Resource in the Rehabilitation of Mental Patients," *AJP*, 98 (1941): 33–41, 53–55; Horatio M. Pollock, ed., *Family Care of Mental Patients: A Review of Systems of Family Care in America and Europe* (Utica, N.Y., 1936); idem, "A Brief History of Family Care of Mental Patients in America," *AJP*, 102 (1945): 351–61; *A Survey of Family Care Practices in Michigan State Hospitals*, Michigan Department of Mental Health, *Research Report No. 20* (1955); Leonard P. Ullmann and V. C. Berkman, "Efficacy of Placement of Neuropsychiatric Patients in Family Care," *Archives of General Psychiatry*, 1 (1959): 273–74; Barton and W. T. St. John, "Family Care and Outpatient Psychiatry," *AJP*, 117 (1961): 644–47; James R. Morrissey, "Family Care for the Mentally Ill: A Neglected Therapeutic Resource," *Social Service Review*, 39 (1965): 63–71.

47. N.Y.S. Department of Mental Hygiene, *AR*, 57 (1944–1945): 128–32, 59 (1946–1947): 22–23; Milton Greenblatt and B. Simon, eds., *Rehabilitation of the Mentally Ill: Social and Economic Aspects* (Washington, D.C., 1959), 157–78; Bernard Berelson to Robert A. Cohen, Jan. 11, Cohen to Berelson, Jan. 23, 1957, NIMH Records, Mental Health Subject Files, Box 72, WNRC.

48. Brete Huseth, "Halfway Houses: A New Rehabilitation Measure," *Mental Hospitals*, 9 (Oct. 1958): 5–6, 8–9; David B. Williams, "California Experiments with Half-Way House," ibid., 6 (Jan. 1956): 24–25; Victor Goertzel, J. H. Beard, and S. Pilnick, "Fountain House Foundation: Case Study of an Inpatients' Club," *Journal of Social Issues*, 16 (1960): 54–61; Greenblatt and Simon, *Rehabilitation of the Mentally Ill*, 169–72; *New York Times*, Dec. 19, 1965; Glasscote, E. Cumming, I. D. Rutman, J. N. Sussex, and S. M. Glassman, *Rehabilitating the Mentally Ill in the Community: A Study of Psychosocial Rehabilitation Centers* (Washington, D.C., 1971), 41–63.

49. Glasscote, J. E. Gudeman, and J. R. Elpers, *Halfway Houses for the Mentally Ill: A Study of Programs and Problems* (Washington, D.C., 1971), 10–24. See also Glasscote, *Rehabilitating the Mentally Ill in the Community*; David Landy and Greenblatt, *Halfway House: A Sociocultural and Clinical Study of Rutland Corner House* (Washington, D.C., 1965); Harold L. and C. L. Raush, *The Halfway House Movement: A Search for Sanity* (New York, 1968); Naomi D. Rothwell and J. M. Doniger, *The Psychiatric Halfway House: A Case Study* (Springfield, Ill., 1966); *Halfway Houses Serving the Mentally Ill and Alcoholics United States 1969–1970* (NIMH, *Mental Health Statistics*, Series A No. 9 [1971]).

50. Glasscote, *Halfway Houses*, 19–20, 175–77; Glasscote, *Rehabilitating the Mentally Ill in the Community*, 8. See also Raush and Raush, *Halfway House Movement*, 56–58, 212, and Barton, *Administration in Psychiatry* (Springfield, Ill., 1962), 160–61.

51. Goldman, D. A. Regier, Taube, R. W. Redick, and R. D. Bass, "Community Mental Health Centers and the Treatment of Severe Mental Disorder," *AJP*, 137 (1980): 83–86.

52. See Goldman, Adams, and Taube, "Deinstitutionalization: The Data Demythologized," 129–34.

53. Edward Eagle, "Charges, Costs, and Other Factors Related to Maintenance of Patients in Public Mental Hospitals," *Public Health Reports*, 78 (1963): 775–89.

54. In 1940 there were some significant differences between private and public institutions. The resident population of the former was 10,678 (2.2 percent of the total institutionalized mentally ill population), as compared with 440,008 (91.6 percent) for state and county hospitals; the remaining 6.2 percent were in VA facilities. Admissions, however, showed a different pattern. Private hospitals admitted 24,347 (16.5 percent); state and county institutions 122,923 (76.7 percent). The latter had a much higher proportion of chronic patients than the former (where the length of stay was much shorter).

55. A. E. Bennett, E. A. Hargrove, and B. Engle, "Voluntary Health Insurance and Nervous and Mental Disease," *JAMA*, 151 (1953): 202–6; "Report and Recommendations of the Ad Hoc Committee on Economic Aspects of Psychiatry Accepted by the Council of the American Psychiatric Association, October, 1954," RMDO, 200-5, APAA; *AJP*, 111 (1955): 931–32; *Financing Mental Health Care in the United States* (DHEW Publication No. [HSM] 73-9117: 1973), 97.

56. "Report and Recommendations of the Ad Hoc Committee on the Economic Aspects of Psychiatry . . . 1954," RMDO, 200-5, APAA; "Blue Cross Coverage of the Mental Illnesses, 1960," JIS *Fact Sheet*, 12 (May 1960); Henry A. Davidson, "Health Insurance and Psychiatric Coverage," *AJP*, 114 (1957): 498–504; JIS, *Insurance Coverage of Mental Illness, 1962: A Special Report* (Washington, D.C., 1962).

57. Data detailing changes in insurance coverage in the 1960s are found in Helen H. Avnet, *Psychiatric Insurance: Financing Short-Term Ambulatory Treatment* (New York, 1962); Patricia L. Scheidemandel, Kanno, and Glasscote, *Health Insurance for Mental Illness* (Washington, D.C., 1968); and Louis S. Reed, E. S. Myers, and Scheidemandel, *Health Insurance and Psychiatric Care* (Washington, D.C., 1972), 45–61.

58. Reed, *Health Insurance and Psychiatric Care*, 32, 35.

59. "Draft of Resolution for the APA Council from the Commission on Insurance," Oct. 31, 1964, "Report of the Subcommittee on Prepaid Health Insurance APA Commission on Insurance," Dec. 1966, "Report of the Task Force on Prepaid Health Insurance APA Commission on Insurance," May 1969, RMDO, 200-30, APAA. The APA and the NAMH were cosponsors of Avnet's *Psychiatric Insurance*. *Health Insurance for Mental Illness* by Scheidemandel, Kanno, and Glasscote, and *Health Insurance and Psychiatric Care* by Reed, Myers, and Scheidemandel were both APA publications.

60. See especially Edward D. Berkowitz, *Disabled Policy: America's Programs for the Handicapped* (New York, 1987).

61. Public Law 86-778, *U.S. Statutes at Large*, 74:991, 1960; *Mental Hospitals*, 13 (1962): 197; *New York Times*, Mar. 6, 1962; *AJPH*, 53 (1963): 653–54. The text of Public Law 89-97 (the 1965 amendments to the Social Security Act that created Medicare and Medicaid) can be found in *U.S. Statutes at Large*, 79:286–422, 1965.

62. Robert Gibson to Blain, Mar. 9, 22, Oct. 7, Blain to John E. Fogarty, Mar. 10, Blain to Wilbur Cohen, Apr. 6, Cohen to Blain, Apr. 14, 1965, Blain Papers, APAA; Frank Carlson to WCM, Sept. 9, WCM to Carlson, Sept. 15, 1965, WCM Papers, MFA; *Mental Hospitals*, 16 (Sept. 1965): 63; Wilbur J. Cohen, "An Outline of Social Security Provisions for Psychiatric Illness," ibid., 16 (1965): 301–6; "Psychiatric Implications of Medicare," *AJP*, 123 (1966): 173–97: "Title XIX: Psychiatric Provisions and Limitations," *Hospital & Community Psychiatry*, 18 (1967): 88–91.

63. *Financing Mental Health Care in the United States*, 146–47; Aviram and Cohen, "Policy Decisions and the Reduction of Mental Hospitalization of the Aged," *Mental Health and Society*, 3 (1976): 315–25. See also Dorothy P. Rice, R. I. Knee, and M. Conwell, "Financing the Care of the Mentally Ill under Medicare and Medicaid," *AJPH*, 60 (1970): 2243–45.

64. The national statistics that show the decline in inpatient state and county mental hospital populations conceal as much as they reveal. The variations among the fifty states are extraordinarily broad. If deinstitutionalization is equated with the year in which the inpatient hospital population in a given state peaked and then declined, we find that seventeen states deinstitutionalized between 1946 and 1954. In 1955 eleven states plus the District of Columbia peaked, and between 1956 and 1969 twenty-two states peaked.

From these data it is evident that the decline in inpatient mental hospital populations was complex and involved a variety of elements, including policies in individual states, federal policies, changing treatment modalities, and attitudes and values. See especially William Gronfein, "Incentives and Intentions in Mental Health Policy," 192–206; idem, "Psychotropic Drugs and the Origins of Deinstitutionalization," *Social Problems*, 32 (1985): 437–53; idem, "From Madhouse to Main Street: The Changing Place of Mental Illness in Post–World War II America," (Ph.D. diss., State University of New York at Stony Brook, 1984); Uri Aviram, S. L. Syme, and J. B. Cohen, "The Effects of Policies and Programs on Reduction of Mental Hospitalization," *Social Science and Medicine*, 10 (1976): 571–77; Aviram and Cohen, "Policy Decisions and the Reduction of Mental Hospitalization of the Aged," *Mental Health and Society*, 3 (1976): 315–25; and Christopher J. Smith and R. Q. Hanham, "Deinstitutionalization of the Mentally Ill: A Time Path Analysis of the American States," *Social Science and Medicine*, 15D (1981): 361–78.

65. NIMH, *Statistical Note No. 107* (1974), *146* (1978): 4; Kramer, *Psychiatric Services and the Changing Institutional Scene*, 80; Gronfein, "Incentives and Intentions in Mental Health Policy," 192–206; Goldman, "Deinstitutionalization," 133.

66. Kramer, *Psychiatric Services and the Changing Institutional Scene*, 81.

67. NIMH, *Mental Health, United States, 1987*, ed. Ronald W. Manderscheid

and S. A. Barrett (DHHS Publ. No. [ADM] 87-1518: 1987), 21, 96–97; Kiesler and Sibulkin, *Mental Hospitalization*, 86ff.; David Mechanic, "Correcting Misconceptions in Mental Health Policy: Strategies for Improved Care of the Seriously Mentally Ill," *Milbank Quarterly*, 65 (1987): 203–30.

CHAPTER ELEVEN
CHALLENGES TO PSYCHIATRIC LEGITIMACY

1. Harry C. Solomon, "The American Psychiatric Association in Relation to American Psychiatry," *AJP*, 115 (1958): 7.

2. Howard P. Rome, "Whence, Whither, and Why—Psychiatry circa 1965," *Current Psychiatric Therapies*, 5 (1965): 1; Krin and G. O. Gabbard, *Psychiatry and the Cinema* (Chicago, 1987), 84–114. The APA presidential addresses in the postwar decades dramatically convey the optimism characteristic of the specialty. See the APA's *New Directions in American Psychiatry 1944–1968: The Presidential Addresses of the American Psychiatric Association over the Past Twenty-Five Years* (Washington, D.C., 1969).

3. "The Social Responsibility of Psychiatry, a Statement of Orientation," GAP *Report No. 13* (1950): 4–5; "Proceedings Meeting of Group for the Advancement of Psychiatry on Urban America and the Planning of Mental Health Services," Nov. 3, 1963, 5, Herbert C. Modlin to Walter E. Barton, June 29, 1966, GAP Papers, AP. See also Henry W. Brosin, "Historical Remarks on the First Eighteen Years of GAP," Aug. 19, 1963, WCM Papers, MFA, and Albert Deutsch, *The Story of GAP* (New York, 1959).

The political liberalism of GAP can be followed in their published *Reports*, 1–79 (1947–1970).

4. "The Psychiatrist and Public Issues," GAP *Report No. 74* (1969): 171–72, 174. See also *AJP*, 118 (1961): 264.

5. Stanley F. Yolles, "Past, Present and 1980: Trend Projections," *Progress in Community Mental Health*, 1 (1969): 3–4. This theme was equally evident in the public pronouncements of Bertram S. Brown, who headed the NIMH's Community Mental Health Facilities Branch. In its origins, the CMHC movement had emphasized the treatment and rehabilitation of the mentally ill; by 1965 the focus was on the improvement of social conditions. See Geoffrey Tooth to Bertram S. Brown, Nov. 10, 1969, and Alan I. Levenson and Brown, "Social Implications of the Community Mental Health Center Concept," paper delivered at the American Psychopathological Association meetings, Feb. 17, 1967, 1–2, Brown Papers, NLM.

6. *AJP*, 122 (1965): 254–85, 123 (1966): 354, 124 (1968): 1015–16, 126 (1970): 1430–86, 1490–92, 1543–54, 128 (1971): 677–87; Milton Greenblatt, P. E. Emery, and B. C. Glueck, *Poverty and Mental Health* (APA *Psychiatric Research Report*, 21 [1967]); *New York Times*, Nov. 19, 1967, May 6, 1969. See also Ronald Bayer's insightful *Homosexuality and American Psychiatry: The Politics of Diagnosis* (New York, 1981).

7. Barton, "Psychiatry in Transition," *AJP*, 119 (1962): 1–15; Gerald Caplan, *Principles of Preventive Psychiatry* (New York, 1964), passim; Seymour L. Hal-

leck, "Psychiatry and the Status Quo: A Political Analysis of Psychiatric Practice," *Archives of General Psychiatry*, 19 (1968): 257–65.

8. Gerald L. Klerman, "Mental Health and the Urban Crisis," *American Journal of Orthopsychiatry*, 39 (1969): 818–26: Robert Coles, "Psychiatrists and the Poor," *Atlantic Monthly*, 214 (July 1964): 102–6, "Southern Children under Desegregation," *AJP*, 120 (1963): 332–44, "Social Struggle and Weariness," *Psychiatry*, 27 (1964): 305–15, "Racial Conflict and a Child's Question," *Journal of Nervous and Mental Disease*, 140 (1965): 162–70, and "The Lives of Migrant Farmers," *AJP*, 122 (1965): 271–85, *Wages of Neglect* (with Maria Piers) (Chicago, 1969), (quotation from 36), and *Children of Crisis: A Study of Courage and Fear* (New York, 1968).

9. Helen Padua, R. Glasscote, and E. Cumming, *Approaches to the Care of Long-Term Mental Patients* (Washington, D.C., 1968); *Rouse v. Cameron*, 373 F.2d 451 (D.C. Cir. 1966); *AJP*, 123 (1967): 1458–60; *Psychiatric News*, 5 (Jan. 1970): 18 (Mar. 1970): 2; Lawrence S. Kubie, "The Retreat from Patients," *International Journal of Psychiatry*, 9 (1970–1971): 693–711.

10. Folder 15 in Box 19 of the Daniel Blain Papers (APAA) deals exclusively with the controversy. See also Blain to Julia Banzon, Dec. 1, 1964, ibid., and the editorial in the *American Journal of Psychotherapy*, 18 (1964): 559–61.

11. Joseph Wortis in *Biological Psychiatry*, 2 (1970): 1–2. The psychiatric literature during these years abounds in discussions of this theme. See, for example, Judd Marmor in *American Journal of Orthopsychiatry*, 40 (1970): 373–74; and Hiawatha Harris in *AJP*, 126 (1970): 132–34.

12. *New York Times*, July 2, 1947; John O'Connor, "Thought Control—American Plan," *Sign*, Nov. 1949, 23–25, 73; D. Bernard Foster to Father Ralph Gorman, Jan. 30, Foster to Archbishop Thomas J. Walsh, Jan. 31, 1950 with enclosed critique, copies in possession of Dr. D. Bernard Foster, Topeka, Kans.

13. A. Robert Smith, "'Siberia, U.S.A.'" *The Reporter*, 14 (June 28, 1956): 27–29; WCM to Philip E. Ryan, June 14, 1961, WCM to Kent Zimmer, Nov. 10, 1964, WCM Papers, MFA; Ed Cray, "Enemies of Mental Health," *Nation*, 192 (Apr. 8, 1961): 304–5; *New York Times*, May 10, 1963; Alfred Auerback, "The Anti–Mental Health Movement," *AJP*, 120 (1963): 105–11; Roger Boyvey, "Mental Health and the Ultra-Concerned," *Social Service Review*, 38 (1964): 281–93; Donald Robinson, "Conspiracy USA," *Look*, 29 (Jan. 26, 1965): 30–32.

14. For general discussions of the antipsychiatry movement, see Norman Dain, "Critics and Dissenters: Reflections on 'Antipsychiatry' in the United States," *Journal of the History of the Behavioral Sciences*, 25 (1989): 3–25, and Peter Sedgwick, "Anti-Psychiatry from the Sixties to the Eighties," in *Deviance and Mental Illness*, ed. Walter R. Gove (Beverly Hills, 1982), 199–223.

15. Limited space precludes a complete listing of Szasz's numerous articles and books. For some representative writings in the late 1950s, see "Commitment of the Mentally Ill: 'Treatment' or Social Restraint?" *Journal of Nervous and Mental Disease*, 125 (1957): 293–307, and "The Classification of 'Mental Illness,'" *Psychiatric Quarterly*, 33 (1959): 77–101. His most controversial books published during the 1960s include the following: *The Myth of Mental Illness: Foundations*

of a Theory of Personal Conduct (New York, 1961); *Law, Liberty, and Psychiatry: An inquiry into the Social Uses of Mental Health Practices* (New York, 1963); *Psychiatric Justice* (New York, 1965); and *The Manufacture of Madness: A Comparative Study of the Inquisition and the Mental Health Movement* (New York, 1970), quotation from xix–xxv. Szasz's ideas were widely disseminated in the popular press. See, for example, Edwin M. Schur, "Psychiatrists under Attack: The Rebellious Dr. Szasz," *Atlantic Monthly*, 217 (June 1966): 72–76, and Maggie Scarf, "Normality Is a Square Circle or a Four-Sided Triangle," *New York Times Magazine*, Oct. 3, 1971, 16–17, 40, 42–45, 48, 50.

16. Cf. Ronald Liefer, *In the Name of Mental Health: The Social Functions of Psychiatry* (New York, 1969); idem., "The Medical Model as Ideology," *International Journal of Psychiatry*, 9 (1970–1971): 13–21 (critique and response on 22–35); Paul Lowinger, "Radical Psychiatry," ibid., 659–68 (critique on 668–92); *American Journal of Orthopsychiatry*, 39 (1969): 720–21. The most extreme antiestablishment statements can be followed in the pages of the *Radical Therapist*, 1–5 (1970–1976).

17. R. D. Laing, *The Politics of Experience and the Bird of Paradise* (London, 1967), 98, 100, 107. Laing's other important works in the 1960s include *The Divided Self: An Existential Study in Sanity and Madness* (London, 1960), *Self and Others* (London, 1961), and *Sanity, Madness, and the Family* (London, 1964).

18. For an insightful study of the process of the popularization of science generally, see John C. Burnham, *How Superstition Won and Science Lost: Popularizing Science and Health in the United States* (New Brunswick, N.J., 1987).

19. See especially Arnold M. Rose, ed., *Mental Health and Mental Disorder: A Sociological Approach* (New York, 1955); Robert A. Cohen and Erving Goffman's contributions in "On Some Convergences of Sociology and Psychiatry," *Psychiatry*, 20 (1957): 199–203; and APA Conference on Psychiatric Education, *Report*, 1951.

20. Erving Goffman, *Asylums: Essays on the Social Situation of Mental Patients and Other Inmates* (Garden City, N.Y., 1961), xiii, 385–86 and passim. See also Bruno Bettelheim, "Individual and Mass Behavior in Extreme Situations," *Journal of Abnormal and Social Psychology*, 38 (1943): 417–52, Gresham M. Sykes, *The Society of Captives: A Study of a Maximum Security Prison* (Princeton, 1958), and Stanley M. Elkins, *Slavery: A Problem in American Institutional and Intellectual Life* (Chicago, 1959).

21. Goffman, *Asylums*, 384. The social and behavioral science and counterculture literature of the 1960s and early 1970s is replete with references to Goffman's work. For subsequent critical evaluations of Goffman's methodology and interpretations, see Roger Peele, P. V. Luisada, M. Jo Lucas, D. Russell, and D. Taylor, "*Asylums* Revisited," *AJP*, 134 (1977): 1077–81; Sedgwick, *Psycho-Politics* (New York, 1982), passim; and David Mechanic, "Medical Sociology: Some Tensions among Theory, Method, and Substance," *Journal of Health and Social Behavior*, 30 (1989): 147–50.

22. Thomas J. Scheff's *Being Mentally Ill: A Sociological Theory* (Chicago, 1966) was the classic statement of labeling theory. The concept, however, set off

a heated and controversial debate among sociologists. See, for example, Walter R. Gove, "Societal Reaction as an Explanation of Mental Illness: An Evaluation," *American Sociological Review*, 35 (1970): 873–84 (and the comments in ibid., 37 [1972]: 487–90); Gove and Patrick Howell, "Individual Resources and Mental Hospitalization: A Comparison and Evaluation of the Societal Reaction and Psychiatric Perspectives," ibid., 39 (1974): 86–100; and Scheff, "The Labelling Theory of Mental Illness," ibid., 444–52. For an overview, see Paul M. Roman, "Labeling Theory and Community Psychiatry: The Impact of Psychiatric Sociology on Ideology and Practice in American Psychiatry," *Psychiatry*, 34 (1971): 378–90.

23. Scheff, "Schizophrenia as Ideology," *Schizophrenia Bulletin*, No. 2 (Fall 1970): 15–19.

24. "Statement on Report of Joint Commission on Mental Illness and Health," *American Psychologist*, 18 (1963): 307; 88-1 Congress, *Mental Illness and Retardation. Hearings before the Subcommittee on Health of the Committee on Labor and Public Welfare ... Senate ... 1963* (Washington, D.C., 1963), 98–99.

25. Roy R. Grinker, Sr., "Emerging Concepts of Mental Illness and Models of Treatment: The Medical Point of View," George Albee, "Emerging Concepts of Mental Illness and Models of Treatment: The Psychological Point of View," and "Letters to the Editor," *AJP*, 125 (1969): 870–76, 1744–46.

26. Foucault's numerous books include *Madness and Civilization: A History of Insanity in the Age of Reason* (New York, 1965), quotation from 259, originally issued as *Folie et déraison, Histoire de la folie à l'âge classique* (Paris, 1961); *The Order of Things: An Archaeology of the Human Sciences* (New York, 1970); *The Archaeology of Knowledge and the Discourse on Language* (New York, 1972); *The Birth of the Clinic: An Archaeology of Medical Perception* (New York, 1973); *Discipline and Punish: The Birth of the Prison* (New York, 1977). The literature on Foucault is already very large; limited space precludes any definitive listing.

27. For a discussion of the historiography of psychiatry and mental illnesses since the 1960s, see Gerald N. Grob, "Rediscovering Asylums: The Unhistorical History of the Mental Hospital," in *The Therapeutic Revolution: Essays in the Social History of American Medicine*, ed. Morris J. Vogel and C. E. Rosenberg (Philadelphia, 1979), 135–57, and Andrew Scull, *Social Order/Mental Disorder: Anglo-American Psychiatry in Historical Perspective* (Berkeley, 1989), esp. chaps. 1–2.

28. Alexander D. Brooks, *Law, Psychiatry and the Mental Health System* (Boston, 1974), xxxi.

29. Clifford Forster to George S. Stevenson, Aug. 30 (with enclosed American Civil Liberties Union Model Commitment and Release Law, Aug. 1945), Stevenson to Winfred Overholser, Aug. 31, Overholser to Stevenson, Sept. 4, 1945, RMDO, 200-10, APAA; "Commitment Procedures," Gap *Report No. 4* (1948); Council of State Governments, *The Mental Health Programs of the Forty-Eight States: A Report to the Governors' Conference* (Chicago, 1950), 46–69; NIMH, *A Draft Act Governing the Hospitalization of the Mentally Ill* (PHS *Publication*

51: 1952). See also Alexander D. Brooks, "Hospitalization of the Mentally Ill: The Legislative Role," *State Government*, 50 (1977): 198.

30. American Bar Association, *The Mentally Disabled and the Law: The Report of the Foundation on the Rights of the Mentally Ill*, ed. Frank T. Lindman and D. M. McIntyre (Chicago, 1961); 2d ed. entitled *The Mentally Disabled and the Law: An American Bar Foundation Study*, ed. Samuel J. Brakel and R. S. Rock (Chicago, 1971).

31. Dr. Zigmond M. Lebensohn, a prominent Washington psychiatrist who testified before the subcommittee, recalled that two explanations of Ervin's actions were current in 1961. First, Ervin's wife was the sister of Dr. J. K. Hall, a southern psychiatrist who served as APA president in 1941–1942. Although Hall had died in 1948, Ervin's interest in the subject grew out of his close ties with his brother-in-law. Second, and perhaps more important, the issue of civil rights for blacks—which had become increasingly central to American politics—posed a dilemma for a southern senator. By convening hearings on the rights of the mentally ill, Ervin could appear as a champion of civil rights and yet avoid the explosive and potentially divisive issue of race. Conversation between Lebensohn and Gerald N. Grob, Oct. 20, 1989; Grob to Lebensohn, Jan. 2, Lebensohn to Grob, Jan. 8, 1990.

32. 87-1 Congress, *Constitutional Rights of the Mentally Ill. Hearings before the Subcommittee on Constitutional Rights of the Committee on the Judiciary . . . Senate . . . 1961* (Washington, D.C., 1961), 2, 273–305. Birnbaum's important article, "The Right to Treatment," appeared in the *American Bar Association Journal*, 46 (1960); 499–505.

Out of the subcommittee's deliberations came the passage of a new hospitalization law for the District of Columbia that attempted to protect the rights of patients by mandating certain procedural safeguards. See PL 88-598, *U.S. Statutes at Large*, 78 (1964): 944–54, and 88-2 Congress (1964), *Congressional Record*, 14548–63, 16005, 20787–92, 21345–46, 21634.

33. "A New Right," *American Bar Association Journal*, 46 (1960): 516–17; *Rouse v. Cameron*, 373 F.2d 451 (D.C. Cir. 1966); *Nason v. Superintendent of Bridgewater State Hospital*, 353 Mass. 604, 233 N.E.2d 908 (Mass. 1968); David L. Bazelon, "The Right to Treatment: The Court's Role," *Hospital & Community Psychiatry*, 20 (1969): 129–35; Alan A. Stone, "Overview: The Right to Treatment—Comments on the Law and Its Impact," *AJP*, 132 (1975): 1125–34.

34. Brooks, "Hospitalization of the Mentally Ill," 198–202. Developments in the 1970s can be followed in Brooks's *Law, Psychiatry and the Mental Health System*, passim, and the *1980 Supplement* (Boston, 1980) to this volume.

35. K. and G. O. Gabbard, *Psychiatry and the Cinema*, 115–44; Frederick Wiseman, *The Titicut Follies* (distributed by Grove Press, 1967); *Newsweek*, 70 (Dec. 4, 1967): 109; Robert Coles, "Stripped Bare at the Follies," *New Republic*, 158 (Jan. 20, 1968): 18, 28–30; Ken Kesey, *One Flew over the Cuckoo's Nest* (New York, 1962); Elliot Baker, *A Fine Madness* (New York, 1964).

36. To document this broad statement by a single citation would be foolhardy, given the magnitude of the debate over concepts of mental illness, the nature of institutions, and the rights of institutionalized patients. For a sampling of re-

sponses to the claims of Szasz, for example, see the following: John R. Reid, "The Myth of Doctor Szasz," *Journal of Nervous and Mental Disease*, 135 (1962): 381–86; C. H. Hardin Branch to Barton, Apr. 18, 1963, RMDO, 100-35, APAA; APA Council Minutes, May 4–5, 1963, 53–54, APA Board of Trustees Papers, Box 20, APAA; *New York Times*, May 6, 1964; Henry A. Davidson, "The New War on Psychiatry," Ralph Slovenko, "The Psychiatric Patient, Liberty, and the Law," and ensuing discussion in *AJP*, 121 (1964): 528–48; Manfred S. Guttmacher, "Critique of Views of Thomas Szasz on Legal Psychiatry," *Archives of General Psychiatry*, 10 (1964): 238–45; Frederick B. Glaser, "The Dichotomy Game: A Further Consideration of the Writings of Dr. Thomas Szasz," *AJP*, 121 (1965): 1069–74; Frederick C. Thorne, "An Analysis of Szasz's 'Myth of Mental Illness,'" ibid., 123 (1966): 562–66; Gene R. Moss, "Szasz: Review and Criticism," *Psychiatry*, 31 (1968): 184–94; Stone, "Psychiatry Kills: A Critical Evaluation of Dr. Thomas Szasz," *Journal of Psychiatry and Law*, 1 (1973): 23–37.

37. George N. Thompson, "The Society of Biological Psychiatry," *AJP*, 111 (1954): 389–91; Jules H. Masserman, *A Psychiatric Odyssey* (New York, 1971), 222ff.; Percival Bailey, "The Great Psychiatric Revolution," *AJP*, 113 (1956): 396, 402. See also the proceedings of the twenty-seventh Milbank Memorial Conference published as *The Biology of Mental Health and Disease* (New York, 1952); R. W. Gerard, "Biological Roots of Psychiatry," *Science*, 122 (1955): 225–30; and Abram E. Bennett, *Fifty Years in Neurology and Psychiatry* (New York, 1972).

38. *Archives of Neurology and Psychiatry*, 81 (1959): 795; Benjamin V. White, *Stanley Cobb: A Builder of the Modern Neurosciences* (Boston, 1984), 260.

39. Although there were numerous publications by individuals associated with the Psychotherapy Research Project, the most detailed report was written by Robert S. Wallerstein, *Forty-Two Lives in Treatment: A Study of Psychoanalysis and Psychotherapy* (New York, 1986). See especially Lawrence J. Friedman, *Menninger: The Family and the Clinic* (New York, 1990), 287–89.

40. Benjamin Pasamanick, F. R. Scarpitti, and S. Dinitz, *Schizophrenics in the Community: An Experimental Study in the Prevention of Hospitalization* (New York, 1967), 271.

41. Judd Marmor, *Psychiatrists and Their Patients: A National Study of Private Office Practice* (Washington, D.C., 1975), passim.

42. *Journal of Neuropsychiatry*, 1 (Sept.–Oct. 1959): 7.

43. Paul H. Hoch, "The Achievements of Biological Psychiatry," *Recent Advances in Biological Psychiatry*, 3 (1961): 10.

44. Fredrick C. Redlich and D. X. Freedman, *The Theory and Practice of Psychiatry* (New York, 1966), 459; Morris A. Lipton, "A Consideration of Biological Factors in Schizophrenia," in *Neurobiological Aspects of Psychopathology*, ed. Joseph Zubin and C. Shagass (New York, 1969), 310–30.

45. For a sympathetic treatment and summary of the work of Osmond and Hoffer, see David R. Hawkins, A. W. Bortin, and R. P. Runyon, "Orthomolecular Psychiatry: Niacin and Megavitamin Therapy," *Psychosomatics*, 11 (1970): 517–21.

46. Linus Pauling, "Orthomolecular Psychiatry," *Science*, 160 (1968): 265–71, and *Schizophrenia*, 3 (1971): 129–33; *New York Times*, Apr. 20, June 16, 1968, Nov. 23, 1969; Dorothy J. Beavers, "The Challenging Frontier: Environmental, Genetic, Biochemical and Neurological Factors in Severe Mental Illness," *Schizophrenia*, 1 (1969): 206–32; David R. Hawkins, "Report of the Academy of Orthomolecular Psychiatry," *Orthomolecular Psychiatry*, 2 (1973): 82–83; A. Hoffer, "History of Orthomolecular Psychiatry," *Journal of Orthomolecular Psychiatry*, 3 (1974): 223–30; *Science News*, 104 (July 28, 1973): 59–60.

47. *Science*, 160 (1968): 1181; *Science News*, 104 (July 28, 1973): 60.

48. Arthur C. Neilsen, "The Magnitude of Declining Psychiatric Career Choice," *Journal of Medical Education*, 54 (1979): 633; George Engel, "Is Psychiatry Failing in Its Responsibilities to Medicine," *AJP*, 128 (1972): 1561–64. A sampling of the reaction to the editorial appeared in ibid., 130 (1973): 223–27. See also John Romano, "The Elimination of the Internship—An Act of Regression," ibid., 126 (1970): 1565–76, and "Problems of Communication between Psychiatrists and Primary Physicians," APA Colloquium for Postgraduate Teaching of Psychiatry, *Proceedings*, 8 (1960).

49. Richard A. Schwartz, "Psychiatry's Drift Away from Medicine," *AJP*, 131 (1974): 129–33.

50. John Maciver and Fredrick C. Redlich, "Patterns of Psychiatric Practice," *AJP*, 115 (1959): 692–97; Fritz Redlich and S. H. Kellert, "Trends in American Mental Health," ibid., 135 (1978): 26; Jeffrey D. Blum and F. Redlich, "Mental Health Practitioners: Old Stereotypes and New Realities," *Archives of General Psychiatry*, 37 (1980): 1253; Sydney E. Pulver, "Survey of Psychoanalytic Practice 1976: Some Trends and Implications," *Journal of the American Psychoanalytic Association*, 26 (1978): 621.

51. APA, *Training the Psychiatrist to Meet Changing Needs: Report of the Conference on Graduate Psychiatric Education . . . 1962* (Washington, D.C., 1964), 8.

52. Ibid., 67.

53. Bernard Bandler, "Current Trends in Psychiatric Education," *AJP*, 127 (1970): 586; Bertram S. Brown, "The Life of Psychiatry," ibid., 133 (1976): 492.

54. Cf. Stanley F. Yolles, "Community Appraisals of Mental Health Practices," *AJPH*, 54 (1964): 1970–76, "Social Perspectives and Mental Health," *International Journal of Social Psychiatry*, 13 (1967): 165–73, "Mental Health's Homeostatic State: A New Territory," *International Journal of Psychiatry*, 7 (1969): 327–32, and "Past, Present and 1980: Trend Projections," *Progress in Community Mental Health*, 1 (1969): 3–23. Brown's views can be followed in his extensive speech files during the 1960s in the Brown Papers, NLM.

55. Brown interview by Blain, 1972, 17–18, copy in Blain Papers, APAA; Brown, "The Life of Psychiatry," 489–95. See also Roy R. Grinker, Sr., *Fifty Years in Psychiatry: A Living History* (Springfield, Ill., 1979), 241.

EPILOGUE

1. See H. Richard Lamb, ed., *The Homeless Mentally Ill: A Task Force Report of the American Psychiatric Association* (Washington, D.C., 1984).

2. Many of those who played leading roles from the 1940s to the 1960s—including Robert Felix and Jack Ewalt—subsequently conceded that their generation had exaggerated both the evils of the old system and the virtues of new policies. See the article by Richard D. Lyons in the *New York Times*, Oct. 30, 1984.

Selected Sources

The limitation of space precludes a complete bibliography of all relevant books and articles. The notes, which represent only a small proportion of the total material examined, should serve as a partial guide. The purpose of this section is to provide information about relevant manuscript collections, government documents, and serial publications, and to clarify some of the research strategies employed in the preparation of this book.

Manuscripts

American Psychiatric Association Archives, Washington, D.C.

APA Board of Trustees Papers (includes the minutes of the APA Council, the predecessor of the Board of Trustees, as well as the Executive Committee).

APA Central Inspection Board Papers.

APA President's, Secretaries, and Treasurer Correspondence. 1941–1950.

APA Records of the Medical Director's Office (includes 100 and 200 series, plus MDO Records, which cover the period since 1948).

APA State Surveys.

Leo H. Bartemeier Papers.

Walter E. Barton Papers.

Daniel Blain Papers.

Francis J. Braceland Papers.

Robert N. Butler Papers.

Donald Ewen Cameron Papers.

Hugh Thompson Carmichael Papers.

Albert Deutsch Papers.

Jack Ewalt Presidential Papers.

Clarence B. Farrar Papers.

Joint Commission of Mental Illness and Health Papers.

Harry C. Solomon Papers.

John C. Whitehorn Papers.

Oral Histories

1. Leo Bartemeier, 1966, 1967 (OH 115).
2. Walter E. Barton, 1965, 1979 (OH 140, 141).
3. Daniel Blain, 1965 (OH 135).
4. Earl D. Bond, 1963, 1965 (OH 131, 132).
5. Karl M. Bowman, 1962, 1965, 1968 (OH 156, 157, 158).
6. Francis Braceland, 1968, 1969, 1971, 1973 (OH 119).
7. Henry W. Brosin, 1978 (OH 122).
8. Dexter Bullard, 1964 (OH 148).
9. D. Ewen Cameron, 1964 (OH 107).
10. Hugh T. Carmichael, 1972, 1974 (OH 113, 134).

11. Dana L. Farnsworth, 1969 (OH 112).
12. Clarence B. Farrar, 1965 (OH 149).
13. Robert H. Felix, 1964 (OH 120).
14. Jerome Frank, 1969 (OH 152).
15. Francis Gerty, 1979 (OH 128).
16. Roy R. Grinker, Sr., n.d. (OH 103).
17. Lawrence Kolb, Sr., 1963 (OH 123).
18. Nolan D. C. Lewis, 1972 (OH 116).
19. Robert L. Robinson, 1977 (OH 129).
20. Harry C. Solomon, 1963 (OH 153).
21. Mary E. Switzer, 1966 (OH 161).
22. John C. Whitehorn, 1972 (OH 117).

Countway Library of Medicine, Harvard Medical School, Boston, Mass.

Jack Ewalt Papers.
Harry C. Solomon Interview with J. Sanbourne Bockoven and Evelyn Stone, 1967–1968, 1980.

John F. Kennedy Library, Boston, Mass.

Myer Feldman Papers.
President's Office Files.
White House Central Files, January 1961–November 1963.
Records of the Department of Health, Education, and Welfare Selected for Deposit in the John F. Kennedy Library (microfilm).
Walter W. Heller Papers (microfilm).
Oral Histories

1. David Bazelon, 1969.
2. Michael J. Begab, 1968.
3. Bertram S. Brown, 1968, 1969.
4. Myer Feldman Interviews, 1966–1968 (fourteen interviews).
5. Seymour S. Kety, 1968.
6. David Ray, 1968.
7. Eunice Kennedy Shriver, 1968.
8. Stafford Warren, 1966.

Library of Congress, Washington, D.C.

Maxwell Gitelson Papers.
Winfred Overholser Papers.

Massachusetts Historical Society, Boston, Mass.

Leverett Saltonstall Papers.

The Menninger Foundation Archives, Topeka, Kans.

Henry W. Brosin–GAP Papers.
Karl A. Menninger Papers.
William C. Menninger Papers.
Mary E. Switzer File.

National Archives, Washington, D.C.

Commission on Organization of the Executive Branch of the Government, RG 264.

National Advisory Mental Health Council. Minutes of Meetings, 1947–1960, RG 90.

NIMH, State and Territory Comprehensive Mental Health Plans and Reports, Community Mental Health Centers Program. 1965–1966, RG 90.

Records Relating to the Historical Development of the NIMH and Its Components, 1947–1976, RG 90.

History of Medicine Division, National Library of Medicine, Bethesda, Md.

Bertram S. Brown Papers.

Robert H. Felix Interview, 1964.

Robert H. Felix Papers.

Mike Gorman Papers.

Lister Hill Interview, 1967.

Lawrence Kolb Papers.

Milton J. E. Senn, Child Development Oral History Interviews (OH 20).
1. John Clausen, 1973.
2. Nicholas Hobbs, 1974.
3. Philip Sapir, 1973.

Milton J. E. Senn, Transcripts and Tapes on the American Child Guidance Clinic and Child Psychiatry Movement (1975–1978) Interviews (OH 76).
1. Spafford Ackerly, 1976.   5. Philip Sapir, 1977.
2. Bertram Brown, 1978.   6. Charles Schlaifer, 1977.
3. Leonard J. Duhl, 1978.   7. George S. Stevenson, 1977.
4. Robert H. Felix, 1979.   8. Stanley Yolles, 1977.

Archives of Psychiatry, New York Hospital–Cornell Medical Center, New York, N.Y.

Group for the Advancement of Psychiatry Papers.

Marion E. Kenworthy Papers.

Vidonian Club Papers.

Rockefeller Archive Center, North Tarrytown, New York, N.Y.

Rockefeller Brothers Fund Papers.

Rockefeller Family Papers, RG 2.

Rockefeller Foundation Papers, RG 1.1 (Series 200, 200A); RG 1.2 (Series 200A); RG 2; RG 3.

Schlesinger Library, Radcliffe College, Harvard University, Cambridge, Mass.

Mary E. Switzer Papers.

Social Welfare History Archives, University of Minnesota, Minneapolis, Minn.

American Association of Psychiatric Social Workers Papers.

Council on Social Work Education Records.

Southern Historical Collection, Wilson Library, University of North Carolina, Chapel Hill, N.C.

J. K. Hall Papers.

Washington National Records Center, Suitland, Md.
National Institute of Mental Health Records, RG 90.

Miscellaneous

Brand, Jeanne L., and Philip Sapir, eds. *An Historical Perspective on the National Institute of Mental Health* (prepared as sec. 1 of the NIMH Report to the Woolridge Committee of the President's Scientific Advisory Committee). Mimeograph. February, 1964.

Reichenbach, Lisa. *The Federal Community Mental Health Centers Program and the Policy of Deinstitutionalization* (prepared as a study for NIMH under Grant MH27738-02).

GOVERNMENT DOCUMENTS

Federal

For congressional documents, the first number refers to the congress; the second to the session. All are printed by the Government Printing Office in Washington, D.C.

HEARINGS

79-1, HR. *National Neuropsychiatric Institute Act. Hearing before a Subcommittee on Interstate and Foreign Commerce . . . on H.R. 2550 . . . 1945.* 1945.

79-1, Sen. *National Neuropsychiatric Institute Act. Hearings before a Subcommittee of the Committee on Education and Labor . . . on S. 1160 . . . 1946.* 1946.

80-1/83-1, HR. Department of Labor–Federal Security Agency, Appropriation Bills, *Hearings before the Subcommittee of the Committee on Appropriations.* 1948–1954 (separate volumes with slightly different titles for each year).

80-1/82-2, Sen. Department of Labor–Federal Security Appropriation Bills, *Hearings before the Subcommittee on Appropriations.* 1948–1953.

80-2, HR. *The Supplemental Federal Security Agency Appropriation Bill for 1949. Hearings before the Subcommittee of the Committee on Appropriations.* 1948.

82-1, HR. *Health Inquiry (Neurological Diseases, Blindness, Mental Illness, Hearing Defects). Hearings before the Committee on Interstate and Foreign Commerce . . . 1953.* 1953.

83-1/91-2, Sen. Labor–Health, Education, and Welfare Appropriations Bills, *Hearings before the Subcommittee of the Committee on Appropriations.* 1953–1971.

83-2/91-2, HR. Departments of Labor and Health, Education, and Welfare Appropriations, *Hearings before the Subcommittee of the Committee on Appropriations.* 1955–1971.

84-1, Sen. *Mental Health. Hearings before the Subcommittee on Health of the Committee on Labor and Public Welfare . . . on S.J. Res. 46 . . . 1955.* 1955.

84-1, HR. *Mental Health Study Act of 1955. Hearings before a Subcommittee of the Committee* on Interstate and Foreign Commerce . . . on H.R. 3458 . . . and H.J. Res. 230 . . . 1955. 1955.

84-2, HR. *Health Amendments Act of 1956. . . . Hearings before a Subcommittee of the Committee on Interstate and Foreign Commerce . . . 1956. 1956.*

87-1, HR. *Health Research and Training. Hearings before a Subcommittee of the Committee on Government Operations . . . 1961. 1961.*

87-1, HR. *Health Research and Training. The Administration of Grants and Awards by the National Institutes of Health. Second Report by the Committee on Government Operations. HR Report No. 321: 1961.*

87-1, Sen. *Constitutional Rights of the Mentally Ill. Hearings before the Subcommittee on Constitutional Rights of the Committee on the Judiciary . . . 1961. 1961.*

87-2, HR. *The Administration of Grants by the National Institutes of Health. Hearings before a Subcommittee of the Committee on Government Operations . . . 1962. 1962.*

88-1, HR. *Mental Health. Hearings before a Subcommittee of the Committee on Interstate and Foreign Commerce . . . on H.R. 3688 . . . H.R. 3689 . . . H.R. 2567 . . . 1963. 1963.*

88-1, HR. *Mental Health (Supplemental). Hearings before a Subcommittee of the Committee on Interstate and Foreign Commerce . . . on S. 1576. 1963.*

88-1, Sen. *Mental Illness and Retardation. Hearings before the Subcommittee on Health of the Committee on Labor and Public Welfare . . . on S. 755 and 756 . . . 1963. 1963.*

88-1, Sen. *To Protect the Constitutional Rights of the Mentally Ill. Hearings before the Subcommittee on Constitutional Rights of the Committee on the Judiciary . . . on S. 935 . . . 1963. 1963.*

89-1, HR. *Research Facilities, Mental Health Staffing, Continuation of Health Programs, and Group Practice. Hearings before the Committee on Interstate and Foreign Commerce . . . 1965. 1965.*

89-1, HR. *Management of Research Grants in the Public Health Service. Hearings before a Subcommittee of the Committee on Government Operations . . . 1965. 1965.*

90-1, HR. *Mental Health Centers Construction Act Extension. Hearings before the Subcommittee on Public Health and Welfare of the Committee on Interstate and Foreign Commerce . . . 1967. 1967.*

90-1, HR. *The Administration of Research Grants in the Public Health Service: Ninth Report by the Committee on Government Operations. HR Report No. 800: 1967.*

91-1, HR. *Community Mental Health Centers Act Extension. Hearings before the Subcommittee on Public Health and Welfare of the Committee on Interstate and Foreign Commerce . . . 1969. 1970.*

91-1, Sen. *Community Mental Health Centers Amendments of 1969. Hearings before the Subcommittee on Health of the Committee on Labor and Public Welfare . . . 1969. 1969.*

94-1, Sen. *Mental Health and the Elderly. Joint Hearing before the Subcommittee on Long-Term Care and the Subcommittee on Health of the Elderly of the Special Committee on Aging . . . 1975. 1975.*

96-2, Sen. *Aging and Mental Health: Overcoming Barriers to Service. Hearing before the Special Committee on Aging . . . 1980. 1980.*

DOCUMENTS

79-1, HR. *Report 1445*. 1945.
79-2, HR. *Report 2350*. 1946.
79-2, Sen. *Report 1353*. 1946.
83-1, Sen. *Report 478*. 1953.
83-2, Sen. *Report 1123*. 1954.
84-1, HR. *Document 81*. 1955.
84-1, HR. *Report 241*. 1955.
84-1, Sen. *Report 869* and *870*. 1955.
84-2, HR. *Document 320*. 1956.
84-2, HR. *Report 2086*. 1956.
87-2, HR. *Report 1488*. 1962.
88-1, HR. *Document 58*. 1963.
88-1, HR. *Report 694* and *862*. 1963.
89-1, HR. *Report 248* and *678*. 1965.
89-1, Sen. *Report 366*. 1965.
90-1, HR. *Report 212*. 1967.
91-1, HR. *Report 91–735*. 1969.
91-2, HR. *Report 91–856*. 1970.

SERIALS

Congressional Record, 79-1/91-2 Congress, 86–116 (1945–1970).
NIMH. *Mental Health Statistics,* Series A, 1–12 (1969–1972), Series B, 1–6 (1968–1974), Series C, 1–6 (1969–1972).
NIMH. *Patients in Mental Institutions,* 1947–1966.
NIMH. *Proceedings of the Conference of Mental Hospital Administrators and Statisticians,* 1–3 (1951–1953).
NIMH. *Statistical Note,* 1–154 (1969–1980).
PHS. *Proceedings Annual Conference of the Surgeon General . . . with State and Territorial Health Officers, State Mental Health Authorities . . .* title varies), 50–53 (1951–1954), 1955–1961.
PHS. *Proceedings Annual Conference of the Surgeon General Public Health Service with State and Territorial Mental Health Authorities,* 1959–1962, 1965–1966.
PHS. *Public Health Reports,* 55–85 (1940–1970).
PHS. Research Conference on Psychosurgery, *Proceedings,* 1–3 (1949–1951).
U.S. Bureau of the Census. *Patients in Mental Institutions,* 1940–1946.
U.S. Statutes at Large, 54–84 (1939/41–1970/71).

MISCELLANEOUS

U.S. Surgeon General's Office. *The Medical Department of the United States Army in the World War.* Vol. 10, *Neuropsychiatry.* 1929.
Science and Public Policy: A Report to the President by John R. Steelman, Chairman, The President's Scientific Research Board. Vol. 1, *A Program for the Nation.* 1947. Vol. 5, *The Nation's Medical Research.* 1947.
Commission on Organization of the Executive Branch of the Government. *Reor-*

ganization of Federal Medical Activities: A Report to the Congress . . . March 1949. 1949.

NIMH. *Mental Health Series,* no. 4 (revised). PHS *Publication 20:* 1950.

NIMH. *A Draft Act Governing Hospitalization of the Mentally Ill.* PHS *Publication 51:* rev. 1952.

President's Commission on the Health Needs of the Nation. *Building America's Health: A Report to the President.* 5 vols. 1953.

Schwartz, Charlotte G. *Rehabilitation of Mental Hospital Patients.* PHS *Publication 297:* 1953.

PHS. *State Mental Health Programs . . . 1954 and 1955.* PHS *Publication 374:* 1954.

Commission on Organization of the Executive Branch of the Government. *Report on Federal Medical Services . . . February 1955.* 1955.

————. *Federal Medical Services: A Report to the Congress.* 1955.

NIMH. *Evaluation in Mental Health: A Review of the Problem of Evaluating Mental Health Activities.* PHS *Publication 413:* 1955.

Kramer, Morton. *A Historical Study of the Disposition of First Admissions to a State Mental Hospital. Experience of the Warren State Hospital during the Period 1916–50.* PHS *Publication 445:* 1955.

————. *Facts Needed to Assess Public Health and Social Problems in the Widespread Use of the Tranquilizing Drugs.* PHS *Publication 486:* 1956.

Bahn, Anita K., and V. B. Norman. *Outpatient Psychiatric Clinics in the United States 1954–55.* PHS *Publication 538:* 1957.

Walter Reed Army Institute of Research, et al. *Symposium on Preventive and Social Psychiatry . . . 15–17 April 1957.* 1958.

NIMH. *Highlights of Progress in Mental Health Research 1958 [1961].* PHS *Publication 659:* 1959 and 919: 1962.

Pollack, Earl S., et al. *Patterns of Retention, Release, and Death of First Admissions to State Mental Hospitals.* PHS *Publication 672:* 1959.

PHS. *Planning of Facilities for Mental Health Services: Report of the Surgeon General's Ad Hoc Committee on Planning for Mental Health Facilities.* PHS *Publication 808:* 1961.

Brand, Jeanne L. *Private Support for Mental Health.* PHS *Publication 838:* 1961.

Cohen, Louis D. *State Activities in Mental Health Evaluation: A Survey of Nine Programs.* PHS *Publication 863:* 1961.

Williams, Richard H., ed. *The Prevention of Disability in Mental Disorders.* PHS *Publication 924:* 1962.

NIMH. *The Treatment of Psychiatric Disorders with Insulin 1936–1960.* PHS *Publication 941:* 1962.

Robertson, Roger L., and E. A. Rubenstein. *NIMH Training Grant Program Fiscal Years 1948–1961.* PHS *Publication 966:* 1962.

NIMH. *Mental Health Activities and the Development of Comprehensive Health Programs in the Community: Report of the Surgeon General's Ad Hoc Committee on Mental Health Activities.* PHS *Publication 995:* 1962.

Geller, Miriam R. *The Treatment of Psychiatric Disorders with Metrazol 1935–1960: A Selected Annotated Bibliography.* PHS *Publication 967:* 1963.

NIMH. *Survey of Funding and Expenditures for Training of Mental Health Personnel 1960–1961*. PHS *Publication 1028*: 1963.

Shriver, Beatrice M., and R. Simon. *Current Professional Status of Mental Health Personnel Supported under National Institute of Mental Health Training Grants*. PHS *Publication 1088*: 1963.

NIMH. *Mental Health Career Development Program. Proceedings of Third Annual Conference . . . 1964*. PHS *Publication 1245*: 1964.

NCMHI. *Digest Progress Reports on State Mental Health Planning 1964*. PHS *Publication 1248*: 1964.

NIMH. *Research Activities of the National Institute of Mental Health*. PHS *Publication 1291*: 1964.

NIMH. *Pilot Project in Training Mental Health Counselors*. PHS *Publication 1254*: 1965.

NIMH. *The Psychiatric Aide in State Mental Hospitals*. PHS *Publication 1286*: 1965.

[Woolridge, Dean E., Chairman, NIH Study Committee.] *Biomedical Science and Its Administration: A Study of the National Institutes of Health*. 1965.

NCMHI. *The Research Fellowship Program of the National Institute of Mental Health: A Source Book of Descriptive Data—Fiscal Year 1963*. PHS *Publication 1303*: 1965.

Goldston, Stephen E., ed. *Concepts of Community Psychiatry: A Framework for Training*. PHS *Publication 1319*: 1965.

Katz, Martin M., J. O. Cole, and W. E. Barton, eds. *The Role and Methodology of Classification in Psychiatry and Psychopathology*. PHS *Publication 1584*: 1965.

Landy, David, and M. Greenblatt. *Halfway House: A Sociocultural and Clinical Study of Rutland Corner House*. Washington, D.C.: Vocational Rehabilitation Administration (HEW), 1965.

NCMHI. *The Research Grant Program of the National Institute of Mental Health: A Sourcebook of Descriptive Data—Fiscal Year 1964*. PHS *Publication 1423*: 1966.

NIMH. Mental Health Career Development Program, *Proceedings of Fourth Annual Conference . . . 1965*. PHS *Publication 1450*: 1966.

Giesler, Raymond, P. L. Hurley, and P. H. Person, Jr. *Survey of General Hospitals Admitting Psychiatric Patients*. PHS *Publication 1462*: 1966.

NIMH. *Community Mental Health . . . A Symposium Ninth Inter-American Congress of Psychology . . . 1964*. PHS *Publication 1504*: 1966.

Arnhoff, Franklyn N., and B. M. Shriver. *A Study of the Current Status of Mental Health Personnel Supported under National Institute of Mental Health Training Grants*. PHS *Publication 1541*: 1966.

NIMH. *Psychologists in Mental Health: Based on the 1964 National Register of the National Science Foundation*. PHS *Publication 1557*: 1966.

U.S. Army Medical Department. *Neuropsychiatry in World War II*. 2 vols. Washington, D.C.: Department of the Army, 1966–1973.

Kramer, Morton. *Some Implications of Trends in the Usage of Psychiatric Facilities for Community Mental Health Programs and Related Research*. PHS *Publication 1434*: 1967.

NIMH. *1966 Final Reports: State Mental Health Planning.* PHS *Publication 1685*: 1967.

Halpert, Harold P. *Comprehensive Mental Health Planning in Six States.* PHS *Publication 1686*: 1967.

NIMH. *Proceedings of the Fifth Annual Conference: Mental Health Career Development Program. . . 1966.* PHS *Publication 1689*: 1967.

NIMH. *Publications Resulting from National Institute of Mental Health Research Grants 1947–1961.* PHS *Publication 1647*: 1968.

Sells, S. B., ed. *The Definition and Measurement of Mental Health.* PHS *Publication 1873*: 1968.

NIMH. *Proceedings of the National Conference on Mental Health in Public Health Training May 27–30, 1968.* PHS *Publication 1899*: 1968.

NCMHI. *Mental Health Benefits of Medicare and Medicaid.* PHS *Publication 1505*: rev. 1969.

NIMH. *Sociologists and Anthropologists: Supply and Demand in Educational Institutions and other Settings.* PHS *Publication 1884*: 1969.

NIMH. *The Nation's Psychiatrists.* PHS *Publication 1885*: 1969.

NIMH. *Better Care for Mental Patients . . . The First 5 Years of a Hospital Improvement Program 1963–1968.* PHS *Publication 1896*: 1969.

NIMH. *The Mental Health of Urban America: The Urban Programs of the National Institute of Mental Health.* PHS *Publication 1906*: 1969.

NIMH. *Private Funds for Mental Health.* PHS *Publication 1985*: 1969.

Sobey, Francine. *Volunteer Services in Mental Health: An Annotated Bibliography 1955 to 1969.* NCMHI *Publication 1002*: 1969.

NIMH. *Staffing Patterns in Mental Health Facilities 1968.* PHS *Publication 5034*: 1970.

NIMH. *Staffing of Mental Health Facilities United States 1972.* DHEW Publ. (ADM) 74-28: 1971.

NIMH. *Utilization of Psychiatric Facilities by Persons Diagnosed with Alcohol Disorders.* DHEW Publ. (HSM) 73-9114: 1972.

NIMH. *Utilization of Mental Health Resources by Persons Diagnosed with Schizophrenia.* DHEW Publ. (HSM) 73-9110: 1973.

NIMH. *Financing Mental Health Care in the United States: A Study of Assessment of Issues and Arrangements.* DHEW Publ. (HSM) 73-9117: 1973.

Bachrach, Leona. *Psychiatric Bed Needs: An Analytic Review.* DHEW Publ. (ADM) 75-205: 1975.

Levine, Daniel S., and D. R. Levine. *The Cost of Mental Illness—1971.* DHEW Publ. (ADM) 76-265: 1975.

NIMH. *Research in the Service of Mental Health: Report of the Research Task Force of the National Institute of Mental Health.* DHEW Publ. (ADM) 75-236: 1975.

Kramer, Morton. *Psychiatric Services and the Changing Institutional Scene, 1950–1985.* DHEW Publ. (ADM) 77-433: 1977.

NIMH. *Research on the Mental Health of the Aging 1960–1976.* DHEW Publ. (ADM) 77-379: 1977.

Bass, Rosalyn D. *CMHC Staffing: Who Minds the Store?* DHEW Publ. (ADM) 78-686: 1978.

President's Commission on Mental Health. *Report to the President.* 4 vols. 1978.

NIH. *1980 NIH Almanac.* NIH Publ. No. 80-5, 1980.

Lerman, Paul. *Deinstitutionalization: A Cross-Problem Analysis.* DHHS Publ. (ADM) 81-987, 1981.

NIMH. *A History of the U.S. National Reporting Program for Mental Health Statistics, 1840–1983.* DHHS Publ. (ADM) 83-1296, 1983.

NIMH. *Mental Health, United States 1983.* Edited by Carl T. Taube and S. A. Barrett. DHHS Publ. (ADM) 83-1275: 1983.

NIMH. *Mental Health, United States 1985.* Edited by Carl A. Taube and S. A. Barrett. DHHS Publ. (ADM) 85-1378, 1985.

NIMH. *Mental Health, United States, 1987.* Edited by Ronald W. Manderscheid and S. A. Barrett. DHHS Publ. (ADM) 87-1518: 1987.

State

GENERAL

Council of State Governments. *Book of the States,* 4-21. 1941/1942–1974/1975.

———. *The Mental Health Programs of the Forty-Eight States: A Report to the Governors' Conference.* Chicago, 1950.

———. *Training and Research in State Mental Health Programs: A Report to the Governors' Conference.* Chicago, 1953.

———. *State Organization and Finance in the Field of Mental Health Research: A State by State Survey.* Chicago, 1959.

———. *Proceedings of the Governors' Conference 1961.* Chicago, 1961.

———. *Recent Developments in the States' Community Mental Health Programs 1960–1961.* Chicago, 1962.

———. *Action in the States in the Fields of Mental Health, Mental Retardation and Related Areas.* Chicago, 1963.

———. *Action in the States in the Fields of Mental Health, Mental Retardation and Related Areas: A Report on 1964–1968 Financial, Legal and Administrative Developments in the States' Mental Health Programs.* Chicago, 1969.

———. *Action in the States in the Fields of Mental Health, Mental Retardation and Related Areas 1968–1969.* Chicago, 1970.

Southern Regional Education Board. *Mental Health Training and Research in the Southern States.* Atlanta, ca. 1954.

———. *Today and Tomorrow: Summary Report of a Panel on Organization and Conduct of State Mental Health Programs.* Atlanta, ca. 1956.

STATE

ARIZONA

Arizona State Plan for Construction of Mental Health Centers. Annual Revision Fiscal Year 1969.

Arizona State Plan for Construction of Mental Health Centers. Annual Revision Fiscal Year 1972.

CALIFORNIA

A Survey of the Mental Institutions of the State of California Conducted by the United States Public Health Service. Washington, D.C., 1943.

The Governor's Conference on Mental Health ... *1949: Preliminary Report of Section Findings and Recommendations. 1949.*

The Governor's Conference on Mental Health ... *1949: Final Report. 1949.*

Senate Interim Committee on the Treatment of Mental Illness. *Partial Report,* 1–5 (1956–1958).

A Study of the Suitability for Outpatient Clinic Treatment of State Mental Hospital Admissions 1957. Department of Mental Hygiene, *Research Report No. 1:* 1957.

The Short-Doyle Act for Community Mental Health Services. 1957.

Welfare Planning Council of the Los Angeles Region. *The Mental Health Survey of Los Angeles County 1957–1959.* Los Angeles, ca. 1960.

Department of Mental Hygiene. *A Long Range Plan for Mental Health Services in California. 1962.*

Senate Fact Finding Committee on Judiciary. *Report and Recommendations on Commitment Procedures for the Mentally Ill January 1965. 1965.*

Assembly Interim Committee on Ways and Means. *The Dilemma of Mental Commitments in California. 1966.*

CONNECTICUT

Care of Patients in the State Mental Institutions of Connecticut: A Report to ... the Governor by the Public Welfare Council Prepared by Raymond G. Fuller ... [and] Embracing a Survey of the State Mental Institutions of Connecticut by the United States Public Health Service. 1942.

Carini, Esta, et al. *The Mentally Ill in Connecticut: Changing Patterns of Care and the Evolution of Psychiatric Nursing 1636–1972. 1974.*

ILLINOIS

A Budgetary Survey of State Mental Hospitals. 1948.

Community and Other Noninstitutional Mental Health Programs. Illinois Legislative Council, *Publication 135*: 1960.

Illinois Legislative Investigating Commission. *Seven Patient Deaths at Illinois Extended Care Center. 1975.*

IOWA

Switzer, Stephen, and H. L. Nelson. *Social Class and Paths to Psychiatric Hospitalization. 1971.*

KANSAS

Survey of Psychiatric Facilities in Kansas, pts. 1–2. Kansas Legislative Council, *Publication 143, 146:* 1946.

State Department of Social Welfare. *Medical Services and Mental Health. 1964.*

Mental Health Needs and Resources: A Report of Regional Citizen Surveys. 1965.

KENTUCKY

Welfare: Mental Hospitals, A Report to the Committee on Functions and Resources of State Government. Kentucky Legislative Commission, *Research Publication No. 24:* 1951.

MARYLAND

Report of the Joint Senate and House Committee to Study the State Mental Hospitals . . . 1949. 1949.

MASSACHUSETTS

Report of the Special Commission on Commitment, Care and Treatment of Mental Health Hospital Patients May 2, 1955. Mass. *Senate Document No. 735:* 1955.

Special Commission on Audit of State Needs. *Massachusetts Needs in Mental Health and the Care of the Retarded . . . July 30, 1958.* Mass. *House Document No. 3250:* 1958.

Mental Hospital Planning Project. *Final Report: Task Force on Geriatrics.* 1973.

MICHIGAN

A Survey of Family Care Practices in Michigan State Hospitals. Department of Mental Health, *Research Report No. 20:* 1955.

Differential Mortality in Psychiatric Hospitals and the General Population of Michigan 1950–1954. Department of Mental Health, Research Section, *Report 28:* 1957.

Michigan Community Mental Health Services. 1961.

MINNESOTA

Care and Treatment of Mental Patients. Legislative Research Committee, *Publication No. 19:* 1948.

The Minnesota Mental Health Program January 1951 [by] Ralph Rossen, M.D.. 1951.

MISSOURI

The Mentally Ill: Their Care and Treatment in Missouri. General Assembly, *Report No. 8:* 1948.

The Mentally Ill: Their Care and Treatment in Four Selected States. Committee on Legislative Research, *Report No. 10:* 1949.

NEW HAMPSHIRE

A Mental Health Program for New Hampshire Submitted by the American Psychiatric Association 1958. Washington, D.C., 1958.

NEW JERSEY

New Jersey State Mental Health Commission, *Public Hearing,* 2–6 (1957–1959).

Conference of County Mental Health Boards. *Proceedings.* 1958, 1960, 1962, 1968.

State Commission of Mental Health, *Toward Better Mental Health in New Jersey: A Report to Governor Robert B. Meyner and the Members of the Senate and General Assembly.* 1961.

Cooperation Toward Mental Health: A Conference of Community Psychiatric Clinics and Family Service Agencies. 1962.

Department of Institutions and Agencies. *New Jersey State Plan for Construction of Community Mental Health Centers.* 1967.

Department of Institutions and Agencies. *Psychiatry in Transition: A Symposium*. 1968.

NEW YORK

Department of Mental Hygiene. *Annual Report*, 53–75 (1940/41–1962/63), 1964, 1966.
Commission to Investigate the Management and Affairs of the Department of Mental Hygiene of the State, and the Institutions Operated by It. *The Care of the Mentally Ill in the State of New York*. 1944.
Temporary Commission on State Hospital Problems. *Insulin Shock Therapy*. 1944.
New York State's Needs in Mental Health Research, Training and Community Services: Proceedings of the Public Hearing on Mental Health Held by the New York State Senate Committee on Public Health . . . 1956. 1956.
Design for Mental Health. 1958.
A Guide to Communities in the Establishment and Operation of Psychiatric Clinics. 1959.
Progress in Psychiatric Research and Education: A Symposium in Honor of the Seventy-fifth Anniversary of the New York State Psychiatric Institute. 1973.

OHIO

Design for a Coordinated System of Services to the Mentally Ill and Mentally Retarded in Ohio: A Report Submitted to Honorable John J. Gilligan. 1971.

OREGON

Oregon State Plan for Construction of Community Mental Health Centers. Revised, Fiscal Year 1970–71. 1971.

PENNSYLVANIA

Report of the Committee Appointed by Honorable Edward Martin to Make a Complete Study of the Mental Hospitals of the Commonwealth of Pennsylvania, July 1944. 1944.

TEXAS

Psychiatric Inpatient Units in Texas General Hospitals. 1958.
Care of Court-Committed Mentally Ill Prior to State Hospital Admission. Texas Legislative Council, *Report No. 57–6*: 1962.

VIRGINIA

Department of Mental Hygiene and Hospitals. *Sixteen Years of Progress 1938–1954*. 1954.

WASHINGTON

Mental Institutions in the State of Washington: A Report of a Survey by Roger Nett. 1948.
The End of the Beginning: A Report on Mental Health Problems in the State of Washington. 1956.

WISCONSIN

Mental Health Advisory Committee. *"Forward" in Mental Health*. 1962.

SERIALS

Two strategies were employed in researching the vast periodical literature of the period since 1940. Those journals that dealt directly or indirectly with mental illnesses or else represented national organizations such as the AMA were examined in their entirety. Since many articles also appeared in the medical and general press as well as in scholarly journals, periodical indexes were consulted. It is of course impossible to list all of the individual items used, but the following publications served as useful guides: *International Index to Periodicals*, 9–18 (1940/1943–1964/1965); *PAIS Index*, 26–61 (1940–1975); *Reader's Guide to Periodical Literature*, 12–35 (1939/1941–1975/1976); *Social Sciences & Humanities Index*, 19–27 (1965/1966–1973/1974); *Social Sciences Index*, 1–11 (1974/1975–1984/1985).

Journals, Proceedings, and Annuals

Administration in Mental Health (NIMH), 1972–1975.
Advances in Biochemical Psychopharmacology, 1–14 (1969–1975).
American Imago, 1–32 (1939/1940–1975).
American Journal of Orthopsychiatry, 10–45 (1940–1975).
American Journal of Physical Medicine, 31–54 (1952–1975).
American Journal of Psychiatry, 97–142 (1940–1985).
American Journal of Psychoanalysis, 1–35 (1941–1975).
American Journal of Psychotherapy, 1–29 (1947–1975).
American Journal of Public Health, 30–65 (1940–1975).
APA Colloquium for Postgraduate Teaching of Psychiatry. *Proceedings*, 2–8 (1963–1969) (first probably not published).
APA Mental Hospital Institute. *Proceedings*, 1–6 (1949–1954) (all subsequent *Proceedings* appeared in *Mental Hospitals* and *Hospital & Community Psychiatry*).
The APA Newsletter, nos. 1–21 (June 15, 1948–June 15, 1950), 3–18 (1950/1951–1965).
APA. *Psychiatric Research Reports*, 1–24 (1955–1968).
American Psychologist, 1–25 (1946–1970).
American Psychological Association. *Research in Psychotherapy*, 1–3 (1958–1966).
American Psychopathological Association. *Proceedings*, 33–65 (1944–1975) (vol. 35 not published).
Annual Review of the Schizophrenia Syndrome, 1–4 (1971–1974/1975) (title of vol. 1 reads *The Schizophrenia Syndrome: An Annual Review*).
Archives of General Psychiatry, 1–32 (1959–1975).
Archives of Neurology and Psychiatry, 43–81 (1940–1959).
The Attendant, 1–2 (1944–1945) (continued as *The Psychiatric Aide*).
Behavioral Neuropsychiatry, 1–6 (1969/1970–1974/1975).
Biological Psychiatry, 1–10 (1969–1975).
Bulletin of the Menninger Clinic, 4–39 (1940–1975).

Community Mental Health Journal, 1–21 (1965–1985).

Comprehensive Psychiatry, 1–16 (1960–1975).

Conference on Psychiatric Education. *Report*, 1951–1952.

Corrective Psychiatry and Journal of Social Therapy, 8–21 (1962–1975) (vols. 19–20 title reads *Corrective and Social Psychiatry and Journal of Applied Behavioral Therapy*; vol. 21 title reads *Corrective and Social Psychiatry and Journal of Behavior Technology Methods and Therapy*).

Current Psychiatric Therapies, 1–15 (1961–1975).

Diseases of the Nervous System, 1–36 (1940–1975).

Group for the Advancement of Psychiatry. *Report*, 1–96 (1947–1976).

Hospital & Community Psychiatry, 17–36 (1966–1985).

International Journal of Group Psychotherapy, 1–25 (1951–1975).

International Journal of Mental Health, 1–4 (1972/1973–1975/1976).

International Journal of Neuropsychiatry, 1–4 (1965–1968).

International Journal of Psychiatry, 1–11 (1965–1973).

International Journal of Psychiatry in Medicine, 4–6 (1973–1975).

International Journal of Social Psychiatry, 1–21 (1965/1966–1975).

International Psychiatry Clinics, 1–8 (1964–1971).

Joint Information Service of the APA and the National Association for Mental Health. *Fact Sheet*, 1–17 (1957–1962).

Journal of Abnormal Psychology, 70–84 (1965–1975).

Journal of Abnormal and Social Psychology, 35–69 (1940–1964) (continued as *Journal of Abnormal Psychology*).

Journal of the American Academy of Psychoanalysis, 1–3 (1973–1975).

Journal of the American Association for Social Psychiatry, 1–2 (1959/1960–1961).

Journal of the American College of Neuropsychiatrists, 1–3 (1962–1964).

Journal of the American Medical Association, 114–234 (1940–1975).

Journal of the American Psychoanalytical Association, 1–23 (1953–1975).

Journal of the Association of American Medical Colleges, 15–25 (1940–1950) (continued as *Journal of Medical Education*).

Journal of Clinical and Experimental Psychopathology, 12–14 (1951–1953) (continued as *Journal of Clinical and Experimental Psychopathology and Quarterly Review of Psychiatry and Neurology*).

Journal of Clinical Psychology, 1–31 (1945–1975).

Journal of Clinical Psychopathology, 8–11 (1946/1947–1950) (continued as *Journal of Clinical and Experimental Psychopathology*).

Journal of Community Psychology, 1–3 (1973–1975).

Journal of Consulting and Clinical Psychology, 32–43 (1968–1975).

Journal of Consulting Psychology, 4–31 (1940–1967) (continued as *Journal of Consulting and Clinical Psychology*).

Journal of Criminal Psychopathology, 1–5 (1939/1940–1944) (continued as *Journal of Clinical Psychopathology and Psychotherapy*).

Journal of Criminal Psychopathology and Psychotherapy, 6–7 (1944/1945–1945/1946) (continued as *Journal of Clinical Psychopathology*).

Journal of Existential Psychiatry, 1–4 (1960/61–1963/1964) (continued as *Journal of Existentialism*).

Journal of Existentialism, 5–8 (1964/1965–1967/1968).

Journal of Medical Education, 26–60 (1951–1985).

Journal. National Association of Private Psychiatric Hospitals, 1–7 (1969–1975).

Journal of Nervous and Mental Disease, 91–161 (1940–1975).

Journal of Neuropsychiatry, 1–5 (1959/1960–1963/1964) (continued as *International Journal of Neuropsychiatry*).

Journal of Orthomolecular Psychiatry, 3–4 (1974–1975).

Journal of Psychiatric Education, 1–7 (1977–1983).

Journal of Psychiatric Nursing, 1–4 (1963–1966) (continued as *Journal of Psychiatric Nursing and Mental Health Services*).

Journal of Psychiatric Nursing and Mental Health Services, 5–11 (1967–1973).

Journal of Psychiatric Research, 1–12 (1961–1975).

Journal of Psychiatric Social Work, 17–24 (1947/1948–1954/1955).

Journal of Psychiatry and Law, 1–3 (1973–1975).

Journal of Social Therapy, 1–7 (1954–1961) (continued as *Corrective Psychiatry and Journal of Social Therapy*).

Massachusetts Journal of Mental Health, 1–5 (1970/1971–1974/1975).

Mental Health Digest, 1967–1968, 1–5 (1969–1973).

Mental Health Scope, 1–9 (1966/1967–1975/1976).

Mental Hospitals, 1–16 (1950–1965) (continued as *Hospital & Community Psychiatry*) (title of vols. 1–2 reads *APA Mental Hospital Service Bulletin*).

Mental Hygiene, 25–56 (1941–1972) (continued as *MH*).

MH, 57–59 (1973–1975).

Milbank Memorial Fund Quarterly, 18–61 (1940–1983).

Modern Health Care, 1–4 (1974–1975).

Modern Hospital, 54–122 (1940–1974) (continued as *Modern Health Care*).

National Conference of Social Work. *Proceedings*, 67–102 (1940–1975) (beginning with vol. 76 title reads *The Social Welfare Forum*).

Neuropsychiatry, 1–6 (1951/1952–1960).

New England Journal of Medicine, 222–302 (1940–1980).

Newsletter of the American Association of Psychiatric Social Workers, 10–16 (1940/1941–1946/1947) (continued as *Journal of Psychiatric Social Work*).

Occupational Therapy and Rehabilitation, 19–30 (1940–1951) (continued as *American Journal of Physical Medicine*).

Orthomolecular Psychiatry, 1–2 (1972–1973) (continued as *Journal of Orthomolecular Psychiatry*).

Pennsylvania Psychiatric Quarterly, 1–10 (1961–1970).

Progress in Community Mental Health, 1–3 (1969–1975).

Progress in Neurology and Psychiatry, 1–28 (1946–1973).

Progress in Psychotherapy, 1–5 (1956–1960) (continued as *Current Psychiatric Therapies*).

The Psychiatric Aide, 3–9 (1946–1952).

Psychiatric Annals, 1–5 (1971–1975).

Psychiatric Communications, 1–16 (1958–1975).

Psychiatric News, 1–10 (1966–1975).

Psychiatric Opinion, 1–12 (1964–1975).

Psychiatric Quarterly, 14–47 (1940–1973) (includes *Psychiatric Quarterly Supplement*, 14–42 ([1940–1968]).

Psychiatric Studies and Projects, 1–3 (1963–1965).

Psychiatry, 3–38 (1940–1975).

Psychiatry in Medicine, 1–3 (1970–1972) (continued as *International Journal of Psychiatry in Medicine*).

Psychoanalysis and Contemporary Science, 1–4 (1972–1975).

Psychoanalysis: Journal of Psychoanalytic Psychology, 1–6 (1952/1953–1958) (absorbed by *Psychoanalytic Review*).

Psychoanalysis and the Social Sciences, 1–5 (1947–1958) (continued as *Psychoanalytic Study of Society*).

Psychoanalytic Forum, 1–5 (1966–1975).

Psychoanalytic Quarterly, 9–44 (1940–1975).

Psychoanalytic Review, 27–62 (1940–1975) (vols. 45–49 [1958–1962] published under the title *Psychoanalysis and the Psychoanalytic Review*).

Psychoanalytic Study of Society, 1–6 (1960–1975).

Psychosomatic Medicine, 2–37 (1940–1975).

Psychosomatics, 1–16 (1960–1975).

Quarterly Review of Psychiatry and Neurology, 1–7 (1946–1952) (continued as *Journal of Clinical and Experimental Psychopathology and Quarterly Review of Psychiatry and Neurology*).

Radical Therapist, 1–5 (1970–1976).

Recent Advances in Biological Psychiatry, 1–10 (1959–1968) (title of vol. 1 reads *Biological Psychiatry*).

Review of Existential Psychology and Psychiatry, 1–14 (1961–1975).

Schizophrenia, 1–3 (1969–1971) (becomes *Orthomolecular Psychiatry*).

Schizophrenia Bulletin, nos. 1–14 (1969–1975).

Science and Psychoanalysis, 1–21 (1958–1972) (continued as *Journal of the American Academy of Psychoanalysis*).

Seminars in Psychiatry, 1–5 (1969–1973).

Social Psychiatry, 1–10 (1966/1967–1975).

Social Work, 1–20 (1956–1975).

State Government, 13–58 (1940–1985).

Year Book of Neurology, Psychiatry and Endocrinology, 1940–1945.

Year Book of Neurology, Psychiatry and Neurosurgery, 1946–1967/1968.

Year Book of Psychiatry and Applied Mental Health, 1970–1975.

Yearbook of Psychoanalysis, 1–10 (1945–1954).

Newspapers

New York Daily Compass, 1949–1952.

New York Star, 1948–1949.

New York Times, 1940–1975.

PM, 1940–1948.

Index

abortion, 276

Action for Mental Health (Joint Commission of Mental Illness and Health), 203–20, 223, 229, 286. *See also* Joint Commission on Mental Illness and Health

Adams, Lynn, 88

Advisory Commission on Intergovernmental Relations, 216

affective disorders, 270

aftercare, 91, 171, 262

aged mentally ill. *See* mental hospitals: aged patients in

Alaska, 280

Albee, George W., 196, 286

Albert and Mary Lasker Foundation, 87

alcoholic disorders, 160

alcoholism, 255

Alinsky, Saul, 242

Allinsmith, Wesley, 198

American Association of Applied Psychologists, 104

American Association on Mental Deficiency, 349n.16

American Association of Psychiatric Social Workers, 11, 117

American Bar Association, 289–90

American Board of Examiners in Professional Psychology, 105, 108

American Board of Psychiatry and Neurology, 98–99, 297

American Cancer Society, 84

American Civil Liberties Union, 289

American College of Physicians, 34

American College of Surgeons, 34, 80

American Hospital Association, 47, 71, 184, 250

American Journal of Psychiatry, 25, 31, 286, 297

American Journal of Psychotherapy, 135

American Legion, 190

American Medical Association, 34, 110, 228, 231, 246; and Joint Commission on Mental Illness and Health, 183, 187, 190; National Congress on Mental Illness and Health, 214; opposes Neuropsychiatric Institute proposal, 46; reaction of to

Action for Mental Health, 213–14; Section on Nervous and Mental Disorders, 46; and staffing of community mental health centers, 247–48

American Medico-Psychological Association: and psychiatric nosology, 96

American Psychiatric Association, 3, 45, 70, 91; and American Psychological Association, 110–14; Arlie House Propositions, 244; Central Inspection Board, 80–81, 163; and clinical psychology, 106–14; Commission on Insurance, 266; Committee on Clinical Psychology, 111; Committee on Medical Education, 99; Committee on Nomenclature and Statistics, 97; Committee on Psychiatric Nursing, 118; Committee on Psychiatric Standards and Policies, 25, 80; Committee on Psychiatry in Medical Education, 98; Committee on Psychotherapy, 135; Committee on the Relation of Psychiatry to Psychology, 106; Committee on Relations with Psychology, 111–13; Committee on Research, 276–78; and Community Mental Health Centers Act of 1963, 227; and DSM-I, 97, 242; and districts, 312n.23; and drug experimentation, 156; and drug therapy, 149; and electroshock therapy, 128; and evaluation of therapy, 133; fights for increased expenditures for mental hospitals, 163–64; and halfway house study, 263; and health insurance, 265–66; and institutional psychiatry, 165; and Joint Commission on Mental Illness and Health, 183, 187, 190; lobbies for federal health construction funds, 186; location of members of in 1950s, 42; and Medicare and Medicaid, 267; membership of in 1940, 17; Mental Hospital Institute, 82, 116, 163; and mental hospital reform, 78; Mental Hospital Service, 82; and mental hospital standards, 9, 74, 78, 80; and National Mental Health Act of 1946, 50; and National Mental Health Foundation, 83–84; and Neuropsychiatric Institute pro-